Serial Killer Cinema

Serial Killer Cinema

An Analytical Filmography with an Introduction

Robert Cettl

McFarland & Company, Inc., Publishers
Jefferson, North Carolina, and London

The present work is a reprint of the illustrated case bound edition of Serial Killer Cinema: An Analytical Filmography with an Introduction, *first published in 2008 by McFarland.*

LIBRARY OF CONGRESS CATALOGUING-IN-PUBLICATION DATA

Cettl, Robert, 1969–
Serial killer cinema : an analytical filmography with an
introduction / Robert Cettl.
p.   cm.
Includes bibliographical references and index.

ISBN-13: 978-0-7864-3731-3
softcover : 50# alkaline paper ∞

1. Serial murderers in motion pictures.   2. Motion pictures—Catalogs.
I. Title.
PN1995.9.S297C48   2008   791.43'653 — dc21   2002011614

British Library cataloguing data are available

On the cover: Lance Henriksen in the 1988 film *Nature of the Beast*

Manufactured in the United States of America

*McFarland & Company, Inc., Publishers
Box 611, Jefferson, North Carolina 28640
www.mcfarlandpub.com*

For my wife,
Lynn Manypenny-Cettl

CONTENTS

Acknowledgments   ix

Preface   1

Serial Killer Cinema: An Introduction   5

Serial Killer Cinema Filmography   33

Bibliography   521

Index   525

ACKNOWLEDGMENTS

George and Anne Cettl
Flinders University Library
Jerry Ohlinger's Movie Materials Store
Louis and Josephine Manypenny
Lynn Manypenny-Cettl
Ngapartji Multimedia and staff
State Library of South Australia
George Anderson
Noel Purdon
Bonnie and Gerald Zimmerman
Nancy Manypenny

PREFACE

Ridley Scott's *Hannibal* was one of the more eagerly awaited releases of the past decade. Audiences wanted to see what a refined, intelligent, cannibalistic serial killer would do with his newfound freedom. They wanted to see how he might continue his potentially romantic attraction to a female FBI profiler. Most disturbingly, perhaps they wanted to see if and how someone would be eaten. The critics predictably were divided in their reaction to the film, and to its solution to the dilemma of audience, and dramatic, expectation. However, the film's box-office performance only served to confirm what many lamented, that the serial killer film was indeed a popular form.

Hannibal was of course the sequel to *Silence of the Lambs*, which soon after its release in 1991 entered the popular lexicon and swept the major Academy Award categories. The critical and popular success of this film legitimized the serial killer movie. It was no longer considered the domain of low-budget exploitation, as was the typical impression of films dealing with such subject matter. Now, "serious" filmmakers, even auteurs, increasingly used the serial killer film for message and money.

Yet these works are examples of a genre dating back as far as the silent era, which focusses on the figure of the repeat sex killer termed "serial killer." In fact, the "question" of the serial killer became prominent in 1888 with the Jack the Ripper slayings. These murders introduced a new type of crime, and insofar as the criminal went uncaught, suggested that such a problem needed new solutions, beyond ordinary police-work.

The unknowable monster and the profiler who seeks to understand him: The ironies and conflicts were considerable. Even television in the 1990s responded to this character pairing, hence the series *Millennium* and *Profiler*, both of which addressed the skills and insights of the person who hunts such monsters. But they did so from opposite ends of a spectrum, the former a darkly stylized noirish psychodrama and the latter a realistic depiction in the tradition of procedural cop shows. The dynamics of the serial killer film entered the living room.

The explicitness expected is the logical outgrowth of a genre from the outset concerned with the experience of, depiction of, and treatment of psychological (sexual) aberration. Indeed, in a climate wherein sex and violence in the media and arts have become major talking points, it

1

is only logical that films which address this union, and with such an aesthetic reservoir, should come under scrutiny, and controversy. As if examining and depicting such atrocious action meant automatically condoning them, as knee-jerk critical reactions would assert.

For, over the course of roughly a century, the serial killer film has indeed evolved a set of operating standards, narrative structures, themes and stylistic choices which qualify it as a genre, or at the very least, a sub-genre, all its own. Although the films are frequently considered horror or thriller, they are often labeled "serial killer films" on the assumption that the audience knows what constitutes such a blanket definition. At the very least, this is based on the shared knowledge of what constitutes a serial killer.

In the early 1970s, FBI agent Robert Ressler coined the term to refer to a particular type of repeat sex killer. This type would harbor homicidal sexual fantasies for a considerable time before turning to murder to make them a reality, then cool off for a certain period of time (days, weeks, months) and then kill again. This killer would never stop, his machine-like regularity making him the popular example in Marxist/Freudian analysis of the evils of Patriarchal Capitalism. Some people, remembering the old Saturday afternoon serial cliffhangers that featured a dramatic climax with a teaser to bring the audience back for another installment, found Ressler's use of the word "serial" disturbing.

These killers have been accorded great status in popular culture. It might be said that they have gone from being merely aberrant evil to being not only the representative but the epitome of a greater, more corruptive and influential Evil, dedicated to preying on the very fabric of society. Furthermore, it could be argued that the killer has been accorded the status of a representative Patriarch in an allegorical

struggle for the salvation of Patriarchy, an institution held up as the ultimate standard, ironically both producing the killer and seeking to purge him from its operations. The profiler has over the years become the sanctioned force responsible for chastising this dangerous threat, and in the process disavowing the role of fantasy. It is a struggle usually confined to males, and it is often a contentious issue, and a further challenge to the operations of Patriarchy, when one or more of the film's central killer types are female. Synopses of the works in this filmography necessarily acknowledge when such a gender switch is made in the formula.

The purpose of this book, after first outlining the development of the serial killer film as a genre, is to list, through 2000, the films (and select television movies) that have tackled the serial killer, and examine how each fits into, or contributes to, the preceding outline. This of course involves a definition of the serial killer film that excludes a number of works some may have thought worthy of inclusion.

There are numerous films dealing with the various sub-types of murderer, but this book includes only those that address the serial killer as a repeat, pattern offender. Most of these killers are sexual predators, but not all of the films to have featured repeat killers chose to explore the sexual angle. In this book, with certain exceptions (see next paragraph), only those films that directly or by suggestion present or explore the killer's aberrant sexual motivations or cravings for manipulation, domination, and control (with subsequent desires to punish women or society) are included. Films that feature killers murdering exclusively for financial reward are therefore excluded unless they affected the development of the serial killer film in some important way, moving it towards the theme of sexual aberration. This is primarily true of films made during the Hays

Code era, when such themes were taboo for filmmakers. Since the definition of the "serial killer" as coined by Ressler refers specifically to sex offenders, whose crimes when based on a form of idealized fantasy empowerment are considered sexual even though there may be no sexual act performed upon the victim, those films in which the killer is driven by such fantasy are included.

Also included are some films that may at first glance seem to fall outside the "serial killer film" definition. These are select films that comment on themes and character types present in the serial killer film, or that make self-conscious reference to and assume a knowledge of serial killer pathology or the serial killer subculture itself, or that have been promoted as having a serial killer connection. It is hoped that these exceptions give an indication of the expanding sphere of influence that the serial killer exerts on an evolving popular cinematic culture.

Some of the films covered in the filmography are impossible to track down, having long disappeared from general release, especially outside of the United States. Some are being re-released from video to DVD, but many of them are so minor and obscure that it is unlikely they will ever be given a general re-release of any kind, their approach to the subject matter precluding their exhibition even on cable. For these items, the Internet movie databases (imdb.com and allmovie.com in particular) and their links to fan sites have proven a valuable source of synopsis and background information, as have the various sources listed in the bibliography. As for the horror genre, which the serial killer film is often linked to, it is the solid fan base that keeps many of these films alive beyond their critical use-by date.

Many of these films deserve broader appreciation. It is the author's hope that by providing an account of these films and their place within contemporary film history, a contribution is made to the understanding of popular culture's response to the psychological and criminological issues surrounding the serial killer. It is meant as an aid for the further analysis of a body of work often referred to in passing but never fully delineated.

SERIAL KILLER CINEMA:
AN INTRODUCTION

Early Serial Killer Figures and Mythos

Taking 1888 and the Jack the Ripper murders as the effective beginning of the modern age of the serial killer, one can say that the cinema has in a certain way grown up alongside this phenomenon. It is no surprise, therefore, that since the silent era, cinema has responded to the new breed of vicious, repeat sex killer in a number of inventive, increasingly complex and problematic ways. This was not always a deliberate choice, at least to start with, but as the characteristics of the serial killer came increasingly under social, psychological and criminological study, it became increasingly clear to filmmakers what the nature of the threat, and indeed heritage, posed by such killers was.

For instance, even as early as the Méliès screen fantasies was there a perhaps Grand Guignol inspired visualization of Bluebeard's chamber of victims. Shock value aside, this was a brief glimpse into the world of a multiple murderer, the quintessential lady-killer, a precursor to Jack the Ripper known throughout Eu-

rope. Be that as it may, it was clear even from the earliest days of the cinema that there was a tendency to address the crimes of the serial killer.

To look at the beginnings of the serial killer film, one must return, as the first stop on a tour through many genres, to the horror film's chilling conceptions of monstrousness and homicidal mania and in particular to films made in Germany during the interwar period. These films attempted to address the phenomenon of repeat sexual murder, exploring the type of victims targeted, the killer's abnormal motives, and the dangers posed to society.

With the term "serial killer" still decades away, for the purposes of this book, the figure causing the social and criminological problem was the repeat killer. This killer murdered (for whatever reason, although sexual aberration was the usual motive — something which fascinated psychoanalyst Krafft-Ebing), cooled off for a period (days, weeks, months) and then killed again in a similar method as before. Although the sexual component would be paramount to the definition of the serial killer, many early depictions tackled instead a killer who killed repeatedly, though not for an overtly sexual motive. They are thus not serial killers according to the strict definition of the term, but their design offers a prototype to which would gradually be added the sexual component of their crimes. Thus, one can trace the emergence of the sexual killer not only in vampire movies (perhaps the most obvious link), but also in mad doctor films, monster movies, werewolf movies, killer ape movies and, of course, other doppelgänger themed films (especially the Jekyll/ Hyde tales). All of these tackle the horror genre's dominant theme of the relationship of Monstrousness (and thus Otherness) to the accepted definition of human "normality" (not intended as a judgmental usage of the term, but merely one that connotes the dominant social consideration — that often targeted by these killers[1]). Inherent in this is the notion of what kind of social response (individual or collective) would be necessary to halt and eliminate these killers — a theme *M* acknowledged most distinctively.

Before looking at the most significant of these films, which, although it's argued herein that they address the problem of serial murder, do not qualify as serial killer films themselves, it is necessary to contextualize them. Although the Ripper case is central, serial sex murder was steadily advancing through Europe. Most alarming were the cases in Germany during the interwar period. Three killers in particular had a tremendous effect on a struggling German society turning towards fascism. Georg Grossmann butchered numerous women and sold their flesh as animal meat on the burgeoning black market, and was finally caught in 1921. Fritz Haarmann, who murdered up to 50 young men and

boys between 1919 and 1924, soon superseded him. Haarmann also indulged in necrophilic sex and dismemberment, and he too sold his victims' flesh as meat for the black market (his case was filmed in 1979 as *The Tenderness of Wolves*). Perhaps most notably, he would bite through his still living victims' throats and lap at the ensuing blood flow. Another killer, Peter Kurten, started his major crime wave in 1924, but it was during his most demented phase, in 1929–1930, that he was dubbed the "Vampire of Dusseldorf" by an outraged media. In truth, however, the vampires of legend had little on Kurten, who raped and butchered women and children, and, like Haarmann, tore at their throats to drink their blood. His youngest victim was five years old.

Authors have outlined a thesis on how the morbidity of German culture fed the growth of fascism, but four central films of this period can be seen also as reactions to the growing menace of serial killers. These films are, in order of release, *The Cabinet of Dr. Caligari* (1919: d. Robert Weine), *Nosferatu* (1922: d. F.W. Murnau), *Pandora's Box*, (1928: d. G.W. Pabst) and *M* (1931: d. Fritz Lang), all made during the time of these killers' operations. Despite their differences, they all feature multiple-murderers who target innocents, and each film serves to define innocence (with victims traditionally gendered feminine and their attackers masculine) and its relation to the Evil represented by the monster.

It is commonly known that Lang's film was based on Kurten, although Lang denied this,[2] but *The Cabinet of Dr. Caligari*, which predated Lang's film by over a decade, was also based on an incidence of child sex murder. As co-screenwriter Hans

---

[1]Hence, an embryonic possibility to see such killers as threats to the dominant social order and thus, almost as revolutionary figures — a tendency which surfaced particularly in US films of the 1970s, amidst an epoch of social upheaval, increasingly violent crimes, and major sociopolitical disillusionment. This notion is discussed further.

[2]As revealed in Nash and Ross (eds.); *Motion Picture Guide* (Chicago: Cinebooks, 1986), p. 1178.

The Invisible Man depicted a scientist's drug experiments gone awry (thus paralleling Jekyll and Hyde), as the quest for knowledge causes mental disintegration, rampant unmotivated homicide and the desire to be known and feared as a famous celebrity: to inspire awe.[17] The mad doctor had become his own monster — no longer were Caligari and Cesare separate. The very title suggests that a mad killer could be lurking undetected within society, perhaps even one of its most respected members— a theme developed in the Jekyll/ Hyde mythos. Like previous mass killers, he was, in terms of physical appearance, removed from normal humankind, although, importantly, he *was* human. But it was the notion of mental illness as the cause of repeat murder which would have the most repercussions for the serial killer film, and something it would forever try to shake.

What is present here is the sense of the corruptive influence of a state of being which once experienced can cause psychological breakdown yet is too appealing to leave. It is almost an arguable liberation from social norms, and even the result of scientific curiosity about the depth of human capability. With such insight into human nature comes an inevitable madness which leads the affected to seek to manipulate, dominate and control all those around him. These unfortunates are little more than toys for his perceived idealized self — perhaps the conscience-less superego capable of the actions of an id. Subsequent films would tackle this transposition of superego and id. This, of course, is the case in Robert Stevenson's novel *Dr. Jekyll*

and Mr. Hyde, which would prove the next decisive factor in the advancement of the serial killer film.

Stevenson's novel was first published in 1886, just two years before the Jack the Ripper slayings. It was soon made into a successful stage play in 1887, which ran during the Ripper's crimes, and made its way onto film as early as 1908. Over the years it became one of the most often filmed novels, with versions in 1910, three in 1915 and then in the USA in 1920, with versions following in 1931 (the year of *M*) and 1941. It also influenced the German film *Der Januskopf* (1920: d. F.W. Murnau), although the doppelganger motif had already been a fixture of German culture.[18]

Here the potential killer co-exists as a separate entity in the same mind as the normal identity. Yet, unlike the werewolf monster initially, they are both aware of each other. The figure of Mr. Hyde was thus an elaboration and qualification of the notion of possession as takeover by another, but no longer takeover by an outside force.[19] It is Dr. Jekyll's suggested sexual repression and curiosity about the dark side of human nature which impels his scientific experiments. Once he takes the drug and becomes the evil, deformed Mr. Hyde, he is free to indulge the desires repressed according to Victorian social dictates. Hyde then prowls the foggy London streets, further tying the film adaptations to Jack the Ripper's legacy.

Yet it still featured the popular image of the killer as substantially different, since the evil Hyde was physically distorted and deformed from the normal Jekyll; the transformation from good to evil still

[17]It's an idea seized upon by the serial killer genre, especially *Manhunter*, wherein the killer claims that society owes him awe, and he kills to achieve this. It has been proven to have some grounding in the mind of killers who murder partly out of rage and frustration against a world/society they feel has let them down or denied them their true place.

[18]See Clarens, C., *op. cit.*, pp. 23–25. The doppelganger motif can thus be seen to influence the conception of the serial killer as discussed in the previous section.

[19]Fleming and Manvell, *Images of Madness*; Fairleigh Dickinson (London: Associated University Presses, 1985), pp. 64–65.

required physical metamorphosis. Significantly though, the fantasy-based supernatural origin of monstrousness that had enveloped the horror movie was done away with. This was more explicit in the 1941 version of the tale, released at the commencement of the aforementioned cinematic vogue for depictions of the mentally ill and their treatment.

As the depictions of Hyde lessened the physical differences between the two identities, the closer the killer resembled normality and the closer the identities seemed to be states of the same mind rather than completely separate entities. Monstrousness was becoming a begrudgingly accepted fact, part of the human condition. But to what extent did Dr. Jekyll know of Mr. Hyde's activities, and how did he react to that knowledge, being a moral, if repressed, man? In particular, did he enjoy it? And did he enjoy it to the point of guilt or remorse?

In that the Jekyll of the novel eventually cannot stop himself from becoming the bestial and monstrous Hyde, Stevenson suggests that the evil side, the murderous side, is inescapable once experienced. It is an addiction, paralleled to drug use (the compound that Jekyll consumes to become Hyde). What is released, however, and what is addictive, is a freedom from constraint, a virtual liberation. Yet this is depicted as a negative, a corruption by warped sexual desires. Hyde thus enjoys sexual sadism (and, by extension, sex murder) as an integral part of the transformed/liberated soul. The negativism associated with the transformation prevents any sense of transcendence. By the end of the story, Jekyll fears (secretly desires?) total subjugation to Hyde. They

may co-exist by the end, but Hyde is inescapable.[20]

Thus, following Hyde, the serial killer figure was now fully human and would enter an altered state of consciousness, murder, and then return to an outward normality for a time before killing again, knowingly and voluntarily. The pattern was set. Hyde was initially switched on and off by drug experimentation, but subsequent killers were turned on by the very lure of Evil. And that Evil was a combination of abnormal sexual desire, misogyny, and a resentment of social norms (although the traditional motives were still persistent).

The notion of the killer's separateness lingered and, since the 1940s, film turned to the rise of psychoanalysis to find a new "reason." The killer wanted to kill, a desire removed from humanity not in terms of physical difference, but in terms of psychological aberration and mental illness. Often this was to allow a kind of diminished responsibility — it was I, but not I: a "defense" locked into the American soul by the end of the 1940s. Even as late as Hitchcock's *Psycho* this notion persisted.

Noir and Post-Noir Criminality

The split-personality motif allowed the potential for the killer to be dormant at times, outwardly at rest whilst the normal human took over and functioned as usual within a recognizable society. It was a form of co-existence. Thus, there was a prospect of the serial killer, though coded as mentally ill or in some way

[20]The studies of the emerging FBI Behavioral Science Unit in the 1970s led investigators to believe that no reform is possible for serial offenders— they are lost causes, driven to murder. After the killer's fantasies are enacted in reality through sexual homicide, murder becomes addictive as a remedy for psychological stress (including that of abnormal sexual desire) and a release akin to a sexual act (even if there is no sexual act performed on the victim).

psychologically afflicted (hence different), occupying the same world as the conventional criminal. The nature of the crime was, of course, divergent and carried with it all of the symbolic baggage associated with monstrousness, but it was still a crime and thus subject to criminological interpretation and response.

One true-life case in particular illustrates the overlap of psychological and criminological factors. In Chicago during 1945–46, a series of burglaries and murderous assaults were committed. The press dubbed the unknown slayer "the lipstick killer" after a note to the police was written in lipstick on a wall at a murder site. The message read: "For heaven's sake catch me before I kill more I cannot control myself." A plain, 17-year-old Chicago University student named William Heirens was arrested for the murders. At his trial, Heirens claimed that his alter ego George Murman (murderman?) had committed the atrocious crimes. The Jekyll/Hyde persona had come to America[21] and was now on the city streets, prowling at night, his homicidal horrors preceded by "normal" burglaries. No mad doctors though, just an inconspicuous everyday monster, a petty criminal with a secret passion.

Therein lay the real terror: that such homicidal evil could rest within conventional society and prey on it seemingly at will. Thus, the emphasis shifted more towards an attempted social contextualization, and the films following tackled not only the psychoanalytical theories behind such aberrant behavior but the criminological impetus. An embryonic, behaviorist approach[22] to portraying such Otherness surfaced in sophisticated depictions of the mentally ill criminal. This idea of the criminal case study, however familiar from gangster movies, would gradually infiltrate portrayals of serial killers through the 1940s and 1950s.

As "madness" became something of a late–1940s vogue,[23] it seemed the switch to realistic depictions of repeat killers would soon follow. However, the "heady" treatment of the mentally troubled protagonist, á la *Spellbound* (1945: d. Alfred Hitchcock), proved not to be a box-office trend, except in comedies like *Harvey* (1950: d. Henry Koster). The mentally disturbed man was left to a secondary, villainous role,[24] albeit, in film noir, a powerful one indeed. It was as a secondary villain that the killer's aberrance became encoded.

The rise of psychoanalysis re-popularized the nature of such aberrance as it redefined it in socially and scientifically significant ways. In particular for purposes herein was the dichotomy between organic and environmental theories of mental illness, or "madness," as the more popular term had it. These attempted to contextualize the root causes not only of mental illness but also of criminality. In cinematic depictions of repeat killers, the psychoanalytical overlapped with criminological theories blossoming since the growth of the city.

[21]See Wilson, C. and D. Seaman, *The Serial Killers* (London: Virgin Publishing Ltd., 1997), pp. 178–182 for an account of the Heirens case and how it fits into the Jekyll and Hyde mode of serial killers.

[22]By the 1950s, psychoanalytic theories of psychopathic action stressed the Behaviorist model, wherein the clash between organic and developmental notions of mental illness that had arisen through the 1930s emphasized the notion of environmental "triggers" instead of simple impulsive behavior. See Fleming and Manvell, *Images of Madness*, p. 102. In addition, this can be seen in the films wherein the impulsive actions of Hyde and his ilk give way to the controlled ruthlessness of the noir psychopaths.

[23]Following on from the suppositions that mental asylums were grim places and to be feared (popular in the horror genre), "madness" began to emerge from these confines as worthy of more exploratory treatment. Hence the likes of *Spellbound*, with its Dali-designed dream sequences and introduction to the emerging science of psychoanalysis, and the combination of docu-drama and noir in *The Snake Pit* (1948: d. Anatole Litvak), which explored the deplorable, near–Bedlam conditions of the psychiatric hospital scene.

[24]For an account of this, see Hutchinson and Pickard, *Horror Movies* (London: Wattle Books, 1983), pp. 144–145.

As the 20th century wore on, it became sociologically popular to hold the criminal as a threat to society, a monstrous figure who operated with different impulses, desires and values than ordinary men.[25] The greater the crime, the more unknowable the criminal. So the process of demonization of the criminal had resulted in depictions of the criminal as Other, from the grandiose gangster to the lowlife hoodlum. But the gangster also was a repeat criminal, and so were his descendants. The conception of monstrousness from horror movies and the conception of monstrousness from crime movies thus intersected in the form of the serial killer as a repeat killer, increasingly sexually motivated. Indeed, the serial killer became the cinematic bridge between psychological and criminological conceptions and depictions of Otherness. This formed a solid basis for longevity and subsequent epochal reinterpretation.

Correspondingly, mad killers were smarter, more inconspicuous, more in control, and more dangerous. In the shadowy world of film noir they could be lurking anywhere, ready to take advantage of the opportunity to kill for pleasure (whatever other motives may be present). And there was no mistake about it; these new noir psychopaths often killed for kicks. Even if this thrill were not overtly sexual in terms of rape or other such violation, as a pursuit of pleasure it had a corresponding sexual component when Eros meets a displaced Thanatos. As the title of Robert Wise's film suggests, it was a world of people seemingly *Born to Kill*,[26] people for whom murder (hence sex murder) is an integral part of their personality, for self-advancement, as self-expression, and even stress relief. These killings were the domain of the psychopath figure. It informs, for instance, Uncle Charlie's murder of landladies in the true-crime inspired *Shadow of a Doubt* (1945: d. Alfred Hitchcock); the bored homosexuals trying murder as something to do in *Rope* (1948: d. Alfred Hitchcock); the giggling hit man of *Kiss of Death* (1947: d. Henry Hathaway; the perfect example of a sadistic criminal killing for personal enjoyment); and Robert Mitchum's demented Preacher in Charles Laughton's 1955 *Night of the Hunter* (a killer with echoes of true-life religion-obsessed killer Earle Nelson, who also inspired *Shadow of a Doubt*).

This murderer was essentially a loner (despite criminal connections), certainly human, tortured maybe, but "one of us" for all appearances, possibly with unsuspecting family and friends. If he had connections with non-criminals, they would always be duplicitous and manipulative, all to keep his secret passions and motives hidden as he sought whatever means to be in control, though with varying degrees of intellectual finesse and, more likely, brutality. The ruthless murderer was an almost accepted part of society in this most pessimistic of genres, and an often commanding presence (though infrequently the protagonist). No wonder then, that Fritz Lang found a second home there.

Structurally and thematically the crime movie intersected the horror film, with the resultant transposition of character

[25]See Morrison, K., "Technology of Homicide"; in Sharrett, C. (ed.), *Mythologies of Violence* (Detroit: Wayne State University Press, 1999), p. 303. The article traces murder as a literary genre founded in developing sociological interpretations of criminality.

[26]Or did society make them that way? Even in the 1940s there was the suggestion that social change, in particular, society's changing attitudes to sexual politics, contextualized a killer's imbalances. Hence *The Lodger* and *Lady of Burlesque*, which both, pointedly, feature killers who murder women partially as a reaction to society's lax standards regarding the expression of female sexuality. Of course, Hays Code restrictions prevented this theme from taking a stronger hold, except in minor film noirs. Killing was almost an impulsive reaction to stressors, signaling a murderer whose loss of control under certain circumstances resulted in homicide.

types and sociological motifs. As film noir story patterns evolved into a central character triptych of investigator/victim/psychopath,[27] so they complemented the horror triptych of savior/victim/monster. However, the resultant hybrid necessitated changes in this character hierarchy. In particular, this resulted in increased emphasis given to the monster/killer as serial murderer, especially as the 1950s stressed a behaviorist model.

Out of film noir's wake there emerged a growing interest in true-crime stories and fictional case studies. Hitchcock did *Shadow of a Doubt*, based on Earle Leonard Nelson, and *Rope*, based on a play inspired by the infamous 1924 Leopold/Loeb murder case. In the 1950s, particularly in two films by Richard Fleischer — *The Girl in the Red Velvet Swing* (1955) and *Compulsion* (1959 also Leopold/Loeb) — the true-crime story centered on murder cases which pushed at the issues of mental illness and sociological conditioning as "the reason" for their criminality. It was a qualification of the programming motif, but one which sought in part to reconcile the organic and the environmental — the killers were predisposed to such crime and, under the right circumstance, would indulge in it. The films thus posed the notion of crime as the result of the natural progression of an abnormal psyche stimulated by usually adverse circumstances.

It was the very question of their aberrant criminality, with its now exclusively homicidal component, that dominated these depictions. Thus, in addition to the tendency to contextualize and attempt to explain such behavior, there was a vigorous qualification of the appropriate social responses to such — qualifications often

lacking amidst noir's pessimism — or, in fact, the inappropriateness of current practice in dealing with and controlling, such monstrousness. It was this yearning for new directions that marked the breakaway point of the serial killer film as the response to an evolving character type.

Importantly, these latched onto a mini-trend of semi-documentary noir films that detailed the organized investigation and pursuit of a conscienceless killer whose threat to a representative society lay in his unwillingness or inability to stop his crimes. This was the manhunt, a race against time to save the next intended, random victim. It expanded the enclosed Chandler-esque detective school. Including *Boomerang* (1947: d. Elia Kazan), *Panic in the Streets* (1950: d. Elia Kazan)[28] and especially *Naked City* (1948: d. Jules Dassin), these films focused on a central two-character polarity — investigator and criminal — with the victim(s) secondary. It was the hunt for a psychopath whose identity is not known to the police or investigators, but is to the audience. Successive films would play with this narrative connection, often withholding the killer's identity until a well-judged moment. They needed to establish the killer's identity relatively early in the proceedings in order to validate a partial case study of the criminal as behaviorist observation — to study the "problem."

The corresponding de-emphasizing of the victim would be a major change in the serial killer film's evolution. The victim was now increasingly random and, as such, had no great dramatic function except as victim. Consequently, the victim received only rudimentary characterization, except when one woman was the killer's real focus

[27] According to narrative patterns outlined in Hirsch, F., *Film Noir — the Dark Side of the Screen* (New York: Da Capo Press Inc., 1981), p. 167.

[28] It's ironic that this film depicts the hunt for a plague carrier rather than murderer. The equation of serial killer to virus would be increasingly self-conscious until the profiler in *Copycat* refers to new killers as viruses, with every one a new variation.

amidst other crimes and surrogate murders. This effectively stressed the killer/investigator function; but insofar as it retained from horror the lack of faith in ordinary police work, it stressed the need for an outside force to be the killer's real nemesis. The more the films probed the nature of the killer in increasing fictional case studies[29] like *Sniper* (1952: d. Edward Dmytryk) and *Peeping Tom* (1960: d. Michael Powell), so too they developed the idea that police alone were insufficient.

"(Ab)Normal Monsters": Peeping Tom, Psycho and Successors

Two films released in 1960 would serve to aggrandize the serial killer film: Alfred Hitchcock's *Psycho* and Michael Powell's *Peeping Tom*. The former premiered to immediate acclaim and controversy in the USA, and the latter to disdain and, for some years, oblivion in the UK. Ironically, although the former was based on a true serial killer case, that of Wisconsin ghoul Ed Gein (whose exploits would also inspire *Deranged*, *The Texas Chainsaw Massacre* and *The Silence of the Lambs*), the latter had more lasting impact on the development of the serial killer film as narrative.

As was unexpectedly evident to all who saw the two films, the portrayal of the mad repeat killer had markedly changed from its horror, noir and thriller counterparts, even though *Psycho* was a variant on the burgeoning multiple-personality motif.

The killers were not only outwardly normal, but were even sympathetic to a degree. They looked plain and everyday, if a little peculiar; they had jobs; and they interacted with other people, although sometimes with difficulty (being withdrawn and vaguely effeminate). They were not the cold and calculating noir killers, although they were capable of such behavior. They seemed harmless and unintimidating, even amusing or pathetic in their occasionally awkward peculiarity. Perhaps they were physically attractive to some. They preferred keeping their distance from people for the most part, however, unless unavoidable — not a giveaway, but an unusual, and even suspicious, trait. Most importantly, each had a perverse sexuality they strove to keep hidden from the rest of the world, but which surfaced in regular homicide. They were, however, coded as neurotic enough to be different from normality[30] and thus descendants of monsters.

What defined these men as characters, and what signaled them as monstrous despite the outward facade of normality, was their pattern of sexual homicide. The key word here being "pattern" — the behavioral details of their killings (murder weapon, preamble, means, disposal, post-homicide actions, sexual expression) revealed their transgressive psyche. The repetition of the killing method became their stamp, their "signature," as modern terminology now puts it; the minor variations with each crime were merely evidence of some kind of refinement. Serial murder was a form of self-definition, self-expression, and even self-actualization that was held by society's moral and ethical codes as abhorrent,

---

[29]Indeed, the case-study aspect of fictional and real killers started in a big way in the 1950s, as did literary accounts and interpretations of true crimes. See Grant, B.K., "American Psychosis"; in Sharrett, C., *Mythologies of Violence*, p. 23. By the 1980s, serial killer memorabilia and true-crime related products, including comic books and collectible bubble-gum cards, had become emblems of a subculture which embraced transgression as communication, birthing a film movement which called itself the "Cinema of Transgression," a movement traced in Sargent, J., *Deathtripping* (London: Creation Books, 1995).

[30]Newman, K., *Nightmare Movies* (London: Bloomsbury, 1990), p. 89.

punishable by confinement or execution. Certainly it was worthy of study.

The films examined the everyday life of a killer, up to, during and beyond the triggers that sent him into homicidal fury. These triggers were now unmistakably sexual circumstances: once desire was aroused, homicidal nature emerged. Sexual stimulation had thus replaced the drugs needed to bring out Mr. Hyde. It was a battle for control over an impulse, in an environment born of abnormal socialization processes (especially an imbalance in parental relationships). There was no hope of a conventional inter-gender connection, and, increasingly, no hope of meaningful interaction or communication, despite the often earnest attempt to establish such. These people were their action.[31] Their life revolved around murder and getting away with it. They did not, or could not, stop.

To an extent, this arguably made them scarred individuals, partial tortured souls, and allowed for the familiar pattern of mental illness or at least mental distress—in Hitchcock's film most of all. Powell's film reveals the protagonist's mental imbalances but stops short of depicting this as an illness per se, and the blame for the killings rests fully on the protagonist's shoulders. With *Psycho*'s lengthy medical-testimony denouement, mental illness was virtually enshrined in the genre: indeed, the next major genre developments examined the consequences of this alliance and popularized the notion of the mad, unstoppable killer. In these films the killer's psychological difference clearly separated him from those around him, and it was often remarkable how he could stay in control. Increasingly, this killer was ever closer to a killing machine. This conception, however, countered the dictates of

the case study, which sought to explore the individuality behind the pattern. They finally resulted in a killer stripped of all personality or identity beyond that of regimented murderer, hence the development of the so-called slasher movies of the late 1970s and early 1980s, as distinct from the serial killer.

Powell, however, was not prepared to simply let mental illness excuse his character's actions. What concerns him more than Hitchcock, and what would soon become of immense interest in a legal sense at least, was not merely the killer's self-awareness, but whether or not they knew right from wrong. In short, whether they chose to act that way despite their past, or were uncontrollably and irreversibly compelled by this developmental deficiency to do so. Did they voluntarily decide to become monsters? It was as if an impulse could be triggered or voluntarily controlled. Were they themselves victims in some way — would they kill if it weren't for mom and pop?

These killers, and their successors, could still remove or conceal the evidence of their crimes to avoid being caught, and thus veil their disturbances and function semi-properly, if marginally sometimes, within the society they preyed upon. They were sane enough to know that they would be in enormous trouble, their lives at risk, if they were caught. If they had an insane motivation, they pursued it in sane and rational steps. The details of their crimes were planned out in advance, and the more practiced at it they became, the more skilled at concealing their involvement to any and all intrusive investigators. All intruders except the filmmakers, that is.

The films thus wanted to observe the killers' behavior as the clues to their char-

---

[31]This murder as self-expression theme would later combine with socioeconomic theory (mainly Marxist/Freudian anti–Capitalist) to depict killers whose murders were treated as their "work" and, later, their "art" (an interesting thematic progression, and most self-consciously treated in the 1990s films following *Seven* and *Copycat*).

acter and its cause and effect relationship to the surrounding social structure. Thus, their depiction of an investigation was in terms of psychological case study and not police procedural. The procedural aspect was thus sublimated, but rarely eliminated entirely. Many of these case studies would be devoid of a police presence until the end.[32] By the next decade, they were increasingly non-judgmental in their depictions of killers. They became controversial films, often talking points regarding social and media standards, as if examining such aberrance were tantamount to condoning or celebrating it.

In the years that followed, psycho movies, as they became known, proliferated. These included the likes of *Homicidal* (1961: d. William Castle), *Paranoiac* (1963: d. Freddie Francis), *The Strangler* (1963: d. Burt Topper), *Dementia 13* (1963: d. Francis Ford Coppola), *Maniac* (1963: d. Michael Carreras), and *Night Must Fall* (1964: d. Karel Reisz). They were clearly inspired for the most part by the enormous success of Hitchcock's films, hence their moniker. Their content was predictably similar and increasingly minimalistic in all departments. Typically, they would detail a psychotic repeat killer as he (later, even she) kills until he/she is finally apprehended and his full mental aberrance unveiled for all to marvel at. However, their motives were not always sexual, and thus the films were not all serial killer movies. The case study was balanced with the trace of the investigative story, although not necessarily involving policemen or private detectives, but intuitive non-professionals, sometimes known to the killer or even potential targets. Traditional investigators

were increasingly of little use in dealing with serial killers.[33] Correspondingly, the serial killer film sought new alternatives outside conventional law enforcement, and thus away from noir.

As these imitations became more common, so they stressed, as a saleable gimmick, the killer's method. Murder by gun, rope and knife soon gave way to axe and even oxyacetylene torch. The more bizarre and novel the type of killing, and even the killer, the more plausible it seemed that these killers were insane. There nevertheless persisted a split tendency once again between emphasizing and de-emphasizing the killer's separation from normality. A spectrum of potential behavior was thus possible, there for subsequent films to draw upon.

Although these killers lived within society and preyed upon it, many were removed from it by an increasing attention to a kind of psycho-dramatic grotesqueness, which owed less to any psychological insight into character than it did to market trends. The more bizarre, the better the gimmicks, the more chance for box-office rewards. Although most films stopped short of celebrating the killer, there was a sobering undercurrent of near glorification, especially in the post–Hays Code 1970s. A sort of wallowing in despair seemed to blossom.

This was important aesthetically, however, for it sought to depict the function of killing in the killer's fantasy as well as in the film's depiction of actuality. The experience of, and the look of, homicide (from killer's point of view, the victim's, and varied mediated perspectives) became a central aspect of the case study, given

---

[32]One remarkable aspect about *Peeping Tom* is that the killer hangs around the periphery of the police investigation into his crimes, filming the proceedings to make a record for future study. This kind of interest — in the impact the killer is having, who is investigating, and how close they are — is a trait that later FBI studies indicated as common to a large number of serial killers.

[33]Analyst Carol Clover in *Men, Women and Chainsaws* (London: BFI Press, 1992), pp. 40–41 charts how the detective plot yielded the "hero plot" of slasher movies by the late 1970s.

added impetus in the development of explicit gore with *Blood Feast* (1964: d. H.G. Lewis). With increasing attention given the role of the killer's fantasies in behavioral science, so arose the possibility of increased stylization. Another spectrum of potential approaches opened up to complement the case study range.

The *Psycho* shower scene and the gross-out mutilations of *Blood Feast* had their influence on the growing emphasis given the moment of murder as a central set-piece in the serial killer film. It was a beat, structurally almost a moment of jouissance, and one bound to be repeated with minor variation, and much desired. It was morally problematic certainly, but a crucial principle in that it allowed narrative strategy to parallel the killer's personal experience.

Thus, out of the films following Hitchcock and Powell there emerged a number of choices in the fields of narrative structure and its corresponding investigative subplot, the emphasis on the case-study aspect, and the aesthetics of murder. Yet, although these options were there, the serial killer film still lacked a singular self-conscious blueprint that contained all possibilities within it. That was soon to change.

The Boston Strangler *and Beyond*

The highest profile serial murder case of the pre–Manson decade was that of Albert DeSalvo, known throughout his 1962–1964 tenure as "The Boston Strangler." During this time, DeSalvo, posing as a handyman sent by the landlord, raped and strangled some thirteen women who had innocently let him into their apartments. His crimes escalated in sexual brutality as he started with elderly women and then chose ever younger victims as his confidence and criminal maturity grew with each "success." He would frequently insert phallic items in his victims' vaginas and deliberately pose the bodies for maximum shock value when they were found. He was flaunting his "talent" in the face of an ever more frustrated police force. DeSalvo was eventually apprehended on other charges and revealed himself as the much publicized strangler. He was later killed in prison. There were those who claimed DeSalvo was a multiple personality whose "normal" side could not remember the murders; many, however, doubt this.

Shortly afterwards, the case was dramatized in a seminal 1968 film directed by Richard Fleischer, a director unfortunately overlooked by many film scholars. More so than any other serial killer film, this one encapsulated the themes and emergent structures to date, and provided a blueprint for successive films to use. Although its influence was not altogether immediate, by the mid–1980s the narrative structures and character types it put forward were indeed central.

It combined the post-noir emphasis on the police procedural manhunt with the emergent case-study approach, and, in its introduction of a third important character type into the mix of killer/detective, pioneered what would become known as the "profiler," a figure paramount in most serial killer films since the mid–1980s. The film clearly showed that current police methods alone were unsuitable in the pursuit of a cunning, remorseless and unceasing killer who murders out of morbid sexual desire, and for whom killing has become an established routine. Indeed, the film suggested that the killer was so well integrated into society (albeit at a comparatively mundane level), and so clever and lucky at his crimes, that good fortune more than solid police work led to his apprehension.

The first act concentrates on the crimes and investigative procedures, detailing the problems faced by investigators and the media, and the social responses of a fearful and resentful populace demanding results. The second act concentrates on the killer's life and behavior, apprehension and final confrontation with the investigator. The film's structure contains a number of issues and scenes that have since become thematic, structural and stylistic conventions of the serial killer film, and are mentioned below in order of appearance. They are not all present in subsequent movies, and do not always occur in the same order, but these numbered points (and possible variations on them) comprise the schema for the modern serial killer film.

It begins with (1) a murder committed (not necessarily the first in the series), as evidenced by aftermath primarily. Soon there is (2) a scene set at the crime scene (or dumpsite in later films) where there is a partially naked female corpse.[34] This is followed by a conventional scene wherein the police chat about the case, involving (3) the confirmation of the same method used in a number of crimes, thus establishing a single killer, and (4) a discussion about the behavior and mindset of the killer as can be deduced from the crime scene details/photographs partially revealed to the viewer. References to the killer as a "full blown maniac" by detectives, who have little to go on, acknowledge the film's heritage. They continue (5)

to pursue their leads and suspect types, to no avail; hence a subsequent (6) press conference establishes the danger to the public, the police relationship to journalists (often antagonistic in later films, sometimes cooperative), and the notion of media responsibility. They follow the clues and leads once again.

When the investigation yields little, (7) pressure (from public and media) on higher authorities leads to (8) the involvement of an outside agent (here a law teacher, played by Henry Fonda, appointed as the head of a new task force). Initially (9) this causes some resentment amongst fellow officers whose jurisdiction they feel has been invaded and whose case they feel has thus been usurped. This refocuses the investigation and narrows the personality type looked for. As the police follow new strategies (including the consulting of a psychic[35]), (10) the killer is introduced in his habitat and social status[36] (or in later films, in the commission of a murder). And thusly, (11) we observe the details of the killer's life and how the pattern of murder fits into it.

Herein lies the behaviorist approach, which is present to various degrees in subsequent serial killer films, sometimes to the exclusion of the investigative plot. In particular, here we see (12) how the killer prowls his community looking for victims. Next comes (13) how he interacts with victims before, during and after the crime (the only time the victims are given char-

---

[34]In many films from the late 1970s onwards, the crime-scene sequence would be complemented by a morgue scene, in which the coroner and the detective discuss the case whilst the naked, or partially naked, female corpse is displayed on the slab (for a necrophilic tease). Often this scene would be used to establish the serial pattern of the offender, as the coroner would compare cases with similar aspects. Sometimes the victim's mutilations were displayed as freely as her nudity, equating necrophilic titillation (and desire) with bodily mutilation in a kind of cause and effect shorthand.

[35]Often in subsequent serial killer narratives a psychic is brought in as further assistance. In a mini-trend of serial killer films, the psychic fulfills the function of outside investigator, or profiler, brought in to supplement the police investigation. Frequently he (more often she) becomes the killer's next intended victim.

[36]Since this film, there have been several which elevate the social status the killer maintained until discovery. Hence the Royal physicians in *Murder by Decree*, the true-life inspired *Docteur Petiot*, the eponymous *Matador*, and, most ironically, Hannibal Lecter in *Manhunter*, *Silence of the Lambs* and *Hannibal*, who was a cannibal to boot. Although these refer back to the Jekyll/Hyde traditions and mad doctor clichés more than (cont.)

acterization is in this context and in introductory preamble leading to the commencement of the crime, unless the victim becomes a living witness/survivor). Herein we are shown what happens prior to the aftermath we had glimpsed before in the crime-scene sequences.

Finally, (14) the killer is apprehended. This leads to (15) a question of the killer's sanity and legal responsibility. Now comes (16) a confrontation between the killer and the appointee/profiler, wherein it is evident that the profiler (17) has throughout been both invigorated and drained by the hunt. The profiler revels in the later chance to confront the killer (here to talk to him, but in many subsequent films to eliminate him via a socially sanctioned killing/execution). This fact later (18) causes him some guilt and distress at his proximity to monstrousness (and/or his frustration at being unable to find the killer for so long) and how this has affected his own personality. This insight, both into the operations of the killer's mind and his self-knowledge in the wake of this, is not gained by the other investigators. This crucial point removes the Fonda character from them: this is the first major time this kind of character, the outside appointee, has featured so strongly in this context.

Correspondingly, just as the horror character division of monster/victim/savior merged with the noir triptych of psychopath/victim/investigator, so now it evolved into killer/investigator/profiler. The victim(s) were no longer a paramount dramatic component: they were functional, designed to further reveal the killer's pathological interests and desires. Surprisingly, the investigator as policeman was not replaced by the outside appointee or "profiler" figure, but complemented and

compared, as if the profiler figure were a bridge between killer and investigator, a theme explored more self-reflexively since *Manhunter* in the mid–1980s.

Insofar as many films concentrated on the killers over the investigators, they actively beckoned the audience into the function of profiler, to observe behavior objectively and deduce what they may. Thus, the dramatic function of the profiler is not only to bridge killer and investigator, but also to mediate between killer and viewer. Thus Fonda's character is obsessed with the idea of confronting the killer and conversing with him.

Most serial killer movies since then readily admit that the killer is sane and certainly does remember the crimes unless pretending otherwise. By the time of *Seven*, the senior detective cautions his younger partner not to make the mistake of automatically dismissing the killer as insane, despite the outrageous and sickening nature of the crimes. Indeed, films through the next decade would feature increasingly outrageous crimes committed by outwardly sane killers, testing the audience's belief in the sanity issue.

Thus, following *The Boston Strangler*, the serial killer film split from its generic heritage into a fully coded subgenre (even potential genre) in need of elaboration and increasingly self-reflexive delineation in terms of character function, narrative strategy, thematic base, sociological contextualization, and stylistic interpretation. All the ingredients were here, yet through the 1970s, rather than consolidate the model, the films seemed to want to splinter it, examining select components of the blueprint only, in response to an unprecedented outbreak of violent crime directed at random strangers. Nevertheless, the

(cont.) others, most serial killer films prefer their killers to be in positions or occupations more low-key. It is the killer's low profile and inconspicuousness which gives them the space to do their "work" or make their "art"—a curious progression well addressed in *Copycat* and prevalent since the mid–1990s.

killer within, who terrorizes a community, would now start to proliferate even more than the rash of *Psycho* imitators. These films sought collective categorization and definition, becoming increasingly inter-textual, as one would expect of an evolving genre.

A Splintering Effect

In the years following the Kennedy and King assassinations, there was a virtual explosion of violent crime in the USA, especially random stranger violence. So much so that by the mid–1970s there was an emphasis on new measures of criminological insight, understanding and control. Intrepid FBI agents began a process of interviewing convicted killers, rapists and other offenders in order to gather behavioral details useful for the categorization of offences and the classification of offenders. This led to the development of the FBI's Behavioral Science Unit, which specialized in the type of offender agent Robert Ressler termed "serial killer," after the cliffhanger structure of old Saturday afternoon movie serials.[37] These serial killers began appearing with alarming regularity, and media coverage made the phenomenon a neighborhood and household talking point.

Ironically, about the time that *The Boston Strangler* was released into cinemas nationwide, a real-life serial predator was stalking San Francisco. Seemingly taking his inspiration from Jack the Ripper, the killer known only as Zodiac, from December 1968 to October 1969, taunted police and press with letters specifically addressed to them. Serial murder had now become something of a game, a competitive sport, between knowing, skilled adversaries—a notion that would become increasingly self-reflexive in the serial killer film. Victims were little more than the trophies of this ongoing battle.

Zodiac made a definitive statement in one such letter, which proved at the core of the new changes in genre direction (and in partial contrast to cinematic depictions of the tortured, driven killers of *Peeping Tom* and *M*). In it he revealed, "I like to kill people because it is so much fun…. Man is the most dangerous animal of all."[38] Based on this last line and other references to movies in the letters, some people supposed the killer was a cinema buff. Zodiac continued his "fun" until inexplicably stopping in late 1969. His exploits were the basis for the influential film *Dirty Harry* (1971: d. Don Siegel), which called for new, forceful measures to deal with such ruthless killers, and was an enormous popular success.

Just as Zodiac was winding down, the Tate/LaBianca murders in Los Angeles received vast publicity. This media coverage would become a phenomenon when Charles Manson (erroneously still considered by many as a serial killer himself) and his Family of outcast hippies were taken into custody and charged with the brutal murders. They were apparently politically and racially motivated. On trial for his life, Manson had said "these children who come at you with their knives, they're your children. I didn't teach them — you did."[39] After months of trial proceedings and enormous public interest, the culprits were found guilty in late 1970–1971.

The increasingly high public profile given to these murders and murderers led films to both document and observe such

[37]Ressler, *Whoever Fights Monsters* (London: Pocket Books, 1993), pp. 45–47.
[38]See Lane, B. and W. Gregg, *The New Encyclopedia of Serial Killers* (London: Headline Book Publishing, 1996), pp. 372–373 for an account of Zodiac.
[39]Campbell, D. and C. Wilson, "Charles Manson," *Murder in Mind*, Vol. 1 (no. 9) (Marshall Cavendish Partworks Ltd., 1997), p. 6.

aberrations as a sociological phenomenon, a response to internal and external triggers, and as a personal statement. Crimes born of amoral abandon and self-indulgence were thus superimposed over, and confused with, murders committed with a seeming need to punish society for its ill treatments (whether real or imagined). The mass killer, the sniper, the serial killer were thus expressing themselves, and were perceived by some even to be social revolutionaries. In the USA of the 1970s, the cult of the anti-hero embraced the murderer as it paradoxically demonized him.

As the cult of the anti-hero thrived, it became dangerously allied to the concept of the personalized rebellion against "the system." The use of violence was a form of empowerment. This was an even more problematic association when considering a sex criminal, for it posited the random sexual killing of a woman to be a revolutionary gesture. Real-life murderer Ed Kemper targeted female college students, beheading them (amongst other necrophilic practices), partially because he wanted to hit society where he thought it would hurt most, "the best and brightest."[40] Ted Bundy, whose case formed the basis for the popular image of a charming, intelligent lady-killer, repeatedly preyed on young female college students. He once entered a sorority house and, in a mad rampage, assaulted any girl encountered in a room to room spree, killing three in dreadfully violent ways (leaving an incriminating bite-mark on one victim's buttock) before fleeing. (This event has been treated as a plot device and structural principle by many college-massacre films.) Bundy expressed no such ideological rationale.

In film, the most interesting aspect of the killer as anti-hero was that in order to qualify for such status, the killer's acts were not overtly sexual. The moment that aberrant sexuality entered the situation, the protagonist so "afflicted" ceased to have even anti-heroic qualities. Once the fantasy of ultimate power over life and death was seized upon by many filmmakers and allied to the concept of explicit sexual aberration, it removed the killer from anti-hero status and placed him in true villainhood. It was as if the sexual dimension (and its component sadism) was the most monstrous of these power-based fantasies. It was ultimately impossible to justify such sex murder as social revolution. The serial sex killer was thus excluded even from the ranks of other mass murderers: he was the epitome of unredeemable Evil.

Thus, rather than a blanket embrace of the homicidal anti-hero, there emerged films which, in response to the rise of mass murder, sought to subdivide the murderer according to the type of murder. Balancing increased criminological classifications and their corresponding application to social codes of conduct, the repeat murderer in film was tackled in many guises: the spree killer, the stalking psycho, the serial killer, and, since the late '70s, the slasher. These cinematic sub-types of killer also had their respective narrative conventions.

The spree killer embarked on a cross-country odyssey and killed those who crossed his path for thrills or for money, although he often professed to be making a kind of social statement/indictment against the perceived ills of a repressive society. He was a brash, forceful man accompanied by a (mostly willing) partner, usually of the opposite gender. Spree killer

[40]This is according to the view of 1970s America as a social climate and culture of violence that spawns mass killer after mass killer in the manner of the machine age. It is related in the documentary *The Killing of America* (1980: d. Sheldon Renan), which offers an up-close look at some of the most chilling real-life inspirations for serial killer cinema.

films were most often variations of the so-called road and youth dropout movies that emerged after *Easy Rider* (1967: d. Dennis Hopper). They are best represented by the remarkable *Badlands* (1973: d. Terence Malick), and later by the bloodily satiric and highly controversial *Natural Born Killers* (1994: d. Oliver Stone). The type is not new, however, and can be seen in noir films such as *Detour* (1945: d. Edgar G. Ulmer) and *Gun Crazy* (1949: d. Joseph H. Lewis).

The stalking psycho was a descendent of the mystery movie. A killer would target one particular potential victim, a woman, and endeavor to get ever closer to her by whatever means were available. Murders would be committed for fun or sexual enjoyment, but all in the context of his fixation on that one person. *Wait Until Dark* (1967: d. Terence Young), *Blow Out* (1982: d. Brian DePalma), and *Blue Steel* (1990: d. Kathryn Bigelow) are variations on this type. Like the serial killer's pattern, it would take place over a lengthy period of time, with breaks between murders; but unlike the spree killer scenario, it was not an odyssey of mixed crimes.

The lone slasher was closest to the conventional definition of a mass killer in that he killed a large number of people in a single small area in a short time (usually in the course of one night). He was often depicted as a punisher of sorts, chastising the young (women especially) for their sexual proclivities. He had no personality of his own and was the epitome of the killer as conscienceless, mindless, motiveless, unstoppable killing machine. Films of the *Halloween* (1978: d. John Carpenter)

and *Friday the 13th* (1980: d. Sean S. Cunningham) mode[41] typify this. It is the most recognizable of the repeat murderer types due to the cyclic popularity of the form. It is also the most despised. Recent slasher films, à la the *Scream* series and *Urban legend* (1998: d. Jamie Blanks), flirt with the serial killer pattern but differ markedly in that all the victims are known to one another, are part of a select group or clique, and thus not the random stranger victims of the serial killer.

The serial killer, to reiterate for the point of contrast, concentrated on people of a certain type, most commonly women. They were random victims generally not known to the killer or to one another. He was motivated by morbid sexual desire (unlike the slasher) and killed intimately. He would cruise for victims regularly, and each murder would be followed by a cooling-off period. The sexual aberration was the focal point of the murders. Although he would never stop voluntarily, he was not unstoppable.

As the serial killer film progressed, it soon embraced what analysts in retrospect would term a postmodern flatness of affect.[42] Killing was no longer only for pleasure, it was a task, a form of work even, and subsequent retrospective analysis would root serial murder in terms of Capitalist commodification.[43] Gone from these conceptions of the serial killer was any sense of the revolutionary. Yet this kind of crime was almost socially inherited in some way: a kind of 20th century social legacy bequeathed by Jack the Ripper. It was almost as if the notion of "the game" had become a

---

[41] See Clover, C., *Men Women and Chainsaws*; for a discussion of the slasher film form on its own terms.

[42] This is analyzed in the many interpretations of the theories of Fredric Jameson, as in Grant, B.K., "American Psychosis" in Sharrett, C., *Mythologies of Violence*, pp. 23–40 (Jameson especially p. 29).

[43] The spokesperson for this view is Robin Wood, whose influential criticism of the horror movie in Wood, R., *Hollywood from Vietnam to Reagan* (New York: Columbia Press, 1986), influences many of the essays in the anthology collection of Sharrett, C.; *op. cit.* Indeed, the confluence of Marxist and Freudian interpretations of cinema and criminality have latched onto the serial killer as the horrendous and inevitable epitome of Patriarchal Capitalism.

prestigious outing and noble pursuit, something for the elite.[44]

The sense in many serial killer films is that this murderous heritage is passed on to newer, more sophisticated killers who learn from the mistakes of others. These killers (in films of the 1980s and beyond) are often aware of other such killers (both factual and fictional), make references to them (as if quoting from acknowledged sources), and seek to experience for themselves what these killers attained from the kill. Ostracized from all, they are a breed of killer in and of themselves[45] who have access to a realm forbidden above all else. With the serial killer thus defined as the absolute nadir of criminality, what nemesis could tackle them?

The Importance of the Profiler Model

The United States was soon referred to as the serial murder capital of the world. The crimes and trials made easy headlines, and lurid tabloids exploited the details, contributing to the growth of a subculture that sprang up around the serial killer, particularly since the 1980s. Trappings include not just films, but comics, so-called fanzines, trading cards and true-crime case accounts. Documentaries, even talk show

spots reflected a fascination with these deliberate transgressors. In both the public mind and the popular cinema, new forces were necessary to apprehend these modern monsters. The direction criminological studies and cinematic interpretations were to take had its roots in an incident that occurred in 1957.

New York City had been the target of a mad bomber since 1940. This unknown culprit was on the most wanted list for some 16 years before police officers, out of desperation, chose to consult psychiatrist Dr. James Brussel. Brussel examined the available evidence (including crime-scene photos and medical records), as well as letters sent by the culprit, and gave the detectives a detailed description, or "profile." This included a description of what he felt the killer would be like (alone and in company), and where and how he lived (down to the details of how he would wear his double-breasted suit — buttoned). Based on his recommendations, investigators narrowed their search and soon the mad bomber, George Metesky, was apprehended — wearing his double-breasted suit neatly buttoned. Many in the profession were in awe of Brussel's skill and almost uncanny insight into the mind and behavior of the bomber.

The press fortuitously dubbed Brussel the "Sherlock Holmes of the Couch."[46]

[44]Correspondingly, there emerged a number of period films that explored history's most notorious serial killers. These included *10 Rillington Place, Town That Dreaded Sundown, The Todd Killings, Time After Time, Murder by Decree* and *Dr. Petiot.* These films offered little hope that such crimes would ever cease.

[45]Indeed, both *Manhunter* and *Silence of the Lambs* feature incarcerated killers consulted by investigators for their insight into an ongoing case. This actually occurred when a captured Ted Bundy offered his "advice," as recounted by investigator Robert Keppel, who consulted with Bundy on the still unsolved Green River case, in Keppel, R., *The Riverman* (New York: Pocket Books, 1985). Ironically enough, Bundy suggested (pp. 257–261) that one way to apprehend possible suspects would be to hold and stake-out a slasher film marathon, taking photos of the male viewers as they left the cinema. Bundy's reasoning was that such films offering graphic depictions of the murder of women attracted men who "want to act out violently [and] also get a thrill out of indulging their fantasies through vicarious means, through media … films and TV" (p. 257). From the killer's own mouth comes an argument ironically shared by the many opponents of violence in the movies.

[46]Wilson and Seaman, *The Serial Killers* (London: Virgin Publishers Ltd., 1997), p. 81. See pp. 81–86 for an account of the case and a consideration of the subsequent development of the art/science of "profiling" and its increased role as a practical criminological tool. Brussel's contribution is readily acknowledged by former FBI Behavioral Science pioneers John Douglas in *Mindhunter* (London: Mandarin, 1996), pp. 33–34 and Robert Ressler in *Whoever Fights Monsters* (London: Pocket Books, 1993), p. 212.

In this equation of detective and behavioral psychiatrist lay the potential solution to the serial killer dilemma. The method was set. Expert crime scene interpretation (of police and medical reports, photographic and forensic evidence, all cross-referenced with compiled statistics of past offenders) was used to determine a set of behavioral characteristics (physical and psychological) which would then enable the profiler to assess the general type of person responsible and deduce his uniqueness. Brussel said[47] that the psychiatrist examines a patient for indicators of his possible reactions to certain situations, and that the profiler in effect reverses this.

The rise of the specialist investigator corresponded to the increased funding and recognition given the FBI's Behavioral Science Unit. Since the mid–1970s the BSU had begun a process of interviewing serial killers, and compiling and cross-referencing the data. These interviews centered on behaviors so depraved that even film representations avoided their overt depiction. It was hoped that this would assist in the tracking down of other such offenders. The categorization of such serial homicides in time led to VICAP, the Violent Criminal Apprehension Program, a multi-million dollar computerized system that stores, collates and analyzes all unsolved homicides from every jurisdiction.[48] Included in this is the PROFILER program, the first computerized attempt to profile serial offenders.

Cinematically, the answer was present in Henry Fonda's part in *The Boston Strangler*, modeled indirectly on the Brussel legacy (indeed, Brussel had been consulted in the actual DeSalvo case, though with less success). Someone with specialized knowledge had to be brought in. In time, this figure would officially be known as "the profiler," a moniker taken from the FBI term for the practice above. In terms herein, the profiler figure refers to the character imported from outside the investigation, or the corresponding experienced specialist when a pair are involved.

The profiler figure was closest to the killer in that he (or she) understood, or was in the process of understanding, the killer. He was brought in as a last resort (in time this would be otherwise prioritized as the genre latched onto the importance of this figure), prompting bureaucratic wrangling in securing the proper jurisdictional clearances.[49] He was then put in charge of the case, often reluctantly. By the time of *Silence of the Lambs*, the Behavioral Science Division of the FBI was the protagonist's home and the source of all knowledge regarding such crimes. Except, of course, the killer's firsthand experience.

The profiler's prominence in the increasingly self-aware genre can be seen in the following cursory examination of some the major serial killer films since 1979, listed chronologically. Twists to the profiler concept occur in *Murder by Decree,* where no less than Sherlock Holmes is brought in to investigate the Jack the Ripper slayings—not by the police, who strongly

---

[47]As recounted by Douglas in *Mindhunter*; p. 34.

[48]See Wilson and Seaman, *The Serial Killers*, pp. 120–126 for an examination of what the system does. This database is the basis for that used in *Virtuosity* as the means for collating and loosing the ultimate serial killer. It has a more realistic function in *Kiss the Girls* as the device that effectively leads to the killers' lairs, although the plot is complicated by the familiar trait of jurisdictional dispute. Nevertheless, it has an increased prominence in the genre. In *Copycat*, through computer files the profiler matches the current killer as imitating the crimes of the past.

[49]This is a popular generic trait often used to place the investigative division at odds with the skilled outsider there invariably to steal the glory of "the collar" from the ordinary detectives or cops who really deserve it. This is a phenomenon Robert Keppel in Keppel, R., *The Riverman* (New York: Pocket Books, 1995), pp. 394–395, calls the "my case" syndrome.

resent the intrusion, but by concerned citizens who find the police both biased and inept. In *Cruising*, after routine investigation fails, a rookie is brought in and assigned a dangerous undercover mission in New York City's S&M gay world. It is ambiguous to what degree exposure to the killer's milieu, and mindset, makes the cop a potential killer himself, as if infected. In *Tightrope* and *Cop*, the policeman is forced to become profiler, as he recognizes his own psyche in the killer's methods and motivations. These two films question the necessity of the profiler by having the lone rogue cop be a virtual outsider and near pervert, much to their psychological detriment, as their chase of the killer seems an excuse to purge themselves. In *Manhunter* the central profiler, a professional in such matters, is brought back from retirement (having quit for being too psychologically corrupted by his insight into the killer's mind) when police are at a loss and time is running out before the next kill. It is assumed that his closeness to aberrance will aid him. In *Black Widow* an agent from the Justice Department tackles a case that the police do not acknowledge at first, and becomes oddly attracted to her quarry. In *Twin Peaks* the FBI agent arrives from another state to investigate a murder that baffles the local police, and in the morgue scene shows the crime to be one of a series when he removes a tiny piece of paper from beneath a fingernail. The killer is now planting clues deliberately to communicate with his nemesis, the profiler. In *Silence of the Lambs* the neophyte FBI profiler, now working for the Behavioral Science Unit, learns from her superior how to track a killer. She receives additional assistance from an incarcerated killer with whom she develops a sort of bond—the same killer responsible for the pre-retirement mental breakdown of the profiler in *Manhunter*. In *Man Bites Dog* a documentary crew do the best job of objective

profiling, they think, when they film the killer himself as he commits the crimes—to the point where they actively join in. In *Copycat* it is the profiler's very profession which makes her the target of the serial killers she studies, and of whom she remarks that they all know her and think of her as their pin-up. The killer bases his crimes on those of previous serial killers, intent on savoring what they did, and targets her personally. In *Seven* an experienced investigator close to retirement detects the links between a series of crimes intended as sermons/messages by the killer. They are ultimately powerless to stop the killer, who has incorporated their presence into his final plan. In *Kiss the Girls* a forensic detective (the same actor who played the older cop in *Seven*, Morgan Freeman) comes to a small town and provides the police with his specialized insight. It is a personal case to him, as his niece has been abducted. The killer expresses the belief that he is merely acting out the profiler's own repressed desire. In *The Bone Collector* a killer implants minute clues at crime scenes, and in codes of bodily mutilation, to speak directly to a near-paralyzed forensic profiler and author in an effort to exact revenge. In *The Cell* police seek the help of a psychologist (and near psychic) who can enter the dreams and psyche of the killer via a piece of mind-transferring equipment. In *The Watcher* a former investigator is brought into an ongoing series of crimes when a serial killer, a man who has followed him from city to city, sends him pictures of his intended victims, almost willing him to share in the crime. In *Hannibal* a cannibal killer strives to reacquaint himself with a female profiler who tried to profile and interview him, and they save each other's lives. When given the chance, the killer refuses to kill the profiler, leaving hope for their continued, almost romantic, relationship.

These examples show that the profiler has become an increasingly central aspect of many serial killer films. In particular, the relationship between killer and profiler has grown into one of near interpersonal communication between adversaries, or even potential lovers. Implied is a certain mutual need, as each gives the other professional and even personal validation through their obsession with one another. The conventional investigators stand by on the sidelines, bypassed in this process.

The profiler figure has evolved from outsider to neophyte agent to specialist. As it originated in a climate of disillusionment with governmental authority, this development is thus a means of restoring faith in a skilled patriarchal representative. In so doing, they have become the last hope of a troubled Patriarchy ripped apart from within by the killers— monstrous Patriarchs or troubled sons, depending on the film's symbolic order. As the killers target women, the profiler has the time-honored role of protector of the innocent,[50] and it is noteworthy that such a US bastion as Henry Fonda played the first effective profiler figure in *The Boston Strangler*: a considered casting decision. The outside appointee assumes responsibility for the whole.

Indeed, the profiler figure is emerging as a mythic figure in that he is cut from two opposite fields, and reconciles in his specialist knowledge the irreconcilable. The profiler knows why and how the killings occur, yet remains free from being a killer despite their understanding and even dangerous empathy for the serial killer. Thus the profiler is capable of restoring the social and ideological balance upset by the killer, and so is sanctioned to eliminate the killer.

There is a stress on the climactic confrontation between profiler and killer wherein the profiler shoots the killer, removing the threat to society and to the profiler's personal physical safety or psychological integrity. Murder and execution are thus often neatly paralleled in the genre as cathartic purification rituals. However, the killer sought transcendence, and the profiler a return to stability. Metafilmically, the killer's death removes audience responsibility for vicarious identification and provides the desirable sense of closure.

If the profiler is the modern savior of sorts, it is because he can get so close to an instrument of death as to know it intimately, and then return. He understands why a particular someone might break society's most upsetting taboos, although does not overtly wish to break them himself. The profiler has an awareness of the killer's very private fantasies. This is heavy baggage for the vulnerable to carry. To be inside the mind of a confirmed killer untroubled by conscience is not a safe place but one to visit by proxy, if the audience can trust the profiler.[51]

The Killer and the Profiler and the Fantasy

In his reinterpretation of the vampire myth in *Martin*, director George Romero contrasts the fantasy the killer, a vampire wannabe, has before committing the murder with the overwhelmingly grisly details of the crime itself: no fangs, just a razor to a woman's wrist and lapping at the resultant blood flow. This returned the genre to its Haarmann-ilk true-crime origins, and

[50]A number of films have recently put women in the role of the profiler (often, but not always, under male supervision), suggesting the incorporation of post-feminist independence into the Patriarchal order, as it is a male psychosis they seek to eliminate, yet a male order they serve.

[51]Hence the genre's movement towards the recent *The Cell*.

saturates it with an examination of the role that private fantasy has in the killer's life.

For the renewed stress on the fantasy life of the killer as a possible motivating force for the crimes, the genre looked to contrast the often banal reality of the killer's life with the flamboyantly stylized act of murder. This act was a dramatization of the killer's private fantasies, as evidenced at the crime scenes. These crime-scene "clues" were increasingly deliberate, left there specifically for the profiler/investigator to decipher.[52] The killer now even acknowledged the profiler as his equal and nemesis. They were attractants.

Distinct films constantly play with expectations about how much of the killer's life will be revealed, adopting a play between case study and psychological thriller. Hence the spectrum between revelations of the banality of the killer's life and the emphasis on its strange, threatening otherworldliness via self-conscious stylization. Even the environment of the captured serial killer is given enormous emphasis.[53]

Correspondingly, there is an expectation as to how much of the profiler's professional and personal life will be revealed in parallel. The profiler is thus frequently depicted as increasingly affected by his immersion in the details of a case, which often lasts a considerable length of time (even years of dedication and frustration). His increasing instability contrasts with the killer's apparent stability. Often dis-

pensed with in the modern serial killer film is that sense in *M* that even the human monster is a psychologically tormented man whose feelings of guilt and self-pity increase with his every lapse into desire. This is a self-conscious play on the notions of transformation and transcendence that influenced the genre's development.

Whereas once the killer's crimes were connoted in terms of transformation, ironically, the profiler also seems in a process of change and transformation, although this to him is undesirable, and he seeks to return himself, and society, to the status quo by the elimination of the transgressor. The profiler is able to resist the lure of Evil and respect society's taboos, unlike the killer, whose transgression-as-transcendence implied to him invulnerability and power.[54] Such was the fantasy: by murder, all was achievable.

This ritual of murder was the essence of the fantasy and would grow more elaborate with each kill as the killer became more confident. Whilst killing, the killer lived in the fantasy and became his ideal self, an invincible force able to act with impunity. Their crimes are thus also clearly at least partly self-esteem killings, born of a need for self-expression. Thus, within the serial killer film conventions, Mr. Hyde is not the increasingly out of control ugly side of Dr. Jekyll, but is his idealized self. But where did this process of the idealization of monstrousness begin?

FBI studies in the 1970s revealed that some level of child-parent relationship

---

[52]This has led many recent post-modern theorists to parallel the investigator in such cases to that of a linguistics expert or semiotician, there to decipher a manufactured text (a regular theme in the anthology collection of *Mythologies of Violence*). This became a thematic and stylistic choice in the films of the late 1990s, with *Seven*, *Copycat*, and *The Bone Collector*. The most controversial subtext in these films is that the act of murder is every bit as involved and complex as the creation of an artwork, and a murder scene deserved such analysis and treatment as a means of interpersonal communication.

[53]As is evidenced in the comparison of the depictions of Lecter's cell in the first two Thomas Harris adaptations, *Manhunter* and *Silence of the Lambs*. The former has the monstrous Lecter in a white, clinical environment, and the latter has him imprisoned in a dank underground modern dungeon.

[54]Recalling the delusions of *The Invisible Man*, this would beget an ontological dimension, with the killer's power over life and death in his mind akin to that of a deity, hence the visualization of the killer's mind in *The Cell*.

rk

abnormality was found in most serial killers.[55] All killers surveyed by the FBI reported suffering emotional abuse during childhood within homes not necessarily broken but severely dysfunctional. Relations between the future killer and his mother were cool and distant, unloving. Fifty percent of the killers interviewed had physically confrontational and brutal fathers, and many lacked a father figure whilst in pre-adolescence and onwards. From an early age, these future killers were drawn into an isolated world of daydreams where their hostility for the society that has so ill-treated them (whether real or imagined) could grow. They correspondingly developed into adults who were incapable of normal relationships and harbored murderous feelings, the ritualistic details of which were repeatedly rehearsed in fantasy for years before the first killing was ever accomplished.

This is, of course, an over-simplification, but these are the points that the films seized on from the real-life tragedy of circumstance. It was precisely the concept of a malfunctioning socialization process, one that fostered fantasies involving sexual aberration and a need for dominance and control over others, that fed the theory-makers. However, it was not violent trauma alone in childhood that led to murder in later life, it was the early development of homicidal fantasy, refined over a lengthy period of time.[56]

Murder was the attempt to bring the fantasy into the real world, and the continuing growth of the fantasy led to repeatedly more involved attempts. It is on the basis of fantasy that the serial killer can justify his actions, at least to himself. They thus became a threat to the very sociological processes that spawned them, processes that needed the interference and abilities of the profiler to restore them to functionality.

These fantasies were by nature marked by a strong visual component,[57] which the films are aware of in their play with point-of-view shots, altered perceptions (wide-angle lenses, color play, shadowy interplay) and compositional stresses. Indeed, the increased emphasis on stylization in the serial killer film can be seen as a partial attempt to explore and depict the role of fantasy beyond its previous limitation to the depiction of the homicide alone. Since many of these fantasies are fueled by pornographic imagery, it is a question which continually pushes the edges of what is acceptable in the genre, and is still a very problematic concern.[58]

The majority of serial killer films attempt in part to deal with the fantasies of the killer as something that the profiler must seek out. The most common way to deal with the killer's fantasy life is to suggest it by revealing details of the killer's method of murder, his behavior during the crime thus providing the evidence as to the role such killings has in his life. The stylization offers clues for the audience to intuit psycho-dramatics. In this sense, the profiler is structured as an inverse parallel

[55]The relationship between early parental bonding and subsequent deviant fantasy is explored in Ressler, R., *Whoever Fights Monsters*, pp. 115–145 and in Douglas also: it forms an increasing part of criminological theories.

[56]See *ibid.*, pp. 134–135 where, in addition, Ressler states that, "[i]t is because these murderers deal in fantasy that we characterize serial murders as sexual homicides, even when [sexual assaults] do not appear to have been perpetrated on the victim. Sexual maladjustment is at the heart of all the fantasies, and the fantasies emotionally drive the murders."

[57]See *ibid.*, p. 135.

[58]For instance, Jorg Buttgereit's much-banned cinema (the *Nekromantik* films, and *Schramm*) openly crosses the line between pornographic violence and a legitimate explicitness in the overlap of such sexual fantasy onto the killer's reality.

of the killer. His task is to probe, analyze and understand aberrance — to look as long into the abyss as possible.

This closeness over time, however, needed a purge, a moment when the profiler figure can eradicate the influence of the killer's mind from his own. Consequently, in the serial killer film there is frequently a final confrontation between profiler and killer, often to save an imprisoned or intended next female victim. Here the profiler kills the serial killer, thus admonishing aberrance and re-balancing his own psyche as he fulfills the role of savior and protector, restoring Patriarchy.

The ritual of murder is a moment of intended catharsis for both killer and profiler, but from opposite sides of the spectrum, with the profiler's purgative actions dramatically and ideologically justified as society's benefit. It is the elimination and denial of fantasy, a process considered as itself inherently transgressive and sexual. The equation of fantasy with homicide disavows its role within the proper operations of a Patriarchy that paradoxically fosters it as a means of (deceptive and hence dangerous) potential empowerment. In the serial killer film, this empowerment must be denied, punished and exorcised.

In this way, the profiler becomes the central figure of a Patriarchy in crisis, his elimination of the killer both chastising and restoring the system that produces such monstrousness to begin with. The irony and ambiguity inherent in this perspective enriches the genre. The ideology-in-crisis subtext of the serial killer film makes it a consistently valid popular forum. The serial killer is thus emblematic of a malfunctioning order, and the profiler the agent of its cure and restoration.

Aberrant desires (sexual, social, political) are thus examined, depicted as a threat, shown to be understood and controlled by suitable individuals, and finally expunged. Of course, there is a counter trend amidst many films in the genre, which takes a bleaker path by presenting the serial killer as the unstoppable force of social and interpersonal disintegration. These films inevitably do so, however, by eliminating the profiler figure. Their effectiveness springs from the audience's awareness of what the profiler figure has come to represent in the serial killer film as a distinct genre with its own set of operating narrative structures, character types, thematic base and stylistic spectrum.

SERIAL KILLER
CINEMA FILMOGRAPHY

Absence of the Good

(1999: d. John Flynn)

scr. James Reid; pr. Brad Krevoy, Kevin Kallberg, Oliver Hess; ph. Ric Waite; m. Richard Marvin; ed. Barry Zetlin; prod d. W. Brooke Wheeler; cast. Stephen Baldwin, Rob Knepper, Shawn Huff, Allen Garfield, Silas Weir Mitchell, Tyne Daly; 95m

Following the accidental shooting of his six-year-old son, a nightmare-haunted police detective (Baldwin) immerses himself in the case of "Mr. Clean," who uses a hammer to bludgeon his victims' heads but cleans up the crime scene and arranges the corpses neatly. The detectives receive profiling assistance from a police psychologist (Daly) who also tries to help Baldwin come to terms with his son's death and his preoccupation with confronting Evil. The investigation uncovers a family headed by a monstrous patriarch whose grown children become the main suspects.

The film tackles the issues of domestic violence and child abuse common to many telemovies, and roots homicidal aberration in faulty socialization: the monstrous patriarch raises the monstrous offspring. It is one's past which shapes one's present. The killer is inescapably trapped in a violent childhood, to the point of returning to previous homes to check on items hidden there when a child. He kills the inhabitants and rearranges the corpses into grotesque versions of "normal" domestic family rituals (including placing the bodies around the dinner table for a meal the killer cooked before leaving).

Director Flynn handles all of this in a coldly efficient manner that tends to negate the horror. Flynn has made intriguing studies of aberration in *Rolling Thunder* and *Best Seller* (from scripts by Paul Schrader and Larry Cohen respectively), and here concentrates on a similar theme of individuals battling determinism, as underpinned by the emphasis on steady narrative flow, a brooding, melancholic, wintry atmosphere and desaturated colors.

The protagonist, an admitted Methodist, believes that a person is either born Good or Evil, and correspondingly has no choice in their actions as adults. However, the more the protagonist learns about the killer, the more passionate he becomes, as if Flynn were suggesting that the real test of humanity is to rise above determining or entrapping circumstances. This anti-mony fuels the film, as it does much of Flynn's work. It is the horror of circum-stance which whittles away inherent Good-ness, a notion expressed by the profiler/psychologist as she observes the protago-nist's obsession with Evil.

Ironically, the only character not trapped in their past is the psychologist. It is hinted that the reason for this is her un-derstanding of the workings of Good and Evil and her ability to dissociate herself from this—her very definition as a profiler. And so the protagonist's road to personal freedom comes with his adoption of the same incisive mindset as the experienced profiler, although this at first frees his emotional expression in unguided direc-tions (he shoots and nearly beats to death the wrong man). The protagonist goes through a cathartic process of over-con-trol and near-psychotic liberation of rage, and becomes a whole character once again, able to save his marriage. This duality, be-tween entrapment and transition, is a cen-tral thematic tension within the serial killer film: the one novelty here is that it is now the policeman's function to rise to the level inhabited by the profiler. Transition is the ability to face Evil and loss, and to move through emotionless professional-ism into emotional release and so back into level-headedness. The killer, trying via murder, cannot attain such transition and is trapped in ritual. Correspondingly, Flynn's visual style stresses entrapment within the frame as contrasted to the pro-tagonist's movements through doors and into and out of rooms, at first directionless but gradually with more assertion as he follows the killer's trail.

Flynn insisted on as much accuracy concerning the procedural aspects as pos-sible, and spent much time in collabora-tion with the Salt Lake City police on lo-cation. However, the final result was considered merely formulaic and was re-leased only briefly before going to video and DVD.

Afraid of the Dark

(1992: d. Mark Peploe)

scr. Peploe; pr. Simon Bosanquet; ph. Bruno De Keyzer; spec eff. John Markwell; cast. Ben Keyworth, James Fox, Fanny Ardant, Paul Mc-Gann, Clare Holman, Robert Stephens. 91m

A community is terrorized by a slasher (and aspiring sadistic killer) who targets blind women (also in *Jennifer 8*). A young boy fears that his blind mother is in danger. The plot concerns this young boy's efforts, his own vision deteriorating, to thwart the killer. The boy's policeman fa-ther also tracks the killer, but seemingly without the same urgency. Slowly the boy realizes the killer's role in his own private fantasies.

This is another exploration of family ties and patriarchal conflicts, with the growth to maturity of a young boy con-fronting the frailty of his own physical predicament and the strength he perceives he can possibly attain through fantasy. It subsequently highlights the socialization process in the kid's relationship to his pregnant mother, and his growing friend-ship with other neighborhood people as he seeks to readjust.

The film seems intended as a treatise on abnormal adolescent psychology more than a procedural, and uses the gimmick of the serial killer as an externalization of the tormented youth's fears and desires when faced with personal trauma and the re-sentments it fosters. Thus, the film's thesis changes at the dramatic midpoint when it is revealed that the preceeding events were indeed the boy's fantasies as he is faced with impending eye surgery.

Correspondingly, the film evokes a young boy's fantasy world and then shows how it is his response to reality. The two interplay as he equates sight with reality, removing his glasses to let the fantasy world blossom. He is faced with perceived separation from his (non-blind) mother, whose attention is drawn to the baby.

Indeed, the film is an analysis of the confrontation with, and appropriation of, the aggressive male gaze as a process of self-definition. In the boy's fantasy, every male is a peeper drawn to gaze at blind women, the unknowing object of desire. All men seek to look, and the boy finally peeps at a naked blind woman posing for a photographer who, revealed to be the slasher/killer, slices the blind woman's skin, tormenting her. The boy then stabs the killer in the eye: fade to ... reality as he puts his glasses on and confronts his own image.

The boy slowly discovers the pleasure and fear in scopophilic actualization as the primary sensory mediator of reality and fantastic desire. In his myopic moments, he projects his fantasy onto reality, with violent repercussions (he stabs a dog and jeopardizes the baby). After the operation he realizes his dependence on sight, admitting, "I like looking," but also realizes the fear of losing it will always be with him.

The film is a fascinating insight into a boy's attempt to cope with possible blindness at a time of realization of the (sexual) pleasure and fear of sight. Thus it is not technically a serial killer film, but one which uses such a figure as the consequence of surrender to the male assaultive gaze, both desired and punished when acknowledged.

This was the film directorial debut for scripter Mark Peploe, who previously won the Best Screenplay Academy Award for *The Last Emperor*. It is a knowing film, drawing on the likes of *Wait Until Dark* and even *See No Evil* for its status as psychological thriller. It attempts more complexity than most, and so plays intriguingly with the notion of the interplay of fantasy and reality. However, it failed to gain a receptive audience.

American Nightmare

(1981: d. Dan McBrearty)

pr. Ray Sager; exec pr. Paul Lynch, Anthony Kramreither; ph. Daniel Hainey; m. Paul Zaza; ed. Ian McBride; art d. Andrew Deskin; cast. Lawrence Day, Lora Staley, Lenore Zann, Claudia Udy, Page Fletcher, Michael Ironside.

This standard slice-of-lifer is about a killer who targets prostitutes, drifters and street derelicts in an effort to both satisfy sexual demands and clean up the streets—the two most common "defenses" in such cases. This Canadian production, filmed in Toronto, suggests that serial killing is perhaps a US plague in danger of crossing the borders. Yet this promising subtext remains undeveloped, and the cross-section of a social order is not nearly as compelling here as in Arcand's *Love and Human Remains* (where the motivation is pure self-indulgence and resentment, an emblem of the lost Generation X).

This combines the slasher use of point of view with Italian giallo trimmings (the razor as murder weapon) and attempts a kind of kitchen-sink pseudo-pornography aesthetic which strikes one as minor Fulci or Lustig. It explores the standard sex-world familiar from countless American films to depict a culture forever verging on the exploitation of the weak. The final revelation of videotaped incestuous abuse serves to underlie an attempt at a dissection of video voyeurism, which sits uneasily with the film's emphasis on titillating female nudity. While it may implicate an evil patriarch, it does not distance itself from those values and winds up an exploitational detective story.

American Psycho

(2000: d. Mary Harron)

scr. Mary Harron, Guinevere Turner; nvl. Bret Easton Ellis; pr. Chris Hanley, Christian Halsey Solomon, Edward R. Pressman; ph. Andrezej Sekula; m. John Cale, Danny Elfman; ed. Andrew Marcus; prod d. Gideon Ponte; art d.

Andrew Stearn; cast. Christian Bale, Willem Dafoe, Jared Leto, Reese Witherspoon, Samantha Mathis, Chloe Sevigny, Justin Theroux, Joshua Lucas; 97m

Bret Easton Ellis' novel was one of the most divisive and controversial works of the past two decades. Many condemned it as violent pornography, and many others acclaimed it as an insightful satire of "yuppie" culture born of the 1980s Reagan era. The novel's blandly repetitive technique matched the character's inner emptiness and dependence on consumer products to enrich his life, to the point where he considers human beings as just another disposable product. Of course, those critics enamored of Freud/Marx analysis jumped at this viewpoint, defending the prolonged descriptions of sex and sadism as reflective of a bankrupt Capitalist soul.

Harron's film is aware of the novel's reception and serves to maintain the satire whilst downplaying the pornography. Harron also considers it a feminist film. It indeed features negative portrayals of men, suggesting that their psychology and Patriarchal Capitalist culture alone are responsible for the creation of lady-killers. Hence the film can almost be considered (as Corliss suggests in *Time*) as a comedy of manners and an indictment of male vanity (according to Roger Ebert). The point is that male immersion in the banal lifestyle of Capitalist "success" commodifies women as victims.

The killer, the impeccable emotionless yuppie, invites people into his pristine apartment, kills them by a variety of means, and then returns to work as usual, as if nothing out of the ordinary has happened. This is, of course, the serial killer enigma, but here it has the trappings of Wall Street culture, although the earlier film *The Banker* tackled similar themes. Serial murder is no longer the act of the aberrant but of the so-called privileged (Guthmann in *SF Chronicle*). Harron

stresses the killer as the epitome of the culture that spawned him rather than as a psychological portrait. Thus, as a running joke, Bale is repeatedly mistaken for another yuppie co-worker.

As usual for killer types, the killer here gradually accelerates his killing cycle as his self-control slips, something Harron represents in the third act, which some accused of over-length and tiredness. The protagonist's psychological breakdown leads him to confess, and he is ironically disbelieved (indeed, throughout the film he has made numerous statements to the effect that he is a killer, and all have been disregarded or unheard in this world of bent communication and facile meaning). Yet the killer is aware of other serial killers and indeed refers to them (Gein, Bundy) when with his friends, who invariably have never heard of them, suggesting a killer aware of heritage. The killer is narcissistic, soulless, bland and forever vacant, psychologically unknowable but culturally explainable (he even watches porno movies and *The Texas Chainsaw Massacre* interchangeably on his VCR, with sex and violence thus mere commodities also).

Harron pursues the notion that the killer is paradoxically hiding from the horrible self-knowledge he ironically seeks to discover. The closer he gets, the more psychotic he becomes. But his real triumph, and an empty one, is the realization of his own monstrousness and that murder will not bring with it the catharsis and transcendence he sought. It is even suggested that repressed homosexuality and subsequent heterosexual overcompensation may be causal factors, although the subplot involving the gay co-worker is not followed through.

Indeed, some have seen the film in part as a development of the conditioning theme in Stanley Kubrick's *A Clockwork Orange*. As Desson Howe (*Washington Post*) points out, the film's voice-over recounting of violent acts recalls that of Alex the Droog. It also can be compared to the voice-over narration in *Young Poisoner's Handbook*. Bale's character even murders a homeless person, as did Alex, and has sex with two women in a scene reminiscent of that in Kubrick's film. Yet the main difference between the two scenarios is that Alex does violent acts by choice, only becoming a victim when that choice is removed from him. However, Bateman's society has conditioned him to become a killer, perhaps beyond any issue of choice (and hence responsibility?), more akin to the conditioning theme in *The Terminal Man*. It is not a rebellion against society as much as it is the logical extension of it. For Harron, society has degenerated into a justifier of transgression without consequence (Smith in *Film Comment*).

Yet there is evidence of the killer's attempts at self-control, knowing that what he is doing is wrong, and knowing further that he is unable to stop himself (although he apparently feels enough to release his secretary from potential death). This awareness triggers his breakdown, but the realization that he can continue to get away with it suggests to him that the crimes were not of as great a magnitude as he thought: his culture can trivialize his acts. Thus he knows he will never face consequences for his murders, although this gives him no real satisfaction.

The film was originally intended for Oliver Stone, with Leonardo diCaprio to star, but that fell through and Harron took over, with Bale starring. However, there were problems filming. It was made at a time of renewed questioning of violence in the media in the wake of numerous school shootings; and Oliver Stone was in court defending charges that he had intended *Natural Born Killers* to incite violence and that the film had influenced various copycat shootings. Harron's film was to be made in Toronto, and there was supposedly (J. Sipe in *Sight and Sound*) a letter-writing campaign against this, citing the case of a real-life serial killer who kept a copy of the novel by the side of his bed. More disturbing, however, was Bale's comment that he had talked to many Wall Street types who not only liked the novel but had no objection to themselves being depicted that way, missing completely the point of the satire.

Amsterdammed

(1988: d. Dick Maas)

scr. Maas; pr. Maas, Laurens Geels; ph. Marc Felperlaan; spec eff. Sjoerd Didden; cast. Huub Stapel, Monique Ven de Ven, Serge-Henri Valcke, Tanneke Hartsuiker, Wim Zomer; 113m

A physically scarred killer in scuba gear uses Amsterdam canals as a hunting ground, coming out to kill women and then returning to his watery hideout. He pursues an investigating policeman who also has a weakness for the ladies. Thus, the two kinds of obsessional lady-killers are brought together amidst pressure on the policeman to solve the crimes before they start to affect tourism. The cynicism is not light.

There is a passing nod to the profiler figure in that the detective's daughter tries to solve the case with the help of a psychic, in order to spend more time with her busy dad. But for the most part the film was considered to be reminiscent of European thrillers of a decade before (almost comparable to the giallo in some gory scenes). However, it has a mordant humor, as did Maas' previous thriller, *The Lift* (which also starred the two protagonists here), and a jovial comic-book approach, full of lurid colors, glossy images and slightly off-kilter angles.

It follows a standard detective plot, intercutting the investigator's efforts (he consults a psychiatrist/profiler off-screen) with the killer's repeated forays. The composition stresses the killer's knife as a substitute penis, although by revealing the killer to be a radiation scarred madman thus removed from humanity, it is finally closer to a hybrid of monster movie and sex killer film, with the profiler as a throw-away cliché.

The film cleverly frames the killings amidst tourist-type shots of Amsterdam, highlighting the museum collections, canals, and the red light district at work. Needless to say, the film was a huge success in Holland and was notorious throughout Europe for its combination of tourist prettiness and scenes such as a glass-topped boatload of boy scouts going under a bridge where the body of a murdered whore has been suspended. Internet responses were positive.

And Soon the Darkness

(1970: d. Robert Fuest)

scr. Brian Clemens, Terry Nation; pr. Clemens, Albert Fennell; ph. Ian Wilson; m. Laurie Johnson; ed. Ann Chegwidden; cast. Pamela Franklin, Michele Dotrice, Sandor Eles, John Nettleton, Claire Kelly, Hanna-Maria Pravda, John Franklyn; 100m

While on a cycling holiday in France through a countryside haunted by an unsolved sex murder two years before, two girls are separated. One is left disoriented and unable to trust the strangers she meets in her search, unaware that her friend has become the victim of a sex killer. The proceedings grow ever more menacing as the protagonist wanders from village to countryside, as the film takes place entirely on a two-mile stretch of road. The film climaxes with the discovery of the missing girl's dead and raped body, with the suggestion that a lone killer still out there will continue to target young female travelers.

The killer could be anyone she meets, and she receives little solace from an uncaring police presence. Her encounters

with people, especially young men, serve to heighten the undercurrent of sexual menace that builds throughout the interplay of innocent and knowing point of view (Boot, *Fragments of Fear*, p. 225). It is almost as if such sexual aberration were inherent in the human male condition. The killer is never found and remains an absent signifier through the understandably downbeat and sinister, if contrived, film. *Variety* found the film's ambiguity about sex-murder repellent.

This film effectively details the discrepancy between the French landscape and the perverse human sexuality that seeps through it: man is unnatural. It is also one of the more interesting uses of the lost object (the dead woman) in the genre. In psychodramatic terms, it is possible that what was unstated sexually between the two friends resulted in the death. That the more flirtatious of the two ends up dead is an interesting precursor to the slasher movie's preoccupation with the punishment of sexually liberated women (a theme which infiltrated the giallo and even the European erotic film with 1969's *The Frightened Woman*).

Director Fuest, a former set designer who emerged from TV's *The Avengers*, as did the film's two scripters, went on to direct Vincent Price's demented revenge killer in *The Abominable Dr. Phibes* and its sequel *Dr. Phibes Rises Again*, and is an underappreciated figure in British horror of the 1970s. Co-scripter Brian Clemens went on to script the similarly low-key thriller *See No Evil*, directed by Richard Fleischer in his crime-mode following *The Boston Strangler* and the UK-set *10 Rillington Place*.

Angel

(1982: d. Robert Vincent O'Neill)

scr. R.V. O'Neill, Joseph M. Cula; pr. Donald P. Borchers, Sandy Howard, Roy Watts; ph. Andrew Davis; m. Craig Sefan; ed. Charles Bern-

A police detective (Cliff Gorman, right) questions teenage prostitute Angel (Donna Wilkes, center) and her street family headed by transvestite Dick Shawn (left) in *Angel* (New World, 1984).

stein; prod d. Luigi Marchione; art d. Stephen Marsh; cast. Donna Wilkes, Cliff Gorman, Susan Tyrell, Dick Shawn, Rory Calhoun, John Diehl, Donna McDaniel, Steven M. Porter; 94m

Primarily about the lifestyle of a fourteen-year-old high school girl who works as a prostitute by night, *Angel* has a subplot about a serial killer targeting the street people she knows. However, unlike most exploitation films, this one ridicules the mother-haunted killer (as Kim Newman points out, p.154) and seems intent on being a character study of streetlife in the vein of Scorsese and Schrader, although more sympathetic, even kind, to its people.

Actually, the film proposes that surrogate family unity, however unconventional it may be, enables the disenfranchised to find some kind of identity on the mean streets. Ironically, the only real loners are the cop and the killer. Conventional family has failed in the protagonist's case, as it has for all of society's outcasts (transvestites, aging street performers), forcing them into makeshift unions of sorts in the effort to catch the killer (shades of the criminal underworld of *M*).

The film is also part of the mid–80s rise in seedy neo-noir à la *Hardcore*, but it fails to achieve the mean-spirited mastery of *Vice Squad*, for instance. However, it has been compared to Ken Russell's *Crimes of Passion*, also about a prostitute with a double life who is stalked by a killer. The main difference is that Russell's film is about the lack of meaningful communication and interaction between people, whereas O'Neill optimistically stresses interpersonal bonds between essentially likeable outcasts. Russell stresses the sex and violence as symptomatic; O'Neill downplays it as aberrance. Still, it was successful enough to rate two sequels, despite its comparative lack of sexual content.

Some scenes eroticize the teenage whore but steer clear of any overt sexual display; as a result, the film is curiously unexploitative. Scenes showing the protagonist at school (in uniform) and then changing into makeup and skimpy clothes (another uniform) suggest the transformation from girl to woman; although it presents such sexual awareness in terms of prostitution, it partially roots this in the absence of a mother figure. It is this trait of a malfunctioning bond with mother that links both protagonist (as potential victim) and killer. She has been deserted by her mother, who abandoned her to go off with a lover, and longs for the return of her father (a function eventually fulfilled by the policeman). The male transvestite fulfills the role of both mother and father in the absence of the real parents.

The killer is obsessed with physical discipline, and is a narcissist who considers himself better than the world around him. O'Neill reverses this, suggesting that although all the characters are products of their environment, the dispossessed and disenfranchised can rise above it, unlike the killer (though he is shown cleaning himself after each crime, as if in a purification rite). In his demented way, he saves victims from the street-life, much as it is suggested the policeman wants to do, to save the protagonist from her lot. Thus, the film establishes good and bad fathers at a surrogate level only. If the killer is a symbol of urban disaffection, then the film comes in favor of victimology and is thus rare in its emphasis on the types of people usually considered "disposable" in the genre in terms of narrative function and characterization.

The film is more complex and interesting than its lack of reputation suggests; it is considered to be let down by mediocre performances. One cannot fault the cinematography by Andrew Davis, later a mainstream Hollywood directorial success story. O'Neill, however, drifted into obscurity, despite helming the sequel, which strains the sense of community found here.

Apartment Zero

(1988: d. Martin Donovan)

scr. Donovan, David Koepp; pr. Donovan, Koepp; ph. Miguel Rodriguez; m. Elia Cmiral; ed. Conrad M. Gonzalez; prod d. Miguel Angel Lumaldo; cast. Colin Firth, Hart Bochner, Dora Bryan, Liz Smith, Fabrizio Bentivoglio, James Telfer, Mirella D'Angelo, Francesca D'Aloja; 121m

A struggling Buenos Aires cinema owner (Firth) needs money to continue to run the cinema and keep his mother in a home. He takes in a handsome American man as a flat-mate and slowly becomes infatuated with him, sensing the same in the roommate. However, this roommate (Bochner) may be a serial killer and ex–death squad member. Once Firth discovers this, he helps conceal a murder and then kills his flat-mate, keeping the body as a souvenir. He turns the ailing cinema into a commercial venture, as if becoming a murderer solved his problems.

In addition to the psychological and sexual depiction of the serial killer, this has a political context. The killer, whose method is identical to that used by Argentine death squads headed by foreign mercenaries, is unquestioningly continuing what he has trained for even after the political use has expired. He is in that sense the individual product of a collective monstrosity that sanctions murder. His mutilation of usually male victims speaks to his own sexual resentments, as if murder were release and purge, whatever political cause he may claim to serve.

The film is saturated with a homosexual subtext, with Firth's infatuation with masculinity reflecting his desire to eroticize and possess. This desire has monstrous consequences when Firth is so swept away that he covers up the murder/mutilation of a friend. Realizing his complicity, Firth's murder of Bochner is not out of guilt or remorse but the desire to preserve what they had: keeping the rotting body with him for some time afterwards, he kills for company (as did real-life homosexual killer Des Nilsen). His sexual expression results in murder. The process of transcendence thus complete, he is more relaxed and confident, changing the movies he screens in his cinema from classics to porno (albeit cult porno—*Cafe Flesh*). He has become another killer, free from repression.

Yet Bochner's easygoing exterior is a pretense, concealing an inner turmoil and fear that surfaces on occasion. His murder is the programmed means of dealing with internal stress, a means of self-validation that paradoxically causes him some remorse—a process in which he initiates Firth. Thus, when his murder is discovered by Firth, Bochner is in a tearful daze, saying that he will go and put on the mask and that everything will be alright: he is aware of his nature and erects a facade to rationalize it, as does Firth. Bochner destroys in order to use rather than confront; Firth destroys to preserve.

David Koepp and director Curtis Hanson reworked this for the Americanized remake, *Bad Influence*. This film submerged the sex killer angle and the political context, and arguably downplayed the homosexual undercurrent.

Apology

(1986: d. Robert Bierman)

scr. Mark Medoff; pr. Les Alexander, Richard Parks, Richard Smith; ph. Phil Meheux; m. Maurice Jarre; ed. Jim Benson; prod d. Ben Edwards; cast. Lesley Ann Warren, Peter Weller, Charles S. Dutton, Harvey Fierstein, John Glover, Richard Zavaglia; 98m

A trendy artist (Warren, playing the combination of independence and vulnerability she essayed so well in *Cop*, another noirish thriller) wants to personalize a sculpture exhibition by playing recordings of anonymous apologies. She thus publicly invites people to call a special number and leave a message, confessing a sin and apologizing for it. One of the callers is a serial killer of homosexual artists who confesses his crimes—and announces more. Of course, she goes to the police. In a twist, they believe the messages are real, but she thinks them fake. It is back to convention, however, as cop (Weller) and killer both fall for her, resulting in a standard triangle fare telemovie which, in its return to killer/victim/investigator prototypes, seems intended as Hitchcockian.

The most disturbing suggestion is that the killer murders partially in order to have something to feel guilty about, and confesses to grab attention, although he clearly loathes homosexuals. The film makes these hate-crimes all the more repugnant for the callousness and sensationalistic intentions of the killer. In so doing, it is one of the comparatively rare number of films to deal with homophobia, although it lacks the intensity of the superior *Cruising*. It does not develop the culture that would provoke such hate crimes, however, preferring to depict art-world stereotypes as mere background. Thus, it never really explores homophobia except as plot contrivance. The killer amidst the art world would be more satirically treated in *Still Life*.

The Arousers

(1970: d. Curtis Hanson) aka *Sweet Kill*

scr. Curtis Hanson; pr. Tamara Asseyev; ph. Edward Anderson, Floyd D. Crosby, Daniel Lacambre; m. Charles Bernstein; ed. Gretel Erlich; cast. Tab Hunter, Isabel Jewell, Angel Fox, John Aprea, Roberta Collins, Sandy Kenyon, Cherie Latimer, Nadyne Turney; 85m

Long before the success of *LA Confidential*, director Hanson helmed this case study of a serial killer (Tab Hunter) in Venice, California, who kills women in a rage, projecting his sense of inferiority onto them as he blames them for his impotence. Murder restores his private sense of potency and is a form of compensatory sexual self-actualization. There are apparent similarities between the killer here and the murderer played by Tom Berenger in Richard Brooks' *Looking for Mr. Goodbar*.

A low-budget, B-movie approach helps to establish this film as one of the first in a trend of 1970s psycho-portraits that would culminate in the early 1980s works of William Lustig. Unlike Lustig, however, this portrait does not immerse itself in the horror genre (although it does contain gore), and seems to aim for a sociological perspective. Hanson would return to portrayals of disturbed psychopaths, notably DeMornay in *The Hand That Rocks the Cradle*, as he segued into more conventional thrillers and mainstream Hollywood acceptance.

The Arrival

(1992: d. David Schmoeller)

scr. Daniel Ljotka; pr. Ron Matonak, Gary Schmoeller; ph. Steve Gross; m. Richard Band; ed. Randy Bricker; prod d. Michael Scaglione; cast. Robert Sampson, Joseph Culp, John Saxon, Michael J. Pollard, Stuart Gordon, Carolyn Purdy-Gordon, Robert Culp; 107m

In between his work for Full Moon head and producer Charles Band, Schmoeller did this remarkable blend of serial killer film and stranded-alien science fiction. The plot concerns an alien who takes over the body of an old man, en-

abling the body to grow younger by ingesting the blood of pregnant women, who are killed in the process. The crimes are considered the work of a sex killer and tracked accordingly by investigators.

It is a film about rejuvenation, however, and elaborately sets up its premise of an old man seeking a new life, at whatever cost. His selfishness, here combined with biological need (recalling the vampire movie origins), leads to the sexual mutilation being almost incidental, and the killer seems to take little additional pleasure in it, accepting it as part of his existence. Thus, like many of Schmoeller's films, it tackles the perversion of the sexual impulse, transcending the genre trappings it exploits.

The need to feel young, and to absorb the life of his victims, turns him into a sexual predator. However, the film explores the serial killer enigma almost as a note of tragedy, as the killer is aware of his monstrousness but cannot bring himself to stop completely. Once he discovers intimacy with a woman (like the killer in *Manhunter*), his perspective is changed, momentarily. However, by having him finally trapped by the pursuing police, using the woman as bait, the film avoids a scene in which the killer is forced to exercise his potential newfound choice. The woman feels affection for him, even when she is told of his monstrousness, and the film teeters into a doomed, even tragic romance story in its second half.

With its alien killer, *The Arrival* is similar to Cardos' *The Dark*, with an emphasis on sympathetic characterization and a clever exploration of how love can almost conquer the monster, a theme found in such a diverse work as Chabrol's *Le Boucher*. Its alien pursuit suggests the film is a more malevolent reading of John Carpenter's *Starman*, and indeed it is a very allusive and mature work, possibly the director's best, although it was generally ignored or dismissed on release. Schmoeller, whom Stephen King has described as his favorite director, tackled the sex killer in the fantasy-tinged *Tourist Trap* and the provocative *Crawlspace*, an equally underrated film.

Arsenic and Old Lace

(1944: d. Frank Capra)

scr. Julius J. and Philip G. Epstein; ply. Joseph Kesselring; pr. Capra; ph. Sol Polito; ed. Daniel Mandell; cast. Cary Grant, Priscilla Lane, Raymond Massey, Jack Carson, Peter Lorre, James Gleason, Josephine Hull, Jean Adair, John Alexander; 118m

This peculiar blend of comedy and domestic monstrousness has two daffy aunts, outwardly shining examples of Brooklyn high society, secretly poisoning their boarders (to save them from misery, it seems) and storing their remains in the cellar. Their nephew (Grant) discovers their method of apparent mercy killing, which has gone undetected for years. All is further complicated when Grant's brother, a murderer on the run, arrives to hide out with the aunts, and is accompanied by a peculiar doctor (Peter Lorre, thus suggesting a link to *M*).

This is an adaptation of a long-running Broadway hit, which Capra directs with a careful eye on slapstick in the latter stages. It was supposedly a much-cherished project for Capra, who adored the stage version and had to work for a different studio (WB) than he was contracted to (Columbia) in order to get it made. What started out as a low-budget comedy became an A-picture when the highly paid Grant agreed to star. Still, Capra worked dedicatedly to retain the theatrical basis, using only the one interior set of the aunts' house and one exterior near a cemetery. Most critics found the film a superb entertainment that captured the morbid spirit of the original play, and another Capra triumph.

Perhaps most notable about it from the perspective of the serial killer film's evolution is the depiction of the home as murder site, however encapsulated in late-entry screwball comedy about secret identity. It shows that serial murder need not be taken solemnly, and that monstrous aberrance can pervert the most benevolent of motives. The sheer incongruity of such harmless eccentricity concealing such horrific monstrosity signals an interest in the depths of human experience.

Art of Dying

(1990: d. Wings Hauser)

scr. Joseph Merhi; pr. Joseph Merhi, Richard Pepin, Charla Driver; ph. Richard Pepin; m. John Gonzalez; ed. Geraint Bell, Paul G. Volk; prod d. Greg Martin; cast. Wings Hauser, Sarah Douglas, Cary Werntz, Michael J. Pollard; 90m

This film has a pair of urban snuff filmmakers attracting young aspiring actresses, then filming their murders, staged as scenes from famous movies (*Deer Hunter*, *Joan of Arc* and *Psycho*, of course), making it akin to the superior *Fade to Black* in that aspect. When a detective on the trail of young runaways finds the corpse of someone he knows, he becomes obsessed with finding the cine-literate killers, even to the point of endangering his current girlfriend.

This woeful attempt at a noir slasher film is the weakest, and at the climax most reactionary, of the numerous depictions of snuff movies in the 1980s, following *Hardcore*, *8MM* and especially the similarly plotted *Special Effects*, which all seek to reveal the sleazy side of Hollywood pornography. In spirit, it is closer to the vigilante-themed Charles Bronson films *Death Wish* and *Ten to Midnight* than it is to the darker implications of its pair of killers, whose joint psychology is almost completely undeveloped. As such, there is little more than efficient formula here, although the self-aggrandizing vigilante motif is common to Hauser's other films as director, suggesting some personal investment in the theme.

Any hope of a return to the truly noir world of Hauser's villainous turn in *Vice Squad* is quickly dashed. In style it is closer to anonymous action fodder and, in fact, was an early collaborative effort from the prolific producer duo of Joseph Merhi and Richard Pepin, who would later jointly unleash a string of generally undistinguished action movies into video stores worldwide.

Its central thesis, which allies film study and ambition to the production of a feature length snuff movie, promises to be an indictment of a genre. However, the film is too routine to develop the interplay of scopophilia and violence, and any hope of a return to *Peeping Tom* is soon lost in amateur performances and merely competent direction. It is, however, an ambitious (pretentious?) debut, exploring the nature of point of view, and there are some on the Internet who consider it a neglected thriller.

Assault

(1970: d. Sidney Hayers)

scr. John Kruze; nvl. Kendal Young; pr. Peter Rogers; ph. Ken Hodges; m. Eric Rogers; ed. Tony Palk; art d. Lionel Crouch; cast. Suzy Kendall, Frank Finlay, Freddie Jones, James Laurenson, Lesley-Anne Down, Tony Beckley, Anthony Ainley; 99m

A serial rapist/killer stalks and strangles schoolgirls who wander unescorted through neighboring woods. A living victim is too deep in shock to be of any help, and the detective (Finlay) is floundering. An art teacher, disturbed by the growing number of victims, offers herself as a decoy to aid the police in luring the killer out from suspects who include a journalist, the principal's sleazy husband and a young doctor.

Although in plot this anticipates the girl's school stalker movies of the post–Bundy slasher film, its use of discreet editing during rape scenes suggests its more English origins. It was considered nothing more than an undistinguished thriller from a once-more-capable director. Nevertheless, it has some tangential interest when compared to the early 1970s films of Robert Fuest, also made in the UK with similar material (most notably *And Soon the Darkness* and its hidden depiction of sex killer psychology). Its view of violent male sexual aberration was thought conventional by comparison.

Hayers limits the locations to the school, hospital and immediate woodland surroundings, stressing the sense of a community under threat from a sex killer, thus echoing many early European thrillers about roaming threats to villages. The limited settings and time frame anticipate the structures of the slasher film of a decade later. It has some historical interest because of this, and as a demonstration of the movement to update English horror in the 1970s as Hammer declined.

The producer is better known for his involvement in the sexual-innuendo-heavy *Carry On* series of comedies, here broadening his scope when he made a deal with Rank to produce other projects (thrillers and romances for the most part). None of these non-comedy efforts has proven to have any longevity.

Atlanta Child Murders

(1985: d. John Erman)

scr. Abby Mann; ph. Victor J. Kemper; m. Billy Goldenberg; ed. Neil Travis; prod d. James Halsey; cast. Calvin Levels, Ruby Dee, Morgan Freeman, James Earl Jones, Alley Mills, Bill Paxton, Felton Perry, Jason Robards Jr., Andrew Robinson, Martin Sheen, Rip Torn, Lynne Moody, Gloria Foster, Paul Benjamin; 245m

This is an excellent, if controversial, account of the case of Wayne Williams (talked about also in both the Douglas and Ressler books as a model case of profiling). This devotes as much time to police procedures as it does to a depiction of Williams, which some critics felt cast doubt upon the guilty verdict found against him. At any rate, one cannot ignore the sociological factors and pressure which serve to contextualize the killer, and the subsequent delineation of public and internal pressures on law enforcement.

The film is careful not to implicate Williams fully, instead examining his actions as both the product of personal arrogance and his resentment of the community he is a part of and thus preys upon. Williams' guilt and calm superiority under immense pressure is explored via his personal response to the charges, that of his disbelieving relatives and a shocked, outraged and equally disbelieving community who feel that one of their own could hardly be responsible. They are forced to confront the monstrousness within their collective self, and forced to seek reintegration in response.

It is arguable to what extent this is racial in origin, with Williams targeting other Afro-Americans, perhaps resenting his own racial stereotypes. However, what is intriguing is the depiction of the automatic assumption that the killer of black children must be a white supremacist, and thus the corresponding misapplication of police efforts. The outside FBI profilers brought in serve to direct the investigation onto its proper course. It is a study in controlled reaction to mounting pressure.

The Avenger

(1960: d. Karl Anton)

scr. G. Kampendonk, R. Cartier; pr. Kurt Ulrich; ph. Willi Sohm; cast. Heinz Drache, Ingrid van Bergen, Benno Sterzengbach, Ina Duscha, Ludwig Linkmann, Klaus Kinski; 100m

This German film, set in England, actually serves as a model of the emerging serial killer subgenre. A killer, complete with gorilla-like servant (a tribute to the demented doctor and crazed sidekick films beloved in European horror), decapitates his victims and then taunts society by mailing the heads randomly. Scotland Yard are baffled by such a new kind of crime, and an outside detective (hence an early profiler figure) is brought in to help stop the killer. A subplot about such efforts involving the rescue of an actress from the madman serves to illustrate the women-in-peril scenario even further.

The Avenger is one of a number of England-set German thrillers filmed during the 1960s (which included *Dark Eyes of London*), yet an expressionistic technique is said to be curiously absent. Klaus Kinski has a cameo role as what Hardy et al. (p. 136) term a misanthropic film director for some meta-filmic subtexts along the lines of the contemporarily released *Peeping Tom*. *The Avenger* has added interest for its continued incorporation of the agent/controller character pattern into the serial killer procedural, a device that remained especially popular in Europe and can be seen in the films of Jess Franco especially.

The Awful Dr. Orlof

(1962: d. Jess Franco)

scr. Franco; pr. Serge Newman, Leo Lax; ph. Godofredo Pacheco; cast. Howard Vernon, Conrado San Martin, Perla Cristal, Diana Lorys, Riccardo Valle, Maria Silva, Mara Laso, Felix Dafauce, Faustino Comejo; 88m

One of the prolific Franco's most enduring films, this is a remake of Franju's acclaimed *Eyes Without a Face*, wherein surreal images become the location of visceral horrors. The title doctor, aided by a devoted, blind criminal named Morpho, kills women and removes their facial skin in order to graft it onto the face of his horribly disfigured daughter. Morpho then disposes of the bodies after, it is suggested, satisfying his necrophilic molestations. A police detective is assigned to investigate the disappearance of five such women. His ballerina girlfriend arouses the killer's interest, and she thinks she can capture him herself. The detective must come to her rescue.

With some scenes constructed as a kind of necrophilic tease (lingering on a naked female corpse), the film effectively links gore with pornography, eroticizing surgical mutilation. The link to Jack the Ripper and to the German Edgar Wallace mysteries (Tohill and Tombs, p. 77) is made explicit as the title doctor, often in a horse-drawn carriage, takes to darkened streets to stalk his next victims, women whose open sexuality arouses him. Whereas Franju preferred the poetic, Franco stressed the graphic component of horror and, with an unusual jazz score, crafted a film that pushed the boundaries of acceptability as he aimed for a Continental audience outside his native Spain.

This film is an example of the European school of surgical horror. It has shades of *Caligari* and features an explicit reference to the Bluebeard legend (which the press inevitably seizes upon). It balances procedural aspects with some style, but central is the theme of how love and passion can warp a "good" person into committing acts of vile, evil cruelty. Thus, it explores the notion of sexual homicide born of obsessive love, the victims as substitutes for that one love. The Sadean corrupts the Romantic. Both policeman and doctor are gentlemen who seek out beautiful women, but only the latter is corrupted by his Sadean impulses; ironically, in the name of the preservation of one's beauty, he sacrifices others. In subsequent films, Franco would be ever more explicitly Sadean in context. Still, it's another good

vs. bad Patriarch movie, with the doctor both loving and resenting his daughter. Typical of agent/assistant European narratives, the servant Morpho, his love-object destroyed, finally rebels against his master.

Franco would make a career out of sex and sadism films, often incorporating hardcore porno footage. However, with few exceptions, he would never equal the noirish morbidity of this film. He flirted with the figure of the serial killer by making his version of *Jack the Ripper* and several sequels to this demented surgeon movie.

There have been those who consider this film part of a Spanish nouvelle vogue in the early 1960s, and the first Spanish horror film. It has been considered a reaction to the growing popularity of Hammer releases, which Franco saw and admired (even though he felt them restrained in their depiction of aberrant sexuality). There are more, however, who consider the film a sensationalistic and offensive piece of exploitation. Two versions of the movie were released, one uncut for the French but the other modified for release in Spain, the United States and the UK.

Baby Doll Murders

(1992: d. Paul Leder)

scr, pr, ed. Paul Leder; pr. Ralph Tornberg; ph. Francis Grammon; m. Dana Walden; cast. Jeff Kober, Bobby Di Cicco, Michael Ennis, John Saxon; 90m

A serial killer strangles beautiful, large breasted women. He leaves a small doll beside each victim, signing the crimes. The cop on the case believes that a recently released ex-con is to blame. He harasses the suspect, until it is revealed that all victims were former patients of a rich Beverly Hills doctor. With this, the investigation changes direction.

This totally unremarkable thriller, in which the female victims are all nude or in the process of undressing when murdered, allies male desire to homicide in the most callous and sensationalistic manner of the worst slasher films. A routine detective story is thus punctuated by sex and violence in the manner of the 1990s rash of mostly video and cable released "erotic thrillers." The killer is the cop's partner, whose wife had aborted his son and who now takes out his resentment on women who have had abortions, a plot hook similar to that in *Criminal Law* and *Sacrifice*. Director Leder is responsible for many exploitation films along these lines, all critically disregarded.

Backdraft

(1991: d. Ron Howard)

scr. Steven E. deSouza, Gregory Wilden; pr. Pen Densham, Richard B. Lewis, John Watson; ph. eff. Mikael Salomon, m. Hans Zimmer; ed. Daniel Hanley, Michael Hill; prod d. Albert Brenner; exec pr. Brian Grazer, Raffaella DeLaurentiis; cast. Kurt Russell, William Baldwin, Robert DeNiro, Donald Sutherland, Jennifer Jason Leigh, Scott Glenn, Rebecca DeMornay, Jason Gedrick, J.T. Walsh, Clint Howard; 135m

This is not a serial killer film, yet it uses elements of it to intriguing effect. Two brothers, both firemen, are forced to deal with a serial arsonist. To learn more about the arsonist's possible psychopathology, they visit an imprisoned serial arsonist (Sutherland), hoping for his insight. This plot point, of an imprisoned offender being consulted, was featured earlier in *Silence of the Lambs* and thus incorporates the profiler mystique into the film's narrative, as well as the suggestion of a classifiable psychology responsible for such acts: aberrance knows aberrance.

Donald Sutherland is meekly chilling as the arsonist whose help they seek (based on the Ted Bundy consultations yet again). He is depicted as a sniveling weakling fully aware of his own disturbance and sexually excited by it. Ironically, he is unable to lie,

although he ceases to be the cowardly milquetoast when talking about the disturbed mind, priding himself on his knowledge of perversity. It is clear that he will never change. Once such crimes are an expression of sexuality, they are inescapable. Despite his assistance in the case, the arsonist on the loose turns out to have a quite different, and even supposedly altruistic, motive — to keep the department on solid ground: the corruption of benevolence. Thus, the two motives are compared and contrasted, yet the arsonist on the loose would divorce his higher motives from those of Sutherland, although the latter has insight into the former.

The Banker

(1989: d. William Webb)

scr. Dana Augustine, Richard Brandes, William Webb; pr. Webb; ph. John Huneck; m. Reg Powell, Sam Winans; ed. Patrick Dodd; prod d. James Shumaker; eff. Wayne Beauchamp; cast. Robert Forster, Duncan Regehr, Shanna Reed, Jeff Conaway, Leif Garrett, Richard Roundtree, Deborah Richter, Teri Weigel; 90m

An investigating officer (Robert Forster) is determined to prove that a prominent financial investor is responsible for the ritual murder of high-priced call girls, all found with a bizarre symbol marking their bodies, suggesting a link to primitive cultural practices. Indeed, the killer's murders are part of a South American ritual as he fanatically smears himself in paint. His weapon of choice is a crossbow, and his stalking practices indicate that serial killing to him is also a kind of hunt. Thus develops the *Most Dangerous Game* potential. A reporter (Forster's divorcee) inserts herself into the investigation. Another criminal uncovers the banker's involvement and tries to blackmail him, but the banker hunts him down.

The sex scenes with call girls are shot with an attempted elegance akin to the "erotic thriller" movement, with the

murder by crossbow as a violently penetrative act from which the killer must
shower in a cleansing ritual purge. Indeed,
the film depicts one of the more heavily
ritualized serial killers. Typically, it is the
crime scene that serves to establish the serial pattern and suggest the supernatural
overtones, serving to define the investigator as nemesis.

The film critiques media involvement
in such cases. The intrepid and ambitious
reporter is contrasted to a caricaturish
dumb blond anchor/host. When the powers-that-be cut off the reporter and put on
a commercial before she can fully finish the
report and warning, she concludes that the
media trivializes murder: a view the film
endorses. Her idealism costs her the job,
though she is later reinstated for the ratings. Yet, interestingly, her persistence as
an outsider equates the role of reporter to
that of profiler, a concept also explored in
The Mean Season. Still, the film questions
her tactics, as she gives away the killer's
method when it would perhaps have been
better withheld.

The killer, who is obsessed with killing, spends his spare time surrounded by
TV screens. He enjoys the sadistic torment
of victims, loosing one in a deserted building and then hunting her down. The cop
is pressured from above to solve the case
and knows that his quarry has the trappings of the rich (money found at the
crime scene). However, their final confrontation lacks the expected sense of
cathartic purge via the killer's execution,
instead having the cop rescue the reporter.

The screenwriter asserts that this film
was redistributed to capitalize on the
Tarantino connection of star Robert Forster from *Pulp Fiction*. However, the film's
main interest lies in its depiction of a yuppie killer and the corresponding link between Capitalist enterprise and ritual sex
murder. This is along the lines of *American
Psycho*, though perhaps more appropri-

ately an extension of the Michael Douglas
character in *Wall Street* and even a dark
take on *Pretty Woman*. The rich murder
women as a kind of modern sport, linked
to occult practices, as a form of personal
empowerment and ritual sacrifice for continued "success." It is in these suggestions,
and the attempt to reintroduce the supernatural into the serial killer film, more
than the execution thereof, that the film
works best.

Barton Fink

(1991: d. Joel and Ethan Coen)

scr. Joel and Ethan Coen; pr. Ethan Coen, Ben
Barenholtz, Bill Durkin, Jim and Ted Pedas;
ph. Roger Deakins; m. Carter Burwell; ed.
Michael Berenbaum, Roderick Jeynes; prod d.
Dennis Gassner; cast. John Turturro, John
Goodman, Judy Davis, Michael Lerner, John
Mahoney, Tony Shalhoub, Jon Polito, Steve
Buscemi; 116m

Only incidentally a serial killer film,
this bizarre comedy concerns a New York
playwright who is invited to Hollywood
(circa 1940s) to become a screenwriter.
Struggling with writer's block in his hotel
room, he befriends an insurance salesman
(Goodman). When he awakens near a de-
capitated lover, his friend helps him. The
police arrive and inform him that his
friend is a wanted serial decapitator, "Madman Munt."

The film tackles the shattering of idealism and the inability to communicate.
The protagonist, in his quest for the soul
of the working man, is unable and arro-
gantly unwilling to listen to the genuine
article when confronted by it. He is too
ready to pre-judge and dismiss, shocked
when his perception is revealed to be false.
Thus, the working class everyman he idealizes is revealed to be a beguiling serial
killer: the film subverts the protagonist's
idea of the nobility of the common man.
Ironically, it is the serial killer who is the
most tormented figure, despite the pro-

Hit playwright Barton Fink (John Turturro, left) with his new friend, a jovial insurance sales-man (John Goodman, right) who is also a serial decapitator, in *Barton Fink* (Fox, 1991).

tagonist's soul searching, at home in the living hell that is the "life of the mind" the protagonist falsely lays claim to. Ultimately, Fink realizes that, as he said, we are all alone in the world: he just didn't know how entrapped.

This is the bleakest of the Coens' movies. It was both hailed as brilliant and dismissed as pretentious when released. Like most of their films, it appeals to a set fan-base. The surrealistic Hotel Hell sequence has the same macabre humor as in the films of their friend Sam Raimi, with whom they co-wrote the ill-fated *Crime-wave*.

Bells

(1981: d. Michael Anderson) aka *Murder by Phone*

scr. Michael Butler, John K. Harrison, Dennis Shryack; pr. Reginald Morris; m. John Barry; ed. Martin Pepler; prod d. Seamus Flannery; cast. Richard Chamberlain, John Houseman, Sara Botsford, Gary Reineke, Barry Morse; 79m

A police officer and science teacher (the profiler figure here as outsider) are hard pressed to stop a killer (an angry ex–phone company employee) who has invented a device which kills those answering the phone (by causing a brain hemorrhage and then transmitting a large electrical discharge). The more the teacher investigates, the more he uncovers possibly conspiratorial research.

The film depicts a revenge killer targeting victims whom he feels have slighted or belittled him in some way. Women are the focus of his anger, his sexual insecurity requiring such a cowardly form of murder as a kind of overcompensation. Director Anderson uses a handheld camera for the killer's point of view shots to suggest his overriding mental instability. When we finally see his home, it is filled with techno-gadgetry, suggesting he is the product of a culture which embraces research at the expense of the individual: a case of misplaced priorities.

It is the teacher (Chamberlain) who picks up on the connection to phone company research and pushes the reluctant investigator into action. Thus, the profiler has the impetus of resolving such cases, with the policeman merely a necessary tagalong without any personal stake, involvement, or curiosity about the case. Anderson suggests that it is the cop's experience with murder which has embittered his idealism, and that the profiler's dedication is in part due to his naive interest, free from having to deal with the regimen of police work. The profiler figure's obsession with catching the killer is, however, not "pure" by any means—he is not so much eager to apprehend a murderer as he is fascinated by the technology of murder.

Thus, nobody in the film operates from any altruistic "goodness"; Anderson suggests that all involved are morally tainted by their selfish response to stimuli, and correspondingly must jointly face the consequences when such erupts into murder. Indeed, the film examines the levels of responsibility faced by individuals and corporations by virtue of their aggressive attitude towards technological possibility. Thus, the corporate experiments by the Telephone Company, in league with university researchers, smack of political thriller conspiracy and science fiction-based technophobia. Murder is the consequence of a widespread climate of depersonalization — the greater the institutional involvement, the greater the potential evil when it spreads down to the affected individual, who merely acts out a corporate design. The film's world is full of malfunctioning patriarchs, with John Houseman's

researcher, mentor to Richard Chamberlain, becoming an ironic counterpoint to his work in *Paper Chase*.

A companion piece of sorts to Don Siegel's *Telefon*, this Canadian film from UK journeyman director Michael Anderson is quite arresting in its own way. Screenwriters Butler and Shryac also wrote the similarly slyly humorous *The Car* and *The Gauntlet*. David Cronenberg, in *Scanners*, further explored the notion of the interaction between phone and human.

Beware My Lovely

(1952: d. Harry Horner)

scr. Mel Dinelli; stry/ply. Dinelli; pr. Collier Young; ph. George E. Diskant; m. Keith Stevens; ed. Paul Weatherwax; cast. Ida Lupino, Robert Ryan, Taylor Holmes, Barbara Whitting, James Williams, O.Z. Whitehead, Dee Pollock; 77m

This noir thriller is about a travelling killer (Ryan), first seen fleeing a small-town community when he discovers the corpse of a woman he has been working for. He goes to another town and gets an odd-job position working for a war widow (Lupino). Mentally unstable, he slowly starts to terrorize her, finally imprisoning her in her own home, the implication being that this is his methodology; but eventually he forgets his murderous rationale and calmly leaves.

Much of what is in this film would become prominent in the serial killer subgenre as it came out of the film noir era. It explores a killer who has a clear mental disorder, and (from his frequent headaches) possibly organic brain damage. He is thus a hybrid of the mentally-ill criminal and the blackout murderer, but is shown with some sympathy amidst the menace — he is a victim of his circumstances and acts according to a dysfunction he recognizes in his more lucid moments but cannot control. He continually flees from the monster he lapses into: as if the psychopath were a transitive state of being, threatening to take over an identity left in tumultuous reaction.

As an itinerant drifter, he is part of a deprived social underclass. His arrival at the home of a widow enables him to retreat into a fantasy wherein he fulfills the traditional male role (a trait later affecting the killer in *The Stepfather*) and helps the frail woman. However, Lupino is far from a dependent woman — raising a potent subtext that such independent women draw resentful males to them. As he holds a photo of her dead husband in uniform next to his own face and peers into the mirror, it is clear that in his mind he would replace the man in all respects, and slowly his intentions towards Lupino turn sexual. His sexual inferiority and resentments are revealed in his mounting anger at the young woman (Lupino's helper) who briefly, and brazenly, flirts with him: he can barely contain his rage at what he perceives as a slight against his masculinity and potency. However, he is so paranoid and insecure that he can only express this sexuality by forceful overcompensation, by dominating the woman and compelling her to be submissive to his will, although there are times when he is in conflict about this.

His inferiority and social resentment is linked to the effects of World War One, as the film is set in 1918. However, although there are initial expectations of the returning disturbed veteran plot line (which would be linked to homicidal action in the post–Vietnam cycle), the film reveals that Ryan was too mentally unstable for wartime service. Thus, never being a soldier in a climate wherein the soldier is a proclaimed hero, he feels that he is somehow less than a male. This insecurity about potency turns sexual, and he seeks out situations wherein he takes odd jobs for single women and kills them when they reject his advances or when he perceives that they have slighted him.

He wants a permanent, stable relationship with a woman, and terrifyingly admits to Lupino that he fears she will be like all the other jobs. Inevitably, he forces her into small domestic rituals (preparing food and drink) and then makes his way upstairs with her, for husbandly duties. Thus, the threat of rape hangs over the film. He desperately tries to remain in control and in charge of the situation around him, doing so by force (as the true expression of masculinity).

His deep-seated sexual insecurity surfaces in violence. His partial amnesia in each case is a means of disavowal, as if the responsibility of his actions were too great for a kind, mild man to otherwise bear. In this way the film develops the amnesia plot line into the realm of sexual dysfunction, clearly moving film noir into serial killer terrain. He is a man in desperate need of psychological help, like the killers in *The Sniper* and the remake of *M*— products of the socially conscious 1950s movies spurred on by Stanley Kramer: but where is this help to be found? Lupino must try to talk her way out of the situation, and professes to understand and want to help him, but this is only under threat, and he takes her concern as another slight against his masculinity. She offers him money, but this type of crime goes beyond that, as he wants to punish the society and gender that look down on him — two motives common to many real serial killers.

Horner was a former production designer (winning an Academy Award for *The Heiress*), and he shot the film in an economic 18 days. Lupino, however, had much creative control and even directed some scenes in Horner's absence. Playwright Dinelli, of course, was known for his work on *The Spiral Staircase*; and the play on which *Beware My Lovely* was based would be remade on TV in the 1950s as *The Man*, with Audie Murphy in the Ryan role.

Beyond Re-Animator

(2000: d. Brian Yuzna)

stry. H.P. Lovecraft; cast. Jeffrey Combs, Bruce Abbott

Third in the series, and the second directed by Yuzna, *Beyond Re-Animator* has scientist Herbert West imbuing dead bodies with other people's souls, thus prompting them to live again. His assistant, Dan, is killed by a serial killer. Once the killer is caught and executed, West transplants the killer's soul into Dan's body. Unreleased at time of writing.

Beyond the Darkness

(1979: d. Joe D'Amato) aka *Blue Holocaust, Buio Omega*

scr. Ottavio Fabbri, Giacomo Guerrini; pr. Marco Rossetti; ph. D'Amato; cast. Kieran Canter, Cinzia Monreale, Franca Stoppa, Sam Modesto, Anna Cardini, Lucia d'Elia, Simonetta Allodi, Klaus Rainer; 94m

This is considered amongst the most repellent of the director's numerous exploitation films. It concerns a young taxidermist who kills and stuffs his wife, and subsequently becomes a sex killer, strangling a hitchhiker after torturing her. He brings young women home and tortures and kills them when they decline a necrophilic threesome. The killer's housekeeper helps with disposal (a trait of many European killer films).

The necrophilic theme suggests *Beyond the Darkness* as a precursor to the equally explicit *Nekromantik* films by Jorg Buttgereit, which are admittedly more serious in intent. It is an unflinching, cynical portrait of aberration, and even comic in its outrageous mix of the grotesque and the gory, realistically depicted for maximum shock value.

D'Amato (real name Aristide Massacessi) apparently padded out the running time with footage of a real autopsy. There are rumors (see Kerekes and Slater, *Killing*

for *Culture*, pp. 233–4) that some of the mutilations filmed were also actually performed on real cadavers (fingernail pulling, for instance). Whether or not this is the case, it exemplifies the exploitation filmmaker's callous servitude to shock value, a charge levelled against Italian exploitation cinema in particular. The film is considered exploitation at its most sensationalistic and opportunistic. Its reputation and popularity amongst genre fans centers on these rumors of actual bodies so used, although the film exists in several versions.

The Bird with the Crystal Plumage

(1970: d. Dario Argento)

scr. Argento; pr. Salvatore Argento; ph. Vittorio Storaro; m. Ennio Morricone; cast. Tony Musante, Suzy Kendall, Eva Renzi, Umberto Raho, Enrico Maria Salerno, Mario Adorf, Renato Romano, Werner Peters, Raf Valenti; 98m

An American writer (Musante) in Rome witnesses the stabbing of a woman by a black gloved and dressed killer, and is subsequently obsessed with finding the murderer, probing his memory of what he saw. He reports the crime and is told that it is one of a series, there having been three similar murders previously. He investigates the case himself, though warned off by two possible killers, and discovers that what he saw was certainly not what it appeared. In the end, it is revealed that the woman is the killer holding the city in fear, and the man who looked to be attacking her was her accomplice husband defending himself.

It popularized the notion of the phantom, gloved serial killer, usually dressed in black, who targets beautiful women before disappearing again into the night. Once again, the killer's psychology is unimportant, and his actions alone are worthy of interest and aesthetic interpretation. Thus, it enters the morally problematic terrain of films dealing with aberrant acts and choosing to depict them. Argento analysts felt it also develops the relationship between killer and outside investigator (Musante is not a policeman and, insofar as he tries to unravel the case and aid police, is a profiler figure) as almost complicit partners in the interplay of passive and aggressive gazing, a theme developed in Argento's subsequent films. This transference of guilt between killer and investigator (Newman, p. 106) of course recalls Hitchcock, and is paralleled to the straight depiction of forensic procedural methodology — all in pursuit of "truth."

The film examines the selective persistence of memory, à la Antonioni, with the protagonist's gradual remembrance of details (used in *Blind Date* and *Blink* also) subverting expectations and gender stereotypes. Hence, the female killer (the inspiration for DePalma's *Dressed to Kill*) has an animalistic sexuality that takes sadistic pleasure in slicing her victims and usurping male power: her husband feels guilty over his complicity but is unable to stop her. She is revealed to have been abused as a child, and when seeing a painting of a sex crime she came to identify with the aggressor instead of the victim, although this last-minute explanation is unimportant except as a prelude to themes Argento would later explore in *The Stendhal Syndrome*.

What is important is the self-reflexive treatment of film style as the embodiment of the process of investigative and affective looking — the combination of objective and subjective perception/truth. The detective plot is the perfect narrative means for such an exploration. Murder as a set piece functions not only as structural beat, but also as a central moment of jouissance, implicating the audience's complicity. The killer becomes a desired object, and the drive that impels the characters' actions becomes an obsession.

This is effectively considered the start of the Italian "giallo" boom and established Argento as a budding auteur and consummate stylist, confirmed by *Deep Red*. Paramount is Argento's emphasis on "the look" and its permutations, echoing Hitchcock, Bava and Antonioni as they probed the notion of cinema as voyeuristic spectacle (Hardy, p. 226), here equated with the desire for suspense and shock. In that, it is a mix of detective story and horror, following the example of the German-produced Edgar Wallace mysteries of the 1950s.

Critics were extremely impressed with this film, and numerous comparisons to Hitchcock emerged, especially regarding the perfectly judged mix of suspense and comedy. As a demonstration of sheer technique, the film is outstanding. It introduces the theme and style common to all subsequent Argento giallo thrillers (including *Four Flies on Grey Velvet*, *Tenebrae*, *Trauma* and *The Stendhal Syndrome*), and is considered the virtual blueprint for the emerging Italian thriller soon termed "giallo."

Black and White

(1998: d. Yuri Zeltser)

scr. Yuri and Leon Zeltser; pr. Ram Bergman, Dana Lustig, Natan Zahavi; ph. Phil Parmet; m. Amotz Plessner; ed. Glenn Garland; prod d. Keith Brian Burns; cast. Gina Gershon, Alison Eastwood, Ron Silver, Rory Cochrane, Ross Partridge, James Handy

In this direct-to-video thriller a serial killer, a man who may be a policeman, embarks on a spree, shooting drug addicts and other social undesirables in the left eye. Investigating are a rookie cop and his experienced partner (Gershon). When her ties to the victims are revealed, she becomes a suspect and has an affair with her younger male partner.

The film tries to tackle many issues: crisis of faith, older woman/younger man relationships, the residual effect of child-hood trauma; but once it raises the serial killer hook, the film gives it only token de-velopment until the resolution. It is back-ground for the character portrait of an in-dependent woman driven to protect her independence and her family secrets, even though this jeopardizes her profession.

She is ready to lie to protect the guilty and so determined to solve every problem without aid that she rejects her own emo-tional needs, though pretending balance, covering up her vulnerabilities and in-volvement in headstrong regimen until she reaches the breaking point. Her compro-mise of professional ethics and personal morality for selfish reasons is the real drama. She is so intent on transcending others' ex-pectations of her that her execution of the killer (her brother, just trying to protect her) purges the possible incestuous desires that had prevented her from cooperating with investigators.

Black Panther

(1977: d. Ian Merrick)

scr. Michael Armstrong; pr. Merrick; ph. Joseph Mangine; m. Richard Arnell; ed. Terry Darvas; art d. Carlotta Barrow; cast. Donald Sumpter, Debbie Farrington, Marjorie Yates, Sylvia O'Donnell, Andrew Burt, Alison Key, Ruth Dunning, David Swift; 102m

Based on the true story of Donald Nielson, this recounts the kidnapping of a young girl by a psychopathic killer. He sus-pends her from the ceiling and leaves her to die until he returns. Though not tech-nically a serial killer film, the socioeco-nomic factors and depiction of an escalat-ing series of crimes (he begins by targeting post offices, then moves on to burglary as a kind of foreplay) suggest the film fol-lowing on from the fact-based case study of Fleischer's *10 Rillington Place*. It is as-sumed that Nielson would repeat this be-havior with another girl if not appre-hended, as it has become for him a sexual ritual.

This is a downbeat case study which avoids any horror in favor of the depiction of a man who feels himself at war with so-ciety and thus granted license to retaliate. He rationalizes and justifies a stream of nuisance crimes, leading to torture and murder. Of course, the girl he kidnaps is not only a sexually desirable teenager (in his view), but comes from a wealthy fam-ily, both factors (gender and socioeco-nomic status) he resents.

The killer is depicted as a gun nut ob-sessed with military discipline to the point of lording over his resented wife and daughter. His dictatorial control over them is a means of compensation for his per-ceived failures in outside life. There is no sex life with his wife, though his repressed desire for his daughter is reflected in his choice of kidnapping victim. His attention all goes into the crimes as sexual expres-sion. He keeps a scrapbook of his acts and meticulously plans each crime. Despite his perceived strength and discipline, he is a sly, cowardly predator who targets those weaker than himself.

Like many serial killers, he is obsessed with control, and the more he perceives his life shifting away from his ideal, the more he overcompensates and targets society, choosing random victims in order to rein-state the sense of control. It is only a mat-ter of course for this psychopathic person-ality, as control is equated with that over life and death. Although financial reward was a contributing factor for the initial kidnapping, it is not shown as the domi-nant motive. When his home life becomes unbearable, he goes out cruising and plan-ning numerous crimes, and so indulges his ongoing fantasies until they are all-con-suming and must be acted out — the serial killer in the making.

His crimes are clearly motivated by sexual fantasy. Hence, as he peeps on a couple making out, the film cuts from a man's hand travelling up a girl's leg to Donald's finger stroking the trigger of the gun he clutches. He immediately goes on to commit a burglary (indeed, fetish burglary is a feature of many real-life serial killers, including William Heirens). He also poses in front of a mirror wearing his guns (recalling *Taxi Driver*). His treatment and humiliation of his victim amounts to his desire for total mastery over her: he perceives that this will in turn give him mastery over the rest of his life. Needless to add, he is completely indifferent to her suffering. His cowardice is revealed when he cries when apprehended, not out of remorse but out of self-pity at being caught.

The film arguably presents its recreations of the killer's life and actions without moral criticism or interpretation (though with some sense of outrage), and thus seems a forerunner of the *Henry: Portrait of a Serial Killer* school, however indebted to Fleischer. It is comparatively meticulous in its attention to character details: an accurate portrait of a psychopath at work. Indeed, much of it is silent behaviorist character observation.

It is shot almost entirely at night or in the dark. The style is equally measured, with controlled movements contrasted with static shots: it favors realism over psychodrama, though it dramatizes those moments where the killer seems to feel internal pressures rising and his control threatens to burst. Nielson was known by the title due to a black slitted hood worn during the commission of his crimes.

The screenwriter wished to avoid any exploitation of the facts and approached the victim's family when writing, so as to avoid causing them undue distress. However, the film was made when the case was still well known to the public, and for legal reasons some story details were avoided. Hence, some reviewers, particularly in the US, found the film hard to follow and too restrained, although admirably earnest.

Black Widow

(1987: d. Bob Rafelson)

scr. Ronald Bass; pr. Laurence Mark, Harold Schneider; ph. Conrad Hall; m. Michael Small; ed. John Bloom; prod d. Gene Callahan; cast. Debra Winger, Theresa Russell, Sami Frey, Dennis Hopper, Nicol Williamson, Terry O'Quinn, James Hong, Diane Ladd, Leo Rossi; 103m

A woman (Russell) marries for money, kills her husband soon after, and then goes in search of another such man to seduce and murder. A Justice Department agent (Winger) follows her trail of dead husbands and hopes to confront her. She comes to admire her and even feels sexually attracted to her. They become close, though the killer is aware of her friend's deceptions. Even though she is close to capture, she cannot resist trying to mate and kill one more time, which she seems to do successfully by implicating the agent, although the agent has, in fact, set a trap for her, saving the next intended victim.

The second neo-noir to emerge from Rafelson (between *The Postman Always Rings Twice* and *Blood and Wine*), *Black Widow* concentrates on the relationship between the two women but leaves the lesbianism rather subdued (unlike the later noir-tinged *Bound*, for example). Instead, it develops the femme fatale as all-things-to-all-men, the studied chameleon whose put-on image of cosmetic beauty is lethal. Although she has a tinge of remorse on occasion, she cannot stop, as if such use of men, even though she may love them on some level, were innate.

Intriguingly enough, she functions as a partial mentor to Winger, and by sharing a man with her, gives her a sexual identity and satisfaction she never had. Actually, Winger was shown as one of the guys at the office; she rejects her boss' advances

A publicity photo from *Black Widow* (Fox, 1987). Justice Department agent Debra Winger (right) trails recent widow Theresa Russell (left), whom she suspects of marrying and murdering a succession of men.

control and exorcism of her sexual insecurities she is able to do the job. The sense that it-takes-one-to-recognize-one is tantalizingly used, but many felt compromised by the happy ending. Nevertheless, by keeping the relationship between the two women somewhat ambiguous, it suggests if not innocence lost, then the consequences of the freedom from repression as betrayal. Sex is a means of manipulative power and self-expression. Is this a form of gender empowerment?

It is a rare look at the serial killer as a woman who seems to equate heterosexuality with murder. She is rich enough not to kill for financial reward, although she gains much from each crime. She kills as part of her design. In the serial killer pattern, she plans and researches each crime well in advance, adjusting her persona and looks accordingly. She embodies the film's central theme of role-playing.

(but in no way jeopardizes their professional relationship). She is intrigued by Russell's beauty, and in one scene she looks at Russell's photo and then toys with her own hair in the mirror, as if wanting to become like her: the narrative strategy in the film's second half. Her inability to be like her, depicted in their respective treatment of the last intended victim, causes her additional resentment. She is angry at the perceived betrayal, both by the male lover (who chooses Russell over her) and by Russell, who uses and frames her.

Her final deception, however, reveals her calculated streak and justifies her as an equal nemesis for the skilled killer. Through

On that level, the film is about a woman who is attracted to one adept at pretense, eventually usurping this power from her. Thus, Russell relishes such role-playing as the domination of and control of men and an expression of personal sexuality, which Winger considers strength akin to liberation and respects as much as she wants to terminate it. Her odyssey of self-discovery and personal empowerment, beginning when she starts to role-play (pretending to be a tourist), thus absorbs the best qualities of Russell and finally purges the aberrant. Rafelson parallels their respective role-playing and the corresponding reversals.

There is no reason put forward as to why Russell kills; instead, the film assumes familiarity with the femme fatale role from film noir and its code of lethal sexuality. However, she targets rich, generally older men; the murders are a means of gender empowerment, the embodiment of the corruption of a feminist ideal — revenge for Patriarchy's entrapment of women. It is her means of control over her own destiny and her own sexuality, driven to kill the one she loves— as opposed to the inevitable surrender suggested by conventional gender roles.

The film's first half is a procedural parallel between profiler and killer, and the second half is their confrontation and the subsequent process of (sexual) empowerment of the profiler figure. The theme of the killer as mentor and possible romantic/sexual partner is also used to different ends in *Silence of the Lambs* and *Hannibal*.

An investigator developing an attraction to a female serial killer was subsequently used in *Eye of the Beholder*; and Jane Seymour played another such killer in the tele-movie *Praying Mantis*. *Prey of the Chameleon* also attempts a discussion of the female serial killer.

Blacktop

(2000: d. T.J. Scott)

scr. Kevin Lund, Scott; pr. Lund, Scott, Josanne B. Lovick; ph. Attia Szalay; m. Ennio Di Berardo; ed. Bert Kish; prod d. Katterina Keith; cast. Meat Loaf Aday, Kristin Davis, Lochlyn Munro, Vicky Pratt, C. Ernst Heath, Amanda Tapping, Doug O'Keefe; 100m

When her boyfriend accepts a stand-up comedy gig over three nights at a truck-stop, a young woman decides she has had enough and hitches a ride with a trucker (Meat Loaf). However, the trucker may very well be a serial killer responsible for the killings of young women like herself. *Blacktop* gives Meat Loaf (who was in *Outside Ozona* and *Fight Club*) a substantial role, and is apparently concerned with killer/victim interaction. The trucker as serial killer also is found in *Clay Pigeons*, which got a far more widespread release than this minor effort. This was unavailable at time of writing.

Blade

(1972: d. Ernest Pintoff)

scr. Pintoff, Jeff Lieberman; pr. George Manasse; ph. David Hoffman; m. John Cavacas; ed. David Ray; cast. John Marley, Jon Cypher, Kathryn Walker, William Prince, Michael McGuire, Joe Santos, John Schuck, Peter White, Keene Curtis, Karen Machon; 90m

This concerns a misogynistic serial killer. When excited, he stabs women to death. The homicide detective on his trail has to solve the murder of the daughter of a politico he strongly resents. Implicated is this man's brother, who seeks to clear his brother's political ambitions from past blemishes (the daughter was a drug addict). Thus the killer ostensibly kills out of moral indignation and self-righteousness, as well as a violent sexuality.

This is considered a rather unremarkable film which fluctuates between killer portrait and procedural as a kind of updated Ripper tale (or so *Variety* said). It balances graphic murder with the usual procedural scenes, and reportedly neglects to develop a subplot about militant Afro-American activists, avoiding the blaxploitation genre then popular.

It was co-written by Jeff Lieberman (who would go on to direct *Blue Sunshine*), and made and set in a sleazy New York. Morgan Freeman appears in an early support role; most of the other actors were theater actors. Director Pintoff was formerly known as an animator. He tries for a verite authenticity, with low-key lighting and shooting with live sound on location, intent on anchoring the film in a sense of place. The urban socioeconomic factors also contribute to a look at faulty socialization, with the middle-aged detective in the role of good father there to punish the bad son.

Blade of the Ripper

(1970: d. Sergio Martino)

scr. Eduardo M. Brochero, Vittorio Caronia, Ernesto Gastaldi; pr. Antonio Crescenzi, Luciano Martino; ph. Miguel Fernandez-Mila, Emilio Foriscot; m. Nora Orlandi; ed. Eugene Alabiso; cast. George Hilton, Ivan Rassimov, Alberto de Mendoza, Edwige Fenech, Christina Airoldi, Carlo Alghiero

In this Italian serial slayer movie, though with more gore and nudity than usual, rich Viennese women are targeted by the "Razor Killer," who slices their throats. A US embassy secretary's wife is an intended victim. One of several men in her life — a former lover, the stranger she has an affair with, and a blackmailer — could be the killer.

Darkly lit, this is generally considered an undistinguished fare from a director who became a minor figure in the spaghetti nightmare boom of the 1970s/1980s after directing *Torso*, which now has a cult reputation. That film was a curious transitional work of the pre-splatter genre, and indeed that hybrid is also perhaps found in this earlier work. It can also be considered part of the emergent giallo movement in Italy at the time, alongside the works of Argento and Fulci in particular. Unlike those two directors, Martino never forged a reputation for himself in the field. Nevertheless, he is not without talent or interest.

Blind Date

(1984: d. Nico Mastorakis)

scr. Nico Mastorakis, Fred C. Perry; pr. Mastorakis; exec pr. D.T. Skouras; ph. Andreas Bellis; m. Stanley Myers; ed. George Rosenburg; prod d. Anne-Marie Papadelis; cast. Joseph Bottoms, Kirstie Alley, James Daughton, Lana Clarkson, Keir Dullea, Marina Sirtis; 100m

In Athens, a man (Bottoms) recovering from a traffic accident loses his sight and is fitted with an experimental device (electrodes in the brain) enabling him to see via computerized impulses fed into his brain. He encounters a psychotic taxi driver who, posing as a doctor, takes women to their own apartments, gasses them and then surgically mutilates them. Being the only person to have "seen" the killer, he thus tries to track him down, leading to a one-on-one confrontation.

Independent producer-director Mastorakis, filming in his native Greece, is obviously enamored of Dario Argento's giallo movies, a style this film follows closely. Hence, the barely glimpsed killer has a homicidal taste for beautiful fashion models (à la Bava's *Blood and Black Lace*), and their death throes are filmed as sexual experiences— for the both of them. Surgical mutilation is thus eroticized (a facet of European horror since Franju's *Eyes Without a Face* and Franco's *The Awful Dr. Orlof*). Indeed, the film self-reflexively looks at portrayals of models as objects in photo shoots and in the media, suggesting a culture of objectification that encourages sex murderers.

The protagonist's altered vision experiences are designed as a combination of psychological projection and the persistence of memory in the pursuit of "truth" (an Argento theme), effectively questioning the perceptual basis for what is termed reality, a theme also of Antonioni. Thus, there is a heavy stress not only on modes of perception but on the commercial forces that mediate perception (i.e. fashion photography, TV, advertising, scientific experimentation), and this incriminates their shaping effect on individuals. The killer's crimes interspersed through the narrative come to represent the consequences of exposure to these modes. The protagonist's altered, unnatural vision is thus a purer and more honest perception of a reality along a spectrum of subjectivity which ultimately denies any possible objective perception. Everything is clouded, and, in a self-reflexive science fiction twist, able to be recorded and thus interpreted and scanned for respective elements of an objective "truth"—akin to decoding a movie.

Mastorakis' familiarity with the Athens setting makes for some superior location work. His expressionistic use of color and concern for reflective surfaces signaled a directorial presence sadly absent from much of his work. The blind witness theme was done later by Michael Apted in *Blink*, and the notion of a recordable vision (also in *Death Watch*) and experience anticipates *Strange Days*.

Blink

(1995: d. Michael Apted)

scr. Dana Stevens; pr. David Blocker; exec pr. Robert Shaye, Sara Risher; ph. Dante Spinotti; m. Brad Fiedel; ed. Rick Shaine; prod d. Dan Bishop; cast. Madeleine Stowe, Aidan Quinn, James Remar, Peter Friedman, Bruce A. Young, Laurie Metcalf; 106m

In Chicago, a blind woman is given an operation to restore her vision. It is a success, but she can see only in a hallucinogenic manner and suffers from a kind of visual flashback wherein she sees people after the fact of their first appearance. One night she sees a rapist killer leaving a crime scene. When she remembers, she goes to the police. She forms a relationship with the detective on the case, although the killer may be closing in on her.

Both protagonists are fiercely independent people. Director Apted devotes much time to their growing attraction and respect, the parallel editing suggesting their destinies are linked (to the killer also), a theme which sits well with the film noir visual design, its interplay of light and shadow corresponding perfectly to the theme of insecure vision. Typical of Apted is the exploration of an individual's potential vulnerabilities and how these become either strengths or self-destructive urges. The characters always seem to be learning and in transition to new self-awareness, all except the killer (in an ironic reversal of the usual murder-as-transcendence motif of the serial killer film), who remains trapped in ritual and unable to progress.

Interestingly, the investigating police treat the case rather self-reflexively, mentioning that they should solve the serial case quickly, before a book can be written about the killer. Appropriately, this conversation takes place during the crime-scene sequence, a central set piece of the serial killer film. It is an acknowledgement of the presence of the serial killer in both law enforcement and popular culture. The reference to VICAP also acknowledges criminological developments regarding the pursuit and classification of serial offenders.

Once the protagonist realizes she has seen a killer, she starts to see him more often, in the periphery of her everyday life. Apted carefully suggests potential danger just beyond the realm of everyday perception. It is the danger of seeing the horrific and objective "truth" of an incident that overwhelms those unable to perceive the true significance of an event. Thus, seeing the killer is tied to Stowe's displaced experience with her mother, whose abuse caused the blindness, an event she in some emotional ways cannot progress beyond. Confronting the killer in a sense exorcises the trauma, and she can begin afresh.

With her vision recently restored, a musician (Madeline Stowe) is pursued by a man (Paul Dillon) but is unsure of his involvement in a series of murders in *Blink* (New Line, 1993).

Thus, if the killer is meant to represent the confrontation with a trauma affecting one's perception, then the film gradually charts not only the protagonist's growing awareness but also her wish and strength to move beyond. The killer enters her apartment, the outside world protruding on the inner, and leaves a message for her (eyes in lipstick on a mirror), thus confirming her fear. Perception = confrontation = danger. Once again, the killer seeks control. But Apted explores the extent to which the desire for control enters interpersonal relationships, with both Stowe and Quinn indulging their fantasy image of each other and feeling threatened when the reality is something different. Self-control is necessary for self-awareness.

The killer's motive is unique, if straining credibility: he murders women who have received transplanted organs from the same donor — the woman he loved.

Consequently, he let the victims bleed to death so the organs would not be salvageable. He holds onto to an ideal image rather than let parts of it contribute to a new life.

Apted favors the relationship over the thriller plot, which is essentially a handicapped woman in jeopardy line. However, the two leads play admirably, and Apted's moody depiction of Chicago (his admitted favored city) certainly impressed Chicago critic Roger Ebert. The film's treatment of blindness is thematically a combination of *Blind Date* and *Jennifer 8*. Quinn and Stowe starred together previously in *Stakeout*.

Blood and Black Lace

(1964: d. Mario Bava)

scr. Marcelo Fondato, Joe Barilla, Bava; pr. Lou Moss; ph. Herman Tarzana; art d. Harry Brest; m. Carl Rustic; ed. Mark Suran; cast. Cameron

Mitchell, Eva Bartok, Thomas Reiner, Arianna Gorini, Dante De Paolo, Mary Arden, Franco Ressel; 88m

This is a disturbing classic from Italian maestro Bava. A masked killer targets fashion models from a house fronting for a drug ring. The plot is a flimsy excuse for the depiction of a faceless male who kills a succession of women who arouse his desire. This is the essence of the sex killer narrative and is here stripped of plot adornments in favor of purely aesthetic thrills.

The killer is a blank everyman of sorts, rather than a deviant. His psychological makeup is secondary, and he seeks to eliminate desire within himself by attacking women in a perverse kind of self-hatred (according to Hardy, p. 166). He represents the psychopathic dilemma possibly inherent in all masculinity. His very blankness anticipates both the giallo trend and the slasher movie. However, Bava's undoubted stylization makes for a self-conscious examination of the sexual drives behind the cinematic process of spectacle (Hardy, p. 166), and the film has a growing stature in genre history. It has been rereleased on DVD and is ripe for reappraisal.

Blood Feast

(1963: d. Herschell Gordon Lewis)

scr. Allison Louise Downe; stry. Lewis, David F. Friedman; pr. Lewis, Friedman, Stanford S.

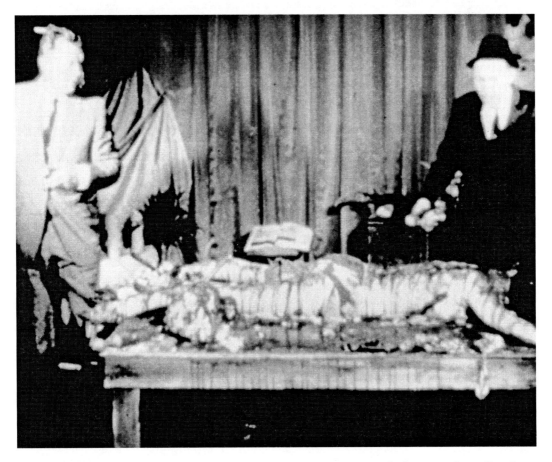

Detectives enter the charnel house of a demented Egyptian caterer to find a woman's mutilated body prepared for a cannibal feast in *Blood Feast* (Friedman/Lewis Prod., 1964).

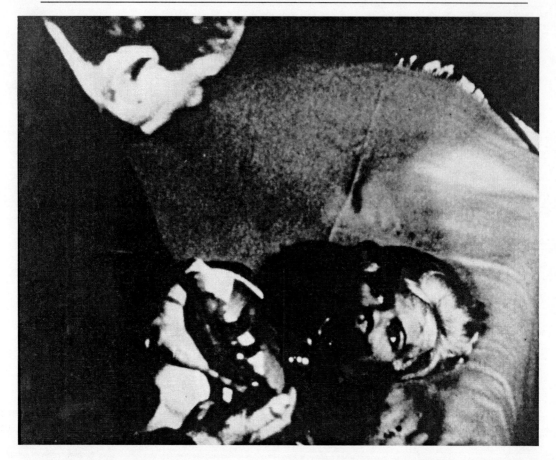

A serial cannibal and necrophilic killer (Mal Arnold) stands over his latest victim in *Blood Feast* (Friedman/Lewis Prod., 1964).

Kohlberg; ph, m. Lewis; ed. Frank Romalo, Robert L. Sinise; cast. William Kerwin, Mal Arnold, Connie Mason, Scott H. Hall, Lyn Bolton, Toni Calvert; 75m

This seminal drive-in horror movie launched the splatter aesthetic and deliberately sought to transgress social taboos regarding sexual violence. It was shot in Miami over nine days for less than $70,000. Its threadbare direction and technical crudity do not disguise the celebration and even Sadean eroticism of bodily mutilation (something Jess Franco was also experimenting with in Spain at the same time in *The Awful Dr. Orlof*). This kind of graphic horror as almost pornographic spectacle (Edwards, p. 112) is further developed by Lewis' casting of a Playboy playmate as the victim. Despite its historical value, the film is, on a technical level, at the very least, dreadful.

The plot concerns a demented Egyptian chef/caterer who kills young women, and disembowels and dismembers them in preparation for a cannibal feast intended to raise a long-dead Egyptian Goddess. The police are on the corpse trail, and eventually they catch up with him and uncover his gruesome charnel house.

Cheap but shocking gore effects (brains scooped out, limbs amputated) barely compensate for amateur acting and bland, unappealing compositions. Nevertheless, this is one of the first depictions in graphic detail of the acts of a serial sex killer and cannibal. In that, it sets the pattern for the

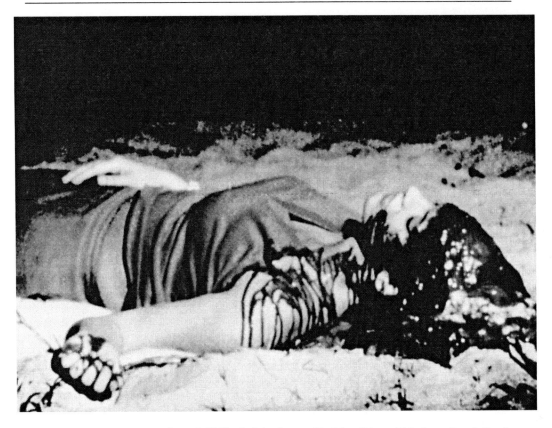

A victim (Ashlyn Martin) of a serial killer left in the sand in ***Blood Feast*** (Friedman/Lewis Prod., 1964).

serial killer film's repetitive murder-as-set-piece structure. It anticipates later canni-bal-themed killer movies like *Welcome to Arrow Beach* and even the comparatively gore-less *Texas Chainsaw Massacre*, al-though the killer in *Blood Feast* is appre-hended (and symbolically eaten by a gar-bage truck) before the title event can be consummated.

Most influential, and disturbingly so, is the application of this pornographic aes-thetic to explicit sexual mutilation. There is no attempt to justify this on any artistic basis; the film was simply intended as a new level of exploitation in its depiction of a killer's methods and charnel house surroundings. However, it is not entirely mindless, developing a theme of aberrant murder as a historically sanctioned legacy (a theme also in Lewis' *2000 Maniacs*). The

lesson of history is the accumulation of the dead, with modern Patriarchy depicted as feeding off such. This renders the film subversive in intent, its gore a deliberate assault on convention. Lewis' sense of irony (the killer worships a goddess of love) and futility saturates the film.

Despite the killer's religious beliefs, it is clear that sexual excitement is the reason for the crimes. Thus he attacks one woman on a bed, his murderous assault tanta-mount to frenzied rape, with her strangu-lation as his climax. Torture of other vic-tims is his foreplay. The dismemberment is the replacement for the porno movies' "cum shot" and "meat shot." The taboos of sex and death are graphically rendered and given a distinct coding.

However, it is too crude (having minimal setups) and even campy to be believable, and any psychological issues are shunted aside in favor of the gore effects. Inevitably, it has become a cult film, and it did extremely well on its first release, especially in the Southern states. Critics detested it almost as much as the publicity campaign, which boasted of its sex murders and mutilations as the main selling point.

Lewis is justifiably considered one of the pioneers of the cheap gore movie, having moved into this when nudies were no longer as lucrative as they once were. His films have a crudely gleeful subversive spirit which is also found in the works of several other directors— Andy Milligan and Ted V. Mikels especially — whose sleazy films seem indebted to him. Jackie Kong's clever *Blood Diner* is a sequel/homage to this film and indulges in the cannibalism to a greater extent. Ironically, the French auteurist critics found Lewis potentially worthy of further investigation, and there has been much attention lavished on retrospective analysis of his work.

Blood Link

(1983: d. Alberto DeMartino) aka *The Link*

ph. Romano Albani; m. Ennio Morricone; ed. Russell Lloyd; cast. Michael Moriarty, Penelope Milford, Cameron Mitchell, Sarah Langenfeld, Geraldine Fitzgerald; 98m

In this psychic-link movie a doctor (Michael Moriarty) involved in mind-control experiments starts to have disturbing nightmare visions, from his point of view, of himself killing naked women. But when he investigates he discovers that the killer is his Siamese twin, separated at birth. He then travels to Hamburg and Berlin to find his monstrous brother, and finds himself a potential suspect.

The film is split between the protagonist's search for the killer, his concern for his own mental health (as affected by his link to said killer), and an analysis of the sex killer's motivations and methods. The killer is a con man/gigolo, first introduced preying on older, lonely women (recalling the male protagonist in *The Honeymoon Killers* and *Impulse*), hinting at his resentment (and even suppressed incestuous desire) for the mother who deserted him. He feels joy as he kills, an experience telepathically shared by his brother (to the brother's guilt and shame). Yet he also preys on younger, more conventionally desirable prostitutes. He is a harsh, cruel strangler who kills for pleasure alone.

The brother, for his part, conducts further experiments with the psychic link by taking drugs (a nod to the Jekyll/Hyde mythos) in an attempt to control memory and pain, as if the two were inevitably bound. The ambiguous ending, with a twin murdered by a woman after sex (poetic justice for a serial killer) hints at a kind of personality and identity transference, which links the film to the Argento giallo heritage of a decade earlier. Indeed, the opening color scheme and certain self-consciously baroque compositions suggest the giallo's dominant theme of altered perceptions, although here they are consumed by an emergent bleak, wintry tone.

It is disturbingly cruel in its treatment of aberration and sex scenes. There are those, John Stanley among them, who consider the amount of graphic sexual violence as making the film almost unwatchable; although, in comparison, there are those who hold the film much less exploitative than it could have been. However, all the major women appear naked and subservient to male desire, however aberrant that may be.

There has been some praise for the effort to study the phenomenon of Siamese Twins, a motif that prefigures *Dead Ringers*. Director DeMartino is a minor influence on the Italian exploitation scene, responsible for US-Italian co-productions/

rip-offs (most notably, from a fan stand-point perhaps, *Holocaust 2000*).

Blood Salvage

(1989: d. Tucker Johnston) aka *Mad Jake*

scr. Johnston; pr. Evander Holyfield; ph. Michael Kemp; m. Tim Temple; ed. Jacquie Freeman Ross; prod d. Rob Sissman; cast. Danny Nelson, Lori Birdsong, John Saxon, Ray Walston, Evander Holyfield, Ralph Pruitt Vaughn; 90m

A demented, Bible-spouting redneck, Jake, and his two sons kidnap people from the highways after forcing car accidents and perform medical experiments on them, selling their organs on the black market. They harass a family led by John Saxon and find that a handicapped girl is harder to control than they expected, although they still subject her to numerous indignities before she starts to turn the tables on them.

This film lifts its sly tone from *Blood Diner*, and *The Cars That Ate Paris*, and seems indebted mainly to the 1970s rural maniac movie cycle which included the likes of *The Texas Chainsaw Massacre*, *Terror Circus*, *Eaten Alive* and *Tourist Trap*. It has a growing appreciative cult on the Internet, though it was unavailable at time of writing. It is included as an example of the rural cycle.

Bloodmoon

(1989: d. Alec Mills)

scr. Robert Brennan; pr. Stanley O'Toole; exec pr. Graham Burke, Greg Coote; m. Brian May; cast. Leo Lissek, Christine Amor, Ian Williams, Helen Thomson; 104m

This is an Australian version of the familiar US formula. A serial killer on the loose around Cooper's Bay, near both St. Elizabeth Girls School and the Winchester School for Boys, stalks and strangles promiscuous teenage girls with a barbed-wire garrote. The killer is revealed to be an impotent and cuckolded high school biology teacher, protected by his promiscuous wife, whose infidelity provides the resentment that is the very motivation for his killing spree.

The teacher kills girls when they are about to have sex, making the film almost a deconstruction of the typical slasher film, as well as a serial killer film in its own right. For its Australian release, it featured a "fright break," à la William Castle's *Homicidal*, making it clear the film was intended as a straightforward exploitation entry. As that, it is functional.

Set mostly in a girl's school beset by the psychopath, who keeps severed body parts as trophies, the film contrasts gender roles (nun, students, teachers) and their respective power hierarchy, implying that the male will resort to murder when his perceived power is threatened or usurped by women. But rather than directly challenge those immediately responsible, he will seek out easier surrogate targets. Parental roles, interpersonal friendships and sexual politics (including lesbianism) mediate this power hierarchy also. The Matriarch prays for forgiveness for the sinners around them, whilst the Patriarch kills them: new and old testament reactions. The comparison of the two power bases yields the suggestion that the killer is in part a projection of the nuns' repressed desire.

The setting recalls that classic of Australian cinema, *Picnic at Hanging Rock*, and the dissection of teen attitudes suggests the sociological documentation streak of *Puberty Blues* with the academic environs of *Devil's Playground*. Thus, it furthers the examination of the consequence of burgeoning sexuality in a restrictive setting, but roots this in malfunctioning Patriarchy. Despite this apparent seriousness, the film ultimately cannot transcend the dictates of the slasher audience, though the attempt is there. Mills doesn't seem bothered by this.

Bloodrage

(1979: d. Joseph Bigwood) aka *Never Pick Up a Stranger*

scr. Robert Jahn; pr. Alan M. Braverman, Joseph Zito; cast. Ian Scott, Judith-Marie Bergan, James Johnson, Irwin Keyes, Jerry McGee, Lawrence Tierney

A sexually frustrated country boy kills a town prostitute when she threatens to tell his mother, and flees to a sleazy New York City where he discovers enjoyment and purpose murdering prostitutes. As a serial killer, he blends in effortlessly; the city is now his home. A police officer from his hometown follows the trail.

The film is structured as a succession of torture-murder scenes interspersed with basic procedural. Characterization is intended to be enhanced by the use of the killer's voice-over narration, as in *Taxi Driver* (about another NYC psychopath). From this, it suggests sex murder as an expression of indefinable rage, both obsessed by and seeking to castigate the dominant urban sex-culture. Thus there is a socioeconomic subtext, as the killer is drawn to the sleazy Times Square area and the wasted lives it houses. However, it avoids the sense of the city as a corruptive influence in that the killer was that way before he found his home there. Nevertheless, it attempts to contrast small-town and big-city mentalities, and their response to sexual aberrance.

Bloodthirsty Butchers

(1970: d. Andy Milligan)

scr. John Borske, Milligan; pr. William Mishkin; ed. Gerald Jackson; ph. Milligan; art d. Elaine; cast. John Miranda, Annabella Wood, Berwick Kaller; 79m

This so-termed bargain-basement cheap horror movie about the Sweeney Todd "demon barber of Fleet Street" killings has three maniacs killing undesirables as Todd slaughters and robs his customers.

He turns over the corpses to a baker and butcher who uses the cadaver's flesh to make meat pies which are sold to unsuspecting residents. So-called "special parts" are kept as pastries for local connoisseurs. A woman goes to the police when her boyfriend disappears, leading to the unmasking of the culprits, who then hack each other to death.

This is Milligan's best-known movie, and one of a pair he did in 16mm in London for producer William Mishkin (the other film being *Curse of the Full Moon*). It is also his goriest work, although the producer edited much out (including a scene in which the butcher scoops out the bowels of a fresh kill). Milligan's cynically grotesque humor is also in evidence in scenes such as a couple finding a severed breast in a meat pie. It is this mordant humor which makes the film both subversive and arguably nihilistic. Milligan is more downbeat than H.G. Lewis, however, and there is little real glee to be had here. Ted V. Mikel's *The Corpse Grinders* is a similarly toned movie, equally low budget, coarse and bleakly (if lethargically) nihilistic.

Blow Out

(1981: d. Brian DePalma)

scr. DePalma; pr. George Litto; ph. Vilmos Zsigmond; m. Pino Donaggio; ed. Paul Hirsch; prod d. Paul Sylbert; cast. John Travolta, Nancy Allen, John Lithgow, Dennis Franz, Peter Boyden, Curt May, Ernest McClure, Davie Roberts, Maurice Copeland; 108m

This is only incidentally a serial killer film. When a sound-recording technician/artist records a possible murder (à la *Blow Up*, but also an extension of *The Conversation*) and saves a female witness from drowning (in a twist on Kennedy-Chappaquiddick lore), a hitman is assigned to kill the witness. The killer intends to make her murder look like one in a series of sex strangling and stabbing incidents in the city by a killer termed the "liberty bell slayer" (because of the shape of the stab wounds), which he himself perpetrates. The chillingly arrogant John Lithgow would be used to good effect in DePalma's later *Peeping Tom*–inspired thriller *Raising Cain*.

The assassin is the epitome of the professional conscienceless killer. He is able to adapt to threatening circumstances, always striving to be in control over the situation, as indeed are all the characters. Ironically, he is the most successful. Yet he is obviously thrilled with his power over life and death, his ability to lure and kill women, ready to mutilate them for both sexual pleasure and to throw the police off the real track. He can rationalize murder and any atrocity in order to get the job done, yet his aberrance is only one end of a spectrum to which all the characters are heading; they all manipulate innocence in order to achieve their own personal self-serving goals. All are complicit in murder. The killer's acknowledgement paradoxically elevates him above the rest — the end of a spectrum maybe, but not a hypocrite.

DePalma would also feature sex murder in *Dressed to Kill* and *Body Double*, the latter tying such sex crimes with the pornography business.

Blue Vengeance

(1992: d. J.C. Ingvordsen)

scr. Ingvordsen, Danny Kuchuck, John Weiner; pr. Ingvordsen, Steve Kaman; ph, ed. Kaman; m. Walter Fritz; prod d. Chris Johnson; cast. Nick Gomez, J.C. Ingvordsen, David Henry Keller, Danny Kuchuck, Jake LaMotta, John Reno, Johnny Stumper; 90m

An ex-policeman, fired for being too unstable and potentially dangerous, is troubled by memories of his partner's murder. When a cannibalistic serial killer, who escaped from an insane asylum, begins killing in the city, the ex-cop suspects that the same man was responsible for the partner's death and wants revenge, an obsession that consumes him.

Despite some interesting footage of a mental hospital for the criminally insane as a modern Bedlam, this focuses on a killer dominated by a fantasy rooted in death metal music culture and medieval imagery. He inconsistently kills according to a ritual message contained in said music, fancying himself an angel of death summoned by his victims. He considers the policeman his rival knight, leading to a motorcycle vs. bike joust akin to *Knightriders*. The film, however, fails to develop a coherent theme, with the motives being too inconsistent.

Bluebeard

(1944: d. Edgar G. Ulmer)

scr. Pierre Gendron; pr. Leon Fromkess; ph. Jockey A. Feindel; ed. Carl Pierson; cast. John Carradine, Jean Parker, Nils Asther, Ludwig Stossel, George Pembroke, Teala Loring, Sonia Sorel, Iris Adrian, Henry Kolker; 71m

This is a much-acclaimed 19th century period piece. In Paris, an artist/puppeteer (John Carradine) hires models for portraits and strangles them once the portrait is completed, as if consummating a sexual process. One potential victim suspects something is amiss and finally unmasks the killer artist.

Artistic endeavor is here equated with sex murder, foreshadowing the murder-as-art/self-expression theme that would feature sporadically since, but especially in numerous 1990s serial killer films (most notably *Copycat*). Artistic expression is depicted as a sexually exciting process. It demands as climax the murder of the real object so that the "essence" is incorporated into the portrait as a lasting impression — a trophy of the murder for the killer to pore over: later films would portray killers taking photographs of their victims in the age of technology. This is also considered

The eponymous killer (Charles Denner) in Chabrol's version of *Bluebeard* (CC Champion, 1962) is faced with the consequences of lady-killing.

as possibly John Carradine's finest role in a 40-year career of villains.

Little violence is actually depicted; Ulmer instead relies on suggestion and suspense. So when the killer strangles his victims the camera cuts away, often to an extreme close-up of the killer's bulging eyes. Since we know the killer's identity right from the start, Ulmer avoids mystery and detective story conventions for a look at the killer's life and psychosis. *Bluebeard* is also a forerunner of the demented artist/sculptor movies à la *A Bucket of Blood* and *Sadisterotica*, and owes much to the early adaptations of *Mystery of the Wax Museum* (itself subject to many revisions, remakes and reinterpretations over the years). Thus it has a firm place in genre history.

Bluebeard

(1963: d. Claude Chabrol) aka *Landru*

scr. Francoise Sagan; pr. Carlo Ponti, Georges de Beauregard; ph. Jean Rabier; ed. Jacques Gaillard; m. Pierre Jansen; prod d. Jacques Saulnier; cast. Charles Denner, Denise Lepurier, Dian Lepurier, Francoise Lugagne, Claude Mansard, Danielle Darrieux, Michele Morgan, Juliette Mayniel; 115 (108) m

In France during WWI, a father of four secretly contacts Parisian women through newspaper personal ads, then seduces and kills them. This is a retelling of the infamous French wife-killer story, but it reportedly lacks the punch of Charles Chaplin's *Monsieur Verdoux*. Part of the killer's motive is to gain money to feed his family, thus adding a sociological aspect to the killings and giving him a convenient justification.

Chabrol treats him as an object of study and contemplation (predating *Henry* to some degree) rather than condemnation (Wood and Walker, p. 76), as an example of the unknowable depth of human motivations. Hence, the film depends upon the accumulation of detail through which the inherent complexity behind such monstrousness within society is suggested. The killer may be unknowable, but there is insight to be gained in depicting his predicament, where work and aberrant sexual pleasure have intertwined (the film was perfect for later championing by Marxist/Freudian critics like Wood). The killer is primarily an enemy of the bourgeois society, although he seems also defined by it, and a refined, even cultivated product of it. A society destroying itself from within seems to be the sociological point here.

Despite the killer's sexual abnormality and his penchant for destruction, his relations with his wife are free from aberration. Although he claims to be murdering for profit (work), all of the victims are sexually attractive, suggesting a deepseated resentment and hatred for female sexuality and beauty. Yet, as typical of many serial killers, he accelerates his crimes and starts to be more indiscriminate in his choice of victims. It is a combination of psychological breakdown and surrender to/consumption by the pressure of work. The questions of guilt and selfawareness are left for the viewer to ascertain, as they never play as great a role as they did in Chabrol's *Le Boucher*. Indeed, it is the killer's lack of self-awareness, of emptiness and monstrousness, which shields him from any guilt or remorse: he is incapable of such insight or such emotion. Even when faced with execution, he remains aloof and self-righteous, unaffected. He is the product of his world and

has reacted to it in a way best to survive as he sees it (Wood and Walker, p. 81).

Bluebeard

(1972: d. Edward Dmytryk)

scr. Ennio di Concini, Dmytryk, Maria Pia Fusco; pr. Alexander Salkind; ph. Gabor Pogany; m. Ennio Morricone; ed. Jean Ravel; art d. Tomas Vayer; cast. Richard Burton, Raquel Welch, Joey Heatherton, Virna Lisi, Nathalie Delon, Marilu Tolo, Karin Schubert, Agostino Belli, Sybil Danning; 123m

The new wife of a respected war hero, akin to the Red Baron, is told to avoid a certain room. She does not listen, and instead discovers the bodies of her husband's previous wives. She listens as he tells the story of how he killed each one of them.

Richard Burton stars as the aristocratic flying ace and wife killer, a portrayal perhaps more in keeping with Vincent Price (then doing the *Dr. Phibes* movies). He is an expert hunter, the implication being that his pursuit and disposal of women is akin to a sport. However, the film reveals more complex personal motivations, revolving around the character's fear of sexual union and his corresponding need to otherwise assert his masculinity — he kills instead of copulating, resenting his own sexual desires but needing to preserve the beautiful object.

The film takes comedic delight in his destruction of a variety of caricatured female stereotypes (incessant chatterer, lower-class fallen nun, vain model, outspoken feminist, uninhibited child-woman), each portrayed by a beautiful international starlet. Burton grows to resent them all, as if femininity itself fuels his innate homicidal (masculine) desires. He considers them all monstrous and unworthy of life, justifying his own atrocities; yet he preserves them, as if in death they have a beauty not in life — a sly necrophilic subtext.

Interestingly, it is the wife who can best analyze and confront him who stays

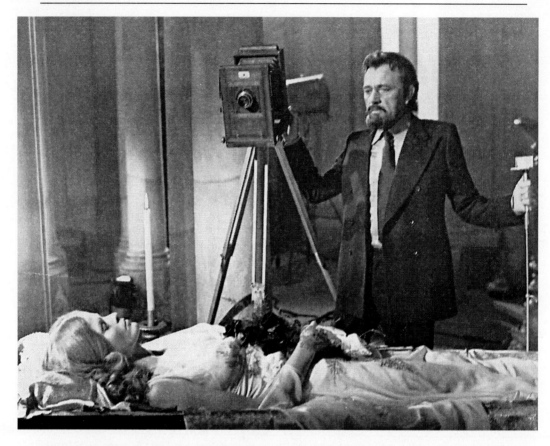

The aristocratic wife killer (Richard Burton) sets out to preserve the deathly beauty of one of his victims in Dmytryk's *Bluebeard* (Cinerama, 1972).

alive. Thus the film addresses the possible survival tactics of women when faced with a misogynistic monstrous killer, a theme rarely given more than a subtext until the crime boom in sex murder in the United States in the 1970s.

Bluebeard here considers women monstrous, and is practically oblivious of his own monstrosity; and he orchestrates in part the greater social madness around him, except when it threatens his aristocratic airs. He keeps bodies as souvenir trophies, frozen in a refrigerated room, reliving their case histories via flashbacks as he relates their stories (falcon attack, chandelier, guillotine, drowning, shooting, suffocation) to his next intended victim. His means is elegant murder, society's is brute force: the old vs. the new, but both

ultimately equally disturbed and consequential, Dmytryk suggests (this perhaps neatly summarizes Kracauer's suggestion in *From Caligari to Hitler* that the morbidity of culture spawned fascism). Burton is, after all, a fascist leader, and, in that, comparable to the serial killer general in *Night of the Generals*.

The premise of the wife discovering a key to a locked room she is not supposed to enter also recalls Lang's *Secret Beyond the Door*. The killer's motive, however, is revealed to be driven by that old standby, motherly love, and Burton keeps the mummified corpse of his mother in a wheelchair à la *Psycho*.

This was a much-touted international production filmed on location in Budapest and Rome. Of course, the main selling point was the promise of naked and near-naked starlets. Dmytryk collaborated on the script, intent on updating the legend to World War II and doubly intent on contextualizing it within the rise of the fascist party (though not directly Nazis, they dress alike and wear similarly colored armbands, but not swastikas). Perhaps this was intended to show the minor murders as symptomatic of a greater collective monstrousness, like that proposed by Chaplin in *Monsieur Verdoux*, Litvak in *Night of the Generals*, and also a theme in the later *Dr. Petiot*.

Dmytryk's bold use of primary colors and some startling compositions of castle interiors lend weight to the film, but the tonal insecurity, although interesting experimentally, fails to gel. It tries for political allegory, camp comedy, European art film and period mystery in a manner approaching post-modernist mosaic fragmentation. In that latter context it is more interesting than successful, and suggests that the film has not received its proper due.

Critics, however, were not impressed by the film's camp humor, and cited it as further evidence for Dmytryk's perceived extended decline after his HUAC testimonials. It was also considered the slightest version of the oft-filmed tale, paling beside the 1944 version, *Landru* and *Monsieur Verdoux* especially. It deserves reappraisal, however.

Bluebeard's Castle

(1970: d. Michael Powell)

pr. Norman Foster; ph. Hannes Standinger; m. Bela Bartok; cast. Norman Foster; 60m

This is one of Powell's lesser-known efforts after the critical disapproval of *Peeping Tom*. This short West German production is based on the Bela Bartok opera about an artful sex killer who seduces and then murders women. By this stage, Bluebeard had become one of the screen's most legendary killers, alongside Jack the Ripper.

The film was completed quickly and went unreleased for several years, due to an unofficial blacklist of Powell on account of the hostility that greeted the shocking *Peeping Tom*. It is now a hard to find item, though it would undoubtedly be of interest.

Body of Evidence

(1988: d. Roy Campanella II)

ph. Frank Beascoechea; prod d. Albert Heschong; cast. Margot Kidder, Barry Bostwick, Caroline Kava, Jennifer Barbour, Tony Lo Bianco; 93m

A small Massachusetts town harbors a serial rapist/strangler of women. The police come under increased community pressure to solve the crimes. The two investigative officers, a police detective (Lo Bianco) and a forensic psychologist (Bostwick), the profiler figure, feel this tension. The psychologist's wife believes that her otherwise mild husband may be the killer: appearance thus hides terror and internal monstrousness.

This tele-movie was first shown opposite *A Father's Revenge* and *The Murder of Mary Phagan* on January 24, 1988. Set in New England but filmed in Calgary, it reveals the incorporation of the profiler figure into television-style procedural stories, and the medium's small-scale melodramatic concern for troubled interpersonal relationships.

The Body Snatcher

(1945: d. Robert Wise)

scr. Carlos Keith (Val Lewton), Philip MacDonald; pr. Val Lewton; ph. Robert deGrasse; m. Roy Webb; ed. J.R. Whittredge; art d. Albert S. D'Agostino, Walter E. Keller; cast. Boris Karloff, Bela Lugosi, Henry Daniell, Edith Atwater, Russell Wade; 77m

This atmospheric Val Lewton–produced thriller is based on the Burke and Hare case, graverobbers who sold corpses to a surgeon and soon turned to fresher prey they killed themselves. The surgeon, the ambitious and proud Dr. Knox, realizes that the killer's taunts will only entrap him in damaging evidence and tries to extricate himself from association with the arrogant killer, who relishes his job more than the money it brings him. The atmosphere of Victorian London provides a clear link to the Jack the Ripper mythos.

The film was noted for its fragmented depiction of Edinburgh as a city of the character's imagination more so than a real place (Hardy, p. 87). The killer is a reflection of the doctor's lost soul, and the descent into evil is one for the both of them, as the film's interpretation of the corruptibility of morals and ethics condemns them both. This interplay of personal and social decay would infiltrate Wise's film noir work, and implicates the struggle for power and control over others as seen in the bleak *Born to Kill*. The ending explores how guilt can manifest itself in action and hallucination.

Numerous UK versions of this tale followed: *The Flesh and the Fiends, Burke and Hare* and *The Doctor and the Devils* (from a Dylan Thomas script) most notably.

The Bone Collector

(1999: d. Philip Noyce)

scr. Jeremy Lacone; book. Jeffrey Deaver; pr. Martin Bregman, Louis A. Stroller, Michael Bregman; exec pr. Michael Klawitter, Dan Jinks; ph. Dean Semler; prod d. Nigel Phelps; m. Craig Armstrong; ed. William Hoy; cast. Denzel Washington, Angelina Jolie, Queen Latifah, Michael Rooker, Mike McGlone, Luis Guzman, Leland Orser, Ed O'Neill; 114m

A nearly paralyzed ex–forensic investigator and author is brought into the ongoing investigation of a serial killer who abducts and mutilates his victims, leaving deliberate clues—and removing bones—for the investigators to follow. An intuitive female uniformed officer becomes involved, and is taken in by the paralyzed man. The protagonists are thus involved in a deliberate battle of wills, trying to locate and save the victims before their set demise. The film balances the pursuit of the killer with the growing admiration between the paralyzed mentor and his young female assistant, which reflects the apprenticeship motif in *Silence of the Lambs*. Indeed, the film alludes to (is derivative of) several recent serial killer movies, borrowing its baroque, gloomy style and morbid attention to crime scenes from *Seven*.

The characters are forever forced to deal in the horrendous aftermath of deliberate sadistic murders, as the killer taunts them to solve the riddles and clues he deliberately plants there for them. The function of investigator is thus akin to linguistics expert (Hunter, S. *Washington Post*, 5/11/99): the profiler's unique skills alone can stop a killer who targets him personally (also a theme in *The Watcher*). That the trail of clues leads to old pulp fiction novels suggests self-consciousness on the filmmakers' parts. By withholding the killer's identity until the end, the film approaches the mystery/thriller at the expense of any case study. It is all style.

The film is obsessed with death, fear and the infernal city. The remnants of an urban wasteland are the sites of horrendous cruelty, framing the study of aberrance in the ruins of a spent culture. Noyce depicts technological advancement as a means of combating and examining a culture dedicated to the examination of death and physical limitation. All characters are subservient to this obsession, which paradoxically gives them an excitement that makes them feel alive. To them, death is a force of transition, and closeness to it is desirable. Perhaps this is intended as a commentary on the genre itself. Correspondingly, there is a visual stress on frames within frames, shadowy spaces and entrapment.

The profiler and killer both feel their lives are over, and their closeness to death is a form of displaced suicide, an equally invigorating prospect. Even the protagonist, who claims to want to die, through investigating the deaths of others, is given renewed life and meaning in his education of a successor. He is thus a substitute father for Jolie, her appropriation of phallic dress signifying her incorporation into Patriarchy. It is the reaction to murder as unnatural death that unites the living and polarizes the killer as an agent of such death instead of its decoder. The theme of confronting death and its agent is a theme in much of Noyce's work, as is the idea of technological obsession: fates are intertwined by murder.

Washington's home becomes the workplace, reflecting the character type's (profiler's) obsession and inability to ever escape the job as both necessity and source of past trauma. The wounded profiler is here physically traumatized by his profession, as opposed to the psychological wounding and facial scarring of the profiler in *Manhunter*. He plays the killer's game: decipher the clues in time and save the victim, a gimmick also used in *The Cell* and *The Watcher*. This raises the issue of predestination, with the study of such murder and death an attempt to cheat potential fate.

The protagonist is nicknamed "Link," making his symbolic association between life and death (alive but immobile) clear. As mobility in cinema is equated with life, the corresponding immobility is a state of limbo between the two opposites. It adds another elucidation to the association between profiler and killer.

The revelation that the killer imitates fictional crimes is both a nod to popular theories regarding the influence of violence in the media and to *Copycat*, wherein the killer imitated real past crimes. It forwards the theme of the past influencing the present. Many critics noted the similarity to Hitchcock's *Rear Window* and lamented the film's contrivance and improbability, as well as its stylistic debt to *Seven*, particularly to those scenes showing the crime scene first detected — scenes here prolonged at length. For his part, Denzel Washington consulted with paralyzed actor Christopher Reeve (who starred in the tele-movie remake of *Rear Window*). Many felt it another in a line of disappointments from a once promising director turned anonymous Hollywood hack.

Bone Daddy

(1998: d. Mario Azzopardi)

scr. Tom Szollosi; pr. Lewis Chesier, Jean Desormeaux; ph. Danny Novak; m. Christophe Beck; ed. Dean Belser; prod d. Jeff Ginn; cast. Rutger Hauer, Barbara Williams, R.H. Thomson, Joseph Kell, Robin Gammell; 90m

An ex–forensic expert and chief medical officer (Hauer) is the author of a fictional account of a serial killer. In the book the killer is caught, but the serial killer he was based on in actuality was never caught. Shortly after the book's publication, the killer resumes his crimes. An extreme sadist with obvious medical knowledge, he removes his victims' bones whilst the poor victim remains alive, leaving the flabby flesh intact. The examiner is forced to investigate on his own, to defend his reputation when it seems the killer has returned just to spite him. The examiner's own son has a motive: he has inherited his father's position and feels himself in constant competition with his father's reputation. Due to his past expertise, Hauer is brought in officially as a "consultant" and teamed with a young female officer. The killer is revealed to be another forensic pathologist, an equally resentful former co-worker.

Saturated with the notion of professional and generational competition as an inevitable (Patriarchal) cycle, the film is competently stylized in the manner of *Seven* and *Bone Collector*. It illustrates the theme of shared responsibility, with the author's fictionalization implicated in this self-perpetuating cycle, but stops short of completely vindicating him. Indeed, all operate from a clouded motive, resentful of their respective interdependence on one another for their continued self-definition. Profiler, killer and suspect son: an embryonic Patriarchy that places the female police officer, and the victims, on the periphery of its own immoral operations.

Born to Kill

(1947: d. Robert Wise)

scr. Eve Greene, Richard Macauley; nvl. James Gunn; pr. Herman Schlom; ph. Robert De-Grasse; m. Paul Satwell; ed. Les Millbrook; art d. Albert S. D'Agostino, Walter E. Keller; cast. Claire Trevor, Lawrence Tierney, Walter Slezak, Phillip Terry, Audrey Long, Elisha Cook Jr., Isabel Jewell, Esther Howard; 92m

This film has the deserved reputation as one of the darkest and most mean-spirited of film noirs. For thrills, and out of wronged pride, Sam Wild (Tierney) murders two innocent people and then pursues a woman (Trevor), even though he is married to her half-sister. Trevor, who witnessed his crimes, is gradually drawn towards the life of this violent criminal, and her self-destructive desires, although providing relief from the boredom of her everyday existence, propel her into contact with evil. Thus she wants him to murder her sister, an act they can both profit from.

Tierney's amoral killer and director Wise's skillful blend of the best of his Val Lewton period Expressionist noir make for an unusually misanthropic view. Even the character of the detective, longtime bastion of law and moral integrity, is corrupt. Ordinary people are ready victims, but it would be hard-pressed to call them innocents since their self-deception is rampant, and they are depicted as almost justifiably insignificant when compared to the killer's animal sexuality, a force that drives the film.

His raging pride differentiates him not in kind, but in degree. His homicidal self-serving abandon is also contagious. He kills without conscience, for personal thrills and not mere financial gain, although Trevor's plan is to use his animalism for said gain. As a portrait of unredeemable masculine pride as thrilling and violently amoral, the film has few equals of this period. The film thus reveals a world of corrupted morals and tarnished ethics, with no place for innocence.

Pride and sexual thrills are the components of homicide, forces that invigorate those under their spell. Even the cold Trevor is warmed by her proximity to evil, a revelation she is aware of and warps for her own means, doing with her icy intellect what Tierney does with brute force. It is a portrait of empowerment through aggression, with killer, accomplice, femme fatale, and detective all sadistically turned on by their deceptively cold monstrousness and ability to manipulate others.

The film's amorality offended many critics, among them *New York Times* reviewer Bosley Crowther, who found it morally and intellectually reprehensible. Indeed, Crowther lamented what is now the film's main achievement — how it probed the limits of the Hays Code's standards of acceptability when dealing with the varied motivations for repeat murder. It insightfully probes the moral abandon of those who hold themselves above any imposed order and free to act accordingly, without conscience, remorse or guilt. Inevitably, there is a dark sexual power play to their motivations.

There is a possibly bisexual component to Tierney's acts. He lives at the start with effete accomplice Cook, who is first seen on a bed with Tierney. Tierney's macho pride could thus be partly motivated by a repressed sexual desire, although he later kills Cook when he feels betrayed. After all, he says to Cook that he can do anything he sets his mind to and isn't interested in dames. He murders women out of hurt pride, an affront to his masculinity, and the murders that begin the film are not his first. He is attracted to Trevor because she has the same hard heart. Pride, self-deception and homicide. The film's thesis is summed up in the detective's last line as he reads about the characters' death in the newspaper before discarding it as trash: "The way of the transgressor is hard." Subsequent films would explore this type of transgressor as serial killer.

The Boston Strangler

(1968: d. Richard Fleischer)

scr. Edward Anhalt; pr. Robert Fryer; ph. Richard Kline; m. Lionel Newman; ed. Marion Rothman; prod d. Jack Martin Smith; cast. Tony Curtis, Henry Fonda, George Kennedy, Mike Kellin, Murray Hamilton, Hurd Hatfield, Jeff Corey, Sally Kellerman, Dana Elcar, William Hickey, James Brolin; 115m

Based on the true story of Albert DeSalvo, this is a seminal serial killer movie and is discussed in the introductory body of the text. It was noted for its non-lurid approach to sensationalistic subject matter. After a detailed investigation, the killer is apprehended partially by chance, and when interrogated in a psychiatric institution reveals himself to possibly be a multiple or split personality with no recollection of the crimes. As he gradually remembers them, he comes closer and closer to psychological breakdown in realization of the monster he is, a process that excites the profiler. The DeSalvo case was also

partial inspiration for *No Way to Treat a Lady*, released the same year.

The Boston Strangler chronicles the city's descent into fear, panic and even resentful suspicion, questioning the motives of the policeman as much as it does the accusers of the innocent. Although it depicts a world of underground practices and sexual aberration (like *The Detective*), it does not seek to condemn such, instead suggesting that many people need psychological help, and their practices are symptomatic of a crumbling society (represented by the ineffectual police). Patriarchal authority needs to reassert itself in proper dealings with such amoral criminality. All people have a dark side; the facade of normality conceals, and it is the most inconspicuous which hides the most monstrous.

It features two profiler figures, brought for purposes of comparison: Fonda as the criminologist, and the psychic. The latter is clearly revealed as fraudulent, and the film thus suggests that the science of the profiler is beyond that of the merely supernatural. This notion, however, of some kind of supernatural insight on the profiler's part would continue as a subtext through many later films — the profiler as witchdoctor.

Fleischer repeatedly uses a compositional trick in the crime-scene sequences: a low angle camera offers fore and midground viewpoints, holds, and then dollies in so that mid-ground — the police — replaces foreground — victim. This is a means of concentrating the film's energies on the investigators, with the split-screen suggesting a perception that highlights specific details and then seeks to place them into a whole view, an exploration of a single killer's impact. The stylistic experiment is both psycho-dramatic and the perfect compliment to the investigative narrative as it moves from procedural to case study. Rarely has the split-screen been so integrated and integral to a depiction of social and psychological dysfunction and the attempt at reintegration. It also suggests a parallel between the investigator's perception and the killer's (made explicit when Fonda inhabits the killer's recollections as onlooker and arguably shaping participant), a link developed in many subsequent serial killer movies.

It was highly praised when first released for its combination of documentary, valid stylistic experimentation, and restraint. The split-screen was hailed as the perfect compliment to the documentary approach. The style follows the steps of the murder via multi-panel shots which allow the viewer simultaneous looks at many places and from as many points of view as possible. Increasing vision, it both directs and fragments it, building to an explosion of perception that fixes itself onto the killer.

Tony Curtis portrays real serial killer Albert DeSalvo in the seminal *The Boston Strangler* (Fox, 1968).

Rare for the genre, police and press cooperate, the press even going so far as to suggest the need for a centralized office to counter the jurisdictional hassles faced by investigators. The police chiefs respond to the suggestion. Real FBI agents Douglas and Ressler would make similar requests in the next decade, leading to the development of the Behavioral Science Unit and the VICAP program, also in response to increased violent crimes of the era. Of course, the creation of such a new force demands the creation of a new head, hence the profiler figure (Fonda) as a means of the proper re-structuring of a Patriarchy otherwise in crisis.

The killer is introduced watching Kennedy's funeral on TV, then leaving in search of another victim. Thus the film an-

chors its criminality as an indicator of a national tragedy (in contrast to the note of national pride — the hopeful astronaut mission — screened on TV at the film's beginning), emblematic of an era. The parallel between TV broadcasts also suggests the film's second half as another investigation, not a police procedural but a behavioral procedural. Correspondingly, the narrative structure is repeated, though the focus has changed. The final confrontation is thus between the killer and the person who bridges both behavioral aspects, the profiler, his intent allied to the viewer's.

The confrontation(s) between profiler and killer in the examination room reveal(s) their mutual interdependence. For complete self-knowledge, the killer needs

Serial killer Albert DeSalvo (Tony Curtis) is a normal, loving family man, despite his homicidal activities in *The Boston Strangler* (Fox, 1968).

the profiler's examination, and this examination prompts the profiler's admission of excitement at completing such. They need to confront each other for mutual closure, born of the pressures of a lengthy investigation. The interior madness destroys and invigorates—the core of the enigma, as both forces battle for control. Later films would dismiss the tortured killer.

Anhalt's script featured over 100 speaking parts and called for 800 extras in its

The first real profiler figure, Henry Fonda (right), is assisted as he heads up the citywide investigation into a serial killer in *The Boston Strangler* (Fox, 1968).

depiction of the varied corners of society. It was an explicit critique of the limits of current police methods (*Variety* noted this, significantly). In her role as living victim, Kellerman depicts the terror and subsequent re-adjustment that the "lucky" must go through — a consideration usually absent in the majority of serial killer films (though central to *Copycat*, where it is the profiler who is the living victim).

It was a call for understanding rather than a wallowing in violence. Indeed, the closing title suggests greater effort is needed in the detection and treatment of such killers before they become dangers to society. It is a call for intervention and treatment over punishment — a liberal sentiment reminiscent of 1950s Kramer liberalism, and one effectively quashed by the irony of *Dirty Harry* three years later.

Correspondingly, Fleischer only shows enough of the crimes to establish the killer's pattern. Despite the filmmaker's care and intentions, the British censors made cuts in order "to avoid the risk of stimulation to potential psychopathic killers who might see the film" (French, p. 7).

Le Boucher

(1969: d. Claude Chabrol)

scr. Chabrol; pr. Andre Genoves; ph. Jean Rabier; ed. Jacques Gaillard; prod d. Guy Littaye; cast. Stephane Audran, Jean Yanne, Pasquale Ferone, Mario Beccaria; 94m

A small-town butcher (a war veteran) falls for a shy local schoolteacher. When the schoolteacher finds, at a crime scene, a cigarette lighter she had given the butcher as a gift, she suspects he is responsible for a series of killings of females (starting with girls and going on to mature women as the killer gains in sexual confidence). Thus revealed, he intends to kill her and comes after her. To her he confides the details of his life that he holds responsible for his monstrousness. Finally, he is unable to kill her and so stabs himself. She is again alone.

The killer roots the cause of his homicidal nature in a horrid childhood complemented by exposure to the horrors of wartime army service, although this does not fully explain the sexual delight in such homicide, instead favoring a thesis of conditioning to murder. This is complicated by the suggestion that the killer is mentally ill to some degree, and that said illness is rooted in a sociological hostility and inability to feel and maintain a genuine and loving communication with another human being. He strives for such a connection with the teacher, but still cannot stop murdering women. The notion that the barbarities of war are acceptable whereas the individual mass killing is considered aberrant is presented as an almost absurd contradiction (and also explored by Chaplin in *Monsieur Verdoux*, by Chabrol before in *Bluebeard*, in *Night of the Generals* and even in the Dmytryk version of *Bluebeard*).

On the subject of contradiction, Chabrol explores the sense of community with a rare conviction, casting locals in an attempt to capture the essence of such a lifestyle and to chart the horror when it is threatened from within. Correspondingly, he stresses communal rituals (feasts, dance, funeral) as dressing in a sense, covering the more bestial heritage of humanity: confirmed in the village's location so close to caves, thus suggesting the close link between surface culture and primitivism (Wood and Walker, p. 132). This raises the issue of what has culture, intelligence and empathetic understanding contributed to the control of bestial rage. Chabrol sug-

gests: very little. However, the two protagonists both separate themselves from the community, despite pressures to integrate, and ironically find a kind of mutual solace in each other.

The killer has a self-awareness and even remorseful self-loathing, which is considerably rare in the latter stages of the genre (and who some have compared to Lorre in *M*). He is haunted by his wartime experience, claiming that it made him a butcher and that he has butchered everywhere (an apt irony). He even voices the question: what is one murder in the context of so many? Thus Chabrol stresses the character's duality—at once capable of warmth and even tenderness towards the schoolteacher, yet capable of murdering a little girl. It is as though, to Chabrol, the killer is trapped by design: part of the human condition exacerbated by social circumstance. This can only result, for those sensitive enough to recognize the need for love but unable to attain it, in an explosion of violence (as in the killer) or the surrender to loneliness (the schoolteacher). Thus the killer, knowing that she knows, asks her why the crimes should stop suddenly, hoping that love will be the answer, although he knows that it won't be.

This is in its way a depiction of a frustrating madness that consumes the killer, and the film slowly descends into ever more shadowy visuals to chart the descent into a psychosis of impossibility. Civilization is only coating an "atavistic darkness" (Hirsch, *Detours*, p. 94). The protagonists are both compared and contrasted, the teacher prepared to take responsibility for the life of children, the killer for their violent death. Lurking in the background is the police responsibility for the protection of all: a social order, no matter how well defined, is capable of housing a monster.

Ironically, it is the teacher who, quoting Balzac, reads of the beauty even in the coarsest of minds, hence her attraction to the butcher and her protection of him — even though she knows what he is capable of doing. Such is their connection, replete with the hope that it will lead somewhere — hence they are often seen walking together, as if on a journey — but, of course, it leads only to tragedy. On a trip to the caves, a boy asks the teacher what a Cro-Magnon would be like in today's world, and she replies that he would adapt — is this the role filled by the killer? Is he then a throwback or even a missing link?

The Boys Next Door

(1985: d. Penelope Spheeris)

scr. Glen Morgan, James Wong; pr. Sandy Howard, Keith Rubinstein; ph. Arthur Albert; m. George S. Clinton; ed. Andy Horvitch; cast. Maxwell Caulfield, Charlie Sheen, Patti D'Arbanville, Christopher McDonald, Hank Garrett, Paul Dancer, Moon Zappa; 90m

This film explores in part the legacy of serial killer violence on today's youth, as it depicts the increasingly violent acts of two young men who leave their small town after high school graduation and become spree killers. It is as an examination of a phenomenon that the film sets itself apart: opening with a compendium of serial killer extracts and showing its two bored killers as imitating the likes of Gacy, Berkowitz, Kemper and Bundy in their sex crimes. This subversive look at Patriarchy's traditions anticipates the likes of *Copycat* and *Natural Born Killers*.

The critics considered the film mainly a curiously violent throwback to 1950s teen morality plays and woefully devoid of any explanation of motive. Of course, this could also be leveled against the comparable *Badlands*. One killer's latent homosexuality was held as motive, since that desire is never sated as the killer goes to increasingly brutal crimes in an effort presumably to satisfy his repressed sexual urges. The

film explores the notion of violence as a self-expression of revolt against cultural disaffection. As told from the killer's point of view, it can be compared to Oliver Stone's *Natural Born Killers*, and it shares its policeman character's sense of despair at the very randomness of these murders. Like that film, it is more a spree killer than serial killer story, although it suggests such crime as the social legacy of the serial killer phenomenon, a theme also present in Stone's movie.

Breaking Point

(1993: d. Paul Ziller)

scr. Michael Berlin, Eric Estrin; pr. Robert Vince; ph. Peter Wunstorf; m. Graeme Coleman; ed. David M. Richardson; prod d. Lynne Stopkewich; cast. Gary Busey, Kim Cattrall, Darlanne Fluegel, Jeff Griggs, Blu Mankuma; 92m

Director Ziller at first brings his experience as a former pornography director to the fore in this erotic thriller about a retired detective who reluctantly returns to duty (à la *Manhunter*) to stop the serial killer known as "the surgeon." This is of dubious morality, since Ziller clearly intends to titillate the presumed male viewer. Ironically though, the killer is revealed early on as a part-time male stripper who knifes women he apparently expects to turn on, paradoxically threatened by and resentful of the sexuality he arouses in them, and they in him.

He taunts an ex-cop (Busey) and threatens to murder his wife (Cattrall). The sister of one of the victims is a police officer who investigates the case in order to avenge the death. The narrative is heavily in favor of procedural aspects and partial case study: unremarkable, though it strives to show individual and societal sexual politics at the title stage.

Bridge Across Time

(1985: d. E.W. Swackhamer) aka *Terror at London Bridge*

scr. William F. Nolan; pr. Richard Maynard; ph. Gil Hubbs; m. Lalo Schifrin; ed. Tom Fries; cast. David Hasselhoff, Adrienne Barbeau, Clu Gulager, Barbara Bingham, Randolph Mantooth; 96m

This is an odd tele-movie that explores the Jack the Ripper legacy. It starts as a period piece in London 1888 as Jack the Ripper dies in the Thames near London Bridge, and then cuts to the replica of London Bridge in Lake Havesa, Arizona, as the rebuilding is complete. A tourist cuts himself, and the bridge absorbs the blood (also a trick in *Hellraiser*) as the Ripper reappears and cuts a woman's throat. A stressed-out policeman from Chicago (Hasselhoff) stays there and finds himself on the trail of a killer who slays in the method and manner of the Ripper. He is contacted by, and in turn romances, a reporter hot for the story, and a mysterious Englishman arrives.

It is cynical in its depiction of a local government more concerned with tourist revenue than saving the lives of its constituent community, and so refusing to close the bridge for forensic examination. In that, the film seems structured along the lines of *Jaws*. Most of the characters are at a point of burnout, where their morality is threatened, and they must fight to preserve it against the homicidal legacy of history. Indeed, Hasselhoff claims a lifelong study of criminal behavior. His pursuit of the killer becomes for him a quest for personal redemption. If he can catch the killer, he has made amends for the death of an innocent boy—the reason he left Chicago. In the end, of course, he saves the girl and fights the Ripper.

Calendar Girl Murders

(1984: d. William A. Graham)

scr. Gregory S. Dinallo, Scott Swanton; pr. James O'Fallon; m. Brad Fiedel; ph. Robert Steadman; ed. Ronald J. Fagan; art d. William Hiney; cast. Tom Skerritt, Sharon Stone, Barbara Bosson, Robert Beltran, Alan Thicke, Robert Culp, Barbara Parkins

This standard mystery gimmick-killer tele-movie has police investigating the murder of models who all worked out of the same agency. The killer targets women according to which month they are associated with, and so the police stakeout the next potential victim.

Again it appears that a culture that objectifies women is partly responsible for the incidence of violence against them. What a male culture commodifies as desirable, so too it seeks to chastise for that elevation — to remove from the pedestal of desirability. The commonality shared by the victims makes this only tangentially a serial killer film. However, it is a common plot hook repeated in the numerous stripper-kill movies.

Cat in the Brain

(1991: d. Lucio Fulci) aka *Nightmare Concert*

scr. Fulci, Giovanni Simonelli; pr. Luigi Nannerini; m. Fabio Frizzi; ed. Vincenzo Tomassi; cast. Fulci, Paul Muller, Malisa Longo, Marco di Stefano, Brett Halsey; 85m

This was shot on 16mm and blown up to 35mm for theatrical release.

Fulci, hailed by some as an auteur second only to Argento, gets self-conscious here playing a director of horror films who suffers nightmares, as someone (himself?) seems to be killing women in imitation of the death scenes in his films. The psychiatrist he frequents becomes a murderer, acting out his patient's visions. Although the killer dies, the director takes up a chainsaw to continue the killer's "work." At this point the film ends, although Fulci's intended ending was apparently to show the killer using dismembered body parts for bait and then have another yacht pull up and reveal the whole thing as a filmed put-on. Balun reports that the studio nullified this meta-filmic intention.

Despite a possible inspiration from *Tenebrae* and the Argento theme of personality transference, this is an excuse for a compilation of clips of murder from Fulci's past thrillers. Thus, there are numerous scenes of "disposable" women, there only to be bloodily murdered and mutilated in a variety of ways. Since they are mostly nude when killed, the film allies murder with the pornographic titillation that Fulci developed in the much-banned and arguably misogynistic *New York Ripper*. Although some considered the film a fitting coda to Fulci's career, it alienated just as many, who thought this vanity production (he not only starred but co-wrote and co-produced) evidence only of a deep and insulting callousness (Balun, p. 55).

The Cell

(2000: d. Tarsem Singh)

scr. Mark Protosevich; pr. Julio Caro, Eric Mcleod; ph. Paul Laufer; m. Howard Shore; ed. Robert Duffy, Paul Rubell; prod d. Tom Foden; cast. Jennifer Lopez, Vince Vaughn, Vincent D'Onofrio, Marianne Jean-Baptiste, Jake Weber, Dylan Baker, James Gammon; 105m

A serial killer (D'Onofrio) is captured but lapses into a coma due to a form of viral schizophrenia. Through an experimental process, a psychotherapist (Lopez) enters the killer's mind in an effort to save the killer's latest victim from a pre-timed death trap. She becomes trapped in the killer's fantasies, and a detective (Vaughn) must also enter the killer's mind to get her out. This was a controversial and visionary debut from a former music-video maker (à la Charbanic, who debuted almost simultaneously with *The Watcher*).

The killer's method is to abduct women, imprison them in a glass cell and slowly drown them by pumping water into the cell, videotaping the proceedings for use in later masturbatory fantasies. He treats, bleaches and prepares the bodies as if making dolls. He lays the body on a table and, in a bizarre necrophilic ritual, suspends himself from the ceiling by chains connected to hooks in his back, masturbating over the corpses as the videotape plays in the background. The film is quite explicit about this process, as it is the spillover of the killer's violent fantasies into real life and thus the key to his mental state. He then dumps the human dolls in the open, where they are found by the FBI. Vaughn intuits that the killer is accelerating, and that he secretly wishes to be caught — views that convince Lopez that she may be able to help them, and even help the killer.

The film is visually allusive and complex (referring to underground performance art and artists). It is this self-conscious quality to the surrealistic imagery which either attracted or repelled the critics. It is a mix of serial killer film (sticking closely to the central character triptych of killer/profiler/investigator), science fiction, and surrealist horror film, and as such is certainly an ambitious hybrid. Inevitable charges of pretentiousness followed, although Ebert held it as one of the best films of the year. Its science fiction aspects, of technology allowing an intruder to enter another's private realm, is related to the virtual reality fantasies of Brett Leonard (*Lawnmower Man*, *Virtuosity*) but without the technophobic aspects. Indeed, here the technology can be used for the betterment of humanity. Lopez not only kills the killer (with his lucid consent, nonetheless, as his experience with the profiler has made him understand himself better) but uses the experience to help a comatose boy. This boy, whose fantasy we see as the film's opening sequence, is

In his private fantasies, a serial killer (Vincent D'Onofrio) imagines himself as the absolute deity of the realm he has retreated into while comatose in *The Cell* (New Line, 2000).

haunted by a boogeyman, and his predicament is paralleled to the killer as a boy, scared and confined by the idealized monster adult.

The Cell balances three narrative strategies: firstly, the investigative race against time to find the killer and then the victim before she dies; secondly, a look into the dream world fantasies of the comatose killer wherein it explores the kind of virtual reality transference pioneered in *Dreamscape*; thirdly a look at the cell of the mind — both imaginative freedom and prison — and the means of responding to it and conquering it/escaping it. The race-against-time structure is a deliberate echo of *Silence of the Lambs*. Like *The Boston Strangler*, it concentrates on firstly showing the crimes and the procedural response to them, and secondly probing the killer's psychology.

In the killer's mind, which he has re-tracted completely into, he exists in three states: the child, the lucid killer, and the idealized deity. Past, present, and intended future coexist in the mix of memory, dream and fantasy that is the killer's mind. The childhood experiences (being beaten for playing with dolls) manifest themselves in perverse acts (turning victims into dolls) which fuel the fantasy of empowerment. Although the lucid state abhors the memory of the monstrous father, the idealized self is an attempt to usurp the absolute power the killer equated with the man. It is this idealized future which is the most lethal aspect of the fantasy, for it demands the real murders as a means of empowerment to gain transcendence. If the killer kills enough times, he will become the fantasy — the very theory expressed by the profiler in *Manhunter*.

To conquer the domination of the fantasy, the profiler must reach the innocent

Another view of the serial killer's idealized fantasy version of himself in *The Cell* (New Line, 2000).

past and appeal to the more lucid, and tormented, present within the killer's mental flux. Momentarily, however, she too is overpowered by the idealized self and believes the fantasy/dream meld to be a reality. Thus the detective, as good Patriarch, must go in to rescue her, in the process gaining an insight into the killer's mind reserved for the profiler and finding the clue that leads to the last victim's rescue. Significantly, the official investigative hierarchy downplays the validity of the process. Equally significantly, it is through the understanding of the killer's mind that the profiler is qualified to eliminate the killer in a possibly benevolent manner.

It is a barrage of imagery that contrasts, juxtaposes and compares visionary beauty and ugliness. Thus, a childlike dreamscape yields images of mutilation and torture (of women) as the film roots the killer's sexual aberration in warped childhood experiences: the child eventually becoming the monstrous father he loved and loathed. This is by now the conventional "reason" for such killers, but rarely has it been as elaborately visualized. The killer's suspension by hooks is partly duplicated in the profiler's laboratory, and is a desire for a floating weightlessness, to be free of the burden of the earth and live in the realm of fantasy. Here pain and pleasure intermingle (hence the emphasis on grisly horror imagery), suggesting the possible influence of Clive Barker.

The killer's mind is nightmarish. The child he was forever hides from the memory of his abusive father, and from the monster adult the child has become. In his own mind, the adult killer is a monstrous deity, the giver of life and death, and the absolute controller of this world. The profiler asserts that if she can end the child's torment, she can bring peace and closure to the monstrous adult. The killer is now totally dominated by the fantasy of himself, except in more lucid and self-reflexive moments: but the killer is not born a monster, he is made one by the fantasy rooted in childhood experience and not by the trauma alone. His schizophrenic ailment originated during his baptism ceremony, a ritual that obviously confused the child and so entered the process of fantasy reconstruction and reinterpretation until it resurfaced in reality as the killer's method of murder — the slow drowning of a woman.

This, of course, reflects the current investigative research of the FBI's Behavioral Science Unit, and *The Cell* is the first mainstream Hollywood film (however daring it may be) to visualize the internal fantasy we have previously been asked to intuit from the killer's behavior. It splits the behavioral study into two aspects: the crimes in real life and their roots in fantasy, charting the horrific spillover. This is a new step for the genre, and the film is also the first, following *Martin*, to attempt to so visualize the role of fantasy in the killer's life and to suggest the treatment of this as a potential remedy.

Inside the surrealist mindscape there is flamboyant camerawork, offbeat angles and deliberately unbalanced compositions, a bold use of color, and imaginative set and costume design. The interior is a mix of the futuristic and the medieval (attempted also by the fantasy *Beowulf*), and seems influenced not only by the surrealists, but also by modern comic-book artists such as Bill Sienkiewicz (*New York Times*). However, it was arguable, according to some, to what extent the provocative imagery was meant to either titillate or to disturb and provoke (the true intent of the surrealist film). *Variety* concluded the film was destined for a cult audience.

Interestingly, the FBI officer, who is traditionally the profiler figure, fills the detective function. Thus the film can also be seen as an elaboration and even sub-division of the profiler. The profiler Lopez is a mix of psychiatrist and psychic (as the film can also be considered a clever variant on the psychic-link subplot of the serial killer movie). It is the self-conscious play with character function that makes it a knowing film.

Centerfold Girls

(1974: d. John Peyser) aka *Centerfold Murders*

pr. Chuck Stroud; cast. Aldo Ray, Andrew Prine, Mike Mazurka, Ray Danton; 93m

Psychotic Andrew Prine kills pin-up girls. An attempt to delineate the sex killer and subsequent changing morality of the 1970s, this is a case study in voracious sexual dysfunction. Yet again is the implication that male sexual commodification of women fosters a homicidal resentment of the very beauty and sexuality it supposedly celebrates.

Prine, usually in secondary roles, here (as in *Terror Circus*) got to probe the sly menace behind the earnest, calculated and authoritative simplicity that made him the Jimmy Stewart of the B movie. He starred truer to form as the police officer tracking a killer in *The Town That Dreaded Sundown*. Alas, this film was one of a string of minor vehicles when independent producers of the 1970s latched onto the psycho and anti-hero trend. It has since disappeared.

Citizen X

(1994: d. Chris Gerolmo)

scr. Gerolmo; book. Robert Cullen; pr. Timothy Marx; ph. Robert Fraisse; m. Randy Edelman; ed. William Goldenberg; prod d. Jozsef Romvari; cast. Stephen Rea, Donald Sutherland, Jeffrey DeMunn, Joss Ackland, John Wood; 103m

This ambitious cable movie is about the case of Andrei Chikatilo, a Russian

The weary Russian investigator and reluctant profiler (Stephen Rea) in *Citizen X* (HBO, 1995) feels the strain.

above and ordered to round up known homosexuals (the same time-wasting strategy seen in *The Boston Strangler*). This gives Sutherland blackmail material enabling him to keep Rea on the case, even when Rea, pushed beyond frustration, has to take leave at a psychiatric retreat. Back on the case, changes in the Soviet hierarchy have enabled Sutherland to get Rea what he initially wanted (including contact with the FBI's BSU in Quantico). They consult a psychiatrist, who gives

serial killer of mainly children, and, with over 50 victims, one of the worst killers of all time. He was also one of the most savage, sexually mutilating his victims whilst they were still alive. As a tele-movie, the film is restrained in its depiction of the killings but graphic enough to convey the cruel, shocking horror of an act so important to the killer.

In Rostov, in Soviet Russia, a new coroner (Rea) is assigned to head the investigation into a number of horribly mutilated corpses. He concludes that a serial killer, preying on children, is responsible, but Soviet authorities refuse to admit that serial killers are possible in the Soviet system maintaining they are a decadent Western phenomenon. He persists, intuiting that the killer is using the slow-moving rural train system, selecting victims from the young and weak at the train stations, and luring them into the woods and then sexually assaulting and murdering them. He gradually wins over an official (Sutherland), although they are hampered from

them a profile of the killer. They set up a surveillance trap and finally apprehend the killer, a communist party member who was taken in before but dismissed when his blood type didn't match the semen sample (a still unexplained event). When he refuses to confess within the time allocated by Soviet law for detention, they bring in the psychiatrist, who merely reads his profile; the killer, reduced to tears at the knowledge of his monstrousness being understood, confesses freely. A bullet to the back of the head executes him, and Rea and Sutherland are applauded for their efforts.

This is a model for the serial killer film, combining procedural and case study. However, it frames this within a chronicle of the collapse of the Soviet system, measured by a deteriorating propaganda poster Rea repeatedly walks by. Sutherland, initially passive, is empowered into decisive action by Rea's efforts and is held up as an example of the new reformed Russia, finally able to fight for justice and

The profiler (Rea, right) and a party official (Sutherland) inspect the forces hunting for a serial killer using the Russian rural train system in *Citizen X* (HBO, 1995).

self-expression: he finds something to believe in. Rea has had this all along and been frustrated by blind Soviet authority (Ackland), which refuses to accept the validity of his investigation and seeks to cover it up and misdirect it to protect party members. It is a measure of Rea's strength and integrity that he continues his investigation, even though the system is against him. The film is thus a story of the varied means to individual empowerment and personal validation, and the processes that can delay justice when the "truth" is politically embarrassing.

The killer is an anomaly which cannot be denied or ignored. The killer's demise is neatly paralleled to that of the Soviet order, as if he were a representative of a malfunctioning system. Yet his motive is apolitical: impotence. Sex murder is a means of compensatory empowerment. Ironi-

cally, his impotence parallels the imposed restrictions on Rea's investigation, preventing him from proper action. All characters seek to escape an initial powerlessness as the personal, sexual impotence is paralleled to the sociopolitical. Meanwhile, the bodies pile up.

True to the film's concern for authenticity, it reveals the importance of the Chikatilo case in Soviet criminological history. For the first time in Soviet history a psychiatrist is brought into the case as a profiler, but only if his involvement is hushed up to protect him from potential professorial retribution, such being the Soviet view of the benefit of psychoanalysis. Indeed, the film neatly encapsulates the importance of this figure, for it is the accuracy of his insight which narrows the investigation and finally gets the killer to admit his monstrousness, a development of Fonda's role in *The Boston Strangler*. The investigator can catch, but it is the profiler who has the final confrontation with the killer and is able to forge a deeper interpersonal understanding, if not empathy, with the monster. The investigator can detect the pattern, the profiler the reason.

City in Fear

(1980: d. Jud Taylor as Alan Smithee)

scr. Albert Ruben; stry. Peter Masterson; pr. Ronald Lyon; exec pr. Masterson; ph. John Bailey; m. Leonard Rosenman; ed. Fred A. Chulack; prod d. Charles Rosen; cast. David Janssen, Robert Vaughn, Perry King, Mickey Rourke, William Prince, Susan Sullivan, M. Emmett Walsh, Mary Stuart Masterson; 150m

When a serial killer is loose in the city, a newspaper editor pressures a disillusioned reporter into tracking him in this ambitious tele-movie/mini-series. The subsequent news reports, however, have the effect of turning the killer into a media celebrity of sorts. Thus he may be continuing to kill simply in order to maintain the media interest in him, getting off on the publicity. This is a lengthy examination of the issue of media culpability and responsibility in the case of a serial killer. It was also star David Janssen's last role. It premiered March 30, 1980. *Crime Time* examines similar themes.

City in Fear is also one of a number of tele-movies that sought to probe and socially contextualize the serial killer within the US demographic. Most of these found their basis in real-life cases, hence *Deliberate Stranger* and especially *The Atlanta Child Murders*, both responses to the 1970s rise in such killers and the possibility that they may not be as anomalous as one would hope. The mini-series *Helter Skelter* (later shortened to movie length), about the Charles Manson case, is probably the starting point for these lengthy studies.

The Clairvoyant

(1982: d. Armand Mastroianni) aka *Killing Hour*

scr. Mastroianni; m. Alexander Peskanov; cast. Perry King, Elizabeth Kemp, Norman Parker, Kenneth McMillan, Jon Polito; 97m

A police officer (Parker) and a talk-show host (King) are each aided by a psychic artist (who has premonitions of murder) in their investigation of a Manhattan serial killer, the "handcuff killer." The psychic (Kemp) has to deal with degrees of manipulation and sincerity from these people, as well as the turmoil of psychic closeness to a killer. The talk-show host plans to have her perform on his television show as a ratings bonus, although the policeman advises her against this, as it may endanger her further. Pursuing a romance with King, she sees a vision in which he participates in the gang rape and murder of a victim. It is revealed that King was part of a group of three sexual degenerates and had murdered the other two lest they turn him in; he intended to continue the sexual sublimation of women on his own.

The film develops the psychic as subconscious witness to every slaying, yet never tries to put forward a reason why. Instead it concentrates on the romantic triangle rivalry between the three protagonists–profiler (as psychic), investigator and (it is revealed at the end) killer. It does, however, hint at a collusion between press and police, which serves as a means of personal self-aggrandizement for those involved, particularly the press. Its cynical view of journalistic showmanship culminates in the revelation of King as the killer. Ironically, King states that society and the individual cannot shield themselves from such violence by running from it or closing their eyes. Yet he represents the perversion of the desire to confront such violence by putting it into practice for his own sexual thrills. The killer is a self-serving, opportunistic sexual sadist — what better representative could the media have in their sensationalist approach, publishing details which could jeopardize the safety of innocents and even hamper the investigation itself? The media make the killer a celebrity, one who revels in his perceived mastery of the situation.

This film is directed with surprising restraint by minor genre figure Mastroianni, although the psychic link plot is conventional and better served by *The Psychic* and *Dead on Sight*. Nevertheless, it is probably his most efficient and effective film, and a better demonstration of his talent than expected. There is some concern for shadowy, dingy location work, suggesting the film as part of an early 1980s rise in seedy neo-noir movies, which included such entries as *Vice Squad* and *Ten to Midnight*, and celebrated the world of urban squalor and vice, post–Scorsese and Schrader.

Clay Pigeons

(1998: d. David Dobkin)

scr. Matt Healy; pr. Ridley Scott, Chris Zarpas; ph. Eric Alan Edwards; m. John Lurie; ed. Stan Salfas; prod d. Clark Hunter; cast. Joaquin Phoenix, Vince Vaughn, Janeane Garofalo, Georgina Cates, Phil Morris, Scott Wilson; 104m

A man stages his suicide to look like murder, implicating his friend (Phoenix) in homicide. The man's wife doesn't care and wants the sex with Phoenix to continue. Phoenix despises her sluttishness and slaps her, an act admired by a visiting trucker. Phoenix's mistress is shot by his adulterous spouse, and he has a second body to dispose of. However, he befriends the trucker (who calls himself Lester the Mo-lester), not knowing that he is a serial killer of seven so far (and a few they don't know about). Soon, as the bodies accumulate, an FBI agent (Garofalo) comes to investigate and Phoenix is suspected. As circumstances implicate him (a homemade porno movie is found by Garofalo), the man finally confesses to a disbelieving policeman (Wilson, who played a less remorseful killer in the classic *In Cold Blood*). He then has to escape from jail to locate the killer and clear his name.

Clay Pigeons reunited Vaughn and Phoenix from *Return to Paradise*, and in retrospect, Vaughn's performance as the killer can be contrasted to his version of Norman Bates in the *Psycho* remake. Garofalo's role as an FBI agent who arrives on the scene is a nod to the profiler archetype and was compared to McDormand's comedic take in *Fargo*. Although here it is big city FBI professionalism vs. small town incredulity and ineptitude: at the end, Wilson resigns, distraught by the profession, and ironically gives a lift and potential employment to the now-drifting killer. The film's tone suggests among its influences *Delusion*, *Breakdown*, *Fargo*, *U-Turn* and *Red Rock West* in its balance of quirky comedy and homicidal menace set amongst a world of lone desert landscapes, confining diners, bars and isolated frame houses.

It is a black comedy about the horror of accumulation (a popular theme in Absurdist drama), as a man is punished for adultery and slowly loses his soul. His morality is but one step away from that of the killer, which the killer recognizes instantly (saying that he sees in Phoenix an early version of himself) and easily. He expertly manipulates Phoenix, seeking and achieving a kinship. To protect himself, Phoenix is forced into collusion with the killer, forever doomed to cover up the crimes of another. Even when his name is cleared and he intends to make a fresh start, he is forever tainted by this association, his soul now as wanderingly bankrupt as the killer he will forever be linked to in his own mind: the killer wins.

This is the directorial debut of a

A serial killer (Vince Vaughn, left) and his new friend (Joaquin Phoenix) discover a corpse floating in the lake, to the dismay of Phoenix, who also has a murder to hide in the offbeat comedy *Clay Pigeons* (Gramercy, 1998).

former MTV maker, and was made from a Writer's Network contest–winning first script from a former journalist. It led to a multi-script deal with Warner Bros. It was only a moderate success, however. It bears some comparison to the gently sardonic *The Minus Man*.

Click: The Calendar Girl Killer

(1986: d. John Stewart, Ross Hagen)

scr. David Reskin, David Chute, Ross Hagen, Hoke Howell; pr. Carol Lynn; exec pr. Clifford Wenger; ph. Gary Graver, Tom Callaway; cast. Troy Donahue, Ross Hagen, Jennifer Sullivan, Daryl Williamson, Jack Vogel, Lisa Axelrod; 86m

A fashion photographer is a murderer of models and, it is implied, women in general. His homicidal nature stems from his being tormented, after caught with girlie magazines, by a stern nurse, who apparently served as the same catalyst as "mother" for Norman Bates, since this killer also dons a wig and drag before he kills.

Although the film's first half shows the killer at work, and apparently cruising for victims, the second half descends into a slasher movie scenario with the killer targeting both genders whilst on an isolated photo shoot. The promotional material suggested the killer is of the same ilk as such true-crime based characters as Albert DeSalvo, et al., but this is merely hype, as the film never really develops the serial killer angle beyond a brief contextualization for the slasher scenes. Some woeful attempts at a hip MTV style do not help this inept mess.

Closer and Closer

(1995: d. Fred Gerber) aka *Terror on the Net*

scr. Matt Dorff; pr. Julian Marks; ph. Peter Benison; m. Micky Erbe, Maribeth Solomon; ed. Ron Wisman; cast. Kim Delaney, John J. York, Scott Kraft

An author's book inspires a serial killer's crimes. The killer then attacks her, leaving her paralyzed. Years later, she publishes a sequel, and the process of victimization begins again, through e-mail. He sends her details of the crimes. She contacts the police and works with them as a profiler, offering her view of the killer based on his imitation of her creation. The killer finally attacks her.

The film seeks to examine the ethical issues surrounding fictional violence and its shaping effect on the real. Thus the killer holds the writer responsible in an effort to divert blame. This is the coating for a look at obsession, with the profiler the real target of a murderer, also wheelchair bound (like the killer in *End Play*), so consumed by the desire to possess her that he kills in an effort to forever link himself to her. His character is thus an amalgam of the stalker, the celebrity assassin who kills in order to have his name forever linked to his quarry, and the serial killer.

The notion of a tormented housebound author follows on from the superior *Copycat*. Another tele-movie, *Writer's Block*, also explored the complicity between author and killer.

Collectors

(2000: d. Julian P. Hobbs)

A documentary that explores the public's craving for serial killer–related material, *Collectors* examines serial killer art works: the artists, the sellers, the collectors, and the people who object to the trade on moral and ethical grounds. It is one of the first nonfiction works to address the burgeoning serial killer subculture and the status given the serial killer as modern communicator as well as abhorrent monster.

Filmed in the South, it concentrates on two people: Rick Staton, a Baton Rouge funeral director who started many imprisoned serial killers painting in order to sell their work (he was Gacy's exclusive dealer); and collector Tobias Allen, who created a serial killer board game banned in Canada. The film follows their road trip on opening night for an art show by killer Elmer Wayne Henley. Also making appearances are renowned artist Joe Coleman and true-crime author Harold Schechter. It was shot on 16mm color film.

Con-Air

(1997: d. Simon West)

scr. Scott Rosenberg; pr. Jerry Bruckheimer; exec pr. Chad Oman, Jonathan Hensleigh, Peter Bogart, Jim Kouf, Lynn Bigelow; ph. David Tattersall; m. Mark Mancina, Trevor Rabin; ed. Chris Lebenzon, Steve Mirkovich, Glen Scantlebury; spec eff. Dream Quest Images; cast. Nicolas Cage, John Cusack, John Malkovich, Steve Buscemi, Ving Rhames, Colm Meaney, Mykelti Williamson, Rachel Ticotin; 111m

A group of convicts on an airplane take over the plane. One of these prisoners, who plays little role in the plot, is a serial killer (played by Steve Buscemi with a mix of menace and charm, and treated with near reverence by the filmmakers).

Of all the criminal types on display (mass murderer, racial/political terrorist, career criminal, serial rapist), it is the serial killer figure who is the unquestioned "worst"— the most awe inspiring, respected and dangerous of them all. He is introduced in restraints akin to Hannibal Lecter's in *Silence of the Lambs* and has the other criminals afraid of releasing him. He has a developed philosophy of killing, saying that most murder is circumstantial necessity, but that the great ones (Bundy,

Gacy, Dahmer) kill because it excited them. Yet when he has the opportunity to kill a little girl, he doesn't. In fact, he is the only major villainous character who does not even want to kill anyone in the entire movie, an irony not lost on the filmmakers who, as a final gag, anarchically celebrate the killer's freedom: he is the only convict to live. The film jokily acknowledges the serial killer's status as potential anti-hero. With the other prisoners in uniform, he is ironically clothed in white. It is by now essential that the serial killer is coded as different even from other criminals. He doesn't participate in their plans, and is the only one to survive.

This is one of the more callous of producer Bruckheimer's films, in as far as it unquestionably caricatures and celebrates the serial killer as a popular icon. Although the serial killer's presence is mere decoration plot-wise, it is at the core of the film's cynically exploitative agenda. Director West has since become a proficient Hollywood technician.

Condemned to Live

(1935: d. Frank R. Strayer)

pr. Maury M. Cohen; scr. Karen de Wolf; ph. M.A. Anderson; ed. Roland D. Reed; cast. Ralph Morgan, Maxine Doyle, Russell Gleason, Pedro de Cordova, Mischa Auer; 68m

This early vampire as serial killer tale encapsulates many of the concerns of the European serial killer films. A professor unknowingly transforms into a lyncathropic creature that preys on a small village in central Europe. His faithful hunchback servant removes him after each kill, before discovery. When the hunchback is believed to be the killer, the professor confesses and then commits suicide, followed by the distraught servant. It is revealed that the professor's mother was bitten in Africa by a bat, thus linking hereditary vampirism to sex murder (the notion of a

woman violated, whose offspring grows into a monster, was also the basis of the later *The Beast Within*).

The professor's reluctant bride is much younger, and it is suggested (by Hardy, p. 61) that the professor's sexual urges are responsible for his transformation into a sex-murdering beast: the consequences of either repression or surrender. The notion of a village terrorized was used again in *Wolf Forest*, and there would be numerous films of demented doctors assisted by deformed servants in the wake of *Caligari* (see *The Awful Dr. Orlof* for an example of this version of the serial killer European style). The vampire as serial killer would move from Europe to the United States in *The Return of Dracula*.

Confessions of a Serial Killer

(1987: d. Mark Blair)

scr. Blair; pr. Cecyle Osgood Rexrode; m. William Penn; ph. Leyton Blaylock; ed. Sheri Galloway; prod d. Robert A. Burns; cast. Robert A. Burns, Dennis Hill, Berkley Garrett, Sidney Brammer, Dee Dee Norton

Inspired by Henry Lee Lucas, who also prompted the superior *Henry, Portrait of a Serial Killer*, this semi-documentary effort is about a man (Burns) who confesses to a string of some 200 murders, some done in collaboration with his killing partner, modeled on the real-life borderline retarded Otis Toole. The police are skeptical until Henry leads them to corpses and shows them Polaroids of mutilated victims.

The success of John McNaughton's *Henry* worked against this film, which was considered minor in comparison, although it has online supporters who hope for its rediscovery. Unlike McNaughton's film, this one actively seeks an explanation for Henry's life of crime, rooted in his horrendous childhood upbringing (indeed, *Henry 2* would also attempt this context).

His lack of proper socialization is held partially responsible for his multi-jurisdictional killing spree.

The killer recounts a childhood spent with a prostitute mother and a disabled father (close to the real Henry), which results in the protagonist's first murder — of a prostitute who rejects his advances—when still a teenager. Scorned, bitter and resentful, he matures into an itinerant drifter who randomly murders (regardless of age, gender or socioeconomic status—unlike most real serial killers) as he crosses the United States. Only suffering comes from contact with this human monster, and, like in *Henry*, there is seemingly little that can be done about it. He is unredeemable.

Like *Henry*, which was released finally in 1990, this film was shelved for some time and, although intended initially for theatrical release, was distributed only on video in 1992, and then without much fanfare.

Cop

(1987: d. James B. Harris)

scr. Harris; nvl. James Ellroy; pr. Harris, James Woods; ph. Steve Dubin, Mikael Salomon; m. Michel Colombier; ed. Anthony Spino; prod d. Gene Rudolf; cast. James Woods, Lesley Ann Warren, Charles Durning, Charles Haid, Raymond J. Barry, Randi Brooks, Steve Lambert; 110m

The quintessential James Woods film: here he stars as an amoral policeman on the trail of a sex killer. His obsession leads him to break ethical standards and exploit a victim's sexual vulnerability, the same quality that affected the killer. The clues lead to a feminist bookstore owner (Warren) and a corrupt street cop. The owner reveals that she was raped in high school (the same one attended by Woods) and deserted by friends, and shortly thereafter was contacted by a secret admirer who sent her letters professing love. The killer apparently intends to take revenge on the women who so mistreated the one he loved. But he butchers them with a sexual pleasure all his own.

Although Woods believes the crimes are related, his superiors do not (also a device in *Jennifer 8*), and he is forced to investigate alone. It is implied that his superiors may believe him but do not want the added pressure of yet another killer to deal with, along with having to explain to the public and internal channels of official accountability. Woods is willing to take the responsibility for such a case onto himself (as would the protagonist in *In the Cold Light of Day*—for differing reasons) but abuses it.

The cop is just as vile as those he pursues, and the film's dark, bleak world enables Ferrara's later *Bad Lieutenant*. The extent of Woods' obsession with police work is depicted in an amusing scene in which he tells his young daughter a bedtime story involving the details of a murder investigation, intending to prepare her for a world which will prey on her innocence. His wife thinks him dangerous and leaves with the daughter. The cop's closeness to the killer, however, is an irony lost on the protagonist, who is so wrapped in his own self-righteousness that he has not noticed the abhorrent specimen he has become.

Woods is obsessed with society's shaping of women's expectations of romance and security with an admiring male, and the film bears out this warped expectation. Such women are fodder for killers and predators as the Romantic is compromised. Ironically, the cop treats women as badly as he seems to resent others doing, and his execution of the killer can also be interpreted as a self-purging act. Indeed, the film is about the end of Romanticism, and the opening reference to Peckinpah violence suggests the corruption of the code of the westerner into sex killer.

James Woods stars as his own brand of justice, self-denial and projection in *Cop* (Ent/Atlantic, 1987).

The film's exploration of the correlation between the cop's sexual exploitation of women and the killer's sex-fantasy makes it a counterpart to *Tightrope* (with Clint Eastwood also as a lone cop with daughters). The bleak tone and the ending in which a policeman cold-bloodedly executes a killer anticipate *Seven*. It is one of the grimmest of modern noir films, not least for the tone of ironic humor accompanying the violence. Harris' style is one of shadowy deglamorization.

Copycat

(1995: d. Jon Amiel)

scr. Ann Biderman, David Madsen; pr. Arnon Milchan, Mark Tarlov; exec pr. Michael Nathanson, John Fielder; ph. Laszlo Kovacs; m. Christopher Young; ed. Alan Heim, Jim Clark; prod d. Jim Clay; cast. Sigourney Weaver, Holly Hunter, Dermot Mulroney, William Mc-Namara, Will Patton, John Rothman, J.E. Freeman, Harry Connick Jr.; 123m

A housebound profiler (Weaver) becomes involved in the pursuit of a serial killer who is duplicating the crimes of other, famous, serial killers, even to the smaller details of the crime scenes. He then deliberately taunts the profiler, sending her e-mails about his next intended victim and even breaking into her house. The detective (Hunter) aids the profiler on the case, their mutual respect growing as they trace the killer's actions. The killer ensnares the profiler, intending to kill the police officer when she comes to the rescue.

The film's parallel of the killer and the profiler is in terms of their knowledge of other killers and their subsequent insight into the mind of a murderer. The killer takes it one step further than the profiler does by actually becoming a murderer in order to feel and understand exactly what previous killers have experienced. This is an alliance of killer and profiler that clearly delineates them in their personal approach to homicidal action, although they are both fascinated students of it (the dilemma facing the profiler in *Manhunter*).

It is a legacy: past crimes provide the base for incipient minds. The film thus develops the sense of kinship between killers, as the killer corresponds with another in prison (the same killer who had previously attacked the profiler), a trait also present in *Manhunter* and *Silence of the Lambs*. This kinship extends to an intertextual canvas wherein murder is an art form and

Serial killer D. Lee Cullum (Harry Connick, Jr.) holds the cord with which he intends to strangle profiler Sigourney Weaver in *Copycat* **(WB, 1995).**

the murderer an artist, with the copycat being an expert forger. The killer is an incomplete personality who latches onto the achievements of others and duplicates them in order to maintain his superiority: he needs to control and torment others to maintain his self-image.

The film also explores the serial killer subculture and plays upon the general knowledge of such killers and their respective milieu. An unusual opening inclusion illustrates this. As Weaver delivers a lecture on serial killers to a crowded auditorium, she asks representative males to stand up and shows them individually on a screen, saying that any one of them could be a killer. Into these portraits is quickly inserted one of actual serial killer Ed Kemper (who killed college coeds). Nothing is said to explain the inclusion, and it is a reference that only those with some knowledge of serial killer history would pick

up — it is in there to illustrate the point to the knowing few and to anchor the proceedings in known fact. The film hinges on the interpretation and interplay of historical fact and fiction as blended in the narrative.

The killer's identity is revealed early on, so the film avoids mystery, concentrating on the intellectual and procedural battle of wits that unfolds. We see the precocious killer at home (with the mother he resents), as he slowly torments a victim, as he hangs about the police station to get added information on the case, and as he prepares for his next crime. This is balanced with a similarly behaviorist study of the profiler-as-victim in her relationship to the female and male officers assigned to the case. It is an interplay of the roles of hunter and hunted and how they affect killer, profiler and investigator as they pursue each other. Each has a perceived tie to the other which entitles them to communicate interpersonally through their response to the act of murder: the film depicting a culture where all have serial killers on the brain — an indictment of contemporary America or of the genre itself?

Contrary to many serial killer films, *Copycat* depicts a world where interpersonal communication is necessary, desired and even dreaded — unavoidable instead of impossible. There are varied means of communication and perception open to all characters. Yet all of these avenues of communication become subservient to the reaction to serial murder: to studying it, talking about

The housebound profiler (Sigourney Weaver) prepares for the worst as she is stalked repeatedly in *Copycat* (WB, 1995).

it, and doing it. The killer's choice of murder is merely one option, the end of a spectrum which carries with it an aggressive perceptual mode that objectifies victims (who are often videotaped by the killer, the tapes altered on computer). Perception and communication are the means of defining an individual in relation and reaction to the surrounding world.

It is only natural for such a world that murder should infiltrate art, film and music. Hence the killer leaves a song (Police's "Murder by Numbers") as the clue to his psyche. The desire for communication and self-expression yield artistic interpretation and identification. This is perhaps Amiel's comment on the serial killer film at that time. This subcultural artistic reaction to serial murder as valid self-expressions would infiltrate many films, among

them the self-conscious treatment in *Summer of Sam* (where a punk band inserts quotes from the Son of Sam killer into their songs). The consequences of heeding these killers' messages, also a theme in *Seven*, is especially prominent in serial killer films from the mid–1990s onwards.

There are two killers featured in the film: one on the loose and the other incarcerated after being captured trying to kill the profiler. Although this killer failed to do the task, he holds onto his perceived control over the situation by harassing the profiler — in a video meeting even asking for her panties in exchange for information about the current killer, whom he refers to as Peter Kurten, a reference to the notorious "Vampire of Dusseldorf" (on whom the film *M* was based). This is another intertextual reference which confirms the notion of such killers as an elite society. The free killer intends his final crime to complete the incarcerated killer's attempt to murder the profiler, and thus continue a line of descent. The final confrontation is between killer, investigator and profiler, the genre's central character triptych, resulting in the socially and dramatically sanctioned execution of the killer. Yet the line is not halted, as the incarcerated killer has a message for the fans and potential imitators that write him in prison. The cycle never stops.

As in the co-released *Seven*, the killer deliberately targets the detectives' weaknesses, finally involving them in his plan for greatness and significance. However, *Copycat* avoids the studied gloom and doom of Fincher's film. Hirsch (*Detours*, p. 283) felt the film reversed traditional gender roles, so that the males are there to be looked at and the central investigators are female, investigating the victimization of women. The computer-literate serial killer would also be featured in *Virtuosity* and *The Bone Collector*.

The Coroner

(2000: d. Juan A. Mas)

pr. Mike Upton; ph. Charles Schnerr; ed. Brian Katkin; cast. Rebecca Gray, Bryn Pryor

A lawyer, after fearing she is being stalked, is rendered unconscious by a blow dart, kidnapped, and tortured in a basement. She escapes and leads police to the location, where the resident turns out to be the local coroner and a friend of the police. Thus he is treated well and she is disbelieved, for no other reason perhaps than that she is a powerful woman and they enjoy her being cut down. Resenting his special treatment and their sloppiness (they get no search warrant), she is determined to make the killer suffer.

The film is apparently intended as a critique of unfair justice when it comes to

victims' rights and an indictment of a certain class and gender bias in the police force. It lays claim to charting the move to empower women and how male society has reacted to such. However, the film was unavailable at time of writing. Again it seems more promising in concept than in apparent execution, having no critical standing or even reception.

The Corpse Grinders

(1971: d. Ted V. Mikels)

scr. Joseph L. Cranston, Arch Hall Jr.; pr, ed, m. Mikels; ph. Bill Anneman; prod d. John Robinson, Laura Young; cast. Sean Lenney, Monika Kelly, Sanford Mitchell, Byron J. Foster, Warren Ball, Patsy Ann Noble; 72m

This zero-budget splatter film in the tradition of H.G. Lewis has become a minor cult item and was a box-office winner for its director. Two owners of a cheap cat-food factory use human corpses as the main ingredient, for economic reasons, and the cats develop a taste for human flesh. They recruit a grave robber at first, à la the Burke and Hare case, and then employ a working strangler to provide fresher produce for their stated clientele, "cats who like people." An investigating doctor and his female assistant trace the subsequent cat attacks back to them.

In its inept way, *The Corpse Grinders* implicates Capitalism as the cause of serial murder. Hence it depicts the deplorable socioeconomic conditions which envelop its protagonists. Those with the power continually exploit — and dispose of — the poor in order to sustain their Capitalist expansion. Indeed, Mikels depicts Capitalist enterprise as merely profiting from the dead. This is typical of Mikels' zero-budget nihilism.

The Corpse Grinders would be an uninteresting and intolerable bargain-basement film were it not for the misanthropic overtones (as McCarty notes, *Guide 1*,

p. 32, it is full of contempt, even for disabled people) and gleeful — if crude — gore. Almost every reviewer consulted felt that it revealed Mikels' callousness and contempt for his own audience also.

Corruption

(1967: d. Robert Hartford-Davis)

scr. Donald and Derek Ford; pr. Peter Newbrook; ph. Newbrook; m. Bill McGuffie; cast. Peter Cushing, Sue Lloyd, David Lodge, Noel Trevarthen, Anthony Booth, Kate O'Mara, Wendy Varnals, Billy Murray; 88m

In yet another variation on *Eyes Without a Face* and *The Awful Dr. Orlof*, a surgeon, somewhat jealous of his younger model wife, accidentally scars her face. He murders and decapitates women in an effort to get the skin he needs to periodically repair the damage. This process becomes both functional and sexual. He kills a member of a hippie group who seeks revenge in a bloody climax that rather disappointingly leads to an it-was-all-a-dream finale.

This film does, however, bring charnel-house gore (severed head in plastic kept in the fridge) into the swinging 1960s youth-oriented London setting. Its view of a corrupt and homicidal older generation preying on the younger echoes Michael Reeves' oeuvre and balances the 1970s work of Pete Walker. Unlike Walker, however, much time here is devoted to the moral and psychological inversion the protagonist undergoes as he segues from lifesaver to life-taker, without any Jekyll/Hyde melodramatics.

Love becomes sadistic homicide too easily. The protagonist's love for his wife is all the more ironic considering the evil bitch the filmmakers consider her to be, at times even more monstrous in her vanity than her husband in his desire to please his trophy bride. Indeed, there is no hint of real love in the film. Even the hippies, supposedly the embodiment of free love, are violent exploiters. There is no innocence left in this world.

The different generational codes of conduct and expectations warp morality. The demands of the younger wife, young enough to be his daughter (suggesting an incestuous dimension), methodically corrupt his spirit. He takes drugs to cope and progresses from removing skin from cadavers (in the name of research) to seeking out prostitutes to murder for their perfect skin. The good doctor thus slowly becomes a Jack the Ripper figure, a link also to previous Hammer versions of the Jekyll/Hyde tale — *Two Faces of Dr. Jekyll* and *I Monster*. As mentioned, the film eliminates the physical metamorphosis that previously accompanied such a psychological change, instead depicting it as perverse, paraphilic progression.

He cannot escape the domination of his wife, whose voice he hears when he talks to prostitutes. The women are surrogates for his wife, his murder and disfigurement of them being a repetition of the moment of trauma in his life, which he slowly begins to eroticize, driven to guilt because of it. His love/hate concern for female beauty enables him to rationalize murder, although the film does not probe this issue as much as Franju in *Eyes Without a Face* or Franco in *The Awful Dr. Orlof*. His wife, in selecting victims for him to kill, becomes his willing dominant partner.

The scripters had previously collaborated on the Sherlock Holmes meets Jack the Ripper movie *A Study in Terror*, and then worked with Davis on *The Black Torment*. These three are considered (Boot, p. 180) pioneers of English sexploitation. Cushing's role as the doctor who discards ethics recalls Dr. Frankenstein and Dr. Knox, as well as Dr. Jekyll. Thus the film represents a bridge to those in the line of 1970s British horror, which attempted to update previous models to contemporary values.

Couch

(1962: d. Owen Crump)

scr. Robert Bloch; stry. Blake Edwards, Crump; ph. Harold Stine; m. Frank Perkins; ed. Leo H. Shreve; art d. Jack Poplin; set d. William L. Kuehl; cast. Grant Williams, Shirley Knight, Onslow Stevens, William Leslie, Anne Helm, Simon Scott, Michael Bachus; 100m

This obscurity was co-scripted by Robert Bloch and Blake Edwards. It concerns a serial killer, recently released from prison, who continues with his "work" as he is undertaking compulsory therapy sessions. He further taunts the police by telephoning them about each new killing. The film reveals a cynical distrust of the penal and psychiatric institutions' ability to treat these killers, and parodies the psychoanalytic process.

Despite the emphasis on analysis of the killer, the film did not probe his motivations and early formative experiences as deeply as many wished for, and so remained more in keeping with straight manhunt narratives, despite the gimmick. The psychiatrist is, however, a substitute father, whom the killer seems to resent as much as his own dead parent. Indeed, the killer views the psychiatrist and the doctor's family as a substitute for his own and develops an unhealthy interest in his analyst's daughter (as *Variety* noted).

The film explores the mindset of a killer whose past, however undeveloped, was serious enough that he seeks out and interprets scenarios that in some way duplicate his family experiences. He is trapped in a cycle of hatred, with murder his main form of expression, not the therapy sessions. It is now rarely screened.

Cover Girl Killer

(1959: d. Terry Bishop)

scr. Bishop; pr. C. Jack Parsons; cast. Harry H. Corbett, Felicity Young, Spencer Teakle, Victor Brooks, Tony Doonan, Bernadette Milne, Christina Gregg, Charles L. Pack; 61m

Women are found murdered and posed in exactly the posture they adopted as models on the cover of "Wow" pin-up magazine. Police finally link the crimes, and suspect an intelligent killer/adversary. The magazine publisher, once a potential suspect, and a pretty model help the police to set a trap for the killer.

It stresses the cultural process of the objectification of women as somehow contributing to the killer's conscienceless disposal of them. The deliberate posing of the bodies reveals the killer's intention for such women to remain the erotic object, which he both loathes and desires. Despite its lack of availability, it would have additional interest as a socially conscious exploitation item that anticipates, at least in thematic synopsis, some of the concerns of those exploitation films that emerged in the latter 1960s to balance Hammer product.

The murder of models/strippers became a regular subplot in the serial killer film, hence *Calendar Girl Murders*, *Click* and the *Stripped to Kill* films.

Crawlspace

(1986: d. David Schmoeller)

scr. Schmoeller; pr. Roberto Bessi; exec pr. Charles Band; ph. Sergio Salvati; m Pino Donaggio; ed. Bert Glatstein; prod d. Giovanni Natalucci; art d. Gianni Cozzo; cast. Klaus Kinski, Talia Balsam, Barbara Whinnery, Sally Brown, Carole Francis, Jack Heller, Joyce Van Patten; 86m

An ex-doctor (Kinski) now runs a boarding house and hires out apartments to primarily young women. He is in reality a sadistic, voyeuristic serial killer who likes to crawl through the ceiling vents and crawlspaces in order to look at the women as they go about their lives. He delights in petty games, experiments he plays with them, blaming rats for the unusual sounds. He enjoys the torture and imprisonment of these woman, and is obsessed with recreating the glory of his father, a Nazi war criminal. The pressure mounts when he is visited by a Nazi-hunter who suspects the doctor of becoming a murderer like his father.

The killer surrounds himself with Nazi paraphernalia and considers his house a mini concentration camp. Thus he keeps a poor, shaven-haired woman prisoner in a restrictive cage. In a perverse way, he has grown attached to her, even admitting that without her he would have no one to talk to. However, his pathology is far more savage. Once he tires of the women, or they discover his secret trap-filled lair, he kills them. After each murder he plays a game of Russian Roulette. Each empty chamber is interpreted as a higher sanction to continue his "work." After all, if he were not meant to kill innocent women, God would have taken his life with the bullet.

The film implicates all males as voyeurs and eroticizes the act of looking from a safe distance. This feeds a fantasy of sexual domination and sublimation that is inevitably homicidal. The gaze is innately masculine and assaultive, and even dooms men to a life of subservience to their sexual desires. It initiates a process of gender role-playing revolving around the duality between the looker and the object of the look. In reality, the killer is all awkward smiles around the women and must compensate through assault — the look and the kill is equated, as in *Peeping Tom*. His observation of women in private, however erotic the act may be, represents the perversion of the behaviorist scientific drive. It enables the killer to fantasize himself a researcher. However, he is aware of his attraction to sex murder, writing in his diary that he is addicted to such murder and that it is an invigorating act. In his mind he is

an amalgam of seducer, lover, father, scientist, and mercy-killing doctor — the ultimate patriarch following in the sanctioned line of Patriarchy. This Patriarchy is here subversively equated with Naziism.

Yet he still has a need for companionship. He must assert his will and macho dominance over these women as a means of staying in control. He thus preys on the common gender stereotype and releases rats to scare the women, delighting in their reaction and perhaps even masturbating as he watches them. It is his escape from an otherwise banal life. His diary entries, as voice-over punctuation, gradually reveal the depths of his monstrousness. It roots his passion in his doctoral practice of euthanasia as a justification for eliminating life, akin to the excuse the Nazis used to eliminate "inferior" races. Like any good researcher, he keeps elaborate records of his actions, perhaps the ultimate act of self-gratifying self-importance. However, he takes this further and keeps victims' body parts preserved in jars as macabre trophies of his actions. Killing for him is the ultimate opiate, and his diary is a document of death. He must in this way constantly reassert his potency. For him, the ultimate form of potency is the control over life and death, itself even a form of omnipotence. It is ironic that this self-proclaimed great man spends much of his time scurrying around like a rodent.

This fascinating low-budgeter was maligned, savaged and dismissed by those critics that bothered to review it. In it, Kinski gives an interpretation of the serial killer that balances the one he essayed in Jess Franco's *Jack the Ripper*.

Schmoeller had treated the serial killer before in *Tourist Trap*, and would return to the character type in *The Arrival*. Both are equally underrated movies, although there are signs of a cult reception for *Tourist Trap*. For some reason, however, even the fans dismiss *Crawlspace*.

Schmoeller is perhaps the best director to carry on with his association with Charles Band, whose Empire Pictures produced this film in Italy.

Craze

(1973: d. Freddie Francis)

scr. Aben Kandel, Herman Cohen; nvl. Henry Seymour; pr. Herman Cohen; ph. John Wilcox; m. John Scott; ed. Henry Richardson; art d. George Provis; cast. Jack Palance, Diana Dors, Julie Ege, Edith Evans, Hugh Griffith, Trevor Howard, Suzy Kendall, David Warbeck; 96m

An antique-store owner (Palance) prays to an African idol, Chuku, in his basement. He believes he will become rich if he makes live sacrifices of prostitutes or sexually independent women to the god. His assistant knows it is happening but is too meek to prevent it, even when the police become involved. Meanwhile, a Scotland Yard detective closes in, finally shooting the out-of-control killer.

The film combines the case study of a psychotic killer with occultism, the killer also functioning as a coven leader, thus reflecting the post–*Rosemary's Baby* witchcraft theme, although it seems a British take-off of the *Blood Feast* school. Despite financially profiting from the crimes, it is clear (McCarty, *Vol. 2*, p. 8) that sexual thrills are the primary reason for the homicides. Palance reportedly overacts, and *Variety* lamented that the film never became the battle of wits between cop and killer that it promised to be.

Like the same team's *Trog*, this is not considered one of Francis' better efforts—despite the good cast. US producer Herman Cohen had previously made five UK-based films. It is functional but lacks the style and commitment that redeems Francis' best horrors. Perhaps *Craze* is best thought of as the UK equivalent of a minor US exploitation movie.

Crimetime

(1996: d. George Sluizer)

scr. Brendan Somers; pr. David Pupkewitz; exec pr. Philip Alberstat, Barry Barenholtz, Mark Vlessing; ph. Jules Van Den Steenhoven; m. David A. Stewart; ed. Fabienne Rawley; prod d. Bernd Lepel; song. Marianne Faithful; cast. Stephen Baldwin, Pete Postlethwaite, Sadie Frost, Karen Black, Geraldine Chaplin, James Faulkner, Phil David; 113m

In the near future, in a media-fixated UK, an actor (Baldwin) is cast in the role of a serial killer on a popular crime-recreation TV show. Considering himself dedicated to the acting craft, he researches the crimes thoroughly, even getting police to show him crime scene details and corpses. He becomes a star, to the delight of the real killer (Postlethwaite), a TV repairman ironically enough, who, in response, is driven to more elaborate and grisly crimes. The killer intends to meet the actor and perfect their symbiotic relationship.

A stab at social satire and the exploration of the interplay between reality and media recreation, the film continues themes present in the likes of *Death Watch* and *To Die For*. It locates the killer's crimes in an unfulfilling home life, where he lives with his blind, child-like, mentally ill wife (Chaplin). The murders are his fantasies, his escape from an entrapping reality, and the media fuel these by recreating them, thus validating his experience and desires.

The killer befriends women and kills them, removing as a souvenir of each crime the victim's left eye, keeping them all in a collection in his basement refrigerator, and taking them out sporadically to gaze at lovingly and reminisce. Indeed, all the characters possess an active gaze, although invariably centered on death, as if to suggest such homicide as the inevitable result of a culture founded on such looking. Such a culture is a self-perpetuating cycle — killing inspires artistic interpretation that inspires ever more grotesque crime — an indictment of the serial killer film of the mid–1990s.

Undeniably stylish and clever in its use of point of view to explore the seamless interplay of fact and fiction, of the real world and the TV recreation, *Crimetime* pulls back on occasion to a more detached, brooding perspective. This contrasts the killer and protagonist, whose efforts to understand result in a dangerous immersion in the details. Graphic murder is just a symptom of a culture that has lost perspective on where and how to look. The killer watches the real victim die; the actor watches the actress die and compares it to the corpse; the TV audience watches the actor; and the film viewer watches it all. These levels implicate the audience's complicity in not only murder, but also its glorified recreation.

Even the killer is concerned with his image, both on TV and in actuality, as he gazes in the mirror, perhaps not recognizing his own monstrous ugliness (recalling that shot in *M*), and pretends he is a glamorous actor. The actor refers to himself as a lady-killer, further contrasting the implications of that statement with the killer's actions, which he starts to pore over, as if sexual conquest can segue into homicidal conquest with media exploitation as the catalyst. The killer leaves messages on the actor's answering machine, furthering their symbiotic association (recalling the killer/journalist relationship in such films as *Mean Season* and *Diary of a Serial Killer*).

The media fuels the killer's fantasies, as he starts to dress fancier, perceiving his intended sartorial elegance as bringing him closer to TV glamour. He fantasizes himself a TV star. Correspondingly, the actor's fantasies become ever more morbid until he desires closeness with corpses, to touch death and see it as the killer did. Finally, the killer is able to implicate the actor in a real murder, and at the climax

wishes the actor to be just like him, a recognition the actor has to purge by stabbing the killer. Cut to: it's all been recreated as a Hollywood movie, with Sluizer himself playing the director — an ending perhaps referring to his involvement in Hollywood's bastardization of his own film, *The Vanishing*.

By so depicting a sinister culture parasitically feeding off murder for profit, Sluizer furthers the concern for self-absorbed egotists enthralled by the prospect of taking lives, and of those obsessed with experiencing such roles for themselves. This is his overriding theme as a director, and amply evident in *The Vanishing*. His fascination with people's desire for empathy with the monstrous is highly self-conscious and complements the theme in *Copycat*.

Sluizer had flirted with the serial killer figure before in both versions of the thriller *The Vanishing*. Baldwin would play an investigator on the trail of a serial killer in the later *Absence of the Good*. Sluizer had greatly resented studio interference over the ending to the American version of *The Vanishing*, but when allowed relatively free rein in the low-budget field, as here, he failed to impress the critics and the film sank into video obscurity.

Criminal Law

(1989: d. Martin Campbell)

scr. Mark Kasdan; pr. Hilary Heath, Robert K. Maclean; ph. Phil Meheux; m. Jerry Goldsmith; ed. Chris Wimble; cast. Gary Oldman, Kevin Bacon, Tess Harper, Karen Young, Joe Don Baker, Sean McCann; 117m

A bright, up and coming lawyer (Oldman) successfully defends an accused serial killer, a spoilt rich young man (Bacon), only to be targeted by the killer who decides to play psychological games with him. He implicates the lawyer in murder, planting a corpse for him to discover, for the thrill and challenge of the ensuing battle of wits. The killer tries to assert his sense of innate superiority, and the ever more humbled lawyer is forced to become detective to extricate himself from guilt by association.

Director Martin Campbell repeatedly compares the two young men as perhaps doppelganger figures, at times suggesting a homoerotic subtext between their adversarial conflicts. Both are arrogant, self-assured and initially self-righteous. Consequently, the actions are a humbling lesson for the lawyer, now forced to confront the monstrousness he made light of by defending so well. Of course, the lawyer is bound by his professional obligations not to reveal what he knows, leading to the inevitable climax.

He discovers that the killer's mother was an abortionist, and that all the female victims had had abortions. This, however, has no real significance beyond a gimmick, and Campbell concentrates on the story of a smug lawyer whom a killer feels needs to be cut down a peg or two (a theme also in Scorsese's remake of *Cape Fear*). The lawyer has to confront his moral responsibility for letting such a killer go free to kill again. In a blatant recognition of the failure of the insanity defense (the film's most sustained theme), the lawyer shoots the killer so that justice is done.

This was Campbell's feature film debut after successful television experience in the UK. He has since gone on to become a professional Hollywood director of action films: *Goldeneye, No Escape, Mask of Zorro* and *Vertical Limit*. His debut did not impress the critics or the public.

The abortionist context would feature as motivation for the killer in *Sacrifice*.

Cross Country

(1984: d. Paul Lynch)

scr. Logan N. Danforth, William Gray, John Hunter; pr. Ronald I. Cohen, Pieter Kroonenburg, David J. Patterson; ph. Rene Verzier; m. Chris Rea; ed. Nick Rotundo; prod d. Michel Prouix; cast. Richard Beymer, Nina Axelrod, Michael Ironside, Brent Carver, Mike Kane; 95m

One of three people travelling across country together is a serial killer. A failed ad executive (Beymer) leaves the city soon after his girlfriend, who had ridiculed him, is found dead, one of a series of murders. The killer tore off the victims' earrings (also in *Love and Human Remains*). The police are on the case. Beymer gets together with a stripper for a cross-country trek, but awakens to find her boyfriend driving. The three of them travel, with the ad executive desperate to retain control over them, and have sexual relations with the stripper. When her boyfriend is found dead, the stripper is revealed to be the opportunistic, resentful killer. The ad exec drives her off a cliff into the grand canyon but jumps out in time to save himself.

This is similar to, indeed anticipates, *Nature of the Beast* and even *Kalifornia* in its combination of road movie, serial killer film and detective story. It portrays a man forever in flight, seeking to escape a life he considers empty. All women remind him of one in particular, and his aggressive sexuality indicates his desire to dominate this type — his life is lived in reaction, despite his perceived control. Correspondingly, the killer feigns a life lived in reaction and submission in order to be in control. As a stripper, sexuality is her weapon, and the stereotypical image of strippers as dumb and childlike is her cover.

As the detective closes in, his brutality and contempt for deviance is revealed. He puts a gay lead's head in the toilet to exact information. His obsession corrupts his moral code, akin to the immorality of the protagonists in the mid–1980s noir serial killer films *Cop* and *Tightrope*. It is as minor noir that this film is best considered, with a dark, shadowy style and duplicitous characters seeking control over their own destiny. They all live in reaction to circumstance, forever trying to assert their personality onto others and the world around them in a quest for identity, however futile — ideal matter for the road movie. The director is a relatively unheralded figure who is a surprisingly capable filmmaker, and this remains possibly his best film and a worthwhile video rediscovery.

Cruising

(1980: d. William Friedkin)

scr. Friedkin; nvl. Gerald Walker; pr. Jerry Weintraub, Burtt Harris; ph. James A. Contner; m. Jack Nitzsche; ed. Bud Smith; prod d. Bruce Weintraub; cast. Al Pacino, Paul Sorvino, Karen Allen, Richard Cox, Don Scardino, James Satorius, Joe Spinell, Randy Jurgensen, Jay Acovone, James Remar; 106m

A rookie policeman (Pacino) goes undercover in the world of leather S&M homosexuals in New York City to find a killer of gays. In the process, his own sexuality is threatened. Condemned by critics, policemen and gay activists alike, *Cruising* is a disturbing look at aberration.

Initially the project was intended for Steven Spielberg and producer Phil D'Antoni (who produced Friedkin's hit *The French Connection*, about another obsessive policeman); but upon reflection, they felt the book too aberrant to film. Friedkin disagreed, resurrected the project and consulted with ex-undercover policeman Randy Jurgenson (Claggett, p. 189) for added authenticity. He demanded genuine New York City locations be used wherever possible. Despite the protests lobbed at the film by gay groups, many gays voluntarily worked on the movie for that much-prized authenticity in the bar scenes. The film was subject to much re-editing and trimming before being finally released to cinemas.

Friedkin deliberately strove for ambiguity, resulting in arguable confusion. There is not simply one killer but several in operation, as if some kind of evil were passed infectiously between them. Indeed, all the killers speak in the same voice — that belonging to the dead father of one of the killers. It was the equation between infectious evil and homosexuality that many condemned. But it is the condemnation of Patriarchy that saturates the film. Even the killer's childish chant, "Who's here. I'm here. You're here" (spoken by different killers), suggests Friedkin was reaching for an allegorical dimension which implicates all as participants in the commonality of such evil-spreading aberration.

Thus, even the cop is treated ambiguously, and we are never sure to what extent he too has been corrupted by his exposure to the hedonistic netherworld the film depicts unflinchingly. He is certainly implicated in the film's final murder (of a sympathetic gay who had forged a friendship with the undercover cop). Perhaps most tellingly, the film equates psychological well being with confidence in one's sexuality, with Pacino's comment that "there's a lot about me you don't know" questioning the dimensions of his identity. Why did he volunteer so easily and say "I love it" when told about the prospect? If your sexuality is threatened, are you likely to become a killer due to Patriarchal expectation? Is exposure to aberration addictive (hence the scene where Pacino is fellated by his girlfriend as he hears the music of the gay clubs in his mind)? Is it a corrupt socialization process rooted in the relationship between father and son? Is the desire to lose oneself in illicit and amoral abandon tantamount to the destruction of that Patriarchal ideal?

Friedkin raises the questions but the film falls short of one coherent explanation. Although this was condemned as the film's failure, it makes it a more thought-

Detective Steve Burns (Al Pacino) poses undercover in the leather-gay clubworld of New York City to gain information about a killer of gays in the controversial *Cruising* (WB, 1980).

provoking examination, however frustrating in its thematic teases. It is certainly among the most provocative, graphic and controversial of serial killer films. There have been recent efforts to provide a unifying account of the film, and to redeem it on social grounds.

The depiction of the police is as harsh as the leather-gays, however, as they are, in fact, repeatedly paralleled as a kind of malfunctioning Patriarchy. The police are hypocritical, violent and homophobic louts, as crass and vulgar and corrupt as they claim the world they police to be. As supposed protectors and enforcers they represent the failure of a system to prevent itself from surrender to self-destroying (liberating?) aberration.

Central to this notion of killing as Patriarchy's legacy is the relation between one killer, the main one investigated by Pa-

cino, and his dead father, whose voice tells him, "You know what to do." The suggestion is that the law of the father has led to such murder. Patriarchy fucking itself. Is this Friedkin's thesis, and is the film thus an allegory? Hence, as the first killer stabs a victim in the back after a homosexual encounter, he remarks, "You made me do that." Pacino is asked, "How'd you like to disappear," a prospect he embraces, and, as such, possibly also becomes a killer: murder as a consequence of the surrender to a corruptive aberration.

The stress on entrances and exits suggests the notion of transferal thus linked to the notion of an infectious evil (this is a pre–AIDS film), and the theme of a journey towards self-discovery—a realization of the killer in all. It is a restless world of sexual compulsion, with horrific consequences for abandon. This world objectifies

The undercover policeman (Al Pacino) is about to leave with a homosexual pickup who may or may not be a serial killer in *Cruising* (WB, 1980).

men as sexual commodities, a function traditionally reserved for women and an inversion of the function of the Patriarchal gaze. It depicts the homosexual underworld as depraved and ritualistic, yet it holds this underworld in collusion with the police as its mirror image, indicators of a systematic failure beyond the homosexual context. The homosexual netherworld is a symptom and symbol of an ideology in crisis, breeding predatory killers.

The ambiguity surrounding the murders (there are at least two killers, possibly three or more) results in a narrative tease which undercuts any conventional structural resolution, even though one is offered. Further complicated by rampant doppelganger motifs, it forwards such homicide as rooted in cultural experience, and that cultural experience is a malfunctioning Patriarchy self-consuming and self-destructing in the effort to preserve itself. The contamination spreads over into conventional heterosexual relations also. In this realm the police force and the bar world are interchangeable (hence precinct night, wherein all the clientele dress up as police officers in leather). Friedkin offers no alternative to immersion in his nightmare world. In its implication of Patriarchy, critic Robin Wood felt that the film developed the very thesis behind the move towards gay liberation (Wood, *Hollywood from Vietnam to Reagan*, p. 67).

The controversial bar scenes explore with a panning and probing camera a world of sexual abandon and degradation (fist fucking, fellatio, groping, torture, etc.). Some background scenes had to be darkened before censors would allow certification, further enhancing the film's bleakly noirish world.

At time of release, practically every review was hostile and condemnatory. *Newsweek*'s David Ansen termed it "a superficially shocking tableaux for the titillation and horror of his audience ... [the film is] a cinematic herpes blister" (Claggett, p. 207). Gay spokesperson Arthur Bell called it "almost a road map on how to kill a gay. It's a product of the grossest dreams of a reactionary gay-hater" (Claggett, p. 201). Friedkin returned to the serial killer for *Rampage*. A gay serial killer would also feature in the film *Frisk*, aimed at the gay audience exclusively.

Cupid

(1997: d. Douglas Campbell)

scr. David Benullo; pr. Clark Peterson, Pierre David (exec); ph. M. Favif Mullen; m. Kubilay Uner; ed. Julian Semilian; prod d. Jodi Ginnever; cast. Zach Galligan, Ashley Laurence, Mary Crosby, Joseph Kell, Annie Fitzgerald; 95m

A young man, consumed by expectations of the perfect female partner, is driven to kill those who do not conform to his fantasy image. His sister desires a continued incestuous union and resents his fixation on a young bookstore owner. He courts this woman until she uncovers the depths of his obsession and kills him in self-defense.

This is a twenty-something coming-of-age movie which seeks to implicate impossible Romantic ideals in the selfish pursuit of fantasy. Fantasy turns the quest for romantic love into a stalking obsessiveness that demands the murder of its fallen object rather than an admittal of the impossibility and unattainability of the fantasy. Thus the film contrasts the killer's expectations of romance with the resulting murders, although not as effectively as did *Martin*. Ironically, the first victim is will-

ing to have sex but not to marry — her "impurity" triggering the killer's rage.

Curdled

(1996: d. Reb Braddock)

scr. Braddock, John Maass; pr. Raul Puig, Maass; exec pr. Quentin Tarantino; ed. Mallori Gottlieb; prod d. Sherman Williams; cast. William Baldwin, Angela Jones, Bruce Ramsay, Lois Chiles; 88m

Produced under the auspices of Quentin Tarantino, this odd piece examines the attraction that serial murders and crime scenes have on a certain subculture of people (known as "gorehounds"). A young woman, fascinated by death and the grisly details of homicide from a young age (when she witnessed a murder), joins a post-forensic crime-scene clean-up business in order to get closer to the murder sites, which sexually excite her. A serial killer/decapitator, the "Blue Blood Killer" (Baldwin), who targets rich women, sees her almost masturbate at the scene of one of his crimes and attempts to forge a relationship with her. Ironically, he is at first repelled by her aberrant sexuality, though he soon realizes its closeness to himself.

This is a weird black comedy, and offers a more restrained, though equally caricaturish, style than *From Dusk Till Dawn*. Indeed, the link to that film is made explicit when the protagonist watches a TV news report of three wanted killers and sees the photographs of Richard Speck (a real-life mass killer of nurses, and an inclusion only those familiar with the subculture would know, thus akin to the inclusion of the photo of Ed Kemper in *Copycat*) followed by those of Clooney and Tarantino. The protagonist not only watches news reports but all manner of violence in the media, and television becomes the agent of graphic horror as the film explores the interplay between violent trauma and the media exploitation of it, linking *Curdled* to Oliver Stone's Tarantino-scripted *Natural Born Killers*. This is only a secondary theme, however, further complementing the stress on the symbiotic relationship between the killer and those who form the subculture around him.

Baldwin is the monstrous lady-killer who kills and pauses to watch his victims writhe and bleed to death. The protagonist imitates these death throes as she seeks to put herself in victim's role and then killer's. In this way she perverts, through warped empathy, the role of the profiler. This process of perversion results in her adoption of the role of killer, decapitating Baldwin as she usurps his power, emasculating him and in the process emancipating her monstrous desire.

Supposedly, Tarantino saw the director's short film at a film festival and used it as the basis for the Harvey Keitel character in *Pulp Fiction*. He subsequently financed the film's expansion to a feature, giving the director his chance.

Daddy's Deadly Darling

(1972: d. Toni Lawrence)

scr. Lawrence; cast. Toni Lawrence, Marc Lawrence, Jesse Vint, Katharine Ross; Iris Korn

A young woman, confined to a mental hospital after knifing her rapist father, escapes in a nurse's uniform to a small town. There she befriends a local farmer, meanwhile killing men who remind her of her stepfather and feeding their bodies to the pigs, who have developed a taste for human flesh — since the farmer is also a serial killer. A sheriff and a private investigator hired by the hospital (to avoid legal ramifications) follow her trail.

Complete with dismemberment scenes and dream sequences, this approaches black comedy, pre–Tobe Hooper style. Odd characters abound, including one woman who believes the pigs house reincarnated souls. As a black comedy about

"love" between two brutal killers, it can be compared with Bechard's *Psychos in Love*. It is a minor addition to the early 1970s rural psycho movie, as better encapsulated by the likes of *Terror Circus* and *The Texas Chainsaw Massacre*. The daughter corrupted by the evil Patriarch whose abuse in turn makes her a sex killer (both to avenge herself and to usurp his power) would be better treated in the later *Eye of the Beholder*. Nevertheless, it remains an early treatment of the female serial killer forever in the shadow of a Patriarchy she rebels against.

Dance with Death

(1991: d. Charles Philip Moore)

scr. Daryl Haney; pr. Mike Elliott; ed. Chris Roth; prod d. James Shumaker; art d. Amy B. Ancona; cast. Catya Sassoon, Martin Mull, Michael J. McDonald, Drew Snyder, Steven Lloyd Williams, Barbara A. Woods; 90m

An intrepid reporter poses as a stripper in order to investigate a series of murders of women from a local strip club. This is a routine entry in comparison to the likes of Katt Shea Ruben's *Stripped to Kill* films and even *Dark Dancer*. It also wants to offer a glimpse into an illicit world, like that portrayed in *Fear City*. It has some interest as an exploration of women's roles within, and an attempt to understand, a Patriarchy that demands subjugation. The idea running through these stripper murder films is that somehow this profession acts paradoxically as a form of female liberation and even gender empowerment. It is this that fuels male hatred and resentment, even though the role of the stripper is a male fantasy. It is a problematic theme.

The Dark

(1979: d. John Bud Cardos)

scr. Stanford Whitmore; pr. Dick Clark, Edward L. Montero, Derek Power; ph. John A. Morrill; m Roger Kellaway; ed. Martin Dreffke;

cast. William Devane, Cathy Lee Crosby, Richard Jaeckel, Keenan Wynn, Jacquelyn Hyde, Vivian Blaine, Casey Kasem; 92m

An alien comes to Santa Monica and murders women for pleasure, decapitating and mutilating them. The police are baffled and consider calling in outside help from the military, while the head detective (Jaeckel) is enraged that a man he sent to jail (Devane) is investigating on his own. The man's daughter was a victim of the killer. A reporter investigates and slowly enters into a relationship with the reluctant Devane. The reporter's editor, however, does not want to sensationalize the crimes. A psychic's insight gives them the clue to locating the killer, and a ferocious gun battle ensues.

The opening script states that not all alien visitors will be friendly, and so the film can be taken as a reaction against the optimism of *Close Encounters of the Third Kind*. Indeed, as the opening spacecraft hurtles to Earth it reminds one of 1950s science fiction updated to the age of the sex killer, the 1970s. Thus it poses the question: what if the likes of Jack the Ripper were not human at all but a malevolent alien visiting the planet for sport (a plot hook which would influence the later *Predator* movies and such other alien killer films as *The Arrival* and *Split Second*)?

Taking place in the Santa Monica fringe of Los Angeles, much of it is set at night, with the implication that this is the time such killers cruise for victims. Such a threat is alien to human nature, and the film thus is a response to the 1970s crime epidemic, resorting to an old-fashioned Otherness as the possible explanation: how could such monstrousness be human? As it fails to characterize the alien as more than a killing machine, the film also ties in neatly to the emerging slasher formula. The cop Jaeckel makes this clear when he says that the shark is termed an eating machine, and that what they are dealing with is a killing machine. This reference suggests the film is in part inspired by the narrative structure of the hit *Jaws*. The alien gains in strength from each kill and must be eliminated before it achieves immortality and spreads its contagion over humanity.

One note of interest is the theme of poetic justice: Devane is an author of violent pulp now reaping the effects of a culture of violence. Although this is raised, it is defeated by the dominant alien visitor theme. Nevertheless, a violent society, fascinated and repulsed by that very violence, gets what it deserves and draws greater violence onto it. Thus the breezy Santa Monica lifestyle is consumed by random, unclassifiable homicide. It is the end of an era, with a horrible portent of what is to come.

The press, of course, latch onto the latest abomination, dubbing him "The Mangler," and the resultant coverage creates a panic and added pressure on the hard-line police to solve the case quickly. Although they rely on forensic means, the results are equally baffling, and at one time the killer is jokingly referred to as a zombie — perhaps a reference to the contemporary success of Romero's *Dawn of the Dead*. The police must choose which details to withhold in the public interest and so clash with the media over the issue of responsibility, a standard theme in the genre.

With a rather contemplative visual style, and a sociological attention to mise-en-scene and people within the urban landscape, *The Dark* is Cardos' best film. In the late 1970s Cardos also made the clever *Kingdom of the Spiders*, suggesting a potential that unfortunately never returned. *The Dark*'s breezy feel and use of open vs. closed spaces is a calculated choice and perfectly compliments the theme of an open lifestyle gradually coming to a violent close.

Dark City

(1998: d. Alex Proyas)

scr. Proyas, Lem Dobbs, David S. Goyer; pr. Andrew Mason, Proyas; ph. Dariusz Wolski; m. Trevor Jones; ed. Dov Hoenig; prod d. Patrick Tatopoulos, George Liddle; cast. Rufus Sewell, Kiefer Sutherland, William Hurt, Jennifer Connelly, Richard O' Brien, Ian Richardson; 97m

This somber fantasy, from the director of *The Crow*, has an amnesiac protagonist (Sewell) pursued as a serial killer of prostitutes by investigators (including Hurt). As he flees, he uncovers a mysterious secret about the world he lives in, in which people's identities are constantly altered and shifted by aliens who are studying the human species in an effort to determine uniqueness. In battling the aliens, who are assisted by a traitorous human psychiatrist (Sutherland), Sewell attains their Godlike powers, able to transform spatial relations by will alone, a process called "tuning."

This film uses the serial killer figure as the epitome of human aberrance, and as an introductory narrative hook. It is a probing treatise on memory and identity, exploring the definition of the soul as an identity separate from that constituted by memory alone. The aliens experiment, switching people's memories to see if they will act according to such a definition, or whether an inherent "self" would rebel against a different, implanted past. The serial killer is held as the absolute nadir of human experience, which imbues the afflicted with a power over life and death that parallels the Godlike aliens (indeed, an alien relishes such experience when

Rufus Sewell stars as the man who has the identity of a serial killer implanted into his own mind by aliens in the somber fantasy of *Dark City* (Roadshow, 1998).

implanted with the killer's identity, though even he finally admits the experience is self-destructive). The protagonist's soul, though implanted with the identity of a serial killer, rebels against such, developing a power for self-expression that, when freed from conventional identity, can shape circumstance rather than be shaped by it. The serial killer identity must be so transcended.

A person is capable of more than the sum of his memories. Though insofar as the human psychiatrist, a mediator who helps the aliens and assists the protagonist to defeat them, is named Schreiber (referring no doubt to the name of Freud's only schizophrenic patient), the film suggests that such a realization and emancipation is akin to the schizophrenic dissolution of reality and the subsequent erection of a delusional and hallucinogenic realm. In that, it is almost a validation of psychotic experience as ontological insight: if one thinks as God is, then one can do what God does—to create as well as to destroy.

Thus the film is a complex and enthralling meditation on the desire to be God. It combines science fiction, comic book fantasy, film noir, and the serial killer genres effortlessly. In fact, its central character triangle (of killer, psychiatrist and investigator) is that of the serial killer film. Here the psychiatrist-as-profiler is reversed, literally concocting the killer's personality based on various ingredients (one part parental abuse, two parts teenage rebellion, etc.) in the effort to control behavior which the investigator reacts to. His understanding is the bridge required for the protagonist to master his power.

The Dark Half

(1991: d. George A. Romero)

scr. Romero; nvl. Stephen King; pr. Declan Baldwin, Romero; ph. Tony Pierce-Roberts; m. Christopher Young; ed. Pasquale Buba; prod d. Cletus Anderson; cast. Timothy Hutton, Amy Madigan, Michael Rooker, Christine Forrest, Royal Dano, Rutanya Alda; 122m

Romero adapts Stephen King (for the first time since the *Creepshow* movies). A writer and academic pens a series of violent novels under the pseudonym George Stark. When he decides to end the books and drop the pseudonym, a series of murders begins, committed apparently by his alter ego, Mr. Stark. Crucial to the issue of his innocence or guilt is evidence that he had an unformed twin surgically removed from him (in a terrifying opening sequence). The killer then apparently pursues the writer as detectives investigate and suspect him.

The Dark Half is an examination of the relation between the creative process and the repercussions on the individual ego when the creative persona is empowered beyond control. King had explored this theme of "character assassination" (Harrington, *Washington Post*) in *Misery*. As a teacher, the protagonist lectures on the duality of man, adding that it is essential to the creative essence to loose such a dark side. Of course this may be the rationalization which enables him to mass-produce pulp thrillers, but it also speaks to the force of his creative energies—that by intensely wishing it so, he believes he could produce an entirely separate personality. Thus the film examines the birth of an alter ego and the consequences when such an amoral force is loosed. It returns the genre to Jekyll and Hyde, although the notion of a double life is familiar to Romero from *Martin*.

As with other films following in the wake of Jekyll and Hyde, the dark side in the protagonist's creative freedom is a form of an idealized self, and the attempt to destroy or bind it is an act of repression. Although, as usual for Romero, the idealized self serves to jeopardize and marginalize the protagonist, and severs the ties to

Timothy Hutton stars as the writer who wants to kill off his alter ego but finds it too powerful in *The Dark Half* (Orion, 1991).

convention (i.e. its own past). The visual emphasis on interiors stresses entrapment, which the protagonist seeks to break through, as the film develops the motif of *Monkey Shines*. The bad self wants out, and gets out, to the detriment of those who would seek otherwise.

The personality transfer is cued by bird song, and gradually the protagonist starts to hear voices as he is forced to confront the monstrousness within him. Or is Stark really a separate entity? Stark does not want to die and strives to find form himself. This thematic stress on discovery is balanced by the procedural narrative, which charts how the investigating officer comes to suspect him. Michael Rooker (who played the eponymous murderer in *Henry, Portrait of a Serial Killer* and the killer in *Sea of Love*) is ironically cast as the investigating policeman (as he would be in *The Bone Collector*).

Since the killings are motivated by revenge and the desire for a new start, more

so than any overt sexual dimension, the film is not essentially a serial killer film. However, the new application of Jekyll and Hyde motifs to the concept of an evil twin illustrates the continued viability of the formula. Still, *The Dark Half* was considered a disappointment from a horror master in decline.

Dark Ride

(1977: d. Jeremy Hoenack) aka *Killer's Delight*

cast. John Karlen, Martin Speer, Susan Jennifer Sullivan, Hilary Thompson, James Luisi; 83m

Dark Ride is one of the first films to explore the Ted Bundy case, although it is heavily fictionalized. A psychotic killer (John Karlen) rapes, tortures and murders women. Three people investigate: a rural policeman, a big-city detective, and a psychologist intent on creating the right profile.

One of the first films since *The Boston*

Strangler to self-consciously develop the profiler figure to some degree, this is a procedural account. It is set in San Francisco but was filmed mostly in Los Angeles. Bundy's case was dramatized for TV, to more attention, in *Deliberate Stranger*. *Dark Ride* is nevertheless a film that responds to the 1970s rise in such crimes—both a portrait of a killer and a social document of the response to such a problem.

Dark Side of Midnight

(1984: d. Wes Olsen) aka *The Creeper*

scr, pr, ed. Olsen; cast. James Moore, Olsen, Sandy Schemmel, Dave Bowling, Dennis Brennan; 108m

A serial killer known as "the Creeper" targets Fort Smith, Arkansas. A detective assigned to the case finds his efforts hampered by the mayor, who impedes progress for financial profit. A minor effort re-released from Z-grade exploitation company Troma, this was unavailable at time of writing.

Daughter of Darkness

(1948: d. Lance Comfort)

scr. Max Catto; pr. Victor Hanbury; ph. Stan Pavey; m. Clifton Parker; ed. Lito Carruthers; art d. Ivan King; cast. Anne Crawford, Maxwell Reed, Siobhan McKenna, George Thorpe, Barry Morse, Liam Redmond, Honor Blackman; 91m

This rare female serial killer movie (based on the play *They Walk Alone* by Max Catto), the story of a "homicidal nymphomaniac," posed many censorship problems. Irish stage actress Siobhan McKenna (in her second film) stars as Emma, a modern siren/black widow who lures men and then murders them for personal sexual gratification. She is the village priest's trusted assistant, and at first no one suspects her double life, except an apparently asexual woman. Gradually the villagers resent and hate her for her effect on men. Thus scorned, she is sent away by the Priest to England, where the bodies start piling up again.

The film posits women's sexual freedom as a threat to the forces of "civilization," with the repressed woman able to spot the unrepressed — and resent such liberation, destructive though it may be. However, the filmmakers depict the civilized people as an intolerant lynch mob and so supposedly generate a certain subversive charge (Bovy, *imdb* comments). The film explores the demonization of this "free" woman also as a function of class politics, as she is Irish destroying the English. She may seem demure, but that appearance hides a fearsome sexuality that seeks to devour her partner — thus in tune with the black widow mythos and the femme fatale persona of film noir (which the film is generally not associated with).

There is nothing in Comfort's filmography to suggest the effectiveness he apparently achieves here, with a hysterical noirist style framing an examination of the grotesque. *Variety* praised the director's courage for bringing a problematic subject to the screen. The film was also the first movie role for Honor Blackman before TV's *The Avengers*, and fame as Pussy Galore in the James Bond movie *Goldfinger*.

Dead Certain

(1991: d. Anders Palm) aka *Murder Blues*

scr. Palm; pr. Mark Cutforth, Palm; ph. John de Borman; m. Richard Derbyshire, Charlie Mole; ed. Roy Burge; art d. Nick White; cast. Francesco Quinn, Brad Dourif, Karen Russell, Joel Kaiser, John Trench, James Davidson; 90m

An obsessed, alcoholic detective believes the killer of a woman he knew is a serial killer (Brad Dourif) and pursues him. The killer ritually disembowels his victims, and the increasingly shabby detective succumbs to heroin addiction. The cop realizes that the crimes are copycat cases. He must go to prison to talk to the re-jailed original offender and gain his confidence, so it will lead to the killer on the loose (who has himself contacted the jailed killer).

This is considered sub-par Thomas Harris plotting, again using the device of the incarcerated killer consulted for additional case input, although the film reportedly predated *Silence of the Lambs*. It is effective at revealing the grim atmosphere of a world populated by tormented people who lose, or are battling with, their moral control. Director Palm is a minor auteur who has found an attraction to the figure of the serial killer, as the march of fate and the agent of death, in his horror/crime films.

Dead Connection

(1994: d. Nigel Dick) aka *Final Combination*

co-d. Thomas Patrick Smith; scr. Larry Golin; pr. Gregg Fienberg, Steve Golin, Gregory Goodman, Gary Milkis, Joni Sighvatsson; ph. David Bridges; m. Rolfe Kent; ed. Henry Richardson, Jonathan Shew; cast. Michael Madsen, Lisa Bonet, Gary Strentch, Tim Russ, Damien Chapa, Carmen Argenziano; 93m

An ex-boxer who uses the names of famous fighters as aliases leaves a trail of sexually assaulted dead women in run-down city motels. An alcoholic cop (Madsen) pursues him. A journalist (Bonet) helps the cop establish the connection between the crime and a similar series a while ago. However, the journalist's motives are dubious, as she is there in part because of a one-night stand the cop spent with her sister some time before, and is more interested in the story than in justice. The killer, for his part, engages in phone-sex encounters, then goes prowling for victims. All characters bring the weight of personal disappointment to their actions.

The protagonist feels that his personal torments will be over if he can apprehend and eliminate the killer. The killer becomes the projected locus of the cop's perceived personal failure. The cop, therefore, is arguably more selfish than altruistic, although he detests the selfishness around him. His one-on-one final confrontation carries with it the full force of cathartic purge and necessary closure.

It depicts a hunting ground of phone sex and clubland encounters. The killer uses sex workers to indulge in a fantasy recreation of women, whom he must then punish for being the sexual objects he makes them. To bring the fantasy woman into reality is to become one with — and chastise — the ideal woman: rape and homicide as a means of absorbing the fantasy object. He constantly cruises for more victims for his possession fantasy. He kidnaps Bonet and reveals to her that he is always let down by women, that they can never live up to the fantasy. Madsen must rescue the kidnapped reporter and thus reassert the values of traditional Patriarchy by eliminating the product of empowering fantasy.

Dead on Sight

(1994: d. Ruben Preuss)

scr. Lewis Green; pr. Roxanne Messina Captor; ph. Levie Isaacks; prod d. Jo Ann Chorney; m. Harry Manfredini; cast. Jennifer Beals, Daniel Baldwin, Kurtwood Smith, William H. Macy; 91m

Daniel Baldwin is a college professor who lectures on serial killers (i.e. it develops the angle of the outside agent as expert, not the detective). He contacts a criminology student (Beals) who believes she has premonitions of new murders committed by the now dead "Clock Killer" of Kingston, Virginia. Her dreams are closely connected to the murder of the professor's wife, leading him to use her to identify the man he has felt all along responsible for the murders, a local cafe owner

(Macy). The cops disbelieve them. Soon she dreams of her own death, seemingly at Baldwin's hands, and goes to Macy for help. She awakens tied up, and Baldwin rescues her, unveiling Macy as the killer all along. The investigating policeman is a stubborn dupe, revealed to have arrested the wrong man long ago.

The film is most noteworthy for its delineation of a split profiler figure in the form of an expert criminologist and an intuitive psychic (usually a surrogate profiler in psychic-link movies), a division made popular on television when considering the difference between the two series *Profiler* and *Millennium*. *Dead on Sight* holds these characteristics as constituent elements of the ideal profiler figure. The detachment possible from both perspectives is eroded, however, by their respective personal involvement in — and closeness to — the killer's design, and their opposition to police views (they are definite outsiders). Hence their personalities are complementary: Baldwin is aggressive, forcing and initiating confrontation, whilst Beals is timid, backing away from those who talk to her. She feels easily threatened, and thus is in need of a protector: the profiler as potential victim.

The film stresses the opposition between police investigator and profiler — the one supposedly objective and with no personal stake beyond professional integrity, and the latter (whose wife was a victim) an obsessed crusader (usually the policeman's role) determined to prove himself right. In the process, it discredits the policeman, with the profiler's balance of professionalism and personal investment championed.

This film offers a neat and relatively fresh encapsulation of the profiler's prominence on the investigative road to the capture of a serial killer. The device of the lecture foreshadowing murder is now common, and infiltrates *Copycat*, *Candyman*, and *Urban Legend*. The plot hook of an investigator having a knowing relationship to the killer, but unable to prove it, was also used in the tele-movie *The Limbic Region*.

The Dead Zone

(1983: d. David Cronenberg)

scr. Jeffrey Boam; nvl. Stephen King; pr. Debra Hill; exec pr. Dino De Laurentiis; ph. Mark Irwin; m. Michael Kamen; ed. Ronald Sanders; prod d. Carol Spier; art d. Barbara Dunphy; cast. Christopher Walken, Brooke Adams, Tom Skerritt, Herbert Lom, Anthony Zerbe, Colleen Dewhurst, Martin Sheen, Nicholas Campbell; 103m

This Stephen King adaptation concerns a man who emerges from a coma after many years, only to find he has newfound psychic abilities. Mindful of the love he has lost in the interim, he sets himself up as a tutor but is approached by those seeking his psychic insight. One such approach is made by the police, as a last resort, who need his help to identify the "Castle Rock Killer" responsible for nine rape-murders. This is only one episode of three such psychic uses in the movie.

The protagonist, whom Hardy et al. (p. 381) consider the typical King everyman, is tormented by his psychic ability, recalling David Cronenberg's *Scanners* (the interplay of the psychic visions and reality is very much a continuing theme of Cronenberg's). *The Dead Zone* explores the fear and responsibility associated with telepathic powers, with the protagonist fulfilling the role of profiler in that he is an outsider with specialized knowledge brought in to assist the stalled investigation. His examination of crime scene details leads him to intuitively ascertain the killer's identity — a superimposition of the supernatural onto established criminological procedure.

The killer, who used his identity as a policeman to cover a seething resentment for the community he was supposed to protect, would rather commit suicide than be captured. He is the epitome of the bad son who warps the Patriarchal values he supposedly is there to protect. His mother covers up his involvement and is a knowing and willing accomplice in her son's corruption of Patriarchy's authority. By identifying the problem, Walken thus becomes the proper agent of a new, restored and even revisionary Patriarchy able to police its own and recognize the self-destructive course it is headed down. The good patriarch can self-sacrificially halt the apocalypse — a theme toyed with more negatively in Cronenberg's previous films.

The singular serial killer is the minor symptom of an ideology that at its worst would correspondingly sanction mass murder. Ironically, it is the politically sanctioned authoritative males who embody the corruption of the ideals they supposedly represent. The psychic gift/curse, and thus the ability to recognize and police monstrousness, ennobles the profiler figure as a suitable alternative and true visionary, able through his insight to change the future.

This is one of Cronenberg and King's more hopeful projects, even if it addresses the need for self-sacrifice for a collective, threatened ideal of humanity as offering the prospect of an unselfish love (which the protagonist strives for). Unlike the self-sacrificial protagonist of the previous *Videodrome*, Walken here is under no delusions, the validity of his insight already established.

The Dead Zone was considered Cronenberg's most conventional film after the critical and box-office failure of *Videodrome*, and an attempt to break through into the US mainstream. His professionalism is much in evidence, although it is his least "personal" movie and so perhaps his most accessible. Some still consider it the best Stephen King horror adaptation to date.

The killer as psychotic policeman is

followed up later in William Lustig's *Maniac Cop* series (with a vastly different tone), and influences the similarly wintery *Kiss the Girls*.

Deadly Force

(1983: d. Paul Aaron)

scr. Ken Barnett, Barry Schneider, Robert Vincent O'Neill; pr. Sandy Howard; ph. Norman Leigh, David Myers; m. Gary Scott; ed. Roy Watts; prod d. Alan Roderick-Jones; mkup. Mark Shostrom; cast. Wings Hauser, Joyce Ingails, Paul Shenar, Al Ruscio, Lincoln Kilpatrick, Bud Ekins, Hector Elias, Ramon Franco, Gina Gallego; 95m

A determined cop (Hauser) follows a serial killer to another city. There the cop starts to harass and plague his ex-wife, a journalist covering the murders. He tries to balance the bi-coastal concerns (though concentrating on LA), and is pressured by a former partner who resents and questions his return with more force than he seemingly uses to investigate.

The film strives to maintain an almost documentary authenticity for its look at the divisive internal pressures on a community and affected officials during a serial murder investigation. Into this use of fluid, slow, minor camera movements are cut the killer's quick attacks, as he lurks seemingly anywhere, his actions breaking the course of life.

Both cop and killer have to confront their pasts (a theme in Aaron's work), although the former seeks reconciliation, however difficult that may be. The latter, who operates a "success training" school (and is more than aware of the irony), kills in order to sever all ties and protect his criminal record from ever becoming known. His sex killing of innocents is an attempt by him to mislead the police. Thus he segues from known to random targets, expanding his pleasure in murder as part of a code of machismo which determines gender interaction.

This was put together by some of the same filmmakers responsible for the excellent *Vice Squad* (1982), which gave Hauser his most memorable role — as a villain. However, *Deadly Force* cannot match the intensity of that earlier film. Co-scripter O'Neill is also responsible for *Angel*, and *Deadly Force* reflects a similar concern for people seeking some kind of community, although driven apart by their rivalries. The notion of a series of sex crimes committed to cover-up an unrelated series also informs *Blow-Out* and *The Glimmer Man*.

Deadly Games

(1982: d. Scott Mansfield)

scr. Mansfield; pr. Raymond M. Dryden; ph. Michael Stringer; m. Robert O. Ragland, H.D. Schudsonn; cast. Sam Groom, Jo-Ann Harris, Steve Railsback, Dick Butkus, Alexandra Morgan, Colleen Camp, June Lockhart; 95m

A music reporter comes back to her small hometown, and discovers it is in the grip of a serial killer who, in a black mask, murders desirable women. As she delves into the case, she uncovers two main suspects: a demented Vietnam veteran now working as a projectionist (in a cinema that screens only horror movies), and the local investigating officer (who's also the projectionist's best friend). Finally, the cop is revealed to be the killer and is shot by the woman; but then his friend attacks her — a rather confusing ending which suggests a personality transfer of evil between males as part of their "bonding" rituals.

Director Scott Mansfield chooses to explore a relatively rare, though central, aspect of the serial killer film — killer/victim interaction and dynamics. This he achieves by concentrating on an unaware victim who enjoys the company of both suspects, contrasting her idyllic expectations with the threat to her life. Mansfield downplays the murders in favor of character and situation. Although *Deadly Games*

came out during the slasher boom, it distances itself from most films of that type. However, it does feature a strongly independent heroine and pays attention to inter-gender communication.

As a prelude to murder, the killer plays a board game based on old horror movies. The film suggests, therefore, that the serial killer is a descendent of such killers and the respective games they play with innocents and Innocence. It parallels the codes of gender interaction — as if such womanhood summons the killer — with his ritual being literally playing a game. Indeed, the killer reveals that he did it at first just to scare women, to relieve boredom and punish those whose attitude and sexuality he finds an affront; but it proved so much fun he continued, unable to stop himself. He kills in a variety of ways, like the slasher figure, but his motive, based on misogynistic resentment and the addictive quality of the murders as feeding his burgeoning fantasies, is unmistakably that of the serial killer.

To play up the presence of former Chicago Bears player Dick Butkus in the cast, there is a scene of a group of men playing football. This is contrasted with a woman's place on the sidelines, stressing the function of gender roles within community definition. The decay and subsequent dysfunction of the male soul is due to long-term stagnation.

A killer motivated by the desire for new experiences was also featured in *Evil Fingers*. The theme of crimes born of boredom and social malaise is often used in spree killer films and forms an interesting subtext for *River's Edge*. Both of these movies are far more effective than the minor effort that is *Deadly Games*.

Deadly Intruder

(1985: d. John McCauley)

scr. Tony Crupi; pr. Bruce Cook, Crupi; ph. Tom Jewett; m. John McCauley, Steve Perry

(Ben Dover); ed. Bruce R. Cook; art d. Lois Shelton; cast. Chris Holder, Molly Cheek, Tony Crupi, Danny Bonaduce, Stuart Whitman; 86m

This is a standard thriller about a serial killer who escapes from a mental hospital and hides out in a small town. Local police wish to stop him before he recommences killing. A mysterious hitchhiker soon fixates on a local woman. This is a terrible slasher movie which barely develops the serial killer angle beyond that of homicidal machine, and is only notable for a cameo by TV's *Partridge Family* star Danny Bonaduce, gratuitous nudity and, strangely enough, a lack of gory scenes or violence.

The compositional stress on medium shots is typical of amateur low-budget works and reflects an overall callousness of approach. The presence of a nomadic, disturbed drifter recalls *Beware My Lovely*, as the killer is unveiled as a new handyman; however, any hope of knowing intertextuality is lost.

Death Valley

(1981: d. Dick Richards)

scr. Richard Rothstein; pr. Elliott Kastner; ph. Stephen H. Burum; m. Dana Kaproff; ed. Joel Cox; art d. Allan Jones; cast. Paul Le Mat, Catherine Hicks, Stephen McHattie, Wilford Brimley, Peter Billingsley, Edward Herrman, Jack O'Leary; 87m

A new stepfather travels with his son across the desert, stopping at what at first appears to be an accident site. The boy finds a medallion there, which he gives to a sheriff investigating the murder of a camping couple. This triggers a reaction from the cop, who relates the murders to an unsolved series from years before. He confronts a suspect and is axed. Staying at a motel, the stepfather hears of the threat to his son and a chase ensues, leading to a showdown at the killer's house and revealing twin brothers as joint killers.

The film strives to contrast locations, cultures and attitudes within the United States— urban vs. desert/rural — and the necessary survival tactics of those who battle circumstance. This is very much a recurrent theme in Richards' work. Correspondingly, he quietly raises the difference in background between the real father (a New York City intellectual who gives his son a book) and the stepfather, who gives the kid a toy gun, and their respective values. The film thus charts the son's gradually growing respect for the stepfather and the realization of the merit of his beliefs, as symbolized in the final freeze frame of the son hugging the stepfather, who is empowered through decisive violent action.

These beliefs are contrasted with the killers', which are the legacy of the Westerner's code of honor transposed into greed and recreational homicide. This examination of a cultural legacy also affected Richards' other films, notably the Foreign Legion movie *March or Die*. Indeed, the killer fancies himself a cowboy, a value system that must be purged if Patriarchy's tradition is to continue appropriately. Ultimately, however, the film becomes an efficient child-in-jeopardy movie, with the stepfather forced into decisive action in contrast to his mild self. Ironically, it is through force, albeit the proper use of same, that he proves his suitability and triumphs over circumstance. Justified violence can empower and ennoble. It is a drama of broken father/son bonds seeking redefinition and reintegration into a modernized set of values; they are able to shed the demons of the past, but such triumph is still based on the use of force.

Death Valley's transposition of horror and western recalls Wes Craven's *The Hills Have Eyes*, which is also concerned with family unity threatened. Craven, however, prefers to show the corruption of Patriarchy rather than its reconstitution. The rural serial killer and western/indian motifs

A young boy (Peter Billingsley) sees a waiter (Stephen McHattie) who has a medallion like the one he found at a crime scene, and suspects him of being a killer in *Death Valley* (Universal, 1982).

are also found in the excellent *White of the Eye*.

Decay

(1998: d. Jason Robert Stephens)

scr. Stephens; pr. Stephens, Al Weigand; ph. Dennis Devine; m. Cynical Swing, Jonathan Price; cast. Tamara Davissi, Raymond Storti, Brian Brock, Robert Z'Dar, Ron Von Gober; 80m

A wife who wants to murder her husband recruits a serial killer and stalker of "exotic women." However, the husband, a dentist, had Mafia connections, and soon the Mob are investigating, as well as the Police and a private detective. This supposed black comedy was unreleased at time of writing.

Deep Crimson

(1996: d. Arturo Ripstein)

scr. Paz Alicia Garciadiego; pr. Miguel Necoechea, Paolo Barbachano; ph. Guillermo Granillo; m. David Mansfield; ed. Rafael Castanedo; cast. Regina Orozco, Daniel Gimenez Cacho, Marisa Paredes, Patricia Reyes Espindola, Julieta Egurrola; 110m

This is a Mexican remake of Leonard Kastle's *The Honeymoon Killers*, itself inspired by the true-life case of "lonelyhearts killers" Martha Beck and Raymond Fernandez. An overweight nurse and single mother of two is consumed by Romantic and sexual daydreams and answers an ad in a lonely-hearts magazine. A Spanish con man/gigolo replies. She falls for him, despite him stealing her money after having sex with her, and abandons her children at an orphanage to be with him. He takes this as a gesture of true love, and the two of them hit on a plan. They pose as brother and sister as he courts women from personal ads. They take their money and then dispose of them before making their way to the next such encounter. After killing a child, they surrender. The police take them to the desert, let them run and shoot them as they flee. They fall together.

Set in Mexico in the late 1940s, this is a sympathetic study of the morally ambiguous passion behind the commitment between two grotesques. The nurse is obese, and the con man is forever concerned about his incipient baldness, worrying more about his hairpiece than about the death of innocents. They are both physical outcasts in some way, both ashamed of the way they look. Indeed, the con man only turns violent towards the woman who teases him about his hairpiece when she discovers it. Ironically, it is the nurse who commits the murders, gaining in emotional, financial and sexual stature with each kill — except the final child-murder, an act so abhorrent that it is the final straw even for them. However, she is so consumed with their homicidal romantic idyll that she cannot stop herself from murdering the child, which she rationalizes as a necessary act of love: after all, love can be painful. Such is the monstrousness here: that love and romantic commitment can justify any moral atrocity. Despite their actions, their vain vulnerabilities humanize them and even make them sympathetic characters, more complexly ambiguous than in Kastle's film. In that way, the grotesque and the Romantic are intermixed and juxtaposed throughout.

Gradually the film reverses gender roles and expectations. The nurse claims passivity to the ultimate Casanova, but her sexual appetite increases as their plan eventuates. As the instigator, she becomes the murderess, coming to treat the mur-

ders as a bond that ties the two of them together practically, romantically and sexually. It is almost a necrophilic stimulus. The con man survives on pretense, showing his lack of strength only to the nurse, who assumes the aggressive role as a means of overcompensation for his lack. He cowers from the murders (one time hiding in a closet), although when his potency is threatened (the wig for him symbolizing his masculinity) he reacts violently. The conventional expectations of gender roles are thus gradually transferred. Together they invert and destroy any conventional normality between themselves, and in their actions.

What perversions lie behind the innocent appearance of people? This is a dominant theme, as the film both begins and ends with reflections—first in life, and then in death. The reflection in the mirror offers an inverse reflection, a truer symbolic appropriation of the monstrousness within the facade of normality. This speaks to the prominence of the mirror scene in the serial killer film wherein the killer contemplates the "normality" of his reflection in the mirror. Only at the end, however, is there any sense that these two characters can see the monsters they have become, as all their other actions bespeak of an all-consuming love.

Both are consumed by Romantic delusions. She for the love of a man, and he for the role of Casanova, preying on the fantasies of lonely women. He cannot escape the role he has set for himself, and is bewildered when she accepts it as an integral part of him and puts it to practical use — as a means of their joint identity. Together they form a monstrousness that would have never happened had they remained separate. However, the victims too (with the exception of the more practical last one) are also doomed by their dreams of love. Hypocrisy underlies these dreams, and the protagonists' constant journey is perhaps a flight from the realization that their love too is doomed to failure. Such is the tragic consequence of the pursuit of fantasy: murder and death. In a paradox, their death is the death of Romantic idealism, however perverted it may have been.

Their union is a liberation for them. Hence the film moves from cramped indoor settings to wide exteriors, away from the constrictions enforced on their lives. Their crimes are a means of escape from a dissatisfying reality. The con man jokes that it is either providence or the Devil that has brought them together. They are propelled by fantasy, a trait which makes the film approach the tragic. However, the movie's tonal balance is far more complex, mixing humor, outrage and a melancholic, even bittersweet charm at times. It seeks always to undercut feeling for them, constantly toying with expectation and audience sympathy to disconcerting effect.

Ripstein is justifiably one of the most prominent of contemporary Mexican directors, having made his first film in 1965, earning instant acclaim. Once an assistant to Buñuel, he has been compared to the late master for his study and insight into the depths and heights of the human soul.

Deep Red

(1975: d. Dario Argento)

scr. Argento, Giuseppe Basson, Bernardino Zappari; pr. Claudio Argento, Salvatore Argento; ph. Luigi Kuveiller; m. Goblin, Giorgio Gaslini; ed. Franco Freticelli; prod d. Basson; cast. David Hemmings, Daria Nicolodi, Gabriele Lavia, Clara Calanai, Macha Meril; 116 (98)m

This worldwide hit, Argento's most high profile giallo thriller, is only tangentially a serial killer film. When a psychic is murdered after sensing the presence of a killer (whom she says will kill again), a visiting American pianist who witnessed the murder (Hemmings) and a journalist (Nicolodi) investigate the homicide. The trail leads to the pianist's gay friend (and co-witness) and his monstrous mother — a death-obsessed but seemingly quaintly eccentric old lady (recalling the dotty aunts in *Arsenic and Old Lace*) who is actually a paranoid schizophrenic who would rather kill than go back to a clinic.

Aberration is partially rooted in childhood experience, the son witnessing his mother's homicidal actions and growing into an accomplice, intent on covering up and denying her nature. His madness stems from the realization of his inability to stop her and his own attraction for altered perceptions, which results in a self-destructive indulgence in booze and sex (though such a rational explanation is secondary). The film seeks to explore how the killings, and the desire to investigate "truth" by scrutinizing them, reflects and unveils a perception beneath the everyday — the literal skeleton in the closet. The deeper involved the protagonist becomes, the more stylized are Argento's compositions, which transform the familiar into the sinister. Added to this is a much remarked on stress on the double motif. This is through narrative structure (death and prefiguring scenes) and visual motifs (mirrors), and a flamboyant style of jagged cuts and odd angles (Hardy, pp. 306–7), which serve to approximate an altered sensory perception acquired by the protagonist as he closes in on the secret. Stylization is an expression of the unconscious forcing its way through — a theme continued in the supernatural-tinged *Suspiria*.

Hemmings' presence, and the exploration of the fragmentation of memory and perception, recalls *Blow-Up* and *The Bird with the Crystal Plumage* (which has a similar structure). But that, and the theme of precognition (Newman, p. 107), is used to stress an irrational realm just beneath everyday perceptions, themes also belonging to *Don't Look Now*. Murder is the means of entry (and immersion) into

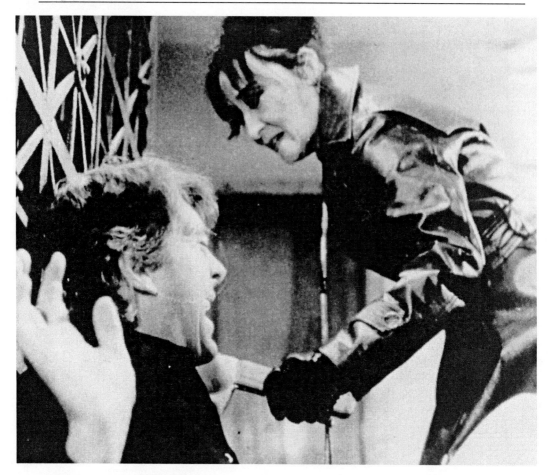

David Hemmings (left) finally reveals the black-gloved serial killer whose case has fascinated him in *Deep Red* (Rizzoli Film, 1975).

this irrational death-obsessed realm (paralleled to schizophrenic psychosis and the corresponding hallucinatory heightening of the senses), and thus a transcendent and empowering act. The depiction of it is therefore a structural moment of jouissance (a theme also saturating *The Bird with the Crystal Plumage*).

Deeply Disturbed

(1995: d. Lory-Michael Ringuette)

scr, pr. Ringuette; cast. Ringuette, Derek-James Yee, Ron Zeno; 82m

A woman disturbed by obscene phone calls mistakenly believes an Afro-American man at her laundromat is responsible. For help, she goes to a salesman, a serial killer who then kidnaps her and takes her to his run-down apartment. She is forced to humor him long enough to survive. Meanwhile, two police officers are on the trail of the caller, thinking he is also the abductor.

This is a San Francisco based low-budget, underground effort which cult drive-in critic Joe Bob Briggs reported played in punk-rock clubs and pornography venues. The director was an actor in low budgeters for some 10 years in Northern California, and cast himself as the killer in this film. It is a virtual one-man show, like many of the dedicated underground horror/transgressive films.

Some attempt at making a psychological thriller notwithstanding, it is deliberately explicit in terms of sexual violence and can thus be seen as continuing the traditions of the Cinema of Transgression in its deliberate embrace of aberration and taboo breaking for non-judgmental shock value. It wants to be a subversive exposure of sexual politics and victimology, but it roots the killer's acts in domination by a horrendous mother, à la *Psycho*, and so is bound in the conventional ideology it seeks to explode. It did not receive a general release.

Deliberate Stranger

(1986: d. Marvin Chomsky)

scr. Hesper Anderson; book. Richard W. Larson; pr. Chomsky; ph. Michael D. Margulies; m. Gil Melle; ed. Lori Jane Coleman, Howard Kuvin, Ronald LaVine; art d. David M. Haber; cast. Mark Harmon, Frederic Forrest (as Bob Keppel), George Grizzard, Ben Masters, Glynnis O'Connor, M. Emmett Walsh, John Ashton, Bonnie Bartlett, Billy Green Bush; 185m

This two-part tele-movie cast Mark Harmon as Ted Bundy. The film considers Bundy a lethally charming, pretty-faced lady-killer and almost an archetypal "All-American Boy," and seems to want to hold Bundy up as an emblem of the age. It covers his crimes, capture and trial, where his immense ego propelled him to act as his own attorney (and get the death sentence). It is a call for cooperation and dedication in such a prolonged case, and a look at the killer's immense pride.

It was first telecast on May 5 and 6, 1986, when Bundy was on Death Row appealing his sentence. As a true-crime mini-series it is perhaps comparable to *The Atlanta Child Murders*. It is in a line of mini-series descended from *Helter Skelter* and *City in Fear*, which used the television format to explore a greater social contextualization of the problem posed by such killers.

Deranged

(1974: d. Alan Ormsby and J. Gillen)

scr. Ormsby; pr. Tom Karr (Bob Clark); ph. Jack McCowan; m. Carl Zittrer; art d. Albert Fisher; cast. Roberts Blossom, Cosette Lee, Leslie Carlson, Robert Warner, Marcia Diamond, Brian Sneagle, Robert McHeady, Marion Waldman, Jack Mather; 82m

This is the closest version to date of the true crimes of Ed Gein, whose gruesome tale inspired *The Texas Chainsaw Massacre* and *Silence of the Lambs*. Explicit gore, mutilation and suggested necrophilia blend with a mock documentary tone that passes for black comedy. Thanks to top-flight acting from Roberts Blossom, it also emerges as a penetrating character study of a demented homicidal necrophile.

A quiet middle-aged man is devastated by the death of his beloved mother, whom he has nursed for many years. He eventually exhumes her rotting body and replaces it in the house. He then exhumes other bodies and bits of bodies—as company for her and material for him, making a costume out of human skin and furniture from bones as he immerses himself in a world of the dead. Necrophilia follows. He soon graduates to live victims, sadistically delighting in tormenting them and keeping their body parts as trophies of sorts, until caught by disbelieving cops and neighbors who had never suspected him (one neighbor even treating the killer's repeated admissions of murder as a joke).

The most remarked on aspect of this film is the dedication to the killer's self-contained world, reconstructed unflinchingly in an effort to probe how his demented fantasies grew out of reality and transformed it once they were enacted upon. Thus, what would seem monstrous has a certain logical progression in the killer's private universe: the immersion in death feeds the fantasy and paradoxically makes him come alive, his sexuality blossoming as if it were another chance at the adolescence he obviously lost to Mother.

As the killer's confidence grows, he targets younger, prettier and more conventionally sexually alluring victims (the first promiscuous, the second virginal), with ever more planning, and delights in psychologically and physically abusing them. This even gives him the confidence to partially go against Mother's wishes and desire sexual intercourse, although his punitive murder of women who arouse such desire echoes Mother's amusingly expressed feeling that women are no good (or "filthy black sluts with pus-filled sores," as she puts it). Ironically, mom is right, but only insofar as when the captured protagonist hears his mother's voice warning him against the perils of sex. It is a note of sarcasm typical of the film's tone.

The seemingly innocuous simple-minded farmer is transformed into a monstrous ghoul, yet all the while maintaining a certain naive innocence in his immersion into depraved mother-dominated psychosis. He was unable to handle reality and so transformed it by fantasy into a nightmare wherein he could compensate for a life denied him.

The narrative is punctuated by the appearance of a narrator, whose tone suggests a parody of the true-crime sensationalist emphasis on case study. He explains, in obvious terms, the progression of the killer's psychosis, and his presence breaks the diegesis, suggesting that he is a deliberately, if comedically, Brechtian device, a chorus of sorts. This layers the film's heavily ironic sense of humor with self-reflexivity.

Although the film is not pornographic, its gorily explicit immersion in necrophilic mutilation anticipates the likes of *Lucker* and the *Nekromantik* films. It is more subdued than Hooper's films (although it has a similar dinner with the dead sequence as *The Texas Chainsaw Massacre*, thus shar-

ing a desire to parody the everyday). But, like Hooper, it concerns the potential interplay of terror and comedy. Co-director Ormsby was known for low-budget creativity, having worked with Bob Clark on the similarly humor-toned cult hit *Children Shouldn't Play with Dead Things*. He would subsequently script Paul Schrader's remake of *Cat People*. *Deranged* also boasts makeup effects by Tom Savini, who went on to acclaimed work in that field, especially for George Romero.

Desire

(1993: d. Rodney McDonald)

cast. Martin Kemp, Robert Miranda, Deborah Shelton, Kate Hodge, Mary Stavin; 120m

A serial killer leaves a bottle of perfume on each of his victims, all beautiful women from Beverly Hills. A police investigator receives help from a female ex-cop, now the security chief for the perfumist who fears her product may be being discredited by a former employee who claims ownership of the scent. In the manner of numerous straight-to-video erotic thrillers, she becomes sexually involved with her quarry. This is a film of no particular reputation, and more of a gimmick-killer movie which uses serial killer pathology without comment. This was unavailable at time of writing.

The Detective

(1968: d. Gordon Douglas)

scr. Abby Mann; nvl. Roderick Thorp; pr. Aaron Rosenberg; ph. Joseph Biroc; m. Jerry Goldsmith; ed. Robert Simpson; art d. Jack Martin Smith, William Creber; spec eff. L.B. Abbott, Art Cruickshank; cast. Frank Sinatra, Lee Remick, Tony Musante, Ralph Meeker, Jacqueline Bisset, Jack Klugman, Robert Duvall; 114m

Frank Sinatra stars as a weary cop who ruthlessly targets the wrong man for a sex crime — the mutilation and murder of a homosexual — which is later revealed to be the work of a self-loathing bisexual killer. Sinatra extracts a confession from the suspect but is troubled by it, although he accepts the promotion that accompanies solving the crime, partial compensation for his faltering relationship with his nymphomaniac wife (Remick). His investigations lead to internal corruption, with his outrage foreshadowing *Serpico*.

The Detective depicts a world of foul language, brutal actions (by both police and killers), widespread corruption, promiscuity and crumbling sexual morality leading to sexual obsession (the wife) and sex murder. Social and sexual mores are hence revealed as in transition. As such, it is a valuable indictment of the turbulent era in which the film was made (released the same year that *The Boston Strangler* sought solutions to the sex killer problem). It is an indicator of Hollywood's attempt to integrate such change into traditional genres, of the self-reflexive contrasting of old and new character types in the search for a new direction.

Although there is only one murder, the killer's tape-recorded admission that he has left this confession in case the circumstances of "that night" repeat themselves suggests that when illicit desire is aroused another murder could follow and thus an addictive pattern would develop. The killer is too consumed by self-loathing to let this happen, and the prospect of how easy and even how attractive it might be repulses him enough to commit suicide. As such, he represents a character type also in transition, balancing that in *The Boston Strangler*, as subsequent sex killers would not feel such guilt and rarely such self-loathing.

The killer is a latent homosexual, but the film's failure to account for the postmortem mutilations suggests sexual pleasure as a motive for the crimes as much as it is resentment and self-hatred on the killer's part. The castration of the victim could be a displacement for a punitive self-castration (an act even found in *Hannibal*, though for different purposes). The film depicts homosexuality as rampant in a world of truck stops and elegantly fronted clubs and salons. It is a cheap, sleazy world of deception and sexual exploitation, with homosexuals invariably troubled people — a theme in part responded to, even countered to a degree, in *The Boston Strangler* — harassed by a restrictive social order.

Indeed, the film examines the respective unsuitability of the tough cop modeled on 1940s noir honor codes to cope with such sexual perversion and corruption. It is a changing world in which the ordinary police officer is threatened unless new measures are taken. This is also the theme of *The Boston Strangler* and *Dirty Harry*. Such a world is too much for the aging policeman, who at the end of the film turns off his police scanner: the end of an era and a character type.

This was the grittiest, and bleakest, of three law-and-order films starring Sinatra, produced by Rosenberg and directed by Douglas, the others being *Tony Rome* and *Lady in Cement*. Its plot of a New York City cop exploring the city's netherworld to uncover a killer of homosexuals anticipates *Cruising*. Although it is only tangentially a serial killer film, its disillusionment with police procedures and human morality anticipates the 1970s gay-killer themed films *Laughing Policeman* and *Freebie and the Bean* and that era's pessimism over an ideology in disarray.

Die Watching

(1993: d. Charles Davis)

scr. Kenneth J. Hall; pr. Vali Ashton, N. Rao; ed. Clayton Halsey; cast. Christopher Atkins, Vali Ashton, Mike Jacobs Jr., Tim Thomerson; 92m

Part of the direct-to-video adult thriller movement, *Die Watching* focuses on a serial killer who earns money as a pornographic moviemaker luring women to auditions and then murdering them. He finds it hard to keep this secret from his neighbor, who hires him to do promo videos and sleeps with him, prompting his confession. It's too late to start afresh, however, as the police are, of course, closing in on him. Rather than be captured or continue his monstrous activities, he commits suicide.

The killer's method is highly metafilmic. He seduces young starlets (à la *The Art of Dying* and *8MM*) and tapes them to chairs, then focuses a camera on them, filming all the time (à la *Peeping Tom*), and places a monitor in front of them, forcing them to watch their own deaths (*Peeping Tom* and *White of the Eye*). The film tackles the issue of the link between pornography and such violence, and seems to want to be topical.

In keeping with the rash of low budget erotic thrillers of the late 1980s and early 1990s, it eroticizes murder. It is arguable as to what extent this is mere titillation or the self-reflexive attempt to probe the aesthetics of murder and its corresponding "look" for killer, victim and viewer. As such, it addresses the genre's inherent aesthetic dilemmas and attempts to humanize the killer as a sympathetic soul who commits suicide when confronted with the monstrous emptiness his life has become, in contrast to what it could have been. In this way the serial killer confronted by real love is almost cured, a theme infiltrating *Le Boucher* and *The Arrival* especially.

Dirty Harry

(1971: d. Don Siegel)

scr. Harry Julien Fink, R.M. Fink, Dean Riesner; pr. Siegel; ph. Bruce Surtees; m. Lalo Schifrin; cast. Clint Eastwood, Andy Robinson, Harry Guardino, Reni Santoni, John Vernon, John Larch; 98m

A sniper, Scorpio (Robinson), blackmails the city, wanting money to cease killing random victims. The eponymous cop is assigned to the case; a brutal, fascistic man, he pursues his quarry relentlessly, intent on stopping him whatever the cost. In capturing the killer, he violates the suspect's civil rights, and so the killer is freed. Scorpio pays for himself to be beaten and publicly blames the cop. Scorpio hijacks a school bus, leading to a final confrontation with the lone policeman. Scorpio is killed and the policeman tosses his badge (in resentment of the system — or in the realization that he too is a brutal and, in his way, sadistic killer).

Scorpio is modeled indirectly on the Zodiac killer, although the character is an amalgam of those random murderers plaguing the era: sniper, sex killer, repeat-killer, racial bigot, and even social revolutionary/terrorist who posits anarchy on the one hand and personal gain on the other. Such new random criminality demands like force in response. From the opening shot, society is confronted by the rule of the gun, from both killer and, in the end, cop.

Scorpio is depicted as an effeminate, cowardly animal. Although he resembles a hippie and wears a peace sign as a belt buckle, his actions speak to the perversion of an ideal into its aberrant opposite. Harry is the resolution both demanded and resented by society: the police officer as modern myth. Indeed, the film continued the depiction of a new type of obsessive and violent response to crime, answering in part the dilemmas posed by *The Boston Strangler* and *The Detective*: not understanding, but elimination.

Harry, seen twice under religious signs (a "Jesus Saves" sign and a park cross), is suggested to be the force of God's Old Testament Law, when the New Testament values of love, peace and forgiveness have failed to reform society for the better.

Scorpio is a symptom of a malfunctioning society which ironically demands sterner Patriarchs. There is no room for the profiler in this world, only killers— on either side of the law; no mediators are permitted. Scorpio is an unredeemable monster; perhaps necessarily, so too is Harry.

The Disturbance

(1989: d. Cliff Guest)

scr. Laura Radford; pr. Guest, Ron Cerasuolo; ph. Angel Garcia; m. Joel Jacobs, Paul Pettit; ed. Nicholas Tsioisias; art d. Nick Farentello; cast. Cindy Millian, Nina Mazey, Joel Jacobs, Jackie Sparke; 81m

This is a film considered to be of dubious import. It is a standard account of a schizophrenic plagued by visions in which he graphically murders women (beautiful women of course). When things start to go wrong in the world, and with new stresses when he loses his job and ceases taking medication, his violent hallucinations could turn real, although he apparently could have a demon in his soul.

Yet another irresponsible link between mental illness and homicidal mania, *The Disturbance* is reportedly little more than another stalking psycho movie with both a pretentious and exploitational attempt to probe psychological aberrance, directed by an MTV personality. It equates mental illness with a kind of modern possession. It has since disappeared after a brief release.

The Doctor and the Devils

(1985: d. Freddie Francis)

scr. Dylan Thomas, Ronald Harwood; pr. Jonathan Sanger; exec pr. Mel Brooks; ph. Gerry Turpin, Norman Warwick; m. John Morris; ed. Laurence Mery-Clark; cast. Timothy Dalton, Jonathan Pryce, Twiggy, Julian Sands, Stephen Rea, Phyllis Logan, Beryl Reid, Patrick Stewart; 93m

Another Burke and Hare tale (see *The*

Body Snatcher and *Flesh and the Fiends*), and the best, despite the harsh critical reception it received when released. It concerns the relationship between surgeon Dr. Rock (Dalton) and his complicity in the murders committed by graverobbers Fallon and Broom (Pryce and Rea), who become murderers in order to obtain fresher corpses.

While maintaining the sense of a corrupted fairy tale, *The Doctor and the Devils* is best when charting the arrogant killers' sadistic sexual joy in murder and the sense of power over others that it gives them. This God-like power over life and death of course parallels Dr. Rock and his assistant (whose admiration of Rock has a homosexual dimension, a concept star Sands would explore in his role in *Gothic*), as the degree of complicity in monstrousness is explored via this doppelganger motif. There is a strong class resentment to this relationship, as it is the killers' hatred and envy of Dr. Rock that prompt them to try to usurp Rock's position in the only manner that they know, by becoming life-takers instead of lifesavers.

Though on opposite ends of this spectrum, both Rock and the killers are ghouls, preying on the dead for their personal advancement. Whatever the altruistic motive Dr. Rock may lay claim to, it is in part self-righteousness which impels his research; and the resentment of the authority that seeks his repression leads to his complicity in murder. Director Freddie Francis has some sympathy for the intricacies of the doctor's plight, rooting the conception of monstrousness equally in personal aberration and in the restrictiveness of a society whose hypocrisy is everywhere in evidence (it is Ripper terrain after all). The obsession with death leads to the equation of murder with sexual desire in the aberrant repressed— hence Fallon seeks to kill women he desires, and Rock's anatomical probings/mutilations are a sexual substitute

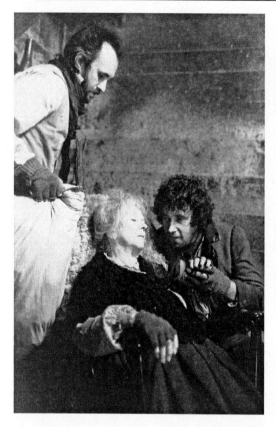

Left: The grave-robbing duo of Fallon and Broom (Jonathan Pryce and Stephen Rea) turn to murdering the innocent to supply a medical researcher in *The Doctor and the Devils* (Fox, 1985). *Right:* Two of the prostitutes (Twiggy and Nicola McAuliffe) are part of the subclass preyed on by killers in *The Doctor and the Devils* (Fox, 1985).

(his wife's sketches of dead bodies arouse him more than she herself as a living woman).

The film contrasts respective class rituals. Interpersonal relationships are warped and jeopardized as morals and ethics are gradually eroded by necrophilic sexual obsession. This social decay spreads like a virus over all entrapped within it. Fallon and Broom delight in luring and tormenting women, Broom crying "give it to her Fallon, give it to her" as Fallon smothers his victim in deference to sexual penetration, their aberrant partnership having contemporary repercussions when considering the actions of the Hillside Stranglers and other killer couples. Fallon desires necrophilic copulation, too monstrous for

him to admit, and is driven insane by his desire for fresh bodies, hoping each time for necrophilic experimentation—that which Dr. Rock enjoys through surgical exploration/mutilation. Ironically, homicide, though transgressive, enables the truly transgressive act of loving the dead.

Francis had photographed the elegant *The Elephant Man* for director David Lynch and producer Mel Brooks, and persuaded the latter to let him direct an apparently long-cherished project, based on the unfilmed 1940s script by poet Dylan Thomas. Nicholas Ray had tried to revive the project in the 1960s but failed. Francis, however, had to compromise his vision, as Brooks had the philosophical script rewritten, by playwright Ronald Harwood, into a supposedly more traditional genre piece than Francis initially had in mind. It is unfortunate that director Francis did not go on to other movies after this, but the film's failure assured his return to cinematography. Despite its rich, busy visual style, the film was considered a flop, achieving neither horror nor poetry.

Dr. Cook's Garden

(1970: d. Ted Post)

scr. Art Wallace; play. Ira Levin; pr. Bob Markell; ph. Urs Furrer; m. Robert Jackson Drasnin; ed. John McSweeney Jr.; art d. William C. Molyneaux; cast. Bing Crosby, Frank Converse, Blythe Danner

Bing Crosby (in his most unusual, not to mention uncharacteristic, role) stars as a small-town doctor who kills those patients he considers disposable and worthless, burying them in his garden. He believes he is doing a socially acceptable thing. A young man he had previously risen as a son returns to town and suspects the bad patriarch. The generational imbalance must correct itself for the smooth functioning of the system.

From a Broadway play by Levin (Burl Ives enacted the role on stage), this was director Post's most ambitious tele-movie, made when he was moving from television to the big screen, thanks to the trust of actor Clint Eastwood. Sadly, it is unavailable and rarely re-screened.

Dr. Jekyll and Sister Hyde

(1971: d. Roy Ward Baker)

scr. Brian Clemens; ph. Albert Fennell, Brian Clemens; ph. Norman Warwick; m. David Whittaker; ed. James Needs; cast. Ralph Bates, Martine Beswick, Gerald Sim, Lewis Fiander, Dorothy Alison, Neil Wilson, Ivor Dean; 97m

In this Hammer companion to *Hands of the Ripper*, Dr. Jekyll (Bates) needs female hormones for his experiments. He enlists graverobbers, taking the needed body parts from them, and they turn to murder to supply the good doctor. Jekyll consumes the drug himself and turns into a sensuous woman (Beswick). To continue, he takes to murdering prostitutes (as Jack the Ripper), extracting the needed parts. Soon the female Hyde is killing women to sustain her gender. Finally, his secret is revealed, and he falls to his death whilst evading capture.

This is in the tradition of the European mad doctor variations of the tale. The sensuous Hyde represents male fantasy constructions of women as a transgressive force (Hardy, p. 232). Importantly for the genre, it links the serial killer directly to the Jekyll/Hyde mythos by having Jekyll, in fact, be Jack the Ripper. Its subplot of graverobbers also recalls the Burke and Hare tale. The film thus touches on the varied forms the serial killer has taken in Hammer projects especially, but also in British horror in general: Jekyll as an amalgam of Ripper and Dr. Knox is unmistakably a founding source in the evolution of the serial killer figure. Indeed, its subplot of upstairs neighbors interested in Jekyll/Hyde is a variation on *The Lodger*, and the visualization of a shadowy London is in keeping with both Hammer and the Ripper mythos.

Jekyll, however, becomes uneasily bisexual as a result of the transformation, auto-erotically caressing his/her body as Hyde and, as a male, making advances towards another male. The film thus roots sexual aberrance in gender identity issues, foreshadowing the transvestite killers of *Dressed to Kill* and *Silence of the Lambs* as it reflects the base in *Psycho*. Hammer films had hinted at issues of androgyny and bisexuality before, notably in *Frankenstein Created Woman*, but this is the first time it became overt (in a context of drug experimentation and sexual abandon perfect for 1970s London audiences). Yet, unlike the films of Walker, Collinson and some Fuest,

The two sides of the bisexually repressed Victorian: Dr. Jekyll (Ralph Bates, left) poses with his alter ego Sister Hyde (Martine Beswick) in *Dr. Jekyll and Sister Hyde* (Hammer, 1971).

it frames its depiction of homicide in period trappings.

Dr. Jekyll and Sister Hyde also explores Jungian issues of anima and animus, as opposed to Freudian notions of superego, ego and id: another rarity in serial killer films. Femininity is an all-consuming collective evil vanity which seeks to subvert individual identity. Thus it is ready to kill to sustain itself. Homicidal gender confusion is the result of self-indulgent amorality. The dissolution of sexual identity through drug use in an effort to sustain pleasure (however rationalized) frees and justifies a homicidal nature. Jekyll's idealized self is the monstrous feminine, a state, as expected, addictive once experienced. This depiction of inter-gender metamorphosis, with Jekyll's body in a corresponding transsexual flux, is the visualization of a tormented sexual identity.

In that a professor is brought in by police for added assistance through the examination and interpretation of bodily mutilation, the film also raises the importance of the profiler, whose closeness to Jekyll, as friend and co-worker, leads to identification and focuses the police methods. He too is corrupted by sexual longing (even if it is heterosexual), as are all the characters to some extent, their fantasies clashing with the horrid reality.

Dr. Petiot

(1990: d. Christian DeChalonge)

scr. DeChalonge; pr. Alain Sarde, Philippe Chapelier-Dehesdin; ph. Patrick Blossier; m.

Michel Portal; ed. Anita Fernandez; cast. Michel Serrault, Pierre Romans, Zbignew Horoks, Berangere Bonvoisin, Aurore Prieto; 102m

This french film is based on the true-life case of Marcel Petiot, a doctor who, during WWII, lured Jewish families into his offices with the pretext of helping them, then stole their money, killed them and burned their bodies, doing on a small scale what the Nazis were doing on a large one. Wonderfully acted and stylishly directed, this is a rich and haunting portrait that incorporates self-consciously expressionistic touches.

The film is so conscious of its roots in German expressionism that the protagonist, in a cinema, steps into the film screened in order to point out how unrealistic is the depiction of such evil as separate from conventional humanity. The film then seeks to remedy this, in the process showing Petiot's systematized murder as a demonstration of the individual's capacity for evil, alongside the good, as human nature. The Nazis turn this capacity into mass atrocity on a grand scale, while Petiot does so in the singular.

Systematized murder is a survival technique for Petiot, as well as a source of pleasure. His routine is set. He lures victims with the promise of helping them escape the Nazi occupation, puts his favorite music on as background, injects them, paints their faces, isolates them, and watches their death throes as he dances around and inspects the private property they brought with them. Then he dismembers them and burns them along with the belongings he doesn't want. He can then return to his unsuspecting wife and child. He is obsessed with control over circumstance, in the process becoming an exploiter of human weakness.

Remarkable is the way Petiot is depicted as always busy, bustling through the labyrinthine world he seeks to control. Ul-timately he goes nowhere, always returning to murder as a form of unquestioned self-definition and self-expression: a mastery over all. That self is unknowable to all but him, though a component sense of transcendence through transgression is reflected in Petiot's final words: "I am a voyager and I take my baggage with me." The Nazi atrocities are not the anomaly we would hope them to be, merely an expression of a horrible, innate potentiality, holding oneself above all others. Self-absorption, despite an apparently benevolent motive, yields the capacity for pleasure in the deception and manipulation of innocents.

Doctor X

(1932: d. Michael Curtiz)

scr. Earl W. Baldwin, Robert Tasker; play. H.W. Comstock, A.C. Miller; ph. Ray Renuhan, Richard Tower; m. Leo F. Forbstein; ed. George J. Amy; art d. Anton Grot; cast. Lionel Atwill, Lee Tracy, Fay Wray, Preston S. Foster, Arthur Edmund Carewe; 77m

This is one of the first US efforts to deal with the serial killer phenomenon, although the film was made partially as an intended rival for Universal's *Frankenstein*. It is a detective horror story concerning the hunt for a "moon murderer" who kills by scalpel and cannibalizes the victims. The title doctor resides in a cliff-top mansion and runs a laboratory with the help of a one-armed assistant. The assistant has discovered secrets of "synthetic flesh," allowing him to don a living prosthetic appendage and become a strangler during full moons (complementing the werewolf mythos).

All inhabitants of the doctor's medical academy are in some way connected to cannibalism (Brottman, p. 161). The cops examine the victim's body in the morgue and there discover the killer's signature, used in several murder cases they are carrying, thus establishing a serial killer at work (the first example of a scene that would become a serial killer film convention). Body parts have been bitten and torn out.

The doctor announces that one of his staff is a cannibal, and so performs experiments designed to explore their respective memories. These suggest that cannibal sex murder is a stored experience common to humankind (Brottman, p. 163). Thus the film roots sexual repression as the cause of such mutilation-homicides— merely the resurfacing of a bestial legacy. The half-eaten bodies in the morgue lay testament to transgressive acts founded in human evolution but repressed by civilization, although ironically made dangerously prominent again by the rise of psychoanalysis. The killer is one-armed and therefore removed from conventional humanity, although his appearance is similar. The phallic significance of the missing limb is not lost on the filmmakers, who suggest that the killer's adoption of a prosthetic arm (synthetic flesh) during homicide is his means of restoring his lost potency, making the crimes sexual in nature. It also refers to the hand-transplant vogue in 1930s and 1940s horror, à la the many versions of *The Hands of Orlac*.

It is a reporter and not the police, however, who finally breaks the case. He is thus an outsider, a forerunner of the profiler figure. His potency is apparently never questioned, in contrast to that of the killer. Unlike most horror films of the 1930s, it is not a period film and is set in a recognizable Manhattan milieu (Clarens, p. 104).

Some first-run prints of this movie were released in an experimental two-color Technicolor process (as were prints of *Mystery of the Wax Museum*), although the majority of subsequent release prints were in black and white. When a color print was rediscovered in 1973, the film was subjected to much critical reappraisal and hailed for its control over atmosphere, with the use of color lauded as more than just a gimmick but a near expressionistic tool in the director's hands.

Don't Answer the Phone

(1981: d. Robert Hammer) aka *Hollywood Strangler*

scr. Hammer, Michael D. Castle; pr. Castle; ph. James L. Carter; m. Byron Allred; ed. Joseph Fireman; art d. Kathy Curtis-Cahill; cast. Red Fulton, Ben Frank, Flo Gerrish, Nicholas Worth; 94m

A serial rapist/killer fixates on the female radio psychologist he phones to vent his rage and complain of his headaches.

The killer is a photographer (à la the real Harvey Glatman), but the film lacks any real examination of voyeurism (besides that now-standard slasher genre use of the subjective camera point of view). He is also a lapsed Catholic, and so is wrapped in sub–Scorsese guilt, and suffering from brain damage. He is also, like in so many depictions, a narcissist obsessed with physical discipline (as is the killer in *Angel* and *Fear City*)— to the point of S&M involvement. His murder method is hence wrapped up in personal religious significance and seems designed as a rite, implicating the Church in such murder. He strangles victims with a stocking wrapped around coins.

Notable is the tendency to depict the killer as irredeemably grotty; he is overweight and into pornography. This reflects an early 1980s trend, present in both *Maniac* and *Henry: Portrait of a Serial Killer*, in which the killer's banality is seen in terms of his class-based socioeconomic predicament. The device of the killer calling a radio talk show was used to better effect in *Martin* and *Outside Ozona*.

The ending justifies vigilante action against such killers, lest they "get off" with the insanity defense, and, as such, is thematically similar to *Ten to Midnight* and *The Art of Dying*. The killer as disturbed

Vietnam veteran is also reminiscent of a late 1970s trend (*Rolling Thunder, Deadly Games*). *Don't Answer the Phone* was supposedly based on the real-life Hillside Stranglers case, itself later filmed as *The Hillside Stranglers*. The original title was *The Hollywood Strangler*, but it was re-titled to cash in on the trend of "*Don't*" titled horror movies.

Don't Go in the House

(1980: d. Joseph Ellison)

scr. Ellen Hammill, Ellison, Joseph Masefield; pr. Ellen Hammill; ph. Oliver Wood; m. Richard Einhorn; ed. Jane Kurson; art d. Sarah Wood; set d. Peter Zsiba; cast. Dan Grimaldi, Robert Osth, Ruth Dardick, Charlie Bonet, Bill Ricci; 82m

A young man, obsessively mothered while growing up, lures women he meets in discos to his house, ties them up in a fireproof room, and incinerates them with a blowtorch. He subsequently dresses the corpses in his mother's clothes and vents his rage on them — the crimes are due to his resentment and aggression towards his dead mother.

The killer is insecure and remote from society. He is also psychotic, hearing inaudible voices and subject to nightmares (rendered incomprehensible). Thus his experience is removed from the normality he preys upon. The director concentrates mostly on the killer's home life, depicting him as almost afraid to venture out, taking refuge in madness from a world he feels inadequate to deal with; he has been "deserted" by his mother and left to fend for himself (like the killer in *Deranged*). His mother used to burn his arms over the stove, a childhood trauma he is now doomed to repeat on innocent victims— substitutes for himself and his hated mother (as he confuses both identities in his own psychosis). When his mother dies, he cremates her and then subsequently

dresses the corpses of his victims in her clothes and places them around the house (à la *Psycho* and *Deranged*, both superior films). The supernatural-themed ending, wherein the corpses return to life and kill him, recalls *Maniac* (in fact, that film's director, William Lustig claimed this movie ripped off his) and EC comics finales.

There have been some recent attempts to find psychological significance in this nasty film, concentrating on the child abuse theme, which many see as mere coating for repellent exploitation. It was only briefly released and poorly distributed before being consigned to video oblivion.

Don't Torture the Duckling

(1972: d. Lucio Fulci)

scr. Gianfranco Clerici, Roberto Gianviti; ph. Sergio D'Offizi; cast. Irene Papas, Marc Porel, Georges Wilson, Florinda Bolkan, Tomas Milian, Barbara Bouchet; 110 (90)m

Along with Dario Argento's thrillers, this was among the first in the giallo series, which developed into a distinct Italian genre that reflected and contributed to the development of the serial killer film and the slasher film in the United States. It shows Fulci as a superior technician, if not quite the visual stylist that is Argento.

In the rural south of Italy, a series of child murders causes a panic, resulting in the wrongful hanging of a local gypsy woman, perhaps targeted for her overt sexuality. The killer is revealed to be a homosexual priest who killed his victims before the taint of sexuality could destroy their purity and innocence. In his own mind he is saving the children from adulthood (a motive shared by the pedophile killer in *In the Cold Light of Day*). The public's reaction shows the populace as being little better than the killer, despite their smug moral superiority.

The film was considered evidence of Fulci's dubious morality — not only for its homosexual killer but for a controversial scene in which a naked mother teases a young boy. The townspeople are all repulsive characters (especially the women, foreshadowing the misogyny of Fulci's later efforts), and all sexuality (particularly feminine) is seen as monstrous. Yet the response to it only reveals the depths of amoral hypocrisy and secret depravity that defines these lives— Fulci apparently depicts them as little better than rural cretins. Scenes of extreme violence and savagery (children without eyes, skulls bashed in) punctuate the goings-on.

Critics considered it a wallow in sensationalism, devoid of Argento's style or any redeeming social comment. However, Fulci fans are ever ready to defend it, and it has been recently revived and rereleased on video and DVD in the United States.

Dressed for Death

(1972: d. Peter Collinson) aka *Straight on Till Morning*

scr. Michael Peacock; pr. Collinson, Michael Carreras; ph. Brian Probyn; m. Roland Shaw; ed. Alan Pettillo; art d. Scott MacGregor; cast. Annie Ross, Claire Kelly, Rita Tushingham, Katye Wyeth, Tom Bell, Shane Briant, Harold Berens, James Bolam; 121m

In this peculiar film about a naive girl desperately wanting a baby, she goes to London in search of a potential impregnating agent. There she is attracted to a man she considers her dream lover but is revealed to be a serial killer. He then plays her the tape recordings of his murders and she is confronted by the harsh reality, ending her romantic dreams.

This is a weird horror movie that suggests director Collinson at one stage could be compared with Pete Walker. The film postulates women's desire as a lure for evil

killers, as part of the mating process. As an allegory of sexual roles, it has some bearing, though it is yet to receive a fully appreciative review. It can be considered a view of the perils faced by innocence in a forum of cultural freedom and the tail end of cultural liberation, which has, as its result, fostered an environment in which the serial killer can live and thrive — and impregnate innocence with his contaminated seed. As such, the film is a bleak view of contemporary social mores, finding no alternative.

There is a heavy irony throughout, as the woman wanting life is attracted to a practitioner of death. The desire for reproduction is thus contrasted to the desire for homicidal sexual abandon (as the ultimate perversion of the reproductive urge). It is a knowing thriller, referring to *Peeping Tom* in the scene where the killer plays his recordings for the next intended victim. Yet it is reportedly filmed in a style more akin to the kitchen sink realism so beloved of UK cinema in the 1960s social resurgence (thanks to directors like Schlesinger, Reisz, Anderson, and Richardson) than to the Hammer tradition. Hence it was Hammer's last horror-thriller effort. It was released as part of a double bill with *Fear in the Night*, and is now perhaps an item strictly for Hammer completists.

Dressed to Kill

(1980: d. Brian DePalma)

scr. DePalma; pr. George Litto; ph. Ralf Bode; m. Pino Donaggio; ed. Jerry Greenberg; prod d. Gary Weist; cast. Michael Caine, Angie Dickinson, Nancy Allen, Keith Gordon, Dennis Franz, David Margulies, Susanna Clemm; 105m

Incidentally a serial killer film, this is a stylish giallo about a transvestite killer who resents his own manhood and kills those women who arouse his desire (as explained at the end, in *Psycho* manner, by

Witness Nancy Allen is menaced by the black-gloved, giallo-inspired transvestite killer (Michael Caine) in *Dressed to Kill* (Filmways, 1980).

the treating psychiatrist). Its play on a male killer thought to be female is a reversal of Argento's *The Bird with the Crystal Plumage*, which plays well upon the assumption of the killer's gender.

When his promiscuous mother (Dickinson) is slashed to death, a young man (Gordon), with the help of a prostitute witness (Allen), stakes out the office of his mother's psychiatrist (Caine). They suspect one of the patients to be the black leather–clad killer and seek to discover her identity. The doctor is the killer, however, and seeks to destroy the prostitute when she tries to arouse his desire as part of a plan to exact the suspected patient's identity.

On one level *Dressed to Kill* explores the inevitably homicidal consequences of sexual fantasy, liberation and frustration, whether heterosexual (the victim) or of a more aberrant nature. The repressed killer is a vengeful, homicidal puritan anchored in self-deception and ready to punish others for his own sexual resentments and proclivities. The hypocrite can thus slide into homicidal abandon as a cure-all. Sex is always lethal in consequence. Ironically, it is the prostitute, the traditional serial killer victim, who is in charge of her own sexuality and emerges victorious, flushing out the killer for police. However, it is that very sexuality which brings out the worst in men.

Hirsch (*Detours*, p. 311) points out that the killer is filmed in blurs and shadows, in the manner of horror movie menaces. She is also, in killing by razor, reminiscent of the murderers in the Italian giallo cycle. The film can be considered a balance of horror and noir — Gothic noir, perhaps.

It has style to burn, as usual for De-Palma, but was accused of being a rather cold and cynically manipulative movie. It was nevertheless a box-office hit, although many critics resorted to their standard dismissal of DePalma as a Hitchcock copycat: all technique. Many objected to the blanket linking of transvestitism, transsexuality, multiple-personality disorder and schizophrenia. The wordless museum sequence was held as a masterful set piece, reminiscent also of Argento (who featured a similar scene of a woman sliced to death in an elevator in *The Bird with the Crystal Plumage*).

Driller Killer

(1980: d. Abel Ferrara)

scr. Nicholas St. John; exec pr. Rochelle Weisburg; ph. Ken Kalsch; m. Joe Delia; cast. Jimmy Laine (Abel Ferrara), Carolyn Marz, Baybi Day, Harry Schultz, Bob de Frank; 90m

A frustrated young man is driven to distraction by the punk band in the next apartment. His limited socioeconomic opportunities and inability to escape an environment he detests slowly drive him crazy and so provide him with the excuse to go out and kill the vagrants and societal drop-outs he fears he is close to. Ironically, he does not target the band that seemingly drives him to madness (a twist most critics thought odd), content with the surrogates. He dresses as a cowboy, with drills instead of guns, and sets out to clean up the streets, à la the great Westerners of old: the corruption of the code upon which the United States is founded — a subversive debunking. Gradually, he cannot keep his violent nocturnal activities separate from his "normal" life.

The killer blends psycho and vigilante aspects (Newman, p. 97) as would the killer of Ferrara's subsequent films — the much better received *Ms.45* and *Fear City*. The story takes place in a world almost devoid of light, a symbolic background for this analysis of the deeper recesses of the soul and the socioeconomic pressures that affect it.

When released, *Driller Killer* was subjected to much critical derision, although director Ferrara's subsequent career has caused its reevaluation and even championing (a Criterion Edition DVD, for instance). In England it quickly became the object of notoriety when it was included alongside such titles as *I Spit on Your Grave* and numerous Italian horrors as "video nasties" and banned.

Ferrara is arguably restrained with the gore and favors a hand-held semi-documentary approach to the social reject lifestyle he depicts. He thus manages to generate sympathy for the victims — even suggesting, through the socioeconomic context, that the term "victim" is indeed relative. It is a challenge for people to rise above their circumstance, and the killer's desire to clean up the streets becomes the warped desire for personal social empowerment through violence as a perceived revolutionary act.

Ferrara contrasts the carefully filmed interiors with the fluid exteriors and with the murders (with one exception), favors showing how the killer performs and enjoys the killing over wallowing in the victims' torment (Hardy, p. 335). *Variety* felt that Ferrara as a director was far from promising.

Dust Devil

(1992: d. Richard Stanley)

scr. Stanley; pr. Joanne Sellar; ph. Steven Chivers; m. Simon Boswell; ed. Derek Trigg, Paul Carlin; prod d. Joseph Bennett; cast. John Matshikiza, Robert John Burke, Terri Norton, Chelsea Field, Rufus Smart, William Hootkins, Zakes Mokae, Marianne Sagebrecht; 125 (US 87)m

This weird film from cult director Stanley (his second, following *Hardware*) is about a shape-shifting killer, drawn by emotional need, who preys on the lonely and lovelorn. Local police are aided by a shaman (the native witchdoctor as profiler) in their efforts to track the murderer. The killer is a demon in human form (who also resembles the Clint Eastwood Man-with-No-Name persona (Hardy, p. 483) who must kill to enter the so-called spirit world. Gruesome crime scenes ensue.

Visually it is said to recall the director's music videos for Goth bands, notably Fiends of the Nephilim. The native shaman (who claims to know the creature's vulnerabilities) is a clever transposition of the modern profiler figure onto supernatural terrain. But despite the killer's supernatural origins, Stanley hammers the point home that he is a lone killer who preys on weakness for his own thrills (however addictive they have become for his perceived livelihood). The premise also seems inspired by Michael Wadleigh's *Wolfen*. Similar Indian-themed serial killers would inhabit *Shadow Hunter*.

Combining the Western (especially Eastwood/Leone) with the serial killer film and the supernatural thriller, this is an ambitious movie whose Namibian desert scenes reportedly have a hallucinatory and post-apocalyptic quality. Although it takes place on the border between South Africa and Namibia, and contains several scenes of white police brutality of black witnesses, it uses this as a backdrop for its examination of the supernatural emerging onto the real, and the continued, systematized exploitation of the weak.

A provocative attempt to enrich the serial killer genre, *Dust Devil* exists in three versions — the European cut ran 125 minutes, the US release 87 minutes, and Stanley's director's cut, 103 minutes. Director Stanley would next be removed from his version of *The Island of Dr. Moreau* (1996) and replaced by veteran John Frankenheimer, a decision the fans lamented.

Dying Time

(1990: d. Allan Kuskowski)

scr. Kuskowski; exec pr. Felipe Mier; ph. Francis Grumann; m. Kevin Klinger; ed. Kuskowski; prod d. Lee Monahan; cast. Jimmy Stathis, Deborah Downey, Paul Drake; 92m

An FBI agent and his partner in New York City are on the trail of a Satanic serial killer who buries his victims alive in a manner recalling a case from 20 years before. In a shootout the partner dies and the killer escapes. When similar murders occur in Los Angeles, the FBI agent journeys there, much to the dismay of the new female head of Special Investigations, who resents the intrusion on her domain. When the killer kidnaps her, the FBI agent has to rescue her and eliminate the killer.

The prologue, wherein a killer is assisted by his son, establishes the sense of ritual serial murder as a tradition spanning the generations. Literally, the bad patriarch rears the bad son, with the profiler having the responsibility to aid the police and restore Patriarchy's balance by punishing the transgressor. The Satanic ritual is just dressing for the killer's sexual inadequacy and subsequent overcompensation: he does not rape the victims, instead videotaping their deaths and masturbating as he replays them. He says that his name is unimportant but his actions are (a similar belief of the killer in *Seven*); yet despite his Satanic aims he tries to use the killings to extort money from the city (as did Scorpio in *Dirty Harry*)—all braggadocio. In one scene he walks into a sorority house and shoots several bystanders in order to get to the one girl he intends to use—a nod to the case of Ted Bundy; the film is conscious of real and fictional killers.

Much is made of a woman having such a high position in the male dominated police force—and the subsequent additional pressures on her to perform to her very best, and so pave the way for others. But rather than portray her as a potential leader, the film chooses to show her as another woman ultimately needing male authority to rescue and protect her, and to sexually dominate her: the film offers a process of female subordination, despite her efforts. Her battle of wills with the profiler serves to illustrate the course of such subordination, as it aggrandizes the male profiler as the real function of a Patriarchy which can take care of itself. The one note of irony is that the profiler is named Ted Bunker, a combination of Ted Bundy and the old slang term "bunko" for FBI agents. This would suggest the profiler is an amalgam of killer and cop, but this promising theme remains undeveloped.

The film seeks to balance depictions of the killer's occult practices with action movie type shoot-out set pieces (both killer and profiler are armed with machine guns, no less). However, this generic crossover has no freshness to it. It is ultimately a film of missed opportunities in its routine following of convention.

Easy Prey

(1986: d. Sandor Stern)

scr. John Carlen; pr. Rene Malo, Barry Rosen; ph. Reginald Morris; m. J.A.C. Redford; prod d. Douglas Higgins; ed. Tony Lower; cast. Gerald McRaney, Shawnee Smith, Barry Flatman, Sean McCann, Susan Hogan, Kate Lynch; 100m

This is a tele-movie based on real-life Australian serial rapist/killer Christopher Wilder (McRaney) and concerns in particular his 1984 abduction of a teenaged girl from a California shopping mall, subsequently forcing her to accompany him on a statewide crime odyssey (though filmed in Canada). Later, the authorities would wonder if the girl was in fact a willing accomplice: a view the film argues against.

The killer takes to rape and murder

when jilted by his girlfriend, thus resenting all women and desperately needing to assert his masculinity through force. He practices deception, pretending to be a photographer to lure naive would-be models into secluded places for the satisfaction of his violent sexuality, and is always on the hunt for potential victims: he has no life beyond the planning and execution of his crimes—they alone give him purpose.

As he crosses jurisdictions, he embarks on an odyssey of escalating crimes, confounding police to the point where an FBI agent (the profiler figure here) offers her assistance. Her profile suggests a man with a violent history who could explode at any moment; the film's tension is based on these implications and the killer's role as monstrous substitute father to the girl he abducts.

The killer/victim interaction is narratively balanced with the procedural aspects, with the killer gaining a kind of respect for the girl over time, despite his rape, threats and sexually demeaning talk. The profiler believes that it is the girl's previous experience with rape (by her father) that enables her to know how to act passively, surrender power and so stay alive. The profiler is treated as an acknowledged expert whose pronouncements serve almost as a chorus as much as an ongoing explanation of the proceedings.

As a crime spree film, *Easy Prey* is in line with *Gun Crazy* and *Badlands*, and the later *Natural Born Killers*. However, it differs from them on two important points: the male killer was a serial offender before the crime spree, and his accomplice is a kidnap victim whose cooperation with her abductor is a combination of survival strategy and the result of psychological battery, torment and threats against her life. The dominant concern for victimology thus sets the portrait of the killer in terms of his actions over others and the clear sense of compensatory power and superiority it gives him.

The makers strove for accuracy in their recreation. Introductory notes claim the film is based on personal interviews, press announcements and other published accounts (i.e. is symptomatic of the true-crime recreation movement that gained tele-movie impetus since the mid–1980s). They claim the FBI personnel represent those actually involved, but it lacks the sociological ambitions and scope of the true-crime based mini-series. It aired first on October 26, 1986.

Eaten Alive

(1976: d. Tobe Hooper) aka *Death Trap*

scr. Alvin Fast, Mardi Rustam; pr. Rustam; ph. Jack Beckett; m. Hooper, Wayne Bell; cast. Neville Brand, Mel Ferrer, Carolyn Jones, Marilyn Burns, William Finley, Stuart Whitman; 90m

This is not to be confused with the Italian cannibal film of the same title.

Tobe Hooper's studio-bound follow-up to his seminal *The Texas Chainsaw Massacre* is another bleakly humorous tale of a psychopath, this time based on real-life circa 1937 serial killer Joe Ball. True-life war hero Brand plays a Louisiana swampland motel owner who kills female (or otherwise troublesome) guests with a scythe and feeds them to his pet alligator kept out back. Trouble arises when a father and daughter come to investigate the disappearance of their daughter/sister, murdered by Brand.

The film continues the Southern Gothic sense of Hooper's previous movie, and satirizes the cowboy macho culture, reflected in the apt, and often remarked-on, casting of decorated war hero Brand as a psychotic killer (indeed, the real Joe Ball was himself a Medal of Honor winner). It is as stylized as one would expect from Hooper, and its critical neglect is shame-ful (genre specialists consider this neglect a backlash against the favorable responses given *The Texas Chainsaw Massacre*). It also has a gleeful EC Comics sense of humor that also infiltrates the films of George Romero. Indeed, the movie anticipates the insane, self-reflexive, heavily ironic comedy that would saturate *The Texas Chainsaw Massacre 2*, and can be considered the centerpiece of a Southern trilogy. More so than its predecessor, *Eaten Alive* borders on knowing pastiche (Newman, p. 54).

The studio-bound film is a baroquely stylized nightmare full of bright colors (especially red, blue and orange); stark lighting; looming, grotesque close-ups that make it an artificially infernal world; and a pervasive atmosphere of aggressive male sexuality. Women are little more than ready victims of male exploiters, and Brand's pathology is merely symptomatic of the inevitable progression of an inherently warped sexual desire — to dominate, control and possess. When aroused, Brand wants sexual satisfaction through force, reflecting an infant's need for immediate gratification. Indeed, despite his monstrousness, he has a childlike quality — though unable to perceive his monstrousness, he recognizes the need to preserve it as secret. Like many of Hooper's overblown caricature villains, he embodies the malevolence of childhood, warped by the world outside, indulging himself without introspection or guilt. His murders (much more explicit than in *The Texas Chainsaw Massacre*) are done as if gleeful play.

The makeshift zoo he keeps is Hooper's acknowledgement of his own treatment of the character in such a studio-bound environment, generating an audience response akin to the scrutiny of gawkers at a circus freak show (a theme Hooper developed in the marvelously garish *Funhouse*). The killer is a sexual degenerate who ironically sees the sexual degeneracy of other locals (the cowboy) and considers them

A motel owner and serial killer (Neville Brand) disposes of another victim via his backyard swamp and pet alligator in *Eaten Alive* (Mars Prod. Corp., 1976).

with hostility—their clashes and power struggles recalling the eccentric familial squabbles of the clan in *The Texas Chainsaw Massacre.*

Hooper undercuts any conventional sense of "normality," as even the most traditional of social orders, the "family," merely offers tension, resentment and hostility. No meaning, mutual understanding, empathy or communication is possible—except the begrudging acknowledgement of one sexual deviant for another. The father and sister seeking their lost relative are also harsh, stern figures, so laughably caricatured as to be devoid of sympathy. Indeed, the film's main failing is ironically its main virtue: by refusing to acknowledge any kind of normality, it thus lacks any dramatic contrast. The film's main suspense is from Brand's pursuit of a little girl who witnessed her mother sexually abused by Brand. Hooper uses this as yet another joke as he deliberately seeks to pile outrage upon outrage, charting his characters' participation in such and systematically degrading them.

It is said that poor distribution wrecked the film's chances, and Hooper was never able to cement a Hollywood career, although he impressed Steven Spielberg enough to be assigned to direct *Poltergeist.* The critics assaulted *Eaten Alive* and its director before the film was even released, further ensuring its commercial failure. The sleazy motel setting, of course, recalls *Psycho* and anticipates *Tourist Trap.*

Eating Raoul

(1982: d. Paul Bartel)

scr. Bartel, Richard Blackburn; pr. Anne Kimmel; ph. Gary Thieltges; m. Arlon Ober; ed.
Alan Toomayan; prod d. Robert Schulenberg;
cast. Mary Woronov, Paul Bartel, Robert Beltran, Buck Henry, Richard Paul, Susan Saiger,
Ed Begley Jr., Dan Barrows; 90m

This is cult auteur Bartel's second flirtation with serial killers (his first was *Private Parts*). It concerns a prudish couple,
named the Blands (Woronov and Bartel),
who take to murdering the "swingers" they
consider morally reprehensible (luring
them by personal ads in sex magazines and
promising to cater to their fantasies) in
order to get the money to open their dream
restaurant. Latin lover Raoul, who disposes of the bodies by selling them to un-
scrupulous sources (pet food merchants),
soon partners with them. It roots crime in
terms of moral outrage and perceived socioeconomic need and resentment; thus,
opening shots of Hollywood are countered
with views of the homeless and the culture
of sleaze that resides beneath Hollywood
glamour. This indicates Bartel's subversive
intent and his apparent disdain for Hollywood mainstream product.

The WASP middle-class are monstrous,
resenting the wealth of those they consider
morally abhorrent, yet equally able to finally
eat the underclass to protect their veneer of
respectability. There is no sympathy for anyone in this film, as all are equally reprehensible. The lead couple is a chaste throwback
to the 1950s who are finally corrupted by the
sexual decadence they claim to loathe and despise. Murder excites them, although the act
itself in their mind also serves to deny such
illicit excitement. They are thus the ultimate
hypocrites and the real sexual perverts.

Normal couple Paul and Mary Bland (Paul Bartel and Mary Woronov) take to murdering
swingers with a frying pan in *Eating Raoul* (Bartel Film, 1982).

Their sex crimes, ostensibly for money, are turned into a profitable Capitalist enterprise; the murders become their surrogate for sexual contact, with the wife finally driven to an affair. They fail to realize that in their sex crimes they too indulge in sexual aberration: the perfection of their means of murder is thus the sexual experimentation lacking in their marriage. Ironically, these bland murderers triumph. They become cannibals in the process of finally realizing their dream. The pursuit of this American Dream thus justifies any atrocity and enables people to be considered disposable commodities little better than garbage. At a swinger's party the comment "happy hunting" implies that the world has become the hunting ground for voracious sexual predators (the decadent party also recalling Woronov's presence in the Warhol Factory escapades). The film thus condemns and satirizes the great US entrepreneurial spirit of productive homicide.

Independent director Bartel had not worked for some time after his work for Roger Corman on *Death Race 2000* and *Cannonball*. He showed the script to Corman, who wasn't taken with it, and so partially financed the film, with additional money coming from friends and, finally, his parents. It was made with an eye on both the exploitation and the art-house circuits. That it did relatively well on both enhances its curiosity value. Bartel himself described the film as "the perversion of middle-class values, the resurgence of Nixonism, Latin machismo vs. WASP fastidiousness, film noir. Finally, however, it's about how financial considerations overpower emotional ones" (Brottman, p. 89). The cannibalism motif is used to demonstrate how the WASP American middle class devours minorities when pressured.

It came alongside an early '80s minivogue for cannibal comedies, hence *Motel Hell* and *Blood Diner*. Bartel and Woronov make cameo appearances as the Blands in the slasher movie *Chopping Mall*, perhaps indicating Bartel's influence over a new generation of independent exploitation moviemakers.

Edge of Sanity

(1989: d. Gerald Kikoine)

scr. J.P. Felix, Ron Raley; pr. Peter A. McRae; ph. Tony Spratling; ed. Malcolm Cooke; m. Frederic Talgorn; prod d. Jean Charles Dedieu; cast. Anthony Perkins, Glynis Barber, Sarah Maur-Thorp, David Lodge, Ben Cole; 85m

This is one of Anthony Perkins' last roles. Yet another version of Jekyll and Hyde, *Edge of Sanity* is decidedly revisionist in intention; and its highly charged sexual content reflects the director's early career as a porno movie director. The young Jekyll is traumatized when he's beaten by his mother's lover after seeing them having sex, whilst the mother laughs at him. This is an imprinting that yields a repressed ocean of sexual resentment as he seeks to identify with the abuser and punish the object of desire that would first entice and then mock him. Once Hyde is loose, he prowls the brothel scene and fixates on a prostitute who reminds him of the trauma. In the meantime, à la Jack the Ripper, he butchers street whores with a scalpel.

This is another of the Jekyll/Hyde films to clearly identify Hyde as a monstrous serial killer, as did the Hammer productions of *Dr. Jekyll and Sister Hyde* and *I Monster*, and to root the experience in the Jack the Ripper mythos. Like in those films, Jekyll here becomes a police consultant in the crimes committed by Hyde — the killer brought in as profiler to diagnose himself.

Kikoine highlights the drug-addiction aspect of the story, with Perkins repeatedly injecting himself, his thin, gaunt appearance contributing to a visual sense

In yet another villainous role, Anthony Perkins stars as the demented serial killer and sexual experimenter Mr. Hyde, free from Dr. Jekyll, in *Edge of Sanity* (Palace/Allied, 1982).

(colors, costumes, make-up) modeled on the heroin chic/punk look of such cult films as *Liquid Sky*. Thus, Kikoine goes behind Victorian doors to reveal a world of sexual perversity and indulgence, a milieu as attractive and addictive as it is amoral. Once experienced, it proves inescapable, corrupting Jekyll's initially supposedly benevolent soul. As Hyde, he is strong enough to enlist a pair of minions to assist him in his homicidal pursuits. The liberation offered by Hyde is one of abandon to sensory experience, and it encompasses bisexual urges. Immersion in the world of sex and drugs is a "freedom," with Hyde thus a visionary social transgressor and worthy anti-hero. It's no surprise that director Kikoine is a former pornographer.

Kikoine concentrates on the seedier aspects of the story, playing up the kinky sex angle, lingering over the display of prostitutes lined up for the perusal of a male audience. Awash in red and blue, the film seems stylistically and tonally indebted to Ken Russell's depictions of sexual decadence (particularly in *Crimes of Passion*, which also starred Perkins as a sexual obsessive and repressed man who turns to murder).

It was filmed in Hungary and released in the United States in both R and unrated editions. It is of chief interest to Perkins completists. Although it is certainly intriguing in light of the origins of the serial killer film, most felt that it failed to live up to expectations.

8MM

(1999: d. Joel Schumacher)

scr. Andrew Kevin Walker; pr. Gavin Polone, Judy Hofflund, Schumacher; exec pr. Joseph M. Caracciolo; ph. Robert Elswit; m. Mychael Danna; ed. Mark Stevens; prod d. Gary Wissner; cast. Nicolas Cage, Joaquin Phoenix, James Gandolfini, Peter Stormare, Anthony Heald, Chris Bauer; 119m

In this controversial follow-up to screenwriter Andrew Kevin Walker's *Seven*, a private detective (Cage) is hired to determine whether an 8mm film showing a girl's death is an actual snuff film or a staged loop. He leaves his family and goes to the hardcore porno underground in Los Angeles, begging comparison to George C. Scott in Paul Schrader's *Hardcore*. He finds himself morally torn and becomes obsessed with seeing what the face of such evil looks like, finally driven to revenge killings—but only when sanctioned by the victim's distraught mother.

Cage is established as a man of solid dependability who treats his work as just that. Seen holding his baby, he is set up as the modern patriarch. The film thus gradually questions and undermines this position as he is corrupted by the taint of aberrant sexual fantasy and must eliminate the bad patriarchs, who put such fantasy into practice, in order to validate his existence and exorcise the fantasies within himself. It is his immersion in this world of fantasy, as well as his subsequent violence, that he feels may have damned him. His final confrontation with the killer is set to the music of Aphex Twin, a song entitled "Come to Daddy," indicating his embrace of a punitive, restorative and disavowing Patriarchy, and his parallel to the killer as monstrous patriarch.

A friend, a porn-store employee (Phoenix) who guides Cage through the pornographic netherworld, remarks that being close to the devil doesn't change the devil, it changes you. Thus the film equates sexual fantasy, and by extension all fantasy (the sexual progressing inevitably to the violent), with Evil. Although this Evil empowers, it is arguable whether it liberates. What is unquestioned is the need for this fantasy to be disavowed and eliminated at all costs. It is the role of the outsider to do so, even at the cost of himself. On behalf of those victims and families destroyed as the result of such loosed fantasy, he is sanctioned to become the executioner he must be in order to purge his own fantasies. However, his descent into violence is a surrender to the fantasy image of himself as avenging angel; he knows this, and before becoming a killer he must call the dead girl's mother and effectively get her sanction to kill the monsters. This fantasy is innate to males and corrupts their soul.

The film is constructed as a detective story/mystery, and as a descent into Hell. Hell here is a pornographic netherworld of exploitation and murder, where basement displays offer an assortment of child pornography, bestiality and violent rape videos. It is the perfect narrative expression of the desire to know the "truth," a desire which affects all characters, however they each define truth — as objective fact, spiritual insight, or amoral abandon and sensorial indulgence. Gandolfini thus admits to watching the young girl's murder simply because he hadn't seen anything like that before and so it was a new experience. His character represents the worst voyeuristic impulses of the spectator, and the side of Cage that he despises within himself.

8mm reveals the seedy underside of Hollywood where naive innocence is exploited and destroyed, even transformed by vice into the realm of lost and damned souls — a realm of people blind to their own banal inhumanity as they seek ever greater depths of surrogate sensation through immersion in pornographic fantasy until, it is suggested, no longer content to passively observe, they must become active participants in the death of innocents, condoning (and paying) murderers. The fascination with Evil leads to immersion, which yields at its end the serial killer (named, appropriately, "Machine") as the nadir and epitome of the consequence of surrender to male fantasy — killing for no other reason than it feels good.

Such moral indifference is everywhere. Even the sympathetic Phoenix is an amoral vacuum of callous hypocrisy who can justify his immersion in Hell (eagerly viewing supposed snuff films without the "purpose" of Cage) and yet claim separateness from it by saying, "I don't buy it, I don't endorse it, I just point the way." He is not damned but is a lost soul, finally used and destroyed by the Evil he courts, which ironically holds him just as disposable as the innocents it consumes: he can offer no resistance.

8mm furthers the scripter's theme of the corruptive influence of evil, as surfacing in his previous *Seven*. By the time Cage becomes a vigilante, it had most critics screaming sensationalism, perhaps even resenting the indictment it makes of the movie industry itself. But is the real evil the killing of innocents for sexual gratification or the filming of it to make such a communally shared experience? Cage is consumed by the need to know why someone would commit such atrocity, and is horrified by the resultant "because I can" motive because he recognizes this within himself. There is no philosophical rationale to the killer here (unlike the self-aggrandizing murderer of *Seven*), no "reason" beyond a corruption of the pleasure principle — the scourge of humankind.

Schumacher had shown a fondness for somber, dark atmosphere in *Flatliners* and even the *Batman* sequels, and here approaches the recesses of Fincher. Its study of an aberrant underclass also recalls *Cruising* in its blend of somber neo-noir and investigative structure. Evil has spread everywhere, as the old man in whose safe the snuff film was found is a rich pillar of the community (in comparison to the lowlifes who carried out his wishes): every male has a guilty secret.

This is quite possibly Schumacher's best film, and further evidence of his ongoing concern for vigilante action as examined in *A Time to Kill* and *Falling Down*, here more concerned with the monstrousness and moral complexity that rests behind such (self-) righteousness. In terms of vigilante justification, this film does not offer the pat resolve of *A Time to Kill*. Although the people exorcised for the betterment of society and the protection of the innocent are reprehensible, the vigilante (the profiler figure here) is of similar stock, both attracted and repulsed by his nature and closeness to porn-junkies and killers.

The Element of Crime

(1985: d. Lars Von Trier)

scr, ph. Von Trier; pr. Per Hoist, Lars Von Trier; m. Bo Holten; ed. Tomas Gislason; prod d. Peter Hoimark; cast. Michael Elphick, Esmond Knight, Me Me Lai; 104m

In this sci-fi tinged murder mystery set in post–nuclear ravaged Europe, small, isolated communities represent the reassertion of civilization. One of them is beset by a serial killer of young girls. The crimes are widely reported as "The Lotto Murders." In the absence of conventional forensic technology, an ex-cop, who returns to Europe after thirteen years in Cairo to solve his own problem with blackouts, must rely on his abilities and wits as a seasoned hunter to track down the killer. To do so he uses the title book, intending to get inside the murderer's thought process (and so make the transition from investigator to profiler). He consults the book's author, who stresses the need for the pursuer to empathize and identify with, and understand the killer he is after.

The director's use of sepia-toned images helps to convey a bleak world and refers back to early European horrors about villages beset by killers, werewolves, vampires, etc. The blend of sci-fi and serial killer film also anticipates such science fiction-serial killer entries as *Dark City* (also seemingly in a nocturnal world) and *Split Second*. The film utilizes constant voice-over narration by the cop and his psychiatrist (i.e. the ideal serial killer investigator/profiler figure examined as a hybrid). It explores the investigator's need to appropriate the profiler's methodology into the science of detection.

Von Trier would later make the highly acclaimed *Zentropa*.

The Embalmer

(1966: d. Dino Tavelia) aka *The Monster of Venice*

A crazed killer uses the Venice catacombs to stalk women, then abducts them and takes them to an underground lair for rape and murder. He then stuffs them to add to his trophy collection. The lair suggests he is a modern beast — an infernal human capable of bestial acts in the pursuit of self-indulgence. Indeed, it thus raises the question of the humanity of such a killer and whether or not he should best be considered a kind of evolutionary throwback.

This serial killer film predates the Italian "giallo" cycle of the 1970s as popularized in the films of Dario Argento. However, it has not received the retrospective attention given to the films of Argento, Fulci and Mario Bava, in particular.

Endplay

(1975: d. Tim Burstall)

scr. Burstall; nvl. Russell Braddon; pr. Burstall; ph. Robin Copping; ed. David Bilcock; art d. Bill Hutchinson; cast. George Mallaby, John Waters, Ken Goodlet, Robert Hewett, Delvene Delaney, Kevin Miles, Charles Tingwell, Walter Pym, Sheila Florance; 110m

Two brothers (one a paraplegic and one adopted) are suspected of involvement in the disappearance/murder of blonde hitchhikers. A process of cover-up and one-upmanship begins between the brothers once they know the police suspect their involvement. This is an engaging Australian psychological battle which indulged director Tim Burstall's trend towards vulgarity, although the *Variety* reviewer felt that it confirmed Burstall as one of Australia's best directors. Despite that, the film has an insecure position in the acclaimed Australian New Wave of the 1970s.

Sex and violence are linked in the minds of both brothers, with the paraplegic saying he would like to talk about sex but instead talks of death and killing. These are compensatory factors for the impotence inherent in his situation, which the able-bodied brother seeks to cover up

without alerting his brother to the fact that he knows he is a killer, thus incriminating himself. The behavior with the provocatively dressed corpse borders on necrophilic longing.

Burstall is at pains to suggest that both brothers have deep-seated reasons for their actions, which they forever seem on the verge of disclosing. This reflects a sexual dysfunction rooted in childhood resentment (and even unconscious homosexual incestuous desires — although the film avoids these implications by revealing one brother as adopted). This psychological dependence on sexuality and the physical inability to express it has led the killer to murder hitchhikers as an expression of a potency he feels swept away from him. The film's psycho-dramatic battle between the brothers is intended to likewise prove potency and restore the killer to the top place in a perceived power hierarchy. This leads to further violence as an expression of mutual resentment.

This was a change in direction for Burstall, best associated with "larrikin" (mischief-maker) movies, here in part condemning the character types he was accused of celebrating. A small-scale film, cast with actors known via their TV work, it did modestly well upon release. Some considered it too talky and contrived, though possessing some effective suspenseful highlights (as when one brother puts the corpse in a wheelchair, takes it to a local cinema screening an odd Australian take on *A Clockwork Orange*, and leaves it there). Burstall concentrates on the brothers' relationship, and the film's success depends upon how involved one gets. Most critics felt it uninvolving and overplayed — a would-be Hitchcockian thriller that falters.

Evil Eye

(1962: d. Mario Bava)

scr. Ennio De Concini, Eliana De Sabata,

Franco Prosperi, Enzo Corbucci, Mino Guerrini, Mario Bava; ph. Bava; m. Les Baxter; ed. Mario Serandrei; art d. Giorgio Giovannini; cast. Leticia Roman, John Saxon, Valentina Cortese, Dante Di Paolo, Robert Buchanan; 92m

This is generally considered the first "giallo" film and is among the director's most stylish works. Nora (Roman) goes to Rome to care for a sick aunt, who dies. She then witnesses a murder. She goes to the police, and a doctor, who do not believe her, given the absence of a body. Subsequent murders are gradually linked to a decade-long killing spree. The victims have been chosen alphabetically by surname.

This film posited the direction of the giallo movie away from straightforward procedural thrillers and more towards stalking and graphic murder scenes. Director Bava would also expound the giallo formula with *Blood and Black Lace* the following year. This film was supposedly a major influence on Dario Argento's breakthrough giallos, *The Bird with the Crystal Plumage* and *Deep Red*. It has yet to see widespread rerelease however, and was unfortunately unavailable.

Evil Fingers

(1971: d. Luigi Bazzoni) aka *The Fifth Cord*

scr. Bazzoni, Mario di Nardo; pr. Manolo Bolognini; ph. Vittorio Storaro; m. Ennio Morricone; cast. Franco Nero, Pamela Tiffin, Edmund Purdom, Renato Romano, Maurizio Bonuglia, Ira von Fuerstenberg, Rossella Falk; 93 (89)m

This is an early giallo. An alcoholic reporter (Nero) becomes a suspect in the string of murders he is investigating. Gradually revealed is a complex plot of illicit sex, blackmail and private sexual trysts/displays (involving a respected doctor) as the underbelly and corruption of Italian life is highlighted. It is boosted by a Morricone score and cinematography by Storaro (who would win the Oscar the next year for *The Godfather*).

Although there is a tentative link between the victims, and the film is structured as a detective mystery, the killer's admission into a tape recorder that he wants to be known and feared as a serial killer reflects the growing perception of the serial killer as the ultimate murderer. The film begins with the tape recording of a man who admits that he intends to commit sex murder, as he has been thinking about it for a long time and already feels the anticipatory excitement. He has no doubt also been fantasizing — as he is later revealed to be a voyeur amidst an underground world of illicit sexual performances, the sex he sees fuelling his violent fantasy reconstructions. He murders. The police investigate. The reporter becomes involved as an outside agent. The killer's second tape-recorded message indicates his thrill at the murder but his disappointment in the press coverage, with a motive for the subsequent murders being to inspire awe amongst the populace.

The film stylishly depicts a world driven by hidden sexual agendas: desire, resentment and retribution. This is ever present, and the killer is the ultimate expression of this world, an awful inevitability. Even Nero feels resentment towards women, striking his much younger lover: he is not as far removed from the killer as he would believe. His uncovering of the killer is a quest to reveal the hidden part of himself and the society that surrounds him and fosters such desires for sexual power.

The killer plans his crimes according to a strict pattern, careful to leave an identifying signature to claim the crimes as his own (a glove with fingers missing, according to the numerical sequence of crimes he intends). Although his motive is finally revealed to be sexual jealousy — to punish desirable women (as surrogates for one woman in particular)—there are links to occult practices. It all begins with personal insecurity.

Indeed, in keeping with the film's stress on secret motives behind aberrant actions, much of the perversity on show is only partly revealed. The true depths of depravity lie there just beyond everyday vision—a theme of the films of Dario Argento in particular, and a dominant concern of the giallo in general. It takes an altered perception to intuit this realm. Yet this perception is dangerous, allied to homicide and mental aberration. Like Argento's work, though lacking its overall stylistic bravura, the film features an occasionally striking use of architectural shapes.

Evil Judgement

(1984: d. Claude Castravelli)

scr. Castravelli, Vittorio Montesano; pr. George Amsellem, Castravelli; ph. Roger Racine, Mario Romanini; ed. Susan Shanks, Gerald Vansier; cast. Pamela Collyer, Jack Langedyk, Nanette Workman, Suzanne DeLaurentiis, Walter Massey

This Montreal-set Canadian/Italian crime drama concerns a young woman who embarks on a private investigation when the police are seemingly unable to locate or identify a serial killer terrorizing her home town. The killer is an escaped lunatic and, as usual for these types, a killing machine (the film coming as the slasher series was petering out).

This escaped lunatic plot dives into sordid sex as a prostitute friend convinces the protagonist to join her in a threesome with a retired judge. Of course, the morally punitive killer's next targets are the whore and the judge. The killer's weapon of choice is a scalpel, at once recalling the European cycle of demented doctors and allowing for a series of shots of women's throats being slashed. The film has no particular reputation.

Evil Obsession

(1995: d. Richard W. Munchkin)

scr. Tom Constantine; pr. Munchkin, Aron Schifman; ph. Michael Goi; ed. Tony Mark; prod d. Allen Tombello; cast. Corey Feldman, Kimberly Stevens, Mark Derwin, Brion James, Stacie Randall, Uma Damon

A serial killer targets cover girl models from calendars and magazines (à la *Calendar Girl Murders* and *Cover Girl Killer*). The principal suspects include a private detective, an aspiring screenwriter, and a sexually obsessed "nerd" (Feldman). A top model fixates on the potential danger to her, and if she might indeed know the killer. The film wants to be part of the erotic thriller cycle but failed to make any impression. Although it updates the theme of sexual commodification and its effects on the male libidinous ego, *Evil Obsession* is, nevertheless, primarily a vehicle for its nominal star.

Evil Spirits

(1991: d. Gary Graver)

scr. Mikel Angel; pr. Bianca Manzo, Sidney Niekerk; ph. Graver; m. Duane Sciagua; set d. Richard Dearborn; cast. Karen Black, Arte Johnson, Michael Berryman, Virginia Mayo, Robert Quarry, Martine Beswick, Mikel Angel; 95m

The tenants of a California boarding house (run by Karen Black) start disappearing once their pension checks have been signed over. A federal agent poses as a visitor to investigate. The killer is revealed to keep the corpse of her wheelchair-bound husband in the basement (a reversal of *Psycho*) and talks to it; she makes room for new boarders by killing males and burying them in the backyard, with the neighbors continually complaining about the smell.

This occasionally sleazy film by a director better known as a pornographic movie producer has some familiar faces, but they have reportedly rather little to do. However, it is eccentric, notably featuring a man chained in the cellar who feeds on human hands (à la *Spider Baby*), and moves towards the stylish Gothic akin to the work other porn-grad horror directors, including Tom DeSimone and Gerard Kikoine. Graver has gone on to more interesting, if minor, work. It is only tangentially a serial killer film, only hinting at the sexual undercurrents, and can perhaps be compared to the likes of *Whatever Happened to Aunt Alice?*, although its sense of comedy is more blatant than that character piece.

The Exorcist III

(1990: d. William Peter Blatty)

scr. Blatty; pr. Carter DeHaven; ph. Gerry Fisher; m. Barry De Vorzon (and Mike Oldfield); ed. Todd Ramsay; prod d. Leslie Dilley; cast. George C. Scott, Ed Flanders, Brad Dourif, Jason Miller, Nicol Williamson, Nancy Fish, Scott Wilson, Viveca Lindfors, Samuel L. Jackson, George DiCenzo; 110m

The official sequel to Friedkin's original, ignoring Boorman's *Exorcist II: The Heretic* completely, this has a cop (Scott) investigate a series of crimes which show signs of bodily mutilation akin to those perpetrated by an executed serial killer (named Gemini, and apparently meant to recall the never captured Zodiac). The killer was electrocuted at the very moment Father Karras (Miller) plunged down the stairs at the end of the first film. The policeman's investigation leads him back to the death of the priest, who may not be dead after all. He finds him alive, sort of— one of many tormented souls (the biblical "Legion") inhabiting a body in an asylum, apparently also possessed by the spirit of the Gemini killer, who may be active once again. The killer has spent the previous 15 years slowly repairing Karras' brain damage. But how does he get out of the asylum?

A fascinating and frustrating thesis on mental illness as ontological insight/despair, *The Exorcist III* continues the themes in director Blatty's *The Ninth Configuration*. Here insight and despair are bedfellows as the policeman has a crisis of faith which, in needing a demonstration of the power of God, is brought into conflict with the force of Evil. This force of ultimate Evil is the serial killer, presented as a kind of wandering soul able to inhabit other minds (only those of the mentally ill) and will them to do his bidding. The film suggests a commonality of experience to the mentally ill, as if it were not physiological illness but a kind of spiritual affliction or malaise. In particular, it holds the rather romantic notion of schizophrenia as psychotic insight, allowing access to a spiritual realm — the realm of the damned and accursed, whose voices and souls inhabit the melange called "Legion" (the biblical curse of madness).

The killer's method is consistent: he drugs victims into paralysis and then creatively mutilates them while they remain conscious. Blatty knows the definition of the serial killer and so has the killer admit that although he previously killed at random, these related killings were a favor to an unnamed demonic power. The killer considers himself an artist, whose pride in his work amounts to the cruel, sadistic domination and torture of his victims. The more elaborate the crime and crime scene, the greater the demonstration of the killer's admitted showmanship. The murders are staged for maximum shock value when they are discovered. Correspondingly, there is no attempt to conceal the body or deny the crime. Such "artworks" demand an admission of authorship. The killer even demands that the policeman inform the press of his return to work. This anticipates the thematic direction of many serial killer films through the 1990s wherein the killers sought to proclaim

A despairing detective (George C. Scott) confronts a homicidal woman (Viveca Lindfors) under the psychic control of an incarcerated serial killer intent on proving his powers in *The Exorcist III* (Fox, 1990).

their presence rather than protect their anonymity.

Blatty's heavy sense of irony is evident throughout, giving the film a kind of cruel humor, which reinforces the intended spiritual shock. It is not merely a clash of good and evil, but also of the necessity to not only admit the presence of supernatural forces that can guide and influence human interaction for better or worse, but to confront it and purge the worst, enabling the good soul to rest. Those who need confirmation of the goodness of God must journey through Legion, the confrontation with Evil-as-madness.

This notion of the serial killer as a supernatural force which can travel from soul to soul also influenced the concurrent release of *The First Power* and the later *Shocker* and *Fallen*, and has some basis even in the notion of a contagious patriar-

chal malevolence in *Cruising*. The killer's description of himself as a traveler, one who moves, inhabits the final words of the eponymous killer in *Dr. Petiot* before his execution: "I am a traveler and I take my baggage with me." What you do in one world affects the next.

The climactic exorcism sequence was tacked on at the producers' insistence, after Blatty had in fact finished the film; and indeed this disrupts the film's thematic continuity, to its detriment. The studio powers-that-be felt that Blatty's cut did not live up to titular expectations. Blatty favors a steady buildup. He tackles the ritual murders in detective fashion, slowly introducing the supernatural theme. He then ties it in to notions of demonic possession and mental illness before concentrating on one-on-one scenes between the jailed killer and the cop, the killer intent on proving the validity of the Evil he represents, ironically providing the confirmation of divinity the protagonist needs.

This confirmation does not have the joy of that in *The Ninth Configuration*. Indeed, that film's star, Scott Wilson, so overjoyed by the confirmation of an afterlife in the aforementioned film, is cast here as a doctor so disheartened by the confirmation of divine forces—as shaped by Evil rather than Good—that he commits suicide. *The Exorcist III* is as despairing as its protagonist.

The Expert

(1994: d. Rick Avery and William Lustig [uncredited])

scr. Max Allan Collins; stry. Jill Gatsby; pr. Andrew Garroni, Barbara Nicols; ph. Levie Isaacks; m. Ashley Irwin; ed. Bob Murawski; prod d. Clay Callaway; cast. Jeff Speakman, James Brolin, Michael Shaner, Alex Datcher, Wolfgang Bodison, Jim Varney; 92m

A tactical defense instructor (and former special operations expert) whose sister has been murdered by a serial killer testifies against the killer and sends him to jail. However, when it seems the killer is to be transferred to a psychiatric institution (at the bequest of a liberal new warden), the ex-commando infiltrates the prison, intending to murder the killer and see justice done.

The film seeks to combine the dictates of the action arena with an exposition of the standard trial arguments in such cases—arguments about free will vs. psychiatric determinism and the aptness of the insanity plea (the killer pleads multiple personality, backed by psychiatric testimony), as well as the appropriateness of prison vs. "luxury" treatment in mental hospitals. It also roots the killer's actions in childhood maladjustments and questions whether or not this excuses his adult actions. Similar themes are found in *Rampage*. The killer however, is fully aware of these issues and able to use them in the manner of a clever manipulator in order to get what he thinks he wants. This cockiness is one feature that further outrages the protagonist, who turns to more vigilante-oriented methods of retribution when he feels the justice system has failed him.

All characters use the issues surrounding serial killers and the death penalty to serve their own agenda, personal or political. No character escapes unscathed, as there are no clear heroes (the liberal advocate and prison warden are both depicted as flawed persons). Each has his own rationale, and for most of its length the film seeks to avoid identification with any one view, in favor of an attempted balanced analysis of multiple points of view. The lack of subtlety and related problems are seen in the casting of a black woman as the liberal, suggesting minorities are perhaps responsible for the relaxation of punitive measures, thus necessitating the actions of a strong WASP patriarch to restore the balance of justice lost. This woman, after being kidnapped and rescued, changes her views (once personally touched by tragedy) and regrets her past leniency towards the killer.

Thus the film resolves in standard vigilante action set pieces what the righteousness of the protagonist has all but accepted (à la Lustig's earlier *Vigilante*), negating much of the preceding discussion. It is ultimately more akin to the likes of *The Art of Dying* and even *Eye for an Eye*, which also advocate vigilante justice in dealing with serial killers.

Exquisite Tenderness

(1995: d. Carl Schenkel) aka *The Surgeon*

scr. Patrick Cirillo, from Bernard Sloane; pr. Alan Beattie, Chris Chesser, Willi Baer; exec pr. David Korda; ph. Thomas Burstyn; prod d. Douglas Higgins; m. Christopher Franke; ed. Jimmy B. Frazier; cast. Isabel Glasser, James Remar, Peter Boyle, Malcolm McDowell, Charles Dance; 96m

The title of this low-budget film (in the *Visiting Hours* vein) about a hospital that becomes the target of a serial killer who steals the pituitary gland from patients to keep his own dying body alive refers to the medical term for "the point where pain reaches its most extreme." Amidst this, doctor McDowell conducts unethical experiments, and a respected surgeon (Glasser) and a proud and arrogant junior doctor (Remar) investigate.

In conception, *Exquisite Tenderness* neatly encapsulates, deconstructs and reinvents the European mad surgeon horror subgenre as popularized by *Eyes Without a Face* and *The Awful Dr. Orlof*. It roots aberrance in past trauma, as the killer as a boy witnessed his brother killed in surgery (perhaps by one of those same mad surgeons in a past movie) and grows to be a monster with a scalpel, continuing a monstrous tradition. The killer is the mad patriarch, ironically coming up against a female adversary who has been sanctioned by the wounded Patriarchy to restore its balance.

The film effectively plays on the dread of surgery, as it contrasts varied types of medical professionals (researchers, students, doctors, surgeons, patients) in terms of their respective humanity — the killer having lost all to selfishness, the very selfishness which can paradoxically result in scientific advancement for the betterment of many. The desire to prove one's knowledge is akin to proving one's superiority, which when accepted can result in inhumanity, with sadism a kind of byproduct. The killer is one who conducted such unauthorized research and now needs to continue it to stay alive and keep his ego intact. He is in the tradition of the Nazi doctors, with grandiose delusions of his own genius and superman superiority justifying murder. His delight in surgical torture goes beyond research, however: the link between genius and sadism, and of illicit research into death and beyond, recalls the work of Stuart Gordon (especially *Re-Animator* and *From Beyond*).

It amounts to a tale of trust and betrayal: from son to father, patient to doctor, and victim to killer and policeman, with the protagonist left to sort out the repercussions when the assumption of patriarchal trust is violated by the rogue killer. Schenkel considers the killer as both the epitome and nadir of the medical profession — the result of early Sadean imprinting. From the abuse of trust comes pain, and the ability to control another's pain is both a God-like power and a contamination of the human soul, which can corrupt and turn benevolence into the Sadean. The killer is aware of the monster he has become but cannot stop killing, so addicted is he to the ritual power he physically gains through the act of murder. The good doctor must purge this corrupted selfishness from the profession.

The scenes set in corridors, from room to room, and on stairs, with doors opening and closing, suggests the theme of transition vs. entrapment so common to serial killer films. The killer's actions are designed to enable his entry into a higher state of being — to transcend the death he inflicts upon others. The good protagonist has to halt the journey and thus disavow the validity of such transcendence, ironically also disavowing the validity of medical research and experimentation to improve the human condition (which, by definition herein, negates the individual). She has the duty, as well as the responsibility, to enact ritual, punitive purge.

With the proverbial "style to burn" (noirish lighting, tilted angles, bold colors, relentlessly mobile camera [in the opening prologue especially]), *Exquisite Tenderness* segues from thriller to comedy and back effortlessly via macabre ironic contrasts (for instance, the 1950s pop music playing as a demented surgeon operates on a boy without anesthetic). It is the work of a self-conscious and deliberate director who loves to contrast angles and camera positions, and jostle tone. Director Schenkel did the equally underrated and effective *Knight Moves*, which also raised the question of professional ethics and the corresponding personality changes when morality is sacrificed.

Eye for an Eye

(1996: d. John Schlesinger)

scr. Rick Jaffa, Amanda Silver; pr. Michael Levy; ph. Amir Mokri; m. James Newton Howard; ed. Peter Honess; prod d. Stephen Hendrickson; cast. Sally Field, Kiefer Sutherland, Ed Harris, Beverly D'Angelo, Joe Mantegna, Cynthia Rothrock, Keith David, Philip Baker Hall; 111m

This is a loaded, blatant endorsement of vigilante action. After being powerless to prevent her young daughter's rape and murder, a mom (Field) sees her daughter's killer (Sutherland) released. She goes to a victim therapy group, where she overhears moves towards private vigilante action. She starts to obsess about the killer and her lost daughter to the point of neglecting her token family. She follows the killer around his neighborhood, stalking him. She seeks vigilante action, and takes shooting and self-defense lessons in preparation. When the killer murders another woman, and is released for lack of evidence, she is distraught and takes the necessary steps to see justice done: she entices the killer into her home (by first ransacking his) and shoots him in "self defense." The investigating policeman knows what she did, but also considers it a justifiable homicide.

The film opens with a harrow-

ing scene of a young girl being raped and murdered whilst her mother, on a car phone, listens in helplessly. The subsequent drama bespeaks of her empowerment through vigilante action, as grief and sorrow segue into aggression and violence. Schlesinger is evidently more interested in the victimology, although he is bound by the thriller dictates (but nowhere near as effectively as in *Pacific Heights* or *The Believers*). The result is calculated commerciality. As an analysis of coping with unimaginable grief, its vigilante solution

Serial killer Robert Doob (Kiefer Sutherland) is freed on a technicality, but soon returns to look for a new victim and mark his territory in *Eye for an Eye* (Paramount, 1995).

is a single-minded cop-out, in reality a drive that too must be surmounted as part of the healing process. Perhaps the film was thus intended as the character portrait of a woman who wants closure above all else, which ultimately emancipates her psychologically and sexually. However, the vigilante drive is nowhere depicted as a corruptive force, but instead a justifiable liberation akin to the revenge-minded actions in Schumacher's Grisham adaptation *A Time to Kill*. It is not only morally justifiable but also deservedly free from punishment.

There is no doubt that the killer is a one-dimensionally reprehensible figure, though Schlesinger makes some attempt to contextualize him in terms of socioeconomic deprivation. He considers women disposable sexual items, and must assert his ego through violent rape and murder as a means of escaping his lot and marking his territory (like a dog, he urinates on the ground of an intended victim's house). He even remarks to the powerless investigating officer that he never does anything he considers wrong. Ironically, his expression of violent will is a form of potency which separates him from most other powerless and effectively impotent males, some of whom (the other victims) seek to restore their lost potency through vigilante violence.

Audience sympathies are with the mother, who gradually befriends other like-affected people who condone secret vigilante retribution against offenders freed by the justice system. She feels so cornered as to have no other choice — once the killer targets other family members. Justice has failed her, and she is thus morally sanctioned to eliminate the threat to herself, her family and other young women posed by this killer; not only is she sanctioned, but, the film posits, morally obligated to. The only questioning of the protagonist's motivations comes in a scene wherein she is so invigorated after the beating of an innocent man that she has more adventurous sex (she gets on top) with her meek husband, who can't explain the change in her.

Social pronouncement at its most dramatically manipulative, this is perhaps intended as a more tasteful version of *Death Wish*, and certainly appeals to the same emotions (though not as successfully and even provocatively as Winner's grotesquerie). Rita Kempley (*Washington Post*) noted the thematic similarity to Field's role in *Not Without My Daughter*; in *Eye for an Eye* she plays a mom now without her daughter. Buehrer (*Magill Cinema Annual 1997*, pp. 173–4) notes that the O.J. Simpson trial is shown on TV during the course of the film's events, but nothing is made of this connection.

Eye of the Beholder

(1999: d. Stephan Elliott)

scr. Stephan Elliott; pr. Nicolas Clermont, Tony Smith; ph. Guy Dufaux; m. Marius de Vries; ed. Sue Blainey; prod d. Jean Baptiste Tard; cast. Ewan McGregor, Ashley Judd, Patrick Bergin, K.D. Lang, Jason Priestley, Genevieve Bujold; 107m

A British agent, the Eye, watches and follows a female serial killer (Judd) across the United States, without her knowing, and even acts to protect her when she is threatened with rape by one of her intended victims and capture by the police. He jealousy sabotages her seemingly genuine love for a rich blind man, less out of concern for the man's safety than for fear of losing her. This was Ewan McGregor's first film after breaking through to stardom in the United States in *Star Wars: The Phantom Menace*. Australian director Elliott is best known for the hit gender-bending comedy of *The Adventures of Priscilla, Queen of the Desert*.

The killer, named Eris (evoking the

goddess of strife and discord, according to Howe in *Washington Post*), is a siren who lures men and then kills them during sex, with presumed necrophilic satisfaction to follow (à la *Matador*, perhaps). She then adopts a new guise, moves to a new state and resumes the pattern (thus recalling the similarly nomadic killers in *Black Widow* and *The Stepfather*). There is a suggestion that she is consumed by an impossible romantic idyll, always shattered by the need to kill. However, there is the possibility that she could have found such an idyll with the blind man, who is symbolically unable to see her truly monstrous vulnerabilities.

The increasingly infatuated agent (suggesting that *The Conversation* might have been an influence) silently observes her over a considerable length of time and with a variety of equipment. It is a study of voyeuristic obsession and the desperate attempt to make a connection with a desired, but ultimately lost, object: they are finally able to touch only before her death. The protagonist, in seeking out her background to understand her character, and compulsively studying her behavior, is the profiler figure here, unable to shed his personal baggage.

Both the killer and the agent have haunted pasts. The killer was abandoned as a child and now kills men in retaliation, and the agent lost his daughter through his own negligence. The haunting is literal in the agent's case, as he is apparently followed around by the ghost/spectcr of the dead daughter and talks to her regularly. This subplot is jettisoned midway, as if the agent somehow made his peace. By protecting a daughter who lost her father, he becomes the father he never was and seeks redemption for his negligence in the loss of his own family. Thus the killer is an amalgam of his lost daughter and wife as a desired sexual object. Until the end they remain physically separated by distance (walls, windows, etc.), with the mobile camera functioning as the force which unites them.

The film's bleak tone is confirmed by the ending, as the protagonist, unable to save his desired object from death — and thus denied redemption — is doomed to repeat the same tragedy of loss that put him in the situation in the first place. This is both a noirish and an absurdist sense of futility, removed from the light touch of Elliott's previous film. Although they start out as both beyond the law and society by choice (one legally), they cannot maintain their separation, as outside forces doom their tentative connection. Fate denies them union.

In a cold and hostile universe, death and murder are inevitable acts of interpersonal communication when dealing with the loss of a loved one. There is no escape from the cycle of death and futility. Hence the characters are always framed and constricted, seeking a freedom of movement in an unattractive world where there is both profound sadness and a perversely erotic beauty in murder, as the protagonist watches the naked killer, who cries after murdering, wash the blood off her body in the rain. Such complex images are indeed captivating and promise more stylization than what is actually present.

A kind of surrealistic noir and would-be art film, *Eye of the Beholder* was generally considered a pretentious failure. The acclaimed novel on which it is based also inspired the French film *Martelle Randonnee*. While most US critics felt it dull and bland, and that Elliott was way out of his depth, reviewers in Elliott's native Australia praised its boldness and ambition.

Eye of the Killer

(1999: d. Paul Marcus) aka *After Alice*

scr. Jeff Miller, Marcus; pr. Tom Kinninmont, Andre Paquette, Tina Stern; ph. Brian Pearson;

ed. Liz Webber; prod d. Taavo Soodor; cast. Kiefer Sutherland, Henry Czerny, Polly Walker, Stephen Ouimette, Gary Hudson; 105m

Ten years before, a police detective (Sutherland) was investigating a serial killer known as "Jabberwocky" who suddenly disappeared, apparently ceasing his murderous activities. His failure to find the killer has left the policeman a tormented alcoholic unable to find and maintain stability in his life. Now it seems the same killer is in operation again, and has sent the police a note requesting the same detective be assigned to the case. The detective agrees but soon finds himself troubled by explicit, potentially psychic visions of the crimes, an ability that started when he was injured in the pursuit of an offender. He enlists the help of a paranormal specialist (Walker) — the profiler here — to catch the killer.

Although the plot suggests some similarities to *The Watcher*, this film benefits from star Sutherland's previous roles as the killer in *Eye for an Eye* and *Freeway*, and is a reportedly competent addition to the psychic-link saga. The killer and cop are both consumed by their adversarial relationship, as if that has in some ways defined their lives, and to the murder of innocents. This bond is so strong that the potential psychic link reflects the theme's genesis in *Manhunter*: the psychological closeness between adversaries, and the desire for purging and closure.

This was originally produced for HBO cable television.

Eyeball

(1978: d. Umberto Lenzi)

scr. Felix Tusell; pr. Joseph Brenner; cast. John Richardson, Martine Brochard, Ines Pelegrin, Silvia Solar, George Rigaud; 91m

In between his notorious cannibal movies, Italian horror specialist Lenzi made this crime drama and borderline giallo about a killer in a red cape and hood who murders tourists by gouging out their eyes. These are the ultimate trophies and the appropriation of another's perception in the hope of enriching one's own — the ultimate act of murder in the giallo form, so concerned with altered perceptions. The murderer operates out of Barcelona and kills beauties he sees on the tourist buses. Gore and lesbian sex reportedly kept it lively enough for the exploitation crowd, but this lacks the style of Argento or even Fulci.

Although a crime drama, *Eyeball*'s advertising campaign promoted it as a horror movie; indeed, it is evidence of their crossover in the giallo. It was originally titled *Red Cat in a Labyrinth of Glass* to match the flamboyance of the Argento and Fulci giallos of the early 1970s. The *Variety* reviewer reported that although some patrons cheered the murder and mutilation scenes, they grew rapidly disinterested in the film after that. Thus it is for completists of the director only, although it partially balances the move towards the slasher movie better appropriated in *Torso*.

Eyes of a Stranger

(1980: d. Ken Wiederhorn)

scr. Mark Jackson, Eric L. Bloom; pr. Ronald Zerra; ph. Mini Rojas; m. Richard Einhorn; ed. Rick Shaine; cast. Lauren Tewes, Jennifer Jason Leigh, John DiSanti, Peter DuPre, Gwen Lewis, Kitty Lunn, Timothy Hawkins, Ted Richert, Toni Crabtree; 85m

A Miami serial killer phones his victims first (telling them they are going to die — thus asserting his power over them and compensating for his personal shortcomings), then stalks, rapes and murders them. An intrepid journalist (Tewes) soon uncovers his identity. She reports her suspicions to the police, who dismiss them, forcing her to take assertive action herself. She then starts to harass the killer with phone calls. Once the killer is onto her, he targets her blind sister. In defending herself against the killer, the blind girl's vision is restored.

By systematically turning the tables on the killer, the film reverses the usual stalking plot of such slasher material. Instead, there emerges a story of female independence, maturation and, as Carol Clover points out in *Men, Women and Chainsaws* (p. 190), sexual awakening through the adoption of an assertive gaze to counter the traditional "assaultive gaze" given the slasher/killer in such films. The blind girl, raped as a child, this times escapes the passivity she seemed resigned to and usurps the phallic power from the killer (blinding him and targeting his genitals). She immediately goes from shooting the killer to looking in the mirror and touching herself sexually — alive in a new-found womanhood.

To deal with internal and external pressures, the killer prowls the streets and strip-bars for victims. He immerses himself in the male objectification of women, allowing him to consider them disposable. It is his recourse, murder being a stress release akin to orgasm. Sexuality is equated with murder as a function of an assaultive male look, dictated and reinforced by an exploitative culture. Women's independence, at least in the slasher film, comes with a punitive adoption of the same.

Although its endorsement of female violence against men recalls the controversial *I Spit on Your Grave*, this film is more complex than most in its treatment of phallic gazing. The cure for blinding in assertive action also recalls *The Spiral Staircase*. The device of having the killer live in the apartment building opposite the protagonists recalls *Rear Window*; and, indeed, the film's knowing treatment of "the look" in the genre elevates it above most. There has been some reappraisal (Clover and Wood) of the film since it was at first dismissed.

Eyes of Laura Mars

(1978: d. Irvin Kershner)

scr. John Carpenter, David Zelag Goodman; stry. Carpenter; pr. Jon Peters; exec pr. Jack H. Harris; m. Artie Kaye; song. Barbra Streisand; cast. Faye Dunaway, Tommy Lee Jones, Brad Dourif, Rene Auberjonois, Raul Julia, Frank Adonis, Lisa Taylor; 104m

John Carpenter scripted this early psychic-link thriller about a fashion photographer (Dunaway) who has premonitions of, or sees, murders through the killer's eyes and contacts the police. A sympathetic detective (Jones) seems to fall for her — until she realizes that he may be involved. Indeed, he is revealed to be the killer.

From the start, with Streisand singing "Prisoner," the film considers visual perception a prison, with characters forced into adopting others' perceptions, whether by looking at their aesthetic interpretations of reality and staged events or by psychic appropriation. Even the killer targets women he sees displayed in violently erotic photographs (resembling crime scenes) in the protagonist's book. To be free from the prison of the gaze, to transcend it, is to kill the object; although this paradoxically amounts to serving it in a cause and effect manner: escape is illusory, as the stimulative gaze is forever reinforced.

The consequence of visually objectifying women as sexual products is sex murder. The film addresses what Clover refers to as "the mechanics of predatory gazing" (p. 183), and thus can be interpreted as addressing the stylistic concern exhibited in scripter Carpenter's own *Halloween*. The female photographer may objectify women via her profession, but such gazing is associated with the male. To make the point clear, the killer stabs women's eyes, punishing them perhaps for their own gaze, lest they objectify him in the same manner. Thus he is drawn to the protagonist as an independent woman who possesses an active, marketable gaze. Ironically, the protagonist claims her photos force one to look at the "reality" of murder and violence (or at least its consequences), but she is terrified when forced to see as a killer sees, devoid of the glamour and distance afforded by her profession.

The film is constructed as a mystery more than a serial killer thriller, with many suspects examined before revealing the killer to be the policeman—the figure associated with the preservation of Patriarchy's functioning. This killer, abused and neglected by a whorish mother, is depicted in terms of a split personality, the good side desiring his own death. It is a sleek and stylish but empty film, although *Variety* felt it to be a step up for its director and a move towards commercial stability.

The Face at the Window

(1939: d. George King)

scr. A.R. Rawlinson, Randall Faye; ply. F. Brooke Warren; ph. Hone Glendinning; cast. Tod Slaughter, Marjorie Taylor, John Warwick, Leonard Henry, Aubrey Mallalieu; 65m

This is a supposedly typical Tod Slaughter vehicle. The menacing Slaughter made several crime melodramas in the 1930s and 1940s, including *Murder in the Red Barn* (1935) and *Sweeney Todd, the Demon Barber of Fleet Street* (1936) which flirt with the serial killer figure. These were not considered horror films, although Slaughter's commanding presence was later appreciated as the bastion of early British horror.

According to Hardy et al. (p. 68), it did depict the lure of horrendous actions and the appeal such evildoers have. Horror tableaux were used to heighten the sense of an aberration on display; yet this Evil was clearly a recognizable criminality rather than the otherworldly monstrousness of contemporary horrors. The Slaughter film(s) thus began to bridge the horror and crime conceptions of the serial killer, a trend balanced in the German Edgar Wallace adaptations.

This is an account of a Parisian killer, circa 1880, known as "the Wolf," who stabs victims distracted by the face of his bestial brother in a window. A Frankenstein subplot concerns a scientist who revives corpses by electricity: one of the corpses reveals the killer's identity. The homicides, despite the pleasure in them, are intended to cover bank robberies. Police investigations and a trap finally undo the culprits.

Fade to Black

(1980: d. Vernon Zimmerman)

scr. Zimmerman; pr. George G. Braunstein, Ron Harmody; exec pr. Irwin Yablans, Sylvio Tabet; ph. Alex Phillips Jr.; m. Craig Safan; cast. Dennis Christopher, Tim Thomerson, Mickey Rourke, Norman Burton, Morgan Paull, Gwynne Gilford, Eve Brent Ashe, James Luisi, Linda Kerridge; 102m

A movie-obsessed young man turns to murder out of personal frustration, staging each killing in imitation of his favorite films. He thus becomes known as the "Celluloid Killer." He dresses up in the guise of movie icons (Tommy Udo—Widmark from *Kiss of Death*; Dracula; Hopalong Cassidy; Cody Jarrett—Cagney from *White Heat*) as he kills, recalling the disguised killer of *No Way to Treat a Lady*. A psychologist is assigned to the police precinct, but his advice and thoughts/analyses of the possible killer are resented by the police detective on the case.

This is a self-conscious blend of serial killer, slasher and the "gimmick killer" as they existed at the commencement of the slasher boom. The victims are unknown to each other, but are all known to the killer before he murders them. In fact, he considers them representative of the factors that have been holding him down. He feels their comments are slights against him (in fact, they all insult him or belittle him in some manner), and he murders them in order to assert his superiority. However, he can only maintain this idealized form of himself by imitating the movie icons he considers representative of a better world. His fantasy is to live in a melange of movie moments. These moments involve stylized, even romanticized, violence, and his attempt to bring the fantasy into real life is to psychologically project it, systematically eliminating those who would stand in its way; in that way he incorporates their deaths as moments in his own derivative movie. He can only become an active participant in his fantasy world through violence.

Although only some of the crimes are sexual (as Dracula he drinks the blood of a prostitute — this is a pre–AIDS film), the film is careful to suggest that the empowerment offered by movie-fueled fantasy is sexual in nature. Hence the protagonist masturbates to a picture of Marilyn Monroe before setting out to kill the Marilyn Monroe lookalike he feels has slighted him, and whose rejection was the catalyst that set into motion his compensatory homicidal drive.

This is a highly effective film, with a superb performance by Dennis Christopher. Its allusions to other films (including *Kiss of Death*, *Night of the Living Dead*, *Dracula*, *The Mummy*, *White Heat*, Western serials) make it a treat for "film buffs" able to spot the references. This knowledge of previous films ironically allows a certain distancing from the action, with the film being thus an examination of the genre itself. The seductive world of the movies only leads to an escapist immersion in violence and final self-destruction: the movies are far from a harmless escape, as they affect a subculture and warp emotions as they transform desire into murder.

Its depiction of police intent on capturing the killer contrasts with that of the psychologist (hence profiler), an ex-hippie intent on treating and understanding him as a product of adverse circumstance. Typical of the film's self-conscious themes, the profiler laments the media imprinting of impressionable youths. However, he too is powerless to prevent it and must deal only with the terrible aftermath, his pleas to the killer and claims of sympathy leading nowhere.

Vicarious identification feeds a fantasy determined to be actualized, with horrendous consequences for individuals and society. The movies offer the killer a validation of his revenge fantasies by setting in progress a process of objectification. However, after his first murder (of his mother, who pretended to be his aunt and had possessively unhealthy sexual interests in him), he confronts his reflection in the mirror and, momentarily unable to reconcile the act with the fantasy, is sick. There is no glamour. Subsequently, he goes to more elaborate, planned-out crimes, ensuring that such murder is the glamorized act he seeks. Consequently, there is a sense of progression and acceleration to his crimes, as he heads towards his revenge against the Marilyn Monroe lookalike.

The film has a mixed, though increasingly favorable, reputation. Several critics (*Variety* included) felt that promising themes were cheated and even betrayed by the film's final resorting to what they considered trendy slasher violence. They neglected to note the movie's examination of itself, and thus the state of 1980s horror, as a product of previous cinematic codes and representations of violence finding a locus in the figure of the serial killer. After the 1970s splintering of the killer into different types, *Fade to Black* was a major move towards the reassertion of the serial killer figure.

Fallen

(1998: d. Gregory Hoblit)

scr. Nicholas Kazan; pr. Charles Roven, Dawn Steel; ph. Newton Thomas Sigel; m. Tan Dun; ed. Lawrence Jordan; prod d. Terence Marsh; cast. Denzel Washington, John Goodman, Donald Sutherland, Embeth Davidtz, James Gandolfini, Elias Koteas; 119m

Like Wes Craven's *Shocker*, and following the line set by *The Exorcist III* and the equally supernatural-themed *First Power* (although much less the comic book), *Fallen* concerns the spirit of an executed serial killer which returns as a demonic force (called Azazel). This force is able to move from person to person through touch, thus making life difficult for the policeman who caught him and now must stop the spirit (assumed male) from murdering again and framing the policeman.

The film posits cop and killer as equal nemeses (recalling Washington's policeman as rival to Lithgow's criminal in Russell Mulcahy's *Ricochet*), each intent on proving their righteousness over the other. It is a game between skilled adversaries, a theme particularly prominent in 1990s serial killer films. The protagonist considers policemen the "chosen people," an ontological Goodness which magnetically draws Evil to it to spite it. The innocents are pawns in this battle, there to be used and abused at will to prove one's superiority in the fight. It is a fight between patriarchs—for nothing less than the fate of the human soul. And this human soul is inherently weak and in need of protection by the justly ennobled few.

Possession by this spirit is akin to a social liberation and empowerment for those so afflicted. It is a freedom from the constraints of Goodness, although this makes them empty vessels for murders they subsequently do not remember. The killer soul inhabits humans but is an Evil essentially alien to the human condition, corrupting it rather than being an innate part of it. This functions as a neat encapsulation and reinterpretation of the themes

On the day of the execution, a jailed serial killer (Elias Koteas) reaches out to shake the hand of the detective (Denzel Washington) who captured him, as the TV cameras look on earnestly in *Fallen* (WB, 1998).

The detective (Washington) and his nephew (Michael Pagan) flee from the influence of a disembodied serial killer spirit in *Fallen* (WB, 1998).

at the foundation of the serial killer film. Correspondingly, the memory loss experienced by those so taken over recalls the amnesia-themed early film noirs, which suggested murder was an act too foul for normal human consciousness to bear.

The crimes are intended as the interpersonal communication between adversaries, beyond the reach and understanding of ordinary mortals, and allow the killer to dictate the course of the investigation. Correspondingly, the profiler figure here is a woman who reveals the spiritual nature of the fight to the policeman, and whose outside help he seeks to battle the supernatural force. Her insight enables the investigator to transform into a knowing agent of the ultimate Patriarchy (God's law) ready to sacrifice himself for the protection of the innocent — although, in the end, he fails to eliminate Evil, and the threat to Patriarchy (civilization) remains in need of divine protectors. By the time of *The Bone Collector*, Washington has made the transition from investigator to skilled profiler.

The notion of homicidal desire as an infectious Evil is a provocative subtext in many serial killer films that target Patriarchy's traditions (although this film doesn't — unlike Hoblit's previous *Primal Fear* and even his follow-up, *Frequency*), such as *Cruising*. The subsequent idea of different killers committing similar crimes informs *Copycat*.

The Fantasist

(1989: d. Robin Hardy)

scr. Hardy; nvl. Patrick McGinley; pr. Mark Forstater; ph. Frank Gell; m. Stanislas Syrewicz; ed. Thomas Schwalm; cast. Christopher Cazenove, Timothy Bottoms, Moira Harris, John Kavanagh, Mick Lally; 94m

This is director Hardy's long-awaited second feature after the acclaimed cult film *The Wicker Man* (one of the triumphs of British horror, in its uncut version). It concerns the "Phone Call Killer" who telephones women and then recites erotic (obscene?) poetry. After thus appealing to their supposed repressions (he thinks), he seduces and stabs them in the back. A young, but independent and strong-willed girl who comes to Dublin captures his attention. The girl suspects a visiting American may be the killer, and the film follows her developing relationship to both him and a local teacher who may also be suspect. The policeman on the case, who not only strongly suspects and resents the American, but also has seemingly strange desires for the woman, further complicates their triangular rivalry.

The killer is not at once revealed and could be any one of these three men attracted to the girl, as if her innocence attracted such sexual predators (a touch of *Pandora's Box*). He considers himself an expert seducer and preys on what he perceives as women's need for emotional connection, leading to sexual domination. The phone calls enable a kind of faceless interaction, a safe distance from which he eventually must draw closer. The killing is a sexual act that consummates the romance and establishes his dominance and intent to make the woman a purely submissive figure. It is a process of objectification, although he seeks to photographically capture the individual beauty of each victim. He poses each victim in imitation of a painting of a nude, but they can never match his ideal conception of beauty.

The Fantasist's theme of a lone innocent in a community of potential decadents recalls *The Wicker Man*, although the film takes pains to equate such innocence with sexual repression. Indeed, the protagonist is a sensual being, a trait that attracts the predators, who are all, in a sense, looking for their ideal fantasy woman and project such onto her. Any male (all males?) could be predatorial by nature, haunted by an unattainable fantasy of womanhood. As such, the film examines how sexual desire and fantasy shapes individuals and even communities (the urban singles scene the film in part explores), a regular Hardy theme. However, at the end of this process lies the killer's homicidal

objectification, revealed in an erotically charged scene which reminds one that Hardy is indeed the director of *The Wicker Man*. Male romantic longing can segue into the Sadean.

Fatal Charm

(1992: d. Fritz Kiersch as Alan Smithee)

scr. Nick Niciphor; pr. Bruce Cohn Curtis, Jonathan D. Krane; ph. Steve Grass; ed. William Butler, Bob Ducsay; cast. Christopher Atkins, Peggy Lipton, Amanda Peterson, James Remar, Andrew Robinson, Ken Foree; 90m

This cable movie thriller has a teen girl trying to prove to everyone, including the police, that the ex-con she corresponded with while he was incarcerated is not a serial killer. When he gets out of prison she becomes a potential target. Hence, she must face the realization that her dream man may not be the perfect ideal she's searching for.

Although it uses pretty-boy Atkins well, recalling his work for Tom Holland and in *Die Watching*, this cynical tract on an irredeemable human nature was much tampered with by the studio, and the director opted for the Smithee pseudonym. *Fatal Charm* is a minor addition to those thrillers that seek to contrast the real with the idealized. Perhaps the realization is even a necessary maturation process.

Fatal Exposure

(1989: d. Peter B. Good)

scr. Chris Painter; ph. Good; ed. Gary Finlan; m. Dean Richard Marino; prod d. Brent Madden; cast. Blake Bahner, Ena Henderson, Dan Shmale, Julie Austin, Renee Cline

A photographer is a descendant of Jack the Ripper (what else would he be with a name like Jack T. Rippington?). He looks for possible women to bear his son and continue the homicidal heritage. In between, he murders women, staging them as artworks (akin to *Copycat* and the snuff-themed films of killers who videotape their quarry). He believes that drinking blood will keep him sexually potent (the film thus tries the serial killer to vampiric lore). He kidnaps and kills models, his girlfriend unaware of what he is doing to the women she supplies him with (and so becomes an unwitting accomplice). Finally his secret is found out and acid is poured over his face in an attempt at operatic grandeur (à la the *Abominable Dr. Phibes* mystique). His girlfriend is no longer his dupe, and is able to exact a just revenge on having been so used. (See Hardy, p. 446, for a look at this minor effort, unavailable at time of writing.)

Fatal Frames

(1996: d. Al Festa)

scr. Festa, Alessandro Monese, Mary Rinaldi; pr. Stefania Stella; ph. Giuseppe Bernardini; m. Festa; cast. Stefania Stella, Rick Gianasi, David Warbeck, Ugo Pagliai, Rossano Brazzi, Donald Pleasence; Linnea Quigley, Alida Valli, Angus Scrimm

A New York City music video maker on assignment in Italy becomes the suspect in the case of a serial murderer who videotapes his victims and sends the tapes to police, sharing his trophies with those who know their real significance as a demonstration of his power. As per the course, he must endeavor to clear his name.

This is a supposedly routine entry which seeks to restart the giallo movement for American audiences. Its concern for altered states of perception and evil realms beneath the everyday bespeak of its heritage, from Argento and Fulci especially. Such realms are accessed through the adoption of the killer's vision, hence the interest in seeing and recording murder as a means of shared illicit communication: an indictment of voyeurism that dates at least as far back as *Peeping Tom*. As a later

addition to the spaghetti nightmare boom, this murder-as-art themed movie (so prevalent since the mid–1990s) perhaps has a ready audience.

Fathers and Sons

(1992: d. Paul Mones)

scr. Paul Mones; pr. Jon Kilik; exec pr. Nick Wechsler, Keith Addis; ph. Ron Fortunato; m. Mason Daring; ed. Janice Keuhnelian; prod d. Eve Cauley; cast. Jeff Goldblum, Rory Cochrane, Rocky Carroll, Ellen Greene, Natasha Gregson Wagner, Paul Hipp, Famke Janssen, Rosanna Arquette; 96m

This is primarily a story of the troubled bonds between an ex-alcoholic father and a drug-using son after the death of the wife/mother. The father owns a bookstore and soon receives a box filled with copies of a strange book. The book is supposedly written by an alien presence, and it has the son enthralled. The son is in the end attacked by a necrophilic bisexual rapist/killer, the "Shore Killer," who has been stalking the area. The son sends telepathic messages to the father, who arrives just in time to save the day.

This uses the encounter with the serial killer as the last stage in a coming-of-age drama of a young man facing up to his psychological and sexual identity, and a father who redeems himself for his perceived failure by finally protecting his son from outside Evil. Thus it is a drama about the restoration of Patriarchy and the acknowledgement of a spiritually valid tradition passed on between Father and Son. Its baffling metaphysics—that humans are capable of a telepathy shared between fathers and sons, possibly the result of an alien imprinting which attracts killers—seem intended to lift the psychic-link movie beyond its considered station. They serve to present the killer as an alien threat to Patriarchy, and not one from within its own functioning. The killer is an undoubted outsider, even an extra-terrestrial presence.

Fear

(1990: d. Rockne S. O'Bannon)

scr. O'Bannon; pr. O'Bannon, Richard Kobritz; ph. Robert M. Stevens; m. Henry Mancini; ed. Kent Beyda; prod d. Joseph C. Nemec III; cast. Ally Sheedy, Lauren Hutton, Dina Merrill, Michael O'Keefe, Stan Shaw, Pruitt Taylor Vince, Kay Lenz, Cliff de Young; 100m

This is a psychic-link tele-movie that explores the interpersonal and reciprocative aspects of the bond between psychically aware people on opposite sides of the moral continuum. Ally Sheedy stars as a psychic who sometimes helps police investigations. Now she sees through the eyes of a serial killer, the "shadow man," and realizes that he too is psychic and conscious of her presence in his mind. The killer uses his power to terrify the woman, forcing her to experience the rush he feels when he murders, and reveals that it is women's fear which arouses him sexually. This killer wants to inspire awe, writing "fear me" in blood at crime scenes for investigators to read and heed. He wants to be known, feared and thus respected.

With the psychic as a compliment to police services, this film examines the profiler as a supernaturally gifted figure. Her insight into the killer's mind comes not from dedicated research but from intuitive psychic visions. To receive such visions she must partially surrender control of her mind to the killer, who is loathe to correspondingly relinquish control of his own (as this would subvert his own perceived power) and seeks to dominate her by sending her visions in return. This makes her the closest to the killer, and the most vulnerable — and useful — aid to skeptical police. The killer's ego cannot stand even the slightest blow, and he must prove himself superior in every way.

From a writer-director who did numerous episodes of the 1980s revised "Twilight Zone," and had previously scripted

Alien Nation for Graham Baker, *Fear* was originally planned for cinema release but debuted instead on cable on July 15, 1990, on Showtime. Intended as a partial showcase for Ally Sheedy's long announced comeback, it failed at that. Most notable for film scholars, perhaps, is the climax in a maze of mirrors, recalling Welles' classic *Lady from Shanghai.*

Fear City

(1985: d. Abel Ferrara)

scr. Nicholas St. John; pr. Bruce Cohn Curtis; ph. James Lemmo; m. Dick Halligan; ed. Jack W. Holmes, Anthony Redman; prod d. Vince Cresciman; cast. Tom Berenger, Melanie Griffith, Billy Dee Williams, Rossano Brazzi, Rae Dawn Chong; 96m

A serial killer, obsessed with martial arts, is murdering exotic dancers. Faced with police ineffectiveness, the criminal establishment takes it on themselves to find the killer, à la *M.* A Mafia Don appoints a club operator/pimp (Berenger) to become the vigilante and deal with the killer before business is too affected. Of course this brings the pimp into conflict with the (hypocritical) police investigator (Williams). It's an ironic view of the profiler-as-outsider in that the outsider is a pimp.

In the vein of post–Scorsese and Schrader 1980s urban noir, the city is depicted as a grim entrapment containing people driven to acts of desperation. This extends the determinism of *Driller Killer* and *Ms. 45*, from the same writer-director team, as it attempts to depict individuals struggling with/against their environment and the monstrosity it births in others. There is no attempt to judge these characters on a moral level, leading to some disturbing ambiguity in the explicit depiction of sexual mutilation. It explores the same sex-club world of such films as *Hardcore*, and recalls the pimp protagonists of *Vice Squad* and *Street Smart*, although *Fear City* is more concerned with morality and worth amongst the blighted. It also touches on themes of *Taxi Driver* and the killer as self-appointed purifier who keeps a diary of his actions and victims. This diary overflows with misogynistic hatred.

The criminal establishment's motivations are far from benevolent, however. The crimes represent a loss of income, as many of the strippers now refuse to dance or travel unescorted. The crimes are an insult to the Mafia's power in the neighborhood, and so it is a matter of pride and economics to apprehend the killer. The criminal powers-that-be, however, continue to objectify and exploit women, giving the killer the very stimulation he requires, and are thus complicit in his murders. The sleazy world they control is central to street life as depicted. No man is immune from violent thoughts towards women under such a world (a development of the themes in *Ms .45*). Even the protagonist harbors violent resentment for his former girlfriend (Griffith, in a role continuing her work in DePalma's *Body Double*), now a lesbian stripper who claims she has no need for men.

Ironically, the strippers have a sexual power over men which fosters resentment as much as desire, and so must be violently dealt with in order to be subordinated. It is a paradox that women's sexuality is thus both exploited and threatening. Their jokes about the fat stripper reveal what slaves they are to their conventional coded sexuality. The killer is consumed by this paradox, driven to watch the strippers for his arousal and then kill them because of the power over him that this gives them. These dancers usurp sexual power. The killer, therefore, feels justified in mutilating them (exorcising their sexuality) and writing about it in diary and story entries (in a work he entitles "Fear City"). He is the modern Jack the Ripper, and there is even a scene wherein the police establish that he has knowledge of anatomy, his slicing designed to prolong death for maximum torment — the ultimate sexual sadist.

There are numerous parallels between Berenger and the killer, particularly in their need for physical discipline (à la DeNiro in *Taxi Driver*). The protagonist is troubled by his past, and flashes back to his days as a boxer when he killed somebody in the ring. Finally, as a lapsed Catholic, he feels that he may have a shot at redemption by saving the strippers and killing the killer. This purges such desires from within himself (ironically, a similar redemption for the protagonist of *Bad Lieutenant* meant giving the youthful rapists a second chance — for their own redemption). After he kills the killer, however, he finds he is denied the redemption he hoped for (also a realization plaguing the *Bad Lieutenant*) and must return to the world of lost souls as a vigilante. The film avoids the confluence of sex and graphic violence of the slasher ilk; and although there is nudity, critics felt it never turned the nudity into a violence-as-sex-surrogate for the audience.

Felicia's Journey

(2000: d. Atom Egoyan)

scr. Egoyan; nvl. William Trevor; pr. Bruce Davey; ph. Paul Sarossy; m. Mychael Danna; ed. Susan Shipton; prod d. Jim Clay; cast. Bob Hoskins, Elaine Cassidy, Peter McDonald, Arsinee Khanjian; 116m

A woman goes to an Irish community where she meets a lonely chef (Hoskins), but there is far more to him than she intuits. He is a local serial killer and has designs on her, apparently from a more benevolent perspective, although he cannot escape what he has become (speaking in part to Chabrol's *Le Boucher*). He takes her into his home, saying that he can help her find the boyfriend who abandoned her, and talks her into an abortion. Before he can kill her, he recognizes her innocence and inherent childlike goodness, and lets her go. Soon after, finally unable to live with himself as he is, he says he is determined to change and so commits suicide.

The killer initially feigns benevolence. A pudgy man obsessed with getting close to a mother he felt little connection with when a boy, he is almost beguilingly childish himself. It is as if evil is a malformed innocence warped over time and born in an unfulfilled childhood. As he preys on young pregnant girls, whose innocence persists even though they may have turned to prostitution, he is both punishing them and saving them from a horrible fate — adulthood, womanhood and motherhood. In his way, he searches for love, believing he has found it with these girls and not wanting to let it go. In death they can never leave him. Hence he holds onto details of his past — products from his mother's cooking TV show (which he views and imitates in an attempt to be close to her) and the videotapes he makes of the victims, kept labeled and neatly filed. He is a collector of objects linked to memories, in an effort to preserve the past and even forego the future.

Correspondingly, the film delves into the past of both the killer and the girl, revealing in gradual flashbacks the events that have taken them to this point in time. Their meeting is thus fated and fortuitous. The opening song promises that hatred and love can be reconciled if one is shown the angelic love of a child. Such is the protagonist's psychosis: murder as a product of the merging of hate and love, needing a redemptive trust, a reminder of what such innocence was truly like, how precious it was, and how monstrous the one who would abuse it. It is a process of delayed self-discovery and self-recognition for a man who has sexualized the vulnerability of Innocence.

Additionally, although the film is set in the present, the interior of his house makes it seem like a period piece, complementing the theme of arrested development that runs through it. Indeed, at times Hoskins has the same charm as the hapless music salesman in the seminal TV series *Pennies from Heaven*, another man consumed by fantasies.

Gradually he begins to feel a kinship and affection for the victim, who has also been abandoned and belittled by parental figures. It bespeaks of his personal paradox that he cannot prevent himself from continuing to manipulate her, in the process forming a trust and bond based on lies, deception and fantasy. Yet, through all his pretenses, she admits that she could always see a troubled man. This insight, both simple and profound, baffles him and forms the catalyst for his reformation of character. He is confronted by the love and understanding of a child, and for the first time he chooses not to destroy it and to begin to heal himself. God's love ironically wins out, though not as the religious fanatics would have it. His only manner of healing himself is to hang himself and rid the world of the aberration he has become.

He becomes a substitute father to the girl. God has given him the responsibility for the life of an innocent, and the film examines what he does with this responsibility, charting the pleasure and turmoil he gains from his power over her innocence. It also contrasts this treatment with the narrow-minded actions of those that claim religious sanction but are blind and unsympathetic in their shallow benevolence. As such, it is in constant play with the Beauty and the Beast fairy tale.

There is enough truth to his manipulations to con the innocent. He is aware of both the wretched irony of his situation (saying that he can't help but be fatherly towards her) and of the aid of circumstance (a sympathetic nurse gives him a bottle of tranquilizers to soothe the girl after the abortion, which he uses to prepare the poisoned drink intended to kill her). He cannot bear to part with his loved one, as he needs to be needed, and manipulates the innocents into dependence on him. Though he may sexually desire the girls, he cannot abuse them sexually, the murders being also a surrogate for illicit sexual contact. The root of his sexual dysfunction surfaces in his admittance that the photograph he claimed was of his wife was, in fact, of his mother.

This is a film concerned with faith, redemption, purity and the triumph of the Innocent making its way into the world of Experience. The human monster is never as unknowably monstrous as to have no hope of redemption, even if it is through suicide as a gesture of self-knowledge. In suicide he finds a final connection to his own inner turmoil. There is catharsis even for such a morally jaded person when confronted by the love of a child (hence the recurrence of the opening song). Astonishing.

The Female Butcher

(1972: d. Jorge Grau) aka *Bloody Countess*

scr. Grau, Sandro Continenza, Juna Tabar; pr. Jose Maria Gonzalez Sinde; ph. Fernando Arribas; cast. Lucia Bose, Lola Gaos, Silvano Tranquili, Ewa Aulin; 102m

A woman believes that she can remain young forever by bathing in the blood of virgins. She poses as her own daughter and lures women to her home. She tries to seduce and marry a young soldier. To stay young, however, she requires ever more such baths; she finally cannot keep up, her body decaying.

As with Hammer's *Countess Dracula*, this utilizes the supposedly true story of Hungarian countess Elizabeth Bathory in combining the vampire and serial killer mythos with the legend of the quest for eternal youth. Blood consumption and the killing of desirable virgins (in order to be one) are the central thematic concerns here. This is only tangentially a serial killer film, but its depiction of a repeat murderer whose actions are rooted in fantasy anticipates more self-reflexive studies.

The director had earlier had more box-office success with the zombie movie *Don't Open the Window*. Although he is Spanish, he is not as widely known or appraised as Jesus Franco or even Eugenio Martin.

The Fiend

(1971: d. Robert Hartford-Davis)

pr. Hartford-Davis; ph. Desmond Dickinson; cast. Suzanna Leigh, Brenda Kempner, David Lodge, Patrick Magee, Ann Todd, Ronald Allen, Madeline Hinde, Tony Beckley, Percy Herbert; 87m

A man, the product of a brutalized youth at the hands of a religious mother, is fixated on her. At night he murders "fallen" women, apparently to save them. He records the crimes and later plays them back for implied masturbatory sexual fulfillment (à la *Peeping Tom* and the later *Henry*). Like the mothers of *Psycho* and *Deranged*, this one believes her son too good for women, and that contact with them would only soil him. His home also houses a religious cult intent on terrorizing the London suburbs. Finally, he murders the cult leader when the leader orders the removal of the beloved and hated mother. The police investigate.

Although the film is synopsized in the relative guides, it remains a dismissed item. It has perhaps some interest in light of the anti-authoritarian, generational disillusionment themes prominent in the work of Pete Walker and even Peter Collinson and Robert Fuest at the time. It is impossible to divorce the film from its contemporaries' reaction to social change and the cynical dissolution of the family unit. It is not widely available.

Final Cut

(1995: d. Roger Christian)

ph. Mike Southon; m. Ross Vanelli; prod d. John Dondertman; cast. Sam Elliott, Charles Martin Smith, Matt Craven, Anne Ramsay, Amanda Plummer, John Hannah; 94m

A mad bomber is loose in Seattle. In desperation, the bomb squad calls on a retired specialist/expert (Elliott), an author of a book on the subject, for help. Soon he is implicated in the crimes and must fight to clear his name and trap the real bomber before more damage can be done. He wonders whether a past offender has returned to the fore.

This film follows on from the serial bombers of *The Mad Bomber* and the serial arsonist of *Backdraft*. It is the least in the series of bomb disposal–themed films of the early 1990s, which included *Speed*, *Live Wire* and *Blown Away*. It is intriguing in its appropriation of the serial killer narrative structure and character typology, especially in its view of the profiler, who claims the best way to diffuse the bomb is to treat it as evidence of the inside of the bomber's head. It is a case of the demolitions man as psychiatrist. Such a killer is, of course, dismissed as a "psycho."

This film would not warrant inclusion as a serial killer movie were it not for the peculiar ending, which reveals the killer's monstrous sexuality as the governing force behind his bombings. He is shown to be working on a human bomb, having previously mutilated women's bodies in an effort to turn them into an explosive device, a perversion of the life-giving functioning of the female reproductive system. His psychosis is thus one of misogynistic loathing as much as it is the desire for superiority and revenge against those with a bigger reputation in the field than he has. The suggestion of necrophilic mutilation intersects with the serial killer film, although the broader implications of and motivations behind this horrible perversion are, unfortunately, left unexplored, and the sexual perversion treated as a throwaway when ideally it should have been central.

Final Judgement

(1992: d. Louis Morneau)

scr. Kirk Honeycutt; pr. Mike Elliott; ph. Mark Parry; m. Terry Plumeri; ed. Glenn Garland; prod d. Colin De Rouin; cast. Brad Dourif, David Ledingham, Maria Ford, Simone Allen, Isaac Hayes, Orson Bean, Karen Black; 90m

An ex-hoodlum, now a priest (Dourif), returns to his gangland roots to prove he is not the killer of strippers, and to avenge the death of his daughter, in whose murder he is also a suspect. Once in the world of the pornography industry, he tries to catch the killer himself, having apparently no faith in police work. He is taunted by the killer and hampered by the police, although aided by a friend of the dead stripper.

The killer, meanwhile, is revealed to be a religious fanatic who paints his victims before killing them (recalling *The Banker* and the notion of private ritual practice as anthropological heritage). This explores the same underworld as *Hardcore*, *Taxi Driver*, *Fear City*, *Stripped to Kill*, and even the later *8MM* but reportedly (Stanley, p. 182) without much distinction, despite an overheated style and pace, again implicating the sleazy sex-culture of a street-based existence in the formation of self-righteous killers. Director Morneau has inched ever closer to conventional Hollywood genre slickness, having attained some notoriety for the silly *Bats*.

Final Rinse

(1999: d. Robert Tucker)

scr. Arthur Schurr, Robert D. Tucker; pr. Dan Reardon; ph. Mark Putnam; m. Knox Chandler; ed. Anne McCabe; prod d. Fred Tietz;

cast. David Cale, Jeffrey Buehl, Frank Gorshin, James McLaughlin; 92m

Internet responses have indicated that this is an odd comedy-horror. A dim, hardboiled cop is on the trail of a killer, called Trojan, who kills rock stars and performs a new haircut on the corpse (as a kind of substitute for necrophilic sex, it seems). Into this "rock 'n' roll pastiche" are mixed the protagonist's LSD flashbacks, which suggest a (possible psychic) link to the killer. Generally unreleased at time of writing, *Final Rinse* indicates a desire to reduce the serial killer to the mere gimmick killer, and is thus included herein with a caution.

Fingers at the Window

(1942: d. Charles Lederer)

scr. Rose Caylor, Lawrence P. Bachmann; stry. Caylor; pr. Irving Starr; ph. Harry Stradling, Charles Lawton; m. Bronislau Kaper; ed. George Boemler; art d. Cedric Gibbons; cast. Lew Ayres, Laraine Day, Basil Rathbone, Walter Kingsford, Miles Mander; 79m

This film details the city of Chicago in the grip of an axe murderer, with six victims having resulted in the arrest of six different mentally disturbed people. The only surviving witness is a not-very-bright woman. However, when a second attempt is made on her life, the protagonist thinks the crimes are not random and that someone has been hypnotizing the mentally ill into becoming homicidal. The culprit turns out to be madman Basil Rathbone, hypnotizing patients at an asylum into axe murderers and doing his bidding. This theme of brainwashing of course recalls *Caligari* but also looks to the generation gap–themed *Sorcerers* by Michael Reeves.

This film, not really a serial killer film, is a curious anomaly. Opening noir-ishly, with police on deserted nighttime streets and the public fearful of an epidemic of axe murders, it soon raises its concern for the mentally ill. Thus, when a decapitator is apprehended, he is shown as clearly deranged and is examined by a psychiatrist (an early profiler) intent on showing the lay person what schizophrenia is. He concludes that such murderers are not ordinary criminals and need special treatment. The mentally ill are responsible for such horrendous crimes, but their accountability is questionable.

However, there is not one lone multiple-killer, but the crimes are committed by various killers, all mentally ill. The film avoids admission of a serial killer, and instead resolves the issue in terms of the old controller/agent characterization, here in the age of noir segueing into serial killer pathology but avoiding true confrontation. Thus, the protagonists talk about "mashers" (the term for lady-killers of the time) as a type of male which is a threat to women, yet the lead is only partially followed through, as the killer has motives beyond the sexual.

The killer is a psychiatrist who has adopted the identity of a famed doctor and is killing those who could disprove that identity, making the crimes look like the random work of the mentally ill. His fantasy is to be a brilliant doctor and seek the truth of the human condition, and he wants this to be true so much that he eliminates those who would challenge the ideal he has now become. His fantasy of being a great man — he tells those he brainwashes that he alone is the voice of truth — makes him the personification of mental illness, and as a psychiatrist, a bad patriarch.

The film is a scathing indictment of the psychiatric profession and the benefits of psychoanalysis. These doctors, buffoons, boring academics or megalomaniacs, do not cure the sick or protect the innocent. They unleash killers and are easily deceived by the protagonist, who feigns mental illness to get to the doctor's files. The film delights in farcically showing them up, revealing a kind of anti-intellectualism that seeks to lampoon the then popular serious treatments of mental illness, in the process equating mental illness with a new kind of apparently random, violent criminality. The movie cannot, however, accept them as truly random, and so shows the need to seek a pattern. Thus the film represents a stage in the evolution of the serial killer genre.

The flirtatious comedy between the two stars undercuts any suspense and is more akin to the light comedies of the 1930s than to the neon world of film noir pessimism that begins the film. The mix of noir and romantic comedy is ultimately an impossible generic mix, and the movie's tone ultimately settles for this mild humor.

Fingers at the Window was intended to start a series of thrillers starring the crime-solving duo of Lew Ayres and Laraine Day, but despite the light comedy being an attempt at *Thin Man* success, a series did not eventuate. Nash and Ross (in the *Motion Picture Guide*) consider this in part to be due to reaction over Ayres being a Conscientious Objector during WWII, and so an unlikely hero in the movies. Director Lederer was a prolific screenwriter, here debuting, and would not direct another film for many years.

The First Deadly Sin

(1980: d. Brian G. Hutton)

scr. Mann Rubin; nvl. Lawrence Sanders; pr. George Pappas, Mark Shanker; ph. Jack Priestley; m. Gordon Jenkins; ed. Eric Albertson; art d. Woody Mackintosh; cast. Frank Sinatra, Faye Dunaway, David Dukes, George Coe, Brenda Vaccaro, Joe Spinell; 112m

Director Hutton took a respite from his usual large-scale adventure movies (*Where Eagles Dare, Kelly's Heroes*) to helm Sinatra's small-scale last movie role. Sinatra stars as a dedicated city detective facing personal problems relating to his ter-

minally ill wife. Adding to this, he has to investigate a random serial ice-axe murderer. He is just a short while from retirement (a situation befalling Morgan Freeman in the later *Seven*) and investigates the seemingly arbitrary murders, although having been advised to stay off and calmly wait for retirement. Once he establishes the murder weapon to be a mountain climber's ice axe, the clues lead to a troubled and insecure, though self-righteous, professional businessman. Lacking evidence, Sinatra follows the suspect, prompting a confession and confrontation.

The First Deadly Sin can be considered as the tail end of the series of cop movies that Sinatra did with director Gordon Douglas at the end of the 1960s, which included *The Detective* and the *Tony Rome* movies. The film alternates the procedural aspects with scenes of Sinatra comforting his hospitalized wife (Dunaway). Many critics considered these scenes to drag the film down to an interminable pace instead of adding character depth.

It was Sinatra's first film in a decade, and Hutton is undoubtedly aware of the Douglas films, especially *The Detective*, to which this film seems almost like a continuation. Sinatra has the same 1940s appearance — out of touch with a modern world that increasingly forces an awareness of mortality and arbitrary death. Like *The Detective* and *Dirty Harry*, the policeman is presented as a modern savior (seen here under the Mt. Pleasant cross, just as Harry was seen under the "Jesus Saves" sign) who has the sanctioned burden of fighting the forces of death (the killer). This is ultimately a futile exercise, however.

The film has many scenes that present the viewer with violent death and its aftermath. There is the explicit autopsy-room scene, with mutilated bodies on the table as the case is discussed around them. Correspondingly, there are many scenes set in the hospital, a world of the dead and

An aging detective (Frank Sinatra, right) on the trail of a serial killer questions the corrupt doorman (Joe Spinell) at the killer's apartment building in *The First Deadly Sin* (Filmways/WB, 1980).

dying, attended by almost indifferent professionals. Doctors and policeman are thus linked, with Sinatra intent to take the case personally in an effort to prove his humanity in the face of its apparent death. Only living victims touched by death close to them feel compassion.

This ironic concern for the prolonged horror of natural death is contrasted with the sudden, final brutality of the killer's decisive actions—an irony not lost on Sinatra. Hutton sets up the film by paralleling surgical violation to prolong life with the act of murder to take it. The killer is a coward who sneaks up on people from behind: death comes up suddenly and strikes when you least expect it. Life is the attempt to cheat this random inevitability.

Indeed, the film is a low-key study in resignation, and the corresponding search

for something to latch onto in order to give life — and death — personal meaning. The investigation into murder provides this for many characters: the policeman, a victim's wife, and an elderly museum curator contemplating his mortality. All are devoid of life until reenergized in part by their ability to aid Sinatra. It is as if the killer's capture would somehow eliminate death from their lives. Sinatra's purging of the killer is a futile gesture aimed towards immortality. Unable to help his wife medically, and thus feeling helpless, he feels that if he can find and stop the serial killer he can save her, and ironically empower him personally.

This parallels the killer, obsessed with physical discipline, and of dubious sexuality, who murders patriarchs as an act of empowerment. He is a tormented and conflicted soul, hardly the stern angel of death one would expect from films made during the slasher boom. He too reflects the frailty (though psychological) of the human condition. He craves sexual contact and communication, claiming that his victims are surrendering their souls to him, allowing him to enter another human being — murder as the warped desire for interpersonal communication. In death, his victims are forever a part of him. Significantly, he was repeatedly beaten by his father, and now as an adult has come to identify with the abuser rather than the abused, although the people he targets may also be surrogates, the focus of his displaced rage.

Thus Sinatra effectively becomes another punitive father, executing the killer when he realizes that there is not enough evidence to convict him. Sinatra sheds the professional to become the personal. But he fails in his imagined task of eliminating death, and his wife dies. In the end, he sits alone at her bedside, a vigilante killer reading a children's book to his dead wife. Like the killer he attempted to chastise, he has become a lost soul.

The film is a complex, bleak, understated examination of a nice, kind man driven to self-sanctioned murder that he feels compelled for moral and psychological reasons to perform. Rather than restoring a threatened Patriarchy or redeeming or empowering himself, his execution of the killer only condemns himself to loss.

Director Hutton would return to large-scale adventures with the subsequent *High Road to China*, while *The First Deadly Sin* faded from memory in an unfortunately indifferent critical and box-office reception. It deserves better.

The First Power

(1989: d. Robert Resnikoff)

scr. Resnikoff; pr. Robert W. Cort, Ted Field, Melinda Mason, David Madden; ph. Theo Van de Sande; m. Stewart Copeland; ed. Michael Bloecher; prod d. Joseph T. Garrity; cast. Lou Diamond Phillips, Tracy Griffith, Mykelti Williamson, Jeff Kober; 90m

This occult-themed movie has an experienced officer (Phillips), who has an expertise with serial cases beyond that of ordinary officers, tracking a seemingly indestructible random killer who murders women according to Satanic ritual. As the result of a clairvoyant's phone call, the cop apprehends the "pentagram murderer," who is correspondingly executed in the gas chamber. However, more crimes suggest that he has returned from the grave with the ability to possess people. The policeman and the clairvoyant (the profiler figure here) must team up to stop this Satanic killer.

The title refers to the power of God and Satan to resurrect their emissaries. The killer thus becomes a kind of disembodied spirit able to inhabit innocents. The murders have been Satanic sacrifices intended to give the killer this power: they thus enabled the transcendence to a higher spiritual realm wherein the killer is all-powerful. The idealized self sought through murder becomes an actuality, in Satan's service. The policeman must track, and the profiler must summon, the powers of a greater Goodness to defeat Evil.

In so doing, they enlist the help of a nun (who has a dagger hidden in a crucifix) who understands the spiritual Evil the killer has become, and consult the killer's mother (?) who reveals the tormented childhood the killer endured, in which she was complicit. Thus, the film posits that one who is abused seeks in adulthood to shed the burden of trauma through repeatedly becoming the aggressor instead of the victim, finally transcending the reality of trauma. This is the alluring path of Evil promising spiritual metamorphosis. Nevertheless, the path to absolute Evil is rooted in human experience and demands that trauma breed trauma.

This promising subtext, however, remains undeveloped in favor of mainstream action thriller highlights—murders, chases, violent confrontation. It is indebted to the psychic link subgenre, and serves to elevate the profiler (here two—the psychic and the nun) to the position of God-appointed agent of absolute Good, sanctioned to purge Evil. The investigator must enable this to happen, and protect the vulnerable profilers, assuming their mission if so able.

The film's blend of supernatural thriller and serial killer slasher motif makes it comparable to other returning-killer films like *Shocker*, *The Exorcist III*, and especially *Fallen* in its plot hook of a returned killer spirit which plagues the protagonist. Action amidst ontological issues makes for an ambitious film, but it failed to impress and was seen as another formula effort from once rising star Phillips. Its use of the urban Hell theme seems noirish, and is influenced by the work of Carpenter and Craven especially (Howe, *Washington Post*).

Five Card Stud

(1968: d. Henry Hathaway)

scr. Marguerite Roberts; pr. Hal B. Wallis; ph. Daniel L. Fapp; m. Maurice Jarre; ed. Warren Low; prod d. Walter Tyler; cast. Dean Martin, Robert Mitchum, Inger Stevens, Roddy McDowall, Katherine Justice, Yaphet Kotto, Denver Pyle, Whit Bissell; 103m

It's a rare Western that touches on the concept of serial murder, and this one has poker players becoming the targets of a killer. Five cowboys who lynched a man for cheating at cards are later systematically killed. A gambler (Martin) who tried to stop the hanging runs up against a new arrival—a gun-fighting preacher (Mitchum)—while trying to solve the crimes. The killer is the preacher, revealed to be the hanged man's brother. The preacher's quest for revenge is aided by the information given him by another card player (McDowall), whose motives are less conventional.

Unlike *Silent Sentence* and the modern Western tele-movie *Pair of Aces*, this is not really a serial killer film, and it is included here as a rare revenge-western that touches on the theme of the hunt for a repeat killer. The murders are framed in whodunit fashion, suggesting a certain attempt to expand genre parameters. It reveals the Western as able to handle the device of the repeat killer, although it emphasizes the moral necessity to have this killer rooted in recognizable motivation, i.e., revenge. There is therefore no sexual motive, although the killer reveals a glee in murder which goes beyond functional vengeance: he is an example of the obsessed morally self-righteous killer (a preacher no less), although in this he is not divorced from, or superior to, the lynchmob. He is not a traditional outlaw, however, but a perversion of the classic Western lawmaker. When he says that "no killer is scared of God," he admits the sense of power a killer has over life and death, though here it is devoid of any inherent sexual sadism.

Mitchum's role recalls his part in *Night of the Hunter*. He hides behind higher sanction. He has the weight of moral justice behind him, for revenge in the genre is often a higher form of justice, held against conventional justice. In this film, conventional law cannot bring order or justice to a community threatened by a repeat killer. It is ironic that the preacher, the ultimate dispenser of moral justice, should be the agent of revenge and in the process become the force that most threatens community stability. Although Mitchum hides and justifies his real motives behind the station of higher sanction, he never fully reveals a psychosis, and is never considered an aberration; rather, he is upholding the code of the West. The more disturbing and provocative quality of psychological aberration is reserved for McDowall.

McDowall's complicity is more intriguing in terms of serial killer pathology than is developed in the film. An early key scene reveals his monstrous pride, and vanity, in subtly sexual terms. In this scene, Martin arrives at McDowall's father's ranch and kisses McDowall's sister (in the film presented as a chaste woman). When they have finished, McDowall stands where his sister stood, and asks Martin, "How do I look?" whereupon Martin punches him to the ground. Martin's action clearly encapsulates the genre's loathing for the threat posed by McDowall's suggestion of unconventional sexuality. From this scene, and the smile that McDowall gives when struck to the ground, it is suggested that homosexual desire and resentment are the factors motivating McDowall to supply Mitchum with the names of the hanging party (except his own).

Mitchum eyes McDowall suspiciously in their first meeting and later states directly, "I killed those men because they killed my brother. Why did you want them dead?" McDowall's answer (that he did it to them before they could do it to him) is a cover for his real motives, to get at Martin. The other men are surrogates in a sense, their deaths intended to punish Martin. Had McDowall been the killer, the film would have truly entered the serial killer field. As it stands, we have to go by the implicit suggestion that the motives of such a man are beyond the understanding of the recognizable moral motivations allowed in the genre, and even beyond the repeat killer himself.

The film does, however, anticipate the dilemma posed in *Dirty Harry* and films that subsequently sought to develop the "urban Western," in that it asks if law enforcement alone (as opposed to vigilante action) can protect a township which fears that anyone could be the next victim. Significantly, the sheriff cannot even begin to solve the series of murders, as they involve a motivation he cannot intuit. The township, in fear, thus relies on guns for protection, and the easy access to weapons only brings further violence.

The film is a sub-textual call for more reformist measures as opposed to reliance on the law of the gun as the great Westerner code, although the problem is ultimately solved by the morally sanctioned use of the gun. Still, the film does question what constitutes such a sanction (personal safety, the communal need for protection). Eliminating the killer does restore Patriarchy's balance through the proper use of force.

Vincent Canby felt the film served best to illustrate the growing prominence of the "buddy movie" in Hollywood and in the Western at that time (following on from *El Dorado*, *The War Wagon*, *Bandolero*, *Villa Rides*). Both producer and director were veterans by this time, and the film follows essentially old-fashioned means despite the casting gimmick. By refusing the real motivations of the serial killer figure, it fails to transcend the Western genre.

The Flesh and the Fiends

(1959: d. John Gilling) aka *Mania*

scr. Gilling, Leon Griffiths; pr. Robert Baker, Monty Berman; ph. Berman; m. Stanley Black; ed. Jack Slade; art d. John Elphick; cast. Peter Cushing, June Laverick, Donald Pleasence, Dermot Walsh, Renee Houston, Billie Whitelaw; 87m

This is yet another tale of the relationship between surgical pioneer Dr. Knox and the pair of grave robbing murderers Burke and Hare. The doctor knows of their murderous actions to get him fresh corpses, but justifies his complicity in the name of scientific advancement, even though he loathes the two vile men. Knox's student assistant falls in love with a prostitute, whom Hare soon murders after she scorns his libidinal advances. When the student sees her body (dutifully purchased by Knox), he goes after her killers but is himself killed. This sets off a chain of events that lead to Burke and Hare's capture. Hare aids the police and is spared although Burke is hanged. The angered townspeople then swarm on Hare and burn his eyes out in a demonstration of mob and vigilante justice.

Cushing plays the role of Knox with the aristocratic detachment of his Hammer work as Dr. Frankenstein. He is the epitome of elegant benevolence corrupted into monstrosity by self-righteousness. His experimentation is a means of personal empowerment, proving his superiority over those who would suppress him. In this, he parallels the killers, whose crimes on one level can be seen as a means of transcending their class and station, in reaction to the morbid, immoral opportunity for advancement enabled by Knox. Although Hare and Burke are despicable people, one wonders if they would have made the leap into murder for profit and thrills if it weren't for Knox. Indeed, Hare spends some of the money on an elegant waistcoat, so that he may look properly distinguished. Hare and Burke nevertheless remain physical grotesques.

Hare (Pleasence) is the sterner of the two and clearly delights in his own sense of superiority over the people he kills. He truly enjoys misleading the people he dupes into Burke's house. Although he starts to kill in order to get more money, his motives are clearly other: power is in the control over the fate of others, and makes him feel God-like (paralleling him to Dr. Knox even more). While Burke strangles the hapless victims lured to his house, Hare looks on gleefully, barely able to contain his excitement, his hand over his mouth. It also gives him a sexual thrill, which he cannot contain, as he soon turns to murdering a prostitute, after which he falls exhausted and satisfied. Sex and murder are thus linked in the killer's mentality, a hideous self-indulgence devoid of the moral and scientific rationalizations that Knox can at least claim.

As Boot points out (p. 76), it is the callousness towards humanity, and the arrogance that would condone murder, which provides the film's core horror, rather than the murders themselves. Indeed, the film opens with a statement that it is the story of "lost men and lost souls." It is a Godless and indeed soul-less world that Gilling depicts. The opening act sets the conflict in terms of class-based philosophical oppositions. The upper, ruling class is stagnant in academic practice and social rituals, and its representative Knox is pre-occupied with death. In contrast, the poor, however crude and uneducated, are lustful towards what they consider life, except Hare and Burke, who turn the lust for life into murder as a means of advancement, though it is only Hare who takes to sex murder as a form of self actualization. In such a class-based culture, sex murder is the inevitable consequence of an obsession with death (a metaphor for aristocratic stagnation) contaminating the celebration of "life," and is an inherent byproduct of British society. Gilling does not view the poor and working class life as an ideal alternative by any means, and it is arguably as stagnant in the end — there is no balance and the only link is achieved through murder.

Through all this, there is nevertheless a moral center. The prostitute Mary and student Chris (Mary and *Christ*, perhaps, if one can argue such an analogy, and there is some evidence there) have a relationship which for a time may transcend the gulf between their stations. However, such is not to be in the film's socioeconomic determinism, for Mary cannot resist the lure of alcohol and sex (though even she draws the line at Hare), alienating Chris, the only man who offered her a way out of her predicament. Finally, she knows what she has lost, and cries as Chris abandons her, leaving her where Hare and Burke, now predators, pounce on her. Should *Christ* abandon Mary (the whore as fallen innocent), she is fodder for the serial killers of the world. Chris is the real innocent in the film, the only hope for moral rectitude, and he too perishes through forces beyond his control, losing his love. This world is perhaps beyond salvation, although in the end Knox has indeed learned a moral lesson about the pursuit of scientific goals at the expense of humanity — but is it too late?

All is set in a studio-bound Edinburgh circa 1820s. In subsequent films, the doctor would no longer need the middleman, and would become homicidal himself (hence the doctor played by Cushing in *Corruption*). The film is rooted in the objectification of people as disposable commodities in 19th century social and ideological conditioning. Attempting to transcend their conditioning, the killers target the people they consider expendable and inferior. Correspondingly, the aristocratic Knox can easily consider himself above all. Knox's reckoning comes when he offers to help a little girl (who does not know who he is), who refuses, saying that he might sell her to Dr. Knox. He is in that moment aware that in the minds of the innocent, he is the real monster, more so than Burke and Hare; his idealism set the process in motion and eventually caused him to betray the core ideals he once held. He realizes the burden and depth of his responsibility.

The story was told in *Body Snatcher* and later remade in *Burke and Hare* and the underrated *Doctor and the Devils*. The film's producers would also helm a version of the Jack the Ripper tale, and director Gilling would do work for Hammer studios.

Follow Me Quietly

(1949: d. Richard Fleischer)

scr. Lillie Hayward; stry. Anthony Mann, Francis Rosenwald; pr. Herman Schlom; ph. Robert de Grasse; m. Leonid Rab; ed. Elmo Williams; art d. Albert S. D'Agostino; cast. William Lundigan, Dorothy Patrick, Jeff Corey, Nestor Paiva, Charles D. Brown, Paul Guilfoyle; 60m

Over six months, a serial strangler who attacks only on rainy nights has terrorized a city. The killer calls himself "the Judge" and believes himself a self-appointed purifier of evil, self-righteously killing those he considers worthless. A determined cop's efforts are hampered by his relationship to a female tabloid reporter. The clues finally lead to the killer's identification and a chase through a gasworks.

This is interesting in part as a minor RKO B-movie noir film but mainly as Fleischer's first real tackling of the repeat-killer motif. It especially shows the director of the later *The Boston Strangler* and *10 Rillington Place* interested in the procedural means employed to catch the killer (the cop builds a special dummy/replica of the killer and spends time contemplating it to gain insight into the killer it supposedly resembles). He balances this with a concern for the interrelationship between real killers and composite (fictional) ones (the killer replaces the dummy in one scene and eavesdrops on the investigation by standing still). This raises the issue of the aberrant psychology that would cause a kind of murder-by-pride (and how this is a form of sexual dysfunction). All of these themes are found in Fleischer's subsequent serial killer and law enforcement crime films.

The most remarked on scene of this film comes when the police are able to reconstruct a mannequin based on witness descriptions and, in darkness, the killer silently sits still where the dummy of himself used to reside. He is thus able to overhear the course of the investigation. The detective also talks to the mannequin, attempting to psychoanalyze the killer it represents. This trait, of an investigator seeking to go one-on-one with an horrific killer whose psychology he can only infer until capture, would, of course, be further dramatized by Henry Fonda in *The Boston Strangler*. The scene speaks of the need for criminological practices to enable a composite profile, both physical and psychological, in order to understand the type and individual responsible. The interplay of real criminal and police interpretation foreshadows the role of the profiler as mediator — in particular, it addresses how police can obtain a physical and psychological "profile" of the killer based on the crime-scene evidence and witness descriptions.

The film also devotes some attention to the husband of one of the strangled victims, thus expressing a care for those affected by the crimes, a notion which remains unexplored in many subsequent serial killer films (although it would be central in *10 Rillington Place*).

Four Flies on Grey Velvet

(1971: d. Dario Argento)

scr. Argento; pr. Salvatore Argento; ph. Franco Di Giacomo; m. Ennio Morricone; art d. Enrico Sabatini; cast. Michael Brandon, Mimsy Farmer, Jean Pierre Marielle, Francine Racette, Bud Spencer; 102m

Argento's second "giallo" movie, following the hit *Bird with the Crystal Plumage*, *Four Flies on Grey Velvet* is the tale of a mysterious killer who murders a drummer's friends. The killer may be his wife, and so the film takes a rare step by dealing with female aggression and dissatisfaction. The four murders lead to the protagonist's house.

Its success was part of the cinema's

embrace of the stalking killer character type, although in the Italian giallo films (and here) the killer was often not technically a serial killer, and the motives were something other than sexual thrills, although linked to a uniquely imbalanced perception of the surrounding world. There is apparently some humor to the supporting characterizations (the homosexual private eye being the most remarked on), but the accent is on mystery and suspense, with isolated set-pieces (a park stalking and a woman hiding in a cupboard) enhancing Argento's reputation as a skilled stylist. It is a film strangely devoid of police presence.

Freeway

(1998: d. Matthew Bright)

scr. Bright; pr. Chris Hanley, Richard Rutowski, Brad Wyman; exec pr. Oliver Stone, Dan Halsted; ph. John Thomas; m. Danny Elfman; ed. Maysie Hoy; prod d. Pam Warner; cast. Kiefer Sutherland, Reese Witherspoon, Brooke Shields, Amanda Plummer, Wolfgang Bodison, Dan Hedaya, Bokeem Woodbine; 102m

A teen runaway (Witherspoon) is picked up by the I-5 killer (Sutherland), a predator who seeks out young female hitchhikers to rape and murder. He gains her trust, enticing intimate sexual details from her, and attacks her. But in a fight she overpowers him, shoots him, is apprehended and then prosecuted for it. She is convicted, imprisoned and escapes, but the crippled killer has revenge on his mind.

In a twist on the Red Riding Hood fairy tale, acknowledged in the film's animated credit sequence, the serial killer is depicted as the big bad wolf of lore (recalling the fact that sex killers have often been compared to wolves, particularly in rural European accounts). The film thus announces itself as a warped, cartoonish fairy tale. However, the girl he targets is far from a likable innocent — she is a foul-

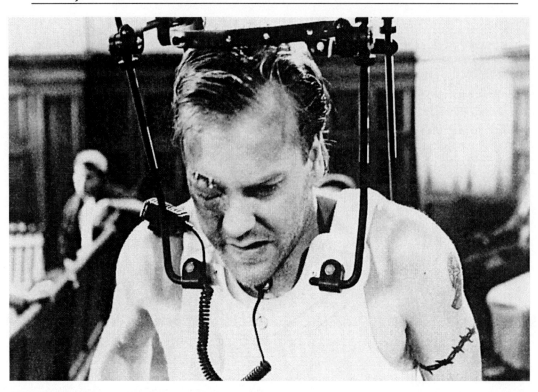

Serial killer Bob Wolverton (Kiefer Sutherland) recovers from a severe injury inflicted by an intended victim he now testifies against in *Freeway* (Globe, 1996).

mouthed, semi-literate, sexually experienced thief whose junkie mother barely cares for her and whose stepfather sexually molests her. She has been victimized all of her life, and subsequently her rage explodes when another fatherly male seeks to exploit her. Her plight is towards a personal empowerment denied her by every form of the establishment (welfare, foster care, education department, and police department), the very forces of a monstrous Patriarchy finally epitomized by the manipulative, predatory killer. The irony is further confounded by the revelation that the serial killer is a child therapist and counselor who uses the appropriate jargon and means to sexually bait the girl into confessing her private history. That way he can cunningly, knowingly (and humorously) manipulate her for his own sexual stimulation. Her rebellion against him is against all those she feels have betrayed

her, and is a revolutionary gesture — she will not be resigned to being the victim society has condemned her to be. However, she is an unsympathetic character.

The blackly comic irony is never-ending, with the wheelchair-bound killer appearing on television in a victim's rights capacity, urging stronger justice for society's scum. He is finally so consumed by revenge as a means of reasserting his hypocritical moral superiority over "Innocence" that all else is secondary. He must assert dominance by consuming his lessors. He is the epitome of the monstrous patriarch, able to conceal his pedophilia from his wife and a society of misplaced values.

Some felt that the film just as strongly resisted any moralizing, constantly undercutting any attempt to see such, although it is there. Bright's style is to constantly subvert the morality and reality established in proceeding scenes. Thus, although it was hailed on the festival scene as a brilliant social satire, many mainstream critics (including *Variety*) dismissed it as vile, grotesque and morally indefensible. An even more demented sequel followed it. Its exuberance and treatment of teen criminality also recalls Rafal Zielinski's *Fun*, another example of a remarked on resurgence of American independent film in the 1990s.

It is a bleak world, full or exploiters and potential exploiters, where innocence is itself an unredeemable illusion. Any atrocity is committed, without care but with equally horrendous consequence, as if goodness is doomed, with only its facades left in place. It is impossible to feel compassion for anyone — the only option left is to champion the protagonist as revolutionary, communicating through violent rebellion. Patriarchy is vile and cannot police itself, and so there is no restoration of order with the elimination of the killer: no socially cathartic purge here. The protagonist is the underdog, the anarchic force of change (and even more so in the sequel), yet is herself finally entrapped in a freeze-frame of her bloodied, laughing face (recalling the ironic liberation in Truffaut's *The 400 Blows*).

An additional knowing wink on Bright's part comes when the girl shows the killer a photo of her father — in fact a picture of Richard Speck (a mass murderer of Chicago nurses), whose picture was also shown in a similar context in *Curdled*. This insertion of real killers into a fictional scenario would also inform *Copycat*, where inserted into snaps of male college students at a lecture is a photo of actual co-ed killer Ed Kemper. Sutherland's casting as the killer also recalls his turn in *Eye for an Eye*.

Freeway 2

(1999: d. Matthew Bright)

scr. Bright; pr. Chris Hanley, Brad Wyman; ph. John Ransom; ed. Suzanne Hines; prod d. Brian Davie; cast. Natasha Lyonne, Maria Celedonio, Vincent Gallo, David Alan Grier, Michael T. Weiss, John Landis; 90m

Equally imaginative as, though more grotesque than, the first *Freeway*, this sequel has two bulimic teen cons (one a serial killer driven by voices) escape prison and go on a murder spree. They flee to Mexico, and the clutches of Sister Gomez, a transvestite nun who professes love but operates a child pornography, murder and cannibalism ring out of her religious practice. The film elaborates on the escape-from-prison climax of the first one.

While the original has slowly earned appreciation as a cult film, the sequel was screened and marketed as a midnight movie. It furthers Bright's black humor, featuring a bizarre world full of atrocities, with characters that accept such as part of the operations of the cruel world. It becomes a search to find what new atrocity can provoke a reaction. The film piles grotesque incident upon violent carnage to show a world out of control, of hypocritical morality, again full of exploiters and hardened youths, where benevolence cannibalizes what it supposedly protects.

The character of the serial killer, a schizophrenic girl, is a product of such hypocritical benevolence (the serial killer Sister Gomez), unlike its representative in the first film. The world manufactures necrophilic sex killers as a self-perpetuating cycle. Sister Gomez preys on a society she pretends to spiritually guide. It is left to the law to attempt to sort out the mess.

The first film promised anarchy as a solution; the sequel explores an anarchic world, even a Matriarchal as opposed to a Patriarchal structure, and shows it as equally horrendous: the protagonist's task is to make sense of this world and, in her own way, restore order. But the only order left is the restoration of a tenable Patriarchy, as represented by the conventional forces of law and justice. The killers must be exorcised and purged from society and the individual as if they were demons. Thus, although the film is more grotesque than the first one, it is not as subversive; it's a twisted *Thelma and Louise*.

Frenzy

(1972: d. Alfred Hitchcock)

scr. Anthony Shaffer; nvl. Arthur Labern; pr. Hitchcock; ph. Leonard J. South, Gilbert Taylor; m. Henry Mancini, Ron Goodwin; ed. John Jympson; prod d. Sidney Cain; cast. Jon Finch, Barry Foster, Barbara Leigh-Hunt, Anna Massey, Alec McCowen, Gerald Sim, Billie Whitelaw; 120m

With his audience diminishing, Hitchcock returned to England to make this story of a serial strangler, the Necktie Killer, and the innocent man implicated in the murders. Thus, it also brought the director back to the wrong man and murder plot of his better known works. With more explicit violence and even nudity than before, the film was more of its era.

The prospect of London beset by a serial killer recalls Hitchcock's earlier *The Lodger*, and the opening scene of a nude body found in the water recalls *Young and Innocent*. *Frenzy* also addresses the potential legacy of Jack the Ripper, whom the public invariably compare the killer to, although the dialogue refers more explicitly to the Christie case. Here the killer seems charming, hiding a sadistic rage that drives him to sex murder. His conscience is not tortured by his need to dominate women, nor by his betrayal of his friend, ironically accused of the murders. He is a rapist driven by the need to dominate women, and for whom strangulation is a sexual coda to the rape. Shown in the commission of a rape-murder, he repeats "lovely" with every thrust and then says that all women are the same, thus all are deserving of their fate at his hands. Yet he is so self-serving that he even willingly

turns his friend over to police. Were it not for the suspicious detective, the innocent man would have been condemned to death.

It is in that plot point that the film refers openly and knowingly to the case of John Reginald Christie, who manipulated an innocent man into taking the blame for the crimes. This innocent was found guilty and executed. In one scene, reminiscent of the hypothetical chat about murder in *Shadow of a Doubt*, two men compare views on the new sex murderer, one saying that there hasn't been a good British string of sex murders since Christie, and that they are good for tourism, attracting Americans especially. The Christie case was, of course, dramatized and filmed by Richard Fleischer as *10 Rillington Place*, released not long before Hitchcock's film, and the above scene is perhaps a sly reference to Fleischer's work. The two films are vastly different in tone, however, with Fleischer revealing a sense of wretched irony, and Hitchcock winking at the notion of justice and innocence (after all, the protagonist, although innocent of the crimes, is an arrogant, unlikable man who perhaps needed a lesson in humility).

It is perhaps the most slyly jovial of the director's thrillers. Much of the humor comes from harsh irony, set from the opening scene of a political rally about water pollution disrupted by a floating nude female corpse. Comedic set pieces are juxtaposed with murder scenes, the two gradually intermingling in the notorious potato scene, wherein the killer has to retrieve an item from a corpse in the back of a potato truck. The scene is riddled with necrophilic undertones. In the manner of a comedy, it is impossible to sympathize with any character, including the victims.

Set in Covent Garden and its surroundings, with studio filming done at Pinewood Studios, and with an emphasis on alleys and a local pub, *Frenzy* dedicatedly explores the location and the intruder/

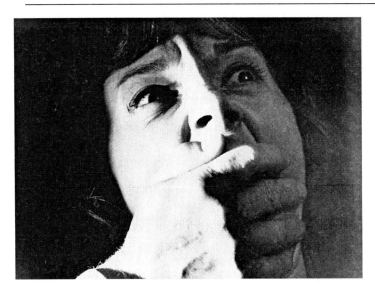

The hand of the London serial strangler reaches out to strike against a victim in *Frenzy* (Universal, 1972).

inhabitants within it, charting the effects of such crimes on the populace and how it reacts. The film was much praised and is often thought of as Hitchcock's last great work, which skillfully manipulates its grotesque humor as a means of generating an overall sense of anxiety: it is an uneasy comedy.

Frequency

(2000: d. Gregory Hoblit)

scr. Toby Emmerich; pr. Hawk Koch, Hoblit, Bill Carraro, Emmerich; ph. Alar Kivilo; m. Michael Kamen; ed. David Rosenbloom; cast. Jim Caviezel, Dennis Quaid, Andre Braugher, Elizabeth Mitchell, Noah Emmerich; 114m

A policeman (Caviezel) uses an old ham radio and contacts his own long dead father (Quaid) from thirty years before, via a time warp caused by the aurora borealis. The son proves himself, and the situation, to his father by predicting the 1969 baseball World Series results. Together they have the chance to undo the father's untimely death. The father does not die, and the son has a new set of memories of growing up with him, realizing instead

that the father would die of cancer much later. However, their efforts have interfered with the time line, and the son discovers that in this altered reality his mother died a victim of the Nightingale Killer, a serial killer of nurses who stopped at three but in the altered time ceased at ten (changing his method to avoid detection). Father and son must work together to stop this killer. As the son discovers the killer alive in the present (and a cop), he instructs the father about how to stop him in the past. But the killer is aware of them and frames the father for the Nightingale killings. At the climax they each square off in their respective times, defeating the killer and in the process changing the future again so that the father is alive in the son's present, rescuing him.

The film is about patriarchal bonds and traditions. It explores the desire for happy memories and fulfillment in family bonds, particularly those between father and son. Caviezel is an alcoholic, troubled man torn by the lack of memories of growing up with the father. The absence of the father is an insurmountable loss, and the film endorses the stability offered by patriarchal bonding. The more memories of life with father attained by the protagonist as he changes time the more conventionally psychologically stable and responsible as a Patriarch himself does he become. As wish-fulfillment fantasy, the film is resolutely clever, restoring the validity of the family and the law of the Father.

The first half is the sentimental tale of a man whose wish to remember and grow up with his father is miraculously granted.

The second half is a thriller about the hunt for a serial killer before he can kill the wife/mother and shatter the family bond. The woman, as wife to Quaid and mother to Caviezel, is a necessary bridge that enables such traditions to flow. The threat to her is a threat to family unity, but not to the father-son bond per se, which the film depicts as of paramount importance. The protection and welfare of the mother allows the father and grown son to work together as a team and so maintain Patriarchy's functioning. This teamwork, as an acceptance of the responsibility of being a whole man and thus a patriarch, ultimately transcends time. Like baseball, it is a necessary, desirable constant through the ages.

Ironically, the serial killer is also a constant through time. As a policeman, he represents the evil patriarch who works from within to destroy the family, including his own. Significantly, he doesn't kill prostitutes but nurses (including his own mother)—a Patriarchally sanctioned view of a womanhood serving men and protecting life (Caviezel's mom is shown rescuing a patient from a doctor's oversight). The killer is, in the father's timeline, a bad son who grows in Caviezel's timeline into the bad patriarch. He must be stopped and purged from the system at all costs before he threatens the proper order. This purge is presented as a social catharsis but not a personal one, as there is nothing of the bad to be found in the truly good.

Here time paradox conventions meet the serial killer film (as they did in the excellent *Time After Time*), exploring the ripple effect theory of repercussions of interference with the time line. However, the interaction of past and present indicates the similarities between the two. The 1969 season is an ideal part of Americana, which can live on through the bonds shared between generations of men. Assuming you could change the past, then it would be

one's responsibility to preserve its glory in the present.

Director Hoblit previously helmed the much bleaker serial killer film *Fallen*. In that too, the killer was a constant presence through the ages, and took on varied guises. Policemen in both films represent the Patriarchally ordained force of Goodness whose ultimate task is to protect Patriarchy. Indeed, all of Hoblit's films to date are examinations of such bonds—good and bad sons—and their corresponding responsibilities. First-time scriptwriter Emmerich was a former music executive at Atlantic records and then New Line. Father and son bonds forged in battling a serial killer had featured in the climax to the offbeat *Fathers and Sons* also.

The Frightened Woman

(1969: d. Piero Schivazappa) aka *Femina Ridens*

scr. Schivazappa; pr. Giuseppe Zaccariello; m. Stelvio Cipirani; ph. Sante Achilli; cast. Varo Soleri, Maria Cuman, Quasimodo, Mirelia Pamphili, Philippe Leroy, Dagmar Lassander, Lorenza Guerrieri; 85m

An independent woman is kidnapped by a rich apparent serial killer (the head of a large philanthropic organization) who systematically tortures and torments her, partially intending her to masochistically enjoy it. Slowly she engages in a battle of wits and wills to save her life. When she attempts to commit suicide, he saves her and admits that he is not a killer. He says that she was his first real kidnap victim (the others he bragged about being prostitutes paid to indulge his whims and be photographed in staged death poses, but emerging alive afterwards), and that he is in love with her. He has apparently been won over by her. She professes love for him too, and the two of them embark on a conventional romantic rural idyll. When they go to make love, he dies of a coronary and she calmly leaves. She is the predatory killer who has planned this all along, and she adds a photograph of the man to her collection of previous victims.

A mix of pre-giallo, Sadean imagery and sexual psychodrama, this is a fascinating, surprisingly stylish discovery: a neglected piece of adult erotica far more slyly complex than its lack of reputation suggests. Indeed, it can be considered a bridge between Italian adult erotica (which in the late 1960s, following this film, had begun to tackle more deviant, sadomasochistic themes) and the giallo movie's stress on sex killers and realms of perception beneath the everyday.

It is a complex examination of sexual power play as a response to the growing feminist liberation movement. Liberated women threaten the male, who claims moral superiority over others. When confronted by a woman from his press office who professes a belief in male sterilization in poverty-stricken areas, he is appalled and kidnaps her, presumably to teach her a lesson in proper gender roles, initiating her, he thinks, in the joys of masochistic subservience to male desire. However, despite his strict regimen and philosophy, he is unsure of his own virility. He achieves a compensatory potency through sadistic domination, claiming to kill his victims at the moment of his orgasm. He fears a world dominated by women, which would make men subservient. His idealized self is thus a killer of such women, who by doing so, restores male, Patriarchal superiority. It is, however, a fantasy, and this is the first time he has tried to put it into practice with a real victim; and he admits being thrilled and excited by women's fear. He cannot go through with murder, however; and by saving her from a suicide attempt, he reverses (he thinks) the situation and sublimates himself to her desire.

Through the first half the victim has been calculatedly playing to his fantasies, moving through passive and aggressive

sexual roles until she can break through them and restructure them according to her own. Thus, she turns the sadist into a passive, romantically teased object. She realizes his love for her and strings him along, leading him through a conventionally romantic courtship — running through fields, etc.— as a demonstration of the opposite to his Sadean fantasies. However, he cannot fully escape his desires and continues to see her as an erotic object. She knows this and uses her sexuality to manipulate him. Just as he took photos of her in a submissive pose to record his victim, she takes a photo of him, their positions now reversed. He has become the victim of a woman who also puts a fantasy into practice, resulting in her total sexual mastery over him through the manipulation of his own impulses, sublimating his desire to her games. She leads him to his death — ironically, just as he feared that all liberated women would do— like the copulating scorpions he saw as a child, the female killing the male. Her photo is a trophy she adds to her collection of kills.

The would-be male killer here is a rich aesthete and a physical disciplinarian of a distinctly Aryan build, indicating director Schivazappa's intention to have the killer in part represent continuation of the Nazi ideal. Indeed, his intellectualization of his own Sadean impulses foreshadows the controversial Nazi-erotica subgenre that would emerge in the next few years in Italy with *The Night Porter*, *Salon Kitty* and *Salo: 120 Days of Sodom*. Incidentally, the Nazi-erotica movement received another early link to the giallo in the otherwise dull and pretentious *In the Folds of the Flesh*.

The female killer is an independent woman whose sexuality revolves around her ability to role-play, according to male conceptions of women's sexuality and essential romanticism, as a means of manipulating the mate. She is revealed to be a rich aesthete also, the female equivalent of the male killer, her masochistic play a means of controlling the male Sadean impulse — and thus itself a sadistic game. This interplay of sadistic and masochistic gender roles informs the film, which finally says that female sexual independence is indeed liberating but produces only monsters just as evil as male killers. The desire to sexually dominate another (whether by sadistic or masochistic roleplaying) is the result of the battle for equality.

It is a rare film that offers a look at the functioning of a serial killer of each gender, subverting any expectations of victimology. *The Frightened Woman* is saturated with a sly, mocking humor (the male sadist listens to a radio horoscope show called "Sexual Aberration and the Stars" —

Cancers under the influence of the moon become necrophiles, etc.). The link of the big with the little death (literal for the male who dies when finally achieving the orgasm he has sought throughout the entire movie), and the theme of an aberrant perceptual realm, would saturate the giallo movies that followed. The film's deliberate stylization, especially the near expressionistic use of architectural shapes, in part anticipates Argento et al.

The Frighteners

(1996: d. Peter Jackson)

scr. Jackson, Fran Walsh; pr. Jamie Selkirk; exec pr. Robert Zemeckis; ph. Alun Bollinger, John Blick; m. Danny Elfman; ed. Jamie Selkirk; prod d. Grant Major; cast. Michael J. Fox, Trini

Ghost-hunter Michael J. Fox (center) and his two special accomplices (Jim Fyfe, left, and Chi McBride) in *The Frighteners* (Universal, 1996).

Michael J. Fox and girlfriend Trini Alvarado must team up to face a deadly spirit, that of a serial killer, in *The Frighteners* (Universal, 1996).

Alvarado, Peter Dobson, John Astin, Dee Wallace Stone, Jeffrey Combs, Jake Busey, Chi McBride, R. Lee Ermey; 105m

A ghost-buster (Fox) realizes that a powerfully evil ghost (of a mass murderer who has become a serial killer) is targeting the small town he has come to work in. Fox sees the number of each victim on their forehead before they die, and when he sees such a number on the forehead of the girl he loves (Alvarado), a recently widowed doctor, he sets out to stop the evil. However, to do so he must himself temporarily die in order to enter the spirit world and confront the ghost. The ghost is driven on by his still-living girlfriend/accomplice.

For most of its length this is only tangentially a serial killer film; it features more of a repeat killer motif, there being no explicit sexual reason for the crimes, which are aimed at both genders. What is paramount to this spectral killer is body count. He reduces the act of serial killing to the pursuit of the highest number of victims. As a mass murderer, he boasts that he got thirteen, one more than (Charles) Starkweather (the real-life spree killer whose exploits were dramatized in *Badlands*). Each subsequent victim enables him to increase his tally, and in so doing becoming the agent of random death. By the end, he remarks to his girlfriend that they got one more than Gacy, and with one more they'd be ahead of Bundy. He adds, most tellingly, that a Russian cannibal was running around saying he got fifty plus (Andrei Chikatilo, whose case is expertly dramatized in *Citizen*

X), but that this kind of record should be held by an American. This is a sly indictment of the US epidemic in serial murder, where it is the mere number of victims which guarantees infamy, public fascination and even cult status.

The film toys with the possibility that it is Fox's out-of-control Thanatosian impulses which powers the killings, but it finally reveals them to be the result of a pair of killers: the ghost and his living girlfriend. Both of these killers had participated in a mass murder at a hospital, to their mutual sexual excitement. Trapped in her house by her stern mother, this woman has no sexual identity beyond that gained through murder. Her outward repression draws the evil to her. Thus, each murder her ghost boyfriend commits is a function of their joint sexuality. Their mass murder spree was the consummation of a couple whose sexuality could only be expressed in a homicidal frenzy. After this initial loss of virginity, every subsequent murder is a means of ongoing surrogate copulation. Through murder they each attain a sexual identity, even though there is no sexual act perpetrated on the victim. They jointly arranged to kill as the expression of their mutual love. Finally, the worm of hell jointly consumes their souls.

This is a frenetically paced and stylishly directed horror fantasy which intersects the serial killer film. All its major characters in some way deal with death, finally having to face the embodiment of death and relentless murder (whatever the motive) — the spectral serial killer. It is arguably about the fascination with death and murder. The killer gains power from his obsession with being the agent of death, and after being executed he finally becomes his fantasy, and is more powerful than when alive. Fantasy has liberated his soul, although it ultimately condemns him to battle with a good soul.

That *The Frighteners* balances comedy and romance so deftly is a testament to Jackson's considerable abilities. There is even a moment of slyly, yet inoffensive, necrophilic comedy, as an old ghost enters a sarcophagus to hump the mummy within. This is paralleled to the killer's spectral caress of his next female victim: sexuality does not end with death. It continues to haunt, as the past ultimately returns to consume the present: it needs a purge.

Frightmare

(1974: d. Pete Walker)

scr. David McGillivray; pr. Walker; ph. Peter Jessop; m. Stanley Myers; ed. Robert Dearberg; art d. Chris Burke; cast. Sheila Keith, Leo Genn, Trisha Mortimer, Kim Butcher, Gerald Flood, Pamela Farbrother, Rupert Davies, Deborah Fairfax; 86m

This is the nastiest, most cynical and effective of the British horror films made by director Walker in tandem with scripter McGillivray in the 1970s. An elderly lady cannibal killer is released from an institution after the governing psychiatric body declare her fit enough to return to society. She resumes her old habits, aided by her long-suffering husband and younger daughter. The mother so corrupts this younger daughter that the two of them intend to kill the eldest daughter, who has tried to take care of them both in the traditional manner associated with motherhood and societal responsibility — all futilely. Indeed, all efforts except the corruptive spread of evil come to naught in this bleak film.

The kindly meek old lady is the dominant force, and the long-suffering husband is powerless to prevent her murderous actions, even when they threaten the life of his own daughter. He is monstrous in his complicity. Walker stresses the irony of this situation, as it is the deceptive rule of homicidal Matriarchy that threatens to consume the Patriarchy (the psychiatric profession) which would seek to contain it. Thus, the serial cannibalism is a revolutionary gesture as much as the exposure of a malfunctioning order. By using a power drill to kill her victims, she usurps phallic power as part of the operations of this new, anarchic Matriarchy. The film ends on a freeze frame of the powerless father, with the voice-over of the sentencing judge saying that society should be protected from such monsters. The real villains are the males unable to contain the monstrous matriarch.

Ironically, she also professes to read the tarot, placing an ad in the newspaper, the lure that brings her a steady stream of new victims to cannibalize (she drills into their skulls and eats the brains). That way, she can ultimately be in control of their destinies, an agent of fate who sadistically delights in manipulating these victims before killing and cannibalizing them. As a portent of the future, she represents the collapse of Institutional Order and the subsequent indiscriminate surrender to quiet anarchy. She represents the individual above the regulations of society, and an individual essentially beyond understanding; ironically, in the end she feeds on the brains of the young psychiatrist (himself following in the tradition of an older patriarch) who sought to psychoanalyze — and stop — her.

The killers inhabit a small cottage, thus recalling the witch and Hansel/Gretel story as the film develops the sense of a grotesque fairy tale, juxtaposing these scenes with those of a decadent, violent, contemporary London (Brottman, p. 184). Such is the clash of values.

Indeed, the film came out in the wake of the swinging 1960s London era and, unlike the same filmmakers' *House of Whipcord*, has no sympathy for generational conflict or for the illusory freedoms won. Such freedoms serve only to provoke violence, always at the bequest of duplicitous women, suggesting a noirish quality. The

older sister claims traditional responsibility, caring for the younger sister — and the mother — in a conventionally maternal manner. The younger sister is a destructive free spirit who rebels (as does the seemingly innocuous cannibal), via homicide, against such expectations. She finds guidance in her real mother, who is a monster.

Kim Newman considers *Frightmare* a rare British horror film in that it captures the bleak desolation of spirit found in American independent horrors, and it furthers the anti-authoritarian themes of *House of Whipcord*. Walker and McGillivray would also contribute the killer-priest movie *House of Mortal Sin* and the ill-informed *Schizo*. Actress Sheila Keith had previously played the warden in *House of Whipcord* and would be the sadistic, repressed nurse in *House of Mortal Sin*. Despite brief claims by Robin Wood that *Frightmare* is a rare and bridging film for its break with Hammer traditions, the film was critically dismissed on UK release by the popular press.

From Hell

(2001: d. Albert and Allen Hughes)

Based on the serialized graphic novel by Alan Moore and Eddie Campbell, this is another version of the exploits of Jack the Ripper. This film was not released at the time of this writing.

Ghost in the Machine

(1993: d. Rachel Talalay)

scr. William Davies, William Osborne; pr. Paul Schiff; ph. Phil Meheux; m. Graeme Revell; ed. Janice Hampton, Erica Huggins; prod d. James Spencer; spec eff. VIFX; cast. Karen Allen, Chris Mulkey, Ted Marcoux, Wil Horneff, Jessica Walter, Brandon Quintin Adams; 95m

A serial killer, the "address book" killer who steals address books and then

A single mother and son (Karen Allen and Wil Horneff) confront the computer-flesh hybrid of a serial killer in *Ghost in the Machine* (Fox, 1993).

murders those whose names are in there, dies following a car crash. His soul enters cyberspace and, via computer and electrical connections in her household, targets a single mother and her computer-literate son. They seek assistance from a male computer technician to rid themselves of the killer, who continues to kill via computer (having the woman's address book in his memory), systematically eliminating her friends and contacts. She deduces what is happening with the help of a former hacker, who is also her friend and possible romantic interest.

The computerized spirit theme and accent on computer graphics are reminiscent of the films of Brett Leonard, notably *The Lawnmower Man* and *Virtuosity*. This interface between human and computer was, of course, predicted in Cronenberg's *Scanners*. It is a dramatization of the fear of the computerization of humanity and the subsequent threat to individuality posed by the age of open communication and technology. The computer liberates Evil from the burden of the physical and sets it loose on the everyday: it deifies Evil and empowers the monstrous patriarch.

The computer-ghost killer is a threat to the fabric of society and the interpersonal communications that bind people. The first on-screen murder has him arrange the corpses of an entire family (around Christmastime no less) on a couch in a grotesque parody of family bonding. He is a threat to the family order. An insecure man who derived sexual power and identity through systematic murder, he, now freed from physical form, can become the unstoppable progression of death he had so idealized — the illusion of purpose thus maintained. He has become the homicidal fantasy of the cyberpunk generation.

This is in contrast to *Virtuosity*, however, where the computer identity seeks

The computerized form of a serial killer seeks a synthetic physical form in order to touch his intended victim (Karen Allen), demonstrating his final need for tactility in *Ghost in the Machine* (Fox, 1993).

physical form to achieve perfection. Indeed, the ending of *Ghost in the Machine* has the computerized soul seek to reenter the physical realm, as an amalgam of data and synthetic flesh, finally able to touch his intended victim for momentary sexual satiation (he had phoned her earlier and expressed his wish to lick her tears). He still needs tactility as a means of reinforcing the fantasy, even though he has progressed beyond the need for physical sensation. The killer needs to feel her fear as a sexual stimulant. The good patriarch has made no such advances, preferring a romantic courtship and friendship.

Director Talalay, as in all her films, stresses teamwork and surrogate family unity as the ultimate solution to the threat posed by a monstrous patriarch. Although a single mother, the protagonist enlists the help of a man (a letdown to feminist readings); together they chastise and eliminate

the evil, thus restoring the family — traditional Patriarchy — to proper, purged functionality. But only after the requisite, beautifully staged death scenes.

The theme of the perils of a computerized society has infiltrated science fiction and thrillers in the 1990s especially. The fusion of man and computer, and the existence of other worlds through virtual reality, are common to the so-termed cyberpunk mentality. With its superior effects, *Ghost* stands as an incorporation of the serial killer into this cyberpunk movement, becoming an intriguing generic hybrid. Perhaps most astounding about the film is its assured control of atmosphere, managing to be both energetic and brooding, with dark, somber colors predominating before erupting into special effects. This makes it in part comparable to the later *Dark City*; and these traits would explode in the multimedia fusion experiment of Talalay's later flop, *Tank Girl.*

The Girl in Black Stockings

(1957: d. Howard W. Koch)

scr. Richard Landon; stry. Peter Godfrey; pr. Aubrey Schenk; ph. William Margulies; m. Les Baxter; ed. John F. Schreyer; prod d. Jack T. Collins; cast. Lex Barker, Anne Bancroft, Mamie Van Doren, Ron Randell, Marie Windsor, John Dehner, John Holland, Diana Vandervlis, Richard Cutting, Stuart Whitman, Larry Chance; 75m

This is more about the potential of multiple murder than it is a serial killer film. In a small Utah township, a visiting lawyer needing time off from work discovers the slashed body of the town's loose woman, a tenant at the Lodge where he too is staying. A series of mutilation murders soon beset the place. The sheriff considers everyone a suspect, including the quadriplegic owner. Fears abound that the killer will strike again, and the lawyer, an outsider, is forced to investigate also.

The Girl in Black Stockings is chiefly interesting as an anticipator of *Psycho* in its small motel setting. The killer is revealed to be a vain woman who apparently kills to ensure that she remains the most beautiful, and desirable, woman there. The film tangentially comments on the cultural codes that affect women's roles and can lead to possible psychosis. The killer's motives are personal vanity, born of inferiority, and arrogant desire (motives which also infiltrate many serial killers)—the desire for authority and control. The killer sees being the most beautiful as a means of being in control, and of sexual empowerment, and so targets those who would take that perceived power away from her.

The Glimmer Man

(1996: d. John Gray)

scr. Kevin Brodbin; pr. Steven Seagal, Julius R. Nazzo; exec pr. William Sandell; ph. Rick Bota; prod d. William Sandell; ed. Donn Cambern; m. Trevor Rabin; cast. Steven Seagal, Keenan Ivory Wayans, Bob Gunton, Brian Cox, Michelle Johnson; 88m

After eight victims are found in Los Angeles, a New York special agent, Steven Seagal, is brought in to investigate a serial killer, known as "the Family Man," who kills Catholic families in a grisly crucifixion ritual (seemingly purificational). Seagal subsequently detects that some of the crimes have been copycated by persons unknown. When a connection between Seagal and a victim is found, he too becomes a suspect. His subsequent investigations yield a plot involving the Russian Mafia and the smuggling of chemical weapons. The serial killer angle is resolved midway, and then the film becomes an action story of organized crime and political corruption (the standard villains of '90s action-thrillers).

One can see this as a slightly personal tract for Seagal, who alleges he worked secretly for the CIA, like his character here, who is also a Buddhist prone to hypocritical cruelty. However, its buddy formula suggested to some a more desperate star seeking to win back the audience who, with the failure of the vanity production *On Deadly Ground*, seemed to have deserted him. Its balance of two types, serial killer investigation and action film, suggests a desperate attempt to both maintain and transcend formula, and the end result is interesting if finally unsuccessful.

The Glimmer Man can be seen as an assembly-line product composed of equal parts of proven Hollywood successes (it mostly follows the buddy-cop routine) and would-be smart dialogue and one-liners (with Wayans clearly the comedy relief). The black cop/white cop team reflects the success of *Running Scared*, *Off Limits* and, of course, the *Lethal Weapon* series. Efficient action set pieces allow the star to show off his abilities, but there is an aspect of deliberate cruelty to his character's treatment of his former boss towards the end, however justified the film makes it seem. Seagal likes the violence he professes to loathe, and his persona as a mythic attempt to reconcile spiritual peace and the use of brute force is an interesting but flawed conception needing more informed guidance if it is not to stalemate.

The second half's emphasis on the evils of Capitalism, a thematic continuation from *On Deadly Ground*, overwhelms the serial killer angle. Indeed, the copycat killer is an assassin, sanctioned by Capitalist enterprise, who appropriates the individuality of the serial killer into his methodology to cover the real reason for the murders (a device used in *Blow Out*). The serial killer is not the product of a bankrupt Capitalism, but an individual aberration (and tortured soul) whose actions are incorporated into the Capitalist operations of corrupt patriarchs. The serial killer is a barely contextualized fixture of society, a self-proclaimed visionary who is exploited; and the validity of his message as psychotic self-expression is appropriated and distorted.

There is an attempt at a psychoanalytic profile of the killer as being obsessed with punishment and purification, intent to convert sinners into martyrs as God intended, but this is raised and dismissed as mere plot function. However, it does enable the profiler (Seagal) to realize the difference between the actual killer's crimes and the copycat's; despite the similarity, the crime is a unique signature that cannot be duplicated, an acknowledgement of the individuality of such serial murder cases.

The film features a noteworthy treatment of the morgue-table scene so common to serial killer films. Two policemen examine a topless female cadaver on display. Seagal asks Wayans for any comments, and Wayans replies that she has great breasts: a tacit acknowledgement of the necrophilic tease of the set piece, treated as a joke. Seagal's response is to touch the breast, make an incision and, from a number (implant?), provide a means of identifying the victim.

The director was better known for his films made for the Hallmark Hall of Fame channel, and critics felt that he was on too unfamiliar terrain here, although that fact actually makes the film more intriguing than many more standard actioners. He had apparently admitted in interviews that this was a major departure for him. The film failed to resurrect Seagal's box-office standing.

The Gore-Gore Girls

(1972: d. Herschell Gordon Lewis)

scr. Alan J. Dachman; pr. Lewis; ph. Alex Ameri; m. Lewis; ed. Eskander Ameripoor; cast. Frank Kress, Amy Farrell, Hedda Lubin, Russ Badger, Nora Alexis, Phil Laurensen, Frank Rice; 90m

A private detective and a print journalist investigate the murders of go-go dancers. Such are the perils of the loose and easy in the 1970s, a moral vacuum for director Lewis, who loves to jovially indict individual and social madness/hypocrisy when he can.

The film is an excuse for excessive, though self-parodic, gore and mutilation scenes. A procession of atrocities unfolds, including a head shoved into boiling oil, a face smashed into a mirror, and nipples cut off (with a breast gushing chocolate milk). All is done with Lewis' customary low-budget humor. Indeed, this was Lewis' last gore movie, and some (Hardy, p. 234) consider it his most extreme. Quite a feat that. But it doesn't make it any better.

The Gore-Gore Girls can be compared to the likes of *Calendar Girl Murders* and even the later *Stripped to Kill* films, which speak of the need to address the effects of the sexual commodification and objectification of women in the wake of the social revolution of the 1960s. It is unlikely that Lewis treats the theme with any solemnity of purpose here, however.

Guilty as Sin

(1993: d. Sidney Lumet)

scr. Larry Cohen; pr. Martin Ransohoff; exec pr. Don Carmody, Bob Robinson; ph. Andrzej Bartkowiak; prod d. Philip Rosenberg; ed. Evan Lottman; m. Howard Shore; cast. Rebecca DeMornay, Don Johnson, Stephen Lang, Jack Warden; 103m

A skillful lawyer (DeMornay) agrees to represent a self-confident, narcissistic, manipulative and cocky womanizer (Johnson) accused of killing his wife. As he tries to seduce her, she realizes his instability and, through his actions, suspects him of being responsible for several other murdered women around the country, something he never denies. She cannot unload the case and seeks to plant incriminating evidence. He discovers this and intends to conquer (and hence kill) her too. He has been playing her all along.

The film unfolds as a battle of wills, as DeMornay is ever more fascinated by her client's sexuality. Of course, this gradually threatens her own, as the attraction/repulsion cycle of confrontations continues. The motivations are more than merely sexual, however, although understated. Sex is a weapon in an egotistical effort to prove one's superiority.

Yet there is more to the killer than there at first seems. On the surface he is a slick Casanova who resents being a kept man by rich women, and so kills them once he is done toying with them. He admits that his talent is getting women to do what he wants them to do, yet slowly his bleaker resentments come through. He says, "God put too many beautiful women in the world," meaning either that there is

not enough time to seduce them all, or there is a surplus in need of culling.

Gradually, however, Johnson adopts an ever more effeminate posturing (at one stage looking in the lawyer's compact mirror). DeMornay's boyfriend remarks to her that Johnson was looking him up and down and checking him out. It is possible that Johnson's sly narcissism encompasses a malevolent bisexuality, a combination of passive and aggressive coding. This raises the issue of possible denial and overcompensation in his role as a lady-killer. He is the epitome of male vanity, finally tiring of its disposable conquests. He thinks so much of himself that he tells DeMornay that he is not a serial killer, and that he takes no pleasure in the act of murder. Yet this is evasive, for in the end he admits that he took his gloves off to kill his wife because "to kill her with gloves on would be like fucking with a rubber." This clearly reveals that to him murder is a sexual act and the consummation of a lengthy seduction-and-conquest process.

He fancies himself too skillful and refined a seducer to be considered a mere sex killer. Yet his ego demands that someone, a woman he considers a worthy rival in the game (as DeMornay considers it at first), know his secret — a lawyer bound by professional ethics not to reveal her client's confidence. Thus he seeks to entrap DeMornay and continually baits her. He even kills the patriarch in her life, her favored confidant and father figure, a private detective — all in the effort to control, manipulate and dominate her.

Guilty as Sin features some of the most striking uses of architectural spaces (large rooms, stairs, buildings, halls, courtrooms, and apartments) in all of director Lumet's filmography. At times it is overwhelming and almost abstract, the bold set design recalling the work of Michael Mann. The off-center compositions stress a psychological imbalance inherent in the protagonists' relationship, and is a device also used in numerous Italian giallo movies to suggest a realm of perception beneath the everyday. The contemplation and exploration of architectural spaces is a definite subtext in this film, which serves to underline the theme of elegant imbalance.

There are similarities, of course, to *Jagged Edge*, which was better received by the critics. Rita Kempley (*Washington Post*) felt that Johnson's combination of suave exterior coating and inner reckless violence recalled Richard Gere in *Looking for Mr. Goodbar*. Johnson, as the sometimes-effeminate lady-killer, plays the role without subtlety, although it can also be seen as a knowing attempt to probe the underside of his persona.

The main hiccup with this film is that although Lumet is a capable director, he is unsuited to the slyly comic mood of Larry Cohen's script, and the film feels unsure of itself. Lumet seems intent on preserving the theme of justice and ethical behavior, whilst Cohen intends to ridicule it. The courtroom intrigue also borrows the incriminating letter device of *Witness for the Prosecution*, and the planting of incriminating evidence against one's own client used in *Class Action* to more ambiguous effect (see Bergman and Asimow, pp. 155–7).

Hand of Death

(1989: d. Anders Palm) aka *Unmasked Part 25*

scr. Mark Cutforth; pr. Cutforth; ph. John De-Borman; spec eff. Image Animation; cast. Gregory Cox, Fiona Evans, Edward Brayshaw; 84m

A serial killer (who wears a hockey mask akin to Jason in the *Friday the 13th* movies) begins to question why he kills when he meets a blind girl who gradually shows him something more than murder. In the meantime, he has been slaughtering teens with abandon. Despite her influence,

he cannot stop, and stabs her too—he is doomed to repeat the ritual of murder.

Underneath this is an attempt at a slasher parody, and even the psychodrama of a young man who imitates his father, himself a serial killer of women. He is thus representative of a Patriarchal legacy, monstrous and yet glamorized on film. It seems the killer is reportedly the star of a series of slasher movies. The ending sees him succumbing to tears at yet another film of his exploits.

Hand of Death is an attempt at satire, one which wishes to tackle the spillover from reality to fiction and vice-versa as the indication of a malfunctioning Patriarchy so consumed by violence and its glorification that sex murder has become an inevitable ritual of both individual and collective self-definition and self-expression. Its suggestion that love may conquer all, but ultimately cannot, recalls Chabrol's *Le Boucher* especially. It is not generally available.

Hands of the Ripper

(1971: d. Peter Sasdy)

scr. L.W. Davidson; stry. Edward S. Shew; pr. Aida Young; ph. Kenneth Talbot; cast. Eric Porter, Angharad Rees, Jane Merrow, Keith Bell, Derek Godfrey, Dora Bryan; 85m

Jack the Ripper's daughter sees her dad kill her mother and has to deal with the trauma. Consequently in certain situations, when reflected light coincides with an embrace, she enters a trance state and kills the one embracing her. A psychiatrist treats her. It is suggested paradoxically that she suffers from a certain incestuous desire towards her loathed father, which makes her identify with the transgressor, although she must disavow this desire as too monstrous for recognition. This is a common theme in later female serial killer movies. The psychiatrist, however, is not able to deal with the complexities of her psychosis. An MP is also interested in her and becomes a rival for her affections. The doctor takes her home, and when he discovers that she is a killer, aids her by hiding the corpses and covering up for her. Finally she stabs the doctor and seeks to continue her father's work (as if possessed), setting out to kill the doctor's son's blind fiancée. In a climactic fight, the blind girl is confused when she hears the male Ripper's voice coming from the woman. Both are in some sense blind.

The film explores seeing as a component of sexuality, and serves to stage each murder in a new way, to suggest an odd progression to the cyclic trap of the killer's mind. The killings are the expression of a tormented mind seeking sexual definition, a similar theme to that found in Hammer's *Dr. Jekyll and Sister Hyde* from the same year.

The woman is unable to reconcile aggression with passivity in gender roles, and so seeks transcendence through transgression, although in so doing she strives to continue the law of the father, herself warped by an inherently destructive Patriarchy which seeks to punish women's sexuality. Thus, it is a tortuous path for a woman to seek an aggressive sexuality, as that involves an embrace of homicidal desire and a repetition of the moment of trauma as the recognition of such desire. It cannot be disavowed, although it must be punished.

Hangover Square

(1945: d. John Brahm)

scr. Barre Lyndon; nvl. Patrick Hamilton; pr. Robert Bassler; ph. Joseph La Shelle; m. Bernard Herrmann; ed. Harry Reynolds; art d. Lyle Wheeler, Maurice Ransford; cast. Laird Cregar, Linda Darnell, George Sanders, Glenn Langan, Faye Marlowe, Alan Napier; 77m

This follow-up to the same team's successful *The Lodger* stars Laird Cregar as a distinguished composer who turns into a killer whenever he hears a certain sound, and prowls fog-bound streets (à la the Ripper), looking for any victim. His crimes are unremembered later. Finally, a psychologist from Scotland Yard (not a policeman) uncovers his disorder.

Set in London in 1903, in similarly Ripper-esque surroundings, this is also another variation on the Jekyll and Hyde mythos in its suggestion of a monstrous side of the personality too abhorrent for the normal side to accept, and loosed only by external stimuli. As per the then current vogue, amnesia results from the clash between the normal and abnormal (by extension, sexually deviant) sides of the personality. The superego still tries to intervene.

It seems that a young singer who deceived him set off his crime spree; i.e. the other victims are random surrogates for a repressed rage and sexual resentment surfacing uncontrollably. The acts are self-expression, however abhorrent they may be. The fact that it is a psychiatrist and not a cop who solves the case makes the film an early depiction of the emerging profiler figure and the recognition that psychiatric issues are at the heart of the dilemma posed by the repeat killer.

This was Cregar's last starring role; the 28-year-old actor died shortly before the film received widespread release and acclaim. Thus, a promising career lamentably ended.

Hannibal

(2001: d. Ridley Scott)

scr. David Mamet, Steve Zaillian; pr. Dino de Laurentiis, Martha de Laurentiis, Ridley Scott; ph. John Mathieson; m. Hans Zimmer; ed. Pietro Scalia; prod d. Norris Spencer; art d. David Crank; cast. Anthony Hopkins, Julianne Moore, Ray Liotta, Frankie Faison, Giancarlo Giannini, Francesca Neri, Zeljko Ivanek, Gary Oldman (uncredited); 131m

Serial killer Hannibal Lecter (Anthony Hopkins) prepares to kill in *Hannibal* (2000).

This is the highly anticipated sequel to the seminal serial killer movie *Silence of the Lambs*. Serial killer Hannibal Lecter (Hopkins) is in Florence, where his identity is discovered by a greedy policeman who reports the find to Lector's only surviving victim, a rich, scarred, wheelchair-bound pervert (Oldman) who wants revenge. Hannibal returns to America and pursues now-disgraced agent Starling (Moore, replacing Foster), who saves him from the rich man's vengeance. She is shot in the process, and Hannibal saves her life. He prepares a grisly dinner to entertain her, eating her colleague's brain whilst he is still conscious, though drugged into a painless high.

The film follows Lecter's romantic attraction for Starling, and his apparent intention to consummate a long-postponed desire. In the time since *Silence of the Lambs*, the FBI agent's graduation has become defeat. She (most disappointingly) no longer seems to work for the Behavioral Science Unit, and has become a disgraced field agent involved in conventional narcotics work who must reacquaint herself with the Lecter case by listening to filed tape recordings and viewing photos. This case, however, has seemingly always been in the back of her mind, as she is now forced to confront Lecter as an amalgam of monstrous father and potential suitor. She has enough respect for him as adversary not to let him die unjustly.

Though Hannibal claims interest in seeing how she has matured, their mutual pursuit of each other, in approximation of the quid pro quo mind games of *Silence of the Lambs*, is a kind of courtship as much as a menacing psychological challenge and suspenseful set-piece. The question running through the film is, what will he do to her, and will, perhaps, she accept him — a theme developed in the novel, whose ending was rewritten for the screen. It is important to her professionalism and personal integrity that he remains a dangerous adversary.

Hannibal Lecter (Anthony Hopkins), in his trademark facemask, carries off the unconscious FBI agent Clarice Starling (Julianne Moore) after she has saved his life. He returns the favor in *Hannibal* (2000).

Although it was criticized for its graphic violence (the supposed reason for Foster declining to reprise the role she made famous), this violence only happens to those characters who, in the film's terms, deserve it. These people — the bitter, spoiled rich pederast/former victim perverted by his desire for revenge; the greedy policeman; the corrupt official who would take Starling's job away from her in part because she refused his sexual advances — are not real innocents, nor are they victims in the conventional sense. Indeed, only the profiler and the killer, ironically enough, are moral people, each put-upon by the exploiters around them. They must overcome this exploitation of their character and in a sense join forces; even though they would seem at opposite ends of a moral spectrum, they are not.

In a reversal of the standard serial killer film ideology, the "victims" are the monstrous patriarchs whom the serial killer has the job of chastising. In the film's subversive agenda, the killer represents the purifying force, although he resorts to psychopathic behavior in response to the threat of exposure. He has controlled his impulses for a decade, and it is on the prompting supplied by the morally dubious actions of others that he allows his "monstrousness" to resurface, almost as if justified. It also implies that the killer has control over his impulses, as his violence is initially self-protective and only later becomes self-indulgent and paraphilic. This monstrousness, however, does not make him a threat to the general populace, despite his presence on the FBI's Ten Most Wanted list.

Indeed, the serial killer is not depicted as a villain. He is a cultured, well-mannered, civil, intelligent, refined gentleman and aesthete. He murders only those whose morals and ethics are tainted, and is in full, selective control of his monstrous urges. The cannibalism is treated more as an eccentricity than a paraphilic psychopathology. The only time its centricity in Hannibal's mind is directly confronted is in the climactic brain-eating scene, though it has been raised jokingly in the movie's course. Thus, it is a much-anticipated event.

This scene exposes Hannibal's full monstrousness for all to see and judge. However, although the scene tests audience sympathy, it does not transform him into a villain. It flirts with this possibility — as Starling is restrained, Lector moves his face in close and snarls as if about to bite/kiss as a sexual gesture, but restrains himself and moves away. Indeed, as the killer recognizes his own monstrous sexual desire at this instant, his response is to purge it from himself in a remarkable moment of symbolic self-castration.

Handcuffed to Starling, without a key, he can escape only by severing either her hand or his. He chooses his own — the same hand that earlier, on a carousel, reached out to brush her hair; the same hand that in *Silence of the Lambs* reached out to touch her finger. He thus eliminates his own sexual desires and punishes himself for having them. He would hurt himself rather than the object of his romantic and sexual attraction/obsession. Nor are the victims surrogates for that unconsummated desire. The film seeks to disavow monstrous sexuality from a sympathetic though awe-inspiring serial killer hero. This is the genre's response to the overwhelming popularity of both the serial killer type and Lecter in particular.

The film is aware of the fact that the serial killer subculture, of both real and fictional killers, has thrived in the decade since *Silence of the Lambs*. Thus, the killer's facemask is now a prized possession, worth a lot of money to select collectors, as indeed are all physical objects associated with the case. The killer's former cell guard profits from his acquaintance with the feared killer by selling such objects. There is a similarly ironic, even morbidly poetic, humor running through the film.

Hannibal was one of the most eagerly awaited films of the past decade and was a box-office hit, despite the expected divided critical response. The objections were mainly on moral grounds, with many finding the brain-eating scene the most repellent display in a supposedly mainstream film. Like its predecessor, *Hannibal* became a popular talking point, and there has been talk of a prequel, again starring Hopkins.

Happy Face Murders

(1999: d. Brian Trenchard-Smith)

scr. John Pielmeier; pr. Ned Walsh; ph. Albert J. Dunk; m. Peter Bernstein; ed. Bill Goddard; prod d. Ed Hanna; cast. Ann-Margret, Marg Helgenberger, Henry Thomas, Nicholas Campbell, Rick Peters, David McIlwraith, Bruce Gray; 98m

Australian exploitation director Smith returns to the serial killer tale (after the supernatural-tinged *Out of the Body*) with this ambitious tele-movie. A detective (Helgenberger) is assigned to work with a young psychologist/profiler (Thomas), a fact she is not happy about. An elderly woman (Ann-Margret) fascinated with TV programs like "Murder She Wrote" and "Matlock" implicates her abusive lover in the murder of a retarded young girl, one of a series. This begins a series of false confessions followed by changes in her story. The more she creates details of the crime based on her conversations with the detectives on the case, the more she implicates herself, and is finally jailed. Of course, she recants her testimony; but by now she has attracted the attention of the real killer who claims, in notes signed with a happy face, that this is part of many such killings he has done. Finally the detective must reinvestigate the case, to the dismay of the get-tough-on-crime District Attorney who prosecuted it.

At first a case of parallel narratives, this proves a constantly invigorating look at how one can use information inadvertently given by police to implicate innocents and oneself in murder. However repulsive the lover may be, and the film makes no attempt to deny this, he is innocent of the crime he has been accused of. The only possible consequences of the woman's constant distortions of the truth are injustices. Yet her motive, to rid herself of a battering lover, is understandable. Her fine-tuned ability to learn from seemingly harmless and innocuous television shows is perhaps meant to represent an American class— bright but aging and put-upon middle–American women who feel they've not been treated by life as they deserve. Hence her attraction to a much younger man, a relationship which finds its parallel in the pairing of older cop and younger profiler. Indeed, the burgeoning older woman/younger man relationship in part recalls *Black and White*.

Happy Face Murders has ambitions as a satire of right-wing, middle–American values: of the DA's "more jail, no bail" mentality and a television culture obsessed with police and judicial methods. Ironically, in the midst of all this due process the killer remains undetected until he sends a note to police admitting his many crimes. The innocent fantasies are fueled by television values, prompting a process of imitation that confuses the real issues and results in increasing fabrications that hamper the true cause of objective justice. The irony of an innocent woman convicted for a crime she didn't commit plagues the killer's conscience and confirms his cynical view of the justice system he despises.

A murderer of innocents, he paradoxically cannot comprehend wrongful imprisonment. The film thus becomes a comedy of repercussion.

The eventual killer is a misogynist who kills women who remind him in some way, no matter how trivial it may be, of his dead ex-wife. He finally has enough conscience, when faced with discovery, to turn himself in. When Helgenberger, finally coming face to face with a real serial killer, asks why, he replies that during his first kill he felt in control over a woman for the first time in his life, and that that feeling proved addictive and reassuring to him. He needs to be in sexual control over a woman in order to feel powerful and a worthy male. In that, he is one step further along the spectrum than Ann-Margret's abusive lover; indeed, the film holds them as kindred spirits in a sense. A process of prolonged violence towards women will turn homicidal.

A compelling, intelligent, involvingly structured and often bleakly amusing film, *Happy Face Murders* is a genuine surprise from a supposed hack exploitation director. In itself it does not suggest that a retrospective of the director's work is warranted, just that he has virtues beyond his customary station. However, he will still be better remembered as one of the founding exploitation directors to counter the art-house trend of the Australian New Wave of the 1970s.

Hatchet for a Honeymoon

(1969: d. Mario Bava)

scr. Bava, Santiago Moncada, Mario Musy; pr. Manuel Cano Sanciriaco; ph. Bava, Antonio Rinaldi; cast. Stephen Forsyth, Dagmar Lassander, Laura Betti, Jesus Puente, Femi Benussi; 93 (83)m

A male fashion designer, impotent when with his wife, is an axe murderer of women in bridal gowns. He has a room full of female mannequins, all dressed as brides. Following each murder, he is aware of one more detail of a repressed childhood trauma. Police investigate him, but he is still compelled to kill, and finally targets his wife, the final remembered detail revealing him guilty of matricide. In the end, he is insane, haunted by the specters of the dead.

The wife resembles the mother, and thus the film is considered a variation on the incest taboo: madness is the result of a passion which society deems abhorrent and must be repressed at all costs, although finally it proves too powerful. However the film reportedly seems more a critique (Hardy, p. 205) of the romantic male lead, and thus a meta-filmic look at narrative — and cinema — as fantasy. Bava here returns to the giallo form he pioneered with *Blood and Black Lace* and *Evil Eye* after his comic-book outing, *Diabolik*.

The Haunted Strangler

(1958: d. Robert Day) aka *Grip of the Strangler*

scr. Jan Read, John C. Cooper; pr. John Croydon; ph. Lionel Banes; m. Buxton Orr; ed. Peter Mayhew; cast. Boris Karloff, Anthony Dawson, Derek Birch, Dorothy Gordon, Elizabeth Allan, Diane Aubrey, Tim Turner, Jean Kent; 81m

A novelist (Karloff) becomes obsessed with the long-closed case of the Haymarket Strangler. A man was executed for five murders, although Karloff feels that the real killer was the surgeon who performed the autopsy, and that the scalpel/murder weapon is buried with the killer to hide the evidence. His daughter feels that Karloff has put himself in danger by investigating the case. Karloff exhumes the body and, finding the surgeon's scalpel, is overcome with strange feelings of homicidal desire and guilt. He soon realizes he is the feared serial killer, returned after a twenty-year hiatus. Even with this new self-knowledge, he cannot stop himself from killing.

The film posits individual violence almost as a product of a culture in transition: hence the film opens with a public hanging, death as public spectacle, and has Karloff consult the police files on the case, stored near those of Jack the Ripper, suggesting both parallel and legacy. It also suggests that the relaxation of codes of sexual morality and the presentation of sexually stimulating acts as a public spectacle (paralleling the execution) are responsible for the liberation and justification of a sex murderer's repellent desires. Such a figure seeks to punish women for arousing him through the open display of sexuality (here a can-can dance, which has Karloff leering slightly), a theme that had also infiltrated both *Lady of Burlesque* and *The Lodger*. The latter especially had a similar scene of a killer attending a burlesque show and barely able to contain his desire and resentment. When the killer side surfaces, Karloff's recourse is to go to the can-can hall in search of women to kill. Murder is his form of sexual expression, but also an uncontrollable impulse as the product of social conditioning.

Karloff as an outsider investigating the case is in part a forerunner of the profiler figure, although his eventual guilt suggests that killers and those who seek them out possess one and the same mindset at the core — a realization they cannot handle. This aspect, realizing after an investigation that oneself is the killer, anticipates the later *Angel Heart*, and utilizes the ever-popular blackout plot, as well as the takeover by another personality (à la Jekyll and Hyde), so that it is not the kindly novelist himself who kills, and blame is displaced. Significantly, Karloff must physically change in the process of becoming the deformed killer. In that way, it acknowledges the actor's persona in many previous genre films.

This was the first of two Karloff films set in 19th century London, the other being

Corridors of Blood; both were filmed on the same sets. *The Haunted Strangler* was released in the US by MGM in 1961. The script had actually been submitted to Karloff years before, and Karloff had wanted to do it, but had had to wait until the opportunity presented itself. It has interest, although its place in genre history is currently without distinction.

The Hawk

(1991: d. David Hayman)

scr. Peter Ransley; nvl. Ransley; pr. Ann Wingate, Eileen Quinn; ph. Andrew Dunn; m. Nick Bicat; ed. Justin Krish; prod d. David Myerscough-Jones; cast. Helen Mirren, George Costigan, Rosemary Leach, Owen Teale, Christopher Madin; 86m

A wife and mother (Mirren), once incarcerated in a psychiatric hospital, suspects her husband of being the title killer, who often targets (and sexually mutilates) mothers, pecking out their eyes with the murder weapon. She is not sure if she wasn't imagining the evidence, and goes to the police. She cannot believe it, however, and nor do they. But she discovers that her marriage is not the ideal she thought and goes back over her husband's business dates to tie them into the murders. The more she investigates, the more her husband is implicated, and the more her sanity comes into question. She stabs him and is arrested. Out on bail, she is determined to prove her sanity, and does so, finally revealing her husband as the murderer after all.

This is an offbeat UK tele-movie charting the protagonist's descent into paranoia and her subsequent attempts to hold onto a provable, concrete reality that runs counter to accepted fact, making the film an odd companion to Mirren's series of *Prime Suspect* UK tele-movies. It charts the breakup of a marriage as the wife realizes the depths of resentment and mon-

strousness hidden behind her husband's facade of caring father, and how her past psychotic history makes her seem the guilty party in the eyes of many. Ironically, the killer suffers from no such illness, nor doubts, as if psychosis were a more humanizing process, allowing a greater appreciation of reality, although hiding the monstrous and incongruous behind human interaction.

He Kills Night After Night After Night

(1970: d. Lewis Force [Lindsay Shonteff])
aka *Night After Night After Night*

scr. Douglas Hill; pr. James Mellor; ph. Dail Ambler; cast. Jack May, Justine Lord, Gilbert Wynne, Linda Marlowe, Terry Scully, Donald Sumpter; 88m

An East End policeman (Wayne) investigates the Ripper-style murders of Soho prostitutes in London. He is sure he knows who the killer is, a teenager, and spends much of his time persecuting the wrong man. Meanwhile, the real killer, revealed as a transvestite judge, continues his purification of the city and personal protest against the swinging 1960s mentality. He dresses in black leather and a wig (akin to the giallo killers in emerging Italian thrillers) as he slashes scantily clad women, be they whores or not. There is some irony to the ending, however, as the killer escapes custody by dressing as a woman but is almost killed by gay-bashers. Although he has a gun in his hand when apprehended, he appeals for help; but he is shot dead by the police.

The film goes over similar anti–Establishment terrain to that found in the Pete Walker/David McGillivray collaborations of the early 1970s, although it stresses the need for sympathetic understanding rather than corrective, punitive measures. It turns the defense attorney into a spokesman of moral reform; and the judge, as self-righteous killer, becomes a representative of a system so founded on repression that it resents any progressive moves, transforming itself into a monstrous deviation worse than what it condemns. He resents the open display of sexuality, even in his younger wife. The killer represents a generation driven mad by repressed lust, unwilling to accept its own sexual desires: an outdated governmental body. The judge is the enemy of progress, however morally flawed that may be.

Considered a long-lost 1960s slasher film, *He Kills* was directed by Lindsay Shonteff, who had a sometime career as a minor horror director (*Devil Doll, Curse of Simba*) and made this sleazy effort before tackling James Bond spoofs. When the film was re-edited by the studio (at the last minute), Shonteff took credit under a pseudonym. Contemporary censors objected to the liberal amounts of nudity and blood, and cut the film even more. Certainly it is much stronger than any Hammer film of the period, and it played in minor exploitation cinemas, often alongside sex films.

The film has a socioeconomic validity as it explores the seedy sex world of Soho, capturing the underside of the "free sex" values of London. As such, it is a sober examination of the consequences of the free love era and the need for understanding the effects of the corresponding social changes on the individual rather than indulging in blanket condemnation.

All characters, even the policeman (equally the ladies' man), are defined by their sexuality and the response to changing morality. However, there are no really sympathetic characters, and despite the call for understanding, there is little sense of any real liberation offered by the sexual revolution. Visually, it is an ugly world, but it is all we have, with the only hope resting on the non-judgmental treatment of consequence in an effort to better society. It is

less the exploitation item than one would expect, and more a film about values in transition. The killer's words to a porn-reading clerk have wide implications: "Overcome it or it will destroy you." The filmmakers suggest that you must understand and treat it, or it will destroy you.

He Knows You're Alone

(1980: d. Armand Mastroianni)

scr. Scott Parker; pr. George Manasse; ph. Gerald Feil; ed. George T. Norris; m. Alexander and Mark Peskanov; art d. Susan Kaufman; cast. Don Scardino, Caitlin O'Heaney, Elizabeth Kemp, Tom Rolfing, Lewis Arit, Patsy Pease, James Rebhorn, Tom Hanks; 92m

A serial killer stalks and murders young brides-to-be. A policeman investigates, believing the offender guilty of a serial pattern and ready to strike again. The killer seemingly attacks anyone connected to weddings. His motive is revenge for having been jilted.

This is more a "gimmick killer" than serial killer film, with the victims random but too indiscriminate, encompassing both men and women, and barely sexual in nature. In fact, the film is sadly unsure of its killer's motives, and so goes through the motions without any real thematic coherence, confusing the killer even further with the slasher figure then popular. Thus, the killer is a barely characterized automaton. It is an opportunistic film, unsure of its own exploitation territory.

The movie has some ambition to be more than the slasher films it was released amidst, as signaled from the opening scene set in a cinema wherein two girls watch a slasher film, and one of them is actually killed. This self-reflexivity signals an interest in the voyeuristic dynamics of the form, as does the killer's sexual violence, but the film fails to self-consciously examine the devices it uses.

He Knows You're Alone is notable

among genre fans for the attention given to the publicity and marketing campaign by a major Hollywood studio, capitalizing on the post–*Halloween* public interest in such gory movies. It was Tom Hanks' first film role, playing a psychology student interested in fear (in another undeveloped self-reflexive subtext), and so has some novelty value, though little beyond that. Director Mastroianni did much better with *The Clairvoyant*.

Headless Eyes

(1971: d. Kent Bateman)

scr. Bateman; pr. Ron Sullivan; cast. Bo Brundin, Mary Jane Early, Gordon Raman; 79m

This is a supposedly minor character study of a New York City sculptor driven to petty burglary for economic reasons. He has his left eye scooped out by a potential victim and becomes a stalker, carving out the left eye of his victims and keeping them in resin for display in a gallery. Thus, his private trophies become the component parts of his artworks, made to share his talent with the world that provokes him. He craves artistic success.

This is a disreputable mix of the revenge-killer movie and Corman's *A Bucket of Blood*, notable mainly for its callousness in the depiction of serial killer trophy collecting. It is also known for the depths of its misogyny and its sleaziness, making *Headless Eyes* perhaps a forerunner of Lustig's *Maniac*, or even *Henry*, and with a socioeconomic subtext better expressed in Ferrara's *Driller Killer*. Scenes of the killer scooping out women's eyes with a spoon anticipate the likes of *Deranged* and Lucio Fulci films. However, this is considered inferior to all of those mentioned, when it is considered at all, and is interesting as an example of the 1970s attempt to seek definitions of the anti-hero which effectively excluded the serial killer. It is currently unavailable.

Heat

(1996: d. Michael Mann)

scr. Mann; pr. Mann, Art Linson; exec pr. Arnon Milchan, Pieter Jan Brugge; ph. Dante Spinotti; prod d. Neil Spisak; ed. Dov Hoenig, Pasquale Buba; m. Elliot Goldenthal; cast. Al Pacino, Robert DeNiro, Tom Sizemore, Val Kilmer, Jon Voight, Diane Venora, Amy Brenneman, Ashley Judd, Mykelti Williamson, Wes Studi, Ted Levine, Tom Noonan; 164m

This is not a serial killer film, although one of the pivotal characters is a loathsome serial killer of young prostitutes. He kills in an effort to prove his masculinity and assert his proud dominance when rejected even by other criminals. He tries to ingratiate himself with a group of professional thieves led by DeNiro, but his actions cause them to want to kill him. Thus rejected, he informs on them. His actions ultimately lead to DeNiro's demise, but only after DeNiro has killed the criminal aberration — and social moral abomination — which is the serial killer.

Heat shows the kind of moral hierarchy that exists among the criminal underclass, with the serial killer the conscience-less worst. The serial killer has no honor code and is therefore removed from conventional criminality, which in turns loathes him as a corruption that must be eliminated in the name of a higher justice and honor among criminals. Ironically, the police must protect the serial killer who has given evidence against the criminals, and target the thieves rather than the real scourge.

The above is a minor subtext in a film which is concerned with the obsessional similarity between professional thieves and the police who pursue them, a development of Mann's previous *Thief*. The serial killer angle is nevertheless interesting, considering that Mann directed the seminal *Manhunter*. The notion of the serial killer as a type separate from conventional criminals was also portrayed, to vastly different ends, in *Con-Air* around the same time, wherein the killer is a respected and feared figure amongst the other criminals, rather than the object of hatred he is here.

Helter Skelter

(1976: d. Tom Gries)

scr. J.B. Miller; book. Vincent Bugliosi, Curt Gentry; pr. Gries; ph. Jules Brenner; m. Billy Goldenberg; ed. Bud S. Isaacs, Byron Brandt; art d. Phil Barber; cast. Steve Railsback, George DiCenzo, Nancy Wolf, Marilyn Burns, Christina Hart, Cathey Paine; 194 (92)m

Although Manson is not really a serial killer, those acting under him (through whatever level of mind manipulation) were — insofar as they committed the same crimes twice and would possibly have continued to do so. However, the case so galvanized public opinion, and became so symptomatic of the end of the free love era, that this television mini-series is included herein.

Under Gries' capable direction, and Steve Railsback's excellent performance, this is a riveting view of the killer cult mentality and its social repercussions. Those who doubt the validity of prosecutor Bugliosi's charges will find it perhaps more inciteful and amusing than insightful. It is also better in the mini-series version than the shorter movie format.

Helter Skelter was the start of a trend of true-crime based mini-series sporadically produced over the next decade, some of which would concentrate on the serial killer problem and the social response to it — notably, *Atlanta Child Murders*, *Deliberate Stranger* and the fictional *City in Fear*.

Henry: Portrait of a Serial Killer

(1988: d. John McNaughton)

scr. McNaughton, Richard Fire; pr. McNaughton, Lisa Dedmond, Steven A. Jones; ph. Char-

lie Lieberman; m. McNaughton, Ken Hale, Jones; ed. Elena Maganini; prod d. Rick Paul; cast. Michael Rooker, Tom Towles, Tracy Arnold; 83m

This slice-of-life film follows the day-to-day Chicago-based life of an illiterate, unrepentant serial killer (Rooker) who murders by a variety of means and independent of gender or socioeconomic status (anyone). He lives with a housemate, Otis (Towles), whose sister Becky comes to stay. Henry educates Otis in the craft of successful serial killing, expounding his minimal philosophy, but ultimately kills him when Otis tries to force himself incestuously on his sister — Henry unable to consummate his desire for her. Henry and Becky leave together, professing love, but Henry kills her too (offscreen) and dumps the body, in a suitcase, on the road. Henry then drives off to continue to kill and get by.

The plot is minimal, in favor of character observation, as Henry demonstrates his remorseless killing machine nature (reflected by his temporary job as an exterminator). The movie seeks to understand and contextualize through nonjudgmental behaviorist observation and study — the filmmaker as profiler. Yet it is aware of the frustrations and even arguable futility in the search for inherent meaning behind such murder, and so continually reinforces the unremarkable banality of these people. Henry is the complete opposite of Hannibal Lecter (the fictional killer who perhaps epitomizes the move to glamorize the serial killer).

The relations between Henry and Otis reveal the easy spread of monstrousness and a hypocritical morality on Henry's part. Ironically, Henry has a certain sexual prudishness. He is awkward with Becky's advances, and he prevents Otis from committing necrophilic acts on one of their victims. It is almost as if this monster is afraid of his own sexuality and kills rather

One of the serial killer film's trademark shots — the mirror shot. Here the illiterate Henry (Michael Rooker) contemplates his reflection in *Henry: Portrait of a Serial Killer* (Electric/Maljac, 1990).

than confront it — the real Henry Lee Lucas on whom the film is based was bisexual, although seemingly not conflicted by it. However, this is not the singular motive driving Henry's crimes, as he kills when feeling insulted or slighted by someone, and for recreational, opportunist thrills. He cannot understand or deal with any emotion, and so kills when stimulated or confronted, as a means of avoidance and compensatory empowerment. His murders give him an identity he otherwise lacks. Again, they are his idealized self, although he seemingly lacks any capacity for self-analysis (and hence, remorse or conscience). Otis is a degenerate whom Henry is able to lure into homicide as a means of

personal empowerment and sexual expression. Henry ultimately resents Otis' open sexual expression, perhaps projecting his own insecurities in his punitive disciplining of Otis. Thus, his dismemberment of his supposed friend and accomplice may be both functional (easier to dispose of the body) and an intended purging of sexual desire.

The most controversial scene was the videotape sequence in which a camera records Henry and Otis killing a family during a home invasion; they then watch the tape (Otis yet again in slow motion) when they get home. It implicates the audience as complicit in murder in their viewing of a homemade snuff film, with

A lighter moment as Michael Rooker clowns around during the filming of the bleak *Henry: Portrait of a Serial Killer* (Electric/Maljac, 1990).

the serial killer as director and actor. Perhaps McNaughton intended to suggest that this is the audience's secret desire in watching serial killer films—to get as close as possible to a recorded portion of the killer's actual acts, as opposed to the mere representation of it. This encapsulates one end of the serial killer's stylistic spectrum — the deglamorizing and intended demystifying docudrama pursuit of "authenticity." Yet, in as far as it is Henry who films the acts, they are in part his orchestrated perception of events, though far from expressionistic. Short of becoming a killer oneself to experience and perceive the act as "pure" (a theme in subsequent serial killer films in the 1990s, especially *Copycat*), there are only representations within representations—the enigma of postmodernism.

Henry has a minimal style, approaching docudrama, with a clever use of the sounds of the murderous incidents playing over shots of the aftermath. It is distanced and non-judgmental, and Hirsch (*Detours*, p. 279) felt it approaches the Naturalistic. Hirsch also stresses that despite its bleak tone, it is not noirish, avoiding the expected stress on entrapment, as Henry moves instead unhindered through the world, in day and night, content to occupy what he has at the moment, killing when unsatisfied. He is a cunning survivor and never shown as a victim. Despite Henry's flat confession of a childhood of abuse leading to matricide (his memory of which is different in its details as he recounts it), the film deliberately avoids any such motivation for the killings. These people's lives are empty, and murder fills the void, allowing them a fantasy empowerment.

There is no police presence nor profiler, as the film is unconcerned with the standard police procedural aspect in favor of the unflinching case study. *Henry* is based on the true exploits of Henry Lee Lucas and Otis Toole. Henry confessed to over 300 murders but later recanted many of the confessions. The actual number of people he killed is debatable.

The film was shot in the winter of 1985–1986 but went unreleased until 1989 due to problems with the ratings board. It was refused an R certificate and so played unrated. It was screened at film festivals and midnight movies before attracting mainstream interest and the corresponding controversy over the film's realism. It was made for $125,000 using actors from Chicago's Organic Theater Company. Star Rooker went on to a mainstream Hollywood career, playing the killer in *Sea of Love* and, ironically, the police officer in *The Bone Collector*. The film *Confessions of a Serial Killer* is also based on the exploits of Henry Lee Lucas.

Henry: Portrait of a Serial Killer 2—Mask of Sanity

(1996: d. Chuck Parello)

scr. Parello; pr. Thomas J. Busch; ph. Michael Kohnhurst; ed. Tom Keefe; prod d. Rick Paul; m. John McNaughton; cast. Neil Guintoli, Rich Komenich, Kate Walsh, Carri Levinson, Daniel Allar, Penelope Milford; 84m

This equally low-budget and grim follow-up is more of a recapitulation, although there is some attempt to make Henry a more conflicted person (he contemplates suicide). After a montage of violated corpses, the film follows Henry as he calmly murders another and then spends the night in a homeless shelter. He is now clearly allied to society's underclass. He

gets a job installing portable toilets and is invited by the boss to stay with him, his wife and her troubled niece. The man is an arsonist who instructs him in the "trade," and Henry returns the favor, giving him lessons on how to kill. The niece also falls for Henry. Thus the film serves mainly to reproduce the character triangle of the first film, with the wife being the only addition to the works (and not offering very much of a difference).

Although it begins in much the same manner, Henry here is more intense and pensive, unlike the illiterate moron he was in the first film. Subsisting as a homeless derelict, he is one of life's losers, with the murders giving him an identity beyond the surrounding banality. His crimes have a more sociological rage than the emotional misdirection and convenience in McNaughton's film. But *Henry 2* has no liberal sympathies for this underclass (one seen homosexually raping an old man in the homeless shelter), and rather considers Henry part of an unredeemable humanity, a man ironically both reaching out for and subverting a role as patriarch.

The film tries for droll irony, with Henry becoming a substitute father for the tortured and suicidal young girl, a responsibility he takes on with some seriousness, perhaps because it offers him a patriarchally empowering role to balance his ideal as killer. These roles are ultimately irreconcilable, creating a tension bound to explode in violence. When she wants to have sex with him, he refuses, a testament again to his hypocritical morality, and to a wish for a conventional father/daughter relationship. She wants him to rescue her and take her away, but confronted by her vulnerability in light of her sexual needs, he rejects her: she has violated the bounds of the patriarchal role that he took such solace in. She intends to kill herself, with the cry, "This is for you, Henry," a proclamation that perhaps provokes Henry's guilt at being unable to save her. His reaction in the light of such emotional turmoil is to murder, and he kills the couple that so graciously took him in, burning their place down. With Henry returning to his aimless existence, the filmmakers postulate that he is a man forever trying to master his circumstances (socioeconomic and interpersonal) but unable to do so, instead murdering to literally remove the problem and then moving on. He is forever psychologically trapped, doomed to react to an unattainable ideal. His joy in murder is his rebellion against the ideal. As mentioned, Henry is characterized as a more pensive individual, and it is ambiguous as to what extent his self-knowledge allows him a conscious expression of that dilemma.

Although it is a flat film, attempting the docu-drama approach of the first *Henry* (but often becoming unintentionally amusing), it is not unintelligent. It uses the figure of the serial killer to examine an aberrant mind that wants to be a patriarch, but rejects this possibility by indulging in grotesque violence for personal pleasure. This violence is paradoxically an admission of failure from which the character seeks to flee but is forever drawn to repeat, as it is the only viable outlet of expression left him.

Hero and the Terror

(1988: d. William Tannen)

scr. Dennis Shryack, Michael Blodgett; nvl. Blodgett; pr. Raymond Wagner; exec pr. Menahem Golan, Yoram Globus; ph. Eric Van Harcn Noman; prod d. Holger Gross; m. David M. Frank; ed. Christian A. Wagner; cast. Chuck Norris, Brynn Thayer, Steve James, Jack O'Halloran, Billy Drago; 92m

A detective (Norris) captures a serial killer called "the Terror" (O'Halloran) by accident and is acclaimed a hero, ending a criminal career that had claimed some twenty victims. When the killer escapes from a psychiatrist and starts killing women

again (breaking their necks and collecting the bodies as if dolls), the cop is forced to track him down lest he be exposed and his image as Patriarchy's hero is undermined.

The killer is depicted as little more than a hulking, predatory animal, an infantile brute, and never speaks throughout the movie's duration. He is an unmotivated, unknowable monster whose physical appearance separates him from the rest of humanity. He is another automaton, though one unlike the slasher in that he spaces his killings and collects victims as trophies. The killer's lair is strewn with the female corpses. He represents the filmmakers' apparent intention to reduce serial killer pathology to the level of the slashers then popular: his flight from prison ties him to the legion of escaped-lunatic films. To gain this animal's scent, the detective must revisit the killer's first lair — just as the profiler visits the jailed killer in *Manhunter* who tells the profiler to smell himself if he wants the scent. Sadly, that implication is lacking here.

This lamentably reductionist mentality is expressed by the film's token nod to the profiler figure, the killer's psychologist (Drago — in a piece of truly weird casting), as he tells the police officer that the killer has no thoughts and merely acts as an animal, killing and taking the corpses home. He avoids explaining or even acknowledging the necrophilic implications behind the killer's acts, and even negates the entire sexual component behind the killer's murder of women. Obviously, therefore, no treatment for such offenders is necessary, nor understanding, as there is essentially nothing to understand. He must be eliminated, pure and simple. Thus, in his final elimination, there is no sense of a social purge, as the killer is clearly an abomination beyond real humanity.

The film parallels the killing of the killer with the birth of Norris' son, suggesting the cycle of life and death. This

A policeman proclaimed as a public hero (Chuck Norris, left) faces his greatest enemy, the hulking serial killer (Jack O'Halloran) known as "the Terror," in *Hero and the Terror* (Cannon, 1988).

raises an undeveloped theme of the killer as an agent of random death, and hence of cruel fate, who sporadically emerges from his underground lair to kill. Perhaps the elimination of this killer is a means of cheating death, of attaining immortality, a theme tackled much more cohesively in *The First Deadly Sin*.

The film also devotes much time to Norris' domestic situation and his troubles with his wife as he seeks to be a more sensitive husband. It is another attempt to broaden Norris' image (as would also be attempted rather more successfully in Andrew Davis' *Code of Silence*). Tannen returned to the serial killer film with the Jack the Ripper tale *Love Lies Bleeding*.

Hideaway

(1996: d. Brett Leonard)

scr. Andrew Kevin Walker, Neil Jiminez; nvl. Dean R. Koontz; pr. Jerry Baerwitz, Agatha

Hanczakowski, Gimel Everett; ph. Gale Tattersall; prod d. Michael Bolton; ed. B.J. Sears; m. Trevor Jones; cast. Jeff Goldblum, Christine Lahti, Alfred Molina, Jeremy Sisto, Alicia Silverstone; 102m

Co-scripted by Andrew Kevin Walker before he wrote *Seven* and *8MM*, this is a fascinating psychic-link movie about a father brought back from the dead (after being dead for two hours) and an experience with the afterlife, who now has a link to a serial killer. He can see through the killer's eyes but realizes that the killer can see through his own in return, and that his own daughter is in jeopardy. Of course, the father is thought psychotic. Brilliant effects and vivid production design add considerably to the portrayal of distraught minds. It seems to foreshadow Neil Jordan's *In Dreams* also.

The film announces its tantalizing religious subtext from the outset. The killer has murdered a woman and daughter (later revealed to be his mother and sister) and posed the bodies in imitation of prayer. Thus, the killer mocks God, deliberately challenging God's law. The killer rejects God and seeks a new life with Satan, becoming his emissary, and suicides. The father discovers all and is faced with an overwhelming despair. His reaction, we learn later, was to take God's law in his own hands and affect the resurrection of his monstrous son. This appropriation is another challenge to God's authority over man and parallels the killer to Christ, a bold subtext that recalls the monstrous cyber–Christ in Leonard's previous breakthrough hit, *The Lawnmower Man*, and anticipates the flesh/data amalgam of *Virtuosity*.

This process of challenging God's authority is countered by the protagonist's growing realization that he has been, in effect, ordained by a heavenly source to battle this evil threat to God, Patriarchy and the family. Thus, Goldblum, as profiler substitute, slowly discovers his potential (he has the power to heal himself quickly) and the corresponding responsibility that goes with it. He is the good Father who must punish the bad son of a doctor/father (Molina) so blinded by love that he would transgress God's authority over death.

The doctor who affects resuscitation and resurrection is in the tradition of the mad scientist, although the film does not condemn him for his actions, as he too is driven by the desire to do good and save his own son. His son, however, prefers damnation and rejects the father's authority. The son's final sin is, logically, Patricide, the ultimate sin as a rejection of God the Father. The killer thus has no hope of redemption. There is a moment, however, as the killer faces a psychic woman, when he betrays a flickering, gestural touch of doubt when confronted by one who knows his secrets and can see into his soul. The

psychic says that he can stop if he chooses to, and he replies that he cannot — he has accepted his fate as an agent of Satan. Evil cannot change its course once the surrender to it has been affected.

In the end, in a special effects extravaganza, the Devil faces off with the Divine, as the killer faces the profiler in the killer's underground lair beneath a condemned showground ironically named "Wonderland," one reminiscent of the horrendous underground lair beneath 'Namland in *The Texas Chainsaw Massacre 2*. The profiler, ordained as an agent of God (and therefore beyond reproach), shoots the killer and restores God's law, Patriarchy's authority and the unity of the family. He is the true deliverer, and the film is an examination of patriarchal responsibility. The killer is impaled on his own sculpture, which he calls his monument to Hell, in an equation of the killer and the artist that would saturate the genre from the mid–1990s.

Hideaway examines the consequences of resuscitative medicine, also explored in Cronenberg's *The Dead Zone*, and the afterlife experience brought back into reality theme of Schumacher's *Flatliners*. But what remains unstated throughout the film is Goldblum's potential identification with the killer when he sees through his eyes — an initial empathetic experience he must control and deny and purge. Thus he sees himself kill a teenage girl, but is shocked and repulsed by the action, as if he must prove himself beyond the contagious lure of such Evil: the good Father beyond such abhorrent temptation. Hence, the visions are symbolically induced through pain, but the stronger a force of Good he becomes, the more he can heal his self-inflicted wounds, with the momentary pain a necessity in combating the abhorrent. His adjustment is to a new spiritual truth, which paradoxically is akin to the process of paranoid schizophrenic

Top: Serial Killer Vassago (Jeremy Sisto) tries to seduce and lure Regina (Alicia Silverstone) after being led to her by a psychic link with her father in *Hideaway* (Tristar, 1993). *Bottom:* The serial killer (Jeremy Sisto) poses at the edge of his underground lair/studio in *Hideaway* (Tristar, 1993).

psychosis—a realm of perception beneath the everyday.

Flashes of violence and mutilation seduce the killer, as he sees his victims, and his world, in those terms only. Tellingly, his pick-up line is to ask young women to go with him in order to "feel something." He is so starved for sensation that he has taken to sex murder as self-actualization, to feel alive, an expression he considers honest and integral in the act of creating his sculpture—Hell on Earth. Art, religion and sex murder. The surrender to illicit sensation is a potential surrender to Satan, a theme also explored around the same time (though in a vastly different context) in Hackford's *The Devil's Advocate*.

Novelist Dean R. Koontz, however, despised the film and wanted his name removed from the credits. Critically, it fared even worse. Director Leonard went on to tackle serial killers and special effects again in *Virtuosity*, though he remains best known for the virtual reality update of *Charly* that was *The Lawnmower Man*. The religious subtext, and an inverse meditation on the execution of a serial killer, would infiltrate Walker's script for *Seven*.

The Hillside Stranglers

(1989: d. Stephen Gethers) aka *Case of the Hillside Stranglers*

scr. Gethers; ph. Ronald M. Lautore; m. Gil Melle; ed. Debra Neil; prod d. Peter Wooley; cast. Billy Zane, Dennis Farina, Richard Crenna; 100m

This tele-movie is based on the real-life Los Angeles killer cousin team of Kenneth Bianchi and Angelo Buono (Zane and Farina). Zane and his cousin share a mutual delight in the subjugation and sadistic torture of young women (even children, in actuality), and team together for repeated rape and murder. Zane is apprehended when he tries a similar crime on his own in an attempt to prove himself to

his cousin. In custody, he sees a movie about multiple personality disorder and fakes this illness, although he implicates his cousin.

The film begins with the killers on the prowl, and it seeks to explore their pre-planned methods (they bring a murder/rape kit with them in anticipation and have a lure ready—they pretend to be undercover policemen). However, it scrupulously avoids any detailed depiction of what the killer pair did with the victims, instead concentrating on the aftermath as a challenge for the dedicated detective (Crenna). It neglects to explore the killer's motivations and does not offer any explanation of how their joint decision to become killers may have occurred, although it implicates the older, sterner Farina as the dominant partner, with Zane almost as an obedient son in the pursuit of sadistic pleasure.

The film actually serves to contrast the bad father (Farina) with the good (Crenna) in scenes that show them with their respective families. It is the socially sanctioned duty of the good patriarch to punish the bad patriarch and son. The good patriarch is dedicated to the protection of the innocent (women and children) and to the restoration of family order. It is the bad patriarch's dissatisfaction with conventional, repressive morality that feeds his desire. He can only express his power through sexual dominance, a sadism that proves equally addictive for the weak-willed uncharacterized Zane. Any attack on Farina's pride, on his image of himself as powerful and superior to all, is enough to send him into a prowling rage, seeking an innocent, weaker victim to kill in order to reassert his superiority.

Pride is, after all, the Devil's sin, and undue pride warps the soul and must be purged from society. It is this pride, when it spreads from Buono to Bianchi, that dooms them, as Bianchi attempts the crime on his own as an attempt to prove his maturity, saying, "See Angelo, I don't need you anymore." The good father can recognize the warped effect of such selfish pride, and it is his duty to police it.

Zane's Bianchi is a moral vacuum who lacks even that reasoned motive, being merely a sexual sadist and disciple of the older Farina. His lack of moral identity makes it easier for him to playact and assume roles when he is captured. His inner emptiness enables him to seek definition via sexual homicide (hence he repeatedly pesters Farina to go in search of more victims) and to deny responsibility. He is forever in a state of seemingly arrested development, an adolescent who indulges his abhorrent lusts without conscience, and who, when caught, seeks to avoid responsibility by increasingly elaborate fabrications.

This routine procedural tele-movie is much milder than it should have been. It is a lightweight account which fails to explore the joint psychology beyond the duo's petty bravado. Gether's script was based on true-crime accounts of the case. It follows the details, but with a minimum of interest, offering only rudimentary characterization. In that, in can be compared to the tele-movie made about Richard Ramirez, *Hunt for the Night Stalker*. A better instance of character portrait in the tele-movie style is found in Brian Dennehy's role as John Wayne Gacy in *To Catch a Killer*.

The Hollywood Strangler Meets Skid Row Slasher

(1979: d. Ray D. Steckler)

scr, pr. Steckler; m. Henri Price; cast. Pierre Agostino, Chuck Alford, Carolyn Brandt, Forrest Duke; 72m

The strangler, a photographer who cruises Hollywood taking pictures of women, kills young female models; the slasher, a female porn-store employee, kills winos and other derelicts. They meet and romance, foreshadowing Bechard's *Psychos in Love*. Most remarkable is the fact that there is no police presence, no news coverage of the disappearances, and no bodies are found, thus depicting an uncaring world where killers roam at will.

In their motives, the killers jointly reflect the sexual component and the sense of moral superiority which characterize many serial killers. As the two killers find solace in each other, these two motives are shown to be complimentary bedfellows. The film, however, is a cult curiosity and difficult to locate.

The Honeymoon Killers

(1970: d. Leonard Kastle)

scr. Kastle; pr. Warren Steibel; ph. Oliver Wood; ed. Stan Warnow, Richard Brophy; prod man. Mike Haley; m. Gustav Mahler; cast. Shirley Stoler, Tony Lo Bianco, Mary Jane Higby, Doris Roberts, Kip McArdle, Marilyn Chris, Donna Duckworth, Barbara Cason, Ann Harris, Elsa Raven; 106m

This is a bleakly hilarious, much analyzed true story, originally set to have been directed by Martin Scorsese. An obese nurse (Stoler) and her gigolo lover (Lo Bianco) plan to rob and kill rich lonely ladies. The gigolo charms them, forever incurring the sexual jealousy of the nurse. They are finally caught and executed after the nurse turns them in, going to their deaths together.

Filmed mostly in long takes and with a static camera, *The Honeymoon Killers* veers between documentary and black comedy effortlessly. Tracks and pans are motivated to search for characters. The stationary camera thus explores spaces between characters. This tonal balance led later revisionist critics to claim the film as one of the first postmodern non-judgmental looks at the serial killer phenomenon. It certainly has a controversial impartiality, and effectively uses the case study to

The killer couple: The nurse (Shirley Stoler) hands a murder weapon to her gigolo lover/accomplice (Tony Lo Bianco) in *The Honeymoon Killers* (1970).

contextualize its look at almost unrepentant aberration.

Peary felt (p. 141) that the film stressed a kind of claustrophobia, with characters most often set indoors in predicaments which act as irritants. With the exception of one woman, the victims are generally unlovable (as were those in *Monsieur Verdoux*). There is no sympathy for anyone in this world, and as the film goes on, the only hint of genuine communication is in the bond shared by the killer couple, as if that itself was a redemptive force despite their crimes.

The film was considered to satirize the notion that no one is complete without a partner, as indeed the lonely are the innocent, and it is the desire to be part of a "couple" which ultimately dooms them,

and indeed makes the nurse a monster. The only loving couple depicted are the killers, themselves far from monstrous in their love for one another. The tone is therefore one of subversive humor, attacking contemporary ideology and partially initiating the 1970s disillusionment with popular ideology and cinematic forms and heroes and values.

Stoler is driven by the fantasy of suburban domesticity, urging her mate to set up house in the San Francisco suburbs. The gigolo, however, loathes this existence, as it is for him a stifling challenge to his own identity (forged in a deliberate challenge to romantic convention — the lethal Casanova), and urges her to resume the seduction and kill pattern. This they do with a renewed vigor, as it clearly has become an expression of their joint sexuality, even though they claim to kill for financial reasons. They exchange knowing glances throughout their deceptions, excited by manipulation and murder. However, the prospect of killing a child proves too much for Stoler to bear, as it is perhaps the ultimate act of monstrosity, done with a coldness that reveals it as an act that destroys their passion. No longer sexually united in their plans, the game is over, and all that is left is to die together. There is no more role-playing.

In this way the American Dream is reduced to a dysfunctional, bland suburban monstrosity — the home as murder site. Although there is an element of social rebellion in their homicidal means, Lo Bianco still refers to it as his "work," and so it becomes a corruption of the American work ethic. The functional and the pathological are combined. The film intends to gleefully subvert the dominant sociopolitical and cultural values of the time, as disillusionment was seeping into the process of social change. They are not revolutionaries, however, but the warped products of cultural expectations and gender roles.

Stoler is a sexual hypocrite, first seen admonishing a couple for having sex on the job, but secretly prone to romantic fantasies to fill the void. She is insanely jealous and possessive of her man (to the point of paranoia and suicide), who in turns claims devotion to her, with other contacts purely in the line of work they indulge in together. She is as blinded by her fantasies as are the victims by theirs, and her paramount fear is that of rejection. Ironically, it is as close to a gesture of love on Lo Bianco's part as he can get that he does not cheat on her, professing an undying love. He does not even reject her when they go to their deaths. Thus, amidst the monstrousness of their actions is a compassion for and commitment to one another that unites these grotesques against the world —

a theme developed more in the remake, *Deep Crimson.*

The male, although a sexual predator, is not a serial killer until he falls in with the woman he professes to love. It is love, and what it is supposed to mean, which corrupts, turning the protagonists into killers who follow their homicidal exploits with lovemaking, as if turned on by the murder of innocents. Murder is an accepted part of their lives, and there is no effort to develop the police procedural, except at the end as an inevitability to such a course of action. Although the film does not condemn its characters, it does not celebrate them, and shows the crimes as truly horrific.

Kastle was a forty-year-old composer, here making his directorial debut. His ironic use of classical music to underscore the murders was much remarked upon. Kastle had apparently always planned it as an art movie (Peary, p. 140), but it was marketed as exploitation. He had written the screenplay after researching the real 1940s Lonely Hearts killers Beck and Fernandez. Unfortunately, Kastle never made another movie. The same case was tackled in the exceptional Mexican film, *Deep Crimson.*

Hampered by inadequate distribution and inappropriate marketing, *The Honeymoon Killers* was expected to fade from sight quickly, until it earned praise from *Variety.* Pauline Kael, however, despised the film. Many subsequent critics have latched onto it as a landmark — see the anthology volume *Mythologies of Violence,* which attempts to posit the film as the start of the modern psycho-movie (which it isn't) and as the start of a new attitude to the subject matter (which it perhaps is). It is still an obscure movie, and its overall influence on film is debatable. Indeed, it arguably develops the black humor of *Pretty Poison* (as cited by *Variety*), and avoids the studied Romanticism of *Bonnie and Clyde*. The notion of the killer couple would also infiltrate the classic *Badlands*. Retrospective interest in the film continues to grow, enhancing its reputation with the knowledgeable, but perhaps not with general audiences. Thus, it is a steady darling of the cult scene.

Horror Show

(1989: d. James Isaac) aka *House III*

scr. Allyn Warner (as Alan Smithee), Leslie Bohem; pr. Sean S. Cunningham; ph. Mac Ahlberg; m. Harry Manfredini; ed. Edward Anton; prod d. Stewart Campbell; cast. Lance Henriksen, Brion James, Rita Taggart, Deedee Pfieffer, Thom Bray, Matt Clark; 95m

This was originally an entry in the innocuous *House* franchise of horror comedies, but in the final cut it was considered too strong for the intended young audience of those films.

A killer (James) is executed and then brought back to life as an electric current (à la *Shocker* and even *Ghost in the Machine*). Thus reincarnated, the killer current finds home in a basement furnace, from where he attacks the family of the policeman (Henriksen) responsible for his capture. The cop is framed for new murders and driven to hallucination and nightmare as he attempts to solve the mystery.

The original director was New Zealander David Blyth, but he was replaced by Isaac due to presumed creative differences after a week. The tone of the film is more in keeping with producer Cunningham, best known for unleashing the slasher hit *Friday the 13th*.

House of Mortal Sin

(1975: d. Pete Walker) aka *Confessional Murders*

scr. David McGillivray; stry. Walker; pr. Walker; ph. Tony Imi; m. Stanley Myers; ed. Matt McCarthy; art d. Chris Burke; cast. Anthony Sharp, Susan Penhalington, Stephanie Beacham, Norman Eshley, Sheila Keith, Mervyn Johns, Bill Kerr; 104m

This time, Walker and McGillivray tackle the Catholic Church in a sardonic tale of a killer priest who strangles promiscuous women (representatives of the permissive society he despises), including those who come to him for guidance and who arouse his repressed sexuality. He tape-records confessions and uses them as blackmail to attain control over the lives of those he tries to save, killing them when his control and power over them is threatened. He lives with his invalid mother, who fears him, and a sadistic housekeeper (Keith), who desires him sexually.

House of Mortal Sin is the follow up to the bleak *Frightmare*, and completes, alongside the earlier *House of Whipcord*, an anti–Establishment trilogy. It has a certain mockingly subversive spirit in scenes that implicate Catholic iconography in murder — the confessional is used as a means of examining prospective victims, a rosary is used to strangle a woman, poisoned communion wafers are given to dispatch the unwanted. The killer priest is warped by repression, transforming his guilt at sexual arousal into resentment and violence. However, he seems unaware of his condition, and so is insane, convinced of his own righteousness, making this an indictment of religious elitism.

He is another monstrous patriarch, and cumulatively corrupts a younger, more liberal priest in touch with the new generation into preserving the horror he represents. This younger priest goes through a crisis of conscience, but, like the demented older man, is convinced that covering up such murder would protect the higher sanctity of the church, and that the older priest is not really responsible after all. Faith blinds those who serve it to the monstrousness within them, which they paradoxically aspire to be freed from. The

Church, fostering repression, is complicit in sex murder.

The female victims are those who have fallen through the new social permissiveness, a world of crumbling relationships and a paradoxical lack of communication, themes also found in the early 1970s British horrors, especially the work of Peter Collinson and Robert Fuest. In a society no longer in transition but facing the aftermath of moves towards liberation, one must face a demented Patriarchy determined to reassert itself at all costs. It is a world of social and physical entrapment (the film cunningly cutting from the confessional to a phone box, both attempts at communication that entrap the individual). The innocents are those who desperately seek an emotional connection in a world which paradoxically praises and denies this. Wronged women look to Patriarchy for support, but the father they find only stalks, torments and kills them — punishing rather than saving them, as he would assert. Children who seek religious counseling leave sobbing.

The killer priest wants to control and possess the object of his desire, and is prepared to go to immoral, manipulative lengths to maintain control, resorting to murder when this control is threatened. He is willing to kill to maintain his ideals, a belief in the need for repression as a civilizing force — the very definition of Patriarchy as put forward. However, this repression only fosters homicidal madness and hypocrisy. The young priest, who supports reform (the lenience of celibacy rules in particular), does not have the strength to fight the weight of tradition.

The priest, too, feels a need to confess when his desires (which he refers to as the old temptations) return. He chooses to confess to his mother, whom he claims is responsible for his return to the priesthood and thus for his mental instability and problems. This mother is far from a monster, however, and, wheelchair-bound and dependent on others, has been living in fear of her son for years. This is the film's real note of horror and pity, as her son is driven to matricide. There is more sympathy for this character, the helpless mother, than there is for any other in Walker's entire horror output.

Ironically, contrary to most horror films, mother is the real victim, unlike the demented matriarch of *Frightmare*, although that film's star (Keith) returns here as the mother's sadistic nurse. Indeed, the film is structurally a variation on the character situation in *Frightmare*: sisters, a young patriarch come between them, one involved with a monster. Keith's final revelation, of resenting the mother who steered her beloved into the priesthood and thus sexual unattainability, is testament further to the film's theme of love perverted into madness. Consequently, the killer murders women who remind him of his youthful lost love (Keith) — they are surrogates for the one woman. Although he finally purges Keith as a lost object, he is still entrapped by desire.

Hunt for the Night Stalker

(1991: d. Bruce S. Green) aka *Manhunt: Search...*

scr. Joseph Gunn; pr. Joel Fields; exec pr. Leonard Hill, Ron Gilbert; ph. Stan Taylor; ed. Mark Rosenbaum; m. Sylvester LeVay; prod d. Barbara Dunphy; cast. Richard Jordan, A. Martinez, Lisa Eilbacher, Julie Carmen, Alan Feinstein; 93m

This tele-movie is about the two LA detectives, Frank Salerno (Jordan) and Gil Carillo (Martinez), who tracked Satanic California serial killer Richard Ramirez. Based on a true story, it was shown on the day that Ramirez' death sentence was announced, an outcome it does not dispute, the killer here being a barely characterized monster.

This is a routine procedural, and

Ramirez is shown as just another prowling boogeyman until the last few minutes. The killings are inexplicably random, and so it's a puzzling case for the compassionate detectives, who, as the killings mount, are assigned to head a task force and deal with an unusually sympathetic journalist who understands ethical responsibilities. The detectives, having had serial killer experience before (and are thus closer to profilers), intuit that there is only one offender and seek the corresponding proof.

The killer is part of an underclass (as is the killer in *Henry: Portrait of a Serial Killer 2* especially). He lives in skid row dumps, high on dope, forever listening to heavy metal as an added impetus (a theme also in the heavy metal fantasy–inspired killer of *Blue Vengeance*), with rotting teeth and no concern for personal hygiene. His strikes against the middle class are as much social resentment as they are self-indulgence. However, the film is weary of depicting him as any kind of social revolutionary. He lacks any ideological basis for his rebellion, and although it is suggested that his crimes were a means of social empowerment, and thus sexual expression, the killer does not realize this. He thinks he kills merely because he wants to, that he likes seeing people die, and that he is serving Satan. His lack of insight undercuts the significance of his acts as a potential expression of sociopolitical discontent. He is consumed by selfish pride, boasting that he is bigger than the Hillside Stranglers because he killed more victims. He wants to be the ultimate killer, part of an elite club, and so transcend his social limitations.

As a tele-movie with true crime origins, *Hunt for the Night Stalker* can be compared to *The Hillside Stranglers* and *To Catch a Killer*, though it lacks the sociological perspective allowed by the mini-series format, as in *Atlanta Child Murders* and *Deliberate Stranger*.

I Dismember Mama

(1972: d. Paul Leder) aka *Poor Albert and Little Annie*

scr. William Norton; pr. Leon Roth; ph. William Swenning; cast. Zooey Hall, Geri Reishl, Joanne Moore Jordan, Greg Mullavey, Marlene Tracy, Frank Whiteman; 78m

The title is supposedly the best thing about this minor horror film from an exploitation director with some longevity, if not a reputation.

An escaped mental patient wants to kill the rich mother who committed him and cancelled his inheritance. Along the way, he is driven to kill "impure" (sexually attractive and independent) women. He becomes enamored of the housekeeper's nine-year-old daughter. She goes with him voluntarily, although the police think she has been kidnapped. It builds to a climax set in a house of mannequins (anticipating *Tourist Trap* and *Maniac*).

The killer is outwardly calm (Hardy, p. 264), but his depravity comes through in sexual violence. The film raises the question of the girl's complicity and awareness of the monster, and her own pre-adolescent sexual awareness of the substitute father that is the killer. Hence, it treats the relationship between man and child as a pedophilic perversion of family values, raising an aspect of subversive social satire. However, by accounts the film fails to embrace its promise. The subtext has more interest and longevity than the film.

I, Monster

(1970: d. Stephen Weeks)

scr. Milton Subotsky; pr. Subotsky; ph. Monty Grant; m. Carl Davis; art d. Tony Curtis; cast. Christopher Lee, Peter Cushing, Richard Hurndall, George Merritt, Mike Raven; 75m

A doctor experiments on himself with a drug that lowers inhibitions. In the process, he becomes the monstrous Blake, who is more physically deformed with each transformation. Finally, Blake is reduced to an animal, trying to kill a friend who knows of his guilt, but falling to his death.

Though a low budget attempt to update the Jekyll and Hyde mythos to the end of swinging 1960s London and the theme of generational resentment (also found in the films of Michael Reeves) *I, Monster* is still bound by period dictates, content to use the Victorian London streets and streetwalkers to suggest the murky world of Jack the Ripper, the old standby. However, it seeks to contrast this to the aristocratic clubs whose inhabitants debate the virtues of repression and Freud. Indeed, the film is an attempt to show the repercussions of the lowering of inhibition as the destructive consequence of the advance of psychoanalysis.

Unlike the protagonist of *Dr. Jekyll and Sister Hyde*, for example, Christopher Lee is in the tradition of the decadent aristocrat, more in keeping with his portrayal of Count Dracula than to previous depictions of Dr. Jekyll. Indeed, the casting of Peter Cushing as his ideological adversary, and thus the equivalent of Van Helsing (the symbolic preserver of civilization and hence repression), further recalls their numerous Hammer antagonisms.

Civilization is acknowledged as the voluntary repression of desires for the common good. Evil is a selfish sensorial abandon to desire. This desire invariably involves sexual homicide. The sex killer, by violating the two great social taboos of sex and death, is presented as the greatest threat to civilization and thus a descendent worthy of DeSade. However, the film resorts to convention and depicts this sex killer as physically deformed, and thus bestial after all, removed from the realms of humanity he was supposed to explore. Experience is damnable. Psychoanalysis only looses the bestial and ultimately provides no understanding of the human condition beyond the acknowledgement of a corrupted baser instinct. The film is intended as a cautionary lesson to those who feel that the release of desires leads to a greater understanding: a reaction against the permissive society.

The compound that the doctor gives his patients, allowing them hallucinatory insight into their own mind, is akin to LSD experimentation, and is capable of inducing good and bad trips, depending on the individual. Exposure to the joys of such a liberating drug brings only the madness of self-indulgent, ultimately meaningless transgression for its own sake. There is no liberation of the soul to be found in the surrender to desire or the freedom from constraint. However, the very emptiness of such sensual abandon is addictive and hence a double threat to the proper operations of Patriarchy. Lee claims such experimentation frees the mind from the policing superego, but it merely redefines it as self-preservatory servant of the liberated id.

"Liberation" results in a random series of crimes, escalating to sex murder, done for the pure joy of committing the crimes. Ironically, the drug-induced, deformed protagonist is named Blake, suggesting that the film also seeks to deny the romantic surrender to a glorified insanity as a liberation of the mind. It produces only ugliness, and Patriarchy is more than justified in eliminating such desire, born in bestial fantasies of transcendence, the film asserts.

The film was begun in 3D, but this was soon dropped. The only scene which would have benefited from this process is the opening shot of a pair of Siamese twin fetuses floating in a specimen jar, intended as an apt symbol of the human psyche in the Jekyll/Hyde mythos.

Ice House

(1969: d. Stuart McGowan) aka *Love in Cold Blood*

pr. Dorrell McGowan; cast. Sabrina, Robert Story, David Story, Scott Brady, Jim Davis, Kelly Ross, Nancy Dow; 85m

A serial killer of women, especially strippers, works in an ice house, where he brings back the bodies for storage. He kills women who reject or snub his advances, resenting what he feels is a cocky attitude slighting him and his sexual prowess. In the process of being investigated, he kills the investigating officer, his own twin brother, and takes his place in the manhunt, then quits the police force and resumes killing.

To maintain his perceived mastery over the situation, he must kill those who reject his efforts at domination. Rejection thus reenforces misogyny and hatred, and rationalizes murder as retribution and the assertion of an otherwise inadequate self. He becomes a powerful man only through the domination and control of others through sex murder.

Impulse

(1979: d. William Grefe)

scr. Tony Crechales; pr. Socrates Ballis; cast. William Shatner, Ruth Roman, Harold Sakata, Kim Nicholas, Jennifer Bishop, James Dobbs, Marcie Knight; 89m

This is an odd obscurity. A child witnesses his mother being abused and stabs the male abuser. Cut to the grown William Shatner, now a paranoid gigolo and con artist who seduces lonely women, obtains their money, and, when the good living runs out, kills them and moves on. When a woman rejects him, he is overcome with anger and kills her, dumping her body in a car into a lake. He tries another woman, whose daughter becomes suspicious.

There is no explanation as to how the grown man has come to identify with the aggressor he loathed. He has come to fancy himself as a ladies man, and is threatened by any challenge or rejection, killing in an uncontrollable rage when provoked in order to preserve his self-image. He is conflicted about such incidents, at least initially, apparently believing that if he pretends that something didn't happen, then it didn't, and memories of it will go away, for all concerned. There is, at least initially, a sense of denial in his character, which he sheds as the film progresses, learning to be more calculatedly predatory. He thus tries to abandon his conscience (and his past) over the course of the film, but is unable to avoid hiding the confused and frightened child he sometimes reverts to. This is the intended theme, though it's barely expressed in the banal, routine direction.

Any reminiscences of, or referrals to, the seminal *Shadow of a Doubt* are in synopsis only, although the tentative links to real killer Earle Nelson are there. Shatner is considered to have overacted badly in this film, hence its Internet curiosity value for fans of terrible movies. Promise is once again undercut by the tired execution.

In Dreams

(1997: d. Neil Jordan)

scr. Jordan, Bruce Robinson; pr. Stephen Wooley; ph. Darius Khondji; m. Elliott Goldenthal; ed. Tony Lawson; prod d. Nigel Phelps; cast. Annette Bening, Aidan Quinn, Robert Downey Jr., Paul Guilfoyle, Dennis Boutsikaris, Stephen Rea; 120m

A married author of books for children has a seeming psychic link to a child-killer, causing her much torment. The police disbelieve her premonitions, and she fears for the life of her own child. When her own child is murdered, she is put away for psychiatric treatment when her behavior becomes increasingly erratic. Her visions have a basis in a drowned town, the site of the killer's childhood trauma as he was abandoned, left to drown there. She is finally driven to track the killer, whom she intuits spent time at the same hospital, when another child is kidnapped. The killer wants her to recreate his lost family, but in the end he kills her too. He is captured but found guilty-but-insane, and sentenced to a psychiatric hospital. He says he can deal with that, but is soon visited by violent hallucinations, seemingly the product of the protagonist's spirit, there to haunt and punish him for eternity.

This is a stylish psychodrama. The killer, of course, as a child was abused by his mother. The town (flooded for a reservoir) is a symbol of the unconscious mind shaped in a very real trauma, and the common ground that thus provides access to the killer's mind and dreams. It represents the point where individual memory becomes a collective experience accessed through dreams, the awareness of which is considered insanity, and the expression of which allows a closeness to a warped childishness. The killer is a case of arrested development, in part a victim of the adult world, which he correspondingly grows into as a misfit and escapee from the mental hospital where he was doomed to spend eternity. In that way, it is a companion piece to Jordan's *The Butcher Boy*, which mostly dispensed with the supernatural theme. Correspondingly, Jordan turns innocent nursery rhymes into menacing portents of doom, suggesting the sly menace in childhood experience which can manifest itself in aberrant actions.

In Dreams examines the overflow and interplay of dream, reality and their union in memory, as the mind is shaped by fear and the desire to integrate and understand the irrational when what was unconscious breaks through into the conscious. Life is lived in reaction to these traumatic forces, which can tear a solid mind apart. The scientific community is quick to dismiss the validity of her experiences and immediately seeks to label, qualify, and isolate her, as if she were a danger. Such insight into an aberrant mind is inherently an irrational experience which the rational society would seek to dismiss as mental illness. Hence the protagonist is subjected to a battery of physical tests (recalling the process inflicted upon the protagonist in *The Exorcist*) to search for organic, recognizable explanations for perceptual and behavioral change. What society terms madness is, however, a valid if inexplicable experience, with a haunting and perverse beauty all its own.

The killer says that he wants a family but is driven to destroy what he professes to need. He is perpetually childlike, shaped by a traumatic fear of abandonment, and correspondingly seeking to recapture the adolescence denied him. He thinks as a spoiled child in an oedipal haze and desperately wants the protagonist to love him as she would her husband. His sex crimes against children are thus a measure of the emergence of an adult sexuality he can no longer deny. As he can relate only to children, he seeks to dominate and manipulate them. Until his encounter with the protagonist, whom he sees as the solution to his emotional and sexual lack, he cannot incorporate adult sexuality into the spectrum and has so given to eroticize children. He is a pedophile for whom all grown women are reminders of the loathed and desired mother who abandoned him.

The film was considered an elegant disappointment from an established talent. Co-scripter Robinson had written and directed the intriguing serial killer film *Jennifer 8*, which featured a killer also tormented by childhood rejection (by a desired object). In addition, *In Dreams* has some parallel to Vincent Ward's afterlife fantasy *What Dreams May Come* released the same year, a return to Romanticism which also failed with both the critics and the public.

In the Cold Light of Day

(1994: d. Rudolf van den Berg) aka *The Cold Light of Day*

scr. Friedrich Duerrenmatt; pr. Haig Brouwer, Arnold Heslenfeld; ph. Igor Luther; ed. Kant Pan; cast. Richard E. Grant, Roger Sloman, Thom Hoffman, Gerard Thoolen, Heathcote Williams, Lynsey Baxter, Simon Cadell, Joanna Dickens; 107m

Somewhere in "a sleepy province in Eastern Europe," a series of child murders is blamed on a dope-fiend. A brutal policeman searching for political advancement forces the suspect into a confession. Another policeman (Grant) believes the killer is still around. When the suspect hangs himself, it is taken as a tacit admission of his guilt. The policeman resigns, a move supported by a local psychiatrist, who becomes a trusted friend when Grant pursues the investigation on his own, now officially an outsider — he balances his investigation with the desire to understand the pedophile killer's mindset, and is thus a bridge between investigator and profiler. He hires a small petrol station in order to take note of the passing cars, as he believes a killer travels to the woods from a local town. He befriends a little girl and her mother, letting them move into his house, at first as bait for the killer, a doctor who indeed falls for the bait and tries to lure the girl to her doom. The protagonist must balance his intent to capture the killer with his growing love for the woman and her daughter, for whose protection he accepts responsibility. Tragedy becomes possible as he faces his shortcomings. The woman also vacillates between suspicion and trust. When the killer lures the girl away again, Grant confronts him. The mother finally shoots the killer, proving herself a worthy protector after all.

When the dead, naked body of a girl is found, Grant has the duty to tell the parents, whereupon he is pressured into promising them that he will catch the killer. He wants to focus on child molesters, but is restricted by official channels. It is as an elaboration of Patriarchy's responsibility that the film underlines. Hence, there are varied father figures and substitutes throughout — the victim's distraught father, the policeman (responsible for the death of the suspect's own father, and who feels such abhorrence runs in the family), the doctor/killer and the protagonist. The protagonist is the bridge between these sanctioned roles within Patriarchy. But this is Eastern Europe, and the get-tough-on-crime mentality is bound in local politics (a theme also found in *Citizen X*), so the protagonist is forced to continue the pursuit of truth as an outsider to the system, although he represents the hope for its proper functioning.

With the pedophilic serial killer as the ultimate threat to Patriarchy from within, the protagonist — as fusion of investigator and profiler (he regularly consults his friend, a psychiatrist) — is the potential solution to the problem. However, he must remain in control over the situation. Hence, the film charts his effort to keep in control in parallel with the killer's similar attempts to maintain control over the situation as he perceives it. This control centers on the treatment of the little girl. Both protagonist and killer are willing to assume responsibility for the little girl's future. Grant feels that he is her protector and is justifiably using her to eliminate the threat to her future growth into the adult world. The killer considers the adult world to be sexually perverse and corrupt, and feels that by killing the girl he can save her pure soul from that horrible future. In that mindset, he can deny the sexual pleasure in his murder of innocents. Both characters react harshly to a threat against their perceived control. Of this, the psychiatrist adds, "It doesn't take much for a man to be a beast," hence the film's use of the woods and the killer's hand-puppet — a dog — to suggest the proximity to a bestial threat. This is, of course, recognition of the serial-killer-as-wolf motif common to European horror in particular.

The killer is trapped in an arrested development. Unable to deal with adult sexuality, he seeks to regress into his idealized state and so become a child again. That this is a sexual dysfunction is clear from two scenes. In one he looks in the mirror and carefully shaves his pubic hair in order to duplicate a pre-adolescent sexual growth (a futile process); and in the second he sits in his underwear surrounded by child mannequins, talking to them as if playing with imaginary friends. His play turns violent, however, when even in his fantasy he fears that his playmates will leave him. He responds as a child would, but in his adult life he holds onto a surface professionalism, although his hand is seen to caress a little girl's exposed abdomen in a shot which slyly reveals the potential for a child to be seen as an erotic object.

Indeed, the film was noted for its subtle sexualization of the daughter to give a glimpse of seeing the world through the pedophile killer's sensibilities. This is carefully controlled, however, and balanced with the protagonist's regular consultations with the psychiatrist, which function both as a means of gaining insight into an aberrant mindset and a self-regulating means to ensure that such understanding does not lead to his approximation of the killer's own desires. This possibility is toyed with, and is an inherent part of the "control" the protagonist constantly asserts he has over every aspect of the situation. He clearly doesn't have this control, as the killer is (even when his presence is known to the protagonist) able to lure the girl away from him. The protagonist considers himself a protector and is able to distract the killer, although it is ultimately the girl's mother who kills the pedophile threat. In part, the film functions as the study of two men's reaction to the process of eroticizing children, and the choice, deliberate or innate, whether to suppress such desires or to foster them. To foster them is perceived as an unnatural development.

The film is actually a remake of the German movie *It Happened in Broad Daylight*. *In the Cold Light of Day* is an extremely rare film in its careful depiction of the dynamics of the interaction between pedophile killer and the child he approaches over time. He does not kill immediately; he slowly gains the child's trust in a process of seduction, with the child's murder as a consummation. He is not content with his mannequins and must seek out real children to satisfy his fantasies. His interaction with, and seduction of, these children are the closest he can get to his fantasy of a return to childhood. He cannot escape his sexual desires, killing victims in an attempt to deny his own aberrance as much as he professes to preserve their childhood.

In the Company of Darkness

(1992: d. David Anspaugh)

scr. John Leekley; pr. Richard Brams; ph. Sandi Sissel; m. Tim Truman; ed. David Rosenbloom; prod d. Robb Wilson King; cast. Helen Hunt, Jeff Fahey, Steven Weber, Juan Ramirez, Dan Conway; 97m

This is a tele-movie that claims to be inspired by real events. A rookie policeman (Hunt) goes undercover as a barmaid in order to lure a serial killer. She becomes his girlfriend, slowly gaining his trust to the point where he confesses his crimes to her, intending to initiate her as his accomplice. Throughout, he has believed himself to be in control, which Hunt accurately senses as the key to his psyche, and is unable to accept that he could have been so duped by a woman.

The film takes its premise of a lone

female officer in a male dominated profession from Jodie Foster's predicament in *Silence of the Lambs*. She goes from parking inspector to an officer experienced with domestic violence and forced to defend herself, to undercover officer, exploiting and mastering the very conception of a mild femininity that the other male officers associate with her. In that, she is shown to use male conceptions of femininity to effectively police their expectations and aberrance, in the process becoming enveloped into the dominant Patriarchy but still able to hold an identity of her own, though in reaction to the male world around her. It is part of the maturation process to recognize the malfunctioning and inequality of the system and do something about it.

She is an amalgam of investigator and profiler in that she seeks to gain incriminating evidence on the suspect, and observe, interpret and understand his behavior as the key to his psyche. She records the conversations, which are later replayed for a psychiatric evaluation/profile of the suspect. But for him to confide in her she must reveal part of herself to him, at least part of who she pretends to be — for he will never know. In the process, she gains insight and strength. The game she plays is to get the killer to confess, triggering his weaknesses, by pretending to have herself once killed someone. The perceived kinship attracts the killer, and it becomes a search for common ground. Hunt must finally purge this closeness to darkness from her heart by confronting the killer and telling him that she was duping him all along. However, by feigning love interest in such a man, she is in need of psychiatric therapy, her innocence gone.

In the process, the film depicts the overall blandness of the killer's humdrum life, as she realizes that murder provides him the excitement he otherwise lacks. He craves power (sexual power) over others

and kills to achieve it — it is a "fix" he needs to maintain his hold over his own stature and to ward off insignificance. This pettiness is the ultimate corruption, and Hunt at one stage feels that she needs to shoot this killer to purge his mindset from her own. This is, of course, the profiler's dilemma, ever since *Manhunter* especially. She realizes, however, that she has a responsibility to the law and a higher justice, and so dedicatedly seeks to lure the killer into an admission, which he makes as a means of demonstrating and sharing his power with another like him.

This is an engrossing work from a director more associated with the sports-themed movie *Hoosiers*. Short of its video release, however, it has not yet found an appreciative reception. Perhaps if Anspaugh is ever subject to reappraisal, this may prove a more intriguing work.

The two *When the Bough Breaks* movies further seek to explore the dilemmas facing a female profiler in a world of male killers. A central tension in these films is the extent to which the protagonist becomes an agent of the very Patriarchy that is in crisis and would initially suppress her.

In the Deep Woods

(1992: d. Charles Correll)

scr. Robert Nathan; ph. James Glennon; m. Sylvester Levay; ed. Mark Rosenbaum; prod d. Jonathan Carlson; cast. Anthony Perkins, Rosanna Arquette, Will Patton; 96m

A body is found in the woods and identified as one victim in a series of killings. The FBI are on the case, as is a sinister reporter (Perkins) who stalks a local woman (Arquette), intent on convincing her that her brother is a serial killer, although he may be trying to divert attention from where it should be. The FBI agent (the profiler) also develops an interest in Arquette as he investigates the crimes.

The killer assembles a murder kit and targets successful women, resentful of their independence and determined to punish them for it. It is almost as if such women magnetically attract insecure yet proud killers to them as a consequence of a perceived threat against the higher functioning of Patriarchy. Such women must be shown their place, a theme in many such films, perhaps especially in *Kiss the Girls*. This is also a displaced rage, the killer unable to (or unwilling to) kill the real object of his hatred and thus seeking surrogates.

The killer's method — he pretends to be crippled — recalls the real killer Ted Bundy; and the real killer Lawrence Bittaker used his means of torture (pliers). Ted Bundy is referred to several times by the characters, and the process of escalation in the killer's crimes (he attacks a dorm room) seems modeled on Bundy. And like the theories behind Bundy's murders, the victims are all surrogates for the one person, in this case the killer's sister (Perkins is right). The killer resents her, his mother's preferential treatment of her, and harbors incestuous desires which he ironically considers too loathsome to confront in himself, and so is driven to proxy as both punishment and denial. This ultimately cannot purge his desires, and his crimes escalate in desperation as he seeks to exorcise his own feelings, doomed to repeat the ultimately unsatisfactory ritual of murder endlessly. It is the object of illicit desire, the sister, who must purge such desire from Patriarchy and restore the proper family balance.

The film develops two profiler figures: the FBI agent assigned to the case and the intrusive reporter (Perkins) who claims to have an insight denied the conventional investigators. Of course, with such a casting choice for a character who justifies stalking as a means of forcing the truth, Perkins is a logical suspect in a film structured more as a whodunit. Interestingly and unusually, it is the object of desire, and not the profiler, who must purge the killer, a trait derivative of what Carol Clover calls the "final girl" in slasher films.

Incredible Torture Show
(1976: d. Joel M. Reed) aka *Bloodsucking Freaks*

scr. Reed; pr. Alan Margolin; ph. Gerry Toll; spec eff. Bob O'Bradovich; cast. Seamus O'Brien, Louie de Jesus, Niles McMaster, Viju Krim, Alan Dellay, Dan Fauci, Ernie Peysher, Lynette Sheldon; 88m

A stage magician, aided by a necrophiliac dwarf (who in one notorious scene uses a severed head as a sexual aid), runs a show involving the torture and mutilation of women as the cover for a sex-slave racket, with the women kept naked and hysterical in cages. It is a world of sex killers which has no conception of an alternative to aberration.

This infamously graphic piece of misogynistic violence is a serial killer film only insofar as the male participants spend the duration of the movie torturing, imprisoning and murdering women for their perverse sexual amusement. Their participation in aberration offers them self-definition through the sexual domination of their lessors. There is nothing in life beyond this. And none of the imprisoned women have substantially developed individual personalities — they exist solely for the pleasure and exploitation of men.

This film is indefensible on any level, and has correspondingly now become a minor cult movie. Perhaps it is best to consider it a demonstration of irredeemably sadistic male sexuality, and a visualization of a supposedly Sadean freedom. There is no attempt to ideologically explain or otherwise contextualize such atrocity. The meta-filmic component of the surrounding stage show is merely a token gesture towards the examination of the interplay of real and fictional violence.

The males indulge in perversity freely (severing fingers, throwing darts at a woman's genitalia, removing a victim's teeth for fear of being bitten during fellatio) as an unbridled expression of their innate sexuality. The film celebrates this, and the ending, wherein freed naked women indulge in cannibalism (eating the offending penis), is merely a gimmick along EC comic book lines. But as it shows that "woman" is inherently an animalistic force, practically incapable of reason or even thought, and thus deserved of such treatment, the finale lacks even the moral poetic justice of the EC tradition.

This is an uncomfortable film to sit through, but perhaps to say so is to unintentionally compliment it. There is no sense of purpose to its deliberately shocking nature, and it seems a throwaway product: atrocity as entertainment. It was banned in Australia for some time, and indeed poses a dilemma for censors everywhere. Its morbid comedy, however distasteful, undercuts any truly subversive potential it may once have had.

Incubus

(1980: d. John Hough)

scr. George Franklin; nvl. Ray Russell; pr. Marc Boyman, John M. Eckert; ph. Albert J. Dunk; cast. John Cassavetes, Kerrie Keane, Helen Hughes, John Ireland, Erin Flannery; 92m

Amidst a small community, women's corpses are found sexually violated, with large amounts of semen present. The local policeman investigates, suspecting a sex murderer but uncovering a potential supernatural force at work.

The opening suggests the film as nature's perception of human interaction, and that the killer is nature's revenge and even a consequence of sexual interaction. The first spoken word is "bitch," signaling the film's developed theme of man's apparent psychological need to subjugate women, the legacy of Puritanism perhaps, and allied to the passage into adulthood as an acceptance of the need for repression, to punish women for challenging such repression by their very sexuality.

This awareness brings a nightmare of homicidal fury to a male youth so afflicted. These sexualized nightmares (including a vivid torture chamber sequence) reflect the dawning of an innate desire to harm women, suggesting male adolescence as a time of guilt and madness at such conflicting emotions. These dreams are an insightful, heightened perception which spills over into the everyday (via wide-angle distorted shots), as if the awareness of an unconscious realm. The heightened sensory experience allies such awareness to schizophrenic processes (as an illness, schizophrenia generally has its onset in adolescence and early adulthood), though the movie does not consider such a mental illness.

Indeed, the film reveals such vision as the result of a psychic link to the sex killer, a woman/monster, as though women's sexuality were an innate monstrousness which drives men to kill them — man's awareness that their sexuality is manufactured in response to the dominant, evil woman. Correspondingly, and Hough leaves these alternatives tantalizingly ambiguous, the supernatural evil woman is the projection of all that is monstrous in men onto women, enabling them to deny their inherent masculine sexuality as abhorrence. Thus Hough has his male protagonists in some way acting against nature. The detective has near incestuous desires for his own daughter. Every touch between Cassavettes and his daughter is replete with the sense of sexual violation.

Her eventual murder suggests the killer (a supernatural evil-gendered female) reacting to secret male desires as a means of her own self-definition. Human sexuality is shown as a repugnant, violent

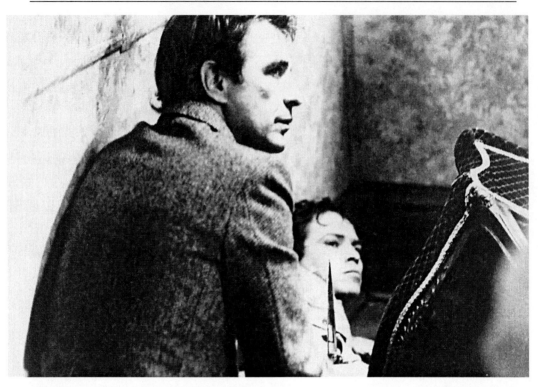

A distraught father and detective (John Cassavetes) must fight for himself and his family against the otherworldly terror of *The Incubus* (ARC, 1980).

interplay of resentment, denial and destructive urges—it is the taint of corruption, both natural and unnatural.

The movie's theme of an evil being able to take a human likeness is echoed in *The First Power, Fallen* and numerous possession-themed films, although *Incubus* suggests in tandem that it is internal pressures and insecurity which affect the emergence of the demon. Similar themes and an equation of supernatural Evil to murder was found in Craven's *Deadly Blessing*. Its implication of the town's founders in monstrosity also reflects Carpenter's *The Fog*.

It Happened in Broad Daylight

(1958: d. Ladislao Vajda)

scr. Vajda, Friedrich Duerrenmatt, Hans Jacoby; stry. Duerrenmatt; pr. Lazar Wechsier;

m. Bruno Canfora; cast. Heinz Ruhmann, Michel Simon, Roger Livesy, Gert Frobe, Berta Drews, Anita Van Ow, Maria Rosa Salgado, Barbara Haller; 97m

To solve a series of killings of young girls, a policeman travels to the region and searches for a child similar to the murdered girls. He finds one and stays with her and her mother in order to catch the killer, but does not inform them of why he is there. A suspect (Simon) commits suicide rather than face the stigma and shame of being branded as a child rapist/killer. The policeman is helped in his search by a psychiatrist (i.e. a profiler).

This Swiss-French co-production about a terrorized forest community (common in European serial killer narratives) draws out the unbearable tension and strain felt by all. It premiered at the Berlin Film Festival and was picked up for worldwide distribution on the basis of the timeliness of the child-killer theme (or so *Variety* felt). The film stresses the natural beauty of the location, in contrast to the horrendousness of the human actions contained within it.

Now hard to locate, it was effectively remade as the provocative *In the Cold Light of Day*, which paralleled the killer's obsession with control to that of the responsibility for the child's life shouldered by the protagonist.

Jack the Ripper

(1958: d. Robert Baker, Monty Berman)

scr. Jimmy Sangster; stry. Peter Hammond, Colin Craig; pr. Baker and Berman; ph. Berman; m. Stanley Black; ed. Peter Benzencenet; cast. Lee Patterson, Eddie Byrne, Betty McDowall, Ewen Solon, John Le Mesurier, George Rose, Philip Leaver, Barbara Burke; 84m

This version has an American detective brought in (i.e. the outsider/profiler figure) to track the suspects. Because of the rudimentary surgical basis to some of the mutilations, they suspect a doctor is responsible. The policeman falls in love with a woman whose uncle is a surgeon. The killer is revealed to be that surgeon, driven insane by venereal disease, who seeks to punish prostitutes and remove their "evil" from society. They are surrogates, in a sense, for the one woman who gave him the disease. After a final confrontation the killer dies in an elevator shaft (in the only scene shot in color in an otherwise black and white film).

The film begins in the midst of the action and depicts six murders before the end. It concentrates on the manhunt and procedural aspects of the investigation, as punctuated by the grisly murders. The romance between a visiting American detective and a local social worker anticipates *Off Limits* and even *Tightrope*. Unlike *The Lodger*, which attempted a psychological portrait of the killer, this film is more of a conventional mystery, withholding the killer's identity (enshrouding him in fog) as he commits his atrocities. The vengeance-for-VD theme was carried on in *Silent Sentence* and *The Ripper* (which had a member of the royal family so afflicted).

The killer combines an innate sense of his own superiority with his hatred and resentment of women. It is as if by eliminating the women whom he feels spread such a disease he can disavow it in himself. His actions cause a panic in the East End, as fear spreads over all. Murder is, in one sense, the consequence of rampant promiscuity and itself a sexually transmitted disease, the killer thus representing the course of the decline of civilization.

The film was given an X rating in the UK (no one under 16 allowed). In the United States, where the movie was considered formulaic, it played on a double-bill with *The Big Night*. Significantly, there is one scene (highlighted by Archer in his *New York Times* review) wherein the coroner criticizes the police as "incompetent, inadequate and inept." This attitude towards police allows the outside agent to evolve as a frequent character type, and so delineates the need for the profiler figure in subsequent serial killer investigations, where the police are ill-equipped to deal with such horrific and unknowable crimes.

Jack the Ripper

(1971: d. Jose Madrid)

scr. Madrid, Jacinto Molina, Sandro Continenza; pr. Madrid; ph. Diego Ubeda; m. Piero Piccioni; prod d. Juan Alberto Soler; spec eff. Antonio Molina; cast. Paul Naschy (Jacinto Molina), Patricia Coran, Rensso Marinano, Andrea Resino, Orqides de Santis, Franco Borelli, Irene Mir, Victor Iregua; 90m

This Spanish version offers some scenes shot in London. The crimes are relocated from Whitechapel to Soho, and updated to the 1970s. From the details of the crimes, police make the connection between the murders and the previous Ripper series. Scotland Yard investigates, implicating a police aid. The killer, the aid, collects body parts as souvenirs, hoarding them in the basement of a country residence. He is found there, amidst his trophies, and killed with the very weapon he used to disembowel his victims.

Each stabbing of an underdressed streetwalker is presented in almost identical manner, as a kind of chorus to the story, a punctuating beat. They are a constant through time, as though passed on through generations of imitators, each intent on perfecting the art. Star Naschy was better known for his werewolf series around the same time, and he became a genre icon in Spanish horror movies, which had limited popularity through Europe.

Jack the Ripper

(1976: d. Jess Franco)

scr. Franco; pr. Erwin Dietrich, Max Dara; ph. Peter Baumgartner; cast. Klaus Kinski, Josephine Chaplin, Herbert Fuchs, Ursuls von Wiese, Lina Romay; 108 (95)m

Franco depicts the infamous killer as a doctor and sex maniac whose mother was a whore, and who now feels compelled to abduct, torture, sexually mutilate (while they are still alive) and kill similar women. He has a complicit female assistant who dutifully disposes of the dismembered corpses by dropping them in the river Thames. A blind witness provides the most useful clues in the investigation. However, the detective seems more interested in his girlfriend than in the case. Finally, in part to protect his reputation, the girlfriend goes out alone to lure the Ripper. He kidnaps her, but the police arrive before he can finish his rape.

The vengeful aspect of this kind of motivation differs from outright misogynist hatred by virtue of a matricidal desire. He stabs women and then has necrophilic sex with the dying bodies in a gruesome series of scenes of sexual mutilation. As with the title character in Franco's *The Awful Dr. Orlof*, such sexual mutilation is the end result of the surgeon's natural progression as he sexualizes his profession, with perversity the only possible result. Benevolence masks hypocritical pathology. Star Kinski would explore this mindset further in *Crawlspace*.

The killer, a doctor, both despises and incestuously desires his whore-mother, whom he sees in hallucinations and hears forever laughing at him. Thus, he fears being mocked and lured by such women, and must punish them, cutting off their sexuality: he removes his victims' breasts—shown in graphic, unflinching detail as a kind of gore-porn. He has sex with the corpses, as he cannot function sexually in "normal" encounters. He kills when aroused (murdering a prostitute as she fellates him, and then, as a post-coital climax, mutilating her breasts).

It is arguable whether he craves a normal relationship, however, although he is capable of tenderness as well as rage towards the landlady who ceaselessly courts him. At times he seems torn between the potential for romantic love and the actuality of homicidal love: as is one of Franco's themes, the Romantic is perverted into the Sadean. That the Romantic is also a function of the Oedipal is Franco's sick joke, one among many. This Ripper is an old man facing the loneliness of age. He is presented with an alternative to his life, but is compelled to continue his destructive urges.

The facts of the case, however, have been almost totally dispensed with by Franco in the drive for greater shocks, resulting in total inaccuracy. Highly explicit, the film borders on the hard-core pornographic (indeed, Franco had started his hard-core films around the same time) and could perhaps have been an influence on the films of German director Jorg Butt-gereit (*Nekromantik* and *Schramm* especially). Love = death = punitive purification: sex murder as personal catharsis.

The killer's fear and resentment of women surface in sexual sadism, a theme prominent in Franco since *The Awful Dr. Orlof*. Indeed, the protagonists of both films are doctors, and Franco similarly eroticizes the act of surgical mutilation. Amidst images of naked and tortured women is the analysis of a man so repelled by desire that he seeks to eradicate it, unaware that this is a monstrous form of sexual indulgence. Consequently, the film was regarded as a rather cynical enterprise, lacking the director's more dedicated style (Tohill and Tombs, p. 117).

Structurally, it is similar enough to *The Awful Dr. Orlof* to be considered yet another remake, down to the scene of witnesses gathered together for a sketch artist to work out a description. Thus, it is evidence of Franco again reworking the formula of his most successful film, though not necessarily to altogether diminishing effect.

Jack the Ripper

(1988: d. David Wickes)

scr. Wickes, Derek Marlowe; ph. Alan Hume; m. John Cameron; ed. Keith Palmer; prod d. John Blezard, Tony Reading; cast. Michael Caine, Armand Assante, Michael Gothard, Ken Bones, Richard Morant, Ray McAnally (as Gull), Gerald Sim, Jane Seymour, Lysette Anthony, Harry Andrews, Susan George, Hugh Fraser; 200m

This television miniseries is considered a highly speculative version, as it introduces all the traditional suspects — the Queen's grandson, members of the Royal Court, mediums, physicians, anarchists, and a US actor — and puts their cases in context. Michael Caine plays the distraught Scotland Yard officer in charge of the case. The pace accelerates gradually, as the film

is an expanded detective story, charting the interconnectedness between the diverse suspects in their relation to each other and the crimes — all as an expression of the potential duality of people.

The duration of the Ripper crimes is considered a "reign of terror" unlike any other in history in that it was a new kind of crime and thus subject to comparatively lavish period recreation. Public pressure on government and police to solve the crimes leads to the appointment of a Scotland Yard inspector (i.e. the profiler as outside agent), as there is no faith in local police. For his part, the inspector realizes the crime is a new kind, and not committed for the usual motives (money or revenge), and realizes that the killer could be anyone. He believes such a killer has a mental imbalance of some sort and goes to an experienced doctor for added insight into the duality of such a killer or killers.

Correspondingly, the film is at lengths to bridge class conceptions, morality and socioeconomic factors in its treatment of the suspects. It knows that the Ripper's identity will remain unknown, and although it promises to identify him, it offers a cross-section of potential killers, all with a side hidden to normal view, partially implicating the restrictive and even hypocritical mores of the time in breeding such murderers. The taint of moral corruption affects all as it reflects a torn psyche seeking a transition beyond the moral status quo.

As it proceeds, the film seeks to incorporate as much of Ripper lore as possible, to be a document not only of the case but of the public response to it ever since. Hence, the detective is overly aware of the far-reaching social significance of the crimes, with a scope beyond mere murder. It is constructed as a tease for knowledgeable Ripper enthusiasts.

The killer is revealed to be a Queen's doctor, assisted by a coachman, with the crimes covered up lest the Royal connection be discovered (also a theme in *Murder by Decree*). This surgeon, William Gull, is a self-proclaimed expert in dementia praecox (the early term given to schizophrenia) whom the investigator consults over the course of the movie for his specialized psychiatric insight (i.e. he too is a profiler figure). Gull admits killing in a pseudo-scientific effort to comprehend why people want to kill—an effort at acquiring greater understanding of the depths of human capability: transgression as a means of transcendence. Ironically, he is blind to the sexual nature of the crimes as an expression of his own sexual rage, and is thus in denial about his own motives. He assigns guilt to his coachman accomplice, whom he considers a little man easily convinced by a strong man (an acknowledgment of the power structure behind dual killers) into performing sexual atrocities, although the coachman presumably experiences an enjoyment beyond the functional. The doctor, like the surgeon Dr. Knox in the numerous versions of the Burke and Hare tale, uses his loftier station and superior intellect to justify and excuse aberrant actions.

In an interesting note, one of the suspects is an American actor involved in a stage production of Jekyll and Hyde. The film thus makes clear the link between the Ripper mythos and the popularity of Stevenson's tale. Director Wickes did his miniseries version of *Jekyll and Hyde*, again with Caine, as a companion piece to this Ripper film, but it lacks the interest he was able to sustain here.

Jack's Back

(1987: d. Rowdy Herrington) aka *Red Rain*

scr. Herrington; pr. Tim Moore, Cassian Elwes; ph. Shelly Johnson; spec eff. John Naulin; cast. James Spader, Cynthia Gibb, Rod Loomis, Rex Ryon, Robert Picardo, Jim Haynie, Chris Mulkey; 96m

On the 100th anniversary of the Jack the Ripper slayings, a copycat killer with some surgical skill murders Los Angeles prostitutes. A doctor (Spader), who treats the poor, discovers his ex-girlfriend butchered after she came to see him seeking a late-term abortion. He blames a colleague, who protests his innocence and strangles Spader to protect it. Cut to: Spader's twin awakening from a dream in which he witnessed the killing. The police want to pin the crimes on the dead brother, so the twin seeks to clear the brother's name, in the process implicating himself. He finally unveils the killer as an older teacher/doctor—the perversion of the mentor.

The film accepts the role that the profiler plays in serial killer investigations as an assist, with the psychiatrist here observing (through a one-way mirror) the suspect's interrogation as regular procedure. However, the psychiatrist is an adjunct, called in to assess a potential suspect. The police are hampered by their desire to make a case stick no matter what, a theme explored in Herrington's later *Striking Distance*. It is up to the outsider to arrive at the truth and uncover the demented patriarch.

This killer is concerned for his power over those he considers underlings at the clinic, who make fun of him and berate him behind his back. He has a long-term resentment at being unable to prove his innate talent and superiority, and so takes to murdering those socially deprived patients he was supposed to treat. He feels himself better than his situation, and yet the only escape he has from a deep inferiority complex is murder. As a doctor, he indulges in the scourge of the profession—the desire to assume God's power over life and death as a means of self-validation.

The film is interesting, to its critical supporters, for the social parallels it draws between Victorian England and the con-

James Spader plays a man, suspected of being a modern day Jack the Ripper, looking into the death of his twin in *Jack's Back* (Palisades, 1988).

from the details, implications and the final confrontation.

Director Herrington was a former gaffer who had primed this project for a long time before finally getting the opportunity to realize it. The film did not do well but received promising notices, which made some critics (Ebert) look forward to the director's next works. Herrington went on to helm the knockabout Patrick Swayze film *Roadhouse* and the conventional serial killer action film *Striking Distance*, which disenchanted those who had high expectations after his debut.

The theme of the actual personage of Jack the Ripper returning to haunt the modern world in some way was explored in science fiction guise in *Time After Time* and in the tele-movie *Bridge Across Time*. In these films he is the horrible, continued legacy of the past.

temporary United States, especially its treatment of the social underclasses preyed upon by the killer. It also, in the doppelganger motif, recalls Jekyll and Hyde and the twin psychic-link movie (as treated in *Blood Link*, for instance). There exists in society a disposable class of people considered valueless by contemporary moral and socioeconomic standards. Like the characters found in Ripper lore, the doctor in part resents this underclass for what he perceives as its paradoxical amoral abandon (although the film does not endorse this, instead stressing such as the consequences of actions born of sociological deprivation). They are thus easy targets for his personal will to power fantasies. However, the film concentrates more on Spader's dilemma than it does on the portrait of a psychotic doctor, which emerges more

The January Man

(1989: d. Pat O'Connor)

scr. John Patrick Shanley; pr. Norman Jewison, Ezra Swerdlow; ph. Jerzy Zielinski; m. Marvin Hamlisch; ed. Lou Lombardo; prod d. Philip Rosenberg; cast. Kevin Kline, Susan Sarandon, Mary Elizabeth Mastrantonio, Harvey Keitel, Danny Aiello, Rod Steiger, Alan Rickman, Faye Grant; 97m

A cop tries to track down the murderer of women (eleven in as many months), all killed in their high-rise apartments. He recruits his brother, an ex-policeman (Kline) now brought back into the case due to his expertise in such matters. Kline agrees, on condition he date the cop's wife, whom he knew before. He does, and they establish a connection. Kline sets up a squad of assistants and must face departmental and romantic pressures. He discovers a pattern in the locations of the apartments and sets a trap for the killer. It segues from romantic comedy in the first half to procedural thriller in the second.

Typical of the post–*Manhunter* narrative, the specialist cop has to be talked into coming back. But his motives lack any psychological reasoning, and he remains at first unaffected by his closeness to atrocity, seeking a balance in romantic entanglements as a means of psychological refreshment before going back to work. Over the course of the film it becomes a personal crusade for him to stop the killer, a development inconsistent with his previous characterization as an irresponsible flake. Perhaps confronting atrocity has clarified his mind and restored a sense of purpose he lacked. Maybe his deciphering of the killer's method (he kills in imitation of a song, leaving the pattern deliberately there for discovery) is a recognition of the pointless frivolity of his own actions, and his pursuit of the killer an attempt to gather meaning and renew purpose. It is never clarified.

The team he assembles is a peculiar nod to the likes of the *Mission Impossible* TV series and the later *Sneakers*. The teamwork of a group of talented outsiders is stressed as a valid complement to established police work. Such a team needs a focused, dedicated leader, a suitable profiler.

The killer's method (the crime scene chosen according to a piece of music) is interesting, but the film tries to cross many genres—thriller, romance, comedy—and as a result is never tonally sure of itself. On the one hand it has a cynical irony (a celebrating crowd is intercut with the strangulation of a victim), yet stylistically it tries to pull away from such a mordant view, immediately countering with a scene of the press announcing the grave threat to women. The content may be routine,

but the treatment is unsure and ultimately (unintentionally) distancing. It seems to want to use the Kline persona established in the hit comedy *A Fish Called Wanda*. Indeed, all characters are marked by a quaint eccentricity that suggests the film is comedic in intention, although even this changes midway as the film's focus alters and it becomes the hunt for an anonymous threat to society.

Once the killer is found, his identity is never shown, the intent being to suggest that he is merely a nobody and not worthy of even that recognition. He could thus be anybody, the monstrous everyman, devoid of any personality or identity beyond that surfacing in his crimes. The elaborate signature he plans is merely a sick joke, a gimmick devoid of any significant social or philosophical statement. The film posits such serial murderers as inadequate, anonymous losers turning to elaborate crime in an effort to prove their superiority.

Although the film improves when it becomes a straight procedural, the critics were unimpressed. Rita Kempley summed up the response when she opined that the filmmakers were way out of their depth; though attempting sensitivity, they induce boredom (*Washington Post*). It understandably fared poorly at the box office.

Jennifer 8

(1992: d. Bruce Robinson)

scr. Robinson; pr. Gary Lucchesi, David Wimbury; ph. Conrad Hall; m. Christopher Young; ed. Conrad Buff; prod d. Richard Macdonald; cast. Andy Garcia, Uma Thurman, John Malkovich, Lance Henriksen, Kathy Baker, Kevin Conway, Graham Beckel; 120m

A city cop involved in a small-town murder case (Garcia as the outsider) believes that the evidence in one case is tied to that in other unsolved local homicides, revealing a serial killer of blind women. He posits that eight women have been

A policeman (Andy Garcia) roughs up a fellow officer who insinuates that he may be a killer or is impinging on the investigation in *Jennifer 8* (Paramount, 1992).

murdered with a .22 revolver and mutilated. No one believes him, including his investigative officer brother-in-law (Henriksen), having memories of the earlier crimes and harboring resentment over his determination to solve a case that they couldn't. He questions a blind woman (Thurman), the roommate of one of the victims, who has possibly met the killer. He falls for her and seeks to protect her when it seems she is in jeopardy from the killer (fearing possible identification, even from a blind witness). When Henriksen is killed in pursuit of a lead, Garcia becomes a suspect.

This is an unusual, but not completely successful, film from a highly regarded screenwriter. The policeman seeks some kind of self-validation in his pursuit of the case and the woman (who is said to resemble his ex-wife). On one level the film seems a self-conscious examination of archetypes (protector, damsel-in-distress, killer), but critics felt it never rose above the level of cliché, culminating in a standard confrontation after a prolonged romance.

On one level it also seems intended, and is visually designed, as an update of film noir. Thus it is often murky and understated. It begins effectively in a garbage dump, where a severed hand is found (memories of the severed ear from *Blue Velvet*). The state of human interaction is symbolically a field of debris, in need of sifting through. For the killer, the victim is little more in the end than disposable garbage. It is this effort to make sense of scattered fragments of the truth that impels the protagonist, the profiler figure here, to the point where dedication yields to obsession. Such is the narrative's direction, with the potential ever there for this obsession to make him a killer: indeed, he is accused of murdering a policeman who doubted the validity of the case.

This works as a study of the obsessive love of an older man for a younger, innocent woman. He increasingly sexualizes her child-woman vulnerability. Indeed, he is told that she is perhaps too naive for him to manipulate romantically, a suggestion he rejects as his erotic fascination deepens. She allows him to be both lover and protective father to her, and thus enables him to fulfill his role as patriarch. He senses the killer as the bad patriarch and the epitome of all he loathes, perhaps even that which he denies in himself (although this is a purely subtextual aspect).

Thurman's connection to the case is the incentive he needs to fuel his investigation, again designed with the need to prove his rightness. He has been emotionally and professionally wounded before the story events, and latches onto this case as his means of professional validation. This quest for validation is as much a motivation as his genuine concern for the girl.

The killer also sexualizes the vulnerability of the blind and innocent. However, the killer's voyeuristic exploitation of that vulnerability separates him from Garcia — not necessarily in kind, but in degree. Thus, the killer lurks in the darkness to take photographs of Thurman in the nude as she bathes, without her knowledge. In the final analysis, the killer (ironically the policeman investigating the original case) is a man who grew up among the blind and who was sexually rejected by them often enough to resent them, killing and mutilating them to assuage his wounded pride and assert his sexual dominance. He is a cowardly bully, coveting his sense of superiority, validated by his power over life and death and his efforts to mislead the investigation. Initial attraction has been warped over time and fantasy into

hatred and homicidal resentment — the Romantic corrupted into the Sadean (a regular theme of Jess Franco and of the serial killer film).

Jill the Ripper

(2000: d. Anthony Hickox) aka *Jill Rips; Leatherwoman; Tied Up*

scr. Kevin Bernhardt, Gareth Wardell; nvl. Frederic Lindsay; pr. Jim Wynorski (as Noble Henry); ph. David Pelletier; m. Thomas Barquee, Steve Gurevitch; ed. Brett Hedlund; prod d. Tim Boyd; cast. Dolph Lundgren, Danielle Brett, Richard Fitzpatrick, Kristi Angus, Charles Seixas, Sandi Ross; 94m

It had to happen. An S&M dominatrix serial killer murders her clients. One of these is the brother of a troubled San Francisco policeman (Lundgren), who leaves the force and goes undercover into the S&M world as a masochist to flush out the killer.

This is a weird vehicle for action B-star Lundgren, courtesy of horror auteur Hickox, the son of director Douglas. It depicts a world of kinky sex and rampant brutality in its exploration of an underground culture based on aberrant power games. The protagonist must confront this in himself as he goes into the world of dark sex (shades of the noirish *Tightrope*). By the time the film gets to the kinky side, however, it has slipped into the routine. Its main selling point is the expectation of seeing the muscular Lundgren (the Russian boxer from *Rocky IV*) as a submissive victim, tied up, suspended from the ceiling and gently tortured.

Jill the Ripper plays with the notion of restraint in compositional, sexual, personal, moral and even rational terms. Imposed restraints on personal liberty, and the greediness of human and financial ambition, saturate the movie. All characters are self-indulgent and hypocritical, even the alcoholic protagonist, who's driven to violence less to avenge his brother than to prove his macho effectiveness in the face of the challenges posed by his masochistic role-playing. As the film explores the underground S&M culture (with aspirations to be a heterosexual *Cruising*), so does it eroticize and fetishize the killer as a desired object, and, for the most part, as an absent signifier. However, it is more complex in its treatment of sex murder, which it presents as a snuff movie film-within-a-film sent to the police, thus almost approaching the ambiguity, self-reference and audience complicity of *Henry: Portrait of a Serial Killer*.

This is, unfortunately, rarely more than a standard detective movie that barely characterizes the killer woman as an incest survivor. To take revenge on the stepfather who repeatedly raped her, she must sexually dominate, humiliate and destroy all men. Her mutilations of the bodies are clearly penetrative sexual acts as she seeks to appropriate the aggressive sexuality usually coded as masculine. Her mild grieving exterior covers intense rage, her revelations shattering the protagonist's idealized view of his dead brother. In a demonstration of sympathy for the killer-as-victim, the protagonist saves her. This is an acknowledgement that their vigilante actions as essentially alike, and it recalls the kinship between vigilante and rogue cop in the *Dirty Harry* sequel *Sudden Impact*.

Just Cause

(1995: d. Arne Glimcher)

scr. Jeb Stuart, Peter Stone; nvl. John Katzenbach; pr. Lee Rich, Arne Glimcher, Steve Perry; ph. Lajos Koltai; m. James Newton Howard; ed. William Anderson; prod d. Patrizia von Brandenstein; cast. Sean Connery, Lawrence Fishburne, Kate Capshaw, Blair Underwood, Ed Harris, Daniel J. Travanti, Ned Beatty; 102m

A Harvard law professor (Connery), opposed to the death penalty, is contacted by a prisoner (Underwood) awaiting execution for the rape and murder of a little girl. They meet and converse. He is convinced the prisoner was beaten into a false confession by a brutal policeman (Fishburne), and a serial killer (Harris) in the next cell claims that he killed the little girl. The prisoner is freed, but he really was the killer and now comes after Connery and his family.

This was co-scripted by action specialist Jeb Stuart, who went on to write and direct the intriguing *Switchback*. It is a film that calculatedly plays on the popularity and awe-inspiring image of the serial killer after the success of *Silence of the Lambs*. Although the serial killer features only briefly, and in a subplot, he is the more intriguing character. He is meant to represent the absolute epitome of evil, and so is the focus of a fascination/repulsion complex by the filmmakers, who clearly model their killer as a less cultured version of Hopkins. Indeed, he is a cross between Hopkins and the country-boy killer played by Harry Connick Jr. in *Copycat*.

Introduced in colored uniform and restraints, he immediately takes issue with his last visitors, the "boys" from the FBI's BSU who came with their questions and surveys. He claims he told them that there is no formula for serial killers like him, just a "predisposition for an appetite." This kind of mock-philosophy undercuts much of the menace intended, and the killer is reduced to being a function of his own raging pride, desperately claiming that he still has influence beyond the walls. Ironically, like Connick in *Copycat*, he *does* have such reach, and is able to affect the death of his family in exchange for lying about Underwood's murders. It is his way of asserting his ego and superiority over all, to the very end. Finally he can't even let Underwood get away with it and admits their joint fabrication.

Connery recognizes this out-of-control pride, perhaps too close to home for

A law professor (Sean Connery, right) confronts a local policeman (Lawrence Fishburne, left) accused of beating a confession out of a suspect in *Just Cause* (WB, 1995).

him, and denies the killer his triumph by refusing to describe the atrocities Harris demanded of Underwood. Connery played the role of smug and righteous patriarch in securing Underwood's release, but he must face the consequences of his own pride when he realizes that Underwood has been gunning for his daughter all along. The twist revelation, that the daughter had prosecuted Underwood for a crime and that, although the case was dismissed, vigilantes castrated him, suggests that Underwood's murder of the little girl was a combination of sexual insecurity and retribution. However, this all exists to show the liberal patriarch resorting to violent justice when threatened, a blatant rightwing message that further alienated critics already lamenting the heavily contrived plot. The violent Fishburne, himself a fa-

ther, was right all along and thus a truly righteous man, despite his questionable tactics. In a world where such killers can so easily manipulate the course of justice, strict measures are demanded in response.

Kalifornia

(1993: d. Dominic Sena)

scr. Tim Metcalfe; pr. Tim Clawson; ph. Bojan Bazelli; m. Carter Burwell; ed. Martin Hunter; prod d. Michael White; cast. Brad Pitt, Juliette Lewis, David Duchovny, Michelle Forbes; 118m

A writer and photographer (Duchovny and Forbes) intend to resettle out west and in the process go on a cross-country tour of famous murder sites for a book project. They advertise for travel companions to share expenses, and are joined by a killer and his girlfriend (Pitt and Lewis) also

Serial/spree killer Early (Brad Pitt) and his partner girlfriend Adele (Juliette Lewis) are soon to go on the road in *Kalifornia* (Gramercy, 1993).

seeking a new life in California. Slowly, the writer develops a fascination for the semi-literate, rough-hewn Pitt, until he discovers his murderous ways.

Kalifornia combines the road movie with the study of banal criminality à la *Badlands*. Indeed, its conception of the killer is closer to a spree killer than to a serial killer, but it was promoted as a serial killer film. Thus it has more in common with *Natural Born Killers* (which also starred Lewis, as a killer equal to her male partner — unlike the naïve, dim-witted waif she plays here, a role she would do more justice to in *The Other Sister*). It concentrates on the clash between a man fascinated with murderers, and a murderer, charting the resultant shattering of idealism as the peaceful Duchovny finds that he is also capable of murder and so not as dissimilar to the killer as he would hope. Indeed, at the end he dearly holds onto the

justification that his punitive, purgative killing of Pitt was a case of justifiable homicide. He finally concludes that the difference between him and Pitt is that he is capable of guilt and remorse, whereas Pitt was untroubled by such emotions. Indeed, the film carries that subtext — a meditation on the fascination of conscientious men for the truly conscienceless.

The collision between the glamorized expectation of serial killers and bland actuality is the thematic basis for this bleak road movie. Those who would romanticize violence (and be voyeuristically, sexually excited by it) are forced to confront the banal, horrific reality of the actual killer, who murders out of wronged pride as much as practical opportunity. Unlike the protagonists, he is under no illusions about the purposes of such violence. Duchovny's illusions are gradually undermined as he feels at first intrigued by his intellectual lesser and then fearful of him. Thus, the road movie is used as a journey towards the recognition of a banal truth. The killer, however socially and educationally deprived, is the most aware (both of himself and of others) of all of them. Although homicidally monstrous, he is ironically the most pure. However, he suffers from a class-based socioeconomic resentment and inferiority, driven to violence as a means of compensatory expression. He thus tries to make Lewis look like Forbes, seeking a sexual conquest. It is a demonstration of his power, although aimless and unfocused. The film is careful not to make him into a social revolutionary, as Duchovny would probably assert. He is part of a disaffected underclass — poor white trash, although that is perhaps where the remnants of the last great American noble savage are to be found.

The killer is also similar to the protagonist of *Badlands* in his relationship to a subordinate female. However, Lewis would seek to deny Pitt's horrendous acts, holding onto the hope that he can change, even though he beats her. She defines herself in relation to him. Forbes, by contrast, loathes the dependent mentality, although she grows to pity Lewis. But all are emotionally distant, despite their proclamations. Interpersonal relationships are always at the point of dissolution. Consequently, the characters' journey for a new beginning in a new land is a futile search for a mythical land of opportunity — America by way of the mythical Kalifornia (the US version of El Dorado). It is an unattainable place, and the film's title refers to a state of mind, of hope in the face of a dwindling ideal: such is the fate of the so-called Generation X.

In the end Duchovny himself becomes a murderer, shooting the real killer and so attaining the experience of murder; but he feels not a sense of self and pride in finally resorting to action instead of words, but an emptiness, the same nothingness he claims he saw in Pitt's eyes. He becomes the killer he once idealized, paradoxically in the act of supposedly denying its validity and purging it. He cannot accept the discrepancy between his idealized killer and the reality he is confronted with, and so he eliminates the reality in an effort not only to purge it but to deny his fantasy, the source of his guilt. Duchovny at first believes that such serial killers are like children unable to distinguish right from wrong, and should be treated and understood, not executed. However, the reality proves too disillusioning to bear, as he learns that there is nothing to understand.

Scripter Metcalfe would tackle the serial killer figure when he directed *Killer: A Journal of Murder*, which fared dismally with the critics and public, unlike *Kalifornia*, which was both praised as an insightful demystification of the serial killer, and vilified as a glorification of nihilistic violence. Sena, who was hailed as a major independent director, went on to mainstream Hollywood — and virtual anonymity — with the slick *Gone in 60 Seconds* and *Swordfish*. His core fans lost out.

Killer: A Journal of Murder

(1996: d. Tim Metcalfe)

scr. Metcalfe; pr. Mark Levinson, Janet Yang; ph. Ken Kelsch; m. Graeme Revell; ed. Richard Gentner, Harvey Rosenstock; prod d. Sherman Williams; cast. James Woods, Robert Sean Leonard, Ellen Greene, Cara Buono, Robert Burke, Steve Forrest, Lili Taylor; 90m

Based on a true story, and set mostly in Leavenworth prison in 1929, this film depicts the relation between serial killer Carl Panzram (Woods) and the prison guard (Leonard) who befriends him and encourages the convict to write down his memoirs, some of which are visualized. The guard tries to prevent the killer's execution but is unable to do so. Instead, he seeks to get the killer's confessions published.

The film is a look at the early call for prison reform and the abuses of the system. However, it does not support the cause either way, instead intended as a balanced look at the attempts to reform an offender for whom no reform or redemption is ultimately possible. It contrasts the expected views: the killer claiming that God created him evil for his own purposes, but the prison guard claiming that horrendous experience and the system makes such killers. The film gives evidence for both sides, showing Panzram as both a reaction to prolonged incarceration and brutality, and an opportunist who commits rape and murder when the situation to do so presents itself.

Panzram, who respects trust, although he can readily break it, is an enigma. Through his confessions, and flashbacks, we get the portrait of a man, raped as a child, who turned to rage as his expression against a world and humanity he considers beneath contempt. His crimes are thus both self-indulgence and an expression of protest. Trust is there to be betrayed, and Panzram takes advantage of a warden's generosity to rape a librarian and so end this paternal man's reform-minded career. Perhaps his regret at betraying the patriarch feeds his relationship with the young officer who considers him a patriarch and worthy of the same trust that Panzram ironically betrayed. Panzram realizes that he cannot be changed, that he cannot resist the lure of violence and wrongdoing, and wants death as an end, a freedom from the Hell he considers his life — and all life — to be.

The portrayal of Panzram as a violent, brutal scoundrel avoids the real man's true repugnance: he boasted of multiple murder for sex and profit, thousands of forced sodomies and rapes, and the prolonged torture of his victims. The film tastefully avoids this, showing a more understandably contextualized monster: the product of adverse circumstance, almost too jaded to acknowledge a kind gesture. His relationship to the guard is in part his last chance at redemption, his confession a cautionary tale and a valuable sociopolitical weapon in the fight for social reform and treatment as opposed to punishment: evidence of the age of indifference. As the disposal of an untamable force, Panzram's death represents the ultimate act of this indifferent world, blind to any joint responsibility. Yet Panzram had his chance and resorted to abhorrence once again, raping an innocent.

This enigma proves attractive, possibly even in a homoerotic sense, to the young prison guard who sees Panzram as both father figure and erotic subject. He can thus neglect marital relations with his wife in order to pore over Panzram's confessions. His obsessive dedication to keeping Panzram alive, despite the killer's own desire for execution, is less professional or ethical than personal. These themes are kept subtextual for the most part, however, in favor of a treatment of the growth of mutual respect in the face of adversity. The guard finds a respect for the career murderer that the murderer treats in kind, for the first time in his life. But if Panzram lived, would he betray this too? Perhaps he knows that he would, another reason he should die.

The film is presented as a series of flashbacks within a flashback. This use of multiple narrators is complex and confusing. The old guard recounts his experience as a young man with Panzram. Panzram relates his own stories in flashback. Does this mean we are seeing the guard's recollections of these flashbacks, and do his moral beliefs and apparent sexual infatuations thus taint them? Can an objective view of Panzram ever be had? All attempts to contextualize him are undercut by the notion of the unreliable narrator's pursuit of "truth." Again, this is kept subtextual.

The film took Metcalfe five years to get from original idea to filmed product, and was hampered by budgetary limitations and an unsure structure which treats the most promising themes obscurely. The film went unreleased for a year after being made, whilst the unimpressed studio determined what to do with it — whether to release it and what type of publicity/marketing to give it. As a result, it received only limited release and slipped by quietly onto video. The only positive critical notices it earned were for Woods' performance. Metcalfe is better known as the screenwriter of *Kalifornia*, and there are hopes that he continues to work, as he can be a provocative talent.

The Killer Inside Me

(1976: d. Burt Kennedy)

scr. Edward Mann, Robert Chamblee; nvl. Jim Thompson; pr. Michael W. Leighton; ph. William A. Fraker; m. Tim McIntire, John Rubinstein; ed. Danford B. Greene, Aaron Stell; cast. Stacy Keach, Susan Tyrrell, Tisha Sterling, Keenan Wynn, Charles McCraw, John Dehner, Pepe Serna, Royal Dano, Julie Adams, John Carradine, Don Stroud; 99m

Director Kennedy is worlds away from his comedic westerns with this story of a sheriff with a split personality, one side being a killer. Although it tries to implicate schizophrenia as the cause, this is closer to a Southern rural Jekyll and Hyde story, as the normal side is confronted with the awareness of the abnormal side's actions and attempts to reconcile them.

The protagonist is concerned with his self-image, his melancholic voice-over identity a mix of memory and hallucination. It is an unreliable inner monologue, forever plagued by intrusive thoughts and recollections (of traumatic childhood) triggered by outside sights and sounds. The film is intended as a visualization of psychological insecurity turning towards violence as a demonstration of coherence, paradoxically avoiding real self-awareness. The protagonist lives in a perceptual limbo: the perception of the everyday is a subjective experience which shatters any hope of the recognizable truth it obsessively seeks. All is projection.

The protagonist cannot communicate his feelings (refusing to participate in sex talk with fellows); when he is confronted by a threat to his ability to control and manipulate, he reacts violently. His loss of control is accompanied by auditory hallucinations, which explain away his murder of a friend in terms of "intellectual superiority" — he feels himself better than others (as justified by his job as police officer and thus moral enforcer) and must prove it through decisive action. However, he ultimately reveals his knowledge of his own paranoid schizophrenia and suggests the crimes are the result of him testing the limits of his mental state and capability. This way he can intellectually justify murder whilst denying his own insecurities.

This is a combination of the Southern Gothic and the psychodrama, though without the grotesquely comic caricature associated with Tobe Hooper's films and the brief vogue for such isolated psychos in the early 1970s. It is an examination of the pressure brought about by psychiatric illness as enabling violent eruptions and then driven to rationalize them as both confirmation and avoidance of moral responsibility: insanity is not an excuse, though it is an explanation.

The film came out the same year as *Taxi Driver*, and is also comparable to Jack Starrett's movies of the same period (*Small Town in Texas*). It can be considered part of a cycle of non-urban set films in the mid–1970s that explored and redefined the potential legacy of the Western hero.

The Killing Jar

(1996: d. Evan Crooke)

scr. Mark Mullin; pr. Crooke, Shelly Strong, Jason Saffran; ph. Michael Wojciechowski; ed. Frederick Wardell; prod d. Don Day; cast. Brett Cullen, Tamlyn Tomita, Wes Studi, Brion James, M. Emmet Walsh, Xander R. Berkeley

A man and wife return to a small town, 20 years after a fatal car accident, to take over the family business. The small community is beset by a series of child murders; and, driving home one day, the husband passes by a murder site and believes he sees more bodies there. The image of the bodies seems to converge with the repressed childhood trauma. Some locals believe that the truth about the car accident was never fully revealed and that this has a bearing on the child killings. Numerous flashbacks revolve around the accident trauma which killed his close friend and injured his younger brother.

This is a reportedly pretentious effort and an exploration of the continued effects of the past on the present, with the serial killer angle decidedly secondary. Hence it never found a niche market and is now an obscurity, even this soon after its minimal release. Generally unavailable at time of writing, Internet sources were not supportive.

The Killing of America

(1981: d. Sheldon Renan)

scr. Leonard Schrader, Chieko Schrader; pr. Leonard Schrader; ph. Robert Charlton, Jon Else, Tom Hurwitz, Willy Kurant, Peter Smokler; m. W. Michael Lewis, Mark Lindsay, Laurin Rinder; ed. Lee Percy; 90m

This is a mondo-style documentary about the rise in random, violent crime in the 1970s. With much stock footage and interviews, it takes a disturbing look at a tumultuous period in American history during which the serial killer came to the public forum more than ever before.

The Killing of America features actual footage of serial killers Bundy, Bianchi, Bittaker, Wayne Henley and an extended interview with Ed Kemper. This footage offers a glimpse at how such killers were treated in the news media, how they correspondingly present themselves, and how they perceive themselves and their respective responsibility.

Kemper (whose picture is used at the start of *Copycat*) in particular demonstrates a remarkable insight into his own homicidal necrophilia and matricide. He knows the depths of his own monstrousness and is aware of the need for his imprisonment to protect society. This is held up in total contrast to Henley, who considers himself a victim of his dominant partner, Dean Corll, and thus seeks to avoid any responsibility or understanding.

The film posits 1962 and the Kennedy assassination as the start in the accelerating cycle of violence that consumed the country for the next two decades. It suggests that since Kennedy, there was a rise in a new kind of killer, not interested in money but in the random murder of a stranger. The narrator adds that in this climate of violence and sexual "liberation," sex murderers appeared with alarming regularity. The film holds these killers as the absolute nadir of Americana, an unknowable symptom of a country consuming itself.

Fascinating but graphic, the movie was produced for the Japanese market where such death culture was enduringly popular (Kerekes and Slater; pp. 198–9). One can see its intentions as an indictment of America's rampant gun culture, as it depicts an out-of-control society heading towards inevitable internal apocalypse. Of the many mondo documentaries made that feature footage of serial killers, this remains the most telling and disturbing. There are signs that it has become a cult film, partly because co-screenwriter Leonard Schrader is Paul's brother.

Kiss the Girls

(1998: d. Gary Fleder)

scr. David Klass; pr. David Brown, Joe Wizan; ph. Aaron Schneider; m. Mark Isham; ed. Harvey Rosenstock, William Steinkamp; prod d. Nelson Coates; cast. Morgan Freeman, Ashley Judd, Cary Elwes, Tony Goldwyn, Jay O. Sanders, Bill Nunn, Brian Cox, Alex McArthur, Mena Suvari; 120m

A forensic psychologist becomes involved in a case involving the kidnapping of his niece. A woman is then kidnapped and imprisoned by the serial killer, who calls himself "Casanova" and collects live women as trophies, setting about systematically breaking their individuality and will, then killing them when he presumably tires of them. She escapes and teams with the psychologist/profiler to find the killer. They discover that the killer may be operating in two locations. Their investigation reveals two killers, in friendly rivalry, who correspond via e-mail. One killer escapes, and they follow the trail back to the original crime scenes and tackle both killers.

This harrowing film, thanks to the casting of Morgan Freeman, can be considered a follow-up to *Seven*. It is a study in personal control, obsession and responsibility, which also seems inspired by William Wyler's *The Collector*. From the opening, where Freeman talks a battered woman out of suicide, interest is signaled in characters who seek control over others and willingly take the responsibility for others' lives as a means of giving them back self-control. The subsequent film develops and contrasts the genre's characters—killer, profiler, policeman, victim, and suspect — in terms of that responsibility.

The profiler strives to remain cool and distant: he values life so much that he is willing to take responsibility for the lives

The profiler (Morgan Freeman) and recently escaped victim Dr. Kate McTiernan (Ashley Judd) jointly delve into the case in *Kiss the Girls* (Paramount, 1997).

Profiler Alex Cross (Morgan Freeman) contemplates the crime scene photographs for links in *Kiss the Girls* (Paramount, 1997).

of those in jeopardy, to preserve their life and eliminate the threat to it. He is the good father and protector, willing to place others' lives alongside, or even above, his own. The killer is the exact opposite: he selfishly wishes to exert his will above all others, and considers those women who seek control over their lives and their sexuality a threat to his masculine control and therefore in need of domination. He assumes that taking responsibility for another life justifies its suppression in favor of his own. He is the danger of excess pride, devoid of moral responsibility, yet the warped end of an order founded on the need for suppression. Both are intelligent adversaries, their rivalry an admitted game between those who seek to free life from constraint and threat by the dominant few, and those few who seek to impose such constraint by the unbridled exertion of perceived superiority. Thus, the killer has a set of rules that he reads to his slaves, a

perversion of the functioning of Patriarchy.

All central characters are faced with a loss of control, their will to survive, whether righteous or perverted, governing their actions and respect towards others. The selfless vs. the selfish displays a moral spectrum of attitudes that forces a choice upon the individual between the liberation and suppression of another's free will. Thus, the film seeks to address the malfunctioning of a shared social compact when warped by excessive pride. Control and pride are bedfellows, with the expression of potency corrupted into the domination of another.

It is arguable the extent to which the killers' actions are a denial of personal inadequacy through over-compensatory sexual domination. Indeed, it is those characters for whom sex and sexuality is not an issue who do not need to suppress or punish others, and can remain in personal and moral control. The killers must turn them into sexual beings, and the killer in the end ascribes his perverse desires for Freeman's niece onto Freeman himself, claiming that it is merely social constraint that prevents Freeman from sexually dominating the girl. Ironically, but most in keeping with the genre's moral dilemmas, Freeman shoots the killer, restoring control, eliminating pride, and perhaps purging illicit desire from within himself. Although this last point is ambiguous, in so doing he arguably becomes an agent of repression and the killer of a liberation society deems abhorrent.

Freeman and Judd, their relationship asexual, seek to be cool and unaffected, as if unmodulated emotional expression were tantamount to aggression (Judd, a doctor who also assumes responsibility for others' lives, boxes, and Freeman almost lashes out at a suspect who boasts of his sexual contact with Freeman's niece). Unless checked, over-control becomes its opposite, a surrender to conscienceless amorality. This raises the issue of whether the loss of control (as an expression of defiance against the social compact) is a sexual expression based on a will-to-power fantasy — the real enemy. Evil rests in this fantasy. Judd's strength comes from escaping the sexual dominance of another and wishing to confront the enemy and remove the threat from society. What is unsaid between her and Freeman is their tacit understanding of the imperative to confront and destroy a force that seeks to define itself as uncontrollable and sexual.

Fleder's style is correspondingly icy and regimented, dramatizing the inevitably intense outbursts of energy he seeks to contain. The suggestion of a shared bond between killers, an elite group of supermen united in their agreed decision to violate the taboos of the social compact, is also found in *Manhunter*, *Silence of the Lambs* and *Copycat*. It is confirmed in a policeman's description of the killer as "a

real student of the game, and [who] likes to play." The film is also cognizant of true-crime cases, particularly that of Gary Heidnik, who imprisoned women as sex-slaves in his basement.

Knight Moves

(1992: d. Carl Schenkel)

scr. Brad Mirman; pr. Ziad El Khoury, Jean-Luc Defait; ph. Dietrich Lohmann; ms. Anne Dudley; ed. Norbert Herzner; prod d. Graeme Murray; cast. Christopher Lambert, Diane Lane, Tom Skerritt, Daniel Baldwin, Ferdinand Mayne, Katherine Isobel, Charles Bailey-Gates, Arthur Strauss; 116m

A small northwestern town plays host to a chess tournament. However, a killer is at work in the community. A champion chess player (Lambert) is implicated in this serial killer's crimes. The policeman on the case (Skerritt), who suspects Lambert, consults a psychiatrist for assistance. She becomes involved in the investigation, monitoring Lambert all the while but unsure whether to believe him, although she is sexually attracted to him, perhaps impelled by the danger. The killer slices his nubile victims' throats, and considers each crime a message and "move" intended for the protagonist to respond to and decipher. It is clear that the victims are no more than pawns in a game between moral adversaries.

The film begins with a blue and white prologue (also used in *Exquisite Tenderness*) which sets up the theme of intense rivalry and disappointment. It then parallels the course of film narrative to the strategic decisions in the game, with each set piece a move in a tacit play between the filmmakers' manipulation and the audience's complicity. There are thus many levels to the conception of "the game" between skilled adversaries, between police and killer, and accused and killer, most directly on the plot level. Developing the procedural aspects to the investigation, the

Chess master Peter Sanderson (Christopher Lambert) realizes the deadly parallels between the game he plays and a killer's tactics as the pressure mounts in *Knight Moves* (Republic, 1992).

film becomes a character study of a man driven to win at all costs who finds his parallel in a killer who considers people as disposable, there to be used in his desire to prove himself the protagonist's better. Indeed, all characters are driven by barely controlled egos.

What separates the killer from the rest is his dependence on fantasy to achieve his ends. In his mind he is a masterful player, but he is no longer content to fantasize it and so must put it into deadly practice. And what greater means of displaying power is there than murder? The profiler asserts that such a killer has fantasized for a long time before mustering the will to carry it through. Once there, he is hooked into a complex revenge fantasy which simultaneously fulfills a dark sexual need to dominate the victims and remove their life force/essence (hence he drains his first victim's blood). In that, the film skillfully combines the two motives.

It is clever, and most noteworthy, in its balance of serial killer and mystery, with a killer who deliberately plants clues at the crime scene. These clues need to be appropriately deciphered and are thus a means of interpersonal communication. In that, it clearly anticipates the likes of *Seven* and *The Bone Collector*, which emphasize the crime as deliberate communication between killer and profiler. Murder is thus a macabre art form, à la *Still Life* even.

This is an engrossing horror film which updates the giallo in much the same revisionist/deconstructive ways that Schenkel would later do for the mad surgeon traditions of European horror in *Exquisite Tenderness*. His stylishly flamboyant camerawork is reminiscent of Argento, though with a more comic-bookish sensibility to the angles and tilts. Schenkel loves colors, with many filters and lights saturating his contrast between hot and cold textures. Strangely, it was considered negligible when it came out, although it and *Exquisite Tenderness* suggest a superior genre craftsman. However, the director's later film, *Tarzan and the Lost City*, did nothing to enhance his reputation.

Lady in Waiting

(1994: d. Fred Gallo) aka *Hollywood Madam*

scr. Dennis Manuel; pr. Brenda R. Kyle, Phil Mittleman; ph. Mark Vicente; m. Robert Ginsburg; ed. Miriam L. Preissel, Omer Tal; prod d. Colleen Devine; cast. Michael Nouri, Robert Costanzo, Shannon Whirry, Crystal Chappell, Meg Foster, William Devane; 84m

A detective known to frequent whores investigates a serial killer of high-end prostitutes/call girls. He soon becomes a suspect when his ex-wife's husband (a rich lawyer) is found dead. The lawyer is also soon linked to the procurement of prostitutes.

An unheralded film which quickly disappeared from view, *Lady in Waiting* apparently develops the common premise of an amoral world wherein male sexuality is linked to the objectification of women as sex objects and possessions, hence the cop's continued interest in his ex-wife. It probably offers little alternative to women beyond definition according to their relationship to the dominant male, and the viewer. Sexuality is not a means of empowerment, although it is both fostered and punished by male culture. This was unavailable at time of writing.

Lady in White

(1988: d. Frank LaLoggia)

scr. LaLoggia; pr. Andrew G. La Marca, LaLoggia; ph. Russell Carpenter; m. LaLoggia; ed. Steve Mann; prod d. Richard K. Hummel; cast. Lukas Haas, Len Cariou, Alex Rocco, Katherine Helmond, Jason Presson, Renata Vanni, Angelo Bertolini, Joelle Jacobi; 113m

A young boy is troubled by his mother's death. Soon the ghostly apparition of a sometime dead girl, the victim of a serial killer, visits him. He sees a murder and realizes that the community has blamed the wrong man (an Afro-American) for a series of child murders (including that of the girl). He searches on his own, developing a caring concern for the fate of the dead girl. Eventually, he discovers that the killer is a trusted family friend.

The film is in part a reaction to Spielbergian romanticized versions of the innocent fantasies of childhood. It repeatedly challenges its audience to interpret the film as a literal ghost story, or as a symbolic psychodrama which treads the ground between remembrance and imaginative reconstruction. The ghost comes to symbolize the union of memory and fantasy in a mystery author's recollection of childhood. His family unity is contrasted with the apparently hostile world beyond it, which seeks to remove innocence from a community identity. He must confront this world, reluctantly, with the killer symbolizing the dawning of adolescent adulthood and the death of childhood. In as far as the victim is a little girl, one can see the dawning of a pre-adolescent sexuality, with a component aggressive gazing projected onto the killer as a form of personal disavowal. This is kept ambiguous and subtextual, and allows the film to be compared to *Afraid of the Dark*, another complex meditation on preadolescent fantasies. It is hence a tale of the realization of Innocence lost.

Correspondingly, the atmosphere, at first filled with the joy of family unity, childhood experience, and small town eccentricity, segues into menace and mystery. Autumnal beauty becomes melancholy. The protagonist begins to perceive this as a realm beneath the everyday, an awareness of the outside world as beyond his limited understanding, and thus greeted with fear and hesitance, no longer a pleasant discovery. What was taken for granted, and the benevolence of people, is not what it seems. It now takes a self-aware courage to pursue what the child comes to realize as an objective truth beyond the surface — a flawed adult world. This theme is also found in *To Kill a Mockingbird*. But as the film is structured as a flashback, it questions the extent to which anything is ever truly objective.

It is a film drenched in the process of change, transformation and maturation. Autumn becomes winter. The turbulent 1960s are lamented by the father, who fears the corresponding change in people's interpersonal regard for one another and sense of community. Hallucination and dream segue into reality. But always, inevitable change brings with it an awareness of horror and disappointment and melancholia.

Lady in White can be compared to the work of Ray Bradbury and even David Lynch in its conception of small towns harboring terrible secrets. Its theme of life processes infiltrating fantasy also informs Bernard Rose's skilful debut *Paperhouse*. The use of voice-over prompted comparisons to *Stand by Me*. *Lady in White* was praised as confirmation of the talent director LaLoggia had shown in the horror tale *Fear No Evil*, and labeled a promising sign of things to come. The critics were kind to this undeniably personal film, particularly to its concern for community values, but it had only a middling box-office reaction, and it was a long time before the director would work again. There is enough in LaLoggia's work to make the receptive wish that he were more prolific.

Lady of Burlesque

(1943: d. William Wellman)

scr. James Gunn; nvl. Gypsy Rose Lee; pr. Hunt Stromberg; ph. Robert DeGrasse; m. Arthur Lange; prod d. Joseph Platt; ed. James E. New-comb; art d. Bernard Herzbrun; cst des. Edith Head, Natalie Visart; cast. Barbara Stanwyck, Victoria Faust, Charles Dingle, Stephanie Bachelor, Marion Martin, Eddie Cordon, Pinkie Lee, Frank Fenton; 91m

This is based on the novel written mostly by Gypsy Rose Lee entitled *G String Murders*. Barbara Stanwyck plays Pixie, the star/main attraction at a seedy Burlesque house. A stand-up comedian courts her. Murder ensues, with a stripper killed by her own g-string. When the murders continue, and the police prove ineffective, the strippers decide to solve it themselves, with the assistance of the comedian. The killer is revealed to be an old misogynist who resents women who use their sexuality for both profit and to subordinate men.

Ironically, the burlesque theater is a converted opera house. And herein lies the film's thesis: that the change in cultural values regarding the free expression of female sexuality (although coded in terms of male desire) produces the sex killer, a theme also in John Brahm's version of *The Lodger*. The killer here resents these women for their open sexuality, determined to punish them for it. He is the self-appointed preserver of what he considers traditional Patriarchy. In that, he represents the product of values in transition. He needs to be eliminated in the name of progress.

On another level though, he represents the hypocrisy of the evolving Patriarchy, threatened with female independence through sexual expression and seeking to codify it and objectify it as a vehicle for male desire — both craved and resented. The sex killer is thus a byproduct of social and moral change. This burlesque world is a precursor to the seedy peep shows and sex culture of the 1970s, which would epitomize the very amoral world the killer fears — and murders to protect society from. He is unaware that his crimes are a demonstration of his own sadistic sexual fantasies of the "loose" women he despises,

The victim of a serial killer in a burlesque hall is found backstage in *Lady of Burlesque* (United Artists, 1943).

perhaps for arousing that desire within him. Ironically, the killer is of the same age and presumed moral superiority of the investigating policeman, who is of limited use in the investigation of such crime.

In that, it shows the serial killer film evolving and clearly addressing the sex killer as a human monster. Wellman makes this clear in that the setting and secret killer recalls *The Phantom of the Opera*, only to have the expectation of a deformed monster undercut by the revelation of the killer as a plain, bland, aging stagehand. Beneath the whodunit structure lies an examination of sex murder. Gone is any hint of glamour or associated Otherness. Likewise, its depiction of the petty intrigues behind the selling of sexual excitement (a profession which paradoxically empowers women, both liberating and objectifying them — a theme common to many subse-

quent stripper-murderer films) is a deglamorization of the backstage musical so popular in the late 1930s.

Lady Stay Dead

(1982: d. Terry Bourke)

scr. Bourke; pr. Bourke; ph. Ray Henman; cast. Chard Hayward, Louise Howitt, Deborah Collins, Roger Ward, Lex Foxcroft, James Elliott; 95m

This Australian sexploitation film is about a gardener who rapes and murders young women. He rapes a famous singer, whom he has long desired, and kills her when she protests. He then seeks to manipulate her newly arrived sister into a similar fate. However, the investigating police intervene, and a shootout/siege results.

The film clearly posits the killer's

rapes as his empowerment fantasy, rehearsed in masturbatory sessions with mannequins and from behind bushes as he spies on his bathing intended victim. He is not content with fantasy and must put his desire for the sexual subjugation of women into practice. When the reality does not conform to the fantasy, he bemoans that this victim was supposed to be different, and when the victim expresses dissatisfaction, the only way he can maintain his control is to kill the victim and attempt to conceal the body from discovery. He thus escalates from rape to murder as a personal ritual he cannot comprehend.

He has a child-like quality and is incapable of normal adult interactions, so consumed is he by fantasy. He also resents being treated as inferior and is determined to prove himself the equivalent of the normal, sexually active, and, in his mind, therefore powerful men that surround his intended victims.

Director Bourke, along with Brian Trenchard-Smith, Richard Franklin, Everett DeRoche and even Tim Burstall, and later Russell Mulcahy, developed and refined the traditions of Australian exploitation following the much-touted Australian New Wave of the 1970s.

Laser Moon

(1992: d. Bruce Carter)

scr. Douglas K. Grimm; pr. Mark Paglia; ed. Ken Koenig; cast. Traci Lords, Bruce Davis Bayne, Douglas Grimm, Harrison Le Duke, Crystal Shaw; 90m

A killer strikes whenever there's a full moon (in a nod to the lycanthropic parallels to serial murders). He kills women via a laser to the temple, then indulges in necrophilic fantasies and mutilation. He is prompted into calling a radio talk show by a DJ (Lords) whose training happens to be as a criminologist, and whose ratings are weakening. The media readily dub the killer "the Laser Moon Killer." The DJ helps the detectives assigned to the case, despite the risk to her safety. When the killer announces his next intention over the radio, the police send her undercover to lure him out.

The notion of a killer contacting a radio talk show was handled more effectively in *Martin*, *Outside Ozona* and the tele-movie *Listen*. The film is notable mainly for being a non-pornographic attempt to make once underage porn star Lords into an actress and B movie starlet.

Last House on Dead End Street

(1977: d. Victor Janos)

note: credit listings have been reported as pseudonymous.

This is a much condemned, even despised, European exploitation rip-off of Wes Craven's controversial *Last House on the Left*, which indeed prompted many European horror/sleaze imitations.

A drug-dealing pimp is released from prison and decides to make snuff movies, partially because straight porn no longer sells as well as it used to. He strongly resents the social values responsible for his imprisonment. He obtains a camera, lures women, and makes his movies. These films are purchased and jointly viewed by a select rich clientele. He pursues ever more gross and explicit atrocities to further his art.

The film is reportedly primarily a succession of atrocity scenes. Hence: a young girl is disemboweled and cannibalized alive, with smelling salts used to keep her conscious; a severed deer hoof protrudes from a woman's crotch and a man sucks on it; actual slaughterhouse footage is shown of cows being brutally killed and their throats torn out; a man admits to having sodomized a dead calf in the slaughterhouse. It is a reportedly unre-lentingly bleak vision of the horrors of people desperate for sensation. Human life has lost all value or meaning in a world of sexual exploiters, for whom sexual vio-lence — whether perpetrating, filming or viewing — is the only experience left which energizes them.

As a demonstration of a low budget imposed realism, the film has been dis-cussed in terms of the pornography of death, which treats the depiction of sexual violence as an act for the consumption and stimulation of its audience. The act is thus shown shorn of judgment (but with some stylization, reportedly), for the reaction it provokes in the viewer — intended as stim-ulation and repulsion. Thus, there is per-haps an arguable celebration, akin to the likes of Jorg Buttgereit and European un-derground horror, which explains the moral condemnation this film and those like it receive.

According to Kerekes and Slater (pp. 44–53; the main objective account of this movie), it was barely released, and then only with minimal marketing as a sequel to *Last House on the Left*. It reportedly was known by reputation alone and, despite a brief US VHS release, is hard to find. It is the minimal critical responses amongst fans (even on the Internet) and objective description of its contents upon which most retrospective criticism is based. It is only tangentially related to the serial killer film, included for its "snuff" there.

Last Victim

(1975: d. Jim Sotos) aka *Forced Entry*

scr. Henry Scarpelli; pr. Sotos, Scarpelli; ph. A. Kleinman; m. Tommy Vig; spec eff. Bob O'Bradovich, Freddy Sweet; cast. Ron Max, Tanya Roberts, Nancy Allen, Brian Freilino; 82m

A garage attendant is a serial rapist and murderer. Tormented by memories of his abusive mother, he spends much time alone cruising for victims and venomously expressing his hostility towards women, whom he considers all to be whores. He breaks into a woman's home and ties her up, but this latest victim, a housewife (Tanya Roberts), tries to manipulate his emotions in order to stay alive. She pre-tends to want to date him, and when his guard is down she stabs him to death.

The film is reportedly seen from the point of view of a serial rapist, and thus lacks any psychological distance from the misogyny on display, becoming decidedly seedy as a result. Although one could argue this as a portrait of unrepentant misogyny, the slow-motion rapes and murders sug-gest an intention to eroticize sexual vio-lence merely for male titillation, as op-posed to any truly subversive intent.

Last Victim anticipates the movement towards the slasher film in its incorpora-tion of a killer who kills using a variety of means. Presumably since his fantasy is never sated, he must constantly seek to make the crime more satisfactory. His be-havior with his final victim suggests that his hatred is the result of an inability to form a "normal" relationship (he kills the women who he feels reject him), the prospect of which momentarily disorients him. It is as if he wants to be desired, and when not, resorts to rape and murder as a means of compensation, asserting his su-periority after all. However, he remains impotent and must use other means, in-serting foreign objects (a beer bottle) as a penis substitute.

This cheap film was repackaged and rereleased in 1984 to capitalize on the brief stardom of Roberts (who went on to TV's *Charlie's Angels*) and a pre–DePalma Nancy Allen (who plays a hitch-hiker victim of the killer). The synopsis indicates a possi-ble similarity to *Beware My Lovely*.

The Leopard Man

(1943: d. Jacques Tourneur)

scr. Ardel Wray, Edward Dein; nvl. Cornell Woolrich; pr. Val Lewton; ph. Robert de Grasse; ed. Mark Robson; cast. Dennis O'Keefe, Margo, Jean Brooke, Isabel Jewell, James Bell, Margaret Landry, Abner Biberman, Richard Martin; 65m

In a small New Mexico town, a series of murders (including that of a child) are seemingly perpetrated by an escaped leopard (brought in for publicity reasons). It is revealed that the crimes are actually the work of a human, who masquerades as the leopard.

This Val Lewton shocker was tellingly advertised as "Women Alone the Victims of Strange, Savage Killer." By revealing the bestial as a front concealing a very human killer, it jettisons the need for physical metamorphosis, commenting on the tradition of werewolf tales to dissociate such sex crime from human capability. The bestial is ironically a facade erected to deny illicit lustful experience unique to humans, who seek to exploit those around them, bringing a moral and physical darkness to the world — the darkness of an essentially human heart, as visually explored in film noir. The film's bleak irony is best demonstrated in a much remarked on scene where a woman locks her little girl out of the house for being late, and the child is then killed, the viewer only seeing blood seep under the door.

The ascribing of horror-monster atrocities to a human being, and the emphasis on shadows and barely seen figures/objects, suggests the film can be considered a bridge from horror to film noir — which also latched onto author Woolrich for inspiration. Despite its retrospective interest, the film was disowned (Hardy; p. 82) by both director and producer as a misfire, a failed experiment.

Life in the Balance

(1955: d. Harry Horner)

scr. Robert Presnell Jr., Leo Townsend; stry. Georges Simenon; pr. Leonard Goldstein; ph. J. Gomez Urquiza; m. Raul Lavista; ed. George Gittens, George Crone; art d. Bunther Gerzo; cast. Ricardo Montalban, Anne Bancroft, Lee Marvin, Jose Perez, Rodolfo Acosta, Carlos Muzquiz, Jorge Trevino, Jose Torvay, Eva Calvo, Fanny Schiller; 74m

The film takes place in the midst of a police manhunt for a serial killer of women in Mexico City. A young man whose father (Montalban) is suspected trails a man he thinks is the real killer (Marvin). Convinced of this man's guilt, he smashes police phone boxes as an intended trail for the pursuing police, hoping that justice will prevail. The killer grabs the boy and a police chase follows, ending at a University campus.

The killer is a self-righteous hypocritical religious crusader who murders those he considers to be sinners, particularly women whose morality arouses and repulses him. The killings' basis in fantasy — that of the killer as avenging angel and purifier — signals them as sexual. The killer has no thoughts about killing (or intending to kill) to protect his identity, and reflects the amorality of tail-end noir, which by the mid–1950s had segued into the socially conscious case study and the law enforcement response story.

Director Horner had flirted with the serial killer figure before in *Beware My Lovely*. *Life in the Balance* also addresses the theme of American Imperialism as spreading corruption, the Mexican setting pointing to the later *Touch of Evil*. The serial killer is arguably a representative of a society and culture founded on religiously sanctioned violence (the legacy of the Westerner and the Puritan's Manifest Destiny). It is perhaps a matter of consequence that the serial killer would emerge as the inevitable result of such a heritage, at once produced by the culture and disavowed by it.

Limbic Region

(1996: d. Michael Pattinson)

scr. Todd Johnson, Patrick Ranahan; pr. George Horie, Tom Rowe; ph. Tobias A. Schlesinger; m. Gary Chang; prod d. Chris August; cast. Edward James Olmos, George Dzundza, Roger R. Cross, Gwynyth Walsh, Don S. Davis, Chris Wilding; 100m

In this ambitious, character-oriented tele-movie about a serial murder case in San Francisco, obsessive cop Olmos does not believe in the same murder suspect as the majority of the force, and so doggedly pursues and harasses the person he feels responsible (Dzundza), and who has indeed been on a serial killing career for over two decades. Olmos waits for the killer to make a mistake, and tries to prompt it to obtain a demonstration or admission of guilt. In the meantime, the two adversaries, cop and suspect, converse with and taunt one another via their shared interpersonal bond.

The killer, nicknamed "The Store Keeper," is supposedly based on the true-life Zodiac Killer (who was also part inspiration for Scorpio in *Dirty Harry*), who also sent letters to police listing the number of victims as a kind of scorecard, lest an incorrect tally be attributed. It is a somber film, with Olmos' voice-over adding a film noir dimension. It postulates a world wherein smart killers can remain relatively safe to carry out their homicidal lifestyle, and the lone cop is a long way from heroic.

The most intriguing aspect of *Limbic Region* is that throughout the film the killer and the cop meet regularly for lengthy discussions. This is part of the "game" between knowing, skilled players, with Olmos ever more frustrated at being unable to prove the killer guilty, a fact which the killer slyly taunts him with, skirting around a full admission of personal guilt until the end. Serial murder as a career has become an interpersonal bond between the two. Subjective camerawork suggests that these scenes may have been intended as psychodrama, and even the transference of guilt and complicity from killer to cop. The cop is aware of the potential for vigilante action but is ethically bound to avoid it, though some of his actions come close.

To further develop this parallel between killer and cop, the psychologist develops a profile of the killer, whilst the film intercuts scenes of the killer and his harsh mother. The profiler concludes that the killer is marked by a lack of human emotion, except weary anger, a possible description of the cop also. Both killer and policeman, and even psychologist/profiler, find personal validation in their interactions. The "game" demands a commitment between them, to the exclusion of much else. It portrays a killer able to easily don masks of reality in between explosions of brutal violence.

The film culminates in the expected confrontation, where the killer finally admits guilt, adding that the greatest thrill was the victim's moment of recognition that they are going to die, this permitting the victim to become a part of the killer with their last breath — fairly common serial killer rhetoric. The moment of his victim's death enables the killer's sexual release — torture (whether implied or depicted) is foreplay — with sex murder therefore a form of personal empowerment.

Liquid Dreams

(1992: d. Mark Manos)

scr. Manos; pr. Cassian Elwes, Ted Fox; m. Ed Tomney; cast. Richard Steinmetz, Candice Daly, Barry Dennen, Juan Fernandez, Tracey Walter, Frankie Thorn, Mink Stole, Marilyn Tokuda, Mark Manos, Don Stark, Paul Bartel; 92m

In a slightly futuristic version of America, a woman journeys to the decaying metropolis to visit her sister, finding her dead in her apartment. She starts work at a sex club in order to investigate further. She gradually reveals a male-dominated internal power structure of ever more perverse and manipulative sexual exploitation. Finally, she discovers that a "Neurovid" center produces porn videos that are designed to control/affect the viewers in ways similar to Cronenberg's *Videodrome* and Bigelow's *Strange Days*.

As such, the film is a mix of Cronenberg and the *Stripped to Kill*–type movies. Its decadent and sleazy world recalls *Hardcore* and balances *8MM*. The entirely self-contained sex-world (workers live and work in the building; porn videos are made in-house and shown to guests and tenants on internal TV) suggests a microcosm of contemporary sexual politics, lauded over, ironically enough, by a man with no genitalia.

The inescapability of TV pornography suggests the film was intended as a kind of Orwellian erotica. The inhabitants have latched onto sex as the only option left them in the harsh world, consuming it literally as the leader kills women to siphon off their endorphins (sex as a drug which inevitably breeds sexual exploiters and sex killers).

It is not really a serial killer film, however, and is included herein for its related depiction of an out-of-control sex-culture headed by killers. Unlike the strippers in many such movies, there is no suggestion that their profession is in any way sexually empowering: it makes them disposable products for an ever more desperate pursuit of sensation. The killer is doomed to murder repeatedly as a means of gaining the sexual release he can no longer achieve naturally.

Despite its low budget, *Liquid Dreams* is an ambitious film that draws on the likes of *The Handmaid's Tale* and *Cafe Flesh*. Its increasingly surrealistic erotica portrays sexual excitement as a demonstration of power, inherently perverse and corrupt, though easily exploitable.

Listen

(1998: d. Gavin Wilding)

scr. Michael Bafaro, Jonas Quastel; pr. Diane Patrick O'Connor; ed. Melinda Seabrook; prod d. Cathy Robinson; cast. Brooke Langton, Sarah Buxton, Gordon Currie, Andy Romano, Joel Wyner; 101m

A woman new to an apartment building discovers that her telephone has a connection that enables her to listen in on her neighbors' conversations. She tells her best friend, and the two of them are slowly enraptured by the secret lives of those around them. The woman is a bisexual and forms a relationship with her neighbors, unspoken sexual attraction influencing the actions of them all. She listens in on the phone sex calls of one neighbor in particular, and starts to spy on his sexual relations. When one involved woman turns up dead, she fears she has uncovered a serial killer. The police are ultimately uncooperative, and the protagonist must pursue the killer herself.

This, like the bigger-budgeted *Sliver*, develops a world wherein hidden sexual desires motivate all human interactions. No one is what he or she seems to be on the surface: the straighter they seem, the more sexually disturbed. In this, the lesbian relationship at first offers a strength and tenderness which allows independence from a heterosexual world that imposes roles and power-politics, which in turn creates a world of sexual predators. These predators are conditioned into becoming killers, and the film's world is based on the assumption that it is inevitable for such killers to be out there.

All human interaction is predicated

on sexual desire. The killer is finally revealed to be a woman who framed a sexually dominant male in order to keep the protagonist's attentions for herself. This is perhaps a "cop-out" ending, for it invalidates the theme of potential freedom from a corrupt heterosexuality and the network of perversity (including snuff film consumption) it fosters. Perhaps the killer has been so conditioned by these gender expectations that her efforts are an attempt to transcend them, unaware that she has become the very thing she resents. There is no alternative to heterosexual role-playing as infectious perversity.

Live! From Death Row

(1991: d. Patrick Duncan)

scr. Duncan; pr. Julie Bilson Ahlberg; cast. Bruce Davison, Joanna Cassidy, Art LaFleur, Calvin Levels, Julio Oscar Mechoso, Michael D. Roberts; 94m

An incarcerated serial killer (Davison) takes a TV newswoman (Cassidy) hostage on the eve of his televised pre-execution interview. The broadcast is maintained, and the killer insists that the reporter interview all death-row inmates in order to give the public a better perception of those whom society considers monstrous. He intends to turn the broadcast into an anti–death penalty forum, ironically culminating in a televised electrocution.

The film is very aware of the subculture that has developed around these killers. Thus, it depicts the people and events attending the expected execution of the killer as a kind of amoral circus, representing the worst in human nature. These people can wear "fry em" T-shirts and condone execution. Even the show's cameraperson laments that the news has become sensationalism, fostering desensitization. This culture makes light of murder and execution as sanctioned murder,

and the killer's efforts are an attempt to force an awareness of moral insensitivity and hypocrisy. He prompts the exploitative reporter to care once again, and is thus a cathartic presence.

This attempt to address the public perception of the serial killer results in a very self-conscious role for Davison. The killer is charming, expressive and intelligent — the very image of the suave killer that had entered the popular imagination since the real Ted Bundy. Indeed, the killer here refers to Bundy, commenting that he, unlike what Ted claimed, has no hidden bodies to disclose. Otherwise, he may be compared, it is implied. However, his ideological agenda is undercut by his spiteful misogyny, a side of himself he cannot conceal; thus, he assaults a female guard and calls her one of the "breeder cows" he has spent his adult life eradicating from the earth. Pathology overwhelms ideology. The guard, in revenge for the humiliation, takes part in his later execution.

It is arguable to what extent the killer is an anti-authoritarian anti-hero (Kerekes and Slater, p. 90), as he expresses his views by similar force. However, his actions have the desired result, as the cameraman will not exploit the killer's suicide by broadcasting it, and the reporter laments her sensationalist drives. The killer is thus an agent of social change, however egotistical his actions may be — his takeover is a means by which he can maintain control, until death. He needs to be in control, as all around him, except the two remorseful prisoners (one a woman) who suicide, cling to idealized conceptions of themselves.

As an examination of TV reality programming and its incipient amorality, the film is perhaps inspired (Kerekes and Slater, pp. 90–91) by tabloid television programs and talk shows (apparently, Geraldo Rivera actually broadcast an episode entitled "Murder: Live from Death Row").

The plot hook of a killer taking a hostage to facilitate an escape was used also in *Natural Born Killers* and *The Expert*.

Lizard in a Woman's Skin

(1971: d. Lucio Fulci)

scr. Fulci; pr. Edmondo Amati; ph. Luigi Kurveiller; art d. Roman Calatayud; ed. Jorge Serralonga; m. Ennio Morricone; cast. Florinda Bolkan, Stanley Baker, Jean Sorel, Leo Genn, Alberto De Mendoza, Silvia Monti, Penny Brown; 105 (95)m

Along with Argento's work and Fulci's own *Don't Torture the Duckling*, this is one of the first in the rash of Italian "giallo" movies. It concerns a lesbian killer who murders in an attempt to keep her sexuality a secret. She is so consumed by fantasies that she is compelled to put them into reality.

The use of dream sequences suggests that a realm of altered perception seeks to seep or force its way onto reality, with horrendous consequences. This reflects the theme of altered perception that runs through the giallo movie. Fulci depicts the clash of reality and fantasy in a protagonist who seeks their potential cohabitation. He would repeatedly tackle the theme, most effectively in *The Beyond*.

This is nevertheless reportedly one of his more stylishly flamboyant efforts, and was praised by *Variety* when released in the United States as an effectively surrealist demonstration of mental derangement and disintegration. It posits such sex crime as a potential consequence of social values in transition, thus incorporating drugged hippies into its array of secondary characters. The protagonist cannot free her sexuality, except through murders designed to validate the necessity of keeping it suppressed.

The film's brutality, a dream sequence involving an eviscerated canine, landed it in Italian courtrooms. Fulci was reportedly saved from a prison sentence only because the special effects man brought proof that it was an effect. This predates the obscenity debate that would greet the Italian horror boom of the 1970s, perhaps most conspicuously in the case of Ruggero Deodato's notorious *Cannibal Holocaust*. The gory obscenities of Italian horror are considered to be epitomized in director Fulci's overall work, and he has become both championed and reviled, though never attaining the auteur status of Dario Argento.

The Lodger

(1926: d. Alfred Hitchcock)

scr. Eliot Stannard, Hitchcock; nvl. Marie Belloc Lowndes; pr. Michael Balcon; ph. Baron Ventimiglia; ed. Ivor Montagu; cast. Ivor Novello, June, Marie Ault, Arthur Chesney, Malcolm Keen; 84m

London is affected by a murderer calling himself "The Avenger," modeled on Jack the Ripper, who murders women (golden-haired girls) on consecutive Tuesdays, his pattern set. A family takes in a lodger whose actions they consider strange; and as the murders continue, they begin to suspect that he is in actuality the murderer. Once a jealous, incompetent and resentful policeman is involved, the lodger is systematically alienated and persecuted by those around him, although in the end he is revealed not to be the killer after all.

Unlike many of Hitchcock's later films, this is not a case study but the depiction of individual and social responses to a grave threat to its secure functioning, as possibly prompting a vigilante response. In that, it can be compared in part to *M*, which added the partial case study. The killer is thus less a real person than a contagion (according to the *And You Call Yourself a Scientist* online site), representative of a new evil which plagues society, a common subtext of early serial killer films. Correspondingly, we never see the real killer, and can gauge his motivations only by implication.

Of course, the media seize upon this threat. Indeed, Hitchcock is at lengths to depict the awesome mechanical apparatus that the print media has become. He initially dwells on shots of giant presses that dwarf human beings, and wire transmitting resources that seem to function independently of human involvement. The sensationalist print media is an immense agency, a new technology able to shape and control people's responses to the threats it chooses to exploit. It is a new force in society and has an awesome responsibility.

Golden-haired models are the killer's targets. Hence, the director also depicts modelling and arguably prostitution as the epitome of female glamour, elegant beauty and presumed feminine desirability, suggesting the killer as a response to the redefinition of gender codes in the 1920s flapper era. Social change brings with it self-appointed, resentful purifiers. The killer calls himself the Avenger, but what exactly he feels he is avenging is left subtextual, although implied to be women's increased independence. In that, the detective comes closer to the killer's psychology than does the lodger.

The detective resents the lodger for taking his beloved away from him. His desire to turn the woman into a kept object is thus frustrated, and his persecution of the lodger is an ability to reassert his lost potency when his desired possession rejects him. He functions out of wronged pride, a corruptive force. Although he realizes the lodger is innocent, and saves him just in time from the actions of a frenzied mob, his turnaround comes less from a sense of legal responsibility than a moral decision to correct what he realizes was a moral weakness on his part. He is willing to admit that he was wrong, and in so doing reveals a willingness to change with the times and respect a woman's choices

towards free will. The lodger admires and embraces the girl's free spirit, the very quality the detective would initially seek to contain. Though the lodger's actions may seem suspicious, he is a kind and benevolent man, and it is a symptom of social paranoia and private resentment that he is misconstrued.

Hitchcock had been to Germany and, impressed by the lighting effects in German fantasy movies (Boot, p. 30), attempted to bring this Expressionist conception to the UK. This resulted in the foggy streets and shadowy, cramped visuals that would become standard for subsequent Ripper films. The director considered this film (his third) as the one in which he got his style together. It is also the first one to reveal his future interest in the theme of the wrongfully accused innocent. Ironically though, this theme was a partial imposition, since matinee idol Novello did not want himself depicted as a murderer.

The Lodger

(1944: d. John Brahm)

scr. Barre Lyndon; nvl. Marie Belloc-Lowndes; pr. Robert Bassier; ph. Lucien Ballard; ed. J. Watson Webb Jr.; spec eff. Fred Sersen; cast. Laird Cregar, Merle Oberon, George Sanders, Sir Cedric Hardwicke, Sara Allgood, Aubrey Mather, Queenie Leonard; 84m

This excellent remake is the start of director Brahm's most distinguished period, resulting in three thrillers for MGM. A heavily atmospheric studio-bound film, it relies on the usual Ripper iconography of harsh lighting and shadows, thick fogs, and class consciousness (as the lodger is in a wealthy family's home, and it is they who suspect him).

Unlike the Hitchcock version, this offers no case of mistaken identity, and the lodger is in fact Jack the Ripper, whose designs may be directed against the landlord's daughter, a provocative dancer. The

Laird Cregar stars as the mysterious tenant who is actually Jack the Ripper in the remake of *The Lodger* (Fox, 1944).

lodger leaves late at night to do his "work," arousing suspicion to the point where a detective is brought in. The detective also has an interest in the daughter. Finally, the killer is uncovered and chased to his death.

The film attempts to define the serial killer with directness rare for the period. The detective is aware that this is a new kind of crime and refuses to accept that such slayings are unrelated, instead searching for the clues that would make them the product of a repeat sex offender, a then-rare type. He strives to fit the crimes into conventional methodologies but cannot, an admission of the different kind of murderer that the emerging serial killer was. He represents the need to impose conventional order onto a situation where none exists. He acknowledges the sexual nature of the crimes, and adds that the killer is sated for a while after killing but is inevitably driven again to recapture the personal satisfaction and release provided by murder. As such, this presents a tacit understanding of the serial killer as a habitual sex killer. Also implied by the detective is the need for someone to predict the behavior set in such a pattern (a function later filled by the profiler). Thus, *The Lodger* has a seminal place in the evolution of the serial killer film as a genre.

The murders occur offscreen, and are only important insofar as they mean something to the killer alone and are apparently unknowable to everyone else. Brahm is aware of this tendency to place such motives beyond human experience, and is careful to provide a recognizable motive in the end. The killer, whose idolized and possibly incestuously desired brother (whose picture he keeps in a locket — Brahm would treat the subject of memory and desire in the classic film noir *The Locket*) was tainted by a prostitute, resents women's sexuality as an evil. Their beauty can then be cut out, although he accepts that this ultimately destroys the beauty also. He demonstrates awareness of the killing as sexual expression and an attempt to punish women for arousing such expression when he says, "man can destroy what he hates, and love what he destroys." He is so compelled by his dysfunction that even when his life is threatened he still tries to kill the woman. Such crime is shown as a balance of irresistible compulsion and sociological "triggers."

Thus, he can rationalize his actions as for the betterment of society, a motive also shared by the killer in William Wellman's *Lady of Burlesque*, which treats a similar theme. Indeed, *The Lodger* has a scene in a can-can theater (a precursor of the burlesque hall, and also a device in *The Haunted Strangler*) wherein the killer is aroused by the dancers and repulsed/shamed by that desire. He projects/transforms these insecure and confusing feelings of his own sexuality into the resentment of women's open sexuality. Is it therefore in part a form of self-loathing also? Like Wellman's film, *The Lodger* suggests that changing cultural attitudes towards sexuality foster tormented and confused sex killers. Thus, Brahm holds on Oberon's bare legs in the dance hall, ironically working in a profession which allows her a sexual freedom that's later codified in terms of male desire, a process the film implicitly acknowledges.

In an ominous early use of the open frame, the film establishes a police presence on the fringes of the action, present but unable to prevent the killings. These crimes and the apparent cleverness of the elusive killer both repulse and fascinate the general public. According to class convention perhaps, the crimes are talked about in dining rooms or in pubs (where they are even joked about, such is the need to make sense of such abhorrence), a device also found in Hitchcock. These are a new kind of crime, one society has not yet developed a conditioned response for, and Brahm is careful to never distance the killer from the real world — he is never made into a monster, despite Cregar's shadowy, bloated menace.

In fact, Cregar makes him into a shy, almost childish figure, akin to Peter Lorre in *M*. Gradually, he reveals his sexual insecurity, turning the pictures of actresses' faces to the wall to avoid their eyes following him and possibly revealing his guilt. He is always framed by Brahm separate from the groups and individuals he comes into contact with — an opposing force, deceptively mild: in appearance hardly the challenge to social order that he is.

Brahm is considered to have utilized the best of German Expressionist techniques, and the film represents the incorporation of the serial killer into film noir, alongside Hitchcock's *Shadow of a Doubt* released the same year. Significantly, the *New York Herald Tribune* commented that the film owes much to Krafft-Ebing's case histories of sex murderers (Mank in *Magill's American Film Guide*, p. 1934), and, consequently, that the sex-murderer is based on a real, human abomination.

The film has been compared favorably to both *M* and *Pandora's Box*. Its theme of a lodger-killer recalls *Night Must Fall*, which also manages to recreate an English feel at a Hollywood studio. The lodger-killer would also be tellingly reinterpreted in *Apartment Zero*.

London Blackout Murders

(1942: d. George Sherman)

scr. Curt Siodmak; cast. John Abbott, Mary McLeod, Lloyd Corrigan, Lester Matthews, Anita Bolster, Billy Bevan, Frederick Worlock; 58m

Amidst the WWII bombing raids on London, in a society beset by constant blackouts, a surgeon turns murderous (metaphorical parallels here to the amnesia narrative). He uses a hypodermic needle as a murder weapon and only kills those he believes are — but never proves to be — enemies. In believing he is killing undesirables for the good of the community, he shares a belief frequently held by real killers.

Once he is captured, the police find that years earlier he had snapped and murdered his wife. As an air raid is in progress, he is tried in a basement, recalling *M*. His crimes are a means of empowerment based

on a fantasy-inspired superiority, and thus arguably a sexual expression, although there is no sexual violation of the victims. It is in the curious suggestion that the criminal career began with a sex crime and segued into self-esteem killings masquerading as patriotism that the film is of interest in the serial killer pantheon.

Love and Human Remains

(1995: d. Denys Arcand)

scr. Brad Fraser; play. Fraser; pr. Roger Frappier; ph. Paul Sarossy; m. John McCarthy; ed. Alain Baril; prod d. Francois Seguin; cast. Thomas Gibson, Ruth Marshall, Cameron Bancroft, Mia Kirshner, Joanne Vannicola, Matthew Ferguson, Rick Roberts; 100m

The serial killer is herein the epitome of social malaise and Generation-X hopelessness and sexual relations. The film takes a look at a number of people, one of whom may be a serial killer of women who rips out their earrings after sex and murder as a trophy and memento. The protagonist is a gay man who lives with a woman (his former lover) who wonders if lesbianism would offer her a satisfaction that she lacks in life.

Arcand once again shows his interest in dissecting a group of loose friends and acquaintances as they attempt to forge an interpersonal bond. Significantly here, they cannot escape their inherent selfishness, a near-sightedness expressed in angst and dissatisfaction with a world that permits them no role and dooms them to loneliness — all except the killer, who has found a self-definition in sex murder as an escape, a surrender to fantasy. It is thus arguably an act of desperation, though he claims it has fulfilled his search for meaning.

Indeed, the film examines the extent to which sexuality enables or fulfills the need for identity. The search for meaning, love and self-acceptance can become the

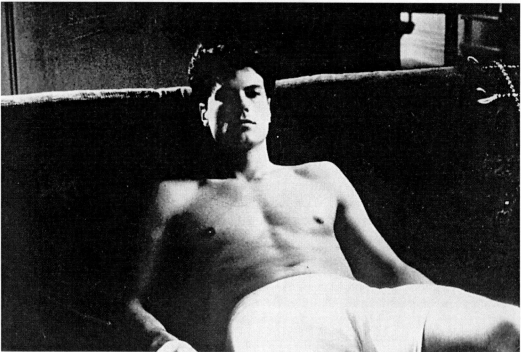

Top: Emotional desperation: Cameron Bancroft, in *Love and Human Remains* (Sony, 1995), in an introspective moment (one of many). *Bottom:* Emotional resignation: Cameron Bancroft in another contemplative moment.

search for sexual fulfillment, the characters mistakenly believing that such an identity offers them a way out of their emptiness. In the world of post–AIDS casual sex, there is literally a killer out there preying on this mentality. It is a sign of the protagonist's maturation that he finally refuses to become a sexual exploiter and does not sodomize a teenage boy who wants him too.

The outside world is one of unattractive urban desolation (an unnamed city). Perhaps this is the only solace allowed the characters. The serial killer's acts are the epitome of passion in this sexually dysfunctional world. Amidst persistent unsafe sex and a quest to transcend gender roles, the film is more about sexual politics than serial killing. It postulates serial murder as an almost social standard, the end result of an aimless culture where sex and violence become interchangeable as disenchantment sets in. Is it a matter of degree?

The killer refers to the homicidal part of himself as "he," separating himself from his monstrous actions. It also implicitly blames male heterosexuality for such a homicidal nature. The killer implies that the protagonist will one day know what he means, as if the journey towards the homicidal monster were inevitable. The "he" is a fantasy construct that permits him an identity beyond himself, and which he ultimately surrenders to, less out of guilt than as a means of immortality. He hopes that he will forever be known and feared as the sex killer, and not the inadequate, hateful being he otherwise is, despite his efforts to appear otherwise. The killer's suicide refocuses the protagonist and ironically gives him a direction, as if his own aimlessness had been purged by his friend's death.

This was Canadian director Arcand's first English-language film, after he achieved international success with *Jesus of Montreal*. It seems to have been an influence on Todd Solondz' *Happiness*. The serial killer reportedly had more of a function in the original stageplay, however.

The Love Butcher

(1982: d. Mikel Angel and Donald Jones)

scr. Jones; pr. Gary Williams; ph. Jones, Austin McKinney; m. Richard Hieronymous; ed. Robert Freeman; art d. Ron Foreman; cast. Erik Stern, Kay Neer, Jeremiah Beecher, Edward Roehm, Robin Sherwood; 83m

A gardener resents his treatment at the hands of the female LA suburbanites who hire him to keep their places beautiful. When he feels insulted, he leaves and returns as his alter-ego, that of his virile brother, and sexually uses and kills the women with the garden tools, punishing them for their superior airs.

The killer is beset by inferiority — he is a cripple (symbolic impotence) — and retracts into a fantasy of himself as a sexually insatiable man. He puts all his energy into this fantasy, satisfied only through sex murder as an act of self-expression. He justifies his response to sexual inadequacy and resentment by claiming that all women serve to emasculate men and thus are deserving of their fate.

Hardy et al. (p. 305) found the film's self-conscious style almost parodic. Beyond that, however, the film seems to have earned no recognition and is difficult to locate, presumably languishing somewhere on video racks. It presumably possesses some similarities to the Australian film *Lady Stay Dead*, also about a psychotic gardener's sexual resentments.

Love from a Stranger

(1936: d. Rowland V. Lee)

scr. Frances Marion; play. Frank Vosper; stry. Agatha Christie; pr. Max Schach; ph. Philip Tannura; m. Benjamin Britten; cast. Ann Harding, Basil Rathbone, Binnie Hale, Bruce Seton, Jean Cadell, Bryan Powley, Joan Hickson, Donald Calthrop; 90m

A woman who wins the lottery is wooed by a gentleman (Rathbone) wanting a room (shades of *The Lodger, Night Must Fall* and even *Secret Beyond the Door*). Once they are married, he tries to get her to sign papers, and she gradually suspects more sinister purposes. A stranger warns her that her husband is not what he seems and is a lady-killer. The husband steadily loses his self-control and hence his sanity. In the end, he is revealed as a charming serial killer known as Fletcher. He tries different ways to kill her, but she is adept at the battle of wits that unfolds. In the end, he believes that she has poisoned him (which he tried to do her) and dies of heart failure, even though he has not been poisoned.

Like *Night Must Fall, Love from a Stranger* paints a portrait of an outwardly ingratiating man who hides a monstrous sexuality. As in *Night* also, the killer becomes involved in a battle of wills with a woman whom he gradually sees as a worthy adversary rather than a mere victim. Many critics acknowledged *Love from a Stranger*'s debt to the Bluebeard legend of a nefarious wife-killer. It effectively concentrates on the horror and mixed emotions of a woman who discovers that her love is not all she thought him to be.

Love from a Stranger

(1947: d. Richard Whorf)

scr. Philip MacDonald; pr. James J. Geller; ph. Tony Gaudio; m. Hans Salter; cast. Sylvia Sidney, John Hodiak, Ann Richards, John Howard, Isobel Elsom, Frederick Worlock; 81m

This Hollywood remake of the hit 1937 UK film apparently has some resemblance to Hitchcock's *Suspicion*, with the heroine not as smartly independent as she was in the first version. The film has additional characters, notably a Scotland Yard investigator, and a more shadowy style in an attempt to transform it from melo-drama into a more conventional thriller or even film noir. The characterization of the killer lacks Rathbone's finesse (according to both *Variety* and the *New York Times*).

Although the killer has victims sign over their money before he kills them, this conventional motive conceals his sexual pleasure at such manipulation and domination. Sadly, the film reportedly does not develop this theme.

Love Lies Bleeding

(1999: d. William Tannen)

scr. Tony Rush; exec pr. Jason Goldberg; cast. John Comer, Faye Dunaway, Malcolm McDowell, Paul Rhys, Emily Raymond

Tannen returns to the serial killer film a decade after his *Hero and the Terror* with this well-cast version of the Jack the Ripper case. It is considered an inaccurate fictionalization of the case, sticking to the barest outlines of truth only. An aristocratic young woman is determined to prove her independence in Victorian London (no easy feat) and gets a job at a newspaper, where she attracts the attention of a veteran reporter (Dunaway). Her intended is a benevolent doctor who claims to support her drive for independence. Meanwhile, the Ripper taunts police, press and a local political activist trying to turn the case into a sociopolitical issue. The reporter suspects her intended, but one of his co-workers is arrested instead. However, after finding incriminating belongings in his possession, she realizes that her intended is the Ripper after all. Unable to kill her (the real target of his anger), he shoots himself.

The film intends to contrast different types of women, from the rare professional to the lowly prostitute, and their respective fates in such a restrictive atmosphere. The prostitute is the innocent dreamer, the mentor (Dunaway) the true realist, and the protagonist the bridge, who tries to gain independence without resorting to gender roles. The protagonist is increasingly aware of a kind of sisterhood necessary to escape from under male domination (which would classify women as sexual beings and resent them for it). As a look at moves towards feminist liberation, the film depicts a Patriarchy intent on the suppression and sexual objectification of women, though its more enlightened members may claim the opposite. Ironically, the most forward-looking is the most hypocritical — the killer. He claims to support his betrothed's moves and to generously treat prostitutes, but secretly resents both for their challenge to passivity.

The film plays specifically on one aspect of Ripper lore: that the mutilations had a certain surgical precision that suggested a doctor may have been responsible (the most popular scenario in the Ripper movies is the demented surgeon). Indeed, a respected doctor (McDowell) is brought into the case for his expert opinion (an outsider, he is thus the profiler figure here). He pronounces that due to a doctor's God-like power over life and death, one in such a profession could be easily corrupted and target the easiest victims — prostitutes. Power, he suggests, is a narcotic. The sexual mutilations are thus the frenzied, orgasmic culmination of a process of eroticizing surgery (a theme in European mad doctor movies especially, hence *The Awful Dr. Orlof*) as a process of sadistic sexual empowerment. As the clearest indicator of the killer's sexual dementia, the mutilations (and removal of body parts) are considered the real outrage of the case and the factor that clearly differentiated it from other sex crimes.

The film's truly horrifying subtext is the growing awareness of the reporter and her elder mentor, who both attend the autopsy of one of the victims, that their sexuality and independence are possibly the factors which draw resentment and hatred upon them: that such crimes may escalate over the years. Is it an us-and-them conflict along gender roles? The movement to end victimization demands due outrage at such acts, but this outrage comes not from the male characters in the film, more concerned with their image as professionals than with actually apprehending the killer, who is, after all, one of them and a representative of Patriarchy.

Lucker

(1986: d. Johan Vandewoestijne) aka *Necrophagus*

scr. Vandewoestijne, John Kupferschmidt; pr. Vandewoestijne; ph. Tony Castillo; cast. Nick Van Suyt, Helga Vandevelde, Let Jodts, Marie-Paule Claes, Martine Scherre; 84m

A necrophilic sex killer, an institution escapee, murders women in their homes. He goes home for several days and then returns to the crime scene to have sex with the rotting corpses. This is shown in graphic, unflinching detail (the killer licks fluid from the rotting female genitalia he lovingly rubs his fingers over) and anticipates the Jorg Buttgereit *Nekromantik* films. The film is thus part of the underground "corpse-fucking art" movement in European genre filmmaking.

The necrophilic component of some serial murders is a rarely examined, though frequently subtextual, aspect of the serial killer movie. Even in as graphic and controversial a film as *Henry: Portrait of a Serial Killer* the eponymous protagonist draws the line at sex with the newly dead, let alone the decomposed. Yet here murder is a form of foreplay for a killer who can only achieve arousal with a decomposing body. It is treated as an objective case study; its non-judgmental black humor and intent to shock makes it a deliberately subversive portrait of transgressive behavior. It is grim Naturalism, perhaps at its most decadent.

Although arguably more provocative, complex, and certainly more technically polished than Buttgereit's films along similar lines, *Lucker* has neither the reputation nor the recognition. It studiously avoids succumbing to horror or thriller status, and its nauseating acts are presented as grotesque sensualities, fascinating in their revulsion. Murder is incidental to true sexual pleasure, the act of necrophilia which follows it being the shattering of society's taboos regarding sex and death, and therefore its greatest transgression. It thus ridicules the social conventions that hold necrophilia as a greater sin than sex murder.

Lured

(1947: d. Douglas Sirk)

scr. Leo Rosten; pr. Hunt Stromberg; ph. William Daniels; ed. John M. Foley; m. Michel Michelet; cast. George Sanders, Lucille Ball, Charles Coburn, Alan Mowbray, Sir Cedric Hardwicke, George Zucco, Joseph Calleia, Tanis Chandler, Boris Karloff; 102m

Lucille Ball stars as a dancer in London whose roommate disappears after answering a personal ad in the *Times*—like several other women, it is revealed (as in the real-life case of Harvey Glatman a decade later). A detective from Scotland Yard prompts her to answer such an ad, hoping to lure the killer out (i.e. she becomes the outside presence). In so doing she encounters many odd people, including artist Karloff whom the police consider the chief suspect. She is courted by a nightclub owner (Sanders) whose quiet business partner is revealed to be the killer. The killer tries to implicate Sanders and kill Ball.

The killer is a quiet man, whose sexual repression has resulted in his elaborate courting of victims. In this manner he can assert his superiority over women, and the police, to whom he sends clues written in

verse. The killer expresses a fondness for the poet Beaudelaire, and his ads for attractive, lonely women suggest his intent to project himself as a great lover, perhaps his ultimate fantasy. In the end, however, he is a self-serving exploiter and predator who resents his partner's success with the ladies. Thus the film elaborates on the concept of the lady-killer as an idealized male fantasy, with lethal consequences.

This was made with some of the same cast members from *The Lodger*, although it's considered Germanic in style. Correspondingly it is not considered part of the noir movement. It is a rare dramatic role for Ball, though with comic asides (she was a dancer also in Arzner's *Dance Girl Dance*), and drew her good notices. However, it is not generally considered one of director Sirk's better films. This early Hollywood mystery tale of a serial killer was based on Robert Siodmak's 1939 French film, *Personal Column*. Sirk claims he never saw Siodmak's movie, and that it was the screenwriter's adaptation. The personal-ad lure would be given a revised treatment in *Sea of Love*.

Lust of the Vampire

(1956: d. Riccardo Freda) aka *I, Vampiri, The Devil's Commandment*

scr. Freda, Piero Regnoli; ph, eff. Mario Bava; cast. Gianna Maria Canale, Antoine Balpetre, Paul Muller, Carlo d'Angelo, Dario Michaelis, Wandista Guida, Riccardo Freda, Charles Fawcett; 90 (71)m

Based on the Elizabeth Bathory legend, as would be *Female Butcher*, this is a seminal 1950s horror film about a contemporary Parisian doctor who drains his patients' blood in order to keep alive his wife. It boosted the mad surgeon range of films in Europe, and is considered to have inspired the likes of *Eyes Without a Face*, *House of Usher*, *Curse of Frankenstein* and *The Awful Dr. Orlof* (Hardy, p. 105).

Director Freda left after 10 days of filming, and Mario Bava shot the last two days.

Lust of the Vampire is also historically noteworthy for its deliberate stylization and eroticism, in total contrast with, and deliberate challenge to, the Italian Neo-Realist movement so beloved by historians. It is considered the first Italian horror film, its lush visuals betraying an increasingly Sadean corruption of the Romantic, a theme frequent in European horror and conceptions of the vampire as sex killer.

M

(1933: d. Fritz Lang)

scr. Lang, Thea Von Harbou, Paul Falkenberg, Adolf Jansen, Karl Vash; pr. Seymour Nebenzal; ph. Fritz Arno Wagner; m. Adolf Jansen; art d. Karl Vollbrecht, Emil Hasler; cast. Peter Lorre, Otto Wernicke, Gustav Grundgens; 118m

Berlin is in the grip of a monstrous child rapist/killer (Lorre). The police seem inconsequential, despite their efforts, and so the local criminal underground, concerned that their reputation is being muddied by association with this new type of killer, arrange their own methods to apprehend him, enlisting the help of a society of beggars. A blind man who recognizes the killer's whistle identifies him, whereupon the murderer flees into a building. He is captured, dragged into a basement and put on trial in a kangaroo court wherein he pleads for understanding for his guilty compulsions. The police rescue him just before the mob of criminals sets upon him.

The killer is a symptom of a sick society — Germany of the 1930s, with Nazism on the rise, and Lang has little sympathy for any characters, especially in their descent to mob vigilante justice. No adult transcends selfishness or displays any real concern for humanity. Innocence is there in this world to be abused, as no one takes the responsibility for truly benevolent mo-

tives. The criminal underworld and the police (paralleled repeatedly as like adversaries) want to catch the killer because he makes them look bad, not to protect other children. The public clamor is to expunge an evil killer they refuse to acknowledge lives within their world. It is a shadowy world, where people often seem consumed by these shadows, of constricted, dingy places.

Indeed, the film moves from exteriors, the streets, finally into the basement at the end, a symbolically infernal journey that yields the monstrousness innate in all humans. The terrified killer is dragged into Hell by amoral, ignorant hypocrites, and pleads for understanding for an evil compunction over which he has no control. There is no movement towards understanding in this mockery of justice. Lang balances the killer's point of view of the world and his victims with that world itself, hostile at worst. It goes from the evocation of a childhood chant about a feared man in black and his chopper to the depiction of a man unable to control his horrible urges — hardly the mere boogeyman of childhood fears. Lang finds an odd pity for his monster, himself in part trapped in childishness, one that demands gratification above all else.

This killer claims that no one knows what it is like to be he, and so they are quick to judge and condemn. Of course he is right, and Lang is aware of past depictions of sex killers which sought to separate the killer from recognizable humanity. Not so the almost baby-faced Lorre, who combines a childlike innocence with the menace of the inevitably demented childlike adult. Hence the inclusion of a most noted scene where Lorre looks at his reflection in the mirror, perhaps searching for a physical monstrousness which isn't there: he must make faces at himself to see the monstrousness attributed to him. The killer is one of us. Indeed, this mirror

The serial child killer (Peter Lorre) brings his next intended victim to a toy store in an effort to seduce and lure her away in *M* (Nero Film, 1931).

scene would be frequently used in serial killer films, and is given particular relevance in *The Boston Strangler*, wherein the killer gazes at his splintered reflection in a broken mirror.

Despite the killer's pleas, there is a monstrousness to him that goes beyond irresistible compunction. He plans his crimes and lures his victims carefully (candy), and he (if it is him) sends taunting letters to the press (as did Jack the Ripper and Peter Kurten), boasting that he will never stop. He has an awareness of his condition and considers himself powerless to stop himself, although he is presumably able to exercise restraint until the opportunity to get away with it arises. Despite his protestations, he is enthralled, even bemused, by the power he perceives it gives

him to destroy innocence and boast of it to those who supposedly prize it.

Typically, the police conclude that the killer is mentally ill—he must be to commit such horrific crimes—and search the criminal underworld accordingly, an association that angers the conventional criminals. The police stage raids on the underworld of usual suspects, although they sense that this may be futile: it makes them appear as if they are doing something. The added police pressure leads the criminals to conclude that such a murderer is bad for their reputation. Thus, the serial killer represents the nadir of criminal activity, separate even from other murderers, as all seek to distance themselves from him. He is a figure unto himself, an enigma that needs to be purged—the ultimate Other.

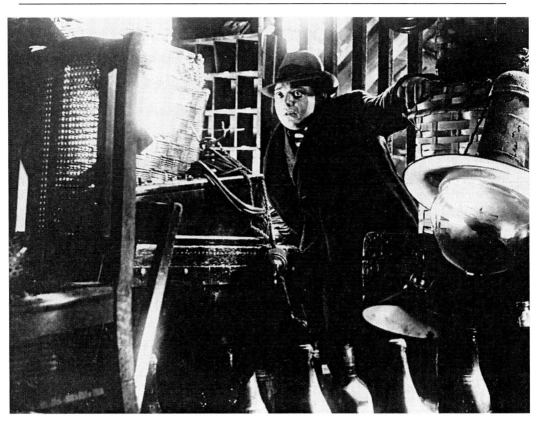

Once his identity is no longer a secret, the serial child killer (Peter Lorre) is forced to flee into a building in *M* (Nero Film, 1931).

This process would be matched in the equally seminal *The Boston Strangler* later, which again sought to stress the killer's conventionality.

The narrative stresses the unusual procedural manhunt, as both cops and criminals pursue various means, each eventually leading to the killer, and the vigilante swell which results from the realization that conventional methods cannot catch such a criminal, and that he preys on the entire city. The police state that they will catch him by luck, as they do not know how to respond. New measures must be taken in order to understand and respond to the threat posed by such a killer, but Lang held contemporary German society too repugnant to offer a valid force. Rather than examine the horror in itself, they would seek to pointlessly and ritualistically expunge it via execution, as if destroying the undesirable (who may be far from innocent) would cleanse what Lang holds an uncleansable society, or redeem an unredeemable humanity.

Lang develops much expectation regarding the appearance of such a monster before finally revealing Lorre. He looks perhaps a little odd, but is able to blend in undetected into the community he feeds upon. He also knows of the pressure for his capture, for the warnings and posters are all over the streets. Indeed, in a note of irony which suggests the killer's mix of compulsion and perverse pride, he lures a victim from under the very sign warning of a killer prowling the streets, his shadow ominously falling across it. It is an added irony that it is a blind man who leads to his capture, given away by a tune he likes to whistle (also a trait of the killer in *Shadow of a Doubt*). In that, we get a partial case study of the killer within his world, a further attempt to remove the sense of mystery initially established, as a move towards understanding, although there is none to be admitted by the characters themselves.

Finally, he is a trapped, pitiful creature, subjected to injustice and forced to plead his case to a hostile populace who have already judged him as an absolute Evil to be exterminated. The court he is subjected to is a parody of the judicial process. It is in Lorre's speech before his "peers" that the serial killer is signaled as clearly different from conventional criminality. He asserts that while they choose to be criminals, he is driven by a deeper compunction that has removed the issue of choice from him. This, arguably, also effectively removes him from conventional responsibility for his actions. He says that there is always an evil force within him, one that terrifies him (was this what he was looking for in the mirror?), and that he cannot escape from himself. The implication is that he is sick and needs a doctor rather than an executioner.

Indeed, Lorre's famous speech would be taken out of context by Nazi propaganda minister Goebbels and used in the supposed documentary *The Eternal Jew* as the confession of a typically perverted Jew admitting his inherent repulsiveness. Thus, what Lang intended to portray as within all human capability was ascribed to the Nazi's Other, the Jew. Goebbels wanted Lang to make films for the Nazis, but Lang (whose mother was Jewish) soon fled, as did Lorre (himself a Jew, and, ironically, supposedly Hitler's favorite actor — Nash and Ross, p. 1782).

Lang went to elaborate lengths to prepare for the film. He interviewed police and criminals alike (employing some to be in the film), and reportedly went to criminal psychiatric institutions for added insight. However, the main influence was the case of real-life serial killer Peter Kurten, who was apprehended two months before Lang announced his intention to make the film. It was certainly a topical work.

M is an influential film and the earliest full demonstration of the serial killer film formula before Richard Fleischer remodeled it in *The Boston Strangler*. A scene missing from many release prints had a group of mothers saying that they should have looked after their children better, and are thus partly responsible for Lorre's crimes. *M* was remade during the McCarthy era and the rise of the social problem film, with the advent of producer Stanley Kramer's liberalism.

M

(1951: d. Joseph Losey)

scr. Norman Reilly Raine, Leo Katcher; pr. Seymour Nebenzal; ph. Ernest Laszlo; m. Michel Michelet; ed. Edward Mann; prod d. John Hubley; cast. David Wayne, Howard Da Silva, Luther Adler, Martin Gabel, Glenn Anders, Karen Morley, Norman Lloyd; 82m

All critics generally, perhaps inevitably, considered this efficient Hollywood remake inferior to the original. Lang had been sought to direct it but declined. Losey relocated the film to contemporary Los Angeles and reportedly (Nash and Ross, p. 1782) stressed the killer's homicidal obsession as sexual perversity (and fetishism) more than in the first film.

It was Losey's last movie before being blacklisted from Hollywood during the Communist witch-hunts of the McCarthy era, and many critics have seen a social consciousness in its depiction of the monstrous outsider-from-within. This subtext can also be found in Dmytryk's films of the period, notably *The Sniper*, and, of course, in the influence of Stanley Kramer. Thus the plot hook of a social outcast persecuted by a bigoted mob can be interpreted as a comment on the anti–Communist furor of the McCarthy period.

The killer here is an older, more blandly Middle American man (Hirsch, *Film Noir*, p. 128), and thus an internal threat, played by an actor usually cast in sympathetic roles in musicals and comedies. He is a warped patriarch, evidence of a malfunctioning system, though a victim. His respectable veneer hides a tumultuous sexuality and a need for sexual power over children. However, the script suggests that he does not sexually violate the children, instead killing them and taking their shoes as trophies for presumed masturbatory fantasies. Fueled by fantasy, the crimes are sexual rituals and inescapable as such, as the killer knows in his final pleas.

Typical of an era that sought new depictions aligning mental illness with criminality, the film has a psychiatrist brought in on the case (and thus a very early profiler) pronounce the killer a "schizophrenic with paranoiac tendencies." This prompted the *New York Times* reviewer to stress that the film more expressly tackles the conflation of mental illness and homicidal impulses. More so than Lang, Losey comes down in favor of the understanding and proper psychiatric treatment of such serial killers. Hence the film's last line has the detective question that if these killers are "psychos," why are they released by the hospitals—a question that would haunt the genre, and the numerous escaped lunatic films of the 1980s especially.

The Mad Bomber

(1972: d. Bert I. Gordon)

scr. Gordon; stry. Marc Behm; pr, ph. Gordon; m. Michel Mention; ed. Gene Rugerrio; cast. Vince Edwards, Chuck Connors, Neville Brand, Hank Brandt, Christine Hart, Faith Quabius, Ilona Wilson, Nancy Honnold; 91m

Chuck Connors plays a man so angry at society and its amorality that he becomes a serial bomber. A serial rapist (Brand, in the act himself) witnesses him, and is then sought by the investigating officer.

The crimes are a sexual surrogate, the vast overcompensation for an inadequate personality who considers himself superior to all. Hence, Gordon compares the bomber to the serial rapist whose eyewitness testimony is sought by the policeman. Just as the bomber targets campuses and has visions and sexual fantasies of the young women there, holding a grudge against their open sexuality, the rapist watches pornographic movies of his own wife, driving himself into a vengeful frenzy. Both are sex criminals, the film implies, part of a spectrum. It is the repressed Connors, who seeks sexual expression through random large-scale destruction (hospitals, schools), whose sexuality is more perverse than the conventional sex criminal, the rapist, though they are not dissimilar. Both hold others to blame for wrongs against them, and seek retribution.

All characters, cop and quarry, are unsympathetic and border on increasingly grotesque caricature — the response to the confrontation of psychological aberrance as a reaction to social mores and values in transition. The heroes of old cannot deal with change and seek to restore the stern order of the father they believe they represent. But Gordon depicts the modern United States of the 1970s as so devoid of interpersonal communication that violence is felt to be a (legitimate) means of personal expression. The policeman is a moralistic sadist blind to the similarity between his brutal tactics and those that he condemns in others.

The violence is the result of a cultural clash, hence the constant bitter irony stressed by Gordon throughout. Hippie love music is used to counterpoint the action as Connors builds his bombs and sets about planting them. In one tellingly cynical scene, Connors stumbles across a meeting of feminists and is so outraged that he plants a bomb—punishing the forces of change and sexual equality, for it threatens the power he maintains in his fantasies. Correspondingly, a verite style breaks into stylized moments of tilted angles.

The cop consults a psychiatrist (the profiler role here) in a nod to the James Brussel case. He posits the similarities of each bombing as a signature, akin to the brutal violence inflicted by the rapist. Hidden agenda segues into ritual, which accelerates as dissatisfaction increases. Despite the killer's initial motive—revenge for his junkie daughter's death—they fulfill his need for sexual expression, a fact which drives him insane, as he is reduced to driving around the city locations of past bombings, planning new ones until he is shot and blows himself up. He is so consumed by his crimes that there is nothing in his life beyond them.

Connors and Brand both had wartime experience and were considered heroes by some, making their casting all the more ironic. Similar casting decisions influence directors Tobe Hooper, who cast Brand as the killer in *Eaten Alive*, and David Schmoeller, who cast Connors as another psychopath in *Tourist Trap*. *The Mad Bomber* is considered as perhaps the best film from a hack exploitation director. Connors' almost self-parodic side would surface again in his work in John Frankenheimer's *99 and 44/100% Dead*. Serial bombing would again be considered a sexual crime in *The Final Cut*.

The Mad Butcher

(1972: d. Guido Zurli)

scr. Charles Ross, Enzo Gicca; pr. Harry Hope, Eugenio Corso; ph. Enrico Betti; cast. Victor Buono, Karin Field, Brad Harris, John Ireland, Franca Polcelli; 83m

Buono stars as the serial killer/butcher who uses human flesh in his products, which he sells from a portable stand. A former psychiatric institution inmate whose doctor claims he's cured, Buono's crimes recommence when he kills his pestering wife, putting her through a meat grinder. To keep up demand, he must kill more. A visiting American reporter hangs around the fringes, suspecting something. Buono is found out when a police officer discovers incriminating objects (buttons) in the sausages he gets from the police station.

The Mad Butcher is sparsely directed and decorated, focusing on character eccentricity and ably making the most of Buono's jovial menace. Despite the odd flourish, the film reflects the minimalist style of Ted Mikels or Andy Milligan, and balances their intense, grubby cynicism. Thus, much is made of the scene where Buono, his temper pushed beyond control, kills his wife and lays the body on the bed and undresses it. The necrophilic intentions are clear. There is a momentary realization of the enormity of his acts, but he is able to rationalize this, ready to dismember the corpse as a sex act. He has become his profession, in the filmmakers' nod to Capitalist enterprise, and jokes "meat is meat" as he commences his grisly task.

This murder and dismemberment frees his sexual appetites, repressed in hospital one assumes. He seeks out prostitutes, despising them but unable to resist, and takes one as a mistress. Ironically, she comes to remind him of his wife, and so he disposes of the mistress too, as he is doomed to repeat this sexual cycle. Rather than liberation, there is only further entrapment. And this is the man the doctors have decreed sane (an ironic attack on the mental health establishment which balances that in *Frightmare*).

This cannibal black comedy was produced in Germany and Austria, and depicts a rather unattractive Vienna. The director was known as a minor parodist. It is based on real-life German killer Fritz Haarmann, also treated in *Tenderness of the Wolves*, and who may have been at least a partial inspiration for *M*. In a jibe at the American audience, the reporter here jokes to Buono that Americans in particular love sex and violence. He goes on to prove this, having easy sexual relations with women, all the while fascinated by the sexual violence around him. Perhaps this was intended as condemnatory, but it does not have the bitterness one might expect in such a caricature. It is more a light parody.

Man Bites Dog

(1991: d. Andre Bonzel)

scr, pr. Remy Belvaux, Andre Bonzel, Benoit Poelvoorde, Vincent Tavier; ph. Andre Bonzel; m. Jean-Marc Chenut; ed. Belvaux, Eric Dardill; cast. Benoit Poelvoorde, Jacqueline Poelvoorde-Pappaert, Nelly Pappaert, Jenny Drye, Malou Madou, Willy Vandenbroeck; 96m

In this controversial Belgian serial killer film, a documentary crew follows a serial killer at work, with family, and as he disposes of the bodies. They are gradually drawn into his lifestyle, to the point of participating in rape and murder at Christmas. The killer and crew are shot in an encounter with a rival documentary crew filming the exploits of another serial killer.

Structured as a mock documentary (a "mockumentary"), which draws comparisons to *This Is Spinal Tap*, this low-budget film proved a talking point both due to its violence and its starkly comedic tone. This grotesquerie was defended as satire and vilified as trendy cynicism, with the film grouped alongside Tarantino's *Reservoir Dogs* as evidence of a renewed non-judgmental emphasis on violence. As a satire of television tabloids, it anticipates the targets and some of the tone of *Natural Born Killers*. There are some (Hardy,

p. 482) who consider the film the epitome of, and a parodic indictment of, the genre's stylistic emphasis on the objective behaviorist observation of a killer, as best demonstrated in *Henry: Portrait of a Serial Killer*. Tellingly, the British censors passed *Man Bites Dog* uncut but insisted *Henry* (which lacks the obvious satire) be severely trimmed, the latter film apparently lacking any socially redeeming merit in their eyes.

At first the serial killer is almost likable, due primarily to his enthusiasm and biting sense of ironic humor. He has no respect for those around him, and is convinced of his superiority and worth, an opinion of himself indeed validated by the attention lavished on him by the documentary filmmakers. He even helps them out financially when money for the film dries up. He talks incessantly, however, and it becomes increasingly clear that there is nothing really insightful in what he has to say. The more he talks about what he finds meaningful, the more his emptiness, banality and even stupidity is evident. He makes pointless sociological observation and pronouncements which inevitably bog themselves down in obsessive trivialities. He is a facile, vacuous, non-stop chattering buffoon who delights in his superiority over the weak. He is only a superficial interest that entices others into participating for the mere sensation of it, eventually leading them to their deaths. His is a wasted life, and any search for meaning in his plight is perhaps destined for disappointment.

Thus the film develops the bizarre notion of the serial killer as a modern fool or court jester. He utters the most mundane poetry, to the delight of the onlookers, and enters a boxing ring only to have himself knocked out the first round, resulting in him subsequently sporting a neck brace. Even with this neck brace, he still tries to kill people, though he falls over and chastises himself as his intended victim flees. Indeed, he reviews the filmed footage to see where he went wrong. In so doing, he slowly becomes a subject of ridicule. Thus, the filmmakers are able to create a distance between themselves and the views of the filmmakers-within-the-film, whose plight lampoons that of the documentarist's pursuit of truth, with death as an occupational hazard.

There are several kinds of random killing indulged in by this serial killer: for sexual gratification, for financial profit and for practical necessity (to silence a witness, for example). All of them, however, are done because they give the killer a pleasure he otherwise finds unattainable. He is a force of pure self-indulgence, as nothing matters to him unless it gives him status or instant pleasure; he is the unbridled pleasure principle, and himself childlike. Such a killer will never stop and so, paradoxically, becomes an object of fascination instead of revulsion to audiences and filmmakers— such is the subculture that has grown around the figure of the serial killer.

The film is one of stylized and calculated verite. One can even see in it comparisons to the technique of the later phenomenally successful horror film *The Blair Witch Project*. The standard scenes familiar from countless TV documentaries here have a bleak edge. Hence the killer interacts with his family, who seem oblivious to his work. Indeed, the family in the film was that of the actor involved and really believed it was about their son (Kerekes and Slater, p. 94). In this sly manner it becomes a parody of what we have come to accept as cinematic "reality." At first beguiling and shockingly funny, it is ultimately confrontational and bleak in its depiction of a world of socioeconomic deprivation and running gun battles between rival killers and their devoted followers.

Man in the Attic

(1953: d. Hugo Fregonese)

scr. Robert Fresnell Jr.; nvl. Marie Belloc-Lowndes; pr. Robert L. Jacks; ph. Leo Tover; ed. Marjorie Fowler; md. Lionel Newman; cast. Jack Palance, Constance Smith, Byron Palmer, Frances Bavier, Rhys Williams, Sean McClory, Leslie Bradley; 81m

This effective remake of *The Lodger* stars Jack Palance as a mild-mannered, reclusive researcher who rents a room in the center of London. Meanwhile, the town's showgirls are being grotesquely murdered. Soon the unbalanced, malevolent Palance develops a potentially unhealthy interest in the landlady's daughter, who spurns him. Again, unlike the Hitchcock film but like the Brahm version, the lodger really is the killer.

The killer here murders women who reject his advances; thus he feels he overcomes his sexual inadequacies, proves himself their superior, and punishes them for their impertinent (sexual) independence. Unlike in the Brahm version, the killer has a genuine attraction for the landlord's daughter, their relationship apparently along Beauty and the Beast lines. Taking the theme from *The Lodger* and *Lady of Burlesque*, changing sexual mores and the resentment of women's open sexuality (even if it were coded for male spectatorship) are contributing factors.

The potential of Romantic love is what this killer seeks, and when faced with this impossibility he is compelled to kill the object who denies it. His desire is that way forever unattainable, although he senses more in his affection for the landlord's daughter. The idea of true love potentially calming a killer, but inevitably failing to do so, was used in *Le Boucher* and *Manhunter*.

Man on the Balcony

(1993: d. Daniel Alfredson)

scr. Alfredson, Jonas Cornell; pr. Hans Lonnerheden; ph. Peter Mokrosinsky; m. Stefan

Nilsson; ed. Helene Berlin; prod d. Kaj Larsen; cast. Gosta Ekman Jr., Kjell Bergqvist, Rolf Lassgard, Jonas Falk, Ulf Friberg, Magdalena Ritter, Ing-Marie Carlsson; 94m

Stockholm is in the grip of a serial killer, an unceasing predator who stalks the parklands and murders young girls there alone. The police are strained and ineffectual. However, their one chance comes when a newspaper stand near a park is robbed about the same time as a murder, and the robber is believed to have witnessed to the murder. The police consult a psychologist to obtain a profile on both criminals.

This is considered a late attempt at a giallo-style thriller. Novelists Maj Sjowall and Per Wahloo were responsible for a number of popular police novels which were made into a series of equally popular movies, of which this is the fourth. It has yet to see widespread release at time of writing.

Manhunter

(1986: d. Michael Mann) aka *Red Dragon*

scr. Mann; nvl. Thomas Harris; pr. Richard Roth (for Dino De Laurentiis); ph. Dante Spinotti; m. Michael Rubini, The Reds; ed. Dov Hoenig; prod d. Mel Bourne; cast. William Petersen, Kim Griest, Joan Allen, Brian Cox, Tom Noonan, Dennis Farina, Stephen Lang, David Seaman; 120m

An FBI profiler (Petersen) is brought back from retirement to investigate the "Tooth Fairy," a serial killer of families who strikes during full moons. The profiler's method is to be alone with the evidence and at the crime scene (the victims' house) until he can psychologically intuit the killer's behavior and motives. To reacquaint himself with these troubled minds, he visits an incarcerated serial killer, the same man who forced him to confront the worst of the abyss in himself (resulting in his need for psychological treatment to recover). That killer was Hannibal Lecter. He

leaves Lecter, running away, but is photographed by an opportunistic reporter. The Tooth Fairy sees the report and corresponds with Lecter in prison. The authorities discover the correspondence and seek to decipher the code used. The profiler teams with the reporter to lay a trap for the Tooth Fairy, but instead the killer kidnaps and tortures the reporter. The killer falls for a blind co-worker but becomes enraged when he sees her with someone else, mistaking her involvement, and plans to kill her as punishment for her betrayal of his emotions. The profiler intuits the killer's profession, learns his identity, and arrives to kill him and save the victim.

This was the first film since *The Boston Strangler* to delineate the profiler figure's importance in the serial killer film. He is separate from the police and is an outsider brought in as a last resort due to his specialized talent. That talent is the ability to get inside the killer's mind through a process of empathy which brings his own mind into contact with the monstrousness, and which can be so distressing as to cause a psychological breakdown — the reason for his retirement. The policeman refers to this process when he suggests, "If you can't look anymore, I'll understand." This equates the act of looking with the behaviorist examination of a serial killer as a means of seeing a monstrous capability within oneself. It also allies the film's narrative to the profiler's plight — to look at a killer and remain as safe from the experience as possible. The profiler is the audience's guide through psychological aberration and the effort to make sense out of such acts.

Director Mann takes care to set up Petersen (as agent Will Graham) as a good father, seen bonding with his son, making love with his wife and promising her that he will not get too deeply involved this time. He treasures family. The killer murders entire families. The profiler has thus

a sanctioned responsibility to go after the killer, despite the threat to his own well-being. But to do so, the manhunter must become a mindhunter, and so isolates himself at the crime scene, poring over the details and photographs and victimology — all to deduce/intuit what the killer did at the crime scene and what that reveals about why, and hence how to go about catching him. Only through such skilled psychological and behaviorist assessment will such a killer be found. Even the other police are surprised at the profiler's abilities and results.

The face of the modern profiler: William Petersen as FBI agent and serial killer specialist Will Graham in the seminal *Manhunter* (DEL, 1986).

He never seems to sleep, and the sense of weary exhaustion is counterbalanced with his dedication and the invigoration at getting ever closer — the perils of obsession. In the absence of a motive, he says aloud that the killer hides his dreams most of all, and that the motive lurks in his fantasies and dreams, which need to be deduced through immersion in the crime scene clues. Significantly, he remarks that the act fuels the fantasy, reflecting the actual theories emerging from the FBI's Behavioral Science Unit. Regular procedural meetings anchor the investigation and allow the profiler space for perspective, which he needs the more immersed in the world of the serial killer he becomes. The police can examine the facts of the case, but the profiler's talent lies in penetrating the all-important fantasy.

The recognition that by being able to ascertain and experience the fantasy and mindset of such killers he in a sense becomes like them troubles the profiler. He visits the incarcerated serial killer Hannibal Lecter for the mindset to return. He says he wants Lecter's help on the case (a plot twist repeated in the better known sequel *Silence of the Lambs*). Their shot/reverse shot talk establishes them as adversaries forever playing mind games. Lecter intuits the reason Graham is there and says, as Graham runs out, "You want the scent, smell yourself." Graham can only flee from this awareness, one too terrifying to know or admit to knowing, as necessary as it is for him to do so.

Lecter's cell is white, pristine. Lecter himself is dressed in white. In total contrast to the more famous dungeon in which the killer is kept in *Silence of the Lambs*, the environmental is clinical, almost abstract

Opposite: The strains of the job show as profiler Will Graham (William Petersen) is now armed in *Manhunter* (DEL 1986). He will use the gun to purge the killer, despite the risk to himself.

in its simplicity. It is the product of a sterile, cold world where men strive to be in control, their perceived professionalism and very adversarial competitiveness giving them self-definition (a theme in all Mann films). This adversarial relationship is all Lecter has left. He uses his considerable intellect and manipulative charm to gain the profiler's home address, and when the Tooth Fairy corresponds with him in prison — likeminded geniuses seeking solace in each other's understanding — urges this new killer to target Graham's family. This theme of killers corresponding with one another as if members of an elite society would recur in 1990s films, most notably *Copycat*.

In Mann's world the protagonists are skilled professionals, repressing any overt emotional display if they can, except when with loved ones. They are obsessive, serious and dedicated to their work. They are willing to cooperate with other jurisdictions and equals in order to get the task done, for they are aware of the seriousness of the matter. The killer is a threat to the social order they represent, ironically also validating their profession — this adversarial interrelationship of cop and criminal would be explored in Mann's later *Heat* especially. Interestingly, Hannibal's treating psychiatrist is not the arrogant, self-serving person he would be depicted as in *Silence of the Lambs*, but another man who takes his responsibilities intensely seriously.

The Tooth Fairy is obsessed with the notion of transcendence. He kills only on full moons, linking his acts to the lycanthropy mythos. He holds himself superior to all and says that Lecter alone knows the glory of what he is becoming. Murder initiates this desired transcendence, and the killer allies himself to the Red Dragon in William Blake's painting of that name. He feels that people owe him awe and that they recognize none of his greatness. But be-

hind his monstrous fantasies is the need to be loved, wanted and desired. He must kill repeatedly to attain this; as Lecter says on the phone to the profiler, "If one does as God does enough times, one will become as God is." The implication is clear: the serial killer acts in pursuit of a fantasy, believing the fantasy attainable if the acts are repeated enough times; of course, the crime is never as good as the fantasy.

Mann allows us to probe the killer's life. We see this physically towering man at work, where he is shy and reclusive, and in his growing relationship to a blind co-worker. It is she who momentarily soothes his savageness (just as he brought her to touch a sleeping tiger — a clear metaphor for his own bind in the killer's mind, and another reference to Blake). She validates the fantasy — perhaps he has killed enough for his dreams of unconditional love and acceptance to come true. It is she who takes the sexual initiative (ironically — in a reference to *Peeping Tom* — as he watches his victims' home-movies, so consumed is he by the prospect of a dream come true), and for the first time in reality he has become wanted and desired. However, when he sees her with another man and misinterprets it, his only recourse is rage: she has crushed the dream and must be eliminated in order to restore it.

It is the fantasy which empowers the killer and which must be purged. Hence, once the profiler intuits the fantasy, he discovers how the killer finds the victims, leading to the killer's identification. However, the profiler does not merely sit back and let the police capture the killer. Instead he charges forth, intent on being the one to apprehend and stop the killer. He must enact this ritual confrontation in order to purge himself and the society he represents of the fantasies and acts he has intuited. Only through killing the killer can he return to psychological stability. Hence, once the killer is shot, and the profiler hugs the victim, he is able to decisively state his name — the threat to his psychological well-being is gone. He will forever bear the taint of the experience though, literally scarred, a cut on his face as a reminder. He can pass the legacy on to his son, telling him openly about his previous hospitalization and his experience with "the worst thoughts in the world."

Mann's visual style is fascinating — a mix of neo-noir Expressionism, the near abstract contemplation of architectural spaces and how people inhabit them, and cold versus hot colors. The use of sudden, striking (often symmetrical) compositions of geometric arrangements recalls Argento and the giallo film's preoccupation with other realms of psychological perception beneath the everyday.

William Petersen played an obsessive, though amoral, FBI agent in William Friedkin's *To Live and Die in LA*, which many critics compared to TV's Mann-produced *Miami Vice*. In that respect, it makes an interesting companion piece to Mann's film.

Maniac

(1980: d. William Lustig)

scr. C.A. Rosenberg, Joe Spinell; pr. Lustig, Andrew Garroni; ph. Robert Lindsay; spec eff. Tom Savini; cast. Joe Spinell, Caroline Munro, Gail Lawrence, Kelly Piper, Rita Montone, Hyla Marrow, Tom Savini; 91m

Controversial due to its explicit violence (Tom Savini scalping effects), this is a forerunner to *Henry: Portrait of a Serial Killer*. It is a slice-of-life depiction of the day-to-day activities of a serial killer who scalps his victims and takes the trophies home to adorn his mannequins and prompt tearful masturbatory fantasies (implied). He is soon interested in a fashion model, but even though she is interested in him (for some reason), meaning his fantasy is attainable, he cannot stop killing. His prized mannequins finally come to life and tear him apart.

The killer has been obsessed with women ever since he was locked in a closet while his prostitute mother plied her trade. Imprinted with sex, fear, resentment and hatred, yet possessing self-awareness of his plight and its monstrousness, he lives in a world of dolls, mannequins, and a shrine. He is fueled by images of female beauty, sex and pornographic fantasy. He is the nadir of the sex-world depicted by the urban inferno work of Schrader and Scorsese in the late 1970s. In this city of moral indifference, he picks up whores but is impotent unless inflicting pain. When the prostitute indulges his fantasy, he is consumed by desire and misogynistic resentment and so strangles her as a substitute for penetration. It is murder as orgasm, followed by Catholic guilt: he cries as he scalps her — a slave to his fantasy. In interior monologue he debates his own sanity but resolves the issue in misogynistic diatribe. Each victim is the mother he resents and sexually desired. His impotence is thus partly the result of guilt at his own incestuous memories, transformed into necrophilic longing.

The film concentrates on the small, banal details of his life and the escape he attains through violent sex murder as a means of self-actualization. It is unflinching and seeks a behavioral profile rather than a condemnation, although its protagonist is grubby and unredeemable. Unlike Henry, he is conflicted about his acts, wanting solace from loneliness but unable to maintain a facade of normality when in private with a woman. Otherwise, he drifts undetected through the city, merely one of the unglamorous many. He is attracted to the photographer, for he sees in her profession a similarity to his desires — to preserve something of the subject/object, possessing it forever.

Lustig does not seek to condemn his

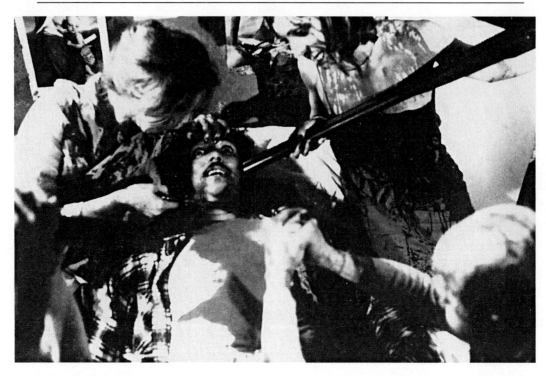

The serial killer and scalper (Joe Spinell) is dispatched by the mannequins who come to life in the EC Comics–style fantasy ending to the otherwise naturalistic *Maniac* (Maniac Prod., 1980).

killer, which makes the EC Comics fantasy ending an anomaly. The grotesque finale visualizes what is implied (mother's hand reaching out from beyond the grave to grab him) and surrenders to the supernatural and the uncanny. As he is overcome with hallucinations, one can interpret it as a psychological projection of his own guilt, and he is thus literally torn apart by it. His mental anguish finally became the reality that consumed him.

The film is part of a bleak revival of film noir in the early 1980s, with the likes of *The Exterminator, Ten to Midnight* and *Vice Squad* especially. These films sought, following *Hardcore* particularly, to mix soft-core sex (bordering on the hardcore in instances) and extreme violence in an effort to explode the perverse undercurrents of classic noir. *Maniac* brings the serial killer into the world of modern neonoir and allies it to a form of stylized violent pornography. Indeed, director Lus-

tig had started out making porno movies in an effort to raise the money to do horror films. His twin interests fuse here, with the murders being the functional equivalent of sex scenes.

Star Spinell had just finished work on *Cruising* in a similarly grubby role of a sexual predator. He teamed with Lustig, and both gave up their own funds to see the film completed. *Maniac* proved more popular on the exploitation scene than expected and garnered a wide release, although all contemporary critics were scathing and condemnatory. However, since its similarities to the celebrated *Henry: Portrait of a Serial Killer* have been more noticed, it has received some reappraisal.

Lustig would go on to initiate the serial killer franchise *Relentless*, drawing out Judd Nelson's better work, and would make several more serial killer–influenced supernatural horror films. He would team with Larry Cohen for a follow-up of sorts,

Maniac Cop and its sequel, about a zombie cop thinking himself above the law and seeking revenge on the department. He teamed with Cohen again for another vindictive zombie movie, *Uncle Sam*. All of these horror films flirt with the repeat killer motif but stop short of being serial killer films.

Mardi Gras Massacre

(1978: d. Jack Weis)

scr, pr, ph. Weis; ph. Jack McGowan; cast. Curt Dawson, Laura Misch, Nancy Dancer; 93m

During Mardi Gras a serial killer ritually butchers women. A policeman, who favors prostitutes, investigates. The killer is an Aztec priest who sacrifices prostitutes to his personal evil Queen, Coatla, Goddess of the Four Directions. He tours the celebration in search of prostitute-sacrifices, going to a bar in search of the most evil woman he can find. He takes her back to his lair, where he performs his private rituals and graphic torture (severing her hands, feet and genitalia).

This is a low-budget imitation of H.G. Lewis' *Blood Feast*. Gore (the victims' hearts are removed as part of the ritual) reportedly counterbalances the expected amateurishness. Possessing barely enough material to sustain a feature, this is another example of the low-budget, semi-underground horror movie's bloodlust, with the serial killer a demented religious fanatic for whom murder-mutilation has become a sexual agenda. He delights in severing what he refers to as a woman's part for doing evil, cutting out what he considers to be evidence of womankind's abhorrence, ironically as a gift for a Goddess. It soon disappeared from release, and rediscovery seems unlikely. It is included here as a virtual footnote to *Blood Feast*.

Martin

(1976: d. George A. Romero)

scr. Romero; pr. Richard T. Rubinstein; ph. Michael Gornick; m. Donald Rubinstein; cast. John Amplas, Lincoln Maazel, Christine Forrest, Elyane Nadeau, Tom Savini; 95m

This seminal movie equates the vampire with the modern serial killer. A sexually insecure young man, who has Romantic vampiric fantasies, murders women and drinks their blood. He comes to live with an uncle and his daughter in a low-rent area of Pittsburgh. His religious uncle believes Martin is indeed a vampire afflicted by a family curse. Martin, meanwhile, pursues other victims, calling in and confessing on a radio talk show where he becomes known as "The Count," and a minor celebrity. When the uncle learns of neighborhood murders, the man kills Martin with a stake through the heart.

Martin is a shy youth corrupted by his Romantic fantasies (in black and white) of a vampiric existence wherein he is a desired, seductive lover, and later a misunderstood object of persecution. This is demonstrated in the extraordinary opening sequence aboard a train where Martin, armed with a sedative-filled hypodermic, fantasizes his victim as welcoming him; he then bursts in, struggles with her, molests her, slashes her wrist and drinks the resultant blood flow. The stark, ugly reality of murder is far from the romanticized glamour of fantasy. Romero's intent to debunk the vampire legend and anchor it in terms of the contemporary serial killer is paramount. The clash between the everyday ugliness and Romantic fantasy is bridged by the killer, who brings a traditional fantasy into the real world, wherein he exists as a banal presence who only finds validity and fulfillment as a killer.

Martin admits his sexual inadequacy on the radio, saying that he is too shy to do the "sexy stuff" while they are awake or

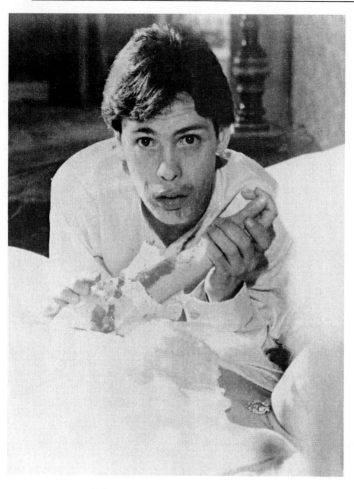

The serial killer who fantasizes himself a vampire: John Amplas in *Martin* (Laurel, 1976).

to do, and that once he has become accustomed to his life as a serial killer it all gets easier — the fantasy allows him control over life.

The real world is the ugly urban deprivation of Pittsburgh. It is suggested that these poor socioeconomic surroundings are a form of entrapment which contribute to the growth of violent escapist sexual fantasies that enable a nobody to idealize himself as a great lover/killer misunderstood by a hostile society. His fantasy is his form of empowerment, and thus the threat to society. But, ironically, although it is the patriarch who kills him (ostensibly to protect society), by becoming such an executioner, the patriarch becomes the fantasy vampire-killer he idealizes himself as in his own private fantasies. Martin realizes this man's dependence on fantasy and sets out to debunk it. Thus, Martin is killed partially for the patriarch in order to maintain his fantasy and remove the threat to it, and not to protect society — that is just a pretense. All male fantasy leads to homicide as a means of actualization — it is inherent in the true functioning of Patriarchy, and to punish it through ritual execution or prosecution is hypocritical.

without the blood. He desires normal relations, with the fantasies a product of a retarded adolescent sexual awareness. He finally achieves normal sex with a (married) woman only to discover her dead by suicide. The momentary tenderness he has desired has been achieved, but any potential change or maturation in his course is ended with her death. His retreat is back into his idealized self as sex killer, justifying his crimes in terms of a thirst (and thus tying into his uncle's fantasy after all), although he is aware of the irony of being blamed for this suicide too. He finally admits to the radio show that in reality he can't get people to do what he wants them

Genre historians have consistently praised the film. Even *Variety* concluded that the film showed evidence of a talent beyond its station. Physically, star John Amplas resembles real-life killer Richard Chase, dubbed the "Sacramento Vampire," whose exploits later inspired *Rampage*.

He is also close to Perkins and Boehm, from *Psycho* and *Peeping Tom* respectively, and is in a line of descent from those sexually troubled killers.

Mascara

(1987: d. Patrick Conrad)

scr. Hugo Claus, Conrad, Pierre Drouot; pr. Drouot; ph. Gilberto Azevedo; m. Egisto Macchi, Franz Schubert, Richard Strauss; ed. Susanna Rossberg; art d. Misjel Vermeiren; cst des. Yan Tax; cast. Charlotte Rampling, Michael Sarrazin, Derek de Lint, Romy Haag, Eva Robbins; 99m

This is a slow Belgian thriller about the investigation of the murder of a transsexual (one of a series) and the people involved in the opera/drag scene. The investigating officer hides his love for a victim's widowed sister, though he is revealed to be a secret transvestite himself, driven to kill the beauty he finds and resents in this spectrum of people. He fixates on one such person and her wardrobe, intent to uncover each.

Mascara tries to balance a procedural thriller with the character study of a man for whom heterosexuality is no longer enough, and provides social observation of rarely examined subcultural values and the subsequent communal and self-definition issues arising from them. It is ultimately more a film about this cultural identity than an examination of a tormented sex killer. It depicts a world of cold sophisticates for whom decadence and sexual deviance is an accepted lifestyle choice, and where the androgyny is almost put on a pedestal (from where the conflicted killer seeks to bring it down). In this world the hermaphrodite or pre-operative transsexual is the ideal of unattainable beauty.

The inspector/killer is obsessed with femininity and the male incorporation of it. He is seduced by the flamboyance of the opera world he investigates. This world of surface flashiness hides torrents of sexuality and incorporates gay S&M erotica. The more the protagonist is confronted by it, the more attracted and immersed he becomes, eventually driven to murder as perhaps a self-purge. However, he cannot maintain his facade of denial and indulges his transvestite whims, hoping to become the union of male and female he idolizes and resents.

The film was a Belgian/Dutch/French co-production with a European elegance in its cold, colorful, reflective surfaces. It was acquired by producer/distributors Menahem Golan and Yoram Globus as part of their bid for status, and to enhance the international reputation of their Cannon production and distribution company. As a supposed study of decadence it is perhaps comparable to the works of Liliana Cavani (in whose *Night Porter* Rampling had starred). *Mascara* has some added curiosity value now for one unveiling scene, which anticipates that found in *The Crying Game*.

Matador

(1986: d. Pedro Almodovar)

scr. Jesus Ferrero, Almodovar; pr. Andres Vicente Gomez; ph. Angel Luis Fernandez; m. Bernardo Bonezzi; ed. Pepe Salcedo; art d. Roman Arango, Jose Morales, Jose Rosell; cast. Assumpta Serna, Antonio Banderas, Bibi Andersen, Nacho Martinez, Eva Cobo, Julieta Serrano; 106m

Two predatory sex killers, one male (a retired matador prone to masturbating in front of horror movies—those of Franco and Bava) and the other female (a practicing lawyer obsessed with bullfighting, and who kills her male lovers with a hatpin dagger at the point of orgasm), develop an attraction. The matador forces his girlfriend to indulge in his necrophilic fantasies in the periods between his murders of young women. The two killers are aware of each other and enter a macabre courtship. Meanwhile, an admirer tries to emulate the killer and become a known and feared rapist/murderer, but he hasn't the ability and is arrested in his place. The two killers, both necrophiles, murder each other as they orgasm together.

This bizarre comedy is often considered Almodovar's most extreme work. It draws on a tradition of European graphic horror exploitation, particularly that of Italian Mario Bava (who is considered to have initiated the giallo) and Almodovar's countryman, Jess Franco (who increasingly mixed horror and hardcore pornography in his Sadean films). *Matador* treats the material of exploitation as comedy and sexual psychodrama, where the little death is equated with the big death as the killers' idealized state. Hence the ultimate consummation for these killer lovers is to die during intercourse.

Unusually, it features both male and female sex killers. And it makes no doubt about the fact that both kill for sexual pleasure, the act of murder being a means for them to achieve a necrophilic bliss. Generally, female repeat killers have a recognizable, conventional motive for committing their crimes and are not often considered sex killers. Indeed, Almodovar makes much of the equation between the protagonists as a means of disavowing traditional gender difference (Smith, p. 74) and associated conventions of passivity and aggression. The matador requires women to be the ultimate passive object — a corpse. In response, the lawyer usurps male aggression and presumed potency by killing her male victims as they orgasm and then achieving her own satisfaction with the passive corpse. It is as if necrophilia were the epitome of the traditional heterosexual roles, though inherently homicidal. The killers seek to transcend conventional sexual power, and recognize such in each other, but are ultimately trapped by their perverted heterosexual longing. It is this interpretation that has been put forth by gay critics.

It was controversial in Spain for its supposed equation of pornography and violence, a theme it treats with black humor. From the opening scene, where the matador masturbates to horror movies and the lawyer has her own necrophilic climax, the film stresses the connection between sexual excitement and representations of sex murder, with sex murder itself becoming almost causal. Watching violence excites these people, fueling their fantasies enough to want to kill: objectification yields dehumanization.

Banderas, as the would-be killer, lives for the fantasy but is unable to put it into practice; unable to differentiate, he is lost in the process of actualization. He wants so much to be a killer that he takes credit for the crimes. In his mind, violent sex murder is a demonstration of one's masculinity and potency, lest the matador (the ultimate male) consider him effeminate or homosexual. This idealized male role model (highly respected in Spanish culture) teaches "the art of killing" and considers women as prey for a masterful killer. The student wants to be like him and embraces his "girls must be treated like bulls" philosophy. Banderas is a sexually insecure young man who equates male desire with violent rape, and will confess to murder rather than be thought of as less than a man. This is his unspoken bond with the real killer.

The matador repeatedly watches videotape footage of the moment when he was injured by a bull. This was for him an emasculating and imprinting moment which he can now overpower only by a repeated closeness to death. He too is concerned with his potency, again underscoring the unspoken bond between all men. In the process of taking credit for murder, Banderas is finally able to achieve violent hallucinatory fantasies, and in his mind he is now one with the matador he admires. He is thus consumed by sexual violence, even though he has failed at perpetrating it — he is on the right path nonetheless.

Mean Season

(1985: d. Philip Borsos)

scr. Leon Piedmont; nvl. John Katzenbach; pr. Turman-Foster; ph. Frank Tidy; m. Lalo Schifrin; prod d. Philip Jeffries; cast. Kurt Russell, Mariel Hemingway, Richard Jordan, Richard Masur, Richard Bradford, Joe Pantoliano, Andy Garcia; 103m

A disgruntled reporter (Russell) is ready to retire from the business, but is talked into taking one more case and cover a serial murder. Soon the killer (Jordan) begins contacting him after each crime. In the process Russell becomes a media celebrity, receiving more press coverage than the murderer. The killer comes to resent this and so targets Russell's wife.

The film explores the relation between the reporter and the killer as one of mutual need. In as far as the reporter is an adjunct to the investigation, and indeed cooperates with the policeman (Garcia) when he's reluctantly brought into the case, he is akin to the profiler figure here. The reporter is the killer's conduit to the attention he craves, but in the process this elevates the issue of journalistic (and all media) responsibility. The killer wants attention, to inspire awe, and when he feels the reporter has usurped this he reacts as a jealous child and targets what the reporter holds dear. The killer, who otherwise chooses random victims as a means of personal, sexual empowerment, here seeks to punish what he, in essence, created.

Correspondingly, the reporter, at first concerned with the case and bringing the offender to justice, starts to revel in the attention lavished on him instead of the jealous killer, considering it a kind of personal and professional validation. In this process of self-aggrandizement and empowerment he fails to realize the dimensions of his close involvement with a resentful serial killer. He crosses the line between reporting and participating, and is thus complicit in murder. Such is the danger of the profession.

The killer is at the beginning of his cycle, leaving a note with each victim. They are intended as his message, a means of justifying his dysfunctional sexuality. They invigorate his existence, just as they do the journalist's. The film depicts a world that seeks to define itself in the reaction to homicidal transgression. In such a world view, the killer is at the center, a belief he holds onto at all costs, his actions justifying reactions which give the connected a sense of purpose.

The killer admits he has two needs — for a victim and a listener — the one having no validity without the other, although he also admits, ironically, that the former is the easier to find. And such is the consulting psychiatrist's advice to Russell — to be non-judgmental, patient and receptive in order to draw out more than the killer would want to reveal about himself. He is thus also a representative of the audience wishing to get inside the killer's private world. The killer, amazed at having gone undetected, wants to be noticed. The journalist is tired of minor bylines and no major recognition — they are kindred spirits, but their egos cannot coexist and are destined to clash violently.

Mean Season was received indifferently by the critics. The basis on reality was acknowledged (the experiences of reporter John Katzenbach, and the correspondence between New York City's Son of Sam killer and *NY Daily News* columnist Jimmy Breslin), but the film was felt to have slipped into cynical, routine melodrama, distinguished only by Jordan's performance. The killer intent to teach a professional a lesson by targeting his family was also conceptualized in the remake of *Cape Fear*.

Mean Season has been considered

Richard Jordan as a serial killer increasingly dissatisfied with the attention given to the reporter he contacts by phone in *Mean Season* (Orion, 1985).

(Good, p. 71) part of an early '80s redefinition of the role of the reporter and professional ethics, as was Pollack's acclaimed *Absence of Malice*. Director Borsos here stresses the sensationalistic tendencies of the media, with the reporter ultimately implicated in the course of monstrousness. It is a world of crumbling ethics and a corresponding absence of morality. Ultimately, decisive violent action is felt to be a valid expression, socially and personally sanctioned in the end.

Messiah

(2001: d. Diarmuid Lawrence)

scr. Lizzie Mickery, Boris Starling; pr. Louise Berridge; ph. David Odd, Kevin Rowley; cast. Ken Stott, Edward Woodward, Michelle Forbes, Jamie Draven, Frances Grey, Neil Dudgeon, Art Malik

A series of mutilation killings in England are interpreted as being related, the victim's tongue removed in each case. A bitter detective with a secret past is in charge of the case and tries to push his co-workers into activity. The investigation deepens, yielding homosexual resentment as a possible motive. However, this is a false lead, and they discover that the killer is murdering people by name, in the manner of the respective apostle's death. The killer is a junior cop, the monstrous son, who keeps a collection of tongues as his trophies. He is a psychotic who intends to resurrect Christ.

This is a British telemovie in the manner of such contemporary successful series as *Midsomer Murders, Inspector Morse* and the *Prime Suspect* films. The American serial killer films of the late 1990s, in particular *Seven* and *Resurrection*, have influenced it. Thus, it invests the style of TV realism with the occasional gory flash or glimpse of perversity. Its exploration of the gay subculture suggests the influence of the controversial UK series *Queer as Folk*; however, the film seeks almost to disavow the sexual nature of the killings in its ultimate revelation of a religious psychosis. But it is aware of the serial killer's overriding definition being based on the presence of fantasy as a motivating force and thus sexual empowerment.

Hence, it seeks to further define the serial killer as distinct from what the detective terms the "same killer." The same killer may have committed several murders, but that killer is only considered a serial killer because the murders speak of a sexual or other fantasy component enacted in ritual. The filmmakers are aware of the evolution of the American serial killer film and here seek to relay the information to British audiences in a more familiar format. The presence of fantasy leads to an investigative response that demands continual informed speculation (of sexual, sociopolitical or other factors) if it is to be kept vital. The film charts how this process of speculation ties in to the lead characters' personal lives; all have secrets in their pasts. Correspondingly, they must repeatedly go over the details as they accumulate in the exploration of the killer's signature as the key to his mind and his art/message. The film postulates that the main dilemma facing such investigators is the search for links between the victims and how they relate to the killer's fantasies.

Microwave Massacre

(1979/1983: d. Wayne Berwick)

scr, pr. Thomas Singer, Craig Muckler; ph. Karen Grossman; cast. Jackie Vernon, Loren Schein, Al Troupe, Claire Ginsberg, Lou Ann Webber; 76m

This is considered a failed horror parody, usually decried as incompetent. After years of constant arguments with his wife over dinner, a construction worker snaps and kills her. He then dismembers, cooks and eats her. Thus acquiring a taste for human female flesh, he seeks out other victims. He lures women to his home and kills them as he has sex with them.

This lost-video item is reportedly overacted and bland. It was supposedly an attempt at comedy but sorely lacked the satiric talents of, for instance, Paul Bartel. The film was actually made six years before it saw a brief release on video only. It is now yet another obscurity on a growing list of minor serial killer films that crossed over into the slasher movement of the early 1980s.

Midnight Killer

(1985: d. Lamberto Bava) aka *Midnight Horror*

scr. Dardano Sacchetti; pr. Mark Grillo Spina, Massimo Manasse; ph. Gianlorenzo Battaglia; spec eff. Amedio Alessi; cast. Valeria D'Obici, Leonardo Treviglio, Lea Martino, Paolo Malco; 90m

Lamberto Bava, son of the great Mario, here tries to mine the giallo vein of his better-known compatriots Argento and Fulci, though without the same impact. As an ice-pick killer murders indiscriminately (surprisingly enough, mostly during the day), various people propose their theories in response to the growing number of bodies.

Midnight Killer is tangentially a serial killer film, with an ending revelation of the killer that was supposedly based on *The Bird with the Crystal Plumage*. This was unavailable at time of writing.

The director expressed dissatisfaction with the movie, complaining that it was miscast (the lead actress was popular but had no thriller experience). Although ultimately released theatrically, *Midnight Killer* was initially intended for Italian television (Palmerini and Mistretta; pp. 25–6). Even fans of Italian horror tend to dismiss this one as unbearably banal. Bava is more at home with supernatural horror than the giallo, although he is perhaps inevitably driven to attempt it as par for the course for all Italian genre filmmakers.

Midnight Ride

(1990: d. Bob Bralver)

scr. Russell V. Manzatt, Bralver; pr. Ovidio G. Assonitis; ph. Roberto D'Ettore Piazzolli; m. Carlo Maria Cordio; ed. Claudio M. Cutry; prod d. Billy Jett; cast. Michael Dudikoff, Mark Hamill, Savina Gersak, Robert Mitchum, Pamela Ludwig

The small California town of Montevideo is gripped by a serial killer, an unbalanced man who takes Polaroids of his victims. He then removes their eyeballs as trophies (like the killer of *Crime Time*, for instance). A policeman's wife runs away from her intense husband (hoping for a later divorce) and picks up a hitchhiker (Hamill), who is in fact the serial killer. Her husband trails her, hoping for reconciliation, and suspects the hitchhiker may be a lover. The killer forces the woman to drive him to the only person he feels he can really trust, his doctor (Mitchum). Once there, however, the killer goes completely crazy and a prolonged fight results. The husband is able to defeat the killer and in so doing prove himself to the woman he claims to love.

Midnight Ride starts off in melancholic fashion as the clash between male possessive pride and a put-upon woman's desire to disappear and be swallowed by the outside world (i.e. for abandon and the dissolution of identity in the hope of finding a greater truth). For her, it is an almost existential quest, but the final destination reunites her with what she was running away from, the possessive male. Indeed, throughout the film she is put upon by Patriarchy. Thus, she is destined to never find freedom, and perhaps surrenders to the stronger rule of the male as an inevitability, even if the male believes he has compromised by agreeing to quit his job for her. It is a battle of wills.

The killer is an inadequate man with delusions of grandeur, prone to acts of sadism as a means of giggling gratification. He has no focus, almost like a lost child in need of a father's guidance. He reaches out for the doctor, but this appeal for help is ultimately sabotaged by his own psychosis, as he now sees the patriarch as his enemy. In that manner, he represents the monstrous son whose aberration challenges the true operations of the system. Yet the film holds no faith in that system and compares the killer to the obsessive possessiveness of the pursuing cop — both need to dominate the women in their lives and to subjugate their independence. Both need to cling to the belief that they have a meaningful interpersonal relationship to the woman.

Ultimately, however, the film becomes a typical genre Mexican standoff as profiler (the psychiatrist), killer and po-

liceman fight each other over the fate of the victim (which she has become, in all respects—despite her bid for independence). Although the killer is a serial killer, out of desperation he segues into the spree killer, a process also explored in *Easy Prey*. Consequently, the film becomes a hybrid of action movie (chase and fight set pieces), road movie and thriller.

This provocative minor film was made in 1985 but remained unreleased until 1990. It is part of a small number of movies that deal with killers-and-hitchhikers, including *Cross Country*, *Freeway*, *Nature of the Beast* and *Outside Ozona*, and the end of *Clay Pigeons*. The theme of the open road as metaphor for spiritual disillusionment and loneliness is prominent in these films also. *Midnight Ride* failed to find an appreciative response, and has instead unjustly found oblivion, even on the Internet.

The Minus Man

(1999: d. Hampton Fancher)

scr. Fancher; nvl. Lew McReary; pr. David Bushell, Fida Attieh; ph. Bobby Bukowski; m. Marco Beltrami; ed. Todd Ramsay; prod d. Andrew Laws; cast. Owen Wilson, Janeane Garofalo, Brian Cox, Mercedes Ruehl, Dwight Yoakam, Dennis Haysbert, Sheryl Crow; 111m

Fancher, best known as the co-screenwriter of *Blade Runner*, made his directorial debut with this profile of a Canadian drifter/serial poisoner (Wilson) affecting a small middle–American seaside community. He boards with a couple (Cox and Ruehl) who gradually see him as a friend and even surrogate son, since they remain unaware that he has murdered the daughter they are missing. The emotionless killer, in voice-over, comments on the repercussions of his actions (some of them comedic) on the locals, as if studying his mark on the world. He gets a job in the post office and finds a romantic interest (Garofalo). After other murders, one of which finds Cox implicated in Ruehl's death, he leaves, presumably to move on to more murders in other towns.

The killer murders in the pursuit of significance; it is beyond sexual expression, as he seems to have no emotional need beyond murder as a means of empowerment. It gives him superiority over those lives he feels he can control and manipulate. He suffers blackouts and daydreams in his pursuit of a fantasy of consequence, all the while revealing a deceptively mild vulnerability. He hopes for a higher purpose, yet his pronouncements are a calm and ultimately hollow recounting of his method, as if a personal confession. They enable his continual justification, reinforcing the validity of his drive for expression and influence — purpose, solace and meaning as an agent of change and even destiny. In this respect, the film bears comparison to *The Young Poisoner's Handbook*.

He is always remote, disconnected and in his own world. Indeed, so are all of the main characters. Correspondingly, all of them try in their own way to forge some kind of interpersonal bond and communication. They search for definition in personal and communal rituals, into which the killer slowly ingratiates himself. Yet, as an agent of change, he is driven to destroy their shared grace, the football star, and watch the response, even participating in a search for the body. As a blank everyman he slowly starts to fulfill whatever role is vacant in the lives of those around him. He is a son for Cox and Ruehl, and a would-be lover for Garofalo (although he is sexually awkward — an instance which questions his gender security, as does his choice of murder means, since poisoning is usually chosen by women). Yet (bi-)sexuality and confusion is still an issue for this chameleon, who indeed strives almost for an asexual state — impulse killing instead of casual sex, perhaps. Hence, after he is unable to sexually act with Garofalo (play-ing too rough with her because he thought that's what she wanted) he immediately goes out to kill. Sex and murder are both components of his fantasy.

He is prone to daydreams of pursuing detectives. He knows that fate awaits him too if he stays too long. These are fantasies designed to compliment his perceived mastery over his own and every situation. He lives in this fantasy of consequence where he is the center of the world. Ironically, he slowly starts to become this in the lives of the people he affects, a reality he shapes and which reinforces the validity of his fantasy. It is a self-perpetuating cycle. Thus, with every urge to kill being an expression of his fantasy identity, he states to himself, "I am becoming a fact." Murder allows him an identity he otherwise lacks.

His voice-over confessions of the means of murder recall *Man Bites Dog* (though with a more subdued satire), and are designed as a self-reflexive commentary on the nature of serial murder as he considers it. He questions responsibility and victimology (in particular, the difference between a random killing and one where the victim invited the killer in) without introspection. It is almost as if his crimes were a kind of experiment in, as opposed to the mere expression of, banal Evil.

The film's sense of weirdness beneath the everyday veneer of small-town America was felt to recall Hitchcock and Lynch. Fancher admitted that he thought the film was about "the proximity of good to evil.... Evil is nothing until it touches good. That is a wild idea, but it's a fact of life" (quoted by Bernstein in *eon magazine*, online). Thus, one can consider the killer's actions as vacant, almost child-like Evil in search of self-definition. Fancher added, "I wanted no pathology because answers are ridiculous and impossible in films."

Fancher had directed plays and short

films before this, but this was his first feature (he was sixty-something at the time, and the film offers a mix of contemplation and resignation that perhaps accompanies age if not wisdom). He was best known for his feature screenplay work on *Bladerunner* and *The Mighty Quinn*. It took him two years and a dedicated producer to get his debut feature off the ground. He said that he wouldn't have done it without the participation of star Wilson, whose droll humor and Robert Redford–like wholesomeness enhance the overall sense of disconnection.

Mr. Frost

(1989: d. Philip Setbon)

scr. Setbon, Brad Lynch; pr. Xavier Gelin; ph. Dominique Brenguier; m. Steve Levine; ed. Ray Lovejoy; art d. Max Berto; cast. Jeff Goldblum, Alan Bates, Kathy Baker, Roland Giraud, Jean-Pierre Cassell, Daniel Gelin, Francois Negret, Maxime Leroux; 104m

A policeman (Bates) goes to a rich man's house and casually exposes him as a serial killer, his tortured, mutilated victims buried in the large back yard. The killer (Goldblum), who admits no remorse, is committed to an insane asylum after refusing to speak. After years of silence, he chooses to speak to a new psychiatrist, and admits to her that he is the devil and intends to make her believe it. He wants to prove that Evil has more power than science or psychiatry. The policeman agrees with him, but the psychiatrist, of course, treats him as delusional—until events seem indeed to have been manipulated by him (a cripple is cured and a patient goes on a killing spree). To save her peace of mind, she admits his power and wants to kill him (thus becoming a killer and lost soul herself—his real corruptive aim). The devil wins.

The killer claims that he is the Devil, and has allowed himself to be captured in order to convince a rational scientist of this

and thus restore fear and awe of him. The question running throughout is whether he is the absolute Evil or the closest a human can get to being equated, even in his own mind, with a more abstract conception of Evil. The serial killer is held as the epitome of this, at a point ceasing to be of human origin. This is, of course, an issue in the serial killer film as a genre. Here, policeman and profiler ultimately cannot rationally account for such a killer, and there is correspondingly no hope of any cathartic purge of an aberration, merely the resignation to its eternal presence.

Mr. Frost possesses a knowingly eccentric humor. Goldblum photographs a cake, then throws the cake out and keeps the photo, claiming to be interested only in the trophy (later horribly revealed in his "little home movies" of child torture and murder). As the film proceeds, it develops into a fascinating psychological examination of the interplay of killer/profiler/cop in response to the enigma of such abominable acts. Central is the notion of who is responsible (physically, psychologically, ontologically) for such a monster, and whether mental illness is enough of an explanation.

Ultimately, the profiler/psychologist cannot account for the protagonist's jovial detachment from his acts. The policeman fears him, and the profiler seeks understanding, where the fear is perhaps the intended response. When the rational is confronted by the irrational (the profiler watches the snuff movies), the rational has no recourse but to crumble and seek to kill the cause of its disintegration, in the process validating its power. The snuff films are not shown (unlike the approach in *Henry*, for instance), with the evil acts left to the viewer's imagination. This implies the function of the gory set piece as jouissance in the genre, but denies the audience such a "pleasure."

The terror spreads: first the killer, then the cop who seeks murder as justice/ purge, then to innocents in the grip of Evil masquerading as mental illness, then to the rational being in a kind of flow. It infiltrates dreams and waking life, corrupting the goodness in all it touches. The only recourse left is to eliminate it, in the process becoming it, even serving it. Evil is timeless, inescapable. The profiler shoots him, but rather than achieving the purge of Evil, she then proceeds to speak with his voice.

This was a French-English co-production from the screenwriter of Godard's *Detective*. Its director claimed it was inspired by a true event in a psychiatric hospital wherein a doctor shot-gunned one of his patients. The notion of a contagious Evil is treated in *Cruising*, *The Exorcist III* and *Fallen*, to different ends. This curious art-house serial killer film never found a sympathetic critic or much of an audience, and was dismissed or labeled as pretentious rather than being acknowledged for its ambiguities.

Monsieur Verdoux

(1947: d. Charles Chaplin)

scr. Chaplin (from an idea by Orson Welles); pr. Chaplin; ph. Roland Totheroh, Curt Courant, Wallace Chewing; m. Chaplin; ed. Willard Nico; md. Rudolph Schrager; art d. John Beckman; cast. Charles Chaplin, Mady Correll, Allison Rodan, Robert Lewis, Audrey Betz, Martha Raye, Ada-May (Weeks), lsobel Elsom, Marjorie Bennett, Margaret Hoffman, Marilyn Nash; 125m

Chaplin stars as a suave lady-killer, à la Bluebeard (whose story was later made by Chabrol as *Bluebeard*). In France in the late 1930s, on the eve of WWII, a bank clerk, married and with one son, loses his job and decides to murder women to support his family. However, his crimes speak of a darker sexuality. He places ads in the companionship section of the local papers to attract rich widows. He then seduces and kills a ready supply of victims. He is caught and tried for mass murder. He explains his work ethic in light of the climate of mass murder around him, but is led to his execution.

Chaplin subtitled the film "A Comedy of Murders," and it is a wicked version of a farcical comedy of manners. However, the initial reviewers were unsure of what to make of the film's ironic, even cruelly comedic, tone. It was correspondingly rejected by viewers unable to reconcile Chaplin's persona, what *Variety* termed the "common man," with that of a droll, calculating sex murderer (even though he claims to murder for profit). Perhaps that was the real point for Chaplin, the incongruence between the image and such acts.

Verdoux is an unrelentingly jovial, busy man. He is a dead man narrating the tale of his demise, as the film opens with a shot of his gravestone. He cheerily states that the "career" of the Bluebeard is not profitable, and that it takes a man of rare optimism to embark on such a path. Indeed, Verdoux is such an optimist, however cynical his particular brand of optimism may be. He adds that he did the crimes for profit alone, distancing himself from any admission of sexual pleasure in the crimes, although there are several moments that suggest otherwise.

He eyes new widows as potential conquests, his gaze lustfully and homicidally contemplating their eventual fate at his hands. His seductive attentions to these ladies are designed to satisfy their fantasies and urges for an attentive, cultured man about town. As the film turns the comedic into the sinister, one senses Verdoux's attraction/repulsion complex for these women, beyond the practical. He can transform sexual disgust into sound business practice to justify his acts. The film neatly suggests his secret perversity in one scene where he enters his victim's bedroom at night and exits in the morning with

Charles Chaplin (right) orders flowers sent to his next intended victim in *Monsieur Verdoux* (C Chaplin, 1947), his real intent hidden from the clerk.

another corpse to dispose of. What happened in the interim?

He has a family of his own, and a wife who is wheelchair-bound and with whom he presumably has no sex life. Their relationship is strained, and the wife admits to worrying about his state of mind, sensing his inner insecurities. If he sees her as a sexual being, he suppresses his desires, again transformed into the attraction/repulsion complex which drives him. He transforms his complex into an immense energy that necessitates murder as a means of fueling itself. Repression and denial are thus channeled into homicide, and without due introspection but with socioeconomic rationalization in the means that he has been conditioned to believe — the work ethic, led by government example. In a cli-

mate of mass murder, why is a single killing considered an atrocity?

Yet he is capable of moral choice, free will and judgment. He assists a young woman he initially intended to test a poison upon, when he hears that she was once in love with a crippled man and would have killed for him. In her he senses closeness to himself and refrains from killing her, giving her money instead. In time, she has manipulated her way into greater social standing, an admittance of their predatory kinship. He is selective, choosing women who know no struggle, as he sees it — the bourgeois. Yet he is of their class values also.

Chaplin politicizes the content, suggesting that socioeconomic circumstances force ordinary people into monstrous acts.

He raises the irony of a situation where large-scale war profiteers are held blameless for the mass murder they sanction, whilst a casual murderer is immediately vilified as a monster. The killer is aware of this and has incorporated it into a philosophy of murder as functional need. His rationalization finally holds mankind guilty and hypocritical for such a value system. He says that in comparison to the war effort he is a mere amateur, and what justice is served by making an example out of him when mass murderers are proclaimed heroes?

He puts into practice a systematized murder for profit operation. He lures gullible middle-aged women to a flat in Paris where he kills them (as sexual consummation — a disavowal of his adulterous nature), burns them in his private incinerator (a device repeated in the French film *Dr. Petiot*), and judiciously invests their money in the stock market — all the while keeping his secret passion from his wife and ailing child. He has become a killing machine, a product of war capitalism. He defends himself during a trial (reminiscent of the killer's final pronouncements in *M*) by saying that his murders are a mere trifle in the state of things. As a Capitalist he is defeated by the stock market crash, and when we see him later, he admits that he has nothing left to fight for and has lost his wife and child. However, one cannot help but wonder about their fate at his hands. He is thus ultimately a failure, and his demise is allied to that of the system that spawned him.

The picketers who congregated outside the theaters that screened it perhaps typified the film's problematic reception. Many bookings were subsequently cancelled, the film even being banned in Memphis (Crowther, *NYT*). Despite the controversy, the script was nominated for an Academy Award. The film was nonetheless soon withdrawn from US release until a Chaplin retrospective in 1964 at NYC's Plaza Theater. The new generation heralded the film as a "superior sardonic comedy," and Chaplin's final break from his famous tramp persona.

Modern critics have attempted to discuss the film in terms of Chaplin's tumultuous private life at the time the movie was made. He was the subject of a paternity suit, and although he won, it damaged his public reputation and increased his bitterness towards the woman responsible, Joan Barry. His leftist political leanings were also criticized by patriotic organizations of the McCarthy period. In addition, Orson Welles, who was paid off when Chaplin commenced the project, proposed the idea, and there was subsequent argument as to how much Welles contributed to the script.

The theme of individual vs. systematized mass murder was also developed in *Bluebeard* and *Night of the Generals*.

The Monster

(1994: d. Roberto Benigni) aka *Il Mostro*

scr. Benigni, Vincenzo Cerami; pr. Yves Attal, Benigni, Elda Ferri; ph. Carlo Di Palma; m. Evan Lurie; ed. Nino Baragli, Franco Fraticelli; prod d. Giantito Burchiellaro; cast. Benigni, Nicoletta Braschi, Michel Blanc, Dominique Lavanant, Jean-Claude Brialy; 110m

An Italian town is gripped by fear after a series of murders (eighteen so far) perpetrated by the "Mozart of vice." A woman is scared by the advances of a harmless con man/squatter (Benigni), who makes a living delivering mannequins and who has mistaken her for a nymphomaniac. She tells the police of him. He is thus believed to be the serial killer, and a policewoman (Braschi) is sent undercover to lure him into rape and murder and either arrest or kill him. She pretends to be homeless and moves in with him, intent to seduce him into activity. She discovers his mild nature, and although she informs her superiors (including a caricature criminal psychologist) that he is not the man they seek, she is ordered to continue with the seduction regardless.

This French-Italian co-production is considered appealing mostly to fans of Benigni (whose real-life wife, Braschi, co-stars). There were those who considered the premise tasteless, however. Although it does not devote time to the actual killer, being more a mistaken-identity farce, it is interesting for its merciless lampooning of the criminal psychologist, the profiler (Blanc), who claims to be an expert and would still consider Benigni a likely suspect.

To that extent, Benigni is a harmless innocent wrestling with an entrapping circumstance and fate. In that respect he is perhaps supposed to be the everyman figure, in the tradition of Chaplin through to Jerry Lewis and even Jim Carrey, although Benigni avoids the aggressive physicality of the latter two clowns. Indeed, to some critics Benigni comes across more as a combination of Jerry Lewis and Woody Allen, a blend of the hysterical and the nervously neurotic.

When it was released in Italy, the film soon became that country's highest-grossing box office hit to that date. In America it was thought a solid demonstration of its star's talent for physical comedy, and was compared to silent clowning, although the reception overall was lukewarm. For all those who had seen Benigni in Jarmusch's *Down by Law*, there were apparently just as many put off by memories of *Son of the Pink Panther*. Subsequently, the Italian comedian did not break through to the United States market until *Life Is Beautiful* charmed the world.

Mortal Sins

(1992: d. Bradford May)

scr. Dennis Paoli; pr. Tom Rowe; m. Joseph

Conlan; ed. Andrew London; prod d. Richard Kent Wilcox; cast. Christopher Reeve, Blu Mankuma, Mavor Moore, Thomas Peacocke, Weston McMillan, George Touliatos; 96m

This tele-movie wishes to be a crisis-of-conscience thriller about a priest who hears a serial killer's confession but is torn over whether to tell the police. Instead, he determinedly tries to solve the crimes himself and catch the murderer of young, church-going women. With the women in his congregation in danger, he puts his life on the line.

Reeve reportedly uses his likable persona well here, but the subject is too familiar, the better examples being *I Confess* and *A Prayer for the Dying*, and the movie apparently too unremarkable, if competent. Screenwriter Paoli is better known for his work for Stuart Gordon, Brian Yuzna and Charles Band. This was unavailable at time of writing.

The Most Dangerous Game

(1932: d. Ernest B. Schoedsack)

scr. James A. Creelman; stry. Richard Connell; pr. Merian C. Cooper, Schoedsack; ph. Henry Gerrard; m. Max Steiner; ed. Archie Marshek; cast. Joel McCrea, Fay Wray, Leslie Banks, Robert Armstrong, Steve Clemento, Noble Johnson, Hale Hamilton; 63m

An aristocratic Russian game hunter, Count Zaroff, rescues shipwreck victims, then lets them loose on his private island and hunts them down for sport and pleasure, the bodies becoming his trophies. (There have been killers like this—Alaska's Robert Hansen, for instance.) His latest victims (a couple, McCrea and Wray) have to defend themselves using harsh tactics.

Revisionist analysts stress the Sadean qualities of this film, which allows its villain much time to voice his reasoning. He is lucid, educated and intelligent, a man who has justified his actions in terms of a personal philosophy which approaches the Nietzschean. Confirmed of his own superior skills, and bored by the lack of challenge, he seeks ever greater indulgences. Indeed, the Count adds, "first the hunt, then the revels," the latter being presumed sexual pleasure with shipwreck victim Fay Wray. He is a portrait of the hunter as murderer as (sexual) predator. It is clear that his hunt is a sexual turn-on for him, as he gains sexual excitement from a sadistic power and pursuit of others. This sexual pleasure demands proof of conquest, and the killer keeps his victims' heads (in scenes cut by the studio to avoid shocking viewers). He tells Wray that when he has lost the passion for hunting (a substitution for seduction and murder) he has lost the passion for life and (pregnant pause) love.

Correspondingly, the filmmakers stress the visceral excitement of the hunt, in the process presumably duplicating the thrill the hunter gets and the invigoration through danger that McCrea finds in himself. Indeed, it is arguable that McCrea finds in himself some of what he despises in the Count, and that his killing of the Count, however justified as self-defense, is also a purge of the savagery in every man. Ironically, before their ship is wrecked, a guest raises the ironic point that a beast that kills for food is considered an animal, but a man who kills for sport is considered civilized. It is this notion of the civilized hunter that the film systematically exposes and condemns. The hunter — soon to be the hunted — defends his position by saying that there are only two classes of people: the hunters and the hunted. Thus, the escapades that follow can be interpreted as fate's way of teaching an arrogant man a lesson, in the process making him a beast and murderer. It explores the dichotomy between civilization and savagery, concluding that they are indeed bedfellows.

The Count has been interpreted as the demented patriarch, the representative of a decadent Old World Europe, and even as an anticipation of the fascist leader (Hardy,

p. 53). In the two remakes, *A Game of Death* and *Run for the Sun*, the Count became a German Nazi to make the point clearer to post-war audiences.

Most Wanted

(1976: d. Walter Graumann)

scr. Laurence Heath; pr. Quinn Martin, John Wilder; ph. Jack Swain; m. Patrick Williams; ed. Jerry Young; art d. Richard Y. Haman; cast. Robert Stack, Tom Selleck, Shelly Novack, Kitty Winn, Sheree North, Jack Kehoe; 78m

This tele-movie pilot is about a detective (Stack) and his assembled specialized unit of early profilers—a computer whiz, a psychologist, undercover detective — assigned to investigate the rape and murder of nuns (a device used later for *Bad Lieutenant*). Some of the co-stars in this pilot, most notably Tom Selleck, did not stay for the brief series that followed.

Although considered an undistinguished venture, it has some novelty interest as an early attempt to incorporate the profiler function (however split it may be into component parts) into the television style cop procedural. Director Graumann was known for his work on episodic television before turning to features in the late 1960s, which included the exceptional *Lady in a Cage*, and then returning to television. At the time of writing it was widely available.

Motel Hell

(1980: d. Kevin Connor)

scr. Robert Jaffe, Steven-Charles Jaffe; pr. Herb Jaffe; ph. Thomas Del Ruth; m. Lance Rubin; cast. Rory Calhoun, Paul Linke, Nancy Parsons, Nina Axelrod, Wolfman Jack; 106m

An elderly man and his sister run Motel Hello (the neon "O" doesn't work). He also makes popular sausage and meat products. His secret ingredient is human flesh. He subdues his victims, buries them

up to their necks, slashes their vocal cords, and keeps them alive in his private farm. He develops a romantic interest in a young guest, to the dismay of his sister (and lover?).

This is an alternately grotesque and endearing comedy about a pair of conscienceless killers. The out-of-the-way hotel recalls *Psycho*, and the cannibalism motif and demented patriarch suggests *The Texas Chainsaw Massacre*. But where Hooper went for caricaturish satire, Connor opts for a kind of melancholy comedy, aware of the tragedy in its patriarch's attempts to stave off inevitable age. This results in a shifting tonality that many critics regarded as uncertainty.

There is a note of pathos to the monstrous irony of the demented patriarch lusting after a younger woman but wishing to take her as his bride to legitimize his desire and relive a lost youth, much to the dismay of his sister, their incestuous relationship kept subtextual. He is concerned with his potency, with his sexual desires transformed into cannibalistic practices. He takes pride in his ability as a cook, though he has transformed his kitchen into a human slaughterhouse. In the macabre climax he dons a severed pig's head and chainsaw and takes to the surviving couple. He has become a mad animal, a caricature of the patriarch, his pig head even recalling the hypocritical fascist authority of *Animal Farm*, oddly enough, and the encapsulation of a human slaughterhouse, wallowing in the viscera of homicidal madness.

Connor's camera veers between overt stylization and a kind of static third-row-center positioning, the result being a distancing effect. Simple pans and functional movements gradually break into odd angles, reality inevitably warping, but it is the seeming matter-of-factness of much of the film's approach which makes the film disturbing and the laughter nervous. The nonchalant narrative pacing reinforces the almost theatrical distancing, but when one seems sure of a remove from the proceedings, Connor will move in for a grotesque moment or an ironic piece of character observation, which redefines the viewer's relation to the unfolding drama. The result is disconcerting and fascinating.

Connor is able to cut from the comical (even farcical) to the tragic within the same scene. The subdued, murkily depressing colors of decay saturate the film and set a mordant, brooding atmosphere to encompass the depiction of a couple whose monstrousness gives them an escape from an otherwise meaningless old age. They have found purpose in sadistic murder and torture of the innocents they literally consume. However, Connor has no real sympathy for the couple's victims either, as they are selfish, unpleasant caricatures themselves. The film is tempted to embrace the old couple's contempt for new social relations and moral changes, but never champions them.

Few films have been as bleak and cynical in their association of comedy and the unbearable suffering of people. It is the bizarre conception of the human farm that pushes the film from the realm of the Grotesque into that of the Absurd. Some critics felt the farm was meant to represent Reagan's America, with almost acceptable monstrousness lightly covered up. Despite the comic exposition of monstrousness, the film never becomes a celebration of the macabre in the manner of the EC Comics

Opposite, top: A rare moment of tranquility as motel owners Vincent and Ida (Rory Calhoun and Nancy Parsons, left) entertain their guests (Nina Axelrod and Paul Linke) in *Motel Hell* (UA, 1980). *Bottom:* The killer's sister also turns to murder as the family way, removing the "prettier" victim in *Motel Hell* (UA, 1980).

The serial killer (Rory Calhoun) dons a pig's head in his home cookhouse/slaughterhouse for the grotesque climax of *Motel Hell* (UA, 1980).

stories that have clearly influenced it. It steers clear of the overt homage that would infiltrate Romero's *Creepshow* and the rash of EC tributes in the early '80s—its jovial cruelty is slyer than that. It remains its director's best film.

Murder by Decree

(1979: d. Bob Clark)

scr. John Hopkins; stry. Clark; pr. Rene DuPont, Clark; ph. Reg Morris; ed. Stan Cole; prod d. Harry Pottle; cst des. Judy Moorcroft; cast. Christopher Plummer, James Mason,

James Mason (left) and Christopher Plummer (right), as Dr. Watson and Sherlock Holmes, investigate the clues left by Jack the Ripper in *Murder by Decree* (Avco Embassy, 1979).

David Hemmings, Anthony Quayle, Genevieve Bujold, Frank Finlay, Sir John Gielgud, Susan Clark, Donald Sutherland, Roy Lansford, Teddi Moore, Ron Pember; 112m

Sherlock Holmes investigates the Jack the Ripper murders. He uncovers a plot to protect the Royal family from a scandal of sexual dalliance and illegitimacy, enacted by supposedly benevolent Freemasons. This excellently cast socio-politically minded and atmospherically directed horror movie is Clark's most enduring film. It's reportedly much better than the similarly plotted *A Study in Terror*, with similarly excellent use of the usual foggy Ripper atmosphere.

It is a film that straddles the horror, detective, period and serial killer genres effortlessly. It intends to measure the responses of a diverse group of people involved in the Ripper horrors. It was the door to the mainstream for director Clark (who would later go on to the much-lamented *Porky's* movies). However, to some critics (Roger Ebert especially) the film followed too closely on the heels of the Sherlock Holmes–meets–Sigmund Freud adventure *The Seven Per Cent Solution*, and the time-travel H.G. Wells vs. Jack the Ripper tale *Time After Time*.

This marked the 134th screen appearance for the famed detective, providing a rich visual tradition for Clark to utilize. Many complimented Clark's almost Gothic approach to sets and atmosphere. Fuelled by recent speculation about the Ripper's identity, the script was dominated by its sociopolitical context. Indeed, it slowly becomes a study of the depths to which sociopolitical hypocrisy will sink in order to protect itself from exposure.

Though the murders can be first in-

The politically radical detective (David Hemmings) is fatally impaled on the sword of one of the fleeing duo (Peter Jonfield) that comprised the joint identity of Jack the Ripper in *Murder by Decree* (Avco Embassy, 1979).

terpreted as either a revolution against society's rules or a preying on its inequality, the film reveals that the murders are committed by those that determine and perpetuate the system of inequality. The elite preys on the disposable underclass unable to find representation in the police force or in government, forcing them to turn to Holmes as a suitable representative. Yet the aristocratic Holmes is hardly a man of the people, a fact he starts to resent as he uncovers the corruption of England's highest representatives. Holmes and Watson are the only characters who do not serve an ulterior motive. The Masons try to protect their beloved monarchy from scandal and their own from discovery. A politically radical detective (Hemmings) suspects the truth but does nothing so that Holmes can reveal all in a challenge to the monarchy's authority. Even the victims seek to conceal the truth, dying for it rather than seeking help, as there is nowhere left to turn in the

class system. The poor are the playthings of the rich, who resort to murder to avoid the consequences of their dalliances and think nothing of it.

In this world of systematized sanction, the killer is a mere functionary. Thus the Ripper, whose actions have a sexual dementia beyond the practical, is denied the power of self-expression when cornered by Holmes, his bloody gloves raised in appeasement. His accomplice is the coachman, similarly deprived of a voice, though with the presence of mind to fight for his freedom. When apprehended, the sadistic torturer of women is in a trance-like state, as if interrupted in a mad transcendence offered by sanctioned, sexually sadistic abandon. The real madness is not in the asylums but in those who run them.

The unrelentingly dark and brooding 1880s London creates a kind of urban determinism resulting in what was felt to be an almost Escher-like depiction of London in the grip of fear. There is no solace from the ideological entrapment the film conveys. Holmes' honesty and concern for human welfare is a bridge between the classes, and his dedication to truth is the only hope left. However, he too finally does not reveal the secret to the public, and will be forever haunted by his part in the death of an innocent woman and his wide-scale horror at the society that he held dear. It is this very society that he too wishes ultimately to protect — and therein lies the real, almost self-defeating irony.

The use of slow motion and wide angle point-of-view distortion suggest the dark malevolence of abhorrence as a prolonged experience of time: in this world, murder may come on suddenly, but death is painful and protracted. Such is the world of the sadist. Yet this is counterbalanced by the gentle warmth and charm between Holmes and Watson, their friendship being the last vestige of a hope in human nature in the midst of outrage and helplessness. Nevertheless, the sense of resignation to an almost omnipotent Evil in the selfish misuse of power and privilege holds sway.

The film is also interesting in terms of its generic mixes. Of course, there is the dark, fog-enshrouded realm of traditional Ripper lore and Hammer cinema, but onto this is grafted a wider political conspiracy thriller akin to those that developed in the US after the 1970s post–Watergate disillusionment. Clark had essayed similar disillusionment with ideology (under the guise of a horror film) in the post–Vietnam terror of *Dead of Night* (aka *Deathdream*).

Murder by Night

(1989: d. Paul Lynch)

scr. Alan B. McElroy; pr. Sheldon Pinchuk; ph. Brian R.R. Hebb; cast. Robert Urich, Michael Ironside, Kay Lenz, Jim Metzler, Michael Williams; 95m

This tele-movie is about an amnesiac (Urich) found at the latest murder site of a hammer-wielding serial killer, termed the "Hammerhead Killer" by police and press. As the man struggles with his memory and identity (a noted artist), he becomes a suspect. Is it possible that he is, in fact, the serial killer but does not remember? The policeman on the case (Ironside) starts to think this may be possible. A police psychologist (Lenz) helps him slowly regain his memory, and he falls for her. He eventually realizes that he is not the artist, but the artist's assistant, and that the killer artist has been posing as his assistant, and so has usurped his identity.

The film calculatedly sneaks in references to the duality of man and the role of memory in identity. It knows its genre heritage; hence the amnesiac is seen watching the Spencer Tracy version of *Dr. Jekyll and Mr. Hyde* as it is interrupted by a news broadcast about the killer's latest victim. The cold surfaces and thematic concern for the duality of appearance and capability recur in Lynch's work, especially in the underrated *Cross Country*.

Murder by Night may ultimately be undistinguished, but it is not as negligible as its lack of reputation suggests. A slow psychological portrait of a man readjusting to a life he cannot remember, it probes his reaction to a growing awareness that he may be a killer. Thus, he is forced to recognize, in the manner of the noir protagonists in 1940s blackout narratives, his own monstrous capabilities. He becomes increasingly obsessed with serial killers, fearing that he may be one of them, a prospect he considers alien. He chats with his assistant about them and is drawn to read about them. But rather than a process of self-discovery, this yields denial, as the real killer is revealed to be the assistant trying to goad the protagonist into taking responsibility for the crimes. Ultimately, a good soul could not take credit for actions it knows are beyond its capability, even if it momentarily doubted its own strength. The identity of an individual is more than the mix of memory and dream: it is also knowledge of capability and restraint.

The film's study of memory and identity finds a parallel in, of all films, *Dark City*.

Murder Elite

(1985: d. Charles Whatham)

scr. N.J. Crisp; stry. Edward Abraham, Valerie Abraham; pr. Jeffrey Broom; ph. Brendan J. Stafford; m. James Bernard; ed. Eunice Mountjoy; prod d. Bert Davey; cast. Ali McGraw, Billie Whitelaw, Hywel Bennett; Ray Lonnen; 98m

A killer is at work in an isolated farming community. Two sisters (McGraw and Whitelaw) argue over the fate of the farm left to them. The sister wishing to sell the farm (McGraw) intends to use the killings as cover for the murder of the other sister. The police investigate the murders and trace them to a simple farmhand (Bennett).

This is a deglamorized look at the drudgery of the England farming lifestyle, but plays as a sluggish melodrama about Patriarchy's legacy. Hence the strongest character (Whitelaw) wishes to keep the farm out of respect for the dead father's wishes. This subplot remains separate from that of the killer, driven by resentment of his invalid mother (a burden) to put women "to peace." The plot strands intersect when it is the killer who foils the bad sister's plan to pin the good sister's death on him. The man who puts women to peace, ironically, saves Whitelaw from wrongful death.

Instead of contrasting Patriarchal and Matriarchal legacies, the film wishes to be a character study of people seeking a place for themselves and a lifestyle to match their contentment and discontentment. The serial killer angle is almost an unnecessary frame for the real drama. It is a slow moving film, with a slight intertextuality in that the innocent-looking Bennett, who played the killer in *Twisted Nerve*, plays the killer here too. Its opening depiction of a killer lurking in the woods speaks to the European tradition of horror films.

Murder in Mind

(1997: d. Bill L. Norton) aka *A Deadly Vision*

scr. Dan Greenburg; nvl. Greenburg; pr. Bernadette Caulfield; ph. Alan Caso; m. Chris Walden; ed. Hibah Sherif Frisina; prod d. Corey Kaplan; cast. Peter Boyle, Ellen Burstyn, Kristin Davis, Jeanine Hutchings, Ed Lambert, Kip Niven

A psychic woman has a link to a killer's mind. When women are found dead, she teams with an older detective (Boyle) and his younger partner in a joint search for the killer.

The killer is a vaguely effeminate religious man and mama's boy who considers himself morally superior to the (fallen) women he kills. His lure is consistent — he cons his way into women's houses, says he wants to date them, forces them to put on music, and instead kills them. He desires romantic union but considers this somehow immoral and himself inadequate to the task, and kills the would-be object of his affection, perhaps stand-ins for a stern mother.

The older/younger detective teaming is better served by *Seven*, and the psychic link substitute for the profiler is unsurprisingly handled and even reminiscent of *Eyes of Laura Mars*. It is perhaps inevitable for one so connected to evil actions to see their own death. Promising material hints at the psychic's root causes in trauma as a parallel to the killer's imprinting process, the film keeps this subtextual, and, after a style-conscious opening, it becomes routine, focusing on the younger cop's potential parallels to the killer.

Murder in My Mind

(1997: d. Robert Iscove)

This is a science fiction–tinged serial killer tele-movie. An agent for the FBI investigates the case of a serial killer of blonde women. The case is considered unsolvable. Determined to solve the case, she utilizes her husband's research into memory transplants. In the process, she affects the transfer of a comatose victim's memories into her own mind.

The admittedly intriguing premise seems not to have made an impact, although a similar premise was used later in *The Cell*, perhaps making this earlier version a noteworthy curio. It was unreleased at time of writing.

Murder Lust

(1986: d. Donald Jones)

scr, pr, m. James Lane; ph. James Mattison; ed. Jones; cast. Eli Rich, Rocky Taylor, Dennis Gannon, Bonnie Schneider, Lisa Nichols; 90m

A Sunday school volunteer and security guard is really a serial killer of teenagers, strangling them and then dumping the bodies. He gets romantically involved with a girl but is impotent unless also killing. He loses his job and is forced to become a jailer, further bruising his ego and sense of superiority, although he wants to get a counseling job at a hotline.

The film depicts a man so unsure of his own manhood that, in response to others' sexism, he goes in search of prostitutes. He uses these women as screens onto which he projects his idealized male power, through sexual violence as a reaction to impotence (a similar ailment experienced by the killer in *Citizen X*). He moves on to younger, more conventionally innocent women as a greater transgression in a world that would divide women's status into virgins or whores, both for the killing.

When his dumpsite is discovered, he gains further prestige in his own mind, finally becoming the man he always wanted to be, although still an anonymous killer. He gains added power and, he perceives, status by torturing and humiliating his victims, rendering them unconscious before he can copulate with them. All is a means of compensation for his lack of social status, something he desperately clings to as a validation. He paradoxically needs social acceptance.

The film is most effective at portraying the discrepancy between the killer's idealized sense of himself as the ultimate mate and the impotent coward he is in actuality, full of contempt for women. Despite this promising contrast and an aware script, the film is undermined by direction that seems only to have used first takes.

Murder on Line One

(1990: d. Anders Palm)

scr. Palm; pr. James Ewart; ph. John de Borman; m. Richard Derbyshire, Charlie Mole; ed. Paul Endacott; prod d. Ged Clarke; cast. Allan Surtees, Simon Shepherd, Dirkan Tulane, Andrew Wilde, Peter Blake, Emma Jacobs, Neil Duncan, Brett Forrest; 103m

In Britain, a serial killer videotapes his crimes for later reexamination and presumed auto-erotic thrills (à la *Peeping Tom* and that episode from *Henry*). Police apprehend a suspect but are unsure of their quarry; and when the killings persist, a reporter tries to prove the police have the wrong man, but she faces resistance.

The film opens disturbingly enough with an eyeball left on a doorstep by a killer who has just slaughtered an entire family. It thus deals with the perception of death by those confronted with it and its investigation. Subsequently, the film becomes a reportedly involving whodunit from minor auteur Palm. This is, like most of Palm's films, not widely available.

Murder Rock

(1986: d. Lucio Fulci) aka *Murderock*

scr. Gianfranco Clerici, Vincenzo Manino; pr. Augusto Caminito; ph. Giuseppe Pinori; m. Keith Emerson; cast. Claudio Cassinelli, Olga Karlatos, Ray Lovelock, Janna Ryann, Cosimo Cinieri, Al Cliver, Lucio Fulci; 92m

A number of dancers at a prestigious dance school are being murdered. The black-gloved killer stabs them carefully with a hatpin after fondling their breasts. The police investigate, and a teacher looks into the case on her own, searching for a man. The teacher is revealed to be the killer, her career destroyed in a long-ago accident, who now kills young and desirable dancers out of resentment.

This is perhaps the best example of the short-lived "disco giallo" subgenre which followed the hit *Flashdance* (and, at its nadir, included the terrible *Slashdance*) and the rap-dance films that proliferated in the early 1980s after *Fame* (*Breakdance*, *Electric Boogaloo*, etc). This is used as an excuse by Fulci to show many leering camera angles of nubile female dancers at the ironically termed "Arts for Living Center," a setting perhaps meant to invoke memories of the ballet academy setting of Argento's *Suspiria*. The dances are presented as erotic spectacles for a male audience. Although the deaths are not as sexually explicit as in Fulci's *New York Ripper*, the same misogynistic, near-pornographic sensibility is present in subdued form. Murder is no longer a hard-core titillation, but a soft-core compromise.

However, this sexist exploitation serves a thematic purpose. By showing the dancers as erotic objects, Fulci depicts a state of desirability the killer feels she lacks. She wants the combination of sexual desirability and grace she sees in these dancers. As she cannot attain this fantasy, she will see to it that no one else will either. In so doing, she has become a killer in reaction to (but not against) the male sexual objectification of women. She wants to be an object, and it is this theme which fully reveals the director's glaring contempt for women. If a woman cannot be desirable, she will seek to prevent others from being so considered, and is an affront against the male's right to commodify women. Yet the crimes are also sexual, an appropriation of the aggressive male gaze; and indeed the person responsible for her accident was a man, whom she intends to frame for the murders. Of course, the dedicated male police officer removes this threat to masculine validity.

The Murderer Lives at Number 21

(1942: d. Henri Georges Clouzot)

scr. Clouzot, S.A. Steeman; nvl. Steeman; ph. Armand Thirard; art d. Andre Andreieu; cast. Pierre Fresnay, Suzy Delair, Jean Tissier, Pierre Larquey, Odette Talazac, Noel Roquevert, Maximillienne, Jean Despeaux; 83m

This was Clouzot's film debut. The film concerns a professional, seemingly detached and efficient homicide detective on the trail of a similarly methodical signature killer (who leaves an identifying card with each victim). He follows the clues to a boarding house. There he adopts various disguises to gain the residents' confidence. When the murders continue with all suspects in custody, he is forced to release them and redirect his investigation towards a possible conspiracy. He finally unveils the crimes as committed by three men, just for fun.

The gimmick-killer film is perhaps noteworthy in the serial killer film's evolution for its ultimate depiction of homicide for thrills (and presumed sexual excitement), and for its consideration of a group identity responsible for such random crimes. Inadequate subtitling reportedly hampered the US version of the film. It is only tangentially a serial killer film.

Murderous Vision

(1991: d. Gary Sherman)

pr. Johanna Persons; ph. Alex Nepomniaschy; m. Joe Renzetti; prod d. Chris Horner; spec eff. Marty Bresin; cast. Bruce Boxleitner, Laura Johnson, Robert Culp; 93m

This is a disappointing tele-movie from an often-intriguing director. A police detective from the missing persons bureau realizes that the mother whose disappearance he has been investigating may be the victim of a serial killer. He gets help from a reluctant psychic (i.e. outsider/profiler figure). It seems the killer is procuring victims for a demented plastic surgeon.

This was Sherman's return to the neon hostility of his neo-noir classic *Vice Squad*. Sadly, any hope of a return to that film's unrelenting bleak action is dissipated by a static, functional style, with only the surprisingly graphic outbursts hinting at the depths of Sherman's melancholic, bleak vision. The killer/procurer, like the protagonist in *Vice Squad*, needs sadism to bolster his self-image. Feeling himself above society and justice, he must keep women and society in its place, humbled before him. He is an organized offender who takes with him a rape-and-murder kit.

Sex murder has been turned into a profitable operation, and the film utilizes the deranged surgeon hook from the numerous Dr. Knox and Burke and Hare plot lines. Despite the novel generic borrowings, the film settles for the portrait of a dedicated officer who does not follow procedure. This was the kind of loner tackled in *Wanted Dead or Alive*, but here forced into a reluctant partnership with a psychic—a plot device that would also be retried in Wes Craven's failed pilot *Night Visions*. The policeman's procedural violations would realistically make it difficult for any successful prosecution to eventuate. Only towards the end, and in its often-comic portrayal of the demented doctor (Culp), does the film raise interesting thematic points.

Most disturbingly comedic is the harrowing scene of the demented killer, a failed doctor desperate to prove himself to the perceived fellows he resents, talking to specimen jars containing the faces of his numerous victims. His need for a trophy of the tangible beauty of the women he uses consumes him. It's a terrible perversion of the notion that beauty is only skin deep, and perhaps reflects the end result of the vanity that drives plastic surgery. The creation of physical beauty is an art, and the face, an artwork unto itself, a collector's item.

Murders in the Rue Morgue

(1932: d. Robert Florey)

scr. Tom Reed, Dale Van Every, John Huston; pr. Carl Laemmle Jr.; stry. Edgar Allan Poe; ph. Karl Freund; cast. Bela Lugosi, Sidney Fox, Leon Ames, Bert Roach, Brandon Hurst; 62m

This is a celebrated Poe adaptation, though it has little in common with his work. A fairground hypnotist has his trained gorilla kidnap young women and bring them to his doctor's laboratory. In the privacy of this lab, he indulges in sadism, sex and surgery. He is determined to crossbreed humans and apes, to create a mate for his prized gorilla: to do so, he injects his victims with gorilla blood. The sideshow is his moneymaking cover. One day, both he and the gorilla develop an interest in a young woman. The doctor intends to operate on her too, but the ape, although kidnapping her, kills the doctor.

Although not a serial killer film in the modern sense, its depiction of a sexual sadist is interesting and comparable. Like many films of the time, it splits the monstrousness in terms of agent and controller. However non-human the ape may look, however, it is the human monster who is the real threat, with the bestial a mere function of a more calculating sexuality. Devoid of a conscience (and thus ultimately unlike even the ape), this sex killer sadistically tortures women in the desire to create an ideal being, and disposes of those he considers unable to live up to his desired ends by dumping them in the river. Despite his scientific pretenses, he is a serial killer; and so the film stands among the first of the mad doctor genre entries to clearly ally such a figure with that of the sex murderer.

This was the third of Universal's horror films of the early '30s, following *Dracula* and *Frankenstein*. It had a troubled history. Florey had wanted a period piece (1840) and the studio a more modern tale. The studio relented but cut the budget. Thus hampered, Florey left the production but was coaxed back by a raise in salary. However, the finished film was reedited by the studio against Florey's wishes and is thus not the version he intended. Despite Florey's objections, the movie has standing in genre history.

It was criticized upon release for its sexual sadism and "unrestrained ferocity" (Clarens, p. 94), the objections mainly leveled at a scene wherein a woman is tied on the torture rack and then bled to death, with the body disposed of in the Seine. Nevertheless, it was a popular box office hit. It was later filmed as the 3D *Phantom of the Rue Morgue* and remade in 1971 for veteran American exploitation studio AIP.

Murders in the Rue Morgue

(1971: d. Gordon Hessler)

scr. Charles Wicking, Henry Slesar; pr. Louis M. Heyward; ph. Manuel Berengier; m. Waldo de Los Rios; cast. Jason Robards Jr., Herbert Lom, Lilli Palmer, Adolfo Celi, Michael Dunn; 86m

In this competent, title-only adapta-

tion of the Poe tale, the daughter of a theater owner (in Paris) staging the title production has a recurring nightmare wherein a man in an ape costume swings towards her and she falls to her death. Murders of the company's actors implicate a man who murders those women who spurn his sexual and romantic advances.

This followed on from the critically acclaimed run of Poe adaptations for AIP by exploitation auteur Roger Corman. In that it takes place in the one area, and most of the victims are related in some manner and not just random strangers, it doesn't fit the serial killer film pattern and is more of a mystery whodunit. However, perhaps in recognition of changing mores, the killer has a recognizable sexual motive — resentment and the desire to prove himself superior. The serial killer as a character type thus enters into other generic patterns.

Murders in the Zoo

(1933: d. Edward Sutherland)

scr. Philip Wylie, Seton J. Miller; ph. Ernest Haller; cast. Lionel Atwill, Charles Ruggles, Kathleen Burke, John Lodge, Randolph Scott, Gail Patrick; 64m

Considered an unusually grisly work for the 1930s, this film concerns a jealous husband (Atwill) who kills those who make advances toward his wife, whom he also seems to resent (the later *Sea of Love* would feature a similarly motivated killer). On board ship, returning from a zoological expedition to capture animals, he plots to dispose of those he perceives as threats.

The unforgettable opening has the sadistic killer sewing a man's mouth shut. This film offended the critics of the day, and as a result scenes were removed from many prints, making a complete version perhaps hard to verify. It is the killer's sheer sadistic pleasure that perhaps elevates the film into the early serial killer pantheon, although like many films of the period, it lacks a true blueprint for such a killer. His true object of resentment may be his wife, and the other killings can possibly be interpreted as displaced surrogates for that one person, another feature in serial killer pathology. Correspondingly, he loathes the desire his wife awakens in others, punishing them for their interest. The film is included here as a footnote.

Mystery of the Wax Museum

(1933: d. Michael Curtiz)

scr. Don Mullally, Carl Erickson; play. Charles S. Belden; pr. Henry Blanke; ph. Ray Rennahan; art d. Anton Grot; cast. Lionel Atwill, Fay Wray, Glenda Farrell, Frank McHugh, Gavin Gordon, Allen Vincent, Edwin Maxwell; 77m

In Curtiz' follow up to *Doctor X*, a sculptor, his hands crippled and forced to wear a mask to cover a facial disfigurement, kills people, removes them from the morgue, encases them in wax, and exhibits them as trophies. He searches for the ideal beauty. Meanwhile, a reporter (Farrell) realizes that the accused, a known ladies man (the lady-killer type), may not be guilty, and so investigates the crimes. Murder is a stage in the creation of an artwork, preserving the beauty of the killer's victims.

The film pushes at the edges of the development of the serial killer film. Although the killer is recognizably physically removed from humanity by his disfigurement, his actions betray a sexual sadism and necrophilia as corresponding psychological human aberration. The movie thus acknowledges the genre's need to physicalize monstrousness as a means of suggesting paraphilic abnormality. To make the point clearer, the film was set in contemporary New York City, contrasting such ugliness within modern surroundings as if it were a contaminant on modern society.

Although it is not a serial killer film, *Mystery of the Wax Museum* interestingly points to the increasing attention given to this character type. Hence, the owner of a wax museum says that his competitors make money because of their exhibits of Jack the Ripper, Sweeney Todd and such like. The implication is that the public wants to see representations of sex killers instead of the representations of high culture that Atwill is so enamored with. Atwill dismisses such a celebration of madmen as reprehensible, perhaps a tacit acknowledgement on the filmmakers' part that they are indeed creating a study of an equally demented madman obsessed with preserving the beauty of a woman, frozen forever in death. Indeed, the sculptor sexualizes this death as part of beauty's transcendence into a kind of immortality. In his search for such bodies, he raids the morgues for necrophilic indulgences and is unable to resist the temptation to murder live women, so consumed is he by his fantasy of the ideal woman's beauty.

With the protagonist a reporter, the film acknowledges the sensationalist clamor for such material. The genre is little more than a search for increasingly bizarre sex murderers, and owes its existence to the public fascination accorded the infamous killers of history. Of course, these are all patriarchs. The association of killer and artist would have surprising longevity throughout the serial killer film's evolution, particularly since the mid–1990s.

On first release, *Mystery* was considered terrifying by some (Agate). Until a print was discovered in the late 1960s, this was thought to be a lost film. Subsequently, it was greeted with some revisionist interest and eventually received a full restoration. Like Curtiz' earlier *Doctor X*, the film is noteworthy for its early use of color. It was remade in 1953 in 3D as *House of Wax*, a movie which is well considered in its own right, but by that time the serial killer film had diverged from such period horror, and the character type evolved into post-noir studies.

Nadja

(1995: d. Michael Almereyda)

scr. Almereyda; pr. Mary Sweeney, Amy Hobby; ph. Jim Denault; m. Simon Fisher Turner; ed. David Leonard; prod d. Kurt Ossenfort; cast. Suzy Amis, Elina Lowensohn, Galaxy Craze, Martin Donovan, Peter Fonda, Karl Geary, Jared Harris; 100m

A young philosophical female vampire, Nadja (Lowensohn), a descendant of Count Dracula and his peasant lover, prowls the streets and bars of New York City in search of male victims. A vampire hunter, Van Helsing (Fonda), whose friend has to bail him out of jail for murder charges, pursues her. Nadja, delighting in her curse/affliction, in turn seduces that friend's wife. Nadja intends to care for her stricken brother, who has put aside his sanguinary ways.

The irony here, and the major twist to the vampire tale, is that the vampire hunter (the forerunner of the profiler figure) has become the obsessed, self-absorbed ritual killer, consumed by his fantasy image of himself as purifier — a development of the uncle in *Martin*. This is, of course, a corruption/subversion of the function of the profiler as sanctioned executioner. He is a paranoid drunk, continually pronouncing his intention to rid the world of "them." He has found a solution to the emptiness of life in his role as a sanctioned killer (in his mind, anyway, although he is a rogue patriarch).

The vampire prowls the bars in search of interpersonal contact, finding only Generation X disillusionment, linking the film to the likes of *Love and Human Remains*. Dissatisfied with the superficiality around her, she seeks to simplify her life. This

Peter Fonda plays a modern Van Helsing — the vampire hunter as near serial killer himself — in the *Dracula* update *Nadja* (21st Century Pic., 1995).

simplification is a succession of sex murders, whereby she seduces a lover, kills him as a kind of foreplay, then consumes his blood as a kind of necrophilic feast. She describes her own life as "the pain of fleeting joy."

The film drew comparison to David Lynch (who appears as a morgue attendant), Jean Cocteau (its use of a modern city and its inhabitants as backdrop for old myth, and the sense of film as a means of magic) and even Hal Hartley (in the use of actors Lowensohn and Donovan). Its style Roger Ebert termed "deadpan noir," a brooding, ironic treatment of aberration, with a morbid, sad humor running throughout. Parts of the film were shot with a cheap child's camera, Pixelvision (for the vampire point of view shots), and it is undoubtedly a style-conscious exercise.

The brooding, sometimes hallucinatory feel and black and white photography make it the first of a mini–new wave of underground vampire movies like Ferrara's *The Addiction* and the vampire-as-serial-killer movie *Night Owl*, which link vampirism to a modern Bohemian lifestyle choice. This lifestyle, that of the so-called Goth, is reflected in the musical choices (the bands Portishead and My Bloody Valentine especially). Its superficiality clashes with the characters' attempts to find meaning in it, which inevitably revolves around murder as an Existential statement. This is not a serial killer film, but it intersects with the themes and character types nonetheless and is therefore included, primarily for comparison to the likes of *Night Owl* and as a line of descent from *Martin*: the noir vampire.

Naked Souls

(1995: d. Lyndon Chubbick)

scr. Frank Dietz; ph. Eric Goldstein; m. Nigel Holton; ed. Rebecca Ross; prod d. Elisabeth A. Scott; cast. Pamela Anderson, Brian Krause, Clayton Rohner, David Warner, Dean Stockwell; 85m

A young scientist experiments with thought transference. He uses a dead serial killer as a subject. One such transference goes awry, and the scientist is imbued with the identity, memories and presumed fantasies of the serial killer. Subsequently, his girlfriend is in peril from the one she loves. There is also a generation gap theme, as the young scientist is bankrolled by an older one (Warner) who wants to share the knowledge, but the younger is more stubborn and, as it turns out, recklessly dangerous. The rich benefactor then uses the device on himself, unaware that the killer's memory cells have occupied the scientist. Now he becomes a killer.

There is an introductory effort to contextualize the film in terms of primitive ritual, equating such with modern body painting for an art exhibit. The theme of evolving cultural practice is used as evidence of a kind of collective unconscious which seeks renewed expression with each generation's attempt at self-definition. The attempt to delve into shared experience, however, yields access to the memories of a killer, almost as a warped individual's experience contaminating the collective soul with a kind of telepathic virus.

The virus consists of a perceptual experience which holds (naked) women as objects to be used. This killer's gaze represents the sexual glorification of violence, the ultimate aberration. Once afflicted with such fantasies, the reality of sex murder is inevitable. It is an altered state of consciousness (indeed, some of the film's design recalls *Altered States*) which absorbs the individual soul as it pretends to liberate it. For the old scientist it is the invigorating essence of perpetual youth, the film also thus referring to the elderly thrill seekers who impel youth to violence in *The Sorcerers*.

The blend of science fiction and identity implanting/transference is treated to better effect in *Dark City* and *The Cell*. It is interesting to see Warner as another serial killer, her recalling his portrayal of Jack the Ripper in *Time After Time*. The director, however, lingers on the often naked and copulating body of starlet Pamela Lee Anderson, signaling the film's real intentions and target audience.

Nattevagten

(1994: d. Ole Bornedal) aka *Nightwatch*

scr. Bornedal; pr. Michael Obel; ph. Dan Laustsen; m. Joachim Holbeck; ed. Camilla Skousen; art d. Soren Krag Sorensen; cast. Nicolai Coster Waldau, Sofie Grabol, Kim Bodnia, Ulf Pilgaard, Lotte Andersen, Rikke Louise Andersson, Stig Hoffmeyer; 105m

A replacement nightshift morgue attendant is implicated in a series of murders when he finds himself looking over the victims' corpses. He listens to the case details as told to him by the investigating detective, and learns of a killer who rapes, scalps and kills prostitutes. The attendant's friend seems strangely interested in these details. Soon, however, after seeing a corpse in the hallway (was it planted there by someone?), the protagonist realizes someone is framing him. The killer is revealed to be the detective, a former night watchman guilty of necrophilia and quietly dismissed, now intent on framing the protagonist. His friends finally come to his rescue, and the detective is shot.

Saturating the film is the theme of exhaustion and the quest for new sensations in order to find meaning and purpose, however ultimately shallow this may be. In that way its protagonists, the two friends, would not be out of place in an American Generation X movie. Starved for sensation, the two enter a game of challenges, each daring the other to perform an act. This involves a teenage prostitute who becomes a link to the killer. The friend batters the prostitute for information and is clearly an exploiter initiating the attendant in the pleasures of such sexual exploitation. In this way the subsequent events are the repercussions of a quest for moral abandon. The protagonist idolizes his dominant, amoral friend, and their friendship recalls that of Leopold and Loeb as explored in *Compulsion*, although they are clearly heterosexual.

The killer is of another generation. He is a sexual deviant intent on framing the substitute son for the crimes of the father. In this way the monstrous patriarch manipulates the next generation into a moral response, like the play between the two friends. The repercussion of the amoral quest for sensation is the erotic celebration of death as the ultimate transgressive act. Hence the scene where the partly decomposed nude female body is displayed before the camera for the characters and the audience to contemplate. In the many US versions of this scene the naked body is unblemished; not so here — she is starting to rot.

The protagonist, despite his fears, is curious, even hesitant and confused, and in a situation that the killer found himself in long ago. The killer preys on the attendant's moral confusion to implicate him in acts he finds both abhorrent and fascinating. Ultimately, however, the two friends effectively distance themselves from the monstrous patriarch, denying his viability as a Devil's advocate, and in a double wedding marry their girlfriends, restoring the moral balance. This arguably undercuts the film's subversive potential in terms of a happy ending. Despite their games, the two friends have learnt their moral lesson and are fit to join adult society, having found marriage as a solution to their initial amoral angst. Order is restored.

Its graphic content and necrophilic themes make *Nattevagten* in part comparable to the underground work of Jorg Buttgereit in Germany, whose *Nekromantik* and *Schramm* sought to depict the acts of such a sex killer. However, it is more self-consciously stylish than these truly subversive, low-budget, naturalistic works. *Nattevagten* proved to be unexpectedly popular throughout Europe, no doubt due to its skillful blend of dark humor and suspense, and was effectively remade in Hollywood by the same director as *Nightwatch*.

Natural Born Killers

(1994: d. Oliver Stone)

scr. David Veloz, Richard Rutowski, Stone; stry. Quentin Tarantino; pr. Jame Hamsher, Don Murphy, Clayton Townsend; ph. Robert Richardson; ed. Hank Corwin, Brian Berdan; prod d. Victor Kempster; cast. Woody Harrelson, Juliette Lewis, Robert Downey Jr., Tommy Lee Jones, Tom Sizemore; 119m

A man and woman (Harrelson and Lewis) run off together and embark on a cross-country crime and murder spree. In the process they become famous media celebrities, with the expected media circus following their every move. An arrogant detective pursues them. They are caught, but with the aid of an overenthusiastic reporter, they escape prison and flee into freedom.

This is not technically a serial killer film but a spree killer film, even though the characters are referred to as serial killers by the press and hailed as such by a league of enthusiastic young serial killer fans. It is thus most noteworthy for its depiction of the response to the growing subculture that would idolize such killers, readily incorporating their actions into an emergent, though barely expressed philosophy which both celebrates and hypocritically condemns anarchic random violence as justifiable social revolution.

This culture seeks to remove the acts from the sociological, psychological and sexual spectrum of events which produced them (except as can be summed up in convenient one- or two-minute sound bites). Indeed, it can codify such experiences as safe entertainment. Thus deprived of dimension, it is impossible to see the acts beyond brief outbursts of intense rage. It is then easy for a culture devoid of satisfactory meaning to attach revolutionary and celebratory significance to acts where none exists. The killers become visionaries in the public eye, their crimes the repressed wish of every disenchanted youth. These people define themselves in relation to the killers; the closer they are, the greater their self-importance, hence the policeman (Sizemore) whose autobiography has become another cultural focus, referring no doubt to the rise in true-crime literature and famed detectives' reminiscences of their time on the job. This kind of literature arguably complements and fosters the fascination with such killers, a self-aggrandizing genre even more arrogant than the killer's acts.

In a society as irredeemably vile as this, where even killers are exploited by greedy, fame-seeking people, what response is there but to celebrate those who would seek to destroy it: to incorporate the aberration as a collective empowerment fantasy. Although authority would deny this empowerment, they cannot prevent it; their punitive means are at breaking point and ultimately validate it through their attempts at suppression. This is the chaos of the culture of violence: nihilistic, hyper, confused, empty but desperate for meaning and conviction, but unable to settle (and visualized in Stone's schizophrenic barrage of images). Although there are motives for the killers, these are not presented as explanations, but rather examples of the cultural response to codify and explain such aberrance.

The film became lastingly controversial. Divided critics praised it as eye-opening satire and (many more) decried it as

Oliver Stone directing a scene from *Natural Born Killers* (WB, 1994).

mindless, incitant violence which degenerates into being the very thing it supposedly criticizes. Real spree killers that followed were often thought to have been incited to violence by the movie, and the film quickly became a scapegoat. Famed author John Grisham attacked the film as "made with the intent of glorifying random murder" (French, p. 234). Oliver Stone was subsequently sued by victims of killers supposedly inspired by the movie, and for a while it seemed to crusaders against film violence that Hollywood would finally have to answer for its spate of violent films.

Stone's version was threatened with an NC-17 (then still perceived as a stigma, and a threat to box-office potential) and was re-cut (150 shots removed or trimmed) into an R-rated version. The uncut "director's cut" was subsequently released onto video and DVD. Aesthetically, it is a fascinating movie, using flashbacks, flash-forwards, TV parody, rear-screen projection, titles, animation, differing film stocks (super 8 and video included), color and black and white, fluid camerawork, shock editing, subliminal editing, and modern music. Despite its chaotic appearance, every frame was deliberately thought out in an editing process over eleven months.

Nature of the Beast

(1994: d. Victor Salva) aka *The Hatchet Man*

scr. Salva; pr. Daniel Grodnik, Robert Snukal, John Tarnoff; ph. Levie Isaacks; m. Bennett Salvay; ed. W. Peter Miller; prod d. Stephen Greenberg; cast. Eric Roberts, Lance Henriksen, Brion James, Frank Novak, William A. Temple; 91m

An uptight businessman (Henriksen) and a brash hitchhiker (Roberts) travel together through the desert roads and attendant road-culture. Through radio broadcasts they learn that one is a serial killer (the "hatchet man" who sexually mutilates his victims) and the other is a thief who robbed a casino. Which is which? That is the dramatic game played with the audience. The brasher man is revealed to be the thief, and the milder man the serial killer. The killer does away with the thief and returns home to his normal family.

The film is slyest with the homosexual undercurrent running between the two men (most notable in Roberts' bravado). Both of them at times break into subtly feminine gestures, and their interplay is intended to assert aggressive and passive masculine roles. This offbeat sexuality is a recurrent theme in Salva's work (and has earned him accusations of sexualizing children in his films *Clownhouse* and *Powder*). They know each other's secret and seek to intimidate, manipulate and control each other, even role playing to achieve this—thus the film plays on the expectation that killers often prey on hitchhikers.

The serial killer (Lance Henriksen) peeks out in *Nature of the Beast* (Cannon, 1988).

They recognize the similarity in each other, though the killer resents it. Roberts suggests that crimes are done for the thrill, to escape the humdrum. Henriksen has rationalized this further, however, and he considers himself an instrument of salvation. The killer is differentiated from the conventional criminal by this philosophical sense of purpose, or so the film suggests. The killer thus tires of what he considers the empty bravado of the thief and finally kills him, as if ridding himself of an irksome pest.

The film ends with a Biblical quotation from Jeremiah 17:9: "The heart is deceitful above all things and desperately wicked. Who can know it?" The film suggests that only the wicked can see such wickedness in others, and that the serial killer's pathology is the nadir of such wickedness and a force beyond the conventional criminal.

Two capable actors and a talented director, though still in the promising category, make this an intriguing battle of wills, although the premise arguably wears thin and soon becomes repetitive. A similar hook (the killer as either driver or hitcher) was used in *Switchback*. The film tackles the same road culture and rural film noir themes as some of the works of John Dahl and J.S. Cardone (especially *Outside Ozona*), and Robert Harmon's *The Hitcher*.

Nekromantik 2

(1991: d. Jorg Buttgereit)

scr. Buttgereit, Franz Rodenkirchen; pr, ph. Manfred Jelinski; spec eff. Alois Vollert, Sammy Bachaus; cast. Monika M, Mark Reeder, Wolfgang Muller, Beatrice M; 96m

In this sequel to the underground hit (dubbed "necro-porn"), a woman exhumes the corpse of her boyfriend (who committed suicide at the end of the first film — a highlight re-shown during the opening credits) for necrophilic pleasure. Soon, however, she tries a normal relationship with a man, but so craves necrophilic sex that she decapitates him during intercourse, tying string around his penis to maintain his erection. She then replaces his head with that of her dead lover. The suggestion is that she has become a serial killer and will repeat murder for sexual pleasure. In a gross punch-line, she learns that she has been made pregnant by the dead man's ejaculate.

The film seeks an art-house quality to counterbalance its scenes of pornographic violence, but it becomes dull when not involved in aberration. There is no fulfillment to be had in life for anyone, and so the protagonist is driven to seek fulfillment in closeness to death. Correspondingly, the film is torn between eroticizing death and non-judgmentally depicting the grisly actuality of the necrophilic practice. Its unflinching view of these practices stood as the most explicit, taboo-challenging depiction of a serial killer's private sexual

fantasies until the same director's *Schramm*. Its intention is present in its opening quote from Ted Bundy — "I want to master life and death": sex murder and necrophilia as transcending death.

From the opening flashback from *Nekromantik*, sex and death are united. A man ejaculates as he commits hara-kiri, his semen turning to blood. Pain and pleasure are one. But such an act can only be experienced once — that is, unless one projects the death experience onto one's lover. The lover is killed so that the killer can become death, and the necrophilic sex which follows is the transcendence of physical death, giving life and meaning to it, allowing a higher state of consciousness — the union of little and big deaths. This other state is fleeting, however, and the acts that precede it need to be forever restaged.

The protagonist exhumes a corpse and brings it home. She slowly undresses it, the camera lingering as if at a striptease. But the scene becomes unflinchingly pornographic (she straddles the corpse, licks the rotting flesh, severs the genitalia and keeps it in the fridge to be found by her later lover), then cuts self-consciously to the next male victim dubbing a conventional porno film. Buttgereit intends to create a kind of pornography of death wherein the acts of the necrophile represent the ultimate challenge to society. In the process he validates this aberration, and therein is the most disturbing aspect, despite the surrounding art-house pretenses.

She goes through a conventional courtship, but this is shown as a stagnant ritual, devoid of any passion or even meaningful interaction. To find this passion she resorts to the grisly dismembering and disembowelment of her corpse lover once he has served his usefulness. She poses her live lover as if he was a corpse and photographs him (strangely, he is still with her even after he finds the severed penis in her fridge). She must find another corpse, and graduates to murder over exhumation. In an ironic ending, she discovers she is pregnant by her activities with the freshly dead — death has found life.

The film is doubly rare for depicting a female sex killer and for the degree of sympathy it has for her morbid desires, arguably even glorifying and condoning them as valid self-expression, whatever the cost. The German authorities certainly thought this way and banned the film after ordering the negatives to be found, confiscated and destroyed. It remains a widely banned film. The documentary *Corpse Fucking Art* features behind-the-scenes footage.

Never Talk to Strangers

(1996: d. Peter Hall)

scr. Lewis Green, Jordan Rush; pr. Rebecca de-Mornay, Andras Hamori, Jeffrey R. Neuman, Martin Wiley; ph. Elemer Ragalyi; m. Pino Donaggio; ed. Roberto Silvi; prod d. Linda Del Rosario; cast. Rebecca DeMornay, Antonio Banderas, Dennis Miller, Len Cariou, Harry Dean Stanton; 86m

A frigid woman, a criminal psychologist (DeMornay), falls for a dangerous stranger who may be a killer. The film intercuts her relationship with the stranger (Banderas) she meets at an art exhibition of sadomasochistic works with her sessions with killer Stanton, whose fabrications (he claims multiple-personality disorder) she must wade through in an effort to determine his suitability for trial. The scenes with the killer are too short, and the film is instead a predictable thriller, more concerned with Patriarchy's sexual politics.

The film derives its female character from the female agents in *Copycat* and *Silence of the Lambs*. It addresses the issue (as in *Copycat*) of an incarcerated killer potentially having an influence on others that reaches beyond the cell confines, as

someone is tormenting her. It emerges in the format of a cautionary tale which adds a twist in that the protagonist also may have a resentment of men, and even a sense of female superiority over them. However, all men are loathsome or dangerous potential killers in this world, validating her views.

Perhaps the movie was intended to show the need for professional women to dissociate themselves from the world (and sexuality) of men. Thus, she is distanced from the accused serial killer and even turns away her own father when he wants accommodation: she rejects the patriarch, but only to a point. Her outward self-confidence is ultimately threatened by her sexual dependence on risk, however she may maintain otherwise. She thinks nothing of taking the risk with a stranger, and so must face the consequences of such an unquestioning and self-deceptive confidence. It is this confidence which the predatory male deems in need of being taught a corrective lesson, and in so doing reinstate male sexual superiority. She must reverse the situation to survive, and so counter the network of abusive males the film connotes.

Director Hall has a tremendous reputation in England as a theater director, having been managing director of the Royal Shakespeare Company and London's National Theater, and was knighted in 1977. Although he had made films before, from 1967 to 1974, these were indifferently treated. The screenwriter was a graduate of SIU-Carbondale. DeMornay spent over a year in development supervising rewrites, and it was she who brought Hall to the project. She later claimed to be thrilled to finally get a film done as she had intended. However, critics and audiences greeted it with indifference, especially considering the impressive credentials of most of those involved with the ill-fated project.

The New York Ripper

(1982: d. Lucio Fulci)

scr. Fulci, Gianfranco Clerici, Dardano Sacchetti, Vincenzo Mannino; pr. Fabrizio De Angelis; ph. Luigi Kuveiller; cast. Jack Hedley, Almanta Keller, Howard Ross, Andrew Painter, Alessandra Delli Colli, Paolo Malco, Lucio Fulci; 93m

This misogynistic film is about a cop on the trail of a violent serial killer who stabs and slices sexily or revealingly dressed, sexually "free" women (shown in explicit detail). The only promising (if ridiculous) lead is that the killer talks like a cartoon duck while committing the crimes or on the phone to police, taking credit for the murders. The policeman enlists a psychologist's help, and the sexual aspects of the crimes fascinate this profiler. When one intended victim survives, she has dreams in which her boyfriend is the killer. Finally, this proves to be true, and the police, who have been following the wrong suspect, must rescue her.

The film presents the victims as almost justifiable targets for predatory men by virtue of their sexual curiosity or snobbish attitude. Such women need to be shown their place, the killer (and, arguably, the filmmaker) feels. Their punishment is sexual torture and mutilation (a woman is sliced from eyeball to nipple in one notorious scene, and another is eviscerated with a broken bottle). This explicit violence is presented with the same obsessive stare found in pornography, and is clearly meant as a sexual act. The crimes are often shot from the killer's point of view, or in extreme close-up, focusing attention on the penetration of flesh. When aroused by the female form, the killer must destroy it, which he does lovingly and graphically. The film does not try to distance itself from such a viewpoint or suggest an alternative.

This makes the movie an exercise in callous sadism, one for male voyeurs. Banned in Australia at one stage, this is a cynical, even nihilistic endeavor which has been interpreted as a near celebration of the murder/mutilation of women. However, Fulci's misanthropic nature never makes the killer into a heroic figure; in fact, every character is treated with almost equal contempt.

The New York Ripper is a vulgar Americanization of the giallo format. The giallo was often concerned with the stylization of a perceptual realm shaped by aberrant sexuality. For Argento, this meant the personality transference between killer and protagonist, as present in *Tenebrae* especially. For Fulci, it is the opportunity to revel in a seemingly relentless depiction of the baseness of the human condition (a theme in part shared with Tinto Brass, although Brass avoids misogyny).

Fulci considers the vast American cityscape with a certain wonderment, contemplating its cold ugliness as if a demonstration of the American character. Hence the streets gradually reveal a network of sex shows, clubs and run-down apartments. The serial killer is the epitome of this world, and a force to be reckoned with, a young man who resents women. Since his invalid daughter will never grow up to be the desired object he feels is every woman's due, he is driven to kill those women who flaunt their sexual desirability. This is a regular Fulci theme and would surface as the motivation for a jealous murderess in the disco-giallo *Murder Rock*. All men consider women as such objects, even in their death. Hence the standard autopsy room scene, with the naked female cadaver on display and an examiner who casually remarks on the damage done to her "joy trail" with "nice, efficient butchery." The callous humor trivializes sex murder.

All women are seen in terms of their sexuality as relative to that of the male. Hence, a main character, a trophy wife, is followed as she masochistically subjects herself to male dominance. Her role in the film is akin to the live sex performers she is driven to seek out. Perhaps in her masochism she seeks to appropriate what she considers a male gaze, but she is doomed by her femininity to retreat into a submissive state. With women so depersonalized, there is no sense of outrage in their elimination and mutilation. It is a true function of the world as it is. Patriarchy, in the form of the profiler, thus characterizes the killer as "a very superior mind"; far from the enemy of Patriarchy, he is part of its design. The union of cop and profiler is a self-policing collaboration forced to eliminate a killer who epitomizes their culture.

Their chief suspect is a man immersed in sexual paraphernalia. But this is a red herring, as Fulci ultimately lays the blame for such sexual rage elsewhere. The killer secretly participates in the sex-culture around him, as the process of objectifying female beauty has irrevocably shaped his ideals. Yet he is from a different social spectrum — he has money, is well educated, and is part of the community rather than the underclass he is drawn to. Nevertheless, he represents the spread of such values beyond the censoring forces of class and other such status. No one is unaffected by the sexualizing of popular culture and gender interaction. Fulci accepts this almost uncritically. In that respect, the director is a bleak fatalist, with his characters doomed by their innate sexual desires, however conscious of them they may be. Fulci treats sexual relations as the basest aspect of the human condition, a theme that contrasts with the treatment of sex as a language in the films of, for instance, Tinto Brass. Fulci runs counter to the European erotic cinema movement.

The Night Caller

(1975: d. Henri Verneuil)

scr. Verneuil, Francis Veber; pr. Verneuil; ph. Jean Penzer; m. Ennio Morricone; ed. Pierre Gillette, Henri Lanoe; art d. Jean Andre; cast. Jean-Paul Belmondo, Charles Denner, Catherine Morin, Adalberto-Maria Marli, Lea Massari; 125m

The giallo apparently spread to France with this film about a Paris policeman trailing a serial killer. This killer first calls his intended victims at night and insults them, ridiculing their lives, before murdering them. He targets "free" women, with the intent of sparing the world from their corruptive influence. The main policeman apparently lets his obsession for a petty criminal distract him from his dutiful pursuit of the killer.

The killer resents women's sexual independence and seeks to punish them. Like many movies of the 1970s, the film in part addresses serial murder as a male response to the pressure of female liberation and its threat to Patriarchy's validity. It is up to such a male authority to police its boundaries accordingly — that is his inherent responsibility (all else is distracting and possibly corrupting). In the process of punishing the transgressive, he restores Patriarchy's validity.

The film proved popular in France. Outside of the European continent, it was considered similar to the American model of the tough, independent police-detective character movie. Screenwriter Veber went on to script a number of successful comedies, many remade in Hollywood. He would tackle a serial killer again in his script work for *Partners*.

Night Cries

(199?: d. M.L. Berhrman)

scr. Berhrman; pr. Berhrman; ph. John H. Burke; ed. Paul Howard; m. Leopold Von

Bagendorff; cast. Jack Klarr, Margot Hope, Dave Shiesser; 91m

This is an obscure minor horror film. A serial killer targets Hollywood prostitutes. A female reporter investigates, uncovering a trail that leads to the associates of a politician on a crusade against pornography and vice on LA streets.

The film is a partial exploration of sociopolitical (Patriarchal) hypocrisy. Thus, while the politicians can claim to want to clean up the streets, morally speaking, in effect this means the unofficial sanction of the murder of undesirables: serial murder as a function of political policy (a theme also touched on in part in *Blade*). The killer lures vulnerable women and kills them as the politician watches, for sexual excitement. This excitement turns necrophilic as the bodies are dissected and dismembered, the spare parts given to lower crooks to dispose of. Thus there is a criminal, male hierarchy suggested, with the politician and killer at the top as monstrous symbolic father and son.

The female reporter must challenge this horrendous authority and attack the pervasive mentality that holds all women as disposable whores and thus validates their murder. She is the real force of potential reform, confirmed by her profession as a seeker of truth. In her is the potential for revolution, the ultimate end of feminism, to escape the monstrous law of the Father. Such would be a desired end.

These promising, even subversive themes are undercut by an unremarkable treatment and a resorting to cliché. Thus, the killer has nightmares of a homicidal mother figure he seems to incestuously desire. The overall tendency, unfortunately, is to treat the material as the lowest kind of exploitation.

The Night Digger

(1971: d. Alistair Reed)

scr. Roald Dahl; nvl. Joy Crowley; ph. Alex Thomson; ed. John Bloom; m. Bernard Herrmann; art d. Anthony Pratt; cast. Patricia Neal, Pamela Brown, Nicholas Clay, Jean Anderson, Graham Crowden, Sebastian Breaks, Yootha Joyce; 100m

This is a Gothic thriller set around a Victorian mansion inhabited by two women, one a middle-aged spinster (Neal) and the other her blind mother. Slowly, their lives are disrupted by their new handyman (Clay), a serial rapist/killer of women buried under roads now re-paved. When the police investigate, the infatuated spinster lies to protect and shelter him.

In this reportedly engrossing look at the lure of the pathological, and how romantic love can become corrupted and enslaved by sexual desire, the killer has a magnetic hold over the spinster, as she sees in her growing relationship to him a chance to finally rebel against the constraints she has lived by all of her life (Nash and Ross, p. 2143). The attraction to Evil paradoxically allows her to experience freedom: hence the attraction is addictive and anticipatory. However, her attempt to create an idyll with him is doomed to failure. The film was compared to both versions of *Night Must Fall* and found wanting in its apparent flat direction (or so *Variety* felt). Due to author Roald Dahl's involvement in the script, it has an interest beyond the genre's confines. However, that has not saved its reputation.

Night Game

(1989: d. Peter Masterson)

scr. Spencer Eastman, Anthony Palmer; pr. George Litto, Eduard Sarlui, Moshe Diamant; ph. Fred Murphy; m. Pino Donaggio; ed. Robert Barrere, King Wilder; prod d. Neil Spisak; cast. Roy Scheider, Karen Young, Richard Bradford, Paul Gleason, Carlin Glynn, Anthony Palmer; 95m

A serial killer kills via grappling hook, and stalks women along the beachfront after each baseball game won by his favorite team, the Houston Astros. A police detective, a former baseball player, is on the case. The policeman's fiancée, who owns a concession stand, is the same physical type as those targeted by the killer, who leaves the bodies by the boardwalk to be found, flaunting his cleverness at not being caught and taunting the police.

In contrast to the movement to sentimentalize baseball, as in *Field of Dreams* and *Bull Durham*, this film juxtaposes the great American pastime with the phenomenon of serial murder. The killer is so enraptured by the team's progress that he celebrates by committing a sex murder. Murder as sport — an indictment of American culture. The killer is hardly an athlete himself though, instead being a fat and bald lowlife whose ideal self only exists when he kills women.

The police regularly discuss the case, adamant in their desire to confront the monstrousness that would mutilate women. The detective in charge stresses the need for outside help, and so a CIA operative is included (the profiler here). Of course, the cops resent the intrusion. In that respect it is a formula procedural, but the film has an unexpected sense of black comedy (even termed gallows humor) which makes for an offbeat, even insecure tone.

Night Must Fall

(1937: d. Richard Thorpe)

scr. John Van Druten; play. Emlyn Williams; pr. Hunt Stromberg; ph. Ray June; m. Edward Ward; ed. Robert J. Kern; art d. Cedric Gibbons; cast. Robert Montgomery, Rosalind Russell, May Whitty, Alan Marshal, Merle Tottenham, Kathleen Harrison; 117m

An Irishman (Montgomery) wins the confidence of an elderly invalid and is taken on as a servant in an all-female household — over the objections of a younger niece. To this niece's dismay, she

suspects that he may be involved in an ongoing murder case and is hiding something from her. Despite this, she becomes increasingly sexually attracted to his charming veneer and is reluctant to involve the police. Finally, he reveals himself to her and is apprehended. The tense, notorious final scene has him wandering around the house carrying a hatbox that may or may not contain a human head (a device used later in *Barton Fink* and *Seven*).

The niece resents her financial dependence on the elderly invalid and is fascinated by any challenge to the complacency that she feels around her. She openly voices her interest in how such can be shaken into an awareness of the dangerous otherness behind people's normal facade. Her interest in such homicidal duplicity, sparked by the ongoing hunt for a murder victim's severed head, almost summons the killer to her household. Is it fate bringing her the confrontation she desired? In that thematic respect, the film anticipates the film noir development of a few years later; oddly, Thorpe's style emphasizes light over darkness, although this is progressively undermined the more the protagonist's suspicions of Montgomery's morality grow. She thus summons not only confrontation, but also darkness to her, testing and tainting her moral resolve.

The killer takes pride in his ability to be charming, and has a need to be liked. He is a manipulative expert at seeming brightly innocuous, even funny. The protagonist claims to be repulsed by his casual attempts at seduction but is entranced by what she senses beneath the charming facade. For him, the facade is all — his vanity and pride consuming him and betraying his arrogance. Thus, when confronted by her in the end, he admits that he wanted to make his mark on the world, that he had big plans and wanted to "be somebody." His ideal sense of greatness and importance has resulted in murder: the control

A seemingly jovial charmer (Robert Montgomery) is a serial killer seeking employment in *Night Must Fall* (MGM, 1937). The younger woman (Rosalind Russell) suspects him, but he beguiles the elderly invalid (Dame May Whitty).

over another life reinforcing his perceived control over his own life — he has become somebody.

The killer and protagonist enter into a complex mind game of role-playing, a process that invigorates and sexually excites, even corrupts, the protagonist. He says he is conceited and always acting, concealing an unknowable and unfathomable monstrous self. She considers herself the superior intellect and seeks to psychoanalyze and profile him. She tells him that he has no real feelings and lives in a world of his own imagination, i.e. he is consumed by fantasy. He knows this awareness excites her and plays into it, although he starts to realize that he is not the clever master criminal he believes himself to be,

an awareness which threatens the validity of his fantasy and makes him more unstable. The more he reveals of himself the harder it is to maintain his sanity.

The protagonist is using him for her own means. Thus, although she suspects he is the murderer, she protects him from the police, verifying that the hatbox is not his. The awareness of being so known by someone finally makes him faint — his defenses have been penetrated. The protagonist, almost sure of his guilt and thus aware of the threat he poses to the old woman, leaves him alone with this woman. In that, she reveals her hope that he may kill the woman she loathes and resents, and her knowledge that she can manipulate the killer into doing so makes her a prototype femme fatale. The killer obliges, and Thorpe brings out the killer's glee at the act of murder, implicating it as a sexual excitement. The subsequent confrontation between killer and protagonist (as profiler here) carries a sexual charge which the killer transforms into guilt and paranoia. The police ultimately catch him, but the protagonist, guilty of complicity (though this cannot be proven) is able to continue her renewed life, free from the tyrannical matriarch.

The film also slyly develops the theme of the public fascination with murder and murderers. Thus the elderly woman sets up tours of the property where the woman's body was found, and charges for the privilege. Of course, the protagonist represents the worst of this fascination, ready to manipulate a manipulator to get what she wants, in the process becoming tainted by her fascination with such duplicity.

The producer Hunt Stromberg liked the stage play and wished to have it filmed, much to the displeasure of MGM head Louis B. Mayer, who despised the property (Nash and Ross, pp. 2148–9). Mayer became even more distraught when Montgomery wanted to star, as the actor was known for his popular comedies. Star Montgomery had to fight with MGM to be allowed to play the role he felt would establish him as a major actor (it did). Mayer restricted the budget, and after the film was released he dispersed disclaimers dissociating himself and MGM from the movie. The movie was a critical and box-office hit, however, and Mayer halted his tactics.

Night Must Fall

(1964: d. Karel Reisz)

scr. Clive Exton; ply. Emlyn Williams; pr. Albert Finney, Karel Reisz; ph. Freddie Francis; m. Ron Grainer; ed. Fergus McDonell, Philip Barnikel; prod d. Timothy O'Brien; art d. Lionel Couch; cast. Albert Finney, Mona Wash-bourne, Susan Hampshire, Sheila Hancock, Michael Medwin, Joe Gladwin, Martin Wyldeck, John Gill; 101m

This is an English remake of the 1937 MGM version. An axe murderer (Finney) infiltrates the home of an elderly woman and her daughter on the pretense of redecorating. He starts to psychologically torment the older woman and has an affair with the daughter. All the while, he plays games with the severed heads of his victims, which he keeps in hatboxes in his room.

This is more deliberately an exercise in serial killer pathology than was the first film, which depicted the subtle shift in power between the killer and the woman who suspects him. Here he is more consciously sadistic and even necrophilic (his sexual use of severed heads is suggested). Unlike the first film, there is no doubt as to what's in the hatbox (indeed, here there are more than one, making the serial nature of the crimes clearer), and so there's no ambiguity to Finney's character. His corresponding psychological disintegration into violence has a sense of inevitability, as he is reduced to a whimpering animal.

The film sits oddly amidst the British revival of the 1960s and the socially conscious dramas that were unfolding. Finney's killer thus has much of the working-class-lad virility that had been popular since the play *Look Back in Anger* (Hardy, p. 165). The killer is very much a lady-killer in both senses—the expert seducer who adapts his personality to what the women expect of their ideal man. Once he has drained their fantasy, he kills them, keeping their heads as sexual trophies. He is therefore perhaps the perversion of the myth of the working class man as modern British ideal, a myth Finney and Reisz take much pleasure in invalidating.

The critics made much of the film's stylistic eccentricity (rare in British film

Night of Bloody Horror

(1969 or 1974: d. Joy N. Houck Jr.)

scr. Robert A. Weaver, Houck; pr. Houck; ph. Weaver; ed. Weaver; mkup. Philip St. Jon; cast. Gerald McRaney, Gaye Yellen, Herbert Nelson, Evelyn Hendricks, Lisa Dameron, Charlotte White; 89m

A man (McRaney) prone to blackouts since childhood, wherein he accidentally killed his brother, becomes the prime suspect when his girlfriends die violently. Although he knows he is a suspect, he cannot remember enough to clear his name.

The killer is revealed to be his mother, intent to punish him for his actions and also deny him his adult sexuality, perhaps usurping it for herself in her presumed adoption, and confusion, of phallic power and maternal justice. She makes her son out to be the worst kind of sex killer, but is she aware of her own sexual resentment? Sources do not say. She keeps the mummified corpses of her dead loved ones (son and husband, who committed suicide). The monstrous mother who suppresses her son's self expression, in the process dominating him, is of course derivative of *Psycho*, which this minor film is considered to be (Hardy, p. 209). It is all reportedly done as luridly and flashily as possible, with psychedelic visuals suggesting the film is aimed at the counter-culture

The serial killer/decapitator (Albert Finney) clutches at a hatbox containing the trophy of his crime in the remake of *Night Must Fall* (MGM, 1964).

before American Richard Lester and the Beatles made the swinging sixties swing), especially Reisz' use of scene transitions, jump-cuts and overlapping sounds. It is a deliberate challenge to the British Realist school from some of its founders. Its stylistic flashiness either alienated or attracted reviewers, with Finney's performance being the most consistently praised aspect, although considered ultimately too showily inferior to Robert Montgomery's. Indeed, the film was only possible due to Finney's enthusiasm and his previous box-office triumph in *Tom Jones*.

of the 1970s, but it wallows in graphic wanton homicidal criminality.

The film is most memorable today for the publicity campaign which glorified the gore as being filmed in "Violent Vision," with TV commercials offering $1000 to the families of anyone who died of fright and claiming that scenes were too gory to be shown on television. It was the kind of campaign that combined William Castle and Allan Shakleton (of *Snuff* fame). Perhaps symptomatic of social change and increased explicitness in exploitation films, it is now a hard-to-find curiosity. It only intersects the serial killer film tangentially, however.

Night of the Generals

(1967: d. Anatole Litvak)

scr. Joseph Kessel, Paul Dehn; nvls. H.H. Kirst and James Hadley Chase; pr. Sam Spiegel; ph. Henri Decae; m. Maurice Jarre; ed. Alan Osbiston; prod d. Alexander Trauner; art d. Auguste Capelier; cast. Peter O'Toole, Omar Sharif, Tom Courtenay, Donald Pleasence, Joanna Pettet, Philippe Noiret, Charles Gray, Coral Browne, John Gregson, Nigel Stock, Christopher Plummer, Gordon Jackson, Harry Andrews; 148m

During the German occupation of Warsaw, a major (Sharif) investigates the death of a prostitute, seemingly killed by a German general. The investigating officer is obsessed with the case and narrows the suspects to three generals. He is so persistent that he is transferred away, to Paris. When another prostitute is similarly murdered two years later, he resumes his inquiries. The killer (O'Toole) murders him, but at a reunion 20 years later the investigator's Resistance friend unveils the killer. This film balances the procedural investigation with a character portrait of the likely killer and a depiction of crumbling Nazi authority.

There is no real doubt as to which of the suspected generals is the murderer.

However, with one exception (when he stares at a Van Gogh painting, perhaps identifying his madness with that of the artist), the killer does not consider himself guilty. After all, in a world of mass murder, of what significance is the sex murder of a prostitute? It matters to no one except the investigator, whose dedication to solving and avenging the death of a simple prostitute earns him the respect of a Resistance member. Obsessed with cleanliness and discipline, the general hides a secretly tortured identity, reinforced by alcohol, which demands he prove himself via murder. This murder takes the form of wartime action and spills over into a sexual preference.

There is also the suggestion that he represses a homosexual longing (indeed, at times he seems effeminate and remarks of Courtenay's "handsome head"), which may surface in a resentment of women's sexuality. He considers the bodily functions "disgusting but inevitable" and wants to see sex in the same way, punishing those who would arouse his desire. In that way, his crimes speak of sexual frenzy, as he inflicts over 100 stab wounds on the first victim. Repression segues into sporadic explosions of violence which satiate only temporarily.

O'Toole and Sharif, of course, had previously starred together in *Lawrence of Arabia*. Indeed, O'Toole's role serves as a counterpoint to his famed performance and stresses rigid over-control erupting into mostly offscreen, almost detached sexual murder. He cannot suppress his fantasies and allies them to decadent artistic impression (a popular theme in the 1990s). He knows that his status brings with it a protection, and so forces his assistant (Courtenay) into taking the blame for the sex murder of a prostitute. Courtenay knows that he must flee, as his word counts less than that of a general. O'Toole dismisses the victim as a mere worthless

A German general (Peter O'Toole) in civilian clothes takes a break from duty in order to prepare to murder a prostitute. His accomplice (Tom Courtenay, background) will be implicated in *Night of the Generals* (MGM, 1964).

prostitute, although she served a useful function by satisfying his sexually homicidal urges. People have no value beyond their role in the life of the dominant male, the ultimate Nazi.

The film compares and contrasts the generals, as two of them consider O'Toole's methods monstrous and are indeed drawn into the failed plot to kill Hitler. O'Toole is thus set up as Hitler's pet — the Aryan as monster, the nadir of the purification ideal. Yet even they consider the prostitutes' deaths as minor and insignificant, Pleasence even considering such as an occupational hazard. Sharif sums up the attitude when he declares, "What is admirable on the large scale is monstrous on the small," a paradox which only he strives to correct,

adding, "Since we must give medals to mass murderers, let us try to give justice to the small entrepreneur." The film's thematic juxtaposition between mass and individual atrocity recalls the killer's defense in *Monsieur Verdoux*. Finally, O'Toole's performance gives a chilling depiction of the Nazi as sexual psychopath, paradoxically identifying with the vision of an artist once confined to a psychiatric facility for treatment. When Courtenay asks O'Toole why he killed, the general asks why he must have an explanation. The act is insignificant except as a function of the killer's desires: a corruption of the interpersonal.

In addition, the film seems to have had an influence in the Vietnam War–set serial killer film *Off Limits*, which also featured officers implicated in a series of prostitute murders.

Night Owl

(1993: d. Jeffrey Arsenault)

scr. Arsenault; ph. Pierre Clavel, Howard Crupa, Neil Shapiro; mkup. Skiba; m. Mark Styles, Rubio Hernandez; cast. John Leguizamo, Lisa Napoli, David Roya, James Rafferty, Caroline Munro; 80m

A young man who picks up women in bars around New York City's Alphabet City district is a vampire who kills the women during sex, biting open their throats and drinking their blood. He dismembers the bodies with a cleaver, keeps choice parts for later cannibalistic snacks, and disposes of the remainder in garbage bags. A man (Leguizamo) whose sister is missing starts investigating and stalks the vampire. Meanwhile, the vampire is getting physically sicker. Finally, the man confronts the vampire and, as a result, becomes one.

Like Romero's *Martin*, the film equates the vampire with the serial killer, the consumption of blood being the sexual consummation of the act of murder. It is orgasmic for the sex killer, who draws power from the relentless torture, humiliation and brutalization of women. This is a ruthless picture of monstrous masculinity. The graphic frankness with which the sex murder is depicted drew criticism from feminist circles, and is somewhat censored in the UK video release. Uncut, it is supposedly tough to watch.

This black and white film was shot on 16mm and is considered part of the New York New Wave, its underground status assured by its graphic violence and a performance by ex–Warhol superstar Holly Woodlawn. Its gritty locations, grainy stock and wholehearted treatment of transgressive acts brought comparisons to the deliberately provocative work of Nick Zedd and Richard Kern — the founders of the Cinema of Transgression movement. It is also comparable to such recent treatments of the vampire myth in *Nadja* and *The Addiction*.

Night Ripper

(1986: d. Jeff Hathcock)

cast. James Hansen, April Audia, Larry Thomas

A serial killer targets fashion models.

This is a film of no reputation, and may be considered a product of the amalgam of serial killer and slasher genres. Once again, it seems that the objectification and subsequent commodification of women inspires sex killers to acts of violence. What is elevated as beauty inspires some to want to tear it down. Whether this is a form of retribution or resentment is arguable. This was unavailable at time of writing.

Night Shadow

(1990: d. Randolph Cohlan)

cast. Brenda Vance, Dana Chan, Tom Boylan; 90m

A TV newswoman returns home after a long absence. On the way, she picks up a hitchhiker. She drops him off in her home town, and soon after a series of murders occur, with the townspeople holding her responsible for cursing their town. She then tries to catch the killer herself.

There is little information to be found anywhere about this film, which plays on the monstrous hitchhiker plot. This was unavailable at time of writing.

The Night Stalker

(1987: d. Max Cleven, Don Edmonds)

scr. Edmonds, John F. Goff, Cleven; ph. Don Burgess; m. David Kitay; ed. Stanford C. Allen; prod d. Allen Terry; cast. Charles Napier,

Michelle Reese, Katherine Kelly Lang, Robert Viharo, Joseph Gian, Robert Z'Dar, Gary Crosby; 91m

An alcoholic cop (Napier) is on the trail of a serial killer of prostitutes (Z'Dar, best known for the *Maniac Cop* films). The killer murders prostitutes and then paints a Chinese symbol on them in an Eastern occult ritual of some sort, seemingly drawing power and perhaps invincibility from each kill (a gimmick also used in *The Banker*). A prostitute teams with the cop to solve the case.

Bullets cannot touch him, a fact that makes for at least one surprising scene when a whore shoots her attacker, only to have him rise and kill her anyway. However, the film does not develop the supernatural killer angle as much as, say, *The First Power* or *Dust Devil*. It does, however, posit the killer as an unstoppable scourge of modern times and a permanent blight on the efforts of policeman. Perhaps facing such a killer is even a rite of passage into Patriarchy's elite unit of enforcers.

The usual scene of a prostitute at work reveals the titillation that equates male turn-on with homicidal consequences, and here combines a tone of sub–*Choirboys* coarse humor with the banal procedural. Napier's role as a robbery investigator brought back into homicide from outside the department allows him to neatly double with the profiler role.

An example of the film's vulgarity is in the conventional morgue table shot offering a topless female cadaver, allowing the viewer one last glance at the naked female form. Again, this is part of a morally questionable set piece, which in part seems a deliberate tease. Finally, in a substandard twist on *M*, and a further nod to the need for outside investigative assistance to lure serial killers, the prostitutes themselves form a union of sorts and work with police, whose presence alone is not enough.

Night Visions

(1990: d. Wes Craven)

scr. Thomas Baum, Craven; pr. Baum, Marianne Maddalena, Rick Nathanson; ph. Peter Stein; m. Brad Fiedel; ed. James Coblentz, Mark Melnick; prod d. Vince Cresciman; cast. James Remar, Loryn Locklin, Mitch Pileggi, Francis McCarthy, Penny Johnson; 96m

In this tele-movie intended as a pilot for a weekly series, a hard cop (Remar) reluctantly teams with a young psychic police psychologist to investigate a series of murders of beautiful women by a serial killer known as "the Spread Eagle Killer." The killer is so named because he positions his victims' legs wide, a sexually submissive pose that also creates maximum shock value when the bodies are found. However, the psychic may very well be psychotic or have a multiple personality disorder, and her visions reflect her own trauma as well, as they seemingly shed light on the killer's identity. The unlikely pair develop a growing respect for each other, perhaps her vulnerabilities bringing out the policeman's softer, caring side, a theme that would no doubt have been developed further in the series.

The psychic's trauma and mental illness allow her to enter other people's minds, a development of the profiler's abilities since *Manhunter* in that she is both psychic and psychologist. She is a novice, a recent graduate expanding her knowledge into a book, and needs exposure to an ongoing case — a similar plot hook to that used later in *The Happy Face Murders*. Such exposure frees her psychic gift, although in the process it threatens her own identity. Her trance states are a form of identity crisis as her mind dissolves into another imposed identity, allowing a psychic empathy. Her ability is the result of childhood trauma, which could alternatively have produced a killer.

She intuits that the killer attacks

certain body parts in a pattern to create a star. He takes photos of his victims' body parts and uses them to make an ideal body (a theme also touched on in *Pieces* and *Resurrection*). He kills in pursuit of a fantasy where, as a God-like power, he can create an image of his perfect woman.

A happy ending was inserted against Craven's wishes. The director was also required to tone down the horror/gore quotient for TV, and the result is a compromised effort. The most interesting aspect is the depiction of the police psychologist as profiler figure with both scientific background and psychic insight. A TV series did not eventuate. However, it can be considered a precursor of such TV series as *Millennium* and *Profiler* (Muir, p. 246) and their accent on individuals with the unexplained ability to enter killers' minds (itself a theme indebted more to *Manhunter*). It is reportedly one of Craven's least seen works.

Night Visitor

(1989: d. Rupert Hitzig) aka *Never Cry Devil*

scr. Randal Visovich; pr. Alain Silver; ph. Peter Jensen; m. Parmer Fuller; ed. Glenn Erickson; prod d. Jon Rothschild; cast. Elliott Gould, Richard Roundtree, Allen Garfield, Michael J. Pollard; 95m

A teenage student tries to convince the Police that his school's most unpopular teacher is in actuality a homicidal Satanist and serial torturer and killer of mainly prostitutes (although he kills the sexy teacher the youth secretly lusts after). When no one believes him, he contacts a retired policeman (Gould), the closest this film gets to a profiler.

This combination of horror and teen comedy recalls Tom Holland's superior *Fright Night* and the work of George Mihalka in the psychic-link field. The young man is conflicted over the future of Patriarchy, as the teacher role model is an aber-

ration, and so the film posits his relationship with the ex-policeman as his search for stability. With the policeman as a proper patriarch, the student can go about eliminating the threat to its future and assume his place within it. He can thus restore his faith in, and need for, the role of the substitute father. Thus, the film avoids any subversive potential. It is considered another negligible video release.

Nightmare

(1981: d. Ramono Scavolini) aka *Schizo*

scr. Scavolini; pr. John L. Watkins; ph. Gianni Fiore; ed. Robert T. Megginson; m. Jack Eric Williams; spec eff. Les Larraine, William Milling; mkup. Edward French; cast. Baird Stafford, Sharon Smith, C.J. Cooke, Mik Cribben, Kathleen Ferguson, Danny Ronan, John Watkins; 97m

This film shows the transition from the giallo to the slasher formula, tangentially intersecting serial killer pathology. A former mental patient, tormented by nightmares, murders innocents before finally targeting one family. The nightmares are rooted in horrendous childhood experience, when he axed his parents to death for participating in kinky sex.

Sex and death have thus been imprinted on the killer's developing mind— he kills when aroused and feels guilty over it, as a means of dealing with an emotional confusion too complex to make sense of peacefully. Sex is terrifying to the killer, and the violent expression is an emotional recourse to avoid the introspective confrontation supposedly provided by the later psychotherapy. The failure of this later psychotherapy represents the genre's distrust of psychiatric authority (best demonstrated in *Frightmare*). Thus, although he is pronounced cured, the killer relapses when he finds himself in a sex shop. The implication is that contemporary sex culture fosters the dangerous imprinting of sex and violence, and fosters serial killers.

The director has a minor place in the spaghetti nightmare pantheon because of this film. When it was screened for the press in England, vomit bags were given to those attending, as a publicity gimmick (Hardy, p. 369). It soon became notorious when included on the UK's banned "video nasty" list. In the United States, it boasted a self-appointed X rating. It proved a box-office success worldwide, although it was not shown in the director's native Italy.

Nightmare Hotel

(1973: d. Eugenio Martin)

scr. Antonio Fos, Martin; ph. Jose F. Aguayo; cast. Judy Geeson, Victor Alcazar, Aurora Bautista, Blanca Estrada, Lone Fleming, Esperanza Roy; 92m

This is a film about a Spanish cannibal motel owner, a situation inviting comparison with it to *Psycho*. A British tourist investigates the disappearance of her sister. She discovers that a motel owner is murdering her male guests, storing them in the food cellar, and then cooking them up for other unaware guests. Sex murder and pragmatism thus intersect. The tourist decides to unmask the killer herself, without police aid.

This is a rare film that explores the mind of a female sex killer; however, her acts are apparently intended to disavow her sexual desires. Thus, she kills men who reveal their desires for her, resenting both their advances and what they arouse in her. The cannibal activities are the sexual surrogate for her, and an expression of her identity, which she must serve to others, perhaps for approval. She literally feeds off the dead, and it is possible that Martin intended the microcosm of the motel to be a sociopolitical allegory.

Underrated Spanish director Martin is responsible for numerous effective horror films (*Horror Express*) and westerns (*Bad Man's River*). However, he has never received the cult recognition accorded Jess Franco, for instance, probably because he worked in multiple genres.

Nightscare

(1993: d. Vadim Jean) aka *Beyond Bedlam*

scr. Jean, Rob Walker; nvl. H.A. Knight; pr. Paul Brooks, Tim Dennison, A and P Georgiadis, Jim Groom, Alan Martin; ph. Gavin Finney; m. David Hughes, John Murphy; ed. Liz Webber; prod. d. James Helps; cast. Craig Fairbrass, Elizabeth Hurley, Keith Allen, Anita Dobson, Craig Kelly; 88m

A police detective still has memories of the serial killer known as "the Bone Man" whom he captured seven years ago. The killer has been the human experiment for a doctor (Hurley) testing mind-calming drugs (known as BFND). However, the drug enables the killer to manifest his hallucinations, which overwhelm the cop and the doctor as they try to stop the killer from having his way beyond the confines of his cell. Reality and illusion intermix as the two protagonists square off against the killer. They defeat him but are perhaps left in this dreamscape world.

The story unfolds mostly at the Institute for Neurological Research, a facility meant to allegorically stand for any institutionalization process, and is depicted as a modern Bedlam. The killer is a contentious issue between cop and profiler. Like the rivalry in *Mr. Frost*, the cop considers the killer pure Evil, while the profiler considers him worthy of study and understanding. Such is the almost irreconcilable polemic facing these character types within the serial killer film. The doctor's plight is allied to the audience's — the desire to see what lies in the killer's aberrant mind (a visualization that proves rather disappointing, if disconcerting, especially when compared to the later *The Cell*). Even the killer voices this, admitting that he knows his aberration holds a fascination for certain people, which he can use to his advantage, so intent is he to control everything and everyone, even to the point of altering objective reality to support his fantasy of how it should be. In the process, the killer becomes a kind of spiritual entity transported into people while they dream, a theme also infiltrating *The Exorcist III*. To defeat this killer, the protagonists must prey on his fear — the loss of power and control.

This has been considered one of the more ambitious British horror films, combining the visual sense of the *Nightmare on Elm Street* movies with the brooding fiction of Clive Barker and Thomas Harris (*allmovie.com*, online). As such, it cleverly makes the serial killer again the subject of the psychological horror movie. Indeed, its premise of cop and profiler interacting with the killer's own fantasy world anticipates *The Cell*. However, it has a fear of the power of the imagination, which denies it any wonderment or affirmative attributes. Perhaps that is a budgetary limitation on visual design.

Nightwatch

(1998: d. Ole Bornedal)

scr. Bornedal, Steven Soderbergh; pr. Michael Obel; ph. Dan Lausten; m. Joachim Holbeck; ed. Sally Menke; prod d. Richard Hoover; cast. Ewan McGregor, Nick Nolte, Josh Brolin, Patricia Arquette, Alix Koromzay, Brad Dourif, John C. Reilly, Lauren Graham, Lonny Chapman; 101m

In this Hollywood remake of *Nattevagten* a student (McGregor) takes a job as a morgue attendant on the nightshift and is implicated in a serial killer case, the victims turning up at his place of work (fueling his own morbid interests). He starts to question the motives of his amoral best friend (Brolin), who repeatedly challenges his conception of morality. On the case is a policeman (Nolte) who seems to suspect the student but who has an unhealthy interest in corpses and is finally revealed to be the killer.

The necrophilic component speaks to the films of Jorg Buttgereit, although the approach, like the original, is more stylized and mysterious. It is a film about the fascination with death, signaled from the opening scene in which a prostitute plays dead for a client finally no longer happy with the compromised fantasy. This man then kills her for real. The protagonist's workplace is filled with the details of death — corpses, preserved fetuses, bins full of collected limbs — and he is eventually contaminated by the smell of it. Being surrounded by death leads to curiosity about the love of death, and for the killer, sexual experimentation with the dead — such is the road the protagonist is headed down once he has been exposed to such surroundings. More so than the first film, this is dark and shadowy, all places imbued with a sense of menace and danger.

These disturbing, mordant themes, and the abrasive mind games played by the protagonist and his egotistical friend, are in total contrast to the light comedy of contemporary horror films à la *Scream* and *I Know What You Did Last Summer*, a point raised by many reviewers. *Nightwatch* has a somber atmosphere with a streak of almost cruel irony. With the opening prostitute's words, "Let me die for you," the film is more clearly an examination of the spectator's role in viewing and desiring such morbid subject matter. Thus, the two friends often refer to a fictional movie made about their predicament.

More so than in the first film, the friend who repeatedly challenges the protagonist is a seductive, Mephistophelean presence. He is closer to the devil's advocate role, and is an amoral, sly manipulator who has no compunction about taking advantage of a young prostitute, delighting in her slow mental torment. In that, he is not dissimilar from the killer, although in the end he acts to dissociate himself from such a murderer. The protagonist is again in a state of moral confusion, and is in a predicament the killer recognizes himself having gone through before. The friend who courts risk and sensation above all else fascinates him. They both strive for "the rush" to invigorate them, and Brolin admits to being too desensitized to feel invigorated by much anymore. Such is the road towards transgression and the violation of taboos, the road of the necrophilic serial killer whose crimes are the ultimate quest for new, illicit sensation. To be close to death is to feel alive. However, the killer says that such men as he are beyond the need to explain or justify their actions. Ironically, in this way they are an essentially meaningless expression of perversity, a sensation-filled chaos beyond normal understanding.

The original Danish version was bought by Dimension Films in order to prevent it being shown in American cinema release until after they produced the English language version. This was both to ensure good box office and to avoid the potentially unfavorable comparisons that had affected the US remake of George Sluizer's *The Vanishing*. *Nightwatch*, virtually scene by scene, is quicker and tighter than the original, and more knowingly malevolent and sardonic in its humor. While the first set up a mood of unease, the remake is somber and suspenseful. This is noted self-reflexively when the two friends talk of films and wonder if people would prefer a contemplative or an actionful treatment of a subject. Perhaps that is how Bornedal sees the difference between his approach there and here.

No One Could Protect Her

(1996: d. Larry Shaw)

scr. Bruce Miller; pr. Clara George, Julian Marks; ph. Peter Benison; ed. Craig Bassett; prod d. Gerry Holmes; cast. Joanna Kerns, Anthony John Denison, Peter MacNeill, Lori Hallier, Dan Lett, Christina Cox, Dan Lauria

A woman whose husband is away is attacked by a serial rapist/killer in her home. She survives, and as police search, many subsequent attacks plague the neighborhood. She becomes preoccupied with finding the offender, and her husband, feeling guilty, is concerned with protecting her (and in the process restoring his Patriarchal validity). The killer, however, considers her a witness to be eliminated.

This feature, from a director better known for tele-movies, was based on a true story written by a rape survivor entitled "Trouble in Allentown" and sent in to the *Reader's Digest*. The serial rapist killed two women and a four-year-old girl before letting one live because a pillowcase masked her head and she was a brunette (he favored blondes). Thus, it is part of a movement, prominent in television, to make a socially responsible treatment of the threat to individual and community identity posed by such random crimes. It also apparently questions the need for socially ordained protectors if Patriarchy is to maintain the safety of its individuals. Is it ultimately up to the individual to face such a threat, and the film posits such an encounter as a possible form of empowerment. It is a measure of the move towards feminist independence that the woman must rely ultimately on herself.

No Way to Treat a Lady

(1968: d. Jack Smight)

scr. John Gay; nvl. William Goldman; pr. Sol C. Siegel; ph. Jack Priestley; m. Stanley Myers; ed. Archie Marshek; art d. Hal Pereira; cast. Rod Steiger, Lee Remick, George Segal, Eileen Heckart, Murray Hamilton, Michael Dunn, Martine Bartlett, Barbara Baxley, Irene Dailey, Doris Roberts; 108m

A mother-fixated, attention-seeking killer (Steiger) who whistles the Jolly Miller disguises himself in various forms (including those of an Irish priest, gay hairdresser, cop, and woman) and murders

The proud serial killer pores over his exploits in the newspaper: Rod Steiger in *No Way to Treat a Lady* (Paramount, 1967).

lonely, middle-aged women. Each corpse is found with a lipstick kiss drawn on the forehead. The policeman on the trail is a similarly mother-smothered man (Segal) whose scenes with his mother (Heckart) add even more comedy to this post–*Psycho* psychological situation and near-parody. When the cop announces to the press that they are dealing with an unusually intelligent criminal, the killer, feeling proud at finally being recognized, phones in messages to the cop, leaving clues to the next crime.

This is a black comedy which allies the repeat, gimmick killer to the sex murderer: he kills women and signs the crimes. The killer repeatedly tries to put his fantasy into practice, all the while role-playing as a means of manipulating victims (before strangling them) and police. He loathes his mother so much that he kills surrogate versions of her. His role-playing is in essence a return to childhood play-acting. Thus, he duplicates his childhood experience as an inescapable trap, gaining temporary relief through murder.

For comedic comparison, the policeman is also dominated by his mother: specialist cop and killer becoming equal, knowing adversaries. So, the killer starts to follow his nemesis, and the policeman starts to bait him (planting a false story so that the boastful killer will phone to invalidate a copycat crime). The film develops their cat and mouse rivalry (Bartholomew, *Magill's Guide*; p. 2376) for a satiric opposition of the character types in detective fiction (Smight had previously made the hit *Harper*, which revived the detective genre).

This is an influential film in its mix of genres (the killer donning disguises anticipates *Fade to Black*), which neatly lampoons the serial killer conventions that were further consolidated the same year in the non-comedic true-crime dramatization of *The Boston Strangler*. Indeed, it is one of the first true comedies of murder, with the pursuit and gleeful strangulation of victims presented as comic spectacles. The characters border on caricatures, and the film is a mix of location-realist style and cartoon (Canby stressed the latter in his *New York Times* review), with a heavy stress on the juxtapositioning and intermingling of comedy and horrific violence.

Director Smight would attempt a quiet, gently mordant humor again in *The Travelling Executioner*, a trait that is found in his best work from the late 1960s and early 1970s before he succumbed to a supposedly flat impersonality. *Variety* noted that the tone was indebted to the Alec Guinness British comedies of the 1950s. It was Steiger, then at the height of his popularity following *In the Heat of the Night*, who carried the film, however. He would play a similarly overblown caricature of a vigilante killer in the comedy/horror *Guilty as Charged*.

Off Limits

(1988: d. Christopher Crowe) aka *Saigon*

scr. Crowe, Jack Thibeau; pr. Alan Barnette; ph. David Gribble; m. James Newton Howard; ed. Douglas Ibold; prod d. Dennis Washington; cast. Willem Dafoe, Gregory Hines, Fred Ward, Amanda Pays, Scott Glenn, Kay Tong Lim, David Alan Grier; 102m

In Saigon in 1968, two plainclothes army policeman (Dafoe and Hines) investigate a series of murders of Vietnamese prostitutes who bore children fathered by American servicemen. Their quest for the truth uncovers sexual promiscuity and seems to implicate officers, mostly American. They soon find evidence of a cover-up. One of them falls for a nun but cannot go through with a relationship.

This unrelentingly sleazy and bleak film depicts a world devoid of morals, where the protagonist's one chance at redemption is thwarted by sexual infatuation that consumes any romantic altruism. The film undercuts the notion of the US winning hearts and minds via the opening scene of a US officer shooting a prostitute (memories of *Night of the Generals*). It is a world in which the US can kill and sexually exploit without repercussion, where drunken, violent, VD-ridden soldiers who seek only sexual conquest and booze frequent whore-strewn bars. In the absence of ideology, the serial killer thrives as the epitome of the US war effort. He kills innocents to relieve the pain of personal resentment, and surrounds himself with photos and press clippings that, in his mind, allow him to be the great officer (a role denied him when his promotion was declined). There is nothing beyond selfishness.

Dafoe (cast with memories of his idealistic sergeant in *Platoon*), the good father, is at first the only hope of ideology or justice, but he is forced to confront the absolute callous monstrosity of the system he enforces. He is forced to confront futility. His partner abandons his ideology when offered the chance to go stateside. By the end, the death of the prostitutes is a minor matter indeed, just as insignificant in such a world as the killer believes them to be.

The film depicts a Hell of lost souls. Even the protagonists are a pair of racist, brutal exploiters who treat their fellows as worthless. In such a world, Dafoe's interest in the nun is doomed to failure. The people they police are foul-mouthed and sex-obsessed, boasting of their sexual prowess and having no regard for the consequences of their actions. The rampant male pride allowed by war degrades women

The two plainclothes military policeman (Gregory Hines, left, and Willem Dafoe) become targets of an angry Vietnamese populace in the Vietnam War–set thriller *Off Limits* (Fox, 1987).

as disposable sex objects. The soldiers who fight for the glory of their country are cocky, self-righteous, arrogant bastards.

Ironically, the nun is the profiler substitute here. She is an outside agent who informs the investigators of the series of crimes, the link between them, and in so doing is the last idealist. Although she too realizes the futility of it all, her faith allows her to persist. Although Dafoe admires this, he knows his interests would eventually corrupt her too, although he persists for a while. She guides him towards the truth behind the American soul, and he is disgusted by what he finds.

Bleak to the point of hopelessness, the film failed to impress with its blend of cynicism and exploitable Hollywood buddy formula. However, it is the unrelenting wallow in ideological despair that ultimately makes *Off Limits* one of the more subversive of the rash of Vietnam War films in the late 1980s. It is visually and thematically indebted to film noir, bringing to the Vietnam War movie genre the post–1970s view of an urban Hell consumed by sex culture. Its neon-lit pessimism and almost uncritical depiction of irredeemable souls make it a deliberately uncomfortable movie experience. Perhaps not unexpectedly therefore, it flopped with the critics, who considered it a sleazy wallow in Hollywood sensationalism.

The Office Killer

(1997: d. Cindy Sherman)

scr. Tom Kalin, Elise MacAdam; stry. Sherman, MacAdam; pr. Pamela Koffler, Christine Vachon; ph. Russell Fine; m. Evan Lurie; ed. Merril Stern; prod d. Kevin Thompson; cast. Carol Kane, Molly Ringwald, Jeanne Tripplehorn, Barbara Sukowa, Michael Imperiolo, Alice Drummond; 83m

A downsized mousy office worker

(Kane) at the bottom of the ladder works for *Constant Consumer* magazine. Reduced to working part-time from home (where she lives downstairs, with her invalid mother upstairs), she is called in to assist her superior at the office. He is accidentally electrocuted. Unsure of what to do and feeling guilty, she takes the body home and sets it up in front of the TV. She soon turns to murder to escape work pressure, and accumulates the corpses at home to relieve her loneliness, now killing for company. She literally brings her workplace home with her. To avoid discovery, she burns down her house and leaves, taking a selection of her most prized body parts with her, in search of a new start.

The killer's murders allow her an escape from her friendless drudgery. They are her means of independence and her revenge against her oppressors, the last act of the disenfranchised. Serial murder becomes a means of feminist expression/liberation. She can indulge in grotesque, and assumed necrophilic, fantasies as she literally makes her world a world of the dead; her liberation is therefore only in her own mind, as she surrenders to her revenge fantasy of interplay and significance. It is in the company of the dead that she finds sexual self-definition, a theme comparable to that found in *Nekromantik 2*.

Her actions are enveloped by her droll voice-over rationalizations on modern life and relationships, as she goes from a put-upon worker to a liberated woman in search of a new start and job (perhaps as a manager, she reckons). Her murders have fulfilled their function as personal revolution, and as the people she kills are all unsympathetic, selfish, arrogant and self-important, it is impossible to feel for them. However, her victory is double-edged, as she now assumes the qualities she resented in others and considers herself capable of the same work. It was only the appearance of a revolution.

The film is most disturbing—and comedic—when depicting the domestic rituals she enacts with the steady stream of corpses. Finally, in death they pay her the interpersonal attention she wanted. In her home she is able to establish the perfect fantasy workplace—and a communal living arrangement—conversing with them, romancing them and even grooming them as they decay around her. She retreats into a childish fantasy of imaginary dead playmates, allowing her the illusion of a maturity she never had. By putting her fantasy into practice, she feels she can affect change, and does so, however hollow it ultimately may be.

Directed by noted photographer Sherman, who had used exploitation motifs in her still work (starting in the 1970s with a series of "Untitled Film Stills"), *The Office Killer* is best taken as a satiric horror film and serial killer parody. The film's equation between yuppie Capitalist work ethics, the constant definition of culture and people as "products," and serial murder makes it comparable to *American Psycho*.

Open House

(1986: d. Jag Mundhra)

scr. David Mickey Evans; pr. Sandy Cobe; ph. Robert Hayes, Gary Louzon; spec eff. John A. Naulin; cast. Joseph Bottoms, Adrienne Barbeau, Rudy Ramos, Mary Stavin, Scott Thompson Baker; 97m

A serial killer, a homeless man dubbed the "Open House Killer" who targets wealthy realtors and their clients (apparently unhappy at rising housing costs in Beverly Hills), contacts a radio talk show psychologist (Bottoms), the host of "The Survival Line." He draws the psychologist and his realtor girlfriend (Barbeau) into the proceedings. To the psychologist, he offers as justification: "Them real-estate bitches deserved it."

The killer oozes resentment and is

presented as the product of socioeconomic disparity. In contrast to the Beverly Hills dwellers, the killer vagrant is shown eating dog food. However, far from being the force of social revolution or protest, he is motivated more by the misogynistic resentment of rich women than by any true conscious ideology. As female real estate agents, his victims represent a sexual, social and political empowerment denied him by his socioeconomic status. Thus, his personal empowerment is achieved through murder: in that he finds an unacknowledged purpose and self-validation. Yet he seeks to draw attention to his plight, and even, by phoning the radio, is perhaps depicted as a kind of spokesman.

The director attempts to spice up the routine proceedings with kinky sex and nudity. The killer/talk show link is also featured in *Martin, Laser Moon* and *Outside Ozona*. Perhaps *Open House* is best considered a partial, failed attempt to turn the likes of *Down and Out in Beverly Hills* into a serial killer/slasher movie.

Out of the Body

(1988: d. Brian Trenchard-Smith)

scr. Kenneth G. Ross; pr. David Hannay, Charles Hannay; ph. Kevin Lind; spec eff. Deryck di Niese; cast. Mark Hembrow, Tessa Humphries, Carrie Zivetz, Linda Newton, John Clayton, Shane Briant; 89m

A Sydney serial killer targets professional women and removes their eyes. The detective on the case is assigned a partner against his wishes. A composer has psychic premonitions of the crimes and tries to warn the victims but is disbelieved. The composer realizes that he houses an entity that takes over his dreaming-freed spirit in out-of-body/astral projection experiences and attacks women.

The film's emphasis on a supernatural entity as the real serial killing force is comparable to that in *Fallen*. If one considers the astral projection phenomenon as psychodrama, then the psychic visions are the dawning awareness of a responsibility too monstrous to accept and so projected outwards. The film neither supports nor denies this interpretation; as such, the mutilations seem motiveless, unless interpreted as the killer's disavowal of the validity of his own perceptual experiences. His dreams enable him to enact violent fantasies which, when put into reality, are too monstrous for him to accept; and so he has possibly concocted the fantasy of possession by another spirit, although the supernatural explanation is ironically supported by his treating doctor. The killer is a constant presence in the universe which preys on the sexual resentment and violent fantasies of dreamers.

This Australian effort by exploitation director Trenchard-Smith follows the US models of police procedural and psychiclink scenarios closely and unremarkably, if efficiently. Smith, along with Terry Bourke, Richard Franklin and later Russell Mulcahy were the bastions of Australian exploitation amidst and since the highly regarded Australian New Wave of the later 1970s. Where Franklin and Mulcahy ultimately escaped their exploitation origins through style, Trenchard-Smith has been unable to achieve their mainstream success. He later did the more intriguing *Happy Face Murders*.

Out of the Dark

(1989: d. Michael Schroeder)

scr. Zane W. Levitt, J. Gregory DeFelice; pr. Levitt; ph. Julio Macat; ed. Mark Manos; m. Paul Antonelli, David Wheatley; prod d. Robert Schulenberg; spec eff. Kevin McCarthy; cast. Cameron Dye, Karen Black, Lynne Danielson, Karen Witter, Bud Cort, Geoffrey

Lewis, Paul Bartel, Divine, Tracey Walter, Tab Hunter; 89m

This would-be stylish film that some consider just slightly above the slasher level is about a clown-costumed killer (à la the real Gacy) who targets "Suite Nothings" phone-sex workers, bludgeoning or strangling them.

It openly raises, but apparently fails to explore, the issues of the phone-sex industry's contribution to the seeming decay of modern America, and instead seems intent to be a sleazy hybrid of slasher and serial killer film. Hardy et al. (p. 437) feels it possesses just enough parodic elements to keep it above the rut, and suggests it is more of a pastiche (of, for instance, *Don't Answer the Phone, He Knows You're Alone* and *Eyes of a Stranger*) than a social commentary. In that there is a clear link between the victims, the film is only tangentially a serial killer movie, though it becomes a study of sexual frustration seeking an outlet but channeled into violence and resentment.

Director Schroeder is considered (Hardy again) a protégé of low-budget auteur Paul Bartel, whose better works straddled the exploitation and the art-house scene. It remains to be seen whether Schroeder will achieve the recognition accorded Bartel. His casting choices, especially that of Divine, indicate that John Waters is also an influence. Editor Manos would branch out into low-budget genre direction with *Liquid Dreams*.

Out of the Darkness

(1985: d. Jud Taylor)

scr. T.S. Cook; pr. Gordon L.T. Scott; ph. Ray Orton, Brian West; ed. John Krish; prod d. Keith Wilson; cast. Martin Sheen, Hector Elizondo, Matt Clark, Jennifer Salt, Eddie Egan, Jenny Tarren, Robert Trebor, Charlie Sheen; 96m

This tele-movie recreates the thirteen month period in 1976–77 when the "Son Of Sam" killer (David Berkowitz) stalked New York City, attacking lovers in parked cars, as well as perpetrating other crimes. It focuses on veteran negotiator Ed Zigo (Sheen), who is brought in to the police task force. A discarded parking ticket finally leads to the killer's apprehension and the revelation of his bizarre reasons for his crimes (the real killer said that his neighbor's barking dog ordered him to kill).

The specialist investigator balances the investigation demands with personal problems related to his wife's illness and death. This suggests a certain similarity to *The First Deadly Sin*, with the killer a force of random death and the investigator's pursuit of him a challenge to mortality. However, it is more a faithful reconstruction of the procedural investigation and the social responses to the presence of a serial killer. The profiler/specialist investigator's role is to bring society out of the title darkness.

Out of the Darkness can be compared to *The Atlanta Child Murders* and *Deliberate Stranger*, both tele-movie recreations of the hunt for serial killers, and both featuring the incorporation of the profiler into the investigation. Taylor also directed the mini-series *City in Fear* about a similar response to such a killer. For that work, he took the Alan Smithee option, and one can assume that *Out of the Darkness* was more to his liking. It originally aired October 12, 1985.

Outside Ozona

(1998: d. J.S. Cardone)

scr. Cardone; pr. Scott Einbinder, Carol Kottenbrook; ph. Irek Hartkowicz; m. Johnny Lee Schell, Taj Mahal; ed. Amanda I. Kirpaul; prod d. Martina Buckley; cast. Robert Forster, Kevin Pollak, Sherilyn Fenn, David Paymer, Penelope Ann Miller, Swoosie Kurtz, Taj Mahal, Meat Loaf; 100m

Over the course of one rough night, on the road between New Mexico and Texas, various travelers interact — a widowed trucker, two bickering sisters, a down and out circus clown and his stripper girlfriend, and a serial killer. The manhunt for the killer forms the background to their separate stories and joint encounters. The characters are variously all tuned to a country and western station playing jazz and blues, punctuated by the DJ's cynical pronouncements (to the station manager's dismay). The serial killer calls in to the radio station to voice his philosophies and hostilities. Finally, a car accident brings them all together.

This is structured more as a series of character vignettes, of lonely people desperately seeking connection with others along the way to a seemingly predestined confrontation/meeting. It takes place in a world called the "badlands" by the DJ, and, as usual for Cardone (see *Shadowhunter*), there is the sense of a malevolent and hostile offscreen space (the only quality of the film that impressed critic Roger Ebert). The loneliness and solitude of the open highway reflects the lives of those who travel it by choice. The DJ's disembodied voice is their only constant companion through the night, a voice that repeatedly baits the killer to call in, as if teasing fate itself.

The killer is the ultimate lonely heart. He murders women and removes their hearts, posing the corpses grasping their vital organ: a portrait of loneliness so starved it becomes hostility and disavowal, seeking to destroy all with whom it interacts. He tells the DJ of his hatred for the evils of Capitalism and how he is serving God. The killer, who may be a psychiatrist, can only find meaning in a self-imposed psychosis he is forever trying to justify, and a sexuality he would disavow.

Indeed, all the characters have reached a point where they are faced with the loss of their goals, dreams and expectations. All that is left them is a need for the warmth of other lost and lonely individuals. They are the flotsam and jetsam of the desert road. They are all hard luck stories, and their inner torment comes from knowing it. The DJ confirms this when he offers a $50 prize for the worst hard luck story. Their luck has run out, all except the murderer's, as the police fear he will merely disappear through the cracks. But luck changes, and the serial killer is killed in an accident which ironically brings these lost souls together. This interrelationship of fate and luck is a regular Cardone theme.

Outside Ozona is an intelligent and calculated, if slow, combination of serial killer film, road movie and desert noir. It can be favorably compared to the films of John Dahl, and to the likes of *Blood Simple*, *Breakdown*, *Clay Pigeons*, *The Hitcher*, *Kalifornia* and *U-Turn*, and be seen as a development of Cardone's similar *Black Day, Blue Night*. *Outside Ozona* was a favored project of actor J.T. Walsh, who attracted most of the cast, but who unfortunately died three days before shooting commenced. He was to have played the trucker (a role inherited by Forster). The film thus lost out on a potentially interesting intertextuality with *Breakdown*, where Walsh played a psychotic truck driver. *Outside Ozona* can be considered an under-rated director's attempt to break through to mainstream audiences. Unfortunately, it failed at that, although it drew supportive reviews. It is dedicated to Walsh's memory.

Painted Heart

(1993: d. Michael Taav) aka *The Paint Job*

scr. Taav; ast pr. Susan Dupre, Jennifer Vian Dennis, Lynn Goldner; m. John Wesley Harding and Sons of Bitches; art d. Ginger Tougas; cast. Will Patton, Bebe Neuwirth, Robert Pastorelli, Casey Siemazko, Mark Boone Jr., Jayne Haynes, John Diehl; 87m

A young woman (Neuwirth) is unhappy with her marriage to a house painter (Pastorelli). She begins an affair with his seemingly unstable co-worker (Patton). One of these two men is a serial killer, traumatized by an abusive alcoholic father. The husband suspects he is being cuckolded and goes out to vent his frustrations by luring a homeless alcoholic to a secluded spot and murdering him. He is seen by Patton, who returns to tell the wife that her husband is the notorious "lipstick murderer" whose exploits have been all over the news. Finally, the two painters fight for Neuwirth's fate, although she is now not interested in either of them.

There are growing voices of support for this movie as an insightful view of threatened interpersonal relationships and the nature of trust. As an independent film and its search-for-connection thematics, it is in part comparable to the likes of *Love and Human Remains*, although tonally it is vastly different. Indeed, it features a slyly comedic romantic triangle. None of the characters are particularly bright, and their dialogue is comically banal at times, although, for them, heartfelt. In that way the film approaches the likes of Dahl, Lynch and the Coen brothers in its search for humor at the ever-evolving outer realms of human experience. Although these characters are funny, there is an underlying menace to their actions, as if there is an instability and uncertainty inherent in all aspects of human dynamics. It is thus wonderfully droll, often at the characters' expense — hence, Neuwirth wipes up her lover's blood (he cut himself to prove his love for her) with her husband's shirt and washes it, to be worn the next day by her husband, who wonders where the faint stain came from.

The film is a view of Patriarchy's malfunctioning traditions. It begins with an incident where a wife refuses a husband sex, so he goes to his son's room and beats the boy for playing with lipstick. The father then says that the son will grow up just like him, a man's man. Of course, this proves horribly true. The son has grown up to be a serial killer of alcoholic derelicts, a disposable underclass. He promises them booze, lures them to a secluded area, crushes them with a bear hug and paints their faces with lipstick. In this way he is getting back at his hated father, unaware of the sublimated homosexual and even incestuous aspects of the crime. His anger at being cuckolded is akin to his father's dissatisfaction with an unresponsive wife, and the violence against a weaker opponent is a compensatory means of establishing his true power. Thus, although the act may seem a symbolic patricide, it is a repetition of a violent socialization process. The son may want to rebel against the father, but ultimately cannot escape his legacy, and is doomed to carry the father's monstrousness even further. There is no escape from this trap.

The happy ending is also ironic, as throughout the film the dreams of these simple people to better themselves and find love are resolutely crushed. With the killer dead, the wife and lover are in the hospital, and the lover pledges his love for the immobile wife, who says she doesn't want him. Unperturbed, he holds her hand. She may have tried to escape a possessive psychopath, but she has only attracted another man who would seek to enslave her. She too is trapped, her romantic fantasies of escape and love have proven futile, and it is a note of defeat that ends this sad, even despairing comedy.

Taav had previously co-scripted the often similarly droll *Still Life*, a film better in the script than in the direction. He had been a house painter himself for some time and thought the comedic possibilities of the profession were there, hence the slapstick final fight between the protagonists. Pastorelli would play another serial killer in *Striking Distance*. The tone of gentle irony and despair has rarely been attempted; its success here is testament to a fine talent. However, Taav has hardly been prolific, and the film has never received much attention.

Pair of Aces

(1990: d. Aaron Lipstadt)

scr. Bud Shrake, Gary Cartwright; pr. Cyrus Yavneh; ph. Tim Suhrstedt; m. William Olvis; ed. Michael Ornstein; prod d. Cary White; cast. Willie Nelson, Kris Kristofferson, Rip Torn, Helen Shaver, Jane Cameron, Emily Warfield, Lash LaRue; 94m

This is a modern Western tele-movie. A Texas Ranger (Kristofferson), with a safecracker (Nelson) in custody, is in pursuit of a serial killer. In addition, he has to protect his two daughters from the killer, who targets cheerleaders. A respect develops between these two old-timers as they eventually solve the case together, perhaps achieving a joint redemption.

This is a rare attempt to crossbreed the Western, albeit the modern Western, and the serial killer film. The protagonists are two aging cowboys and two Western archetypes—the sheriff and the good-hearted, honest outlaw. In this world the serial killer is an anomaly, and is not a product of the same Western honor code these types cling to so desperately. The investigation thus represents the clash of the old and the new (twentieth century criminality). Indeed, it contrasts varied types of outlaws, juxtaposing Nelson with a motorcycle gang (the modern banditos) and the offscreen killer (as a presence which ultimately taints them all). The serial killer, and the sexual nature of his crimes, gives traditional outlawry a bad name and has no real presence in the code of the West (hence the rare appearance of such killers in the genre).

The killer is part of the new genera-tion, a football hero, the proverbial "clean-cut kid" whose religious obsession is founded on the resentment of women's sexuality and the need to suppress it, perhaps even from within himself. However, this theme is subtextual only, and derived from the killer's possibly insecure presence in a world saturated with such macho codes. He considers his victims disposable, dirty little women—the macho identity gone crazy in the search for a sexual identity. In that, he is possibly the descendent of a traditional Patriarchy who violates that tradition and is subsequently disavowed.

Cult director Lipstadt (best known for the low-budget sci-fi *Android*) treats this film, despite the subject matter, as a light comedy, making innocuous jabs at Texas machismo and spending time characterizing the local eccentrics. Even the killer's accomplices, corrupted by this new kind of crime, are just "good ole boys" to whom the fun-loving lifestyle has turned deadly—they are corrupted cowboys.

Pale Blood

(1990: d. V. Hsu and Michael Leighton)

scr. V. Hsu; pr. Tony Brewster, Leighton; ph. Gerry Lively; m. Jan A.P. Kaczmarek; ed. Leighton, Michael Kewley; prod d. Shane Nelson; cast. George Chakiris, Wings Hauser, Pamela Ludwig, Darcy de Moss, Earl Garnes, Frazer Smith, Michael Leighton; 93m

A serial killer (Hauser) wants to believe he is a vampire (à la *Martin*), even using fake incisors on his victims, and comes into contact with a real vampire. Ironically, the real vampire (outside agent) wants to stop the serial killer from giving the vampire community a bad reputation. He teams with a female detective obsessed with vampire lore (and who herself romanticizes such aberrations). They develop a psychic intuition. The killer wanted all along to attract a real vampire, and to be bitten and so become a vampire, his ideal fantasy image.

The film is aware of previous screen depictions of the vampire and the serial killer, and seems intent on rescuing the Romantic conception of the vampire from the taint of the serial killer, counter to the trend in such works as *Martin* and *Night Owl*. Thus, the vampire, although preying on humans out of biological need, ironically possesses a humanity the serial killer lacks. The director cuts from the vampire's fangs to *Nosferatu* playing on the TV set he has brought his date/victim home to watch. The killer films the crime scenes from above (making a documentary about himself, à la *Peeping Tom*), so intent is he on his own greatness and on becoming his ideal: the vampire. Of course, his home movies also serve another purpose — snuff pornography (recalling Hauser's role as the anti-snuff vigilante of *Art of Dying*).

The killer uses high-tech equipment to duplicate the vampire's blood-drawing ability. He is the force of a new, twentieth century Evil, intent on callously appropriating a misunderstood myth for self-aggrandizement. The serial killer, not the vampire, is the real taint of Evil, yet they are close enough to recognize each other and even summon each other psychically. The vampire is aware of such killers as a threat to his continued existence and to the reputation of his kind. The detective also senses this, the theme being that the vampire is a dying breed slowly being replaced by such serial killers, the human attempt to duplicate something inherently inhuman, and in the process unduly sexualizing and debasing a Romantic act. This is, of course, a self-conscious theme in light of the development of the serial killer film.

In the end, the old (vampire) must fight the new (serial killer) in order to restore the purity of the image. Thus while the vampire is real, the serial killer is confined to a criminal psychiatric hospital: the film divorces the two and restores, to the delight of Goth cultists everywhere, the Romantic conception of the vampire (who has now taken the detective as his lover and partner). The detective has also been seduced by her closeness to the fantasy ideal male lover, the vampire, but without the taint of psychic decay and moral corruption that accompanies the serial killer.

This is a curious Hong Kong–backed action-horror movie more akin to the pioneering work of a somber Robert Clouse than to the stylized world of John Woo or Tsui Hark. It is a calculatedly cold film, with blues and reds predominant, and despite this calculated-ness, seems breezily acted, even oddly improvised in parts. It seems designed to counter the demystification of *Martin*, which sought to equate the vampire with the serial killer. Does this mean the film can be considered as a re-mystification?

Pandora's Box

(1929: d. G.W. Pabst)

scr. Pabst, Laszlo Wajda; plays. Franz Wedekind; ph. Gunther Krampf; ed. Joseph R. Fliesler; art d. Andrei Andreiev; cst. Gottlieb Hesch; cast. Louise Brooks, Fritz Kortner, Franz Lederer, Gustav Diessl; 97 (105)m

Now highly regarded as one of cinema's all-time classics, *Pandora's Box* centers on a flower girl and mistress of several men (Louise Brooks) who becomes the wife of an editor and flaunts her sexuality. She is turned into a dancer and becomes the era's major sex symbol, drawing all men to her. The husband dies, unable to deal with the open sexuality he has so unloosed, and she is blamed for the death. She is tried and found guilty, and forced to flee with his son, who is also infatuated with her. After he loses all their money gambling, she takes to prostitution when they move to England. This has unexpected consequences, as she becomes a common streetwalker and ends up a victim of Jack the Ripper, whom she invites to her flat for sex even though he admits having no money.

The film depicts the protagonist's sexuality as a kind of innocence that draws Evil (tortured male sexuality) onto it. This tortured male sexuality desires and loathes the object of desire, a process at its worst spiraling into guilt and compulsive sexual homicide. Despite her sexually free ways, her demise is not interpreted as a punishment for her wickedness. It is her free and open sexuality which is a magnet for others, particularly exploiters. Those who fall for this open sexuality are doomed to disappointment or even death, but is she responsible? Or is she a true innocent, attracting the inherently self-destructive to her?

She means no harm, and loves men, saying at one point, "You'll have to kill me if you want to get away from me." This is perhaps a challenge, however unknowing on her part, to all mankind who have manipulated her into a cultural icon and desired object. There lies the film's puzzle: that she is both so desired and resented that the only way to remove her sexual identity is to kill her, as if purging her from a higher male order. In this way she may be a catalyst for all that happens, but she is not the seductively malevolent femme fatale of the film noir works that followed. She may lure and control men by her free sexuality, but that leads only to her doom. Innocence is lethal in this world, which seeks to define women sexually and is then consumed by that definition.

The film delineates the 1920s vamp image from the flapper days and lays the groundwork for such to be later twisted into the manipulative femme fatale. She knows that people would condemn her for her sexual behavior (Peary, pp. 247–251) but makes no effort to control or suppress

it: she is a true free spirit. Thus, she rejects conventional morality, which in a time of social change would preach both indulgence and repression, resulting in the true sexual perversity of Jack the Ripper, to whom murder is a crime of passion. For the Ripper, murder is an act of sexual love and punishment, as he can only achieve release when stabbing the woman with a knife he finds nearby. Paradoxically, she is used by those around her rather than achieving a true sexual freedom.

She is made into a victim by one to whom passion has become homicidal psychosis, one who is himself a victim of a world that feeds and condemns such amorality—both are obsessed with their own sexuality and, in part, find solace in each other (so Peary found). Ironically, she is relieved that his hesitancy at not following her was the result of his not having any money, and not because he didn't sexually desire her. Far from a manipulative woman, by the end she has become a victim. She and the killer are slaves to their sexual desire, and even sympathetic in that. Louise Brooks said of her character's end, "It is Christmas Eve and she is about to receive the gift which has been her dream since childhood: death by a sexual maniac" (quoted in Peary, p. 251).

The Ripper is first seen as a sorrowful man. His eyes meet hers, and it is clear that he longs for a connection. She recognizes this and gives him a flower. Pensive and melancholy, he searches rather than prowls the foggy streets. Perhaps he is the agent of fate and a functionary of male sexuality, compelled to kill what it sought connection with, in the process destroying part of itself, as indeed all males are depicted as self-destructive to a relative degree.

Pandora's Box was critically savaged and then forgotten upon its initial release, but film historians in the 1950s "rediscovered" it and proclaimed it a masterpiece. Its depiction of German decadence was found scandalous, and its non-judgmental view of sexual promiscuity and prostitution angered moral activists. Scenes involving the lesbian countess were cut for the initial British release but restored to the 1950s rerelease. Its consideration of changing cultural mores resulting in the sexual resentment of women's newfound sexual liberation finds its echo in the 1940s American films *The Lodger* (also about Jack the Ripper) and *Lady of Burlesque*. The film's considerable reputation as one of the best of the silent era continues to grow.

Partners

(1982: d. James Burrows)

scr. Francis Veber; pr. Aaron Russo; ph. Victor J. Kemper; m. Georges Delerue; ed. Danford B. Greene; prod d. Richard Sylbert; cast. Ryan O'Neal, John Hurt, Kenneth McMillan, Robyn Douglas, Jay Robinson, Denise Galik, Joseph R. Sicari, Michael McGuire, Rick Jason, James Remar; 93m

A staunchly heterosexual police officer (O'Neal) is forced to pose undercover as a homosexual, accompanying a gay police clerk (Hurt) in order to investigate a series of murders in the gay community. They have to act flamboyant enough to be noticed. Of course, the film charts the growing respect between the heterosexual and the gay, who inevitably develops a romantic interest in his handsome companion. Finally, Hurt saves O'Neal's life but is wounded in the process.

The film examines the role one's sexuality has on one's humanity and self-definition. Much of the comedy centers on O'Neal's fish-out-of-water scenario as he experiences social prejudice, but the real subject of the movie is not his tale of threatened identity and progressive, respectful sympathy, nor the serial killer narrative, but Hurt's story as an example of gay empowerment. For Hurt, who has tried to hide his sexual identity, the film becomes an out-of-the-closet tale. He

steadily moves from mousy passivity to forceful aggression, a process of emancipation, although it involves control over a gun, the symbol of male potency. Ultimately, as a gay, however, he cannot end up in full possession of such phallic power, and is shown fumbling with it at first, then shot in the attempt. His move towards gay potency cannot go uncountered, and so the killer wounds him. He does kill the killer, however, thus purging from the homosexual community the threat to its collective sexuality.

This killer represents the sexual resentment of such homosexual empowerment, which is to him embodied in the male model as an idealized sexual commodity. His actions also speak of denial and the societal need to suppress such desire. However, the killer is not alone, as he is aided and blackmailed by a woman who sought to exploit such sexuality for her own financial gain. It is she who is the most predatory of the characters on display, and the most threatening. As a photographer in charge of the male models, she controls the conception of male homosexual fantasy, just as males would commodify female sexual identity. She controls the look, making men objects of the gaze, for the consumption of other men, an end the killer resents.

Thus, in its use of point of view the film attempts to jostle perspective according to sexual identity—heterosexual, homosexual and even bisexual—as all revolving around the display and commodification of the male body (personified by O'Neal). It is the display of the male body, the reaction to that display, and its function within Patriarchy—and even as a threat to that Patriarchy (which the killer feels)—which forms the film's subtext. It is more intriguing in that than as either comedy or light, otherwise formulaic thriller.

The script is by French comedy writer/director Francis Veber in the mold of his

Left: The reluctant partners: John Hurt (left) and Ryan O'Neal are told to pose as a gay couple to infiltrate the homosexual community beset by murders in *Partners* (Paramount, 1981). *Right:* The two undercover officers (John Hurt and Ryan O'Neal) posing as a gay couple in *Partners* (Paramount, 1981).

script for *La Cage Aux Folles*, and debuting director Burrows is best known for his TV work on, among others, *Cheers*. It was panned on release for its shallow, cliched stereotyping. However, the partial attempt at a celebration of gay culture and identity can be seen as an answer to the despair of Friedkin's *Cruising*, with the filmmakers intent on depicting positive gay characters, however stereotyped and condescending the results may be. A policeman becomes sympathetic to the gay cause instead of being corrupted by it, and a gay becomes both an agent of gay liberation and, as a policeman himself, Patriarchy.

Peeping Tom

(1960: d. Michael Powell)

scr. Leo Marks; pr. Michael Powell; ph. Otto Heller; m. Brian Easdale; ed. Noreen Ackland; art d. Arthur Lawrence; cast. Carl Boehm, Moira Shearer, Anna Massey, Maxine Audley, Bartlett Mullins, Shirley Ann Field, Jack Watson, Nigel Davenport; 109m

This seminal serial killer film is about a young, retiring man named Mark (Boehm) who kills women, filming their fear-filled expressions as they watch themselves die, to replay later in his apartment for masturbatory excitement. He works for a film studio and doubles as a soft-core porno photographer. Hidden in a tripod leg is a long blade which he uses to impale his victims, filming all the while. He even films the police investigating his murders, in the process making a documentary about his activities, so egocentric has he become.

The overt linking of violence and

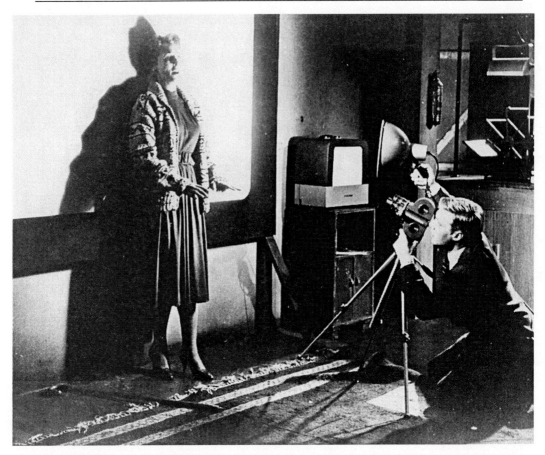

Serial killer Mark (Carl Boehm) sets up a lethal shot for his next intended victim in *Peeping Tom* (Anglo-Amalgamated, 1960).

sexual pleasure in *Peeping Tom* provided a definitive step forward in the evolution of the serial killer film as a genre. No longer was the killer physically removed from the outside world, but an intelligent, obsessed man to whom the sexual fulfillment offered by scopophilia has become violent. This violence is inherent in the act of looking, and Mark's actions are the end of an extreme. His use of the camera is a sadistic act of looking — the filming process thus hurts its object. To gaze is to assault, and the looker becomes a predator (see Clover, pp. 168–181). Such sadism, inherent in the cinematic process, is the rule of the father, and is challenged only by the blind mother, a tenant who senses Mark's discomfort.

He is sexually attracted to fear, his sadistic acts designed to provoke in the victim the fear of her impending death as she looks at herself being killed by Mark. The moment of death is almost orgasmic for this killer. But he does not defile the corpse, rather screening the films at home for solitary and presumed autoerotic excitement. Violence is a sexual release, and the film souvenirs are his attempts to keep the excitement going — until he is driven by sexual desire to perform another murder. He admits that he plans each murder to be his last, but that he never gets the details right (i.e. it never fully lives up to the fantasy in his mind), and so he is driven to repeat the act to attain the perfection of the imaginary.

The film roots the problem in Mark's

Serial killer Mark (Carl Boehm) demonstrates his murder apparatus (the spiked tripod) to the only girl (Anna Massey) with whom he has had a "real" relationship in *Peeping Tom* (Anglo-Amalgamated, 1960).

childhood experiences with an obsessive father. Such homicidal scopophilia is the result of years of systematic abuse by such a father, providing an imprinting process by which the son becomes like the monstrous parent. The son adopts the father's aggressive gaze, finding its locus in the camera he uses. Thus, Mark is treated with sympathy and care: he is a sexually tormented obsessive, deserving of care and treatment, and is far from an inhuman monster. He has been conditioned into becoming such a sex killer, and is aware of that fact, adding to his introspective torment, a torment that only leads to reinforcement through successive murder. As the film depicts the start of his homicidal

career, so too does it reveal how such has entered his fantasies over many years, developing until the desire to put them into reality is too great to resist any longer.

There is no way out for Mark, and the real villain is not Mark but the father (ironically played by Powell himself). However, Mark bears his Dad no ill will, and indeed has idealized him. His victims all resemble the woman who married his father six months after the death of his mother (Peary, pp. 252–255). It is this woman, who tore the beloved father away from him, he resents most of all, the crimes possibly being intended to punish them both. Indeed, Mark has a picture of the mother's successor in a bikini. With her thus clearly a sexual object, it is possible that Mark would have equated resentment and desire with such feminine "perfection." His homicidal desires could have emerged out of confused emotional responses in a developmental adolescent sexuality appropriating a male process of assaultive gazing: to both identify with and punish the father. As a soft-core photographer he takes girlie pictures of women in staged poses, not unlike the stepmother.

He is attracted to soft-porn representations of women, perhaps even more so than real women, whom he compulsively views through his camera (from the film's very opening) as objects. Only the downstairs neighbor's attentions offer a challenge to this. The film thus also partly addresses the changing social values of England as it enters the 1960s, and the consequences of the emerging sex industry/culture. Powell inserts a tellingly sly joke (one of many) at this point: an old man pays five pounds for pornographic "views," whereas the real prostitute from the opening would have only charged two pounds. Ironically, the objectified representations of women are more desirable and valuable than the real thing. In this way, the culture fosters male masturbatory dependence.

Mark desires a normal relationship but is too far gone to be able to maintain one, though he desperately seeks to share his childhood torments at the end and in a sense unburden himself. His normal girlfriend persuades him once to leave his camera behind, perhaps initiating a change from his sexual dependence on it. She represents his possible normal life beyond the camera, and thus he is adamant that it will never see her (he says "see" rather than "photograph," tellingly enough). He says to her that whatever he photographs he loses.

His sexual self is inescapable, however, and he is a doomed lost soul. In a near constant state of scopophilic sexual arousal,

ironically even suppressing "normal" desire, he lives in an anxious state, always clutching or carrying his camera as his substitute penis. This pain is relieved only in the acts of murder when he is able to enact the sexual identity that plagues him. He defines himself by his actions, which have evolved into a pattern, and, although aware of the alternatives, he is compelled to return to that pattern. In the end he battles to resist the impulse to kill the very love interest that could offer him a way out (a theme also in *Le Boucher*). He kills himself instead, aware of his impending arrest, and perhaps as the ultimate sexual thrill, putting himself masochistically in the position of the victim, surrendering male aggression and his own sexual identity.

Mark's retreat to his darkened rooms are a retreat from the bright colors of life outside, which he only experiences fully through films. This heightened sense of color, which Powell had explored in earlier films, reflects the protagonist's perceptions of the world, with so much to see and so many sources of visual stimulation and beauty. He locks onto women's faces in this world, intent to shape them to his will, almost as an artist (or, specifically, a film director) would. The outside world is thus almost frightening and fascinating in its intensity (Boot, p. 130).

Hugely controversial in England when first released, *Peeping Tom* almost ended the director's career, but has since been subject to vast reappraisal as an exploration of the relationship between viewer and cinematic spectacle (Hardy, p. 135). However, that the spectacles were the acts of a serial killer, and a sympathetic one at that, made the film morally problematic for viewers at the time. It was treated as a horror film, a label which Powell resisted, claiming it was instead "a film of compassion, of observation and of memory, yes! It's a film about the cinema from 1900 to 1960" (quoted in Clover, p. 169).

It flopped with the public. Consequently, the British especially detested the film and held Powell accountable for it. Formerly acclaimed as one of England's best directors, he was ostracized and remained out of work for a lengthy time (doing supposed hackwork like *Bluebeard's Castle* in the meantime). The film was recut by the studio for a brief US release. Thanks mostly to Martin Scorsese, a restored print was released in the United States in 1979.

Personal Column

(1939: d. Robert Siodmak) aka *Pièges*

scr. Jacques Companeea, Ernest Neuville, Simon Gantillon; pr. Michel Safra; m. Michelot; ed. Yvonne Martin; art d. G. Wakhevitch; cast. Maurice Chevalier, Pierre Renoir, Marie Dea, Erich Von Stroheim, Jean Temerson, Andre Brunot; 120m

A killer uses lonely-hearts personal ads to attract victims. Does he loathe women's romantic and sexual needs? Paris police convince the latest victim's roommate, a dancer, to assist their undercover investigations and trace the man who placed the ads the victims answered. She thus goes through many men seeking female employees until meeting a nightclub owner. Her interest soon turns romantic however, as she falls for him. Despite their plans to marry, the police still suspect him of being the killer and he is arrested. She goes undercover further to prove him innocent, and unmasks the real killer.

This film was smuggled out of France for US release. It was among the last films made in France before the outbreak of WWII. The US censors, however, were disapproving of several reported scenes revealing details of the victims' sex lives, however integral these were to revealing the killer's motives and inspirations/resentments, and trimmed these scenes. Nevertheless, the film was remade as *Lured*.

Director Siodmak relocated to America, where he contributed to the emergence of film noir and examined serial killer pathology again in *The Spiral Staircase*.

Phantom of the Rue Morgue

(1954: d. Roy del Ruth)

scr. Harold Medford, James R. Webb; pr. Henry Blanke; stry. Edgar Allan Poe; ph. Peverell Marley; m. David Buttolph; cast. Karl Malden, Claude Dauphin, Steve Forrest, Patricia Medina, Allyn McLerie, Dolores Dorn; 84m

Mad scientist/zookeeper Malden uses a trained killer gorilla to revenge himself on the women who spurn his advances. Each woman is given a bracelet with a bell that summons the ape. A professor of psychiatry (early profiler/outsider figure) investigates but is arrested by the police. In the end, the animals are loosed in the zoo, and Malden goes totally insane.

The symbolic finale, with the out-of-control zoo representing the protagonist's bestial condition, seeks to encapsulate homicidal madness as the expression of an innately animalistic (and hence destructively sexual) force. Sexual resentment causes the accumulation of corpses, and the film seeks to have its murders as set-piece structural beats. The act of killing only temporarily satiates the killer, whose pathology demands repeated sexual superiority over women: this is still depicted in terms of agent and controller, however, an outdated device. The homicidal drive is still considered the function of something other than twisted human nature, although ultimately rooted in it.

The 3D effects were considered unsubtle and now reportedly make the film gimmicky when shown flat. Although the 3D process suggests a link to *House of Wax*, this is more a remake of the 1932 version of *Murders in the Rue Morgue*. It was considered efficient horror exploitation and far from a serious Poe adaptation. It is representative of a state of transition in the evolution of the serial killer film, and is included herein to follow through the plot line.

The Phantom Speaks

(1945: d. John English)

scr. John E. Butler; pr. Armand Schaefer; ph. William Bradford; ed. Arthur Roberts; art d. Russell Kimball; cast. Richard Arlen, Stanley Ridges, Lynne Roberts, Tom Powers, Charlotte Wynters, Jonathan Hale, Pierre Watkin; 69m

A reporter investigates a series of killings. He discovers evidence that implicates and suggests a killer already executed. The killer's spirit has returned to Earth and taken over the body of a gentle scientist (profiler/killer link here) at that scientist's experiment/arrangement. The killer thus sets out on a series of revenge murders.

Although not really a serial killer film (more of a repeat revenge killer motif), *The Phantom Speaks* is notable for foreshadowing the *Shocker/Fallen* serial-killer spirit-returning subgenre, and a variation on the possession motif. The strong-willed killer is able to exert his influence over the weak-willed host. Typical of the era, the weak side does not know what the stronger is doing. The film can be seen as a partial examination of the role of conscience in the commission of murder, a theme also in the Jekyll/Hyde tales, which did away with the amnesia device.

The Photographer

(1975: d. William Hillman)

prod d. Kirk Axtell; cast. Michael Callan, Edward Andrews, Susan Damante-Shaw, W.B. Hinman, Barbara Nichols, Betty Anne Rees, Isabel Sanford; 94m

A soft-core photographer lures pretty women with the promise of modeling jobs. He then photographs and murders them.

As usual for killers who take visual records as souvenirs and trophies, he uses the photographs later for presumed self-gratification. Two elderly detectives investigate. Meanwhile, the killer's resentment for his mother grows, as it is clear that she still exerts an influence over his mind. He is not conflicted about his crimes in any way, however, as he plans each in advance, and has indeed turned the photography studio into a profitable enterprise and not merely a ruse for the victims.

Any hopes of *Peeping Tom* insights are quickly dashed in this inept, disastrous, risible attempt at psycho-dramatic horror. With an immobile camera forever in medium shot or close-up, the film devotes much time to the killer's rants as he justifies his atrocities and reveals his hatreds, petty resentments and mother-driven madness. The killer's "work" is all he thinks about, and he is a man consumed by voracious sexual desire and the need to keep stimulated. His homicidal desires stem from the night he saw his mother having sex with a man who caught him watching and choked him. Since then, he has developed the kind of gazing that equates scopophilic power with sex murder. Strangely, he blames the mother for instigating the beating rather than the man.

Pieces

(1983: d. Juan Picher Simon)

scr. Dick Randall, John Shadow; pr. Randall, Steve Mansian; ph. Juan Marino; cast. Christopher George, Lynda Day George, Edmund Purdom, Paul Smith, Frank Brana, Ian Sera, Jack Taylor, Gerard Tichy; 85m

A killer dismembers his pretty co-ed victims, taking select pieces home for his private human jigsaw puzzle. Police investigate and set up a woman as a decoy to lure the killer into action. His jigsaw woman comes to life in the end to exact a horrible revenge (à la *Maniac* and EC comics), clearly intended as poetic justice.

A prologue set in 1942 has a young boy doing a jigsaw puzzle of a nude woman, only to be found out and berated by his mother who threatens to kill him and his absent father. This supposedly accurate encapsulation of the childhood of the future serial killer is treated as a comedy, as indeed is much of the film, which subsequently descends into gory set-pieces as the boy axes his mother to death and dismembers the corpse in imitation of the puzzle. Forty years later he has grown into a serial killer of women, dismembering his victims and removing select pieces for his home project of an ideal woman. His necrophilic sexual pleasure with the dismembered limbs is implied.

The visualization of the barely-glimpsed killer is indebted to the gloved killer of numerous Italian giallo movies, but the film sadly lacks the necessary style to convey this sort of homage and subsequently exists only for its beautiful victims and graphic gore. A bland style — a wandering camera and a preponderance of close-ups and medium shots — sinks the film, as rarely is there even suggested an alternate way of seeing the world. Even the music seems to imitate the Italian band Goblin, who scored many successful European horror films, including a number by Dario Argento.

Pieces incorporates the murder-to-murder structure of the then-current slasher boom into its standard police procedural investigation, with many murders centered on a campus populated by loose, sexually amoral co-eds who deserve what they get, the film disturbingly suggests. However, the killer has a sexual pleasure in mutilation that is not present in the slasher figures, as these often seem asexual (although they may kill women). Once the police and decoy go undercover, the director uses the premise to fall into the slasher pattern of teen sex followed by death/punishment.

More attention is given to showing the killer's pathology as more than a mere slasher boogey-man, and the director dwells on scenes of the killer's charnel house, complete with a freezer to store his precious body-part trophies, to be used as fetishistic stimulants. The film is thus chiefly interesting for its eroticization of bodily dismemberment, recalling the gleeful mutilations in the films of H.G. Lewis. The story of a dismembering killer was handled more effectively in the genuine Italian giallo *Torso*, which anticipated the split between the serial killer and the slasher.

This was a Puerto Rican production filmed in Boston and Madrid by a Spanish director known for Jules Verne movies and the documentary *The Wild Wild World of Jayne Mansfield*, which recreated her car crash and decapitation. He had developed a reputation for minor schlock.

Play Nice

(1992: d. Terri Treas)

scr. Chuck McCollum, Michael Zand; pr. Luigi Cingolani, Don Daniel; cast. Bruce McGill, Hector Mercado, Chuck McCollum, Mimi Maynard, Prince Hughes, Ed O'Ross, Amy Steel, Angel Ashlay; 90m

A policeman specializing in serial killers is on the trail of a female killer who shoots her male victims in the mouth with a pistol, following sex. The bodies are discovered naked in New York City hotels. He soon discovers a link between the victims–they all had forced incestuous relations with their daughters. Thus he suspects the killer was an incest survivor. He goes for assistance to an incest counseling center, and becomes sexually involved with a frail, girlish woman there. Soon she becomes a suspect.

Like the female killers in *Basic Instinct*,

Nekromantik 2 and *Eye of the Beholder*, she kills during intercourse. In her fantasy she goes from passive to aggressive and exacts revenge on her sexual tormentor — the father. She is an expert at manipulating what the film considers as every father's inherently incestuous desires. In the film, Patriarchy is a reprehensible institution, reduced to a process of incestuous sexual sublimation of women.

All men carry such a pedophilic fantasy for young girls— it is an inherent aspect of a masculinity that seeks not to condemn such but merely to police and regulate its indulgence. The perpetrating patriarchs are hardly punished, and the only justice can be attained through revenge. The incest survivor's killing of men is thus a revolutionary gesture. The protagonist says to the cop that she could pretend to be his own daughter. He indulges in this fantasy sexual role-playing, revealing his own incestuous fantasy and becoming the bad father. The killer is a threat to the bad father and so to all Patriarchy, as she is the object of its darkest sexual desires who uses that sexual identity against the ones who forced it on her. The killer is one identity of a multiple personality — a constructed identity in reaction to abhorrent male sexual fantasy.

Playbirds

(1978: d. Willy Roe)

scr. Robin O'Connor, Bud Tobin; pr. Roe; ph. Douglas Hill; m. David Whitaker; ed. Jim Connock; art d. Peter Williams; cast. Mary Millington, Glynn Edwards, Gavin Campbell, Alan Lake, Windsor Davies, Derren Nesbitt; 94m

A serial killer targets the cover models of a successful girlie magazine. Two investigating detectives are thus drawn into the UK porno underworld of nudie bars, massage parlors, porn magazines and sex shops, allowing much nudity in the film. The chief suspect is the magazine publisher, a "pornocrat" whose magazine recently featured a Satanic porn photo spread. Other suspects include a religious figure, a photographer, and an anti-porn Member of Parliament. Much was made of the scene where the police "audition" female police officers to go undercover as porn starlets, rating their desirability as a measure of their effectiveness.

The film is considered notable mostly for its depiction of a British subculture rarely explored. Indeed, the magazine's Satanic photo spread is actually based on a real 1970s magazine entitled "Witchcraft," and a mock trial is intercut with the killer burning a crucified woman to death. This supposedly passes as social comment. Ultimately, *Playbirds* settles into the familiar rhythms of police procedural and investigation into the lifestyle of a porn czar (Gavcrimson, *imdb.com*). However, as an attempt to broach the topic of changing social mores (à la *He Kills Night After Night After Night* and the Schrader/Scorsese United States inferno movies), it is reportedly a curio. It is fascinated with lives consumed and affected by the porn culture: from porn czar to killer as a potential cause and effect trickle.

Playbirds was unusually popular when released, mainly due to the presence of starlet Mary Millington shortly before her untimely death at age 35. Millington was a nude model with no acting experience, but was put into the film to capitalize on her beauty. It was also one of the last movies produced by Tigon before they floundered in soft-core porn. As such, it perhaps has some significance as an example of the tendency to equate the horror serial killer film with the "adult" movie, disturbingly considering women's roles as relative to male sexual demands.

The Playgirl Killer

(1966: d. Enrich Sartamaran)

pr. Max A. Sendel; cast. William Kirwin, Jean Christopher, Neil Sedaka, Andree Champagne; 90m

A demented aspiring artist kills nude models and stores the bodies in his meat freezer. A rich, lonely woman hires him as a handyman. Meanwhile, a determined police detective sets up a woman as bait to lure him out.

In this type of standard plot, women are constantly in jeopardy, and it is arguable whether they are in control of their own will, as the male desire to objectify them literally removes them of life beyond this. This is, of course, a common theme which dates back to the origins of the genre. It remains a popular means of charting changing sexual mores and the increasing definition of female roles within Patriarchy.

This is further evidence of the ripple effect of the commodification of women. It is equated with the notion of murder as art, a theme gradually infiltrating the serial killer film. Here the corpses are the real artworks worthy of preservation, and presumed necrophilic pleasure. This is a supposedly campy Canadian horror film and was not released in the United States. It chiefly holds interest now only because it features songs by Neil Sedaka. It's currently out of circulation.

The Possession of Joel Delaney

(1972: d. Waris Hussein)

scr. Matt Robinson, Grimes Grice; nvl. Ramona Stewart; pr. Martin Poll; ph. Arthur J. Ornitz; m. Joe Raposo; ed. John Victor Smith; prod d. Peter Murton; cast. Shirley MacLaine, Perry King, Michael Hordern, David Elliott, Lisa Kohane, Barbara Trentham; 108m

A wealthy divorcee (MacLaine) lives with two kids and dotes unnaturally on her brother (King), although her brother prefers the East Village to her upscale lifestyle. Unaccountably, the brother is prone to violent attacks on people, which he cannot remember afterwards. Although he is put into a psychiatric institution, she moves him into her apartment and gets him psychiatric help. He deteriorates and soon cannot communicate about anything except a Puerto Rican man. The maid believes him possessed by the spirit of a Puerto Rican serial killer/decapitator. A seance is tried, but to no avail. Finally, as the brother dies, the killer's spirit enters MacLaine.

The theme of revenge for racial mistreatment is submerged beneath the calculated post–*Exorcist* melodramatics. However, by depicting a killer as a member of a racial minority, the film reportedly jostles a racist, reactionary posture (Hardy, p. 265) which holds, like *The Omen*, that evil is foreign and essentially un–American, contaminating the pure of heart. However, there is still the reportedly unexplored subtext of incestuous desire and resentment.

Correspondingly, it locates socioeconomic conditions (and resentments) as dominant contributing factors, over any psychological reasons. The underprivileged and the disenfranchised will seek to corrupt the innocent WASP responsible for their socioeconomic entrapment. However, the killer's crimes (sexual beheadings) are a means of sexual empowerment more than a sociopolitical statement. Only when the killer spirit works through another vessel does the material become so politicized.

The film was shot for little money, as part of star MacLaine's arrangement with British TV producer Lew Grade. It was made at a time when MacLaine was recovering from the flop movie *Desperate Characters* and a failed TV series, *Shirley's World*, and is generally considered as evidence of her career low-point. Nevertheless, in light of her stated beliefs, it is clearly a work of some personal import, perhaps reflecting the star's personal beliefs in past lives. Indeed, she fought (presumably for the validity of her message and the seriousness of tone) with the initial producer, Martin Poll, who subsequently left the production. The film's concern for ethnographic spirituality (which intrigued *Variety*) partly anticipates John Schlesinger's thriller *The Believers*.

Postmortem

(1998: d. Albert Pyun)

scr. John Lowry Lamb, Robert McDonnell; pr. Tom Karnowski, Gary Schmoeller; ph. George Mooradian; m. Anthony Riparetti; ed. Natasha Gjurokovic; prod d. Pat Campbell; cast. Charlie Sheen, Michael Halsey, Ivana Milicevic, Stephen McCole, Gary Lewis, Dave Anderson; 105m

This is a brooding and stylish film about an American ex-cop-turned-author (Sheen) unwillingly brought into a serial murder investigation in Scotland (his adopted home to get away from the pressures of the United States) when a body is found on his rural property. The Scottish detective (Halsey) in charge of the investigation at first resents the American profiler's presence. The killer sends the profiler fax messages (obituaries of his intended victims). The investigation yields a necrophilic serial killer. This offender has been draining his victims' blood postmortem, then dumping the naked bodies.

The killer is obsessed with death, both romanticizing and sexualizing it. He can quote Shakespeare ("In that sleep of death, what dreams may come") and has an infernal subterranean lair that allows him the time he feels is his due with his corpses. He has been imprinted with necrophilia from an early age when his mother died and he (revealed in flashback) incestuously fondled his mother's body. Thus, his burgeoning preadolescent sexuality was equated with death. A subsequent disgraced career as a mortician, covered up by his rich father, furthered his transgressive obsession until, no longer content

with corpses alone, he presumably added homicide to his sexual arsenal. Thus, he could fulfill his ideal image of himself as the personification of a sexualized death. Now he meets his future victims in funeral homes.

Sheen is the reluctant profiler, estranged from his family and from his profession (where he has been blamed for the death of a girl), and who seeks escape in alcohol. His ability to seemingly peer into the killer's mind casts him in the tradition of William Petersen in *Manhunter*. As an American expert on a criminal phenomenon associated almost exclusively with America, he has a responsibility to fight it no matter where it may be. Thus, the film reveals him as unable to run from his professional duty as patriarch. He may dislike his work, and the closeness it brings him to aberration, but it gives him purpose. Ironically, that links him to the killer–both find quasi-religious meaning in facing death.

Sheen's obsession leads to a growing respect from the detective in charge, who urges him to continue when Sheen balks at getting too close. The policeman accepts the value of the profiler's intervention. The detective takes it upon himself to prevent the inevitability of death, and sees in the profiler a means of doing this. He recognizes that the profiler is a potential deliverer. But all seek meaning in dealing with death: once the investigators all recognize this, they can function as a team, with each member having an assigned place in the hierarchy. Such is the film's subtextual agenda — to stress the need for a hierarchical structure to combat the threat posed by the serial killer, and the corresponding responsibilities of those so ordained. It is almost a religious organization, a Church of sorts in its own right, with the profiler as fallen priest seeking redemption. To beat the force of death is to see God.

It is correspondingly a cold, somber

film of drab blues, greens, browns and grays, saturated with death and decay and the psychological toll it takes on those who accept and challenge it. The film is therefore a neat encapsulation of the issues and structures of the contemporary serial killer film. Pyun was better known for his post-apocalyptic science fiction work, some of which has the bleak, wintry and brooding quality he brings here. *Postmortem* is one of the prolific director's best films. It is an engrossing and stylish addition to the genre in the manner of a low-budget David Fincher. The link between mortician and serial killer was also explored in both versions of *Nightwatch*.

Praying Mantis

(1993: d. James Keach)

scr. William Delligan, Duane Poole; stry. Delligan; pr. Marjie Lundell, Robert M. Rolsky; exec pr. Keach, Jane Seymour; ph. Ross A. Maehl; m. John Debney; ed. Stanford C. Allen; cast. Jane Seymour, Barry Bostwick, Chad Allen, Frances Fisher, Colby Chester, Michael MacRae; 90m

A woman (Seymour) seduces men, pretending to be their ideal woman, and then kills them after marriage as a bizarre honeymoon ritual consummation. She changes her identity and then moves on to the next town and the next victim. A dedicated FBI agent detects a pattern and concludes that the case proves that serial killing is no longer exclusively a male domain, and that the killer is thus a significant criminological case. The agent follows the trail. The next intended victim's sister-in-law suspects something is amiss, and looks into the case.

The killer has a cold and impenetrable psychosis, a mixture of the elegance associated with star Seymour and her feigned vulnerability. She is adept at role-playing, finding purpose and arousal in manipulating men, killing them as a means of sexual conquest. She kills in order to feel something, her emotions having been stripped as a result of child abuse. But her acts are ultimately empty, providing only temporary satiation, and she must move on.

This is a routine tele-movie in the *Black Widow* manner, with a similar stress on role-playing as a means of establishing a sexual identity. Such role-playing enables men to project their codes onto the woman, which the woman gradually usurps and turns against the male. She refuses to let male fantasy define her, killing men rather than succumbing to their conception of how she should be. She is thus a major threat to the sanctity of the male.

Pretty Maids All in a Row

(1971: d. Roger Vadim)

scr. Gene Roddenberry; nvl. Francis Pollini; pr. Roddenberry; ph. Charles Rosher; m. Lalo Schifrin; cast. Rock Hudson, Angie Dickinson, Telly Savalas, Roddy McDowall, Keenan Wynn; 95m

This black comedy from the giallo age is set in a University campus beset by co-ed murders. Hudson stars as a promiscuous football coach/guidance counselor who takes sexual advantage of the young women who come to him for help. A cheerleader threatens to expose him, so he murders her, part of a pattern. An insecure male goes to him for pointers so he can romance older teacher Angie Dickinson.

Hudson is the killer who kills any woman that rejects his ego. Although they are intended to protect his secret from discovery, he takes pleasure in the murders beyond the functional. They too are part of the turn-on. He has built his ego around manipulative conquest and cannot assimilate any threat to that ideal image of himself. The vain lady-killer becomes the literal lady-killer in a satirical jibe at the morality of promiscuity that began to consume the 1970s, and the glorification of sex as an expression of eternal youth. He fancies himself the ultimate Casanova and a mentor to a younger male student. Casanova has become a serial killer. Thus, at the end, as Hudson drives into the sea, the younger student is ready and primed to take his place. Patriarchy's legacy of the serial killer is passed on through generations as a reaction to changing sexual mores—the film becomes a black comedy/sex farce.

Roger Greenspun of the *New York Times* considered the film a kind of American High School Gothic, the condemnatory view of a European perception. Thus, Vadim brings his eye for beautiful women (he made *And God Created Woman*, lest we forget) into a landscape rife with generational exploitation and resentment. In that respect, the film anticipates the numerous co-ed slasher movies that would proliferate a decade later. The pursuit of pleasure has its consequences: it is perhaps inevitable that the way of the libertine would lead to murder as a function of said pleasure.

Produced and scripted by Gene Roddenberry, of *Star Trek* fame, this has since been considered one of star Hudson's attempts to break out of the image fostered by his comedies with Doris Day. He had earlier tried to broaden his range and toy with his image in John Frankenheimer's bleak *Seconds*, but the public would have none of it. His casting as a heterosexual Casanova is ironic in retrospect, although it represents the pinnacle of his screen image, which Vadim gleefully undercuts by revealing the matinee idol to be a secret sex killer. This was Vadim's first US movie, and was considered a disappointment and one of his lesser films.

Prettykill

(1987: d. George Kaczender)

scr. Sandra K. Bailey; pr. John R. Bowey, Sandy Howard, Martin Walters; ph. Joao Fernandes; m. Robert O. Ragland; ed. Tom Merchant; art

d. Andris Hausmanis, Jimmy Williams; cast. David Birney, Season Hubley, Susannah York, Yaphet Kotto, Suzanne Snyder, Germain Houde; 95m

A detective assists a brothel madam who wants him to find a prostitute who has a multiple personality disorder. One of the personalities is a serial killer. This personality (that of her father) kills other prostitutes. The detective is interested in restarting a relationship with the madam (they were formerly married), to the case's detriment.

Despite a sometimes Altman-esque interest in multiple characters, *Prettykill* is a merely functional and competent melodrama. Most interestingly, it attempts to portray a cross-section of the modern types and classes of women. However, all are eventually drawn to the domain of prostitution, as the epitome of the modern woman's plight — a life lived in reaction to male sexual commodification. Young women, in perpetual supply, are thus subordinated to male sexual desire, which is even incestuous in design — a theme elaborated on more subversively in *Play Nice*. The killer comes to embody the worst of this male abhorrence, becoming an empty vessel devoid of a coherent personality except that of her dead father, reconstituted in her own mind as the shaping force in her private life.

In this world, vice and exploitation are hidden by the trappings of a rich and sophisticated allure. This concern with surfaces seems a regular Kaczender theme, although it can also be considered cut-price Altman. Kaczender then contrasts the lifestyles of the honest policeman with the indulgent rich. Despite some characters revealing a growing disenchantment with their self-indulgent lifestyle, all are trapped in a world where the violent destruction of the lifestyle from within is inevitable.

To this extent, the killer is both a

purge and a monster. The murderer is revealed to be a whore with a multiple personality complex, the killer personality being the reincarnation of her dead and abusive father (providing an inversion of *Psycho*). As such, serial murder is the product of an abusive Patriarchy, and it purges this Patriarchy of what it feels are the symptoms of illness—women. The theme of the killer as victim of child abuse is, of course, a common one, but is here little more than a tacked-on subplot, as the film is more concerned with the relationship between the investigating officer and the madam, who were formerly married to each other. The two plot lines serve to encapsulate the theme of reconciliation and its impossibility.

The film always threatens to become more involving than it does. As mentioned, it is inspired by Altman but lacks the complex use of open spaces, favoring a bland, enclosed style, trapped in constant medium shot, reminiscent of the tele-movie style. *Prettykill* is, however, thematically rich, though undeveloped.

Prey of the Chameleon

(1991: d. Fleming B. Fuller)

scr. Fuller; April Campbell Jones; pr. Patrick Peach; ph. Randolph Sellars; m. Shuki Levy; ed. Karen Joseph; prod d. Clare Scarpulla; cast. Daphne Zuniga, Alexandra Paul, James Wilder, Patricia Place, David Powladge, Michele McBride, Lisa London; 91m

This is a rare female serial killer cable movie, although the theme seems more prominent on television, perhaps due to the advent of gender programming and stations especially for women. A returning mercenary finds his ex-girlfriend (Paul) now a deputy sheriff. She still feels bitter and resentful at his having left her. He takes a job offer in a nearby town and drives there. He picks up a female hitchhiker (Zuniga), who may be a patient—a serial killer known as "the chameleon"—recently escaped from a psychiatric hospital and on a wave of killings. Her ability to assume the identities of each victim confounds the FBI agents trailing her, who come into Paul's investigation of related homicides.

Like many depictions of female serial killers, this one frames her in terms of role-playing akin to multiple personality. The thesis seems to be that while a male serial killer tries to become the fantasy ideal image of himself, the female serial killer has to forever adapt herself to male fantasies of the ideal woman to lure her prey and then kill. This film adapts that slightly, in that the killer kills women and absorbs their personalities, identities and sexuality as she seeks self-definition. Many real serial killers have expressed the belief that their victims are forever a part of them, and take trophies to enhance this. Zuniga can only find self-definition through her role as a killer forever in a state of transition, however ultimately directionless this may be. As she adopts a male persona also, this transitive state she desires seems to be genderless, although it allows her an aggressive, if temporary, sexual identity.

The film seeks to capture the menacing, desolate nuances of such rural film noirs as *Blood Simple*, especially *Clay Pigeons* and *Delusion*, but even *Outside Ozona* and the films of John Dahl. However, it lacks the tonal complexity that enhances these movies. Its main film noir quality is the equation of the femme fatale with the serial killer, a rarity acknowledged by the FBI agents on the case. However, unlike the duplicitous, controlling femme fatales of noir, Zuniga does not lure men to their complicit doom.

The film posits the FBI as earnest manhunters forever on the trail of such serial murderers. In the process, they educate the local police about the nature of crimes that would otherwise be baffling. Thus, the cop and the profiler are posited as the best team to catch this kind of killer.

It culminates in a female killer vs. female cop showdown, as the cop tries to talk about the killer's childhood trauma (a tormenting mother) to save her life. Unlike the killer, the cop has a sure sense of herself in relation to others, and it is this quality that the killer finally seeks to absorb. Although it is a cohesive identity the killer seeks, the film doesn't fully explore the sexual expression or pleasure of the killings, leaving this aspect subtextual, instead verging on a spree killer movie, as the killer commits other crimes of convenience as she goes along. Nevertheless, it is more thematically provocative in its exploration of personality absorption as a consequence of role-playing (the usual theme in female serial killer movies) than perhaps expected, and thus one of the more interesting variations on the female serial killer mystique.

Private Parts

(1972: d. Paul Bartel)

scr. Philip Kearney, Les Rendelstein; pr. Gene Corman; ph. Andrew Davis; m. Hugo Friedhofer; ed. Morton Tubor; cast. Ayn Ruymen, Lucille Benson, John Ventanonoi, Laurie Main, Stanley Livingston, Charles Woolf, Ann Gibbs, Len Travis, Dorothy Neumann; 87m

One boarder at a dilapidated boarding house run by the peculiar Aunt Martha is a serial killer. The film follows many relationships, including that of the landlady's daughter forced to grow up and dress like a man (a plot hook that would affect the killer in *Deadly Blessing* and *Unhinged*). The killer, a photographer interested in the daughter, keeps an inflatable sex doll, apparently filled with blood, in his room, which he uses as stimulation between murders.

The film is too slyly knowing for outright horror, and is full of allusions, especially to *Psycho*, *Peeping Tom* and the homoeroticism of *Midnight Cowboy*. It parades its sexual kinks proudly (full of peep holes and leather outfits) as it depicts a world overrun with sexual dysfunction and perversity from which there is no respite. Thus, it reportedly vacillates between gag-filled social satire and titillation, a balance also attempted in Bartel's subsequent films. There is no sense of normality in the film, as all characters are kooks or caricatures.

This was cult director Bartel's debut. He considers it an artistic and financial flop (McDonagh, p. 53) which the distributor, MGM, did not know how to release, nor indeed who the target audience really was. The kinky sexual component caused harsh reactions at a preview screening and caused MGM to take their name off the production and replace it with Premier Productions. Bartel himself took the film around the festival circuit for a year before returning to Roger and Gene Corman for the production money for his next film, the exploitation classic *Death Race 2000*. Bartel would return to the serial killer motif, and the sex-mad world subtext, for *Eating Raoul*.

Profile for Murder

(1997: d. David Winning)

scr. Steve Fisher; pr. Dan Redler, James Shavick; ph. Bruce Worrall; m. Barron Abramovitch; ed. Michael John Bateman; art d. Lana Kozak; cast. Lance Henriksen, Joan Severance, Jason Nash, Jeff Wincott, Fawnia Mondey, Ryan Michael; 95m

This is an attempted erotic crime-thriller about a millionaire (Henriksen) accused of being a serial killer responsible for the deaths of a number of Los Angeles nightclub ladies. He intends to seduce the criminal psychologist (Severance) assigned to asses him. She starts to have sexual fantasies about him; such is the erotic appeal of the ultimate transgressor the film implies:

the serial killer as a sexual turn-on in women's fantasies. This is a fascinating, if morally problematic, theme, and is suggested here rather than explored. It was also tackled in *Writer's Block*.

Profile for Murder attempts to capitalize on Henriksen's persona as the profiler on TV's *Millennium* and features much nudity, simulated sex, and masturbation and violence. Perhaps it can best be thought of as a swinger, soft-porn take on *Silence of the Lambs* for the erotic video market. It has no reputation to speak of, beyond curiosity value. It seeks to explore the role of private sexual fantasies in an individual's demonstration of self, a regular justification for soft-core titillation. This was, unfortunately, unavailable at time of writing.

Psychic

(1991: d. George Mihalka)

scr. Miguel Tejada-Flores, Paul Koval; pr. Tom Berry; ph. Ludek Bogner; spec eff. Brock Jolliffe; cast. Zach Galligan, Catherine Mary Stewart, Michael Nouri, Albert Schultz, Ken James, Clark Johnson; 88m

A youth with powers of ESP believes the teacher he craves is to be the next target of a serial killer/strangler. He believes this killer to be a respected psychology teacher at the college he attends. The police, of course, do not believe this, and neither does the intended victim, and so he sets out to stop the killer himself. He is also romantically interested in the next victim, a teacher herself, and she considers him jealous and does not heed his warning. When she goes off to an encounter with the professor, he follows them, convinced that the professor will try to kill her and so expose his real nature. His concern for the woman's fate is balanced with his intent to prove himself right, and he perhaps loses sight of the truly benevolent motives.

Mihalka cleverly draws out the stu-dent's resentment of the teacher. The teacher is smarter, more successful with women, and from a more affluent socioeconomic background. In that sense, their clash is generational. The protagonist resents the patriarch. He attributes sexual maturity to this teacher, while he himself still indulges in adolescent sex talk with his roommate. Ironically, the teacher he resents and considers a murderer is his idealized male role model: the film thus charts the process of maturation as the disavowal of the flawed father figure as role model and sexual competitor. At first, the protagonist wants what the teacher has, and his outward sexual confidence (in asking the desirable female teacher out) covers his insecurity.

The psychic ability is thus equally a form of projection, however valid it is in the conventional ending. It is also a sign of his maturity. At first he uses it to guess cars passing by and to pick up women by feigning insight into their lives (recalling the irresponsible Dennis Quaid in *Dreamscape*). His confrontation with the killer is ultimately a confrontation with what would be his idealized self if he kept on the irresponsible, egotistical and exploitative path he was headed down.

Ironically, the professor is brought into the investigation by the police in order to give a profile of the likely killer. He profiles the protagonist who suspects his guilty secret. Thus, the film is among the first to experiment with the profiler as killer motif, an obvious but sparingly used device because it invalidates the symbolic importance of the profiler. Nevertheless, as used here it is a knowingly ironic twist on the genre's central character triptych. Indeed, the film compounds the irony further, as the protagonist is arrested and the psychiatrist sent to evaluate him as the profiler/killer. And, of course, with the profiler such an esteemed icon, who would disbelieve him?

This novel work is generally dismissed as a made-for-cable psychic-link effort, though some (Hardy, p. 485) considered it evidence of Mihalka's vast improvement as a director. Indeed, there is enough of interest in his body of work to warrant further attention. Editor Ziller is a minor director himself.

Psycho

(1960: d. Alfred Hitchcock)

scr. Joseph Stefano; nvl. Robert Bloch; pr. Hitchcock; ph. John L. Russell; m. Bernard Herrmann; ed. George Tamasini; prod d. Joseph Hurley, Robert Clatworthy; cast. Anthony Perkins, Janet Leigh, Vera Miles, John Gavin, Martin Balsam, John McIntire, John Anderson, Mort Mills, Patricia Hitchcock, Simon Oakland, Frank Albertson; 109m

A bank teller (Leigh) steals money from work and flees the city. She takes refuge at an out of the way motel run by the neurotic Norman Bates (Perkins). As she undresses, he spies on her through a peephole. As she showers, she is murdered by what seems to be an old woman. Norman blames his mother for the murder. The thief's boyfriend (Gavin) and sister (Miles), and a private detective (Balsam), trace her steps to the motel. It is revealed that the killer is Norman, whose identity is taken over by his reconstitution of his mother as part of a multiple personality disorder. He correspondingly dresses up like his mother (whose corpse he keeps in a wheelchair) to kill the women who turn him on, and so reveal themselves to be the corruptive filth his mother despised.

At first, the film develops as a feminist challenge to Patriarchy's authority. Leigh is a sexually independent woman who steals from an older, drunken patriarch who can offer only money to ward off the world. By stealing, she plans to usurp his position and prove herself independent, if fallen (at first seen in white underwear, she is then in black, the change complete). For this challenge, in the Hitchcock world she needs to be punished. The film is ostensibly set up as a conventional crime movie but soon segues into something far more sinister and malevolent, as Hitchcock piles irony upon irony.

It is Norman who (unknowingly) convinces her to return the money, and is, in that sense, a deliverer and a force of benevolent justice (punned on further in *Psycho III*, where the homicidal Norman is seen as a divine angel by his intended victim). He is the agent of change who turns an unrepentant woman into a repentant one. Yet Norman, at first polite and accommodating (if awkward), is tainted by a ferocious sexuality which begins in voyeurism (and thus is linked to the audience) and culminates in the punitive murder of the object of desire. At the root of this psychosis is, of course, the domineering mother who haunts her son long after her death. Indeed, he is so dominated by her that he must reconstitute her in his own mind in order to be with her: the murders he can thus ascribe to her will, denying and chastising his own sexual perversity. There are sly cues to danger that precede the crime: the stuffed birds, Norman's talk of everyone having their personal trap and the impossibility of escape, his mounting instability conveyed in gesture and tone of voice.

The shower murder scene is one of the most celebrated in cinema history. Aside from the technical brilliance of its construction, it was a deliberate challenge to the accepted narrative structure of American film: it killed off the heroine midway through. And it transferred audience sympathy to Norman, the devoted son cleaning up the crime in order to cover for his beloved mother. Although little is shown of Leigh's nakedness during the scene, it establishes the genre's stress on the set-piece murder of a beautiful, naked woman (presumably then at her most vulnerable

Norman Bates (Anthony Perkins) in *Psycho* (Universal, 1960).

and desirable) as a major moral problematic in successive films. It makes Norman at least complicit in murder, and aware enough to cover up and dispose of the corpse (although this is still to protect "Mother," it is a self-preservatory gesture also).

Significantly, it is not the police who are on the woman's trail, but affected outsiders. In a deliberate challenge to the im-

portance of the detective in such murder narratives, the character is also killed off by Norman/Mother. It is a calculated narrative strategy, flying in the face of convention as it were, and a testament to the film's historical interest and longevity.

There is a note of pathos to Norman, a poor soul drawn ever deeper into cover-up and the attempt to conceal Mother from discovery. He says to the detective that he is unable to be fooled, not even by a woman — another irony, in retrospect (the film exists to be seen at least twice). This is a comment that introduces the possibility of such murder as a response to the threat against one's manhood, a disavowal of desire ironically climaxing it.

Norman exists in a limbo, both desiring and seeking to chastise that desire. "Mother" has effectively become his superego. Yet the acts Mother sanctions are abhorrent products of the id. Thus, one could argue that it is the malfunctioning superego transposed over the id that leads to sex murder in Norman's case. And that this is such an abhorrence that it results in psychological incoherence and the emergence of a multiple personality. Such is his trap: "Mother" is both his escape and the agent of his entrapment.

The lengthy dénouement, which equates mental illness with such serial murder, has a psychiatrist explain Norman's condition. Norman killed his resented mother but was so conflicted that he erased the crime in his own mind and tried to preserve the body and reinvent her personality, trying to be his mother, who now went crazy whenever Norman felt sexually attracted to other women. It has since been argued that this scene was intended as a mockery of the psychoanalytic process.

Despite this killer's tumultuous inner world, he was able to maintain an outwardly normal, orderly world. Such would be the enigma of the serial killer in many subsequent films. The clash of the inner and the outer is the fantasy impinging on reality, transforming it in the process as an exercise in the assertion of the will. Mental illness was, for many subsequent films, the battleground in which fantasy and reality fought, with lethal consequences to innocents.

Although the film was made for Paramount, it was self-financed by Hitchcock and shot in black and white on a Universal back lot by his TV crew. He personally participated in the marketing and publicity, notably refusing to let people (even critics) enter the cinema once the movie had started, and asking that no one reveal the ending. Many attacked what they thought was a questionable morality and an exploitation of mental illness: why had a major director stooped to such a level? As a joke, no doubt. Hitchcock stated, "The only way to remove the numbness (of civilization) and revive our moral equilibrium is to use artificial means to bring about the shock. The best way to achieve that, it seems to me, is through a movie" (Nash and Ross, p. 2484).

However, the film has since proven to be seminal and arguably subversive in its taboo-breaking subject matter (encompassing transvestitism, sex murder, necrophilia, even schizophrenia). Its controversy was matched in the UK the same year when *Peeping Tom* was released. The emphasis on murder in both of these films as a gory set piece would dominate the horror and thriller crossovers that followed and become central to the serial killer film as it evolved.

The film was based on the true story of necrophilic ghoul Ed Gein, who exhumed his mother's corpse, dressed in women's skin and body parts (notably using a vulva in his underwear to cover his own genitals), and went on to sex murder. Gein's case would also influence *Deranged, The Texas Chainsaw Massacre,* and *Silence of the Lambs.*

Psycho

(1998: d. Gus Van Sant)

scr. Joseph Stefano; pr. Brian Grazer, Van Sant; ph. Chris Doyle; prod d. Tom Foden; ed. Amy Duddleston; m Bernard Herrmann, Danny Elfman; cast. Vince Vaughn, Julianne Moore, Viggo Mortensen, William H. Macy, Anne Heche, James Remar; 100m

Director Gus Van Sant contemplates the *Psycho* remake (Universal, 1998).

This was a generally panned scene-by-scene, virtually shot-by-shot remake of the Hitchcock classic for a generation presumed to be unfamiliar with the original. The original script is repeated almost verbatim, with Vaughn in the Perkins role as Norman Bates.

The film is more sexualized than the Hitchcock original. Hence, Heche is pixie-ish, Moore is aggressive, Mortensen's buttocks feature teasingly, the opening hotel room features the sound of a fornicating couple in the adjoining room, and as Norman peeps on the showering Heche, he

Producer Brian Grazer (left) and director Gus Van Sant (right) discuss the making of the *Psycho* remake (Universal, 1998).

visibly and audibly masturbates. Important are two choices: one is to clearly imply Norman masturbating as he spies on his next victim, and the second is the concurrent eroticization and distancing of the shower scene. Heche's body is more an erotic object than was Leigh's (particularly in the way her newly dead body leans over the bathtub). The insertion of a shot of an approaching storm breaks the scene's diegesis and is an arguable attempt at de-eroticization, a portentous comment on it as an act of sex murder, the killing of an innocent, and a function of contemporary heterosexual politics.

Van Sant thus makes the film more knowingly and openly about sexual polemics than did Hitchcock. Van Sant is scathing about contemporary male-female relations as a function of sexual power games, a corruptive force that impels transgression as a means of establishing a counter identity. Norman is therefore more explicitly a challenge to the process of gender definition. Correspondingly, Van Sant stresses the gay subtext of the first one, a decision more attributed to his personal sexual preferences than to any thematic examination. Norman is arguably more of a repressed homosexual who needs voyeuristic sexual stimulation to assert a declining heterosexuality that finds its assertion and disavowal in the act of murder. Hence his assertion that he cannot be fooled even by a woman.

Van Sant stresses the notion of the workings of a guilty conscience. He emphasizes the inner voices that Heche hears as she drives, later to be contrasted with the mother's voice as the dominant superego. The troubled conscience impels the characters into a mutual tragedy of sorts. Vaughn's Norman is similarly tinged with self-recognition and self-deception, suggesting not so much instability as a barely controlled rage, which speaks to frustration. This frustration is linked to the need

for sexual fantasy in order to maintain a gender identity.

The presence of Mother is almost incidental, although it shows that Norman's wish in this context is to be a woman, a realization which he cannot reconcile except through the murder of women who arouse in him a desire which would challenge that gender identity. In that way, Van Sant is doing a remake of Hitchcock's *Psycho* as informed by the DePalma of *Dressed to Kill*. The remake thus brings with it the weight of every subsequent variation of the motif since the original film.

Van Sant plays some interesting games with color (the curtains and lights of the hotel eerily match Heche's dress) and object association, and, like Hitchcock, plays up the sense of accumulation, the snowball effect as a balance of fatalism and farce. His Norman tries to preserve a childhood that was itself beset by confusion (hence he preserves his attic room, complete with the soft-core magazines of a yearning adolescence). However, due to Van Sant's public persona, such as it is, it is perhaps impossible not to look for increased emphasis on the sexual identity dilemma, for in that way a shot-by-shot remake can become a personal film. Indeed, many responses to the film centered on the nature of the remake phenomenon itself.

Psycho 2

(1983: d. Richard Franklin)

scr. Tom Holland; pr. Hilton A. Green; ph. Dean Cundey; m. Jerry Goldsmith; ed. Andrew London; prod d. John W. Corso; eff. Syd Dutton, Albert Whitlock, Melbourne Arnold; cast. Anthony Perkins, Vera Miles, Meg Tilly, Robert Loggia, Dennis Franz, Hugh Gillin, Claudia Bryar, Robert Alan Browne, Tom Holland; 113m

This long-delayed sequel is effective, as Norman slides back into his old psychosis. He is pronounced sane and released after 22 years in a mental hospital. However, he soon starts to feel the presence of Mother, and bodies accumulate. The killings, however, are the result of an aunt, and exacerbated by Miles, who wants to have Perkins recommitted as a murderer and sends her daughter Tilly in to mislead him and provoke his return to madness. In the end, Norman discovers that the woman he saw as an aunt is his real mother, and responsible for the murders in the film, and kills her. However, he once again answers in her voice: "Mother" is back.

In this intriguing sequel, only tangentially a serial killer film by association, Norman is, until the end, portrayed as a victim. The final murder is the only means left him to break free from victimization, although again it is a repetition of his original trauma and so reinstates the psychosis. He sought to break out of the trap but instead is overwhelmed by it. In the end, he becomes the murderer, and threat to society, that Miles always considers him to be and sought to prove. There is a note of doom and genuine pathos to Perkins' plight here which overwhelms the black comedy.

The film depicts a Norman Bates willing to return to the site of the original trauma, and to escape its influence, with the help of a good doctor. It is therefore an examination of the United States' beloved belief in rehabilitation, the hope that a murderer can reform and overcome his compulsions by interaction with normal people and society. However, this normality is ultimately deceptive, with characters full of hidden agendas and ready to exploit Norman. Norman being Norman, the odds are stacked against him, but he tries desperately to overcome them, although he's ultimately resigned to his fate and the inescapable past: Mother.

Significantly, he is not a sex killer in this film, although he would resume that role in *Psycho 3*. There are sly moments that suggest his tortured sexual identity has not been suppressed, however. For instance, he hesitates over saying the word "bathroom," in recognition of its place as a murder site and a voyeuristically spied-upon place.

That is the real horror: the gradual slide back into monstrous habit, the realization of such, and the final knowing surrender to it. The plot shows how circumstances repeat themselves and that life resolves itself ultimately in the recourse to the habitual manner of dealing with similar circumstance. Trauma is inescapable. Tilly, whom Norman spies upon and intends to befriend, is named Mary, close to Marion — Leigh from the first film — the similarity preying on Norman's mind as he seeks to make sense of renewed conflicting impulses brought on by circumstances and the dictates of others. Norman says that people don't change, and, unfortunately, he is right.

Director Franklin's style is a sly allusion to Hitchcock, playing masterfully on audience expectation and stressing visual entrapment and odd angles. In addition, Holland's witty script surprised many critics. Perkins here develops the childlike vulnerability of Norman more than in the first film. *Psycho 2* was thus considered a worthy sequel and a break from the surrounding slasher boom of the early 1980s. There were inevitably some objections, but Perkins always defended Franklin's approach. Original author Robert Bloch published a book entitled *Psycho 2*, which did not follow the plot of the film — he was not actually asked to contribute to the movie, which may have disappointed some fans. Franklin had previously helmed the thriller *Roadgames*. Screenwriter Holland went on to a career as an accomplished genre director himself.

Psycho 3

(1986: d. Anthony Perkins)

scr. Charles Edward Pogue; pr. Hilton A. Green; ph. Bruce Surtees; m. Carter Burwell; ed. David Blewitt; prod d. Henry Bumstead; cast. Anthony Perkins, Diana Scarwid, Jeff Fahey, Roberta Maxwell; 93m

Perkins himself directed this third film, which takes place shortly after the end of *Psycho 2* and sees Norman disposing of adolescents and infatuated with a fallen nun. In the end the nun dies and Norman stabs his mother's corpse, claiming he is finally free as he is led away by the police, although he cradles her severed hand — he is forever in her grasp.

Despite the engagingly stylized opening, this quickly falls into a succession of knife killings as Norman goes about murdering those women who arouse him. However, he is depicted as the least morally objectionable presence in the movie. In so doing, the film almost makes Norman Bates akin to a teen slayer of the slasher ilk (though with more depth and personality), the very typing *Psycho 2* flirted with but sought to avoid. But it ultimately transcends this mere reduction.

Although he is no longer the near-victim he was in the preceding film, he is still fighting to take control of his own destiny, but losing. Mother by now is an accepted presence, part of his signature, but with little psychological significance beyond that: she represents the homicidal compulsion, whatever the motives behind her existence to begin with. Norman is forever in conflict with himself, knowing that he is forever driven to kill by Mother, and so has a personal dimension and complex motivation the slasher lacks. Thus, Norman balances the slasher persona with the tortured murderer of the likes of *M*, and the film is a hybrid of a past and then currently popular form. That conception of Norman reveals the character's influence on the development of the horror film.

The most novel scene is the variation on the shower scene. Here, Norman, as Mother, pulls back the curtain to reveal the intended victim, a fallen nun, in the bath, having slashed her wrists. She has a hallucination and sees Mother as the Virgin Mary, and thinks she is there to save her. Indeed, Norman saves the woman he has come to kill. He has become the savior he was ironically presented as in the first film (where he inadvertently triggers Leigh's conscience). He can then find some solace in her company, as they are both psychologically troubled, lost souls. They need love, but that need ultimately dooms them, and the nun is killed when she is impaled on the arrow in a statue of Cupid. In that respect, the film is about the search and need for salvation and atonement in a despairing world which does not reward the faith in God. Indeed, such faith is a torment. Despite the comedy, *Psycho 3* is a bleak film — there is no God, only Mother.

Perkins made his debut as director with this film, and it has a consistent, quickly paced sense of the stylized and the grotesque. His job as director and actor were praised, but most felt the script, with minor exceptions, was a letdown. Perkins presented the film at its world premiere at the Seattle International Film festival in June/July of 1986 and said that he felt the franchise "represents the excessiveness of emotions most people feel for their mothers" (Hartl, *film.com*). By then, critical attention towards the series was diminishing, however, and the next installment was on the small screen, although it proved a worthy project.

Psycho 4: The Beginning

(1991: d. Mick Garris)

scr. Joseph Stefano; pr. Les Mayfield, George Zaloom; exec pr. Hilton A. Green; ph. Rodney Charters; m. Graeme Revell, Bernard Herrmann; ed. Charles Bornstein; prod d. Michael Hanan; cast. Anthony Perkins, Henry Thomas,

Olivia Hussey, CCH Pounder, Warren Frost, Donna Mitchell, Thomas Schuster, Sharen Camille; 96m

Original screenwriter Joseph Stefano and star Perkins return for this cable movie prequel. A paranoid Norman Bates recalls his childhood with "Mother," as he talks with a radio talk-show host. The film explores the frustrated Oedipal relations and yearnings between young Norman (Thomas) and his sultry, wanton, teasing and punishing mother (Hussey). Norman fears that he may kill again, and since his new girlfriend is pregnant, he also fears that his legacy will be passed on to the child. He wonders if he should kill his pregnant wife rather than let his homicidal legacy continue. This last is a comment on the horror film franchise phenomenon.

Although novelty value is certainly a factor in this sequel, the undoubted lure is not the study of a young Norman as much as it is a depiction of the mother that would shape a future serial killer. Their relationship, as the source of Norman's dilemma, is presented as a perversion of adolescent yearning via an illicit sexual desire that Norman realizes is wrong but cannot control. He is finally driven by conflicting impulses to matricide in an effort both to punish the provocateur and purge the desires from within himself. It is not simply the incestuous desire, but the mother's conflicting signals regarding it, and her later rejection of her son for an older man, that create the ground for Norman's sexual imagination to turn to violence and murder as a means of control and resolution. Director Garris is obviously fascinated by the theme of mother/son incest, as he would return to it in the Stephen King–scripted *Sleepwalkers*.

The young Norman is a bookish nerd with an adolescent's sexual curiosity about a young girl who enjoys leading him on. He is unsure of how to react to such a provocative, teasing girl, and is torn be-

tween his desire for her and his concern for his mother's health. His mother, also provocatively clothed (with Norman's gaze drawn to her bare skin), is played by Hussey as a childish, spoiled disciplinarian (the perversion of her role as Juliet from the Zeffirelli version of Shakespeare's play)—another tease. She wants to be the only woman in her son's life, with Norman thus forced to part with the object of his desire, but cannot. The clash between keeping the desired object and sending her away results in later years in murder as a means of both—she is gone but stays with him (for potential necrophilic experimentation). Sexual curiosity and denial have also apparently resulted in Norman's tortured sexual identity, which finds expression in transvestitism.

He is in a constant state of emotional and sexual confusion, fueled by his mother (even years later, as he recounts the tale, he must still make excuses for her). From an early age he has fixated on his mother: his father died early and he has perhaps taken his father's place—an Oedipal drama of which he is increasingly aware—as he enters adolescence. At his father's funeral he is more concerned with the way his mother looks than with anything else. In retrospect, he admits that she made him unsure of everything. This is revealed in a scene wherein Norman is in bed with his mother, both nearly naked, and he has an erection (and ejaculation?) and leaves, only to be berated by his mother for being dirty.

She too has desires for her son, and resorts to violent denial in response—so much so that she would prefer to suppress Norman's burgeoning manhood and sexual identity rather than face the consequences of her actions and desires. Thus, she dresses Norman as a girl in an attempt to get rid of his horrid "thing" (the desired and loathed penis). Her attempt to deny and punish his sexuality (inflamed by her taking another lover) is the final straw for

Norman, who in turn has made the desired object into a loathed object. Norman's second murder is thus an older woman who attempts to seduce him — a clear substitute for his mother. His crimes are working their way up to the eventual matricide, an event ultimately too conflicting in consequence for him to interpret cohesively.

Finally, teasing and rejection result in matricide, as Norman poisons his mother. But he needs her presence (as the only one who can provide the illusory cohesion and reconcile his desire/repression complex), so he is driven to taxidermy (itself an act of incestuous necrophilia, and a move towards the consummation of his desire). Ironically, in retrospect, Norman warns the DJ not to take his memories merely as an incest tragedy, although that is clearly where his psychosis is rooted. Garris imbues the scenes of Thomas and Hussey together with a genuinely illicit erotic charge (which he would do again with the mother/ son sex scenario in *Sleepwalkers*).

Norman is a sympathetic character capable of introspection and, later, mature clarity. He is not a complete victim, however, as his choice to kill his mother, however explainable, is still deliberate, cruel (he watches her slowly die, thus voyeuristically eroticizing her death throes) and spiteful. Nevertheless, there is a genuine hope that, as he finally burns the Bates house down, Norman will finally be free of his past.

Stefano's script is an intelligent and clever account of the character's development, and a valuable backstory to the original *Psycho*. It is therefore a more rewarding psychological probe of aberration than the intervening sequels. Indeed, *Psycho 4* can be seen without parts two and three having any real bearing on the proceedings. Garris wisely serves the script and treats Norman's sporadic conversations with a radio DJ as encounters which function as a kind of Brechtian chorus to the

flashbacks, allowing a contemplative distance.

Psychomania

(1963: d. Richard Hilliard)

scr. Robin Miller; pr. Del Tenney; ph. Louis McMahon; ed. Robert Q. Lovett; m. W.L. Holcombe; cast. Lee Philips, Shepperd Strudwick, James Farentino, Carol Bishop, Lorraine Rogers, Sylvia Miles; 90m

A Korean War veteran and martial arts expert becomes a painter of nudes. When local college girls are found dead, victims of an axe murderer, he becomes the principal suspect. He then works with a lawyer to clear his name.

Psychomania is perhaps most noteworthy for its embrace of the depiction of sex murder (of "attractive" young women) as a set piece and accepted structural beat, presumably devised for the titillation of a male audience. Indeed, the setting, mostly at a girls school, although a convenient excuse for female nudity, anticipates the slasher boom of over fifteen years later. The film's construction, alternating sex and murder, also reduces the burgeoning serial killer narrative to the slasher-like succession of sex and violence, with rudimentary characterization of assorted weirdoes tossed into the mix. Women's adolescent sexuality almost summons the predatory male to it.

This came out too soon to be considered part of the returning-vet subgenre, and was the directorial debut of the screenwriter of *The Horror of Party Beach*, another film seeking to equate predatory male violence with youth sexuality and culture. Although perhaps considered tame by today's standards, the amount of nudity in the film caused it to be considered almost pornographic by *Variety,* and the film was dismissed as crude sexploitation. As such, it perhaps reveals the gradual coarsening of the exploitation industry's attitude toward sex and violence.

Psychos in Love

(1987: d. Gorman Bechard)

scr, pr, ph, m, ed. Bechard; cast. Carmine Capobianco, Debi Thibeault, Frank Stewart, Cecilia Wilde, Donna Davidge; 90m

This is a cheap, amateurish effort about two serial killers, one of each gender, who date, reveal themselves to each other, and fall in love. They indulge each other's taste for victims, bringing their "hobby" to their home for necrophilic sessions, as they profess love for each other. They participate in the equivalent of homicidal courtship rituals.

This is an explicit low-budget, pseudo-underground comedy about people who find meaning in murder and death. Such killers are kindred spirits, and in each other they find a validation of their necrophilic perversity: true love. Despite their interest and solace in one another, their life still revolves around their victims and crimes. Their lives are ultimately too ritualized to allow them any alternative, not that they would desire one. They inhabit a world of sleaze, wherein women are objects. The female killer has appropriated the male domain, seeing her male victims as passive objects: she is thus an equal to men on their own terms. The partial equation of heterosexuality and necrophilia finds an echo in, oddly enough, *Matador*.

Both killers reveal the same pettiness. Once they find each other, they talk about why they do it, with a kind of Woody Allen neurosis. They describe it as a hobby, although it is clearly more central to their self-definition than that. Their residence becomes a charnel house, as they can casually make dismemberment jokes and cannibalize body parts.

It starts as a partial mock documentary, with the male killer videotaping himself as he reveals, in pornographic fashion, his sexual obsessions. This graphic frankness is intended as shocking comedy. It is balanced by the first person confessions of the female killer. These scenes function as narrative interruptions and a deliberate distancing technique: one can almost see them as a device akin to that found in *When Harry Met Sally*. The killers' awareness of participating in a documentary anticipates the theme in *Man Bites Dog*. In the end, the killers comment on the script they are reading, a self-aware humor that pre-dates the self-consciousness of Kevin Williamson's scripts (particularly the *Scream* series for Wes Craven).

Psychos in Love's crude humor has some novelty value, along the lines of Paul Bartel (indeed, a frying pan killing alludes to Bartel's superior *Eating Raoul*), although it lacks his bent social satire. Nevertheless, it remains its director's best known film, and one aware of its independent heritage. Bechard was scheduled to work for producer Charles Band until they had a falling out. He has continued to work nonetheless, as a dedicated do-it-yourselfer with a quirky sense of humor, a demented joviality also indebted to H.G. Lewis.

Pure Killjoy

(1998: d. Aaron Downing)

scr. Downing; pr. S.P. Downing, Dale Downing, Lane Soelberg; ph. Keith Smith; m. Eric J. Ray; ed. Michael Matzdorff; prod d. Jan DeHartog; cast. Gregg Rubin, Christina Gulino, Mark Phillips, Brian Frank Carter, Melanie Hall; 87m

In near future Los Angeles, a serial killer is loose. Meanwhile, a stand-up comedian is dumped by his girlfriend. Distraught, he finds solace in wandering the streets, frequenting seedy nightclubs. He has disturbing, vivid nightmares which make him think he has a psychic link to the killer — or may even be the killer himself. He struggles with the realization that he is turned on by these visions of women being murdered, an admission of the inherent dark side to male sexuality.

This blend of film noir and science fiction was screened at the Santa Monica "Dances with Films Festival of the Unknowns" and has had moderate success on the film festival circuit, where some Internet responses have hailed it as a combination of *Eraserhead* and *Barton Fink*. Certainly it has the hallmarks of post-modern allusion common in the avant-garde in its self-consciously claustrophobic atmosphere. It has yet to surface beyond this minimal audience, however, and was unavailable at time of writing. It presumably would have interest for its admission of the potentially destructive and often suppressed role of violence in male sexuality.

The Rain Killer

(1990: d. Ken Stein)

scr. Ray Cunneff; pr. Stein, Rodman Flender; ph. Janusz Kaminski; m. Terry Plumeri; ed. Patrick Rand; prod d. Gary Randall; cast. Ray Sharkey, David Beecroft, Tania Coleridge, Michael Chiklis, Bill LaVallee; 94m

A Los Angeles serial killer targets rich single ladies, all ex–drug addicts, and kills only when it's raining. An alcoholic detective (Sharkey) is reluctantly teamed with an FBI agent to catch the killer. The detective believes the agent is obtrusive. The killer is revealed to be the FBI agent, the ex-husband of one such woman, taking revenge against the "rich cunts"— women who embody the fight for female independence and reformed attitude he despises and resents.

The movie intends to depict a world of sexual and socioeconomic resentment, the residual of the modern film noir. However, it follows the expected procedural pattern, with the revelation of the killer being the FBI agent (and hence profiler) the only real novelty in this cheap, practically style-less movie. Hence, it has only its numerous sex scenes to punctuate the overall mediocrity.

This is one of the most lackluster of the 1990s serial killer films before the reinvigorating boost of *Silence of the Lambs*. It strives for film noir (wet streets, seedy strip bars, saxophone music) but falls back on the simplest of repeat killer motifs, and fails to flesh out the killer's motivations beyond greed and resentment. The romantic subplot is telegraphed well in advance and has faint echoes of Ridley Scott's *Someone to Watch Over Me*, as a poor cop is romanced by a rich woman. Correspondingly, the film is easily dismissed as routine.

Rampage

(1987: d. William Friedkin)

scr. Friedkin; pr. David Salven; ph. Robert Yeoman; m. Ennio Morricone; ed. Jere Huggins; prod d. Buddy Cone; cast. Michael Biehn, Alex McArthur, Nicholas Campbell, Deborah Van Valkenburgh, John Harkins, Art La Fleur, Billy Green Bush, Grace Zabriskie; 92m

A serial killer (modeled on real-life "Sacramento Vampire" Richard Chase) enters people's houses, slaughters the women and children there, mutilates them and consumes their blood. A suspect is soon identified and the killer is apprehended, his basement lair of his mother's house storing Nazi paraphernalia, pornography and body part trophies. A DA who finds his views of the death penalty changing in light of the serial killer's presumed insanity prosecutes him. A trial ensues. However, the killer commits suicide in custody, and the DA is thus freed from facing the consequences of his own beliefs.

This is a solemn examination of the legal and ethical aspects of the serial killer enigma, yet it remains ultimately ambiguous about both the sanity/insanity of such killers and the death penalty as a deserved fate/punishment. The initial reaction when faced with such atrocity is to want to condemn and purify through ritual execution.

The serial killer (Alex McArthur) ready to randomly invade a home and strike out at the inhabitants in *Rampage* (Miramax, 1992).

The DA at first disapproves of the death penalty. The sheer abhorrence of such actions as beyond human understanding and thus the result of an abnormal mind, upon reflection suggests that incarceration, treatment and study may be a better solution, although not as socially cathartic or as satisfying to the victims' relatives. However, when faced with the graphic consequences of such unaccountable monstrousness, the DA holds it heinous enough to warrant the death penalty as justly punitive. The liberal changes his mind when confronted with the horrible truth.

The DA's office, even before the killer is apprehended, say they will seek the death penalty no matter what, the reason given being that that is what the public wants. Is this an ethical compromise? The issue here for Friedkin is prejudgment, how a society has already shaped its view of such killers and how to deal with them. The DA admits, however, that the case has "not guilty, insanity" written all over it. Thus, Friedkin questions what his moral and ethical responsibilities are, and to whom is he accountable. Is the prejudging and execution of such killers in order to placate the public, and victims, real justice? Is it possible to keep one's personal feelings separate from one's professional responsibilities?

The killer has a pathological need for blood, believing that his own is being poisoned. With such a clearly delusional belief, his sanity is the central issue, and whether that in itself is enough to allow him a reprieve from the death penalty, or even responsibility, despite the callous, deliberate, and therefore evil nature of his offenses. It is up to the most reliable and expertly sanctioned of patriarchs—the law enforcers, lawmakers and psychiatrists—to decipher this enigma and interpret it accordingly.

The serial killer (Alex McArthur) is finally imprisoned in *Rampage* (Miramax, 1992).

Yet the killer has a calculated side and is capable of dispassionate murder, and is aware enough of his condition and possible legal fate to say that he needs a doctor and that the police do not understand him. Thus, he is subject to a battery of tests to detect and diagnose a possible abnormality (begging comparison to the plight of the possessed girl in Friedkin's earlier *The Exorcist*), revealing no organic mental illness. However, a subsequent test later does reveal an abnormality. The psychological profile that emerges is also inconclusive: a broken home, watching his stepfather repeatedly abuse his mother, forced hospitalization by his mother (for signs of mental illness) and subsequent resentment.

Friedkin presents this information in a second-hand manner, via psychiatrists after the fact, and so we initially never see or hear the killer talking about himself. In that way, Friedkin again centralizes the question on the means and reliability of the interpreters, and, correspondingly, enforcers, faced with deciphering the facts and making sense of the motive and the madness. Thus, the defense, through legal maneuvering, is able to pressure the prosecution's doctor into a diagnosis (the ultimate scapegoat — paranoid schizophrenia) which fits the legal issues they intend to raise. Friedkin suggests that the elevation of the psychiatric diagnosis to a legal function, which alone has the power over the killer's potential life or death, impugns and contaminates the validity of the diagnosis. There is no absolute standard possible in such cases, and so, perhaps, neither is an objective view possible.

When we finally see the killer talk to a professional, he says he does not want an insanity defense and did the crimes because Satan told him to, by radio. He wanted their blood; killing them was incidental to that ends. The devil told me to: a remarkably common excuse, and ironically, perhaps, the only believable explanation (after all, Friedkin is the director of *The Exorcist*) when science and law are so inconclusive. Indeed, when the killer escapes, he breaks into a church at night, naked, and screeches "Where's the blood?" amidst sound effect distortions which recall *The Exorcist*. It is an act of sacrilegious desecration. Yet there is one incident that suggests that behind it all, despite whatever psychosis may exist, is sexual fantasy — thus, during the trial the killer daydreams that the stenographer is enamored of him.

The ending, however, with the killer committing suicide for no explained reason, is an irony that leaves these issues ultimately unresolved. Did the killer feel remorse? Did he not wish a life in captivity? Is the suicide an indication of his knowledge of the seriousness of the events? Yet, when he escapes earlier, he cannot flee fully and finds another victim before being apprehended. Is he therefore driven by a compulsion to kill? More so than he did in *Cruising*, but without the tantalizing narrative ambiguities, Friedkin treats the killer as an enigma.

Patriarchy here is in a state of disarray, unable to deal with a problem that threatens to undermine its continued functioning. Unlike in *Cruising*, the killer is not fostered by that system but an almost analogous threat to it — an abomination. It is the duty of Patriarchy to rally around the threat. However, it cannot understand, explain or contextualize the serial killer to its satisfactory resolve. Thus, it is ripped apart, reflected in the protagonist's disintegrating marriage and professional insecurity due to his obsession with the case. The killer murders women and children, thus threatening the propagation of the species and undercutting the validity of the Patriarch. Why he does this is ultimately unfathomable.

The film is an examination of a society ill equipped to deal with aberration and its consequences, and thus doomed to perpetual confusion and reaction. Friedkin said of the matter, "It's a failing of psychiatry, which is one of the most insidious influences on the breakdown of the legal system. There is no general consensus on what constitutes insanity" (quoted by Hartl, *film.com*). How can such confusion put forward a means to make such a killer accountable or pay for his crimes? Friedkin's narrative strategy is to deliberately undercut any hint of certainty that may emerge. No solution is possible, except for such killers to do away with themselves and spare society the ethical debate.

The film was initially the property of DEL (DeLaurentiis Films), who gave Friedkin the go ahead to film with a small budget. It was shot in 26 days and with what Friedkin referred to as "no discernable visual style" (Clagett, p. 249) to counter the stylized polish of his previous film, *To Live and Die in LA*. Although the film was first screened at the Boston and Seattle Film Festivals, it went five years unreleased and in litigation, immersed in the studio's bankruptcy. When it was finally released, the critical responses were indifferent, many considering it flat and reminiscent of a bland, functional tele-movie. Friedkin would return to legal issues in his subsequent work in *Jade*, *Twelve Angry Men* and *Rules of Engagement*.

Ravenous

(1998: d. Antonia Bird)

scr. Ted Griffin; pr. Adam Fields, David Heyman; ph. Anthony B. Richmond; prod d. Bryce Perrin; ed. Neil Farrell; m. Michael Nyman, Damon Albarn; cast. Guy Pearce, Robert Carlyle, Jeremy Davies, Jeffrey Jones, John Spencer, Stephen Spinella, Neal McDonagh, David Arquette; 97m

Only incidentally a serial killer film by virtue of its treatment of the nature and appeal of transgression, this is a fascinating combination of vampire and cannibal mythos. In the snowbound Sierra Nevada wilderness, soldiers at a small fort discover a man (Carlyle) with a strange tale of cannibalism. When the soldiers investigate, the stranger kills all but one (Pearce), who escapes to the fort — but only after resorting to cannibalism also. There he tells all but is disbelieved, and is further frightened when the cannibal reappears as the new commanding officer. Once human flesh is tasted, an insatiable hunger for it takes over those affected, who are driven to kill and eat in order to achieve the same high.

Bird, who had essayed sexual difference and social transgression in the homosexual longing of *Priest*, again tackles the theme of transgression. Cannibalism invigorates the killer but makes the curious (and experimental) protagonist feel guilty, as if it's a form of sexual deviance, a lust which the protagonist seeks to disavow. Indeed, in the end, killer and protagonist are bound together in a deadly embrace.

In that, cannibalism is allied to a sex crime, an addictive, insatiable experience which must be continued for self-definition, indeed self-actualization. By cannibalizing, the killer becomes an idealized figure, his physical health restored — in the process becoming a supernatural figure, the Native American Indian myth of the Wendigo. According to this myth, the eater possesses the victim's past and assumes his strength. This sense of a victim forever being a part of the killer is common to many serial killers who ingest their trophies and are driven to kill again to achieve the same "virility" (as the cannibal Carlyle describes the aftereffects of killing and consumption, adding a sexual dimension).

Once again, this is not a serial killer film but rather a clever generic hybrid of horror and Western, playing on the true-life story of the Donner party, whose themes intersect serial killer pathology on a metaphorical level. Indeed, part of the film's appeal is that the cannibalism can be taken (or stretched) as a metaphor for many things, among them homicidal sexual deviance. It's a sly criticism of the principals of Manifest Destiny, and indeed cultural appropriation, as potentially permitting a clique of such killers to selectively consume the country's pioneers and feed off its foundation (a rare superimposition of serial killer themes onto the Western).

However, the film's tone is one of sly horror-comedy. Hence, the opening quote from Nietzsche, "He that fights with monsters should look to it that he himself does not become a monster" (also appropriated for the title of FBI profiler-pioneer Robert Ressler's book *Whoever Fights Monsters*), is followed by a quote from anonymous: "Eat me." The movie's wintry, isolated setting makes it a treatment of the inhospitability of the human soul when faced with the seemingly inescapable. Faced with despair at the end of a quest for rejuvenation, invigoration and virility, all that remains is to consume each other. New life and pleasure can be achieved only by consuming and usurping that of another.

The thematically rich film premiered at the Sundance Film Festival but was generally released to an indifferent, even hostile (though curious), reception. Those not repulsed by the subject matter and graphic gore were bemused by the sly comedy and impressed by the wintry tone (and Slovakian settings). Bird, not surprisingly considering the way meat is depicted in the film (though not quite as slyly off-putting as that in the cannibal-comedy *Parents*), is a self-described vegetarian.

Reason to Die

(1989: d. Tim Spring)

cast. Wings Hauser, Arnold Vosloo, Anneline Kriel, Liam Cundill; 86m

A tough bounty hunter (Hauser) searches for a razor-using serial killer of prostitutes. He is so determined he is prepared to use his own girlfriend as a decoy; thus, his morality is dubious and arguably corrupted by his pursuit of the killer.

Hauser is much better suited to being the villain of the piece (and he played a serial killer in *Pale Blood*). However, it is perhaps better to consider this film in the light of the obsessed near-vigilantes he would play in *Deadly Force* and *The Art of Dying*, as this type and theme attracts him as both actor and sometime director. In *Reason to Die* he once again examines the personal consequences of such an obsessive pursuit. However, this film has the lesser reputation of those mentioned.

Redball

(1999: d. Jon Hewitt)

scr. Hewitt; pr. Philip L. Parslow; ed. Cindy Clarkson; cst des. Lisa Collins; cast. Belinda McClory, John Brumpton, Frank Magree, Peter Docker, Anthea David, Neil Pigot; 88m

A disillusioned police officer is assigned to a case of child sex murders committed by "Mr. Creep." Progressively disgusted by the abuses of power and widespread corruption she sees (ranging from sloppiness to violent rape), and even condones, on the police force, even by those she considers friends, she is further shocked when the evidence points to the killer being a cop. Meanwhile, her associates on vice come across information and a possible suspect, whom she beats up in interrogation in order to get information. Her partner abandons her when another cop (his former partner, it turns out) is implicated. When it seems that the killer cop will go free, she confronts him. He is about to beat her when her partner shoots him, but not before the killer has implicated her partner. She aims her pistol at her own partner, who is also ready to shoot back.

The film's cynicism is set from the opening scene of two Melbourne policemen finding a dead body floating in the Yarra river and then calling in the plain clothes detectives, who feel that if they wait long enough, the body will float into another jurisdiction and be someone else's problem. This is turned into a running joke, as the body turns up at various places throughout the film, and is pushed aside or ignored by superior officers who force their uniformed subordinates to look the other way, thus perpetuating an attitude which fosters corruption and indifference. This portrayal of the Australian police force won the film few allies.

The protagonist works from a barely controlled fury, regulated by alcohol and disillusionment. She is a troubled person, and far from the feminist ideal in a world of overbearing male psychosis, as she lives forever in reaction to that definition of authority. Indeed, she works to uphold the Patriarchy that secretly condones the horrors she investigates and is rife with violence and corruption. Is she the purifier, the answer to this Hell? Is her anger with the killer and her implicated partner out of outrage at such crimes, or frustration at the personal betrayal of her pride and trust?

Its rawness was considered comparable to early Abel Ferrara, and equally confronting as a portrait of bleak depravity in the police force as was *Bad Lieutenant*. However, the rapid editing and hand-held, close-in work searches for the stylized authenticity of TV's *Homicide: Life on the Street* (referred to in the homicide department shot of a white board with a name in red erased and rewritten in black — a punctuating mark in the TV show) and the intensity of *Romper Stomper* (which a policeman rents from a video store).

The title is police slang for a high priority, high-pressure case. Yet no one has any sense of outrage at the crimes except the protagonist. Her partner supplies illegal pornography to video stores, such is the hypocrisy of the police force and the total disregard for the sexual exploitation all around them. Unlike in Ferrara's films, there is little hope of even an illusory redemption; society is too immersed in the moral quagmire, and even the police are driven to kill each other, partially as a matter of personal pride.

The police's corruption and brutal treatment of suspects is the epitome of the vile, tough Aussie code of machismo; though it's no longer limited to men alone, as female officers are equally implicated (corrupted) by their servitude to the male-dominated police force. However, the female police psychologist stands up for the protagonist but is ultimately overruled by a male authority who considers her a threat.

The protagonist has not given in completely to the stress and temptations of the job that has corrupted her fellows. Power corrupts, inevitably eroding the sense of social responsibility that should go with it. The film is therefore presented as a succession of scenes, each section given its own title, which reveal an endemic, systematic corruption as it exposes a netherworld of sexual exploitation (ironically condoned and practiced by the police). In this world the serial killer police officer represents an untouchable nadir, the inevitable end of such abuse and moral indifference to suffering.

Yet throughout the film is a questioning of such corruption as perhaps a necessary evil and a matter of unavoidable degrees. Thus, the protagonist, who knows her buddies are corrupt, must draw the line somewhere and attempt to end the slide. She realizes she has become tainted by association, and seeks to extricate herself by killing the killer and those associated with him: to escape the abyss before being consumed by it; thus she is always under psychiatric review.

Redball was shot on found locations over ten days and weekends on digital video by independent exploitation filmmaker Hewitt (who had applied for grant money to make the film and been refused, and so self-financed it). It was then transferred to film for theatrical release, preserving the gritty, low-budget hand-held look desired. There were some favorable reviews, notably from David Stratton, but it failed to obtain a prolonged run and seems destined to become a cult film (as was the previous *Bloodlust*), as Hewitt's career as "Australia's last cinematic outlaw" (Free, *Film Ink*, pp. 26–28) continues to evolve.

Hewitt wanted TV actress McClory for the role all along, and claims that he wrote it for her and that she resembled a young Helen Mirren (then in the English *Prime Suspect* tele-movies popular on Australian television). She agreed to participate, considering his work a vital part of the Australian underground. Her participation reportedly attracted other professionals to the low-budget, independent project.

The Reflecting Skin

(1991: d. Philip Ridley)

scr. Ridley; pr. Dominic Anciano, Ray Burdis; ph. Dick Pope; m. Nick Bicat; ed. Scott Thomas; art d. Rick Roberts; cast. Viggo Mortensen, Lindsay Duncan, Jeremy Cooper, Sheila Moore, Duncan Fraser, David Longworth, Robert Koons, David Bloom; 95m

An eight-year-old farm boy with a rich imagination is convinced that a recently widowed neighbor lady is a vampire and responsible for the murder of several young local boys. He is determined to apprehend the apparent serial killer stalking and killing his playmates. The police suspect his father, so torn over his own homosexuality that he emasculates himself. The boy's brother, however, falls for the lady, and the boy is determined to expose her as the killer, even if tragedy should result.

The film charts the growing boy's perception of the creepy, almost otherworldly menace of the adult world around him. It also questions his conflicted response to his own preadolescent sexuality (thus making the film thematically comparable to *Afraid of the Dark*). Beneath the outside beauty lies inward corruption and destructive forces, and the characters are all grotesques (Hartl, *film.com*). The protagonist's confused awareness is a necessary rite of passage, a loss of innocence that creates fear as a means of confrontation — recognition beyond projection. Ridley thus delights in contrasting beautiful exteriors with graphic horror.

This is Ridley's directorial debut. He was best known previously as a painter and playwright, and for scripting Peter Medak's hit *The Krays*. On the basis of his debut, he had several English critics comparing his work to the weirdness of David Lynch. *The Reflecting Skin* is also considered to challenge the romantic idealization of childhood, and can be contrasted to such treatments as *Lady in White*. It is still generally thought of as a bizarre curiosity, more popular on the festival scene when initially released than subsequently.

Relative Fear

(1994: d. George Mihalka)

scr. Kurt Wimmer; pr. Tom Berry, Stefan Wodoslawsky; ph. Rodney Gibbons; m. Marty Simon; ed. Jon Webster; prod d. Patricia Christie; cast. Darlanne Fluegel, Martin Neufeld, M. Emmet Walsh, Matthew Dupuis, James Brolin, Denise Crosby; 89m

Police suspect that a very young autistic child, obsessed with "the Crime Channel," is responsible for a series of murders, to the mother's dismay. However, it is discovered that the child's real mother is a now-imprisoned homicidal maniac, partner to a supposedly dead serial killer (the boy's father), and that the babies were switched due to a hospital mix-up. The mother then goes in search of her real son. She discovers that the serial killer father is still alive and has been living in their house, and is responsible for the deaths. The child shoots the bad father.

With its baby-switching premise, this film clearly examines the theme of whether such homicidal criminality is hereditary. This is established clearly at the outset when the new mom cradles her presumed son, only to be scratched by the baby. Born bad? From then on, parental expectation and reality diverge, as the child seems strange and, to the mother, other than her own, although she still loves him. It stresses the bond between mother and son as a telling form of identification and possible psychosis when the parent does not receive the reaction expected. Indeed, when faced with such disappointment, the parent may act by disavowing the child. However, this theme is not really confronted in that the mother discovers the child is not hers after all.

The film carefully establishes the potential that the boy may indeed already be a killer, or will grow into one. He is distant and wrapped in his own world much of the time. He is tormented by the other kids and may be harboring deep-seated revenge fantasies. This seeks to demonstrate infantile sexuality as rooted in a retributive power fantasy — hence, the budding killer retreats to fantasy and the assertion of it as a means of dominance over others.

Is the child's fascination with gory crime reenactment a sign of his true heredity? Does he imitate what he sees on TV? Is it possible that an incipient criminal mind would latch onto depictions of violence and incorporate these into his budding fantasies? Thus, his friend finds a father's gun and gives it to the kid, saying, "We could blow someone away, just like on TV." These issues are unsubtle and topical, and almost undercut by the ending.

On another level, the film is a look at a hopeful family's attempts at cohesion when threatened with an abnormal child, and the corresponding blow to their expectations. This theme is common enough in tele-movies, and is here logically turned into a thriller. However, the ending, which has the parents discover their true child after all, who meets expectations and so validates the mother's dissatisfaction with the other, puts the blame squarely on the monstrous patriarch.

Hence, the child's real father, a serial killer, has been looking after his offspring with the intention of having him grow up to embrace his homicidal legacy, killing those who he considers have been bothering his kid and standing in his way. He represents the monstrous father, a product of foster homes, who considers mothers a dime a dozen, and the real bond to be that between father and son. The son must shoot the father, the act of patricide being an act of self-expression that purges the homicidal legacy from within. However,

the final shot of the murderous child, now adopted, playing war with the real son suggests that he has been imprinted by this cathartic violence and is perhaps doomed after all. This ambiguity means the issue of heredity may win out (after all, the couple's real son is the bright, talented reflection of his intelligent parents).

This is a careful meditation not only on heredity, but also on the social expectations and conventions that frame it. It is further evidence of Mihalka maturing as a minor genre figure (*My Bloody Valentine*, *Psychic*, and *The Blue Man*) in the Joseph Ruben tradition. This Canadian thriller is indeed knowingly comparable to Ruben's *The Good Son* (itself a tangential serial killer movie), in that it deals with a homicidal child. As such, it can also be compared to *The Bad Seed* and *The Omen* (which also had a mother doubting that a child was hers).

Relentless

(1989: d. William Lustig)

scr. Jack T. Robinson; pr. Howard Smith; ph. James Lemmo; m. Jay Chattaway; ed. David Kern; prod d. Gene Abel; cast. Judd Nelson, Robert Loggia, Leo Rossi, Meg Foster, Patrick O'Brien; 93m

A displaced New York cop (Rossi) finds himself in LA with a new partner, old-timer Loggia, where he must search for a serial killer (Nelson) dubbed "The Sunset Slayer" by the voracious media. The reluctant partners' respect for each other grows as the killer perfects his ritual of murder and becomes interested in the police investigating him.

The killer represents a generation without a voice, and thus one struggling against Patriarchy, a society that fascinates and repulses him. He hears his dead father's voice when he looks into the mirror — the voice of a brutal policeman obsessed with disciplining the child. In that,

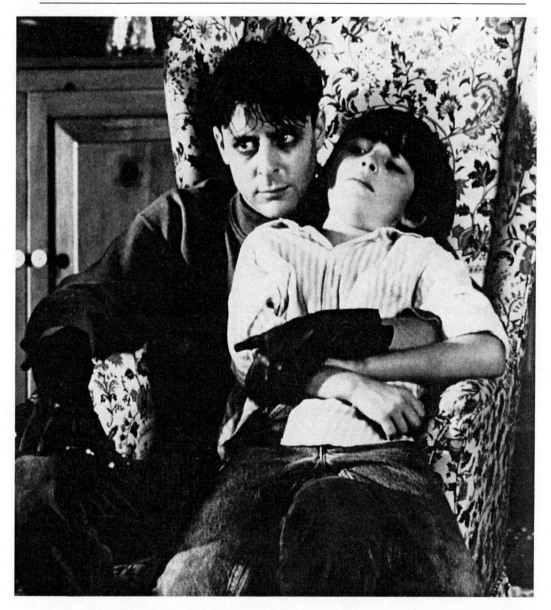

A serial killer (Judd Nelson) holds a detective's son (Brendan Ryan) hostage in order to facilitate a confrontation in *Relentless* (New Line, 1989).

the film recalls *Cruising*, but whereas the son in *Cruising* sought to continue Patriarchy's hatred and so live up to the father's legacy, Nelson here kills both to challenge that authority and to inherit its dysfunction. He even has a shrine to his dead father (just as the protagonist in Lustig's earlier *Maniac* had a shrine to his dead mother). Nelson's flashbacks serve as a lesson in the perversion of Patriarchy's legacy, as once again the killer's formative years are characterized by his love/hate relationship to a domineering parent, with murder the result of the inability to reconcile his emotional reactions.

His method reflects this fascination/repulsion complex. When he feels the urge to murder, he selects a victim from the phone book with a name similar to his, phones them to establish they are at home, drops by, and forces them to participate in their own deaths. He attaches to the body the phone book page with their name underlined and with a taunting message for the police. These messages speak of his need to confront the authority the police represent (hence he writes, "Why are you taking so long?"), and a need to be punitively disciplined once again by the father, specifically by the good father as represented by Rossi, the profiler. His murders therefore are a deliberate challenge to the law of the father (he even kills men, suggesting a possibly repressed and tortuous bisexuality — an insecure, conflicted identity). They are the work of the bad son, perhaps needing to be caught (indeed, when finally caught he has a note which reads "thank you"). The profiler and detective are the good fathers, with the responsibility to chastise the offspring, and Rossi's home life is intercut into the procedural investigation as a means of validating his socially sanctioned function.

Rossi is the determined figure whose experience with previous serial killer cases (the New York City Son of Sam) separates him from conventional police and elevates him into the profiler category. He is thus in a line of descent from the figure in *Manhunter*, and in the sequels he would be successively affected by his psychological obsession with such killers. His recourse and moral balance are in his procedural regimen. However, his obsession affects him personally, and he must violate such procedure to get the job done, in so doing becoming a virtual vigilante figure. He proves his own self worth by stopping the killer.

Director Lustig (*Maniac* and the *Maniac Cop* series) here returned to serial killer terrain, with former brat-packer Judd Nelson a standout as one of the first of the so-called Generation X serial killers. However, he is a long way from the yuppie

wannabe of *Love and Human Remains* or the full-blown yuppie of *American Psycho*. After the success of *Maniac Cop*, Lustig was approached by exploitation producers Shapiro/Glickenhaus (*Slaughter of the Innocents*) to do another film. He selected a script by Phil Alden Robinson (who had completed the hit *Field of Dreams*), retitled it *Relentless* and took it to the producers. The subsequent film was successful enough to spawn three sequels, though without Lustig. It is, in effect, the first franchise based on the profiler figure as opposed to the serial killer.

Although it contains graphic murders (stabbing, strangling with piano wire, gunshots), Lustig's visual style is more nondescript and functional than expected. Critical responses were surprised by Nelson (at the end of his brat pack days) but indifferent to the film. Nevertheless, it boosted the minor career of Rossi, who returned for the diminished sequels.

Relentless 2

(1991: d. Michael Schroeder)

scr. Mark Sevi; pr. Lisa M. Hansen; exec pr. Paul Hertzberg; ph. Jamie Thompson; ed. Alan Baumgarten; m. Paul F. Antonelli, David Wheatley; cast. Ray Sharkey, Leo Rossi, Meg Foster, Miles O'Keefe; 90m

Rossi, estranged from his family (and son, who carries over the trauma from the first film), must now face a new serial killer who disembowels his victims. Rossi's increasingly erratic and disturbed behavior leads to increased personal problems and draws the attention of FBI agent Sharkey, who knows more about the case than Rossi. Indeed, Rossi begins to wonder if indeed it is a serial killer, and starts questioning the case.

The profiler is increasingly psychologically unbalanced by his work and the constant exposure to such abhorrent crime. Yet he has a need to pursue the dark side, although perhaps failing to realize the appeal and fascination it has for him. His pursuit of such killers is a means of avoiding introspection, projecting his own dysfunction onto that of the killer. Yet he knows enough to have to be drawn into such investigations, almost against his will — a trait explored in the remaining sequels. Here Rossi is paradoxically haunted by memories of his wife in jeopardy from Nelson in the first film but still neglects her, perhaps unable to respond to her in any other terms except as memory.

The killer kills both genders and is oddly, jokingly, homo-eroticized — the camera follows two transvestites leaving prison, one of them remarks "nice ass," and we cut to a shot of the killer's bare buttocks as he is about to take an ice bath (regulating his own hyper desires?). This subtext is not followed through, as the film reveals the killer's real motivations are beyond the sexual (although that does not deny his obvious pleasure in murder). However, in that he kills both genders, rare for a serial killer, one can see a tormented bisexuality at work (in a nod to Nelson in the first film too). However, these leads are effectively jettisoned by the final revelation of the killer.

Whatever the killer's motives, his pleasure in murder is beyond the functional. He is revealed to be a Soviet Special Forces officer, murdering people in FBI witness protection, giving only the appearance of a serial killer. Indeed, it is Rossi's knowledge of serial killer pathology that allows him to intuit the difference (a development of the protagonist's empathetic abilities in *Manhunter*). Thus, he wants a psychological profile, but the FBI, keen to protect the truth, do not. This plot device, of a killer covering up the real reason for his crimes by disguising them as serial murders, is also found in *Blow Out* and *The Glimmer Man*.

Relentless 3

(1993: d. James Lemmo)

scr. Lemmo; pr. Lisa Hansen, Paul Hertzberg; ph. Jacques Haitkin; ed. Nina Gilberti; prod d. Richard Hummel; cast. Leo Rossi, Felton Perry, Catherine Paolone, Jack Knight; 84m

A necrophilic serial killer (William Forsythe) sends his female victims' body parts through the mail to police. He is set to go after Rossi's lady friend. Rossi, however, does not want to be personally involved in the investigation and agrees only to act as a consultant (i.e. here he makes the full transition from investigator to profiler in the genre hierarchy). However, he cannot maintain this distance when it seems the killer is someone he has arrested before and has been staging the murders to provoke Rossi's involvement.

This sequel reflects the formula of the *Relentless* series, concentrating on cat-and-mouse games between cop and early-identified killer instead of any mystery. The cop, of course, takes each new case personally, his life otherwise increasingly empty. He pretends to loathe the material at hand, but it is the only meaning he has left in his life, a fact acknowledged by the killer. Critic John Stanley feels that the series increasingly turned towards a kind of "nihilistic inevitability" (p. 423) to its repetitive structures. Rossi's status as a consultant seems designed to make him a representative of the serial killer expert profilers like former FBI agents John Douglas and Robert Ressler, the former especially, who worked as a consultant after leaving the force.

Time is devoted to studying the killer at home, probing his dissatisfaction with his wife, whom he criticizes for gaining weight and staying home in bed, and for no longer catering or appealing to his sexual fantasies of what a woman should be: desirable object. His murders are, again, a form of sexual empowerment enabling him to be the fantasy dominator not permitted him in real life. A cross-dresser (a gratuitous revelation), he is revealed to have escaped from a hospital for the criminally insane due to lax security, a clear message that such serial killers should be in prison.

The film is an improvement over the second part due to its efficient, back-to-basics blend of procedural and killer character portrait. It draws out the parallel fates between killer and profiler (both ostracized from their home life) doomed to forever interact. Both are dissatisfied individuals who rally around murder for their self-definition.

Relentless 4

(1994: d. Oley Sassone)

scr. Mark Sevi; pr. Russell D. Markowitz, Rossi, Catalaine Knell; ph. Russ Brandt; m. Terry Plumeri; prod d. Jeannie M. Lomma; cast. Leo Rossi, Famke Janssen, Colleen Coffey, John Scott Clough, Christopher Pettiet

Rossi (now also a co-producer) again has to stop a serial killer. This time he also has to contend with two women, his new partner and an additional police psychologist/profiler, concerned over his interpretation of taking the law into his own hands. The profiler is now slowly becoming the vigilante. The killer this time targets women who have had near-death experiences, apparently rectifying the error of their survival. The investigation leads to a psychiatrist (a self-proclaimed Thanatosian) who may be hiding some information about the killer. Rossi develops a romantic interest in her, and also tries to manipulate her into giving him the relevant information.

This is considered a step down in quality, and is the last of the series to date. With a common link between the victims, it suggests more of a gimmick-killer scenario than before, and the overloading of investigators suggests the profiler forever faced with a hostile reception from other agencies and even other specialists. In that way it recourses to the standard "my case" conflicts that recur in the genre. Its most interesting aspect is its stated acknowledgement that each of the main characters defines themselves in relation to death — always a subtext in the genre, but particularly in this franchise.

The ritual nature of the serial killer's crimes almost has an occult significance. Indeed, the killer is a religious lunatic who suffers auditory hallucinations. Clearly mentally ill, he epitomizes the threat to "normal" humankind. He is obsessed with death and the associated cultural practices linked to it, and is murdering in imitation of such practices. A diagnosed paranoid schizophrenic (this is a banal recourse at this stage), he is the doctor's half brother, and she has been driven by family loyalty to protect him, even though this leads to their deaths. The doctor too studies death, dedicating her life to such. The profiler too dedicates his life to fighting the agents of death, represented by the killer and those in collusion with the killer (clearly meant to represent both an inhumanity and a life's apposite). It is as though their closeness to death may enable them to cheat fate and attain a kind of transcendent immortality, a state the killer in particular envies.

There is a subgenre of films in which a killer who may be one of them individually targets the patients in a group therapy session. Including the likes of *Schizoid*, *Phobia* and the exceptional *Color of Night*, these are generally not serial killer films in that the victims are not chosen at random. However, the subgenre has also spawned the intriguing *Trail of a Serial Killer*, which explores the premise more provocatively than here.

Resurrection

(1999: d. Russell Mulcahy)

scr. Brad Mirman; stry. Mirman, Christopher Lambert; pr. Howard Baldwin, Patrick D. Choi, Lambert, Nile Niami; ph. Jonathan Freeman; m. Jim McGrath; ed. Gordon McClellan; prod d. Tim Boyd; cast. Christopher Lambert, Leland Orser, David Cronenberg, Barbara Tyson; 108m

This follows the thematic and narrative patterns set in motion by *Seven* and *The Bone Collector* in particular. A Chicago detective (Lambert), newly arrived from New Orleans, investigates a serial killer who cuts off body parts from his victims (leaving them to sanguinate, and writing messages in their blood—"he's coming"). We learn that the killer takes the body parts home and puts them together in the belief that he can create the body of a new Christ that will come to life at Easter. The cop's troubled relationship to his wife stems from the death of his son; all are factors weighing in on his religious faith or lack thereof.

Lambert, a loner partnered by Orser (who was in *Seven* and who played the killer in *The Bone Collector*, and thus becomes an interesting intertextual link), goes through the usual scenes: consultation with superiors, the morgue scene, not talking about the case with an increasingly estranged wife. As with the protagonist of *Absence of the Good* (which also, as did *Postmortem*, tackled the theme of ontological despair), dreams and memories of his lost son torment him. He blames himself for the son's death and feels that this has sapped his role as patriarch. He projects this anxiety onto his work, feeling that if he can somehow stop this killer he may be absolved from responsibility for the death, and possibly even restore his lost faith. Like Morgan Freeman in *Seven*, he studies the case in an effort to get at the motivation and decipher the Biblical references deliberately left by the killer for the police.

This has become a dominant theme since the late 1990s, which has resulted in increasingly vivid production design of the crime scenes, and the centrality of forensic investigation.

To his dismay, his superior brings in an FBI profiler to give his opinion of the killer, which at first offers little to go on. Reluctantly, the profiler becomes part of the investigative team. It emerges that, like in *Seven*, the killer is preaching and, if not caught, will finish his sequence and disappear uncaught (although ultimately he needs to be identified in order to take the credit for his sermons).

The killer's need to be remembered, and to prove himself superior to his lessors, proves his undoing. Unlike in *Seven*, the killer is finally denied his triumph, and the protagonist's faith is healed as he saves a baby boy from death, making amends for his guilt over the death of his own son: God has given him another chance, and he has proved his worth. In that respect, the killer was the personification of the protagonist's despair, and the film a search for a restorative Christian faith. The killer was literally rebuilding his Christ, just as the protagonist's obsessive pursuit of the killer was a means of rebuilding personal faith. The protagonist becomes the true savior of life, a Christian patriarch sanctioned by God.

The presence of the FBI agent is the film's major departure from the narrative structure of *Seven*, which it otherwise follows closely. Indeed, the film is that rare one (in a possibly increasing trend) in which the profiler is revealed to be the killer (a plot line in *The Psychic* also), or, more accurately in this case, the killer poses as a profiler. In that way, acknowledging the adversarial closeness between killer and profiler, the killer can guide the investigation to his will. Once his deception is uncovered, it becomes a race against time to gather enough evidence to charge him with the crimes.

This may be derivative, but it is undeniably stylish. Australian director Mulcahy is an early graduate of music videos who started directing in the early 1980s (and who worked with star Lambert previously on *Highlander*) in a brooding MTV manner — rain-soaked, shadowy, and full of somber, earthen colors to frame its story of despair. This film received a theatrical release in Europe, but was shown only on HBO cable in the United States. It is an intelligent, compelling work which has been dismissed due to its similarity to better known films, although it makes much of its intertextuality.

The Return of Dracula

(1958: d. Paul Landres)

scr. Pat Fielder; pr. Jules V. Levy, Arthur Gardner; ph. Jack MacKenzie; m. Gerald Fried; ed. Sherman Rose; art d. James Vance; cast. Francis Lederer, Norma Eberhardt, Ray Stricklyn, Greta Granstedt, Virginia Vincent, John Wengraf; 77m

Although this is a vampire film, it is included here due to its similarity to the earlier *Shadow of a Doubt*. Dracula kills an artist and assumes his identity to travel to the United States and Carleton, a small town in southern California. There he poses as the distant relative of a California family, the Mayberrys, and seeks new victims. The Mayberrys' daughter is infatuated with him; though, following her friend's death, she is entranced by his hypnotic control. Meanwhile, an Immigration Department investigator on behalf of vampire hunters doggedly pursues the vampire. Dracula is alerted to their presence and tries to turn the girl into an undead vampire, but her boyfriend aids her and Dracula fails into a pit, impaled on a stake.

This is an early instance of the movement to equate the vampire with the sexual predator and serial killer, most curious for its reactionary views of sexual matura-

tion and sanctioned punishment. It starts with the expected Gothic atmosphere, and then introduces its vampire into a recognizable, everyday reality and examines the process of adjustment as the Old World vampire segues into the new surroundings. Although he can metamorphose into a wolf (only the end result is shown), for the most part he is suave and disarming, a charmer. Thus the film overtly reconciles the vampire and werewolf into the one serial killer figure.

The vampire, however, is from Old World Europe and so represents the threat of foreign contamination more than a domestic problem: the film thus recalling pre-war isolationist themes. The vampire hunter has the unassailable and indisputable responsibility to purify America from such contamination. And the contamination is in the form of sexual awakening. Vampirism is equated to sexual expression, and the vampire hunters are the agents of civilization and repression. If the vampire hunter is the proto-profiler, then Patriarchy's sanction means repression, suppression and punishment. Though this is a common subtext, particularly in the Hammer horrors, here it is accepted without question, in the end condoning the actions of the mob as they drive a stake through a blind girl whose sight has been restored through sex with the vampire. She is punished for sexual maturity. Innocence must be preserved, and the vampire/serial killer is the symbol of true Evil, for he would seek to destroy Innocence (or even aid in its transition to Experience). There is no hint of any male character, except perhaps for the adolescent boyfriend (also hypnotized by Dracula in part — an acknowledgement of adolescent bisexuality), having any sexual desire, for all such desire is tainted.

The Return of Dracula is also an interesting addition to vampire lore in that a blind girl gains sight when she becomes a vampire, almost as if this were a form of sexual liberation, implying the victim's complicity. Indeed, this blind girl welcomes Dracula into her bed as a lover, and becomes by implication a mature woman in the end and a servant of the sexual male. Vampirism is equated with sexual awakening, and the vampire is clearly an egotistical sexual predator attracted to innocence and seeking to destroy it. Unlike most vampire films, there is no obvious sign of a bite or other such penetration: the vampire's seductive conquest is an openly sexual one, removed of the need for blood. Indeed, Dracula's biological need for blood is downplayed and only briefly referred to as part of his attempt to seduce the protagonist. He is able to use the young protagonist's infatuation with his slick sexuality to manipulate and control her. And that is the basis of his power kick — he wants to dominate all around him.

The American family he comes into is missing a father figure. Thus, it is as a substitute father/lover that Dracula is most threatening to America. Every man must join together to remove this dangerous presence, as it is such sexual desire which would erode conventional society. The sexual predator is the ultimate evil transgressor, and all sexuality is dangerous and corruptive of an inherent, American, goodness.

The black and white film has a note of color at the end. The audience is allowed to see the flow of blood as a wooden stake is driven through the blind girl's heart by the vampire hunters — repressed males, sanctioned by the Church and the police, communally punishing her for her sexual desires and mature awakening into womanhood.

Return of the Family Man

(1989: d. John Murlowski)

scr. John Fox, Murlowski; pr. Johan Van Rooyen, Kari Johnson; ed. Steve Sandrock; m.

Colin Shapiro, Barry Bekker; cast. Ron Smerczak, Liam Cundill, Terence Reis, Michelle Constant; 87m

This South African–produced effort is about an escaped serial killer, the eponymous "Family Man" (who designed the Star Wars defense system, the script suggests and then drops) who butchered entire families. He returns to his house, where the corpses of a castigated family are in a walled-up room, and sets about the killing of the teens who have mistakenly rented the place as a vacation spot to flee an earlier shooting in which they have been involved.

The killer, like many slashers, is depicted as a kind of eternal child, appearing in a perpetual daze, who merely wants to go home and return to his family, even if they are all mostly decomposed corpses. However, after showing the killer having massacred another family and thus returning to a pattern, the film abruptly changes tack and moves toward standard slasher formula, with the escaped killer, in the course of one day/night, systematically eliminating the teenagers who have invaded his home crime scene. Thus, it is hardly a serial killer film at all (no profiler, no investigation), with only the sole novelty value of being filmed in South Africa, though set in the United States.

The Ripper

(1986: d. Christopher Lewis)

scr. Bill Groves; pr. Linda Lewis; spec eff. Tom Savini; cast. Wade Tower, Tom Savini, Mona Van Pernis, Randall White, Andrea Adams; 90m

A ring once belonging to Mary Kelly, victim of Jack the Ripper, has supernatural powers that may transform a college professor (who lectures on Famous Crimes on Film) into the reincarnation of the infamous killer — or at least prompts visions of the graphic disembowelment of women.

But are these visions attractive or even seductive?

This is a regional production from Tulsa, Oklahoma. The director also made the film *Revenge* the same year, about killer cults, and seems to have an affinity for the notion of murder as an inherited tradition of sorts. The only novelty here is Tom Savini's reportedly moustache-twirling performance as the Ripper. It can be considered a more graphic Ripper legacy film than *Bridge Across Time*. It flirts with the possession motif, in the process equating the Ripper with an absolute Evil forging a presence on Earth.

The Ripper

(1997: d. Janet Meyers)

scr. Robert Rodat; pr. Allison Lyon Segan; ph. Martin McGrath; m. Mason K. Daring; ed. Elba Sanchez-Short; prod d. Tim Ferrier; cast. Patrick Bergin, Gabrielle Anwar, Samuel West, Michael York, Adam Couper, Essie Davis; 120m

In this Australian/US tele-movie filmed in Melbourne, an Inspector (Bergin) hunts for Jack the Ripper in 1888 London. His search leads to Prince Eddie, the oldest son of the Prince of Wales, and Queen Victoria's grandson. This film explores a part of Ripper lore in that it posits the Prince as the killer of prostitutes in revenge for having contracted venereal disease. It premiered on the Starz! cable channel on December 6, 1997.

The murderer's identity is fairly evident from the start, and the film actually concentrates on systematically stripping the detective's admiration for the upper classes and their manners, clubs and social practices. Thus, the Inspector is introduced fixing his tie by looking at a chart that gives the proper way to tie one's tie for each occasion. Although he comes from the working class the killer preys on, he aspires to the gentlemanly elegance and superficial sophistication of the aristocracy. His involvement in the case allows him an opportunity to fraternize with the social elite, but his respect for this elite is gradually eroded the more he learns of the pettiness of mannered society and indeed the monstrousness that it would protect. Such a class considers him an inferior, and it is only when he threatens to expose the killer's identity that they proclaim him as "one of us now," a phrase that cynically brings to mind the chant in *Freaks*. Indeed, the upper classmen are arrogant, hypocritical parasites who sexually exploit and despise the underclass they should protect.

The aristocrats are not free from the ravages of a sexual disease commonly equated with the lower class, however, as the Inspector discovers when he obtains a list of privileged patients from a VD clinic. By so revealing the snobbery, racism and stagnancy of the upper class, Bergin no longer feels proud to be amongst Royalty. Indeed, he feels almost ashamed at having so longed for this. Instead, he returns to his roots and develops an interest in a young woman (a former prostitute who witnessed the killer and eventually identifies him). By saving her, he feels that he can redeem himself in her eyes and dissociate himself from the class that would condemn her to certain death. Thus, he gives her the money that had been given to him as a reward for his services to the crown, enabling her to go to America. Finally fed up with the corruption that is England, he too leaves for America.

The film suggests that this Royal Ripper, though ravaged by the mental degeneracy associated with syphilis, wanted to be caught, and specifically selected this Inspector to achieve those ends. He is obsessed with formal cleanliness and cannot stand the taint of dirt that has infected him. Thus he seeks revenge on the women that have contaminated him, cutting out their sexual obscenity in a demented frenzy. He even rationalizes this as performing a social service and ridding the proper society of its filthy underclass. His contamination is for him a social humiliation, an assault on his pride as a God-ordained Royal. It is a shame that demands vengeance. He cannot stand even a minor humiliation, and so burns alive the horse that threw him from its back. In the end, although intending to kill the girl, he recognizes the aberration that he has become and lets himself be arrested by Bergin. He is then taken away to a private sanitarium. Bergin nonetheless has a begrudging respect for the man, although he has lost such for the system he represents, a system that would maintain difference and privilege as its intended aims.

The film contrasts the rituals of high and low society, and revels in the depiction of a future King of England — a "gentleman of quality"— as a vile murderer. This scathing indictment of the English Monarchy as diseased, perverse, corrupt and self-serving is hardly surprising when considering that Australia at the time was involved in a debate and referendum regarding the country's separation from the Monarchy and declaration of itself as a Republic. In a referendum two years later, Australians rejected the move to Republicanism, a move that can't have pleased the Australian makers of *The Ripper*.

Ripper Man

(1996: d. Phil Sears)

scr. Sears; pr. Sanford Hampton, Andy Howard, Tony Mizrahi, Aaron Norris, Valerie Norris, Tom Steinmetz; ph. Blake T. Evans; m. Jim Ervin; ed. Peter Lonsdale; cast. Mike Norris, Timothy Bottoms, Robert F. Lyons, Charles Napier, Bruce Locke, Carey Scott

A stranger (Bottoms) asks a former-policeman-turned-hypnotist to bring out, under hypnosis, the man's alter-ego, George Chapman, here held as the real Jack the Ripper. The stranger soon becomes a ser-

ial killer of women, and the hypnotist attempts to track him down before more bodies turn up.

A possible subtext for this effort is the presence of Jack the Ripper as a symbol for the abhorrent part of the collective unconscious, that which may propel the id. Such destructiveness when aroused in one can never be fully suppressed, resurfacing under duress or when the situation presents itself. This curious subtext infiltrates many of the Ripper films which seek to present the Ripper as a constant force through the century — timeless in his everyman anonymity, and the Father of the modern sex murderer. The killer thus represents a rival Patriarchy founded on the liberation of the id as opposed to the repression deemed necessary by civilization.

Roadgames

(1982: d. Richard Franklin)

scr. Everett DeRoche; pr. Barbi Taylor, Richard Franklin; ph. Vincent Monton; m. Brian May; ed. Edward McQuinn-Mason; cast. Stacy Keach, Jamie Lee Curtis, Marion Edward, Grant Page, Thaddeus Smith, Bill Stacey, Stephen Millichamp; 101m

Somewhere on the Australian outback roads, and consistently evading police capture, is a murderer (strangulation and dismemberment) of female hitchhikers (a plot hook also found in another Australian serial killer film, *End Play*), who drives around in a van. A truck driver (Keach) who has linked the van's presence to the crimes wants to catch the killer himself, picks up a hitchhiker (Curtis) whose presence draws the killer out. The killer kidnaps Curtis, and the truck driver must tail him, forcing a confrontation and saving the hiker.

Keach's main companion is his unusually adept mind. On long trips he tries to keep busy by playing mind games — counting cars and imagining what their

A long distance trucker (Stacy Keach) inspects the meat he carries in his trailer, under suspicion that a serial killer may have entered there in *Roadgames* (Avco Embassy, 1980).

inhabitants' personalities are like. He is intrigued by the van driver's sexual escapades, and intuits, through deductive observation, that he is responsible for the murders. We see the man is the killer who murders his naked victims when aroused: homicide as intercourse. Fueled by news reports of the crimes, Keach is increasingly drawn to the killer who prowls the lonely highways as he does.

The film is a leisurely-paced examination of the loneliness of the profession, and a sly thriller. Keach is intrigued by the killer's psychology, and, with Curtis, plays amateur profiler, trying to intuit the killer's mind and method. He is increasingly fixated on the van's elusive driver, a killer who provides the lonely Keach with a challenge to his intellect. He thus enters into a game of presence and absence on the road (memories of *Duel*), as the killer is aware of Keach's at-first half-hearted pursuit of him, and may have even added a skinned, disemboweled torso to Keach's truckload of meat. This note is left ambiguous, as it could be a product of Keach's admittedly active imagination, which propels him into contact with the killer primarily in order for Keach to validate his intellect. In the end, he proves himself right.

The film's jigsaw puzzle structure — of the accumulation of small details in order to arrive at a larger picture — stresses the need for a sharp intellect to survive, a theme that had infiltrated Franklin's cult hit *Patrick*. *Roadgames* is not interested in procedural, instead being concerned with imaginative reconstruction and deductive reasoning. On a self-reflexive note, Keach's reading material consists of *Hitchcock's Mystery Magazine*, and his observatory pursuit of the killer takes its impetus in part from the Hitchcock protagonist's inquisitiveness. And like the fate of many Hitchcock protagonists, Keach realizes that he has been implicated as the killer, and that the mind game has turned suddenly more serious.

Keach's attraction to Curtis is due to her equally sharp mind, something she finds just as fascinating about him. Although she has a formal education and he is self-taught, they develop a mutual respect and even a flirtation as they discuss the killer. However, while Keach is studious from a distance, Curtis is more confrontational, which eventually lands her in trouble, although it finally turns Keach from a man of thought and words into a man of decisive action (as an adjunct to his mental prowess). Intellectual excitement thus gradually becomes physical excitement and invigoration for a man whose job avoids confrontation with people, yet who is driven by a desire to communicate with others. In the end, he joins Curtis hitchhiking, while a cleaning lady finds a severed head in his truck — had the killer left that torso after all?

The interesting casting, regarding not only Curtis' fame as a post–*Halloween* scream queen, but memories of Keach's role in *The Killer Inside Me*, adds to the intertextual tension. It can thus be considered an intriguing, even fascinating, Australianization of the American thriller. It has been called Hitchcockian, and indeed it was on the basis of this film that Australian-born, US-trained (University of Southern California) thriller director Franklin (the cult *Patrick*, *Link* and *F/X*) next went on to helm the much anticipated *Psycho II*.

Franklin represents a transition in Australian exploitation towards mainstream acceptability. He provides a bridge from the likes of Terry Bourke and Brian Trenchard-Smith to the style-conscious Russell Mulcahy.

Roots of Evil

(1991: d. Gary Graver)

scr. Adam Berg; pr. Sidney Niekerk; m. Duane Sciacqua; cast. Alex Cord, Deanna Lund, Delia Sheppard, Charles Dierkop, Jillian Kesner; 95m

This is a remake of a hardcore porno movie, *Trinity Brown*. Two detectives (Cord and Lund) are assigned to the case of a serial killer of Hollywood prostitutes and strippers. They get involved in underworld drug slayings and have to find the related killers in that case also.

This is played off as broad comedy, and verges on the self-parodic, with the killer a cliched bad son tormented by memories of his mother rejecting him: the imprinting event that drives his resentment of women. It has a callous humor, hence the scene where a whore gives the killer the finger (the bird), so he cuts it off to teach her a lesson. The film thus indulges the same kind of casual misogyny which affects such exploitation, with women portrayed as cock-teasing arrogant bitches who deserve what they get, a theme in Fulci's *New York Ripper* especially. The killer phones his mom after each kill to confess and torment. This comedic undertone bespeaks of a bleak world of social despair where cop and killer are comparable (both are alcoholics). Criminality is everywhere, feeding off itself, with the killer an ineffectual male (he runs away when he can't overpower) to whom murder achieves a sexual power he sorely wants.

This is an action video with much soft-core sex (as usual from exploitation figure Graver, who has considerably less ambition even than most low-budget toilers possess). Graver's work here, with its emphasis on titillation and action, suggests comparison to David DeCoteau's straight action work. Indeed, the film features a brief appearance by future scream queen Brinke Stevens, who would feature regularly in DeCoteau's films. In that *Roots of Evil* does not enter into an analysis of the eroticization of murder, it avoids tackling the genre's themes in favor of conventional action and murder mayhem, and is thus easily dismissable. This film was once advertised as an upcoming Michael Pare project, but the nominal star backed out, to be replaced by Reb Brown, who also left the production to be replaced by Cord.

The Rosary Murders

(1987: d. Fred Walton)

scr. Elmore Leonard, Walton; pr. Samuel Goldwyn; ph. David Golia; m. Bobby Laurel, Don Sebetsky; ed. Sam Vitale; prod d. W. Stewart Campbell; cast. Donald Sutherland, Charles Durning, Josef Sommer, Belinda Bauer; 105m

A priest (Sutherland) tries to help solve a series of murders of priests and nuns. Naturally, he hears the killer during confession and is torn whether or not to share this knowledge with the police. He struggles with doubt and the narrow-minded opposition of the Church superiors. He is finally confronted with perhaps the ultimate act of unforgivable Church hypocrisy.

Although the material recalls, of course, *I Confess*, and the premise was better treated in *Prayer for the Dying*, *The Rosary Murders* still has a certain perennial hook. Walton has proved a capable, if nondescript, director, having helmed *When a Stranger Calls* (which also starred Durning) before returning to unheralded mediocrity. Sadly, *Rosary* is a case of one film that could have been so much more provocative.

This is not really a serial killer film, although it tangentially treats a revenge killer, one who ironically judges those that he considers moral and sexual hypocrites. He punishes them for their sanctioning of sexual abuse, and is thus a self-appointed deliverer. The killer was practicing incest with his daughter, confessed this to a priest and was absolved. He now feels guilt over her subsequent fate and his own pedophilia, and has focused his anger on the priest who could so easily forgive the sin he feels so conflicted about. The killer would deny his sexuality and put the blame elsewhere — the crimes being the indirect result of sexual perversion, although they are not in themselves sex crimes. *Rosary* is included in this book only for its undertones and as a point of comparison (see below), although technically it doesn't fit.

The Rosary Murders was based on a novel by an ex-priest. However, it stops short of implicating church authority as more than accessories to murder, whose easy forgiveness could just as easily have justified a pedophile's continued career. Thus, it lacks the anti-authoritarian subversiveness of Walker/McGillivray's *House of Mortal Sin*, which sought to probe the moral hypocrisy as deep-seated psychosis (as opposed to the almost indifference which affects Durning here). Nevertheless, *Rosary* is intriguing for the way in which Catholic iconography becomes a murder weapon, again a theme better treated by Pete Walker.

Rough Draft

(1997: d. Joshua Wallace) aka *Diary of a Serial Killer*

scr. Jennifer Badham; pr. Kandice King, Lance King; ph. Keith L. Smith; m. Stephan Edwards; ed. Christopher Koefoed; prod d. Ladislav Willieim; cast. Gary Busey, Arnold Vosloo, Michael Madsen, Julia Campbell, Reno Wilson, David Michaels

An out-of-work journalist (Busey) witnesses a crime, and contacts the murderer, a slick, lounge lizard–type (possibly bisexual) serial killer of women (Vosloo, who would become known as the villain in the Stephen Sommers *Mummy* movies) intending to write a feature article on his activities. They come to a mutual arrangement, and the journalist follows the killer at work, even interviewing him for a profile, in the process becoming complicit in sex murder. Meanwhile, a dedicated police officer (Madsen) is on the case.

After the amusing opening sequence, which sees Busey in drag (as he was in *Under Siege*) in a dedication to the pursuit of authenticity in his stories, the film is primarily concerned with the corruption of the journalistic code of ethics. Busey considers it important to immerse oneself in the material he writes about, as if such immersion would access a greater, purer truth.

The killer sees in Busey a similarity to himself, as he admits that the real thrill is not in the killing, but immersion in the pursuit of said end. The killer and the journalist-as-profiler are of the same ilk, and both are guilty of the perpetuation and

glorification of the serial killer in popular culture. Both have lost their morality in their obsession. Although Busey stops the killer and writes the book in the end, his guilt is never in doubt, and it is ironic that he seems not to be ultimately troubled by that fact. He has done away with his conscience in the pursuit of "truth" and "authenticity."

Despite the subject matter, surprisingly little is made of the killer's sexuality (besides revealing that he has a gay lover). Although the resentment of women may be a factor, and murder a demonstration of his loathing of the heterosexual process, he is comparatively unmotivated. Sexual aberration remains the undeveloped subtext here, with characterization thus affected by its absence. *Rough Draft* is sadly unprovocative.

The Ruling Class

(1972: d. Peter Medak)

scr. Peter Barnes; play. Barnes; pr. Jules Buck, Jack Hawkins; ph. Ken Hodges; m. John Cameron; cast. Peter O'Toole, Harry Andrews, Arthur Lowe, Alastair Sim, Coral Browne, Michael Bryant; 155m

A titled member of the British aristocracy hangs himself while dressed in a tutu. His successor (O'Toole) is a paranoid schizophrenic who thinks he is Jesus Christ. His greedy relatives wish to have him certified insane and take over the estate, but a doctor (who isn't English and so looked down upon by the snobs) believes he can cure O'Toole. In a radical experiment, he brings in another delusional patient who also thinks he is Jesus Christ and lets the two of them fight it out. O'Toole loses and seems to respond to his own identity. He passes a sanity test, to the consternation of his relatives. However, he again retreats into delusion and believes himself to be Jack the Ripper. Setting about a secret career as a sex murderer, he is accepted into high society, who suspect nothing is wrong, even taking his place in the House of Lords where his views of a return to sterner punishment and discipline make him a spokesperson.

Long but often hilarious, this farce doubles as the study of a man who so resents his own identity that he would reject it and seek a substitute at all costs. However, he has no moral core and can segue from Jesus to the Ripper, acknowledging the contradiction but unhampered by it. It is ironic that as the Ripper he is accepted and thought cured, but as Christ he is dismissed as a mere lunatic, albeit a highly privileged lunatic. Thus, the film exposes the emptiness and superficiality of the English upper classes, who often boast of England's proud heritage, whereas in reality that heritage is epitomized by the legacy of Jack the Ripper, whose views are still endorsed by the ruling class.

One can feel sympathy for O'Toole as Christ and his views of the liberty of mind and body, until the film explores the underside of this liberty as fostering a sex murderer. Indeed, amidst the comedy and outrage is a penetrating look at the folly and horror of the schizophrenic thought process. As Christ, he searches for the love and acceptance of all, but is forced to realize that it is a duplicitous, loveless world, and that he has been betrayed rather than blessed by God.

Perhaps that recognition sets his mind on an alternate path that leads to another kind of libertine, one fit for a "proper England." As a killer, he is ready to assume the proper duties of his class and uphold their hypocritical moral righteousness. He thus turns against even those who have shown care for him. No longer thinking he is one with God, and so no longer a Good Shepherd, he must be its opposite, a man from Hell, sent to destroy. There is no middle ground, nor is there any compromise for him. He retreats into a fantasy of sexual purification, intent on restoring moral discipline and fear onto a lax populace. Where once he wanted a kiss from his aunt, he now kills her. The forces of repression project desire outwards, making one seek to punish the object rather than the true internal source.

The film cleverly undercuts any preceding sympathy, stranding the viewer in the recognition of the abhorrence of both the ruling class and even of human nature itself. It is a Comedy of Despair.

Sacrifice

(2000: d. Mark L. Lester)

scr. Randall Frakes; nvl. Mitchell Smith; pr. Dana Dubovsky, Mark L. Lester; ph. Bob Steadman; ed. Christopher Roth; prod d. Peter Kanter; m. Steve Edwards; cast. Michael Madsen, Bokeem Woodbine, Jamie Luner, Joshua Leonard; 92m

A convicted bank robber (and murderer, though this is justified — in the film's terms— as a mercy killing) learns that his daughter has been viciously raped and murdered by a serial killer known as "Sweetwater" (who enjoys slashing his victims' throats). Madsen breaks out of FBI custody while being transported to prison. He wants to find the killer, in order to exact vengeance and vigilante justice. Although he is pursued by an FBI agent (Woodbine), the con is assisted by an ex–call girl, now a gangster's moll. Madsen discovers that all the victims, including his daughter, had had abortions. The killer is revealed to be the abortionist.

Madsen takes it upon himself to investigate the killer, and in effect becomes the profiler, poring over the police files (which he obtains from a corrupt detective) in order to ascertain motive. However, this subtext, like most in the film, is mentioned as a simple plot function and then dropped before it can become a theme. Consequently, we never get into

Madsen's motivations beyond revenge for the daughter he lost. She seems to represent the ideal life that once was his but is now gone. Perhaps he turned to crime in order to better his circumstances and is now being punished. It is never clear whether he pursues the killer in the hope of some redemption or merely out of a vindictive honor code among criminals, which the serial killer is removed from.

The killer targeting women who have had abortions also infiltrated *Criminal Law*, although *Sacrifice* represents the extreme side of the raging anti-abortion debate: the murderers are murdered. Thus, the killer is set up as doubly enigmatic, as a symbolic pro-life advocate who is hypocritically perverted into a murderer. Such is the possible perversion of benevolence and justice. Indeed, in that regard, both protagonist and killer are similar in their self-justified vigilante actions. However, these promising subtexts are undercut by the film's resolution.

The killer is revealed to be a psychotic abortionist, a woman who was raped at thirteen by her own brother and who aborted her own fetus only to hear the dead infant's voice. Later, she kills because motherhood is sacred, and she is reuniting the mothers with the souls of the dead babies to ease the babies' suffering. The killer's clearly psychotic rationale (including occult rituals involving severing her victims' breasts to bury with the aborted fetuses—so they can forever feed, one assumes) effectively downplays any confrontation with the pro-choice movement, a topical theme in US society, in favor of mad killer melodramatics.

This is yet another tele-movie, this time from a director whose career has forever straddled exploitation and the mainstream (*Class of 1984*, *Firestarter*, *Commando*). The plot hook of a convict breaking out of custody is the opposite of *The Expert*, where the protagonist sought to break into prison to punish the serial offender. Director Lester's better works have a sardonic view of justice and the workings of an unjust society that demands vigilante action as a necessary purification of internal corruption. However, the vigilante action is itself morally aligned to an abuse of power.

Sadisterotica

(1967: d. Jess Franco) aka *Red Lips*

scr. Franco, G.G. Hoffmann; pr. Pier A. Caminnecci, Adrian Hoven; ph. Jorge Herrero; cast. Janine Reynaud, Rossana Yanni, Adrian Hoven, Michel Lemoine, Chris Howland, Alexander Engel, Jess Franco; 92 (79)m

A sexually independent female private investigator, who marks her cases and presence with the imprint of her lipstick coated lips (sealing the territory with a kiss), is partnered by an equally "liberated" assistant. Together they investigate a serial killer artist who abducts women and paints them while his thuggish assistant, a kind of ape-man, murders them. The artist then pours plaster over the bodies to preserve them forever as trophies, *Bucket of Blood* and *House of Wax*–style.

The killer is a villain in the traditions of the Poe adaptations of the late 1930s through the 1950s. Like most of Franco's killers, he is a passionate man whose love for and appreciation of female beauty has been corrupted by his inherently sadistic desires. This sadism is, for him, innately voyeuristic: thus, it is his ape-man assistant who actually kills, while he watches, his aggressive gaze willing the events to happen without his direct participation. Like the killer of *Peeping Tom*, he is obsessed with the look of fear on women and seeks to artistically capture the moment. Once again, the Romantic is corrupted by the Sadean, with voyeuristic pleasure the agent of such perversion. The male gaze is inherently sadistic and so violates its object.

The film borders on soft-core titillation, with the two central women often revealingly dressed. It features a lighter, more-sprightly pace than usual for Franco, and is a comedy. However, counter to expectations, perhaps, it is the two women — intelligent, unashamed, funny and sexy — who dominate the film. They clearly love life, unlike the death-obsessed killer (perhaps representative of all males) who seeks to snuff out such liberation (although he is fascinated by it and seeks to codify it in terms of male desire).

Perhaps such is the reaction of a male society challenged by the open display of female sexuality. Indeed, the male characters in the film are either hopelessly ridiculous or monstrous, as if male sexuality imprisons one in a death-obsession. Correspondingly, feminist liberation is a potentially purifying force in the world, an emergent force that would seem to have as its new responsibility the task of patrolling and regulating the destructive male desire that would suppress it. In that way the film is oddly progressive, a positive response to the social changes of the 1960s, which sees feminism as a desirable challenge to a repressive, stagnant male authority.

This was the first of a three-film deal Franco had with German production company Aquila. He followed this with a sequel, *Kiss Me Monster*, and then with *Necronomicon*, which some consider the prolific director's best film. All three starred Reynaud. Franco next moved on to more explicitly sexually violent (and pornographic) films, never again achieving the hopeful lightness of touch seen in this film and its sequel.

Sanctimony

(2000: d. Uwe Boll)

scr. Boll; pr. Paul Colichman; ph. Mathias Neumann; ed. David M. Richardson; art d. Tyler Jones; exec pr. Stephen Jarchow, James Shav-ick; cast. Casper Van Dien, Eric Roberts, Michael Pare, Jennifer Rubin, David Millbern, Catherine Oxenberg; 86m

In a small, anonymous American town (a kind of anywhere United States), a serial killer removes his victims' eyes, ears and tongues. He is apparently obsessed with the proverb "See no evil, hear no evil, speak no evil," and so is labeled the "Monkey Maker" by police and press. The two detectives on the case (Parc, Rubin) have to face added pressure from higher up (Roberts). A handsome, intelligent yuppie stockbroker (Van Dien), soon to be on a TV talk show, comes in for questioning as a potential witness. His arrogant demeanor makes the investigators suspicious. The detectives seek to prove him the killer before the FBI take over the case (and steal the glory). He *is* the serial killer, and has taken to that in an effort to prove his intellectual superiority and satisfy his taste for sensation and a challenge. Sex murder is a game for him.

This follows on from the soulless yuppie killer of *American Psycho*, and suggests a contemporary existence so deprived of meaning, interpersonal communication and experience that those who materially have everything find expression and sensation (and thus invigoration and fulfillment) in homicide. It is almost the only spiritual act in their lives. It is their relation to death and murder that allows adversaries to compete and thus find meaning in their adversarial relationship. Serial murder is therefore a knowing lifestyle choice, a means of personal empowerment devoid of any true compulsion or root cause in mental illness — an increasingly prominent motif, and a developmental counterpart to the society-is-responsible theme of anti–Capitalist interpretations of the genre.

The credit sequence, graphic mutilation murders, brooding style, urban Inferno and religious theme are all indebted to *Seven*. Like the killer in that seminal film, Van Dien here works to a finite pattern, almost as if serial killing were a temporary project rather than a defining ritual. Aptly, Pare remarks that there is nothing like a serial killer with a little bit of personality, a comment on the genre's search for bizarre, grotesque, stylized offenders with more of a gimmick to their pathology than rape murder. It is nevertheless a spoken understanding between police officers that the killer will only stop when apprehended, despite the pattern hinting otherwise. This comment sets up he film's self-referential narrative strategy as a comment on the genre's current status. Its awareness of the history and codes of the serial killer film make it clear that it is indeed treating such as a distinct genre.

The killer represents the bankrupt soul of the soured, material American Dream. Like the killer in *American Psycho*, but without even that killer's conscience, Van Dien's actions are a combination of the conditioned response to Capitalist commodification, and a desire for new sensations—to feel alive. He perceives any doubt, guilt or emotion as a sign of weakness. Paradoxically, he can rationalize his crimes as a justified indulgence earned by his success as an American superman. His lifestyle of elegant, self-indulgent excess speaks to the issue of over-control and its repercussions. This is paralleled to Pare's middle-class existence in a partial attempt to delineate the class structure within contemporary American society.

Monetary success has brought with it the desperate quest for new experiences. Thus, the killer journeys to an underground club and watches the death of a young woman during the production of a snuff movie. The drive for sensation has turned murder into a spectator sport for an elite and discerning clientele, a theme also covered in *8MM*. It even recalls the private sex club in *Eyes Wide Shut*. With

Van Dien's fantasies and desires thus excited by the performance, he goes home and forcibly rapes his girlfriend. He only enjoys it when it hurts her, and so when her outrage turns to enjoyment (itself a morally questionable development), he stops. In a highly aroused state, he then goes out in search of someone to kill, the act that alone presumably brings him to orgasm. He has violent fantasies about every woman he sees, including the female police officer, and is driven to see them become reality.

The detective admits a fascination for such normal-seeming killers, a curiosity about why they do what they do. Therein lies a dominant theme, the interrelationship between curiosity and free will (as modulated by the conscience) as a shared bond between profiler and killer. The latter willingly gives in to curiosity, and the former studies such by proxy (and is therefore dependent on the killer for self-definition). Sex murder in this way has become in the modern world a quasi-religious ritual form of individual and collective definition for those who qualify themselves in reaction to such incidences. It is the central, defining moment of an entire subculture.

The killer acknowledges the interpersonal link between detective and killer and enters into a "quid pro quo" arrangement with the female officer (in homage to *Silence of the Lambs*). He admits that he delights in the game of constant one-upmanship with his pursuers, as initiated by the murders. The crimes are his means of practicing a kind of enslavement of the everyday in service to his needs, a process of further self-aggrandizement. On a daytime talk show he says that rape-and-pillage is a justifiable and necessary reaction to any institutionalized corporate practice, a theme that dates back as far as *Monsieur Verdoux*. Finally he snaps, resenting even his so-called equals in status, and turns from a serial killer into a spree killer, murdering his friends at a party until Pare guns him down. He has become an unceasing murder-machine: Capitalism consuming itself.

This is a German/United States co-production from a director better known for comedy.

The Satan Killer

(1993: d. Stephen Calamari) aka *Death Penalty*

scr. Edward Benton, James Brandauer; pr. Ross Borden, Joel Silverman; ph. Cotter Ward; m. Jim Attebury; cast. Stephen Sayre, Billy Franklin, James Westbrook, Belinda Borden, Cindy Healy; 90m

A widowed, alcoholic policeman whose fiancée is murdered becomes a vigilante obsessed with revenge. He teams with an elderly private eye. Together they hunt for the killer. This murderer is a jovial man, pleased with himself and his work, who has taken to riding a Harley Davidson motorcycle and murdering desirable, bikini-clad women. He is thus punishing them for their open sexuality, and allowing for the filmmakers to exploit the depiction of sex murder.

There is much graphic violence towards women featured in this reportedly cheap and inept film set in Norfolk, Virginia. Supposedly incoherent, this revenge-driven melodrama flirts with the serial killer figure and the theme of the perversion of authority, as responsible men have no option but to take the law into their own hands. Of course, these are standard themes of the vigilante vs. serial killer subgenre, and are more provocatively and effectively dealt with in the collective genre appearances of Wings Hauser. This was unavailable at time of writing.

Satan Returns

(1996: d. Allan Lam) aka *The Devil 666; 666 Satan Rebirth*

pr. Wong Jing; chor. Donnie Yen; cast. Chingamy Yau, Donnie Yen, Francis Ng, Yuen King Tan, Ivy Leung, Si Man; 90m

This thriller was advertised as Hong Kong's answer to *Seven*. A male police detective and a female police psychologist investigate a serial killer. This religious psychopath targets women born on the 6th of June, then crucifies and surgically disembowels his victims according to cult practice. It seems the psychologist is the next intended victim of a killer revealed to be a disciple of Satan in search of the reincarnation of Satan's daughter on Earth. The killer is caught and intends to get the detective to believe that his female partner is the devil's daughter, which she may believe herself.

The film segues from serial killer thriller to supernatural demonic horror in the latter stages. Interestingly, the profiler's abilities and psychological insights are linked to supernatural abilities, which threaten to overwhelm her personality. This develops a neat encapsulation of the character type's split origins in science and superstition.

The film explores the lady-killer mentality in Hong Kong society. In a nod to the popularity of Category Ill films (Hong Kong sex films), the killer is obsessed with women as sexual objects. His lair is riddled with cut-out pictures of women, and his paintings of women and snakes. He has equated women with Evil, and has been corrupted by such a warped Christianity within his tortured soul. He must punish women for arousing desire in him, a desire he is so intent to purge that he has resorted to religious delusion to validate his killings as necessary ritual. Sex murder would allow him to become the spiritual ideal. In a neat collision of East and West, such murder would permit an ideal enlightenment and the death of Christ.

Seven symbols are drawn on the bodies, according to the Lamb in Revelations—

a realization which prompts one man to joke that this lamb is a sequel to that in *Silence of the Lambs*, revealing the film's knowledge of its American genre counterparts. In another intertextual joke, a cop, on learning of the seven qualities the killer intends to achieve through murder — authority, wealth, power, wisdom, honor, glory, and responsibility to the killed lamb — remarks that the killer should watch *Seven*. These references create an odd, knowing distance from the film itself.

This can be considered an attempt to blend Christian mythology (à la *The Omen* and *Seven*) with the demands of the Hong Kong kung-fu action film (à la John Woo) and possessed-evil-woman supernatural fantasy subject matter. The result is an unusual hybrid which also feeds into the apocalyptic, millennial messages of the likes of the later *End of Days* and *Stigmata*. The Hong Kong cinema had previously intersected the serial killer film in *Pale Blood*.

Savage Intruder

(1973: d. Donald Wolfe)

scr, pr. Wolfe; ph. John A. Morrill; m. Stu Phillips; ed. Hatwig Deeb; prod d. Norman Houle; cast. Miriam Hopkins, John David Garfield, Gale Sondergaard, Florence Lake; 90 (85)m

This odd, critically neglected retake on the classic *Sunset Boulevard* has an aging ex–movie star living in an increasingly dilapidated mansion. Various eccentrics attend her. She hires a male nurse to tend to her needs, but he soon proves to be a sadistic psycho who enjoys dismembering his victims as he kills them.

This is perhaps intended as a psychodrama, with much concentrating on the relationship between the two central characters. A now rarely screened film, it can also be considered a development of the themes in *Night Must Fall* in the context of the decaying memories of old Hollywood types and even formulas. The old become targets of a new youth (which they perhaps perpetually seek to recapture), as what starts out as seductive becomes menacing and dangerous. This has disappeared from release and was correspondingly unavailable. It is included here as evidence of the 1970s concern for potentially antiheroic psychopaths, although the film itself has no reputation.

Schizo

(1977: d. Pete Walker)

scr. David McGillivray; pr. Walker; ph. Peter Jessop; m. Stanley Myers; ed. Alan Brett; art d. Chris Burke; cast. Lynne Frederick, John Leyton, Stephanie Beacham, John Fraser, Jack Watson, Queenie Watts, John McEnery, Colin Jeavons; 109m

An old man, recently released from prison, is obsessed with a young figure skater; and when she gets married, a string of violent deaths follow as he stalks her. A twist ending has her revealed to be a multiple-personality killer, and the man only wishes to confront her with the realization of what she has done, including the murder of her own mother — the crime the man had been imprisoned for. She kills him and resumes a new mastery over men.

If one can excuse the misinformation about schizophrenia (another equation of it with multiple personality disorder and violent behavior), one can see the film as an attempt to restore the faith in Patriarchy that had been eroded in the previous Pete Walker/David McGillivray collaborations (see *Frightmare* and *House of Mortal Sin*). Hence, it starts out as a thriller about a demented father figure intent on doing harm to a young woman he seems to sexually obsess about. But by the end, it proves that this patriarch has been wrongly imprisoned and is merely trying to prevent a murderer from going undetected.

Although he ultimately fails at his task, the intent is there.

His journey is a confrontation with a past, even a rendezvous with fate, as it were. The narrative built around the two characters' near confrontations moves with certain inevitability towards its final "surprise" ending. The two characters are thus repeatedly paralleled. He is haunted by memories of an event that the woman has suppressed as too terrible, except for the homicidal side of her personality, which kills to avoid detection. (Although this motivation means the film is ultimately outside the serial killer field, the preceding implication of a male sex killer plays on its conventions and expectations deliberately, and it is therefore included here.) Both are driven by an inner hostility: he with a desire to confront the truth and she to avoid it. He is from a lower socioeconomic order than she is, though it is hinted that part of the reason for her marriage is that it enables her upward mobility, suggesting a more cunning presence and the first hint of ulterior motives.

Indeed, the narrative serves to provide clues that undermine the protagonist's innocence and psychological well-being. She hears voices in a supermarket, and has memory lapses and even two names. Knowing of her distress, she talks to a psychiatrist, who proves at first as ineffectual as usual in Pete Walker films, not clueing in to her disturbance. Throughout the film she is surrounded by Patriarchy, and it is possible that her homicidal personality (emerging perhaps to punish her mother for sex with a dominant man) is a deliberate challenge to an authority that would suppress women. Finally, the homicidal personality takes over (is allowed to?) as the true maturation of a woman and the end of a self-deceptive innocence. The woman is the real predator, and will kill to avoid discovery and the subsequent suppression deemed necessary by Patriarchy.

The film has a title and shower scene reminiscent of Hitchcock's *Psycho*, and its brash marketing reminds one of William Castle (some showings promised free smelling salts for affected viewers). Indeed, Walker had earlier drawn comparisons to Hitchcock for his work on *Die Screaming Marianne*. *Schizo* is the least provocative of the Walker/McGillivray collaborations which invigorated British alternative horror in the 1970s. Significantly, McGillivray was brought in as a script doctor on this project. The duo have done much better, though the final scene of the little girl holding the knife anticipates the murderous boy in *Halloween*.

Schramm

(1994: d. Jorg Buttgereit)

scr. Buttgereit, Franz Rodenkirchen; pr. Buttgereit, Manfred O. Jelinski; ph. Jelinski; m. Max Mueller, Mutter, Gundula Schmitz; ed. Buttgereit, Rodenkirchen; cast. Florian Koerner von Gustorf, Monika M., Micha Brendel, Xavier Schwarzenberger, Michael Romahn; 75m

This film observes a serial killer's acts and private psychosexual torments without judgment. The "lipstick killer," so called because he adds lipstick to his victims' lips after prolonged necrophilic intercourse, is in operation. Although the film only depicts two murders, these are shown repeatedly, and from different angles, to represent the killer's obsessive thought patterns.

Buttgereit continues the deliberate assault on convention. His gratuitous taboo breaking, however, results in another morally problematic assessment of its serial killer protagonist. Rather than condemn the killer's actions, the film arguably celebrates them as a deliberate challenge to a stagnant sexual morality. Continuing on from the themes in *Nekromantik 2*, the act of necrophilia is a sexualization of death, which demands murder as its functionary. As such, the killer spends his time in a state of sexual excitement, posing the corpses for his pleasure. However, he is still driven enough by socially-ordained guilt to seek to punish himself, leading to his mutilation of his own genitalia as a manifestation of his awareness of a perverse sexuality. Perhaps it is also a desire for redemption through pain.

This socially-ordained, stifling guilt is the real enemy of sexual freedom and self-definition, however aberrant that may be. Ironically though, as is Buttgereit's intent (explored in Kerekes and Slater's *Sex Murder Art*), the killer is the epitome of an inner emptiness driven to transgress as a means of attaining an identity. Yet this identity is inherently purely self-indulgent, and although it ironically represents the freedom from all constraint, it is an entrapment in desire. Such liberation is ultimately doomed, and the serial killer becomes a truly tragic figure. It is this notion of the tragic anti-hero that is the film's boldest suggestion.

It is an intimate portrait (the camera is kept close in to the subject and his actions) of a man who has sexualized death and the functional act of murder. The film explores his thoughts and inner fantasies, and how the murders function as an expression of these tormented and obsessive desires as an idealized self conceived in sexual expression. It is a brave film to graphically explore such aberration, and perhaps braver not to condemn it.

The film took two years to complete, and was made with the participation of friends and business associates. It is the director's most technically polished work to date, as attempts at stylized interior psychodrama disrupt the otherwise observational style. It walks the line between art-house product and pornographic exploitation, and received some festival screening. Buttgereit continues to improve as an underground filmmaker, after the problematic *Nekromantik* movies. Indeed, recent DVD and mainstream UK VHS releases of his work has made him perhaps the highest profile European underground director, a reputation enhanced by increased coverage given his films' continued censorship problems.

Screamplay

(1985–6: d. Rufus Butler Seder)

scr. Seder, Ed Greenberg; pr, ph. Dennis M. Piana; spec eff. Seder; cast. Seder, George Kuchar, Katy Bolger, Nina Piana, Eugene Seder; 85m

A policeman investigates brutal murders. A serial killer is at work, murdering those people written about in a frustrated screenwriter's masterwork. The screenwriter writes about the people who upset or denigrate him. Is the killer an idealized projection? Or is it an alter ego?

This is considered a minor serial slasher film with some underground interest due to the casting of celebrated avant-garde filmmaker George Kuchar (who merged horror and pornography in the cult hit *Thundercrack!*) as the killer. Thus, it perhaps has an intertextuality with other peculiar underground efforts, an aesthetic choice it apparently deliberately flaunts (Newman, p. 134) with a stylized use of black and white, and painted sets, which suggest a deliberate nod to German Expressionism as the root of horror and the avant-garde. The meta-filmic subtext, and the film's notion of a tormented writer plagued by a serial killer, finds its echo in, of all things, *Barton Fink*.

Sea of Love

(1989: d. Harold Becker)

scr. Richard Price; pr. Martin Bregman, Louis A. Stroller; ph. Ronnie Taylor; m. Trevor Jones; ed. David Bretherton; prod d. John Jay Moore; cast. Al Pacino, Ellen Barkin, John Goodman, William Hickey, Michael Rooker, Richard Jenkins; 112m

A publicity photo of the detective (Al Pacino) and the woman (Ellen Barkin) who may be a serial killer of casual pickups in *Sea of Love* (Universal, 1989).

A serial killer murders men contacted through personal ads in a magazine. The investigating officers (Pacino and Goodman) place their own ad and then screen and secretly fingerprint the women that respond, thinking one of them may be the killer. They cannot get prints from one woman (Barkin), who later forms a relationship with Pacino (who suspects that she may be a killer). He almost prefers to believe this, as it adds a tantalizing thrill to his relationship with her. Finally, it is revealed that her ex-husband (Rooker) is the killer, murdering the subsequent men in her life out of sexual jealousy.

Pacino's weary cop is invigorated by his sexual relationship with Barkin. The illicit danger involved is an excitement he craves, to the neglect of duty and better judgment. In that he knowingly chooses to sleep with a woman who may kill him after it, the film can be interpreted as an AIDS allegory. Indeed, it is her previous sexual partner who proves the death of her current lovers. The serial killer is the personification of the perils of casual sex at the end of the 1980s. The insomniac, lonely protagonist is driven by a desperate emotional and sexual need for connection, and is willing to risk his life to achieve it. Barkin too is impelled by this need for connection.

The killer seeks to disavow that need now that he no longer fulfills the desired role of sexual confidante, punishing those that have usurped this role from him. Love and death are forever linked. Hence the killer, struggling with repressed homosexual longing, plays the title song as he forces the naked male victims, face down in an anally receptive position (Hirsch, *Detours*, p. 200), to simulate intercourse, and then shoots them in the back. Ultimately, it is the male obsession with sexual partnership that both kills and lures the afflicted self-destructively to their deaths.

Pacino's role as a policeman gone undercover in a sexual subculture (the singles personal ad scene) recalls his role in *Cruising*. That film's homosexual killer is also neatly echoed in the killer here, who punishes males for their heterosexual desire for a person who used to be his object alone. In that sense, once again Patriarchy devours itself. In the end, Rooker forces Pacino face down on the bed and sits on his ass (as if about to sexually penetrate him), such is the killer's barely controllable desire (which would murder the male erotic object rather than consummate an illicit desire). Indeed, Rooker's repressed homosexual obsession surfaces in the joke he tells his co-workers.

Sea of Love portrays a world that speaks of secret desperation and the encounter with "strange trim." Need has resulted in a hunting ground for lost tormented souls. The film was generally well received by the critics and popular at the box office, and, along with the earlier *The Big Easy*, made Barkin into a star and sex symbol. Screenwriter Price had previously tackled a middle-aged man's pursuit of reinvigoration in his script for *The Color of Money*, and director Becker's functionality established him as one of Hollywood's most proficient craftsmen. Rooker, of course, played the eponymous character in *Henry: Portrait of a Serial Killer*, and would be self-reflexively cast as a police superior interfering with the course of a serial killer investigation in *The Bone Collector*.

Secret Beyond the Door

(1948: d. Fritz Lang)

scr. Sylvia Richards; stry. Rufus King; pr. Lang; ph. Stanley Cortez; m. Miklos Rozsa; cast. Joan Bennett, Michael Redgrave, Anne Revere, Barbara O'Neil, Natalie Schafer, Paul Cavanagh; 98m

A wealthy socialite (Bennett) marries a handsome but emotionally unstable man (Redgrave in his first American role). She gradually comes to question his deep distrust of women, in actuality a deep hatred he can barely contain. She suspects that her husband may actually be a murderer (à la *Suspicion*) and fears she may be murdered in her sleep, even though she remains loyal to him. He has warned her never to open a particular room, and, of course, she does, discovering the depths of his homicidal resentment of women. He is obsessed with the effect of place on human action and has rebuilt the rooms in his house as replicas of rooms where famous murders have occurred. When she opens the door, she discovers a replica of her own room. Apparently he can no longer keep his fantasies and urges under control.

The would-be killer reveals that he was once locked in a room by his mother, who then left him and sped off with her lover. He admits his desire to kill his new wife, in retaliation, and is also aware of the battle raging within him over such homicidal impulses. Ultimately he claims that no man is responsible for his unconscious impulses, although he is aware of such impulses enough to feel guilty and conflicted about them (he hallucinates himself on trial, for instance), and to strive to eliminate such guilt. This would be the true stepping stone to this budding serial killer — the elimination of a conscience as a necessary step in the process of self-actualization. This dichotomy, of guilt vs. compulsion, is a theme which had infiltrated the trial scene in *M* also, wherein the killer gave a similar rationale/excuse for his murderous habits.

Bennett, even knowing of the potential threat to her life, is so intent on preserving the love she feels (as *Variety* interpreted it) that she risks death in an effort to cure the man, with some last minute confrontational psychoanalysis. She would rather live in self-deception, and even possibly die, than admit the failure of her ideal. But can love truly conquer such deep sexual resentments and bitterness? Not in film noir's bleak and conflicted world is such a resolve possible, and one is left feeling that Bennett will forever be in jeopardy.

Recounted in Bennett's voice-over, *Secret Beyond the Door* is a film of romantic infatuation (as opposed to love, perhaps), with the wisdom that comes in hindsight, intermingling with memory, dream and romantic fantasy. Redgrave recognizes her need for such fantasies, and calls her a sleeping beauty needing to be woken up, as if in a trance. Yet he too lives in a fantasy, albeit a far more sinister one than her longing. Both hope for romantic satisfaction, and the film becomes an insecure, even melancholic mix of melodrama and psychodrama. As they seek an idyll together, the film examines a woman's growing recognition that she hardly knows the man she married and is driven to constant introspection as a means of self-reassurance.

Redgrave is also wrestling with such introspection, and therein lies the path to homicide as a means of avoidance. He can claim that no man is responsible for his unconscious, but this amounts to surrender to homicidal impulse. He can see the pieces but cannot go beyond them to counter what he feels he has been, in effect, programmed towards by circumstance. Hence, he says that all his life he has been dominated by women, and grew up harboring violent and homicidal fantasies, which became too powerful to suppress and too attractive to resist. With an impulse to kill so fostered over time by fantasy, he says it was inevitable that he turn to murder. Such a state of mind would feature prominently in the descriptions of serial killer pathology that emerged following the FBI Behavioral Science Unit's investigations and interviews.

This is considered a Freudian version of the *Bluebeard* tale, and is an addition to the group of psychoanalysis-themed movies in vogue in the 1940s. However, both Lang and Bennett considered this the least of their collaborations (following *Man Hunt*, *Woman in the Window* and *Scarlet Street*). True to Lang, the film portrays a shadowy, secretive world of aberrant motives where nothing can be accepted at face value. Less a serial killer movie than a partial exploration of a man predisposed to becoming such a killer, it is one of Lang's least involving films.

Secret Life of Jeffrey Dahmer

(1993: d. David R. Bowen)

scr. Carl Crew; pr. Bowen, L.P. Brown III, Crew; exec pr. Bill Osco; m. Bowen; cast. Carl Crew

This is a supposedly factual blend of exploitation and documentary-inspired recreation. Young Dahmer has a death obsession, and even a fear of abandonment that leads to murder, mutilation and necrophilia in later life.

Information about this film is as hard to come by as the film itself. It is an apparently underground low-budget recreation, perhaps intended along the lines of the films based on Henry Lee Lucas. Although it may have interest as a true-crime recreation, it has failed to make an impression. It was unavailable at time of writing.

See No Evil

(1971: d. Richard Fleischer) aka *Blind Terror*

scr. Brian Clemens; pr. Martin Ransohoff, Leslie Linder; ph. Gerry Fisher; m. Elmer Bernstein; ed. Thelma Connell; art d. John Hoesli; cast. Mia Farrow, Dorothy Alison, Robin Bailey, Diane Grayson, Brian Rawlinson, Norman Eshley; 87m

The killer is identified to the audience only by his boots, and is a depersonalized killing machine who has just slaughtered an entire household, for no apparent reason, except for a young, recently blinded woman (Farrow), a guest in her uncle's house. Gradually she realizes the situation she is in, as the bodies are visible to the audience but not to her: the suspense increases when the killer returns to retrieve a lost bracelet, a presence of which she becomes increasingly aware.

Much of the film is dedicated to the protagonist's discovery of her situation and the gradual realization that her family is dead. There is no initial motivation for these crimes, although Fleischer gradually reveals the killer's broad resentments: of the class system, of the old, of women. He stands defiantly in front of a luxury vehicle until the driver, who will later be killed, acknowledges his presence. He is a social nobody who resents being treated as nothing. He sees his crimes as a means of sociopolitical revolution and sexual empowerment, as his advances are also scorned. Although he is not technically yet a serial killer, it is implied that he would have moved on to another family in time. He is arrogant, convinced that his superiority has been unheralded, and is fascinated by pornographic imagery which fuels his deeds.

He is first seen emerging from a cinema showing a double feature of sex murder movies (entitled "Convent Murders" and "Rapist Cult"). He is thus influenced by a culture centered on depictions of sex murder, perhaps even pornographically validating them. His fantasies thus inspired, he would put them into practice. And the film suggests that murderous fantasies are harbored from an early age and are ingrained as part of the childhood socialization process; hence, he pauses at a toy store whose window display consists of toy guns. He next passes a TV store, each screen offering a violent act. This opening montage is a neat encapsulation of the cause and effect cycle of violence in modern culture, forming a society in effect consuming itself (a theme later visualized in the cannibalism motif of Fleischer's *Soylent Green*). In this way the film is also linked to the director's 1970s studies of the conflicts faced by law enforcement officers in response to murder.

The film is awash with confrontation and clash as evidence of society and personal intercommunication in decline. Gender relations have boiled down to pornography in the killer's mind, and he seeks to have what he feels social injustices have denied him. He thus avoids any admission of personal inadequacy. Until the end, he is identified by his boots, signaling his intent to stomp on anyone and anything. In that way he poses a challenge to the process of class socialization, a symbol of a disaffected youth (who resents not being one of the hip crowd), and a force of social change. Ultimately his crimes are too personal to be socially cathartic, however. He must convince himself of his superiority, in the process giving him license to teach society a lesson. The film develops this characterization of the killer mostly in his absence and from his status as a put upon worker.

The isolated setting and theme of home invasion suggest comparison to Peckinpah's *Straw Dogs*. Indeed, Fleischer's depiction of the vengeful boyfriend taking to horseback to pursue a nomadic band of gypsies (the substitute Indians) he thinks responsible even speaks in part to the Western. However, it concentrates on Farrow's plight as she wanders through a violated home, even falling asleep next to the raped corpse of a relative. As she realizes her predicament, so too does she realize that her life is still in jeopardy, as the killer has returned to remove incriminating evidence and correct his oversight once he realizes that he has left one alive. Fleeing for her life, she is rescued by her boyfriend, a man whose class status ironically makes him the agent of a repressive class, no matter how justified his recourse to vigilantism may be.

Although not a serial killer film, *See No Evil* is included for the purposes of completion. It was considered a suspenseful minor thriller, and drew comparison to *Wait Until Dark*, though Roger Greenspun (*New York Times*) objected to the class-based subtext and the killer's motivations as facile. Nevertheless, its examination of the consequences of the UK social changes of the swinging 1960s era make it an intriguing addition to a cycle of British exploitation cinema adjusting to a more sociological impetus and away from the Hammer traditions.

Self Storage

(1997: d. Tony Spiridakis) aka *Tinseltown*

scr. Spiridakis, Shem Bitterman; pr. Randy Lippert, Bitterman; ph. Scott Henriksen; m. Harry Spiridakis; ed. Pamela Martin; art d. Rusty Smith; cast. Ron Perlman, Arye Gross, Tom Wood, Kristy Swanson, Joe Pantoliano, John Considine; 91m

Two aspiring screenwriters, one convinced to stay in Hollywood by the other, are in need of a place to stay and work. They break into a house used for storage, and are allowed to stay by the building manager (Perlman). They suspect he is a serial killer and write a script about the possibility.

This was shown at the 1997 Montreal World Film Festival but has since received scant attention. It may be considered another of the independent cinema's often-comedic attempts to incorporate the serial killer as a culturally affecting individual. There seems to be a self-conscious concern for the interplay of fact and fiction, and the salability of such subject matter in Hollywood. It remains to be seen whether this offbeat comedy is an intended indictment, as it is currently unavailable.

Serial Killer

(1995: d. Pierre David)

scr. Mark Sevi; pr. David; ph. Tom Jewitt; m. Louis Febre; ed. Julian Semilian; prod d. Whitney Brooke Wheeler; cast. Kim Delaney, Gary Hudson, Tobin Bell, Pam Grier, Marco Rodriguez, Joel Polis; 94m

An agent from the FBI's Psychological Profile Unit (à la *Silence of the Lambs*) tracks a serial killer (the "Picasso killer") who has murdered many women in Los Angeles. He attacks her before he is caught. Two years later, as she recovers from the wounds, the same killer escapes. She is forced to rely on her psychological ability to intuit the killer's behavior and motivations, a process she calls "mind-walking," to trap him again. Once again, he has designs on her, his previous intentions being unfulfilled.

This is a bland, functional tele-movie that takes the material of the Thomas Harris adaptations *Manhunter* and *Silence of the Lambs* and reduces them to standardization. As such, it is an effective, dispassionate summary of the modern serial killer formula, devoid of interpretation or development. Perhaps most tellingly, the film falls into the trend of depicting such serial killers as educated, intelligent individuals, even philosophical in their justification of sex murder. Thus, the trick for interpreting the killer lies in the incorporation of their savagery as a function of their refined intellect. It is as if intelligence and education bring with them an increased awareness of the temptations of Evil. This needs to be disavowed and purged, and it is almost poetic justice that the profiler has been punished by that which she sought to prevent. The film is therefore arguably anti-intellectual and reductive in tone, but too flat to develop this theme with any conviction.

The film's central concern is the obsession people have for such killers, and the desire to understand what motivates them, although this draws the attention of the killer onto the profiler as his equal adversary and nemesis. It also provokes an affinity for aberration, which, through empathetic association, allows an enjoyment of such closeness to Evil, and subsequently provokes guilt, again a theme of *Manhunter* especially. However, there is little sense of the psychotic passion of such aberration and the despair of the fascination with it.

Canadian director David is better known as a producer, having been associated with the early works of David Cronenberg. He has been unable to forge a substantial directorial career, and has had to play up the Cronenberg association (hence his direction of *Scanner Cop* in reply to Cronenberg's provocative *Scanners*). The title *Serial Killer* promises something more insightful and definitive than is ultimately offered here.

Serial Killing 4 Dummies

(1999: d. Trace Slobotkin)

scr. Slobotkin; pr. Mathew Davidge, Harry John Trube; ph. John P. Tarver; cast. Stuart Stone, Lisa Loeb, James Asmodeo, Elise Ballard, Thomas Haden Church

An unambitious high school student intends to become a serial killer but cannot bring himself to actually commit murder. He meets a Goth girl, and together they attempt to learn the secret pleasures of being able to kill randomly and repeatedly. In the meantime, he thinks he knows the identity of a real serial killer operating in the area.

This attempt at satire can perhaps be considered an examination of the status that the serial killer has achieved as role model, revolutionary and even spokesperson for a generation. In this way, the "serial killer" is almost a movement, a desired ends and identity. It is unremarked on whether or not the film has the requisite cynicism and underground aesthetic that usually accompanies such satire. It is another hard item to track down, having only minor Internet mentions (even the plot summary on *imdb.com* was provided by the director). At time of writing, it was generally unreleased.

Serial Mom

(1994: d. John Waters)

scr. Waters; pr. John Fiedler, Mark Tarlov; ph. Robert M. Stevens; m. Basil Poledouris; ed. Janice Hampton, Erica Huggins; prod d. Vincent Peranio; cast. Kathleen Turner, Sam Waterston, Ricki Lake, Matthew Lillard, Mary Jo Catlett, Patricia Hearst, Mink Stole, Suzanne Somers; 89m

A suburban housewife/mother (Turner) who likes to cook and clean, is always cheerful, and loves her husband and two kids, is a killer of anyone who crosses the family or offends her delicate sense of common decency. She is caught, put on trial, and becomes a money-spinning celebrity attracting a media circus. She is found not guilty.

This is a satire of the mad housewife subgenre, the more known examples being *Images* and *Diary of a Mad Housewife*, and the more contemporary being the equally satiric *To Die For* and *Positively True Adventures of the Alleged Texas Cheerleader-Murdering Mom*. The routine of suburban life and the obsession with conventional normality is enough to provoke psychosis. As a kind of mad melodrama, the housewife is so programmed with cultural expectations as to attempt to eradicate any difference, any slight against her perceived true order of things, in the process ironically becoming an aberration herself: a perpetual paradox.

She is obsessed with ordinariness as a perfect ideal, but behind closed doors is thinking and reading of other serial killers (championing Bundy and Manson, both of whom also became [in]famous through their actions), is sexually aggressive and turned on by her actions. She is spurred on by minor inconvenience (losing her parking spaces, anger at people who don't rewind videotapes) and has been driven mad by the trivial minutia of the everyday she champions.

Ironically, however, the society that would spawn such aberration is fascinated by its difference, and the son (a horror movie junkie) asks his father if he's seen *Henry: Portrait of a Serial Killer*. Even in decent suburbia, the serial killer has become a breakfast talking point, and the young male especially is raised on horror images. Ironically, the horror movie–obsessed son is the last to suspect his own mother, although he's quite ready to make money from it. Of course, the mother denies that anything about her kids' possible dysfunction is her problem and kills the teacher who suggests otherwise. Such is Waters' systematic attack on the conventional family as a self-deceptive monstrosity, revealing the rottenness behind the facade. It is a culture saturated with visions of horror beneath the surface.

Thus, the serial killer can easily become a profitable commodity, and her daughter sells souvenirs as the son negotiates a television deal. The mass commodification and celebration of the criminal perhaps negates and even excuses the acts, in the futile effort to contextualize them, when the killer becomes a famous celebrity, ironically a spokesperson for self-indulgence, although motivated by a desire to maintain her sense of decency. Such ironies are ultimately irreconcilable, and the world that tries to do so is ultimately in a hypocritical chaos. In that aspect, the film is a satirical companion to *Natural Born Killers* in its condemnation of the killer-as-celebrity media mentality of modern society. Such a society needs to celebrate what it condemns, another paradox.

Waters' attempt to combine his subversive humor with more professional Hollywood production values, à la the previous *Hairspray* and *Cry Baby*, has his usual stock company (Patty Hearst, Traci Lords, Mink Stole, Susan Lowe). It also has a greater emphasis on shock value (including graphic hit-and-run and disembowelment deaths, and an impaling which recalls the jovial grossness of the Warhol/ Morrissey *Flesh for Frankenstein* movies). Although it stops short of the celebration of the infantile gross-out of Waters' earlier cult films, it represents the same subversive intent. Its exposure of monstrousness beneath plain suburbia also recalls David Lynch and *Blue Velvet*, and the caricaturish tone of Paul Bartel (especially *Eating Raoul*).

Seven

(1995: d. David Fincher)

scr. Andrew Kevin Walker; pr. Arnold Kopelson, Phyllis Carlyle; exec pr. Lynn Harris, Richard Saperstein; ph. Darius Khondji; prod d. Arthur Max; ed. Richard Francis Bruce; m. Howard Shore; cast. Morgan Freeman, Brad Pitt, Gwyneth Paltrow, Kevin Spacey, R. Lee Ermey, Leland Orser; 126m

An elderly detective (Freeman) on the verge of retirement is teamed with a brash young detective (Pitt) to investigate a series of murders he soon realizes are sermons based on the seven deadly sins. They track the killer, through legally dubious means, but he gets away. He subsequently surrenders and agrees to plead guilty if the detectives agree to his terms. They do and are subsequently led out to the desert where Pitt discovers that the killer has murdered his pregnant wife (and unborn baby). Unable to restrain himself, Pitt shoots the killer, as the killer had always intended him to do. The killer gets what he wanted, Pitt is arrested, and Freeman can only despair.

This is a modern noir: dark, gloomy, dank muted colors (especially black and brown, the earthen colors), decaying atmosphere, rain soaked and shadowy. Such is vital to the depiction of a cruel and brutal world, with a killer and detective driven by their search for meaning. Freeman struggles with surrender to the absence of a greater moral meaning or purpose in life, surrender to cynicism in a sinful world. He no longer sees the righteousness of his job as able to affect change, and is waiting for retirement (the clock literally ticking away). However, Pitt eventually intuits that Freeman desperately wants to disbelieve that cynicism, and that his job offers him a means of cheating that resignation to defeat. Pitt is outraged by the violent madness he sees in the world around him, as is the killer, who is determined to affect change in a direct, punitive manner. Pitt has found solace in the everyday normal life of marriage and his job, and holds onto both as moral absolutes—by the film's end, he will lose both, and perhaps even his soul (he does not pass the test). The killer is so repulsed by the moral, sinful degeneration around him that he is determined to purge the sinful and affect moral change — in God's name. He too is a moral man, and envious of Pitt's life (and perhaps sexuality), which he must also destroy in a most disturbing and much remarked on ending. Both Freeman and the killer have reacted to despair, the killer to challenge it and Freeman battling with surrender to its inevitability.

The killer is obsessed with the sinful, and has found solace in religious sanction. He claims that the Biblical seven deadly sins (gluttony, greed, sloth, lust, pride, envy, and wrath) are tolerated by society, looked on as normal and everyday. He therefore murders the sinners in the manner of their sin, to bring God's law back into the world. By punishing supposed transgressors, he is a perversion/subversion of religious sanction. His crimes are sermons, a means of communication that he feels will be studied and followed. He is unshakably confirmed of his own self-righteousness. He dies convinced of this: his victory is his ability to make his desired fantasy an actuality. Yet he is envious of Pitt's normal life, a symbol of what has been denied him and which ultimately he must destroy.

He needs to control destiny, such is his idealized self as an agent of a greater power and beyond the lustful urges he seeks to chastise in the sinners. Ironically, he tells the detectives that he is nothing special, but that his "work" is—he has gained meaning, purpose and self-expression in cruel, systematic murder, and escaped an otherwise inevitable despair. He is paralleled to Freeman, who paradoxically finds such actions as evidence of the despairing absence of God rather than its confirmation as the killer intended. The killer's desire to shape destiny leads him to play his elaborate final game with the police, maintaining control until the very end. He is indeed so adept at it that he gets exactly what he wanted, in the process dragging down Pitt (testing his moral character and convinced of his fallibility) and reenforcing Freeman's despair. He is independently wealthy and an educated, intelligent man—a rival of sorts to the type of killer popularized by Hannibal Lecter. He also knows that it is more comfortable for people to label him insane (as Pitt does, even though Freeman urges him not to). In an awareness of the serial killer subculture, Pitt tries to lower the killer by saying that he is not a messiah and is a T-shirt at best. The killer is a test of humanity's resolve.

Brad Pitt stars as the detective who will become a vengeful executioner in *Seven* (New Line, 1995).

The killings/sermons are meant to illustrate the depths to which modern society has sunk in its condoning of sin and aberration. It is a foul, dystopic world forever in need of literal and metaphorical cleansing. Hence the perpetual rainfall until the ironic end. Until the end, where Pitt becomes a vengeful vigilante killer, there is no act of murder shown, only the terrible aftermath—visualized in elaborate, intense production design, and often illuminated by the detectives' probing flashlights. The emphasis on the crimes as means of communication and the importance of the crime scene as an artwork to be decoded as to clues about the artist would develop following this film into a potent theme, hence *The Bone Collector*, *Postmortem* and *Resurrection* especially. It is also a choice in production design that enhances the stylized apocalyptic undertones.

The theme of inevitable apocalypse is stressed from the outset, as Freeman listens to time ticking away. Perhaps it is lost time, or even wasted time, for a man whose existence he fears has been reduced to waiting for the next human atrocity. What is the solution? A lyric in the opening credits song speaks of getting closer to God. Perhaps by tackling the evil in human nature around him Freeman can attain not redemption, but an awareness of a higher purpose, which would give his life a sanctioned validity in the face of apparent futility. In that way the world would be worth fighting for, even if it were a troubled, horrible place beset by sin. It is the desire to affect change that is equated in the film with the desire of humankind to be one with God, an aspiration propelling the killer into sadistic murder, with the intention of forcing people into a recognition of a higher meaning. Murder is an act of communication in an age wherein sin is tolerated and accepted.

The killer's apartment, congested and dimly lit (like most rooms in the film), is filled with hand-written volumes—a mind on paper. Throughout the film, Freeman has been reading and researching the seven deadly sins, and the art and literature that has interpreted and utilized them (Dante, of course, and Chaucer). Ironically, it is the killer who comes closest to being a visionary and artist in the tradition of even Thomas Aquinas, in his dedication to putting his mind across, in reacting to the everyday, and creating a message intended to warn society and affect change. He has left a legacy behind in his crimes/artworks and his autobiographical ramblings. Equally ironically, the killer's reading matter, tracked illegally by the FBI, leads to his early iden-

tification. It is the killer who affects change in this world and culture of hellish vision: transgression as cultural artifact, a theme followed up by screenwriter Walker's subsequent *8MM*. The legal system is even implied to somewhat hamper the detective's progress, evidence of a stagnant bureaucracy which Freeman believes at its worst reduces the detectives to being virtual file clerks of evidence.

As the two protagonists work together, they develop a mutual understanding based on an interpersonal appreciation of one another, as initiated by Pitt's wife (Paltrow). Their awareness of each other as human beings is the only positive note in this bleak film. For Freeman, his advice to Paltrow allows him to fulfill the role of substitute father and friend in a way he presumably never has. It is a moment of interpersonal communication which validates his role as a patriarch, although this is undercut by the killer, who decapitates Paltrow and leads Pitt to his doom. In the process this eliminates the effectiveness of the Good Patriarch, but perhaps not his validity, or so Freeman would desperately cling to at the end.

Fincher had directed music videos (including "Vogue" and "Express Yourself" for Madonna) and TV commercials before debuting with *Alien 3*. His second feature was *Seven*, and it established him as a preeminent stylist. His subsequent works (*The Game*, *Fight Club* [again with Pitt]) have confirmed him as a major American auteur. His works are eagerly anticipated. An extraordinarily rich film, *Seven* was a highly praised, surprise box-office hit, further confirming the box-office high profile of the serial killer figure. Its influence on the serial killer film since its release continues to be felt, and the film has been justifiably much written about.

Seven Orchids Stained in Red

(1972: d. Umberto Lenzi)

scr. Roberto Gianviti, Paul Hengge, Lenzi; nvl. Edgar Wallace; pr. Horst Wendlandt; ph. Angelo Lotti; m. Riz Ortolani; ed. Eugenio Alabiso, Clarissa Ambach, Jutta Hering; cast. Uschi Glas, Antonio Sabato, Marisa Mell, Pier Paolo Capponi, Petra Schurmann

This is a giallo which, in its character design, apparently bridges the popular series of Edgar Wallace mysteries and the serial killer slasher aspects of the multiple killer movies in Italy. A killer intends to kill seven women by different methods, and the investigators must hurry to stop him before he can finish his intended series.

Lenzi is better known for his successful Italian cannibal movies in the 1970s exploitation boom in Italy. Serial murder as a personal thrill is a common factor in the giallo, influencing the killer of *Evil Fingers* also. What is perhaps noteworthy about *Seven Orchids Stained in Red* is the implication that the killer embarks on a limited series of murders as a personal project rather than the lifestyle choice it is for the actual serial killer. But could such a killer merely stop after the project is complete, or would he go on? This aspect would be in part explored in the late 1990s with *Seven* and *Sanctimony* in particular. In this way, the serial killer and the gimmick killer slowly become allied figures.

Shadow of a Doubt

(1943: d. Alfred Hitchcock)

scr. Thornton Wilder, Sally Benson, Alma Reville; stry. Gordon McDonnell; pr. Jack H. Skirball; ph. Joseph Valentine; m. Dimitri Tiomkin; ed. Milton Carruth; art d. John B. Goodman; cast. Teresa Wright, Joseph Cotten, MacDonald Carey, Henry Travers, Patricia Collinge, Hume Cronyn, Edna Mae Wonacott, Wallace Ford, Irving Bacon, Charles Bates; 108m

A serial killer (Cotten) of rich widows runs from pursuing detectives. He goes to his sister and niece in a small town in California. There the niece (Wright), who shares his first name of Charlie, idolizes him. However, detectives have tracked him there and pose as census takers in order to get his photograph. One detective voices his suspicions to Wright, who disbelieves him; but after investigating, she realizes that her beloved uncle is indeed the "Merry Widow Strangler." She still protects him, however, on the promise that he will leave soon. When another suspect is arrested, Cotten now considers Wright a threat to his safety and intends to kill her. He tries to throw her from a train but falls to his death. He is buried as a regular man, with Wright having to keep the burden of knowing his terrible secret, lest it shock her fragile mother.

This is commonly considered one of Hitchcock's darkest films, and reportedly is a favorite of his. It is thought of as an examination of the potential evil that lies behind the superficial charm of a beguiling everyman, a psychological case study thereof, and a scathing indictment of the US middle class. Thus, the director delights in gradually undermining the trust assumed between family members in particular and human beings in general. Two friends talk of the best way to murder one another and get away undetected, completely unaware of the true murderer in their midst. But what appeals more to Hitchcock is the process by which the young woman realizes that her idealized patriarch is a monster. Initially convinced that she has a telepathic bond with this man, she finally realizes that there is only an unknowable darkness to the human condition. That is her unfortunate rite of passage into womanhood, the awareness of the patriarch as monster.

The killer's view is chilling — that the rich widows he kills are nothing but bloated swine, and since it is a hellish world, it makes no difference what happens in it anyway. He considers the world a bad joke, an attitude which first alerts Wright to the fact that not all is well with her uncle. He has an attraction/repulsion complex for the older women he murders (for more than their money), offering a parallel of sorts to the psychology behind the killer in *Monsieur Verdoux*. He is a resentful man who seems to have fond memories of childhood, so fond in fact that he loathes the interpersonal rituals of the adult world, in particular that of the matriarch. He has only a moment of shame, looking away from Wright when he knows she knows. Perhaps that influences his decision to kill her. Not so much that she knows his secret, but that he felt a moment of shame at that recognition.

Also ironic in that context is how the young Charlie believes that she summons the older Charlie, as if calling the angel of death. What she learns of him is the ultimate betrayal of their unspoken bond. Yet out of a family loyalty she would still protect him, even when she knows that he is trying to kill her. In that way she becomes partially complicit in a transference of guilt (Hirsch, *Film Noir*, p. 140) — always considered a paramount Hitchcock theme. A fatalistic subtext, it implies that his presence is her passage into maturity. Their relationship is one of many instances of the film's use of pairs and doubles to reflect the duality of Good and Evil (i.e. two Charlies, two detectives, two suspects, two conversations about murder techniques, the "till Two" bar, two unsuccessful attempts on Charlie's life, Charlie's two friends, etc).

Shadow of a Doubt was filmed in Santa Rosa, California, as representative of wholesome middle-class American values hiding dark inner corruption. Thus, the detectives ironically pose as census takers in search of the average American family. Such is Hitchcock's intention — to subvert the appearance of stability and the faith in human bonding. In this way Uncle Charlie is the killer within all, and a development from the Jekyll/Hyde persona.

The screenwriters based the character of Uncle Charlie on the true-life serial killer Earle Leonard Nelson, who went from town to town, staying at rich widows' boarding houses and then murdering them after taking their money. The film also fits neatly into the burgeoning film noir and its morbid, pessimistic take on human nature. It was remade as *Step Down to Terror*, *Return of Dracula* and a television adaptation.

Shadows and Fog

(1991: d. Woody Allen)

scr. Allen; pr. Jack Rollins, Charles Joffe; ph. Carlo Di Palma; m. Kurt Weill; ed. Susan E. Morse; prod d. Santo Loquasto; cast. Woody Allen, Mia Farrow, John Malkovitch, Madonna, Donald Pleasence, Lily Tomlin, Jodie Foster, Kathy Bates, John Cusack, Kate Nelligan, Julie Kavner, Fred Gwynne; 86m

In a 1920s city, nerdy clerk Allen is awakened one night and forced into joining a mob hunt for a serial strangler on the loose. There he falls in with a former sword swallower now turned to prostitution. He is mistaken for the killer and pursued by the mob. Finally, he joins the circus as an apprentice magician.

The unspecified European city (everycity?) is perpetually dark, murky, fogbound and an unavoidably menacing labyrinth. The characters search desperately, always on the verge of themselves being lost, perhaps a moral statement on the human condition as it existed in cinematic works of that period. As such, it is impossible to remove the referential frame of homage and reinterpretation from the movie. It is all studied atmosphere, full of characters seeking connection and an overall meaning.

Shadows and Fog is primarily considered as Woody Allen's version of German Expressionist horror and psychodrama, and Kafka. It is grotesque, shadowy and full of bizarre characters (some from a circus, prompting comparison to Browning even), all set to Kurt Weill music (from "Threepenny Opera") and featuring the necessary specter of *M*. Despite its visual cleverness, *Shadows* was seen by most critics as merely an academic exercise, devoid of real personality, and indulgent of Woody's philosophical asides. Riddled with amusing cameo appearances, which some felt were distracting, it concentrates on Woody and Mia.

It is only tangentially a serial killer film, in that the murderer is a mostly unseen force that motivates the proceedings—perhaps the sum total of the characters' projected disillusionment, although he appears as a menacing hulk. Thus, even the pursuers are not sure of his method, as he is referred to as a strangler who cuts throats. He is also the communal boogeyman of myth, to which community definition is made in reaction against. Initially part of this community, Allen leaves it in a gesture of disavowal when it turns on him (in this hostile universe the illusion of love and interconnection impels people into caring activity). Only the prostitutes seem truly contented in this world of self-deception and illusion. Hence the killer is almost trapped in a magic trick but gets away, himself perhaps an illusionist's trick. If one can interpret the director as the master illusionist, one has a sense of the film's meta-filmic dimension. There is only uncertainty. Hence, the doctor says that what could inspire one to artistic expression could inspire another to murder, and that there is a point where insanity stops and evil begins (a position confirmed by his murder). The taking of another life is that boundary.

Although *Shadows and Fog* is not quite the descent into sardonic nightmare that was Scorsese's *After Hours*, it is perhaps Allen's most guardedly bleak comedy. Nevertheless, it is still considered a negligible addition to an astounding body of work.

Shadows Run Black

(1984: d. Howard Heard)

scr. Duke Howard, Craig Kusaba; pr. Eric Louzil; ph. John Sprang; ed. Raul Davalos, Davide Ganzino; cast. William Kulzer, Elizabeth Trosper, Shea Porter, Julius Metoyer, Kevin Costner; 89m

A serial killer known as the "Black Angel" (Costner) dresses in a black jumpsuit and mask, and uses a meat cleaver to murder college coeds. A cop investigates, although he doubts the seemingly randomness of the crimes. The nameless women are killed in various states of undress: many teasing shots result.

This supposedly unremarkable almost–slasher film was made in 1981, at the height of the slasher boom, but went generally unreleased until 1985, and now is only treated as a footnote due to Costner's presence. It is included for the purposes of this novelty value, although it is an example of the trend to treat the sex murderer as gimmicky automaton, and an excuse for nudity.

Shadowhunter

(1993: d. J.S. Cardone)

scr. Cardone, Duane Poole; pr. Scott Einbinder, Carol Kottenbrook, Brian Parker; ph. Dick Bush, Michael Cardone; m. Robert Folk; ed. Ralph Brunjes, Thomas Mashelski; prod d. Susan Longmire, William Maynard; cast. Scott Glenn, Angela Alvarado, Robert Beltran, Tim Sampson, George Aguilar, Beth Broderick, Benjamin Bratt; 100m

The film begins with the familiar aura of sleazy city life, until a mysterious woman commits suicide (shooting herself) in front of her children. Glenn investigates and discovers the world of a homicidal dominatrix. Disillusioned and beset by personal problems (his wife recently left him), Glenn argues with his superiors over the case and is assigned to a "lesser" case. He is sent to an Indian reservation to pick up and escort back a Navajo serial killer, the "Coyote Man," considered a supernatural force by the natives. This killer escapes and stabs the cop with a magical bone, allowing the Coyote Man subsequent access to the policeman's dreams. The cop is then partnered with a tribal officer and a tracker, and all go in pursuit of the killer. The killer uses the cop's gun in more crimes. The killer harasses them as they pursue him, and may be entering into Glenn's mind via a supernatural thought/ dream transference method.

The killer is an intriguing amalgam of conventional killer and mystic Indian outlaw, as if a Native American presence was corrupted by a Western sin — pride. He wants to be feared by the locals and to inspire awe (a telling trait of serial murderers, and affecting the killer in *Manhunter*), in the process becoming a boogeyman of sorts, as if such murders have elevated him to the status of a supernatural being — and are thus a means of transcendence. Murder, necrophilia and cannibalism invigorate him, much as it does the killer cannibal Wendigo of *Ravenous*, as a means of attaining supernatural strength and power.

There is hence a mystical Indian interpretation of the serial killer offered: as a soul-taker and dream-stalking presence who can affect possession. The protagonist's growing confusion can thus be taken as a sign of his takeover by the spiritual force. It is his confrontation with the validity of a spiritual rationale other than his own. It is symptomatic of a psychological breakdown, and is the dissolution, and subsequent reconstitution in reaction to external pressures, of his ego. When he faces the killer, he finds only a laughing, sadistic man confirmed of his own superiority. The protagonist can only reconstitute his ego by killing the killer, who has come to represent and embody his own psychological despair.

Cardone likes the sense of isolation that the road and the rural towns offer. His later films, beginning with this one and encompassing *Black Day, Blue Night* and *Outside Ozona*, have explored the effects of such a lonely landscape on desperate characters, and the subsequent kinship felt as the human presence redefines the spatial relationships. He repeatedly probes a state of physical and psychological desolation, with characters faced with an unenviable despair.

Aerial shots of Navajo country give way to a modern Western or pursuit, bringing to mind *Tell Them Willie Boy Is Here*. When with the Indians, Glenn at first feels some WASP arrogance and even moral and religious superiority (recalling his work and character in *The Challenge*). Thus, he at first can deny the supernatural spiritual beliefs of those around him, until confronted by the killer's presence in his own mind. Cardone's descending camera conveys the sense of an otherworldly force descending to influence the party. Thus, the killer plagues them repeatedly as they track him.

Director Cardone is an interesting case of a director of genre and low-budget items whose works all evidence considerable intellect and ambition, but who has been unable to break through into mainstream success, coming closest with *Outside Ozona*. *Shadowhunter* went similarly unheralded, although it drew some comparison to the contemporary *Thunderheart* and *Dust Devil* (Hardy, p. 485). The Native American mysticism also offers an interesting parallel to *White of the Eye*.

She-Wolf of London

(1946: d. Jean Yarbrough)

scr. George Bricker; stry. Dwight V. Babcock; pr. Ben Pivar; ph. Maury Gertsman; ed. Paul Landres; cast. Don Porter, June Lockhart, Sara Haden, Jan Wiley, Dennis Hoey, Lloyd Corrigan, Martin Kosteck; 61m

In early 20th century London, an elderly aunt tells her niece that the young woman is tainted with werewolf blood and is responsible for a series of murders. Distraught, the niece breaks off her engagement, but her fiancé investigates on his own and finds the real, non-werewolf, killer.

The film reportedly balances the supernatural potential with a straight investigation and multi-character whodunit; the conclusion is most interesting in light of the developing serial killer film because it has the crimes attributed to a werewolf committed by a very human monster. The London setting and fog-bound streets also link the film to the Ripper legacy. Thus, it may be interpreted as a film that sought to explore the human sex killer and dispense with the lycanthropy myth, which it raises but barely develops. There is some interest (*Variety* felt) generated by the dilemma of a protagonist mistakenly believing herself guilty of murder, but this is a red herring in the overall mystery structure.

Although this is a Universal release, it was made at the end of the horror cycle and is not usually included in discussions of horror's "golden age." Fans of veteran exploitation director Jean Yarbrough (one of the first, and who now has a cult following thanks to fanzines and the obscure-video retailers who advertise in them), here given a modestly budgeted venture, may wish to seek it out more than others. Its theme of a series of murders blamed on an animal but committed by a human finds its echo in *The Leopard Man*, another film to address the lycanthropy myth in relation to the human serial killer.

Shocker

(1989: d. Wes Craven)

scr. Craven; pr. Marianne Maddalena, Barin Kumar; ph. Jacques Haitkin; m. William Goldstein; ed. Andy Blumenthal; art d. Randy Moore; cast. Michael Murphy, Peter Berg, Mitch Pileggi, Cami Cooper, John Tesh, Heather Langenkamp, Jessica Craven, Richard Brooks; 110m

A young man has dreams of a serial killer, a TV repairman who slaughters entire families, at work. His visions include the death of his own family. The psychic link enables him to identify the killer and, with his policeman father, apprehend him. The killer is executed, but as part of a demonic pledge he returns as an electrical current, moving through television broadcasts and able to possess innocent people.

The climax, as killer and protagonist battle their way through TV shows, is an interesting demonstration of violence in the media, and suggests the film as a satire of the channel-surfing American mentality (Muir, p. 156). This theme is also explored in Ted Nicolaou's low-budget satire *Terrorvision* and Peter Hyams' *Stay Tuned*. *Shocker* is more caricaturish and comic in tone than previous Wes Craven films, and is possibly best considered a bridge to the tonal complexity of *People Under the Stairs*.

The killer is obsessed by images of individual and mass destruction on television, watching multiple sets in a kind of demonic shrine. He also delights in news reports of himself as an intelligent killer. He is a media-fuelled threat to Patriarchy, finding his token demon in TV waves (a nod to the *Poltergeist* films). It is up to the stepfather-and-son combination to sort out the mess in the bad patriarch's wake and uphold Patriarchal justice, and, amusingly enough, restore television, the functionary of Patriarchy, to a non-threatening, supposedly innocuous and zombifying barrage. Executing the killer purifies television.

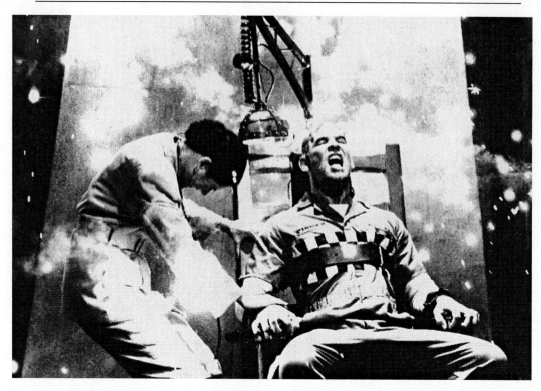

The serial killer (Mitch Pileggi) in the process of being executed in *Shocker* (Universal, 1989). He will return.

The killer's revelation that he is the protagonist's real father, hence validating the psychic link at a plotline level, suggests the necessity of a punitive patricide. The father would seek to destroy the son, who in turn must rebel against the real father and preserve the stepfather (the policeman and symbol of authority) in order to chastise the monstrous patriarch, and himself prove worthy of the role of his stepfather. It is hard to decipher whether the film is a subversive attack on Patriarchy or a call for its redemption. Craven's tone denies any character the validity of a spokesperson, and the film is thus a hit-and-miss parody of the system's restorative process.

This was Craven's attempt to create another franchise success after his hit *A Nightmare on Elm Street*, whose narrative structure it follows closely, with a TV netherworld becoming the dreamscape of the earlier film. It was not popular with ei-

ther critics or fans. However, it was an influence on the later *Fallen*, which effectively jettisoned the media subtext.

Silence of the Lambs

(1991: d. Jonathan Demme)

scr. Ted Tally; nvl. Thomas Harris; pr. Edward Saxon, Kenneth Utt, Ron Bozman; ph. Tak Fujimoto; m. Howard Shore; ed. Craig McKay; prod d. Kristi Zea; cast. Jodie Foster, Anthony Hopkins, Scott Glenn, Ted Levine, Anthony Heald, Frankie Faison, Roger Corman, Kasi Lemmons; 118m

A trainee FBI agent (Foster) is recruited by her superior at the FBI's Behavioral Science Unit (Glenn — modeled, they say, on real-life profiler and author John Douglas). She is sent to question an incarcerated serial killer, Hannibal Lecter (Hopkins), in the hopes of, unknown to him, getting the killer's assistance in an ongoing serial murder case, that of Buffalo

Bill (Levine). Lecter only helps her on condition that she reveal personal details about herself. He escapes, and she confronts Buffalo Bill, rescuing his next intended victim in time.

This taut combination of psychodrama, thriller and procedural is the film that established the serial killer movie in the public consciousness: the box-office and critical reception legitimized the form. Although the character of Hannibal the Cannibal (as he is referred to) was characterized by Brian Cox in the earlier Thomas Harris adaptation *Manhunter*, it is Anthony Hopkins' interpretation of the character which endures (and that is not meant as a slight against Cox's performance in any way). Hopkins plays the refined, intelligent killer with a charm that eerily undercuts his malevolence, his character a balance of restraint and ferocity (overcontrol), in contrast to Cox's chillingly clinical interpretation of a genius master manipulator. Lecter here too is an expert manipulator who can turn events in his favor in order to facilitate his escape.

His control over the people who seek to impose control over him, and his subsequent ability to shape and even control their destinies, anticipates the killer in *Seven* who was also able to manipulate circumstances to his desired ends. Indeed, this manipulative struggle for control is a perpetual mind game played between killer and profiler, and again stems from *Manhunter*. This battle for control and manipulation of others is the knowing state of affairs at the adversarial level. It is a skill that Foster at first lacks— it is part of her professional maturation that she learns to manipulate, and to play the corresponding mind games that the patriarchs are so adept at.

Hence, Demme develops four male authority figures in particular, all using varied techniques to enforce their will and manipulate a situation to their own ends.

Agent Crawford is the most refined, and Lecter's real nemesis, despite the claims of Dr. Chilten, the least subtle operator (whose techniques Lecter refers to as "petty torments"). They all conceal agendas and information to serve their own ends. It is Foster's honesty and transparent techniques which prove attractive to Hopkins. Demme contrasts Lecter's desire to personalize her, finally resulting in the most fleeting of touches (his finger brushes hers, a brief sexual contact?), with Bill's depersonalizing of his victims (referring to his captive as "it") and subsequently easier mutilation — and incidental killing — in the pursuit of their skin. Manipulation and deception vs. honesty are regular Demme themes.

Like the Tooth Fairy in *Manhunter* (though with far less sophistication), Bill is concerned with transformation and transcendence, and kills to maintain this process. He believes that he is in a process of becoming. Hence, he places the moth in the mouths of his victims, his signature, as it were. Lecter, however, is motivated by no such desires: indeed, we can barely glimpse at his motives or the causes for his aberrance, beyond the desire to assert his superiority. He arguably represents the attractive unknowable, and is separated from Bill's sexual deviance. Even in *Hannibal* the filmmakers take steps to remove sexual aberration as a motive for Lecter's cannibalism and murder, as if somehow he is better than "the rest" (and in Scott's film is even restored, ironically enough, to the level of an admirable patriarch).

Despite the presence of two serial killers in the film, Foster's tale is central. A diminutive woman in an all-male world (she is often framed surrounded by groups of larger men), she possesses a driving ambition and vulnerability. She is intent to prove herself to the good and bad substitute fathers she encounters— her superior profiler at the FBI's Behavioral Science

Novice FBI profiler Clarice Starling (Jodie Foster) has the weight of Patriarchy looking over her shoulder and on her back — the serial killer Hannibal Lecter (Anthony Hopkins) and the FBI's Behavioral Science Unit expert Jack Crawford (Scott Glenn) from *Silence of the Lambs* (Orion, 1991).

Lecter is played both for shock value and contrast, as Demme constantly plays with audience expectations of a serial killer. He is introduced, well dressed and groomed, in a virtual dungeon, the cultured centerpiece of a bizarre freak show. (This is totally the opposite of his presentation in *Manhunter*, where he is dressed in white in a white, pristine, isolated and orderly cell). His dialogue reveals his cold monstrousness: "I ate his liver with some ... beans ... [followed by a sucking sound]." As chilling and disarmingly humorous as this may be, it is far from the philosophical rationalizations of both killers in *Manhunter*. It is direct and shocking, but as an insight into character it reveals little. Nevertheless, it is the anomaly posed by Lecter, especially in comparison to the brash deviance of Bill (the serial killer equivalent of low culture), which elevates his character to modern myth.

Unit, for whom she wishes to work, and, increasingly, Lecter. Indeed, her relationship with Lecter evolves into one of mutual trust and confession, the beginnings of a romantic attraction, and which had some critics referring to a Beauty and the Beast relationship. She is surrounded by monstrousness and asked to keep a level, objective head, and it is a measure of her strength that she seems to. Although at the end, when an escaped Lecter phones her, speaks briefly and hangs up, she is left repeating his name — the depths of his influence made clear.

The key to Lecter's monstrousness is revealed in his breakout scene, the film's most operatic and celebrated set piece. Lecter calmly disposes of the guards and (we see only the aftermath) arranges the corpses for maximum shock value, as if creating a demented artwork. In *Manhunter*, Lecter creates disarray in the outside world from within his cell confines, partially by corresponding with the free serial killer as kindred spirits. Lecter here would be unlikely to have anything to do with the lowlife Bill, as he considers himself innately superior to such deviants (hence his treatment of Miggs in the next cell) and feels little if any kinship with them, although he uses information again to get what he wants. This set piece would have implications for many subsequent serial killer films, which treated the crime scene as an artwork needing to be decoded. It is a civilized ferocity, a demented brilliance that is arguably treated as almost attractive, mythic in its inherent contradictions; hence the scenes between Hopkins and Foster filmed often in close-ups and medium shots as an odd intimacy develops.

Buffalo Bill lacks any such refinement. He is an immature sexual deviate who often resides in the basement of his house, an aspiring transsexual who is fashioning himself a body suit out of the skin of his victims. He is modeled on real-life killer Ed Gein, who was also the basis for *Psycho*, *Deranged* and *The Texas Chainsaw Massacre*). He has a certain childlike quality at times, but is prone to savagery — without the civilized component. He is closer to an animal.

Silence was only the third film to that date (following 1934's *It Happened One Night* and 1975's *One Flew Over the Cuckoo's Nest*) to sweep the five main Academy Awards — Best Film, Director, Adapted Screenplay, Actor, and Actress. The eagerly awaited sequel, *Hannibal*, appeared a decade later, with Hopkins reprising his role but with Julianne Moore replacing Jodie Foster (who objected to the violence, among other things). Neither Demme nor screenwriter Tally returned for the sequel.

Silent Madness

(1984: d. Simon Nuchtern)

scr. William P. Milling, Robert Zimmerman; pr. Milling; ph. Gerald Feil; cast. Belinda Montgomery, Viveca Lindfors, Solly Marx, David Greenan; 97m

A computer error sets free an incarcerated homicidal maniac, a diagnosed "paranoid psychotic," responsible for the "Sorority Slaughter," but spared the electric chair as a result of mental illness. He returns to his old hunting ground, a sorority, and resumes killing nubile young women. While the hospital tries to cover up the blunder by sending hired killers to dispatch the offender before the release is discovered (with only a passing thought to any additional victims that may result), a doctor goes in search of the killer, à la *Halloween*.

Although this is an undistinguished slasher film, it is included here as an example not only of the Ted Bundy sorority-slaughter legacy (the house of women as a magnet for mentally ill killers), but a demonstration of the incurable nature of the serial killer and mass murderer. Those convicted of murder and treated in a psychiatric institution for the criminally insane, if released, no matter how liberal or punitive the treatment (here it is the latter, much to the dismay of the liberal doctor), will resume their homicide. Such killers are imprinted with sexual sadism from an early age (hence the obligatory flashback, here to the janitor-protagonist being sexually humiliated by the sorority sisters, revealing revenge and sexual resentment/inferiority to be his real motives).

There is some explanatory treatment of the mental health system as beset by budget cuts and forced to release unstable patients in order to preserve bed space. The mental health system is riddled with hypocrisy, claiming such releases are safe for the community, while at the same time devoted to the torture of humanity's most miserable specimens. However, the film suggests that these specimens ultimately deserve their treatment. Psychosis is shown as a silent condition which finds expression only in acts of the most abhorrent sexual violence: the mad speak in acts, not in words, and have no personality beyond those acts.

The doctor (female and hence a liberal, according to the low-budget movie arena) advocates treatment, while the police she runs up against favor sterner punishment. This theme of understanding vs. punishment seems a subtext in Nuchtern's work; however, it is resolved in a reactionary and reductionist manner in this case. The killer may have the motivations of a serial killer, but he is reduced to a mass murdering automaton, turning the film into more of a slasher movie than a serial killer film (although it addresses in part the common ground).

Director Nuchtern (encased in seedy exploitation fodder) was a friend of Romano Scavolini, and was involved in the production of *Nightmare*, hence a minor link to the Italian horror boom. This film was shot in 3D, following the popular example of *Friday the 13th Part 3D*. However, the gore scenes lack the comical, grotesque exuberance of the Warhol/Morrissey films *Flesh for Frankenstein* and *Blood for Dracula*, for instance.

Silent Sentence

(1973: d. Larry G. Spangler) aka *Jack the Ripper Goes West*

scr. George Arthur Bloom, Seton I. Miller; stry. Miller, Robert Shelton; pr. Spangler, Stan Jolley; prod d. Jolley; cast. Jack Elam, Ruth Roman, Jeff Cooper, John Kellogg, Gene Evans, Diana Erwig

This is a rare Western serial killer film. A small mining town is beset by the murder/mutilation of prostitutes. When the sheriff (Elam) is unable to solve the case, the town leaders invite an outside agent. This creates tension with the sheriff. Various townspeople (all Western archetypes—whores, barber, bartender, etc.) could be suspects.

This follows a procedural story in the Western setting. However, unlike *Five Card Stud*, which concerned a non-sexual repeat killer, the sex killer fully enters into the Westerner's code. Brothels are a common occurrence in the Western, and prostitutes are often manhandled, but this is the first time they have been targeted by a sex killer. Interestingly, he too, like many great Western heroes, is motivated by revenge. But, in that it is revenge for having contracted venereal disease, it is a transposition of honor code and sexual dementia.

The film is best at depicting scenes of venereal horror (should one compare them to the sexual madness in Cronenberg's earlier films?), with the killer in the advanced stages of syphilis, and its condemnation of mother/son bonds. It is revealed that the mother, so resentful of her son's illness, has been bringing him prostitutes to kill and mutilate (a sexual frenzy), which she then watches for voyeuristic excitement — a displaced incestuous desire. Sex madness has consumed these characters and cost them their stability.

Far from anomalies, they are presented as part of the fabric of the town, a family and value system of civilization founded on sexual exploitation and its violent consequences. Patriarchy and law thus serve only to regulate sexual practice and chastise what it fosters (as prostitution is legalized and celebrated within the foundation of US authority). The West here only yields disease and madness, and the perversion of idealism. The film is an interesting grafting of 20th century serial killer pathology (and cinematic codes of exploitation) onto the codes of the West. It reveals sex murder as an exposition of the madness at the core of US society, in the process suggesting a deep-rooted evolution of the sex killer as part of the modern fabric. Jack the Ripper would have been just at home on the Frontier.

Knowing of Ripper lore (the killer's motive as revenge for catching VD), this was released firstly as *A Knife for the Ladies* and then (when no one noticed) retitled and rereleased as *Jack the Ripper Goes West*. Still no one noticed. However, it is a rare generic hybrid, and thus an interesting video discovery. It is a genuine shame, considering its subversive potential, that the film is not better than the disappointing curio it is. Still, it's worthwhile nonetheless.

The Sinister Urge

(1960: d. Edward D. Wood Jr.)

scr, pr. Wood; ph. William C. Thompson; ed. John Soh; cast. Carl Anthony, Vic McGee, Reed Howes, Duke Moore, James Moore, Conrad Brooks, Jean Fontaine; 82m

Murder in the porno world: when three models are found dead in a park, two police detectives investigate. They discover a failed filmmaker reduced to making such smut, and are determined to bring down the pornographic empire they discover (headed by a so-called Queen). Meanwhile, a young man exposed to pornographic imagery is slowly driven mad, becoming an aspiring sex killer as he attempts to rape and murder his date, and others.

In the manner of such cautionary fiascoes as *Reefer Madness*, this film develops the proposition that prolonged exposure to pornographic imagery (even "harmless" nudie pictures now no longer even considered pornography) will turn even the most wholesome of American men into psychotic sex murderers. As is usual for Wood, this is supposedly developed with unshakable conviction (Nash and Ross, p. 2943), although the depiction of sexual aberration (which Wood had attempted in *Glen or Glenda*) leads to the unintentionally funny moments expected of this director. Ironically, it contains an autobiographical component in the character of a filmmaker now reduced to sleaze, whose office is decorated with posters of Wood's own films—a clear statement of his own fate.

The Sinister Urge was the cult director's last feature film. It was made for veteran producer Roy Reid and released on a double bill with the Wood-scripted *The Violent Years*. Apparently it proved Wood capable of making an easily releasable item (Hanke in *Sleaze Merchants*, pp. 30–32), but did not result in a career boost. Thus, Wood subsequently turned to industrial films financed by government bodies, his feature career over. Like most of Wood's films, it has a ready-made cult audience today, composed of fans of so-called bad movies.

Sketches of a Strangler

(1978: d. Paul Leder)

scr. Leder; pr. Leder, Tom Spaulding; cast. Allen Garfield (Goorwitz) , Meredith MacRae, Jennifer Rhodes, Clayton Wilcox, Frank Witeman; 91m

A mother-fixated art student (Goorwitz), living with his sister, is obsessed over the beautiful young women he considers unattainable, to the point where he begins to kill prostitutes. A victim's sister looks for him.

This is remembered on the Internet as one of Goorwitz' more bizarre and kinky 1970s films, but is otherwise an unknown, minor psycho movie at the start of the slasher era. Once again the serial killer verges on the automaton (though characterized here in the expected horrible-mother scenario), and is a man seeking expression of pent-up rage and resentment.

Reportedly, however, the film could not escape convention and even mediocrity. Director Leder is a regular figure in exploitation films, best known for *I Dismember Mama*. His humor is submerged beneath bare competence. This was unavailable at time of writing.

Slash Dance

(1989: d. James Shyman)

scr. Shyman; pr. Andrew Maisner; ph. Geza Sinkovics; m. Emilio Kauderer; ed. Larry Rosen; art d. Wayne Lehrer; cast. Cindy Maranne, James Carrol Jordan, Jay Richradson, Joel von Ornsteiner, John Bluto; 83m

A serial killer targets scantily clad dancers who audition for a musical show, and leaves the bodies in an old theater, which seemingly has a special place in his heart. A detective poses as a dancer to lure the culprit, and captivates a man whom she believes to be the killer.

With little nudity or violence, one wonders what the expected exploitation market made of this minor thriller, intended perhaps as a slasher parody of the hit *Flashdance*. However, as comedy it is inept and too restrained in its approach to the subject matter. Thus, it only timidly frames the goings-on in the world of illicit sex-culture, instead focusing on poor routines and a barely characterized killer — lured by the dancers' apparent combination of innocence and sexuality (as virgin-whores).

Owing to the developments of a distantly remembered *Phantom of the Opera*, by way of the vastly superior Michele Soavi thriller *Stagefright* and even Fulci's disco-giallo *Murder Rock*, this film never takes fire as an intended US giallo. It may aspire to this Italian form, but it emerges as a most rudimentary movie whose conception of a sex killer is more akin to that found in an anonymous slasher film.

The Slasher

(1974: d. Roberto Montero) aka *Slasher Is a Sex Maniac*

scr. Montero, Lou Angelli, I. Fasant; pr. Eugene Florimont; ph. George Gaslini, F. Rossi; cast. Farley Granger, Sylvia Koscina, Susan Scott, Chris Avram; 88m

A serial killer slays adulterous women and leaves photographic proof of their infidelities at the crime scene for the investigators to find, apparently meant as a justification to excuse his punitive actions. Police investigate.

This is a minor US-Italy giallo co-production, with Farley Granger as the head cop. Reportedly undistinguished in every respect (with few reports of it at all), it is considered to have predated the slasher boom, and is perhaps more important in its title (which posits the US direction of the giallo interpreted as slasher film) than in much else. Nevertheless, it does testify to the popularity of the giallo and its increasing applicability to American exploitation formulas. It has disappeared from release.

Slaughter of the Innocents

(1993: d. James Glickenhaus)

scr, pr.; Glickenhaus; pr. J. Richard; ph. Mark Irwin; m. Joe Renzetti; ed. Kevin Tent; prod d. Jack Ballance, Nicholas T. Preovolos; cast. Scott Glenn, Darlanne Fluegel, Zakes Mokae, Zitto Kazann, Kevin Sorbo, Jesse Cameron Glickenhaus; 103m

A Cleveland-based FBI agent (Glenn) is assigned the case of a Utah serial child molester/killer. A Bible-spouting religious fanatic and cave dweller is a chief suspect. He is revealed to be building a replica of Noah's ark in his cave and collecting things in twos. He believes he is doing God's bidding. Despite the agent supposedly being an expert on such monsters, it is his fifteen-year-old son who runs away and solves the case.

This is considered, on the Internet, as merely trading on star Scott Glenn's recent appearance in *Silence of the Lambs* (with Glenn here cast again as an FBI specialist), and an excuse for director Glickenhaus to cast his non-actor son in a major supporting role. Glickenhaus had been partly responsible for Lustig's *Relentless*, and applies a similar functional tone here, balancing suspense and a kid's struggle with his father's reputation, the child determined to prove his own worth on the same scale. It is thus an examination of father and son interactions and its dynamics when faced with such a responsibility as that posed by the killer's continued actions.

Unlike Lustig, who arguably condemns the monstrous son, Glickenhaus here celebrates the son as both an independently willed young man and the just inheritor of Patriarchy's traditions. The boy is a regular wonder kid, unusually talented, and ready to become the next generation of profiler and serial killer pursuer, even upstaging his father. Many serial killer films do not share this faith in the ability of a subsequent generation. It takes a near child to really stop a child killer, and the film thus develops its notion of poetic justice.

The movie shows the child systematically adopting the methodology of his elders (in a nod to VICAP, he develops a program on his home computer designed to track the serial killer), and the son is able to talk about the forensic details of the case with his father without outrage. He is held up as the all–American boy and the future of the country — baseball-playing, respectful and strong-willed, clever and cunning. He is more than a match for the demented killer. Had the director's son not played him, perhaps the film would have been better received by genre fans.

Sledge Hammer

(1984: d. David A. Prior)

cast. Ted Prior, Steven J. Wright, Doug Matley; 87m

A killer, who when a child murdered his mother and her lover, now bludgeons teen girls to death. He returns home to the scene of his imprinting and creates havoc in an otherwise tranquil town. The au-thorities investigate after several bodies are found. The only novelty here, reportedly, is the murder weapon, which the killer conceals under his coat.

This was made on videotape by a minor exploitation figure and released without fanfare. It has yet to find widespread release or a receptive audience. Once again the killer functions as a menacing automaton with only a traumatic childhood and subsequent sexual resentment of women (the most common nod towards characterization in the lower echelons of the slasher/serial killer spillover) distinguishing him from the more unmotivated slasher figures. The killer returning home may be a sign of the desire to confront the source of the trauma, but he resorts to murder as a solution.

Snapdragon

(1993: d. Worth Keeter)

scr. Ashok Amritraj; exec pr. Barry Collier, Barbara Javitz; ph. James Mathews; m. Michael Linn; cast. Steven Bauer, Pamela Anderson, Chelsea Field, Irene Tsu; 96m

Two men are killed during intercourse by a young prostitute. A young woman (Field) transferred from vice to homicide asks her boyfriend (Bauer, a police psychologist) for an analysis of the killer. He later meets a blonde (Anderson) who tells him of her nightmares in which she kills her lovers; he falls in love with her, to his girlfriend's dismay. She also suffers from amnesia. The killer is revealed to be Anderson's sister.

The film offers a harsh depiction of male sexual obsession, as at the beginning a child is sold into white slavery and tattooed (with the snapdragon symbol) as property. Men seek to exploit and suppress women, as the police officer discovers when she goes undercover and busts men who like to rough up prostitutes, or obsess about them and shape them into their private fantasies (as Bauer does), hiding their real, exploitative motives.

Unlike many female serial killers, the killer actually murders during intercourse (as would the killer in *Nekromantik 2* and *Eye of the Beholder*) and presumably copulates with the corpse. The victims are revealed to have ejaculated after death (the little death thus equated with the big death)—providing her a satisfaction beyond revenge. This makes a mockery of sex as love and reproduction: it is an act of power and dominance. Necrophilia is thus a deliberate challenge to Patriarchy's romantic and sexual conventions, and hence a societal taboo.

The female police officer respects the killer as making a feminist statement of sorts in her usurping of male aggression; thus, she plays killer with her boyfriend as a means of sexual role-playing. The killer is therefore a fantasy devourer of men, a combination of sex killer, vampire and black widow. She is seeking retribution for a lifetime of sexual exploitation, and so is a deliberate challenge to Patriarchy's system of gender authority and definition. Such a woman sticks up for her sister in a gesture of feminist unity. She reacts against her definition in relation to men by severing the source of that definition and its corresponding sexual sublimation.

The killer's weapon is the "dragon's tongue," a Chinese razor concealed in her mouth under her tongue (a similar weapon is used by whore Pam Grier in *Fort Apache the Bronx*). A great title, marketable premise and better-than-expected direction from Keeter (perhaps best known among horror fans for the 3D *Rottweiller*) make *Snapdragon* a moderately effective addition to the rare female serial killer subgenre. Terri Treas, who would later direct *Play Nice*, an equally harsh condemnation of male sexuality, scripted it.

The Sniper

(1952: d. Edward Dmytryk)

scr. Harry Brown; stry. Edna Anhalt, Edward Anhalt; pr. Stanley Kramer; ph. Burnett Guffey; m. George Antheil; ed. Harry Gerstad, Aaron Stell; prod d. Rudolph Sternad; cast. Adolphe Menjou, Arthur Franz, Gerald Mohr, Richard Kiley, Frank Faylen, Marie Windsor; 87m

A young man takes out his sexual frustrations with his rifle. He hates his mother, and shoots at women with his long-range rifle, clearly a metaphor for sexual dysfunction and frustration: a form of rape-murder even. The killer is aware of his illness and seeks psychiatric help, but when faced with general indifference he surrenders to fantasy. A policeman (Menjou) is assigned to the case, and suspects that a mentally ill man, as opposed to a conventional criminal, may be responsible, although his superiors are dissatisfied with this explanation and, in conjunction with the media, pressure him into action. In the end, with the killer facing off against armed police, the killer finally believes he is being given the recognition he deserves.

The reputation and "importance" of this film has recently been reassessed. Indeed, in the anthology *Mythologies of Violence*, the film is considered as one of the first American movies to tackle the serial killer in a case-study manner, with the killer not the embodiment of all evil (as per the horror film), but as a psychologically and even socioeconomically explainable problem in need of treatment and understanding if progress is to be made. In that, the film is a bridge from the film noirs of the 1940s to the case-study mentality of the 1950s criminal portraits, via the social-problem genre beloved of producer Stanley Kramer. Thus it emphasizes locations (San Francisco—the same terrain to house another rifle-shooting serial killer, Scorpio, in *Dirty Harry*) and factual police procedures in response to the new threat posed by such a killer. It does not, however, abandon the noir-stylized psychodrama that Dmytryk had essayed in his earlier work (*Murder My Sweet* and *Crossfire* among them).

Appropriately, the police psychiatrist (an early profiler figure, as he is brought into the case) provides the most rational explanation (according to Ruben in *Mythologies*, p. 43). The police are confounded by such an unclassifiable crime, and it is the psychiatric profession that can offer solutions and effectively profile a still-at-large killer. Dmytryk's style then seeks to frame such psychological imbalance, and its Expressionist legacy, in a recognizable milieu. It is doubly interesting then as a companion piece to the Losey remake of *M*, also a product of the early 1950s social-problem film: how should society deal with such a problem? Although the crimes are sexual in nature, it is arguable to what extent Dmytryk conveys the killer's sexual pleasure in his crimes (the *New York Times'* Bosley Crowther felt it wasn't explicit enough about this).

General indifference to mental disarray is held in part responsible for the killer's violent crimes. He has a record which clearly indicates his current path, yet when he has the sense enough to avoid it, he is greeted with indifference; a clearer checking of the facts, and concerned analysis, would have detected the problem before it resulted in homicide. And motiveless homicide founded in such mental distress proves a problem beyond contemporary police practice (as *Variety* noted in a review also praising the film's intelligent approach over sensationalism). The sympathetic policeman feels both the need to capture the killer and to do something for him, to understand him (Nash and Ross, p. 2990), and is thus a synthesis of police detective and concerned police psychologist — an early profiler.

The style-conscious Dmytryk employed a sketch artist to elaborately storyboard the film in advance, finally shooting it over eighteen days. At the time, Dmytryk had been blacklisted, although he was invited by Kramer back to Hollywood. Consequently, much was made of his working with a politically conservative actor, Menjou; and the Communist newspaper the *Daily Worker* even went so far as to claim Dmytryk had sold out to Big Money and betrayed his ideals (as recounted in Nash and Ross, pp. 2990–1). Ironically, Menjou apparently also was criticized by those sharing his political beliefs for working with the liberal Dmytryk.

So I Married an Axe Murderer

(1993: d. Thomas Schlamme)

scr. Robbie Fox; ph. Julio Macat; m. Bruce Broughton; ed. Richard Halsey, Colleen Halsey; prod d. John Graysmark; cast. Mike Myers, Nancy Travis, Anthony LaPaglia, Amanda Plummer, Brenda Fricker, Matt Doherty, Charles Grodin, Phil Hartman; 92m

This is an early Mike Myers comedy. He stars both as a young man (a sci-fi author and poetry performer) romantically involved with a local butcher, a woman who may be an axe murderess, and that man's hyper–Scottish father (a forerunner of the Fat Bastard character he would play in *Austin Powers — The Spy Who Shagged Me*). He brings his new girlfriend home and soon sees in her a resemblance to a "black-widow" type (she lures men and kills them on their wedding night). Normality soon breaks down as Myers must face the possibility, with the protagonist left to decipher the remains, and rediscover hope. The killer is revealed to be her meek and mild sister.

Myers plays a performance artist immersed in the remnants of the San Francisco Beatnik scene. His policeman friend (LaPaglia) is tired of the drudgery of police work, having joined the force with expectations based on the film *Serpico*. His friendship with Myers is the film's warmest note, as it is partly the policeman's triumph that he uncovers the killer's identity and rushes to save Myers, in the process becoming the decisive agent of action and change that he wished to be. In short, his role in Patriarchy is validated by his response to his friend's jeopardy, although he at first thought that Myers' suspicions were merely an expression of a fear of commitment.

Myers plays a likable, good-natured man. He longs for commitment but is afraid of it, and has a history of sabotaging his relationships when they get too serious. In fact, every character is essentially likable, a decision which separates the film from the truly black comedy work of *Eating Raoul* and *The Young Poisoner's Handbook*, and even the Dmytryk version of *Bluebeard*. However, the film does play with the notion of the duplicitous female, with the protagonist justifiably mistrusting the two sisters. Amidst the light romantic comedy is a sly questioning of the perhaps inherent duality of women, a legacy from film noir. It is too innocuous to manage a statement, however.

Star Myers had broken through to the big screen in *Wayne's World* after coming to public attention on television via *Saturday Night Live*, and this was his moderately successful attempt to further forge a big-screen identity (this would come in the two *Austin Powers* films and his superb "serious" role in *Club 54*). He has since gone on to become one of Hollywood's most successful comedy performers.

The Sorcerers

(1967: d. Michael Reeves)

scr. Reeves, Tom Baker; stry. John Burke; pr. Patrick Curtis, Tony Tenser; ph. Stanley Long; ed. Ralph Sheldon; m. Paul Ferris; cast. Boris Karloff, Catherine Lacey, Ian Ogilvy, Elizabeth Ercy, Victor Henry, Susan George, Dani Sheridan; 86m

This is not a serial killer film, although it does intersect the genre in interesting ways. An elderly couple, a former stage hypnotist and his assistant, invent a machine which allows them to control the thoughts of others, effectively hypnotizing them. They take over young men and begin to live vicariously through them. Twisted with the bitterness and resentment of age, and craving ever more voyeuristic thrills and sensations in the midst of the swinging 1960s era of youth revival, the old woman drives her young male to sex murder. Her more responsible husband is outraged but cannot stop her from her pursuit of transgression.

The treatment of voyeurism, implicating the audience as complicit in sex murder, even willing it to happen, is a cynical tract that brings to mind *Peeping Tom*. The generational theme, of a hypocritical, monstrous elder seeking to control youth, also anticipates the work of Pete Walker, perhaps *Frightmare* in particular. It is as a reaction to changing times, and outdated horror role models and formulas (the all-powerful Hammer studios were by now in their decline), that the film is a bridging work. The monsters here are far from the alluring and sophisticated lady-killers of Hammer (as Newman points out, pp. 12–14); nor are the young completely innocent, as it is suggested that the hypnotic control looses their innate capability, and that they correspondingly must battle with guilt and pleasure over their actions.

The central theme is control, and so the film cleverly adopts the agent/controller dynamic of earlier horror films. As the characters seek freedom and experience, they gradually lose control over themselves and seek to assert their will over others. The social revolution has loosed only resentment, megalomania and the sensationalist desire to experience transgression.

The old may ascribe these qualities to the youth and condemn them, but this is a hypocritical stance, as they seek to revel and exploit these sensations.

Despite Karloff's good intentions, his wife dominates him, and he is unable to prevent her sadism and resentment from overpowering his will. This monstrous, dominating matriarch would also feature in the Walker/McGillivray *Frightmare*. Indeed, the film features a similar condemnation of the family, here consisting of the monstrous parents and the surrogate rebellious son who in the end serves their monstrousness. It is the desire of the old to control the young which leads to sex murder as merely another experience to be had in the quest for sensation fostered by social change and the cultural celebration of youth.

Special Effects

(1985: d. Larry Cohen)

scr. Cohen; pr. Carter DeHaven, Paul Kurta; ph. Paul Glickman; m. Michael Minard; ed. Armond Leibowitz; cast. Zoe Tamerlis, Eric Bogosian, Brad Rijn, Kevin O'Connor, Bill Oland; 103m

A film director (Bogosian) in need of a hit, in a rage kills a girl on film. He decides to make a movie about the subsequent investigation, enlisting the detective as producer, though he gradually wishes for more control. The director hires a lookalike actress (Tamerlis) to take the murdered girl's place, prompting her to recreate the dead girl's personality (a nod to Aldrich's *Legend of Lylah Clare*—Newman, p. 114), and becomes obsessed with killing her too, so he can use the snuff footage, even though police investigate. The dead woman's husband, whom the director tries to frame for murder, in the end wants the actress to replace his wife and be mother to his kids.

Although there is only one murder,

the film's examination of the fascination with real and recreated death, a development of the themes of *Peeping Tom*, makes it a topical inclusion here. Even if it is not technically a serial killer film, it concerns a protagonist increasingly obsessed with sex-murder and its attendant details. He seeks to turn this obsession into financial profit, even though it may cost the actress her individual identity.

With its opening photo shoot of a nude model with an Uncle Sam hat, the film announces its thematic concern with the snuff pornographic ethic of an American culture obsessed with sexuality and murder. Thus, once the director kills the girl, he indulges in necrophilic fantasy, filming himself bathing the corpse. He has become obsessed with sex murder and its corresponding representation as a cultural artifact. To him, murder has become a self-aggrandizing gesture, providing him with a new life and goal. It has served as transcendence, and as an imprinting event which makes him want to re-experience the moment, an incipient serial killer who will attempt to manipulate reality to serve his own need for power and superiority. Murder as an art form — the ultimate condemnation of US film, and an eerie anticipation of the 1990s thematic direction in the serial killer film, further showing Cohen as a provocative independent filmmaker.

Species 2

(1997: d. Peter Medak)

scr. Chris Brancato; pr. Frank Mancuso Jr.; char. Dennis Feldman; ph. Matthew F. Leonetti; prod d. Miljen Kreka Kljakovic; ed. Richard Nord; des. H.R. Giger; m. Edward Shearmur; cast. Michael Madsen, Natasha Henstridge, Marg Helgenberger, Mykelti Williamson, George Dzundza, James Cromwell, Justin Lazard, Miriam Cyr; 89m

This is a fascinating hybrid of alien threat and serial killer film in the AIDS era.

During a mission to Mars an astronaut (Lazard) is infected with alien DNA. On earth, he has a voracious sexual appetite, his alien form killing the women he mates with as they bear his alien offspring, which he keeps as a brood. The crimes are interpreted as sex killings and reported on the news as the result of another serial killer on the loose. He is tracked by a scientist (Helgenberger), assassin (Madsen) and another alien/human crossbreed (Henstridge), who is used to lure him out, despite fears of what could happen if they breed.

There is some sympathy for the killer, infected with an alien virus, who tries to commit suicide at one point, as a man who cannot control the destructive force inside him which seeks sex as its means of expression and power. Devouring the human female is an instinctual part of the male alien mating process. But this hypersexual craving is not unique to the astronaut. Indeed, all the astronauts seem to be in perpetual heat, a state of constant, insatiable craving, which the dutiful patriarchs, and those who function in their name, repress. Thus, the scientists and military order the astronauts to refrain from sex for a test period (which they do not), and isolate Eve (the alien, symbolically named) from male contact lest she be turned on and wish to mate and procreate.

In this context, the alien DNA is a sexually communicable virus, and thus the film becomes an AIDS-era science fiction movie to rank alongside the undervalued *Lifeforce*, although it falls short of Hooper's manic grandeur and depiction of mass hysteria. The scientists discover the alien presence as a blood abnormality and track it accordingly, as they would the course of a viral contamination. They ultimately kill the alien by introducing another, human, virus into its system, linking such viral outbreaks to bacteriological warfare advances.

The film's tone suggests deliberate genre parody, set from the opening note of a spacecraft bearing US corporate logos—the commercialization of space. But such references, with conspiracy comedian Richard Belzer cast as the President, are throwaway gags undermining any solemn reading of the material, and suggesting the slyly subversive tone characteristic of Medak's better works. This subversive intent is far from subtle, and the characters are caricatures. The plot and dialogue may often be silly, but it is the film's thematic skill which makes it interesting and a vast improvement over the original *Species*, which was the most blatant of Hollywood's assembly-line product.

Hence, the protagonist is presented as the all–American hero for "these imperfect times," a football hero with a politically ambitious father. He is the product of a self-congratulatory Patriarchy and heir to its legacy. Ironically, he is also the infected agent that threatens to tear it apart and destroy its pure image of itself. It is telling that the threat to Patriarchal stability is considered by the press and general public to be a serial killer, and that the serial killer once again is an alien presence, a modified humanity essentially non-human — a return to the horror origins of the serial killer figure.

Yet this alien knows human weakness — sexual desire — and voraciously prowls the streets, cruising for women to impregnate (and kill in the process of subsequent birth, the alien/human offspring spreading the viral contamination over the world), choosing the serial killer's favored easy target, prostitutes. In that, he is a perversion of the heterosexual desire to procreate, and the film is filled with genuine revulsion at the prospect of copulation. It culminates in a pornographic sex scene between the aliens which shows sex as a repugnant power game devoid of "love." It is a depiction of lust gone mad, and destroying

Patriarchy from within, driving the hero son into committing patricide to protect his sexual secret against the forces of repression. The killer kills in the process of self-actualization.

Director Medak is better known for the crime drama *The Krays*, but he had tangentially tackled the serial killer in *The Ruling Class* (about a paranoid schizophrenic who is deemed insane when he thinks he is Jesus Christ, but becomes an influential Parliamentarian when he thinks he is Jack the Ripper). Screenwriter Brancato is known for his work on TV's *X-Files* (scripting the first season fan favorite "Eve" episode). He admitted an admiration for Frankenheimer's *Manchurian Candidate* and its plot premise of a man who returns a hero, but has a changed agenda, "a demon inside" (MGM DVD liner notes).

The Spiral Staircase

(1945: d. Robert Siodmak)

scr. Mel Dinelli; nvl. Ethel Lina White; pr. Dore Schary; ph. Nicholas Musuraca; m. Roy Webb; ed. Harry Marker, Harry Gerstad; cast. Dorothy McGuire, George Brent, Ethel Barrymore, Kent Smith, Rhonda Fleming, Gordon Oliver, Elsa Lanchester, Ellen Corby; 83m

Circa 1906, an old New England mansion may be harboring a killer. A young mute woman (made so by childhood trauma) is employed by an elderly invalid with a son and a stepson (Brent) who seems infatuated with her. The girl loves this well-educated stepson, who is overly concerned for her welfare. A doctor offers the girl therapy, and she falls in romantically with this doctor, whose reputation and abilities are doubted and questioned by those around him. Meanwhile, their town is terrorized by a serial killer of disabled or weak women. The mute girl is therefore a potential future target. The killer is finally revealed to be the seemingly compassionate stepson she has so trusted. She is finally forced to flee him. His invalid stepmother, who has warned the girl throughout to leave this place lest it consume her, shoots him.

This is an early demonstration of the perversion of the Romantic obsession with beauty into Sadean practice, as the killer wishes to eliminate physically disabled or disfigured women. He is obsessed with an ideal image of feminine perfection that enables him to rationalize his actions as for society's betterment — to purge the weak. He can then deny them as a function of his own perverse sexuality and his cowardly need to dominate the imperfect. His psychological aberration is suggested through the point of view shots of McGuire as he sees the mute girl literally without a mouth on her face, a detail he cannot escape. He visualizes what he perceives as physical aberrance, and a sign of inferiority and weakness, to disfiguring proportions, and fixates on it. Perhaps we are all driven to seek out details that have personal meaning (as the camera selects details of story and thematic importance).

Murder gives him a purpose and definition he otherwise lacks. And, significantly for the era, these murders are rooted in sexual aberration, fueled by cultural and community standards of physical perfection. In this film, the sex murderer entered the shadowy, visually encoded world of film noir. In such a world, characters are inevitably trapped between shadows and light, and amidst reflections, with women the object of a male gaze, both eroticizing and punishing the perceived inferiority it is drawn/attracted to. The killer, as an agent of cruel fate, has planned the details of the evening to suit his homicidal agenda. Paradoxically, the traumatic experience he puts the girl through enables her to regain the power of speech and end her disability. In effect, he has purged it after all. The realization of it all reduces her to tears.

The mute servant girl (Dorothy McGuire) realizes that her benevolent employer (George Brent) is a serial killer of disfigured and "imperfect" women, and intends to kill her next, in *The Spiral Staircase* (RKO, 1945).

The depiction of the killer reflects a case study in psychosexual aberration, and an attempt to reintroduce the aberrant humanity into the movies. Significantly, it is an abnormal relationship with his father that has driven the killer to kill the weak in an effort to prove himself strong, to prove himself to a stern father (is he thus supposed to represent an individualized Nazi threat?). It is the law of the father, as a malfunctioning socialization process based on rampant masculinity, which would destroy those who do not conform. He kills the weak, coded as female, in an effort to remove his own vulnerabilities and sexual attraction to those other than those to whom he should have been programmed to respond. He must disavow his own difference, and the process of disavowal offers a transgressive, addictive sexual release.

The first murder is intercut with an early cinema screening of a woman-in-jeopardy movie, the difference between the two perils reflecting the developing tradition of women in danger as social expectations continue to evolve. It is with the third murder that the investigators announce that it could be anyone: that no male is safe from the desire to exploit women. Thus the film cleverly maintains every male as a suspect, no matter how benevolent they seem. Indeed, it reveals such benevolence as a ruse concealing a sexual infatuation. Both Brent and the doctor are infatuated with McGuire, but only Brent transforms this into homicidal desire, the doctor professing true love. Male human nature therefore has the capacity for both: to love an object for its beauty and imperfection, and to seek to destroy it. Later, Michael Powell would flirt with this theme of attraction to the imperfect in *Peeping Tom*, wherein the killer is attracted to a woman with a facial scar.

The relative unity of time — all in one night — is a theatrical conceit later adopted by the slasher film. It enables Siodmak to explore the strained character dynamics of the family, and the killer's desperate need to be the head of such a family. This position is partly threatened by the return of his half brother, who rejects the father's view of the strong surviving and the weak perishing, as he considers the both of them to be weak men, despite their apparent success. Ironically, he is right, as what the killer holds as strength is a terrible psychological weakness.

The film is additionally interesting as a kind of cross between *Night Must Fall* and *Shadow of a Doubt* in its conception of a serial killer lurking in the same residence as a protagonist who is infatuated in some way with him. The protagonist's idealized image of herself and another finally results in a confrontation with the other. It is not as cynical as *Night Must Fall*, however, where the protagonist sought in part to manipulate the killer, and perhaps is closer to the innocent obsession of little Charlie for big Charlie in *Shadow of a Doubt*. Hitchcock's film also postulated the killer's death as a rite of passage in the maturation of a vulnerable heroine.

A German director who came to America to avoid the Nazi regime, Siodmak never received the critical appraisal of other German directors, especially Fritz Lang, although Siodmak's film noirs are a considerable body of work. Recent reappraisals of film noir, however, have devoted attention to a select number of his works. Still, he perhaps remains best known for his work with Burt Lancaster on the pirate movie *The Crimson Pirate*.

The Spiral Staircase was the first of a number of intended co-productions between RKO and David O. Selznick's Vanguard Films. English director Peter Collinson remade it in 1976, and updated it to contemporary England, to much critical hostility.

The Spiral Staircase

(1976: d. Peter Collinson)

scr. Allan Scott, Chris Bryant; pr. Peter Shaw; ph. Ken Hodges; m. David Lindup; cast. Jacqueline Bisset, Christopher Plummer, John Philip Law, Mildred Dunnock, Gayle Hunnicutt, Sam Wanamaker, John Ronane, Ronald Radd, Sheila Brennan, Elaine Stritch; 89m

This is a capable, if unremarkable, remake. A mute nurse (Bisset) attends to an elderly invalid, unaware that there is a killer (Plummer) lurking amongst the group of inhabitants in the large suburban house.

Collinson stresses reflective surfaces and shadowy compositions, and often shoots from outside windows looking in, to capture the reflections of the outside world and suggest an intrusive gaze. He stresses entrapment within the frame as a bind of the modern world. But his stylistic flourishes seem overstressed gimmicks. Collinson stresses the act of looking as an aggressive gaze, essentially masculine by definition and perverse, forever unstable. He links sight to memory and the influence of the past, in that way suggesting it forever remains subjective.

Ironically, with the exception of the killer, the people seem oddly out of their element, a regular theme of Collinson's, even in his comedy work. By stressing looming foregrounds and figures in the background, he further implies a menacing separateness to human interaction. As it explores a group of people bound together by circumstance, the movie becomes an old-fashioned melodrama, never achieving the modern relevance perhaps hoped for — with reviewers thus considering it an

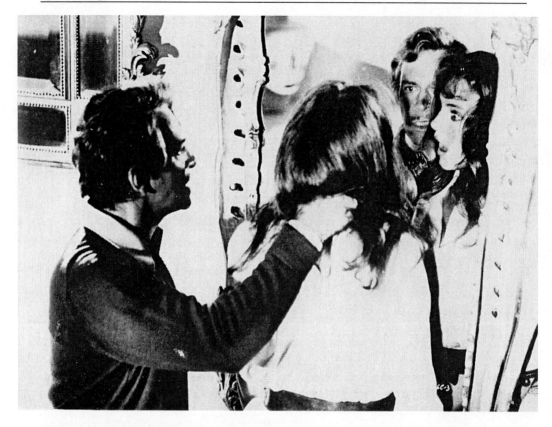

The serial killer (Christopher Plummer) of "imperfect" women and the object of his rage in the remake of *The Spiral Staircase* (WB, 1976).

unnecessary remake. Still, Collinson tries for modern relevance (for UK audiences) in the depiction of a monstrous aristocracy in decline, its traditional social structures coming apart. One could hardly call it Chekovian, however. Indeed, at times it seems to become a parody of manners, with its refined, gentlemanly killer once again striving to eliminate imperfection from the world, the legacy of his father's intolerance. The lack of genuine communication between people enables such a killer to thrive.

Collinson further tries to update the material to contemporary England by setting it in the suburbs instead of the original's isolated retreat. As a director, he tried to shape the horror thriller to his own ends but was unable to make the lasting impact of Pete Walker in the early 1970s, to whom

he can perhaps be compared. He tried another old dark house–style melodrama in his update of Agatha Christie's *And Then There Were None*, but will perhaps always be best remembered as the director of the highly regarded caper comedy *The Italian Job*.

Split Images

(1996: d. Sheldon Larry)

scr. Pete Hamill, Vera Appleyard; nvl. Elmore Leonard; pr. Zev Braun, Ken Gord; art d. David Orin Charles; cast. Gregory Harrison, Robert Collins, Maury Chaykin, Rebecca Jenkins, Steve Whistance-Smith, Nahanni Johnstone

A wealthy playboy murders people and videotapes it, forming a collection of homemade snuff movies for later playback and presumed masturbatory thrills. A journalist probes the related evidence between killings, and she confides in a detective. The killer hires an ex-cop for protection, and initiates him in the process. Soon the ex-cop is holding the camera for the killer.

The killer is obsessed with the "look" of murder and the "feel" of killing. He holds himself superior to all, and so justifies his exploitation of what he considers a dying culture, unaware that his obsessions epitomize it. Just so there is no doubt as to the killer's sexual delight in murder, the filmmakers include a scene whereby his watching of snuff is intercut with the ex-cop's viewing of pornography. The film's direction suggests that the latter, a symptom of cultural disillusionment, leads to the former. The killer is bored with privilege and so preys on the disposable for additional thrills.

The film is an unfortunately minor addition to the snuff cycle of serial killer films, which include *Peeping Tom*, *Art of Dying*, *Special Effects*, *Henry: Portrait of a Serial Killer* and *8MM*. In addition, novelist Elmore Leonard would tackle murder, pornography and the snuff aesthetic in *52 Pickup*, master filmmaker John Frankenheimer's welcome return to form. *Split Images'* ending, as the killer watches his own death, is a clear nod to *Peeping Tom*. Despite its intertextual interest, this is a minor tele-movie. It seems to want to be a criminal indictment of voyeurism but lacks even the impact of *Sliver*.

Split Second

(1992: d. Tony Maylam)

scr. Gary Scott Thompson; pr. Laura Gregory; ph. Clive Tickner; m. Francis Haines, Steve Parsons; ed. Dan Rae; prod d. Chris Edwards; cast. Rutger Hauer, Kim Cattrall, Neil Duncan, Michael J. Pollard, Alun Armstrong, Pete Postlethwaite, Ian Dury; 91m

This is a considerable improvement over Maylam's previous slasher film *The Burning*. London in the near future (2008) is a flooded city, the result of forty days and nights of rain (itself the result of global warming, but a possibly biblical warning). In this world of perpetual night, a policeman (Hauer) trails a cannibalistic serial killer/alien monster. This killer eats his mostly police officer victims' hearts and adorns their chests with carved astrological symbols.

It is an England plagued by the Jack the Ripper of the future, where the loner cop is reinstated to the job, even though he is considered distraught. An expert in serial killers partners him. This serves to contrast the two responses — the practical, forceful cop who prefers ruthless pragmatism as opposed to the intellectual profiler. Ultimately the violent pragmatist wins out in the face of such an unstoppable enemy. This is an ironic subversion of the profiler figure, in the process depicting the policeman's violent response to the world along the lines of it-takes-one-to-know-one. In such a world, occultism, Satanism and psychosis are interchangeable. As usual in films involving cannibalism, the eating of flesh can be considered a sexual surrogate, although the film stresses the occult angle more, a means of empowerment and the hunter's rite, to consume the hunted and so ingest his trophies as they become forever a part of him.

Despite the profiler's attempt to make sense of such a random killer who strikes out at both genders, the cop merely replies that the killer is a beast, pure and simple. This reductionist view proves correct. Indeed, the alien killer is perhaps the ultimate beast, incorporating in his genetic structure the DNA of all of his victims, human or otherwise, reminiscent of the alien in the John Carpenter remake of *The Thing*. In that way, the killer is the sum total of all of his adversaries, a theme also infiltrating the computer-designed killer of *Virtuosity*. The profiler insists there is a connection between the victims, but the cop insists that there is none. He is right, and the profiler finally resorts to larger guns as the proper response to the essentially inhuman serial killer. However, the killer works to an astrological pattern, suggesting him as a functionary of a higher purpose.

The film is part of the alien serial killer subgenre of such works as *The Dark* and *The Arrival*, and the killer-alien of the likes of *I Come in Peace* and *The Hidden*, informed by the alien hunter of the *Predator* movies and the science fiction film noir of *Bladerunner*. It was unfavorably compared to Richard Stanley's cult hit *Hardware* as part of a British science fiction revival and a rare non–Clive Barker inspired horror film. As social criticism it can also be compared to *Shopping*. Originally set in Los Angeles, the location was changed to London, and correspondingly set in the future, when the US producer brought it to her UK counterpart.

Spooks Run Wild

(1941: d. Phil Rosen)

scr. Carl Foreman, Charles Marion, Jack Henley; pr. Sam Katzman; ph. Marcel Le Picard; ed. Robert Golden; prod d. Ed W. Rote; cast. Bela Lugosi, Leo Gorcey, Huntz Hall, Bobby Jordan, David Gorcey, Sammy Morrison, Donald Haines; 65m

This is an early horror movie of only incidental interest to the emerging serial killer film.

The East End Kids are sent to a mountain camp in an effort to stop their slide into criminality. There they become convinced that a magician (Lugosi), who is aided by a dwarf assistant, is the homicidal sex maniac responsible for scaring the local community. They seek sanctuary in an old mansion which belongs to the suspected killer.

Although the Lugosi plotline is eventually revealed to be a red herring, the film is interesting for its acknowledgement of the problem of the serial killer, and for its final suggestion that such a killer is inconspicuous, lurking within the community, and not the usual horror movie icon of difference.

Screenwriter Foreman went on to a reputable career as a mainstream screenwriter with *High Noon*, *Bridge on the River Kwai*, *Guns of Navarone* and *McKenna's Gold*. Regarding his script for *Spooks Run Wild*, reportedly the kids improvised much of the dialogue (Hardy, p. 78).

Star Time

(1992: d. Alexander Cassini)

ph. Fernando Arguelles; m. Blake Leyh; ed. Stan Salfas; prod d. Dave Jensen, Carey Meyer; cast. John P. Ryan, Maureen Teefy, Thomas Newman, Michael St. Gerard; 85m

This is supposedly intended as a combination of social satire and the Faust mythos. It is about a suicidal, mentally ill young man obsessed by television. He is both fiercely angered and sent into despair when a favorite TV show is removed from the airwaves. He wants to commit suicide but is talked out of it by a mysterious man (the devil's agent), who then promises to make him into a TV star if he kills people. Thus, he becomes the "Baby Mask Killer."

Star Time addresses the drive to fame of such killers, who embark on their murders specifically to build a public recognition and escape the desperation and personal entrapment of their own inferiority. Strength, sexual expression and identity in murder are less a sexually transgressive challenge to their resented society than a function of its process of social marginalization. However, the real motive — seeking infamy — is far removed from any revolutionary interpretation. Media fame and the serial killer of course influences the satire of *Crime Time* and *Natural Born Killers.*

Star Time can be seen also as a modern variation on the old agent and controller formula of old-style horror depictions of early serial killers, here updated to incorporate a Mephisthophelean dimension. Hence, a strong man uses a weak-willed, disturbed and psychologically vulnerable other to do his functional homicidal bidding, in the process creating the serial killer as an idealized state for disenchanted youth. Although the film played at the Sundance Festival, it is only on limited video release that it seems to have found any recognition.

The Stendhal Syndrome

(1996: d. Dario Argento)

scr. Argento; pr. Argento, Giuseppe Colombo; ph. Giuseppe Rotunno; m. Ennio Morricone; ed. Angelo Nicolini; art d. Antonello Geleng; spec eff. Sergio Stivaletti; cast. Asia Argento, Thomas Kretschmann, Paolo Bonacelli, Luigi Diberti, John Quentin, Julien Lambroschini, Marco Leonardi; 119m

A detective suffers from the title affliction, which causes her to react in bizarre, hallucinogenic ways when she looks at paintings. She is on the trail of a serial rapist/killer who lures her into an art museum and then takes advantage of her when she reacts to a painting, imagining herself falling into it and the killer as her rescuer. He uses her disillusionment to later meet and rape her. He then rapes and kills another woman in front of her eyes, but she escapes and seeks psychiatric help. She then tries to catch him again.

The title syndrome refers to that reported of a French author in the 19th century who, whilst examining Italian architecture, was so overwhelmed by the artistic beauty of his surroundings that he entered a trance state, taking days to emerge fully. Argento juxtaposes smooth, fluid camerawork with unsteady, rapid point of view shots, their clash in the recognition of an artwork becoming the entry into a hallucinogenic, schizophrenic realm. Memory and identity are lost in prolonged exposure to this state. It is a world of fantasy, allying artistic creation and the schizophrenic reorganization of "reality" according to an internal logic triggered by external factors. It is a transcendental state, surrealistically visualized by Argento who plays with the killer's real and fantasy role in her mental chaos, a point of comparison perhaps to *The Cell.* The identity of one so affected is thus forever in flux. Yet this state is triggered by violation, one that is paralleled to the killer's rape. For the rape victim, the addictive state is triggered also by a masochistic surrender which she must struggle to disavow.

Raped and used by the killer, she admits to a psychiatrist that the idea of sex repulses her unless she "fucks like a man" and identifies with the aggressor. It is possible that by being so victimized she has grown to loathe her female sexuality. She is driven to find other survivors in the hope of a commonality of experience that will lead to an identification of the killer, a means of confronting the agent of trauma. In the process, the active killer overpowers her once again. As she is tied up, to be raped again and tormented, Argento raises the possibility that this degradation fulfills a masochistic need too repellent for her to admit, let alone accept. It strengthens the perceptual change and her aggressive response in reaction to it. Does she need it? Thus, she fights back and disables the killer both in self-defense and to deny her masochistic relationship to him. The arrogant rapist/killer indeed believes that he has a special relationship to the protagonist, and that his violation of her is a repeated means of consummation. He is an agent of change whose violation paradoxically enables her to seek a coherent identity.

After so removing the killer, she finds that she has recovered from the title syndrome. She now surrounds herself with paintings, daring her perceptions to return. However, she believes that the killer is still out there. She takes a new lover, and is the sexual aggressor with him, almost as if completing a form of personality transference initiated by the rape. The film's end implies that she has become the killer, now residing within her and ordering her to do horrible things. Left raving and wandering the streets, she is carried off sympathetically by the police.

Argento at his stylish best here returns to elements of the giallo, as he did in part in *Opera* and in *Trauma*, this time directly confronting the serial killer. He is here concerned with the violation of the human body as an experience that can trigger the entrance into another perceptual realm and initiate a schizophrenic dissolution and redefinition of one's identity. Sex and pain trigger perceptual insight, obsession and manipulation. The rapist/killer is an agent of this process. Just as many real killers have admitted the belief that their victims are forever a part of them, so too in this film the living victim gradually, psychologically becomes him, as he is forever a part of her. The film is thus a rare glimpse into a living victim's response to her experience with a killer.

Step Down to Terror

(1958: d. Harry Keller)

scr. Mel Dinelli, Czenzi Ormonde, Chris Cooper; stry. Gordon McDonell; pr. Joseph Hershenson; ph. Russell Metty; ed. Frank Gross; cast. Colleen Miller, Charles Drake, Rod Taylor, Josephine Hutchinson, Jocelyn Brando, Alan Dexter, Rickey Kelman; 75m

A serial killer (Drake) goes home to stay with his mother and widowed sister-in-law (Miller) after being away for six years. He is welcomed back into the fold. The sister-in-law's suspicions of the man are fostered when a pursuing detective visits them and asks questions. She then digs into the case and uncovers his true criminal past. The killer tries to kill her to protect his secret, but the detective saves her.

This is a capable remake of Hitchcock's *Shadow of a Doubt*, although the studio downplayed this connection when the film was released. This is remembered as a competent thriller (*Variety* felt) but nowhere near the source quality. *Variety* also felt the film was distinguished by the noirish aspects of veteran cinematographer Metty. Interestingly enough, the same material featured in the horror film *The Return of Dracula*, which perhaps proved a more remarkable version. Co-screenwriter Dinelli treated the theme of a killer within a family in *The Spiral Staircase*, here combined in part with the demented intruder theme of his work on *Beware My Lovely*. As such, it feeds into his theme of the clash between appearance, expectation and reality.

The Stepfather

(1986: d. Joseph Ruben)

scr. Donald E. Westlake; stry. Brian Garfield; pr. Jay Benson; ph. John Lindley; m. Patrick Moraz; cast. Terry O'Quinn, Jill Schoelen, Shelley Hack, Charles Lanyer; 88m

A man (O'Quinn) in search of the perfect family, as embodied in the sitcom mentality of US television-based ideology, goes from family to family, marrying single mothers and then murdering them and their children when they inevitably fail to live up to his impossible ideals. He wants to be the ideal father, and cannot tolerate any imperfection in his scheme of true family values as the embodiment of a true Patriarchy.

This is a remarkably subversive film in that it equates the patriarch with the serial killer as the inevitable end of such a

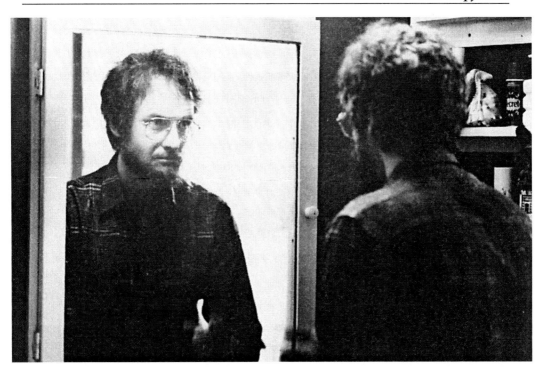

Another mirror shot. The killer (Terry O'Quinn) prepares to change his identity and his name, and move on to a new family in *The Stepfather* (New World/Vista/ITC, 1986).

value system. Under this system everybody has his/her place, and difference, let alone deviance, cannot be tolerated. However, the inflexibility of such rules makes them essentially unrealistic values and indefensible — except through the ritual purgation of those who do not "fit in" to the impossible ideal. The nuclear family is an impossible ideal which corrupts those who aspire to it. The American Dream fosters serial murderers by design.

The film tackles a man's need for absolute control over every aspect of his life and those who intersect it. Of course, this leads to frustration and disappointment in the quest for perfection, and the protagonist can only resort to purging the impurities and starting again. In the process, though, of going from assumed identity to assumed identity, the chameleon killer starts to lose his own sense of self, at one point wondering aloud, "Who am I here," his real identity forever threatened with submergence into those he pretends — except in the act of murder, which gives him the invigorating God-like redefinition that his fantasy of absolute control ultimately demands. Thus, his homicides are followed by what film noir theoretician Foster Hirsch (*Detours*, p. 276) calls a "post-orgasmic calm," the killing being also his form of sexual expression, an aspect he would deny. Indeed, he can find little sexual satisfaction with the women he courts, almost as if it were a chore.

He considers that the absence of a father as head of the family is a crucial lack, which his fantasy compels him to fill. He has to be the authoritative last word. When his authority (i.e. control) is undermined, he treats this as an intolerable imperfection, and is propelled again into his fantasy image. When his acquaintances read of the murder of a family and question why someone would do that, he coldly responds, "Maybe they disappointed him."

His new daughter disappoints him by being sexually active, and can intuit his sexual dysfunction. She must be purified. Yet through it all he remains a lonely man desperately seeking the pleasures of family. The daughter finally stabs him before he can kill her and her mother. By killing the patriarch, a new bond can form between mother and daughter which does not rely on the male for its relative growth. The rule of the father is an outmoded, corrupt and perverse tradition adhered to only out of a process of cultural and sociopolitical reenforcement.

Although it was at first dismissed, praise soon grew for this skillful thriller, the first film to confirm Ruben's maturation as a director following the intriguing *Dreamscape*. It is a measure of cold style and restraint hiding the potentially explosive. Its depiction of Our Town Americana drew comparison with Hitchcock and especially *Shadow of a Doubt* (the *Washington Post*'s Hal Hinson, in particular, was highly praiseworthy). Ruben continued to refine his abilities, etching his way into the mainstream with *Sleeping with the Enemy*, *True Believer*, *The Good Son*, *Money Train* and the highly acclaimed *Return to Paradise*. He remains another director worthy of greater attention.

The Stepfather's reputation as a scary psychological thriller continues to grow, and studies of 1980s cinema are bound to uncover its subversive subtexts. On that note it has already been held up as the opposite of the reactionary *Fatal Attraction*, which was released at the same time, to greater box-office returns and critical acceptability.

Stepfather 2

(1989: d. Jeff Burr)

scr. John Auerbach; pr. Darin Scott, William Burr; ph. Jacek Laskus; m. Jim Manzie, Pat Regan; ed. Pasquale Buba; prod d. Byrnadette Disanto; cast. Terry O'Quinn, Meg Foster, Caroline Williams, Jonathan Brandis, Henry Brown, Mitchell Laurence; 88m

This is an effective but unspectacular recapitulation of the first one. The killer father escapes from a mental hospital and assumes the identity of a psychiatrist and family therapist. In another small town he again seeks his ideal family, courting a divorced real-estate agent and attempting to ingratiate himself with her son. He kills those who would stand in the way of this union.

Stepfather 2 dissipates the tensions of the first film, with the killer murdering those in his way rather than the soured objects of his idealized fantasy. In that way, it also shifts the figure away from the enigmatically menacing, yet even sympathetic, serial killer he was in the first film. Instead, there is a tone of knowing humor and the kind of irony (the killer watches the TV show "Dream House") unique to sequels calculatedly aware of their predecessor's achievements. Nevertheless, O'Quinn's sinister performance is continually interesting. Overall, however, the film adds nothing.

Stepfather 3

(1992: d. Guy Magar)

scr. Magar, Lee Wasserman; pr. Magar, Paul Moen; ph. Alan Caso; m. Patrick C. Regan; prod d. Moen, Richard B. Lewis, Laurie Scott; cast. Robert Wrightman, Priscilla Barnes, Season Hubley, David Tom, John Ingle; 110m

The monstrous father again escapes from the mental hospital. He goes through plastic surgery (without anesthetic) and, with a new identity, resumes his old habits: new town, new family. Additional morbid touches, such as the killer using human mulch on his garden, fails to enliven this tele-movie sequel which reduces a potent concept to the most routine of horror franchises. Without O'Quinn's unsettling interpretation of the character, there is little left.

Stepfather 3 seeks to restore the balance of Patriarchy eroded by the first two films. Thus, the killer becomes father to a boy in a wheelchair. The boy in the end is able to walk, saving his mother, jointly eliminating the killer, and restoring the future of Patriarchy. Throughout, the killer has been urging him to walk, for his affliction is an imperfection that threatens the killer's fantasy of the pure American home. By restructuring the film's central character struggle between father and son instead of father and daughter, *Stepfather 3* removes any subversive charge in favor of conventionality.

Still Life: The Fine Art of Murder

(1992: d. Graeme Campbell)

scr. Campbell, Michael Taav, Dean Parisot; pr. Paco Alvarez, Nicolas Stiliadis; ph. Ludek Bogner; m. Jeff Danna, Mychael Danna; prod d. Ian Brock; cast. Sam Malkin, Stephen Shellen, Jessica Steen, Jason Gedrick, Gary Farmer; 83m

A serial killer fancies himself an avant-garde artist and uses fresh victims posed to create living (dead?) artworks. He becomes a hit in the art world and a media celebrity. He signs the work "AK" for "Art Killer." A TV reporter follows the trail, but the killer plants clues that implicate her pianist roommate. It seems the man who hired the musician to compose a work may be the killer.

This is an early film to tackle the murder-as-art theme that would saturate the self-reflexive 1990s genre works. Thus, the elaborate crime scenes, deliberately staged to be found and deciphered by police/onlookers, anticipates the emphasis of such in *The Bone Collector* especially. As satire, *Still Life* explores the ultimate perversion of the philosophy "art-for-art's-sake," with many

in the art world claiming the killer is making a valid statement which should be given as much consideration as any other creative act. The fact that someone died in the process is almost incidental, a valid means to an end. In a nod to serial killer fandom, the killer has a loyal following who claim that all meaning has gone out of contemporary art, and that the Art Killer is restoring passion and complexity to artistic statement.

In this way the film is about the popularization of the serial killer as a cultural spokesperson. In a subculture of people struggling for their own voice, and disillusioned about contemporary society and their own sociological entrapment, it is tempting to view an apparently intelligent, artistic killer as a modern social revolutionary and visionary. In that way, this is one of the rare serial killer films to treat the killer as an anti-hero, although it views this with the necessary postmodern satiric distance.

Such a killer becomes the spokesperson for the rootless 20-something Generation X. Like many portraits of this generation, perhaps most notably *Love and Human Remains*, this reveals a neo–Bohemian lifestyle in which people desperately search for purpose and expression but ultimately are unable to make sense of the chaos around them. Thus, the protagonist is asked to put music to a montage of apocalyptic imagery — to find the art in the chaos of inevitable destruction — a metaphor for this generation's values. Of course, the Art Killer spawns his own brand of copycats, or murder forgers, and in that way has spawned the beginning of an artistic movement.

Though critically neglected, this is of more interest to the genre than its lack of recognition and reputation suggests. Screenwriter Taav next went on to direct the comically offbeat independent film *Painted Heart*, again tackling the importance of the serial killer in defining interpersonal and social relationships.

Strange Days

(1995: d. Kathryn Bigelow)

scr. James Cameron, Jay Cocks; pr. Cameron, Steven-Charles Jaffe; ph. Mathew F. Leonetti; prod d. Lilly Kilvert; ed. Howard Smith; m. Graeme Revell; cast. Ralph Fiennes, Angela Bassett, Juliette Lewis, Tom Sizemore, Michael Wincott, Vincent D'Onofrio; 145m

On the eve of the millennium, an ex-cop turned dealer of memories recorded onto discs patched into the human brain is involved in the killing of a prominent Afro-American celebrity by racist cops. In the process of escaping them and bringing the recording of their actions to the proper authorities, he discovers that a serial killer has been killing women and recording their death throes as they feel his pleasure at their deaths.

Only the subplot makes this a serial killer film, and a variation on the self-reflexive dimension of *Peeping Tom*. The premise develops a kind of technologically enhanced voyeurism — it is now possible to experience recorded segments of another's life as they felt to that individual: to relive another's life. The devices necessary to achieve this have been declared illegal, and the experience is considered an addictive drug. Of course, the equipment has been used for negative purposes, for pornography and snuff (termed "blackjack," these episodes record someone's death). In such a chaotic view of human interaction as here, it is ironic that a technology which theoretically could bring people together through rare empathy has been abused and trivialized, although it is ultimately unveiled as a vehicle of truth. If the equipment can be considered to represent film itself, then the movie serves as a revalidation of the form's power in the means of mass communication and tech-

nological interaction (when does virtual reality become reality? — a theme also addressed in Cronenberg's *Existenz*), equally evident in Bigelow's energetic, forceful direction.

The most controversial aspect of this film is its scene of rape/murder recorded from the killer's point of view. In this scene, a young woman is blindfolded and handcuffed, her genitals are stun-gunned, and she is slashed to death, her own death experience recorded for the killer's playback. Such a killer seeks not only to kill but to experience the victim's fear at the killer's own power, doubling his intensity at murder. This, of course, also doubles his sexual enjoyment and is the ultimate trophy of such a crime — the victim's experience of the killer would be forever his to savor and re-savor. He can experience another's perception of him as a supremely powerful, awe and fear inspiring man. But, of course, the temptation to use the equipment in murder is as addictive as the murder itself. In that way the film addresses the misuse and perversion of the potential for increased human empathy. Joy becomes sexual excitement becomes snuff as an inevitable human progression.

The killer has gone beyond despair into pure self-indulgence. He is a lost, corrupted soul — the emblem of all that ails human interaction. His closeness to the protagonist suggests he is a potential devilish presence in an ongoing battle for the protagonist's soul (or so E. Guthmann in the *San Francisco Chronicle* thought). Significantly, the protagonist is an ex-policeman, a failed patriarch who has shunned responsibility in favor of chaos. In this, Bassett represents the forces of stability and reason, vying for the protagonist's well-being.

The Strangler

(1941: d. Harold Huth)

scr. J. Lee Thompson, Lesley Storym; nvl. Gordon Beckles; pr. Walter C. Mycroft; ph. Claude Friese-Greene; cast. Judy Campbell, Sebastian Shaw, Niall McGinnis, Henry Edwards, George Pughe; 75m

In London's Soho district a strangler uses silk stockings to kill women. A female crime reporter believes the killer is a visiting US millionaire. A detective-story writer, however, persuades her otherwise, and the two search for the real killer before the accused American can be executed for the crimes.

This was co-scripted by future director J. Lee Thompson (who would tackle the serial killer and police response to his aberrant personality in the rather reactionary *Ten to Midnight*), and has some aspects of Ripper lore to it. It addresses the Americanization of British culture, and as a film made during World War Two, may have some interest as a demonstration of allied cooperation — saving the reputation of the US, assuming the film can be taken allegorically. Unfortunately, this has disappeared from circulation and was unavailable at time of writing.

The Strangler

(1964: d. Burt Topper)

scr. Bill S. Ballinger; pr. Samuel Bischoff, David Diamond; ph. Jacques Marquette; m. M. Skiles; ed. Robert S. Eisen; cast. Victor Buono, David McLean, Diane Sayer, Davey Davison, Ellen Corby, Michael Ryan; 89m

A mother-fixated hospital orderly's mother has a heart attack, and a young nurse is assigned to care for her. The nurse's presence drives her son (Buono), an overweight lab technician and a future killer, to distraction. He becomes jealous of the attention lavished on his mother — which triggers a killing spree: he strangles women, especially young nurses. He collects dolls, perhaps as representatives of the living dolls he murders. He accidentally leaves one such doll at a crime scene, leading to his capture.

Based on real events of the then-unknown Boston Strangler Albert DeSalvo, and thus covering terrain also addressed in Fleischer's seminal *The Boston Strangler*, this quick exploitation film was rushed into cinemas to take advantage of the city's then-widespread fear. It correspondingly has a reputation only as cynical exploitation. Taking the route of *Psycho*, it depicts a man warped by a monstrous mother figure, with the tubby Buono essaying the menacing innocence he embodies so well and would tackle again in *The Mad Butcher*.

Streets

(1990: d. Katt Shea Ruben)

scr. Andy Ruben, Katt Shea Ruben; pr. Andy Ruben, Roger Corman, Rodman Flender; ph. Phedon Papamichael; m. Aaron Davis; prod d. Virginia Lee; ed. Stephen Mark; cast. Christina Applegate, David Mendenhall, Ed Lottimer, Kay Lenz; 90m

A drug-addicted teen prostitute (Applegate) lives an aimless existence. She befriends a middle-class rock star wannabe who has journeyed from the suburbs to the streets of Venice, California, in order to follow his dream. He saves her from a beating by a client who wanted rough sex. She gradually reveals the seedy side of the community to him, a community also terrorized by a psychotic cop, secretly a serial killer. This psychopath delights in the rape and torture of young prostitutes.

Director Ruben had explored similar terrain in her *Stripped to Kill* films, and here presents a harrowing picture of a futile existence where young women are subject to heroin addiction and sexual exploitation, and seemingly fated for horrible, random death. Unlike the subtext of the *Stripped to Kill* films, this one lacks the exploration of the topic found in *Fear City*, that the sex industry can paradoxically liberate those it may enslave to male objectification. *Streets* explores the unseen, hidden side of such a Patriarchy's tendency towards exploitation and sexual sublimation. There is some hope that the young man so educated in the injustices of the world may be able to change the ways of the substitute fathers.

Female liberation has come to this horror, with the killer the result of a culture of male objectification and sexual sublimation of women. In that the killer is an authority figure, he is a function of a monstrous Patriarchy which seeks to suppress women and punish them for the very sexuality it hypocritically fosters. It explores the sex netherworld of post–Scorsese/Schrader/Ferrara terrain. The friendship between outcasts brings to mind the substitute community of *Angel*, again about teen prostitutes: the patriarch is a threat even to this.

It is a world of lost souls, where redemption seems possible only through genuine human interaction and empathetic non-judgmental treatment. The young and innocent are perpetual victims fighting for survival, and the protagonist seeks both escape in drugs and an identity in the only avenue left her — prostitution. This furthers Shea's interest in how young women may use their emerging sexuality as a means of mastering their circumstances — a theme she essayed well in *Poison Ivy* and *The Rage: Carrie 2*, also about the problems facing young women maturing quickly. Star Applegate is better known for her role as the teenage girl in the TV sitcom *Married with Children*. Lenz's presence here gives the film a connection to the original *Stripped to Kill*.

Striking Distance

(1993: d. Rowdy Herrington)

sci. Herrington, Martin Kaplan; pr. Arnon Milchan, Tony Thomopoulos, Hunt Lowry; ph. Mac Ahlberg; prod d. Gregg Fonseca; ed. Pasquale Buba, Mark Helfrich; m. Brad Fiedel; cast. Bruce Willis, Sarah Jessica Parker, Dennis Farina, Tom Sizemore, Robert Pastorelli; 98m.

Willis is a former policeman (and informer on his brutal partner, a relative), now a member of the river coast guard, who publicly criticized the police force's opinion of the identity of a serial killer responsible for the death of his father. Two years later, now a recovering alcoholic, he believes that the same killer is still dumping bodies in the river. He knows these new victims, as it seems the killer is personally pushing him into action. With a new partner (Parker), he investigates and finds the trail leading to his own family.

The killer plays the song "Hey There Little Red Riding Hood" by Sam the Sham over the phone to the police before he kills. Although this recalls *Sea of Love*, it also reveals the killer's predatory mentality, identifying him as the Big Bad Wolf of the fairy tale, an aspect explored more vigorously in *Freeway*. As such, it is a partial exploration of an out-of-control cult of machismo embodied by the family of cops as a malfunctioning Patriarchy that is in need of the purifying actions of the good son. However, this is ultimately submerged beneath the assembly-line combination of honest cop, buddy movie, serial killer thriller, procedural and action movie set pieces.

It ultimately concerns the bonds and responsibility between fathers and sons. Willis, given a second chance to catch the killer, is able not only to avenge his father's death, but to live up to his memory and creed. Significantly, the film ends with Willis, now married to Parker and with a young son, visiting his father's grave. He has proven himself a worthy father/patriarch at last, and has chastised the killer.

The killer is the bad son, finally driven to patricide when his own father (who spared him earlier) wants to turn him in and restore a functioning Patriarchy. However, this father (Farina) has soiled such

A demoted and disgraced police officer is now a river rescue operator (Bruce Willis) with a new partner (Sarah Jessica Parker) in *Striking Distance* (Columbia, 1993).

an order and is no longer a representative of the true order, and thus ultimately unable to do his duty. He tries, but it is too late for him. He is the fallen patriarch, living and dying with his inability to uphold the honor code challenged by his own son. This code, expressed by Willis' father as "loyalty above all things, except honor," is suggested to be that which should bind Patriarchy together and which it must uphold for a fair, just society to function, and for in-squabbling to cease.

This is thought of and dismissed as a fair-to-middling film from the director who tackled the serial killer figure more provocatively in *Jack's Back*, but who is better known to critics as being responsible for the knockabout Patrick Swayze vehicle *Roadhouse*, a film vilified by the press. Although competent, overfamiliarity with the subject matter and plot hooks doomed *Striking Distance*. It failed to boost star Willis' career after the successive box-office flops of *Hudson Hawk* and *Bonfire of the Vanities*.

Stringer

(1992: d. Michael DeLouise) aka *Prime Time Murder*

cast. Laura Reed, Tim Thomerson, Sally Kirkland, Anthony Finetti; 95m

A photojournalist and an ex-cop working for the six o'clock news uncover a serial killer intent on cleaning up the streets by targeting homeless derelicts. Cynically self-serving, they treat it as their breakthrough story. In so doing, the film raises the issue of press responsibility and the media's quest for easy headlines at the expense of the innocent.

In plot synopsis, some of the social comment recalls Ferrara's *Driller Killer*, and even brings to mind the killer in

Painted Heart, though *Stringer* remains unremarked on even on the Internet. Another obscurity, it tackles the theme of the apparent disposability of an American underclass. It is currently unavailable.

Stripped to Kill

(1987: d. Katt Shea Ruben)

scr. Andy Ruben, Katt Shea Ruben; pr. Mark Byers, Matt Leipzig, Andy Ruben; exec pr. Roger Corman; ph. John Le Blanc; ed. Zach Staenberg, Bruce Stubblefield; cast. Kay Lenz, Greg Evigan, Norman Fell, Tracy Crowder, Athena Worthy, Carlye Byron, Debbie Nassar; 88m

This is considered a surprisingly effective and unusually stylish thriller about a policewoman (Lenz) who voluntarily goes undercover as a dancer at the "Rock Bottom" strip club in order to flush out a serial killer of dancers. The policewoman wants the case in part to satisfy her own ambitions, as does her male partner. In the process, she is made aware of the dimensions allowed the expression of female sexuality.

More forthcoming and with more nudity than the mainstream stripper-portrait *Striptease*, *Stripped to Kill* pays more attention to elegantly filmed and erotic dance sequences. Indeed, these dances are the most beautiful aspect of the world these women inhabit, where the sign on the change room reading "women" has been crossed out and rewritten "sluts." Yet the women there, through their actions, ultimately transcend those circumstances that would for them have been a trap. Hence the film is apparently more humorous than expected. However, the killer that plagues them would continue their entrapment and deny them even the individual identity they gain through their profession. In this respect, the film perhaps examines similar subtexts to *Fear City*, wherein the strippers gain a paradoxical liberation through their sexuality, however codified it may be by

male desire. Perhaps it can even be considered an update of some aspects of *Lady of Burlesque*. *Stripped to Kill* can also be compared to *Slash Dance* and Fulci's disco giallo *Murder Rock*.

Director Ruben, who was an actor in Roger Corman–produced movies, would go on to direct a sequel and then the similarly themed, although more socially conscious, *Streets*, before flirting with the mainstream in *Poison Ivy* and *The Rage: Carrie 2*. Unfortunately, she has never received the attention of Lizzie Borden or even fellow genre toilers Mary Lambert and Rachel Talalay, although she warrants it.

Stripped to Kill 2

(1989: d. Katt Shea Ruben)

scr. Katt Shea Ruben; pr. Roger Corman, Rodman Flender, Andy Ruben; ph. Phedon Papamichael; m. Gary Stockdale; ed. Stephen Mark; prod d. Virginia Lee; cast. Maria Ford, Ed Lottimer, Karen Mayo Chandler, Birke Tan, Marjean Holden; 83m

This is considered to lack the humor, suspense and eroticism of the first film, and be just another lurid thriller. A razor-wielding killer is murdering strippers in Los Angeles back alleys, and a psychic is commissioned to assist. The film depicts strippers as forever walking the line between personal security (physical and psychological) and an omnipresent world of sex killers: these people are more aware of the threat to their lives as an inherent danger of the profession.

Online critic Linda Rasmussen (*allmovie.com*) considered the film evidence of Shea's low-budget mini-auteur professionalism, but noted that the film still does not transcend the crass exploitation level that the first installment managed to avoid due to its humor and conviction. Once again, it can be compared to *Slash Dance* and the disco giallo of *Murder Rock*.

A Study in Terror

(1966: d. James Hill) aka *Fog*

scr. Donald and Derek Ford; pr. Henry E. Lester; nvl. Ellery Queen; ph. Desmond Dickinson; m. John Scott; art d. Alex Vetchinsky; cast. John Neville, Donald Houston, John Fraser, Robert Morley, Cecil Parker, Anthony Quayle, Barbara Windsor, Adrienne Corri, Judi Dench, Frank Finlay; 95m

Sherlock Holmes (Neville) and Dr. Watson (Houston) take on the case of the missing son of a Baronet. As they investigate, they uncover ties to the ongoing Jack the Ripper case. A doctor's daughter (Dench) suspects the missing man's brother of unhealthy involvement.

This first Sherlock-Holmes-meets-Jack-the-Ripper movie, though it is thought of by some as a disappointment in comparison to the later *Murder by Decree* (Hardy, p. 174), certainly lacks the political subtext and implications of Clark's film, and does not suggest a widespread conspiracy involved in the criminal cover-up. Instead, it reportedly concentrates subtextually on the sociological factors which underlie prostitution and entrap individuals, and on the people (the doctor — Quayle) determined, it appears, to save them from their lot. But once again, what motives underlie seeming benevolence?

The film depicts a wasted, fated UK underclass (Boot, pp. 177–178) of lost souls beset by alcoholism, despair and moral abandon. The attempt to impose and police order only reinforces the self-destructiveness of such overcrowded angst in need of clearer focus and direction. Yet part of this underclass is an open sexuality which beckons the exploiters to it. It is therefore the responsibility of those with much to care for the underprivileged — or at least such should be the priority. The killer (not surprisingly, given the social context here) is an intelligent man who masquerades as a concerned, benevolent member of the upper class (indeed, the missing man's brother), but who is consumed by homicidal lust, exploiting the underclass' easy sexuality.

There is evidence of a destructive male sexuality and resentment affecting and corrupting all classes; thus, the plot encompasses an acid-scarred prostitute within the aristocracy. Such a sexuality is perhaps a consequence of a paradoxical sexual liberation (tying the period film to the swinging 1960s climate in which it was made) scorned and resented by the powers that be, and a product of the class system.

The second Sherlock Holmes film to be made in color, this was also the first to deal with a more sexually explicit subject matter. As a manhunt/procedural, it was also unusual for its combination of a fictional detective investigating a real crime (as an adjunct to the police, who seem, again, ill-equipped to deal with such sex crimes). Finlay reprised his role as Inspector LaStrade for Bob Clark in *Murder by Decree*. The screenwriters went on to write *Corruption*, which addressed the changing morality, generational conflicts and sexual longing that were also subtexts here. Unfortunately, *A Study in Terror* is not readily available.

Summer of Sam

(1999: d. Spike Lee)

scr. Victor Colicchio, Michael Imperioli, Spike Lee; pr. Jon Kolik, Lee, Imperioli, Jeri Carroll-Colicchio; ph. Ellen Kuras; prod d. Therese DePrez; ed. Barry Alexander Brown; m. Terence Blanchard; m sup. Alex Steyermark; cst des. Ruth E. Carter; cast. John Leguizamo, Adrien Brody, Mira Sorvino, Jennifer Esposito, Anthony La Paglia, Ben Gazzara, Bebe Neuwirth; 136m

With a framing introduction by columnist Jimmy Breslin, the film is the account of several lives within a tight-knit ethnic community during the summer of 1977, when the Son of Sam killer (David Berkowitz) was in operation, shooting

Hairdresser Vinny (John Leguizamo) and his punk friend Ritchie (Adrien Brody) still hold on to the vestiges of their friendship amidst a tumultuous community in *Summer of Sam* (Buena Vista, 1999).

lovers in parked cars. The quintessential long hot summer also saw a record heat wave and looting amidst widespread black-outs, and seems emblematic of a social col-lapse (anticipating the treatment of the blackout-affected community in *The Trig-ger Effect*).

The film is less the study of a serial killer than a portrait of a community in turmoil as the free-sex-without-conse-quence era of the 1970s explodes into vio-lence, and disco gives way to punk. Thus, there is no insight into Berkowitz' charac-ter as such, and he remains an unknow-able lunatic whom Lee often shows flailing around in his gun-and-garbage-strewn hovel of an apartment. However, his progress as a killer is paralleled repeatedly to the amorality that surrounds him. He is not characterized enough to give an indi-cation of his crimes as a knowing personal

reaction/statement beyond psychosis, al-though this seems likely.

One of the film's subtexts parallels the disco and punk scene's respective ignoring of and incorporation into subcultural definition the killer's activities (the lyrics of a punk band's song are based on the let-ters Son of Sam sent to the police). Indeed, Lee develops the different ways in which the killer's actions affect community defi-nition and instigates community collapse, as vigilante action and riots eventuate. As in *Do the Right Thing*, the troubled com-munity finds self-definition in mob action. Once again, Lee observes without overt judgment, though he shows the potentially disastrous course of such action, as an in-nocent is targeted.

It shows that hostile or indifferent cir-cumstance, where interpersonal commu-nication means anonymous sex, brings out

Vinny (John Leguizamo) and Gloria (Bebe Neuwirth) read of the killer's exploits in their neighborhood in *Summer of Sam* (Buena Vista, 1999).

the worst in these people. The protagonist, a philandering hairdresser (Leguizamo), recalls Warren Beatty in *Shampoo*—a film that also seems an inspiration for Lee's structure here. He is led to betray everything in his life that is important to him — wife, best friend, job — all through environmental pressures and a vehement sexual appetite.

It is as a determinist anthem that the film emerges: all characters are affected by the world around them; and when this comes into disarray, they collapse into a sexual or violent haze of private resentment and rebellion that the community cannot understand or tolerate. In this world, the killer, although psychotic as depicted by Lee here (receiving orders to kill from a talking dog), is part of the community he preys upon. The film serves to show that anyone is capable of horrendous actions (always a Lee theme since *Do the Right Thing*) as the process of subcultural definition and socialization is eroded from within. So the film dances with the issue of whether the killer is a symptom of collapse or its agent. Ironically, the killer is almost a public celebrity by the film's end, as if Lee is saying that society had entered a new stage of definition in the wake of the 1970s

The neighborhood guys and Vinny (John Leguizamo) are increasingly convinced that the killer is within their community, and start to plan a violent response in *Summer of Sam* (Buena Vista, 1999).

serial killer epidemic, as epitomized here by Son of Sam.

The voice-over taken from the killer's actual letters further reveals him as deeply psychotic, a man who feels himself apart from everyone and everything, and lives for the hunt. Quick, anonymous sex has translated into quick, anonymous violence. It is in his reaction to the world of drugs, anonymous sex and random-violence-as-social-rebellion that the killer is paralleled especially to the aspiring punk (although to each of the main characters also) whose slide into pornographic amoral-ity makes him a suspect in the community. The killer is, ironically, the only one who does not dive into the rampant promiscuity around him, though his motives in shooting women are clearly related to sexual dysfunction and rooted in the amorality of the world around him. To further stress the determinist theme, Lee has the punk at one point say that everyone has two personalities, one you're born with and the other the world gives you; and so when they clash, an explosion occurs.

Its depiction of a community falling apart, of connected lives spiraling out of control, and Lee's visual style, recalls Paul Thomas Anderson's triumph *Boogie Nights*, and even anticipates *Club 54* to a degree. It is part of a mini 1970s nostalgia wave in film and television at the beginning of the 21st century.

Superstar Female Serial Killer

(2000: d. Chris Morrissey)

scr, pr, ph. Morrissey; ed. Vickie Velvet; cast. Vickie Velvet, Filberto Ascencio, Share Fantasia, J. Daniel Mesta, Matt Miyahara, Christina Muzyk, Polyester, Lenii Reed, Veneta

An ambitious film student (Velvet) decides to enter the industry by making a documentary about Hollywood prostitutes, but she kills her first subject and stages the crime scene to look as if an enraged male client did it. When another body is found, the media react and publicize the murders as the work of the "Vice Stalker." Soon her attempts to keep it all a secret unwind as she is stalked and people she knows (her crew) are murdered.

This is the feature directorial debut of a Los Angeles based filmmaker who reportedly sells his films on his private website. It was shot in black and white in an intended documentary style over four months, mostly on weekends, and stars local singer Vickie Velvet. It has no reputation beyond its maker's self-promotional exercises, and is generally unreleased at time of writing.

Switchback

(1997: d. Jeb Stuart)

scr. Stuart; pr. Gale Anne Hurd; ph. Oliver Wood; m. Basil Poledouris; ed. Conrad Buff; prod d. Jeffrey Howard; cast. Dennis Quaid, Danny Glover, Jared Leto, R. Lee Ermey, Ted Levine; 118m

A rogue FBI agent (Quaid) is doggedly on the trail of a serial killer that has kidnapped his son. The killer is one of either a railway worker (Glover) or the hitchhiker (Leto) he travels with. The agent is assisted by a sympathetic sheriff (Ermey) in the midst of an election campaign, even if this puts him in conflict with the FBI. The hiker saves the worker from death, but discovers him to be the serial killer. The agent tracks the killer to a certain snowbound railway community. The killer has deliberately guided him there and has left a clue specifically for the detective to decipher.

It is in its subplots, and careful delineation of the warmth between people (illusory in the serial killer's case, although he too seems at first a kind man), that the film excels. It depicts people reacting differently to life's challenges, striving to keep their personal worth and sense of self-definition in the face of circumstance. These people need to communicate with others, and seek connection, even though, like the hiker, they may be fleeing some aspect of their lives which they ultimately cannot escape, as the killer brings them together.

Switchback's pace, concern for the road, and isolated settings having their effect on the people within them recall the work of J.S. Cardone, especially *Outside Ozona*. However, it pays more attention to the process of subcultural definition (especially among the railroad workers) that allows people connection and happiness. There is no place for the loner, and it is ultimately humanity that triumphs over the real enemy — indifference.

The killer is treated as an anomaly, a freak of nature. He feeds on people's need for connection and manipulates it to his will. The film begins with his murder of a young girl, a knife between her legs clearly indicating his desire for sexually violent domination. He has taken the substance of heterosexual interpersonal contact, sex as love, and turned it into a disposable commodity, hence his car is decorated in pornographic pictures. He is a rootless, nomadic killer, seeking to destroy those who have found definition and stability. He thinks of himself as a cruel, random fate.

Indeed, as fate, the killer influences and shapes the course of those around him. He knows his nemesis, the FBI agent (and profiler), and so seeks to involve him personally in what he considers a game, forcing the agent to consider it a personal crusade to purge a malfunctioning patriarch (who would kidnap a son). There is no meaning in the killer's acts, as he can dismiss them as a game, and is incapable of connection with another. The role plays calculatedly with Glover's likable image: he is the epitome of indifference, all pretense and essentially unknowable and enigmatic.

This is Stuart's directorial debut after a long time as a successful screenwriter of mainly action movies. Although *Switchback* was his first script, written when he was a student, it took the success of *Die Hard* and *The Fugitive* to see him given the chance to visualize it. Perhaps unfortunately, it failed to make a lasting impact.

Tale of Sweeney Todd

(1998: d. John Schlesinger)

scr. Peter Buckman, Peter Shaw; pr. Ted Adams Swanson; ph. Martin Fuhrer; m. Richard Rodney Bennett; ed. Mark Day; prod d. Malcolm Thornton; cast. Ben Kingsley, Joanna Lumley, Campbell Scott, Selina Boyack, John Kavanagh, Katherine Schlesinger; 120m

This is a heavily fictionalized version of a homicidal 19th century barber (Kingsley) who murders his customers. He then sells their jewelry and, most horribly, sells the corpse meat to a neighboring chef (Lumley, with an industrial-size meat grinder) renowned for her meat pies. Both of them have an affluent, unsuspecting clientele. An insurance inspector (Scott), on the trail of some $50,000 worth of missing diamonds through the city, probes the crimes, as does an innocent young woman. He gradually uncovers widespread corruption throughout the urban spread.

This is a comedic film which tackles the horror of accumulation (long a standby of farce), with protagonist and killer faced with increasing complications in their smooth functioning system. The killer relies on his ritual of murder to relieve himself of stress, as well as serve his business interests—as the film criticizes commercial enterprise as inherently corrupt and perverse. Thus, the society founded on it can only profit off the dead, and reproduce the corruption and perversity so imbedded in it. Is the killer an aberration? To run smoothly requires surrender to aberration as definition.

This more Europeanized effort knows the previous versions of the demon barber legend. These range from the Victorian penny dreadful by Christopher Bond, "The Story of Pearls," to the stage play by Dibdin-Pitt, and the Tod Slaughter film *Sweeney Todd, the Demon Barber of Fleet Street* to the 1979 Stephen Sondheim stage musical *Sweeney Todd* (which was turned into a musical television production with George Hearn and Angela Lansbury). The story has also influenced low-budget US horrors by Andy Milligan and Ted V. Mikels.

Filmed in Dublin, this tele-movie was seen by some as a return to form for the ailing Schlesinger. It is certainly more tonally and thematically complex than the straightforward theatrical release *Eye for an Eye*. The comedic undercurrent is confirmed by the casting of Lumley, better known for the UK sitcom *Absolutely Fabulous*. *Tale* debuted on ShowTime cable in the United States on April 19, 1998.

Ten Monologues from the Lives of Serial Killers

(1994: d. Ian Kerkhof)

scr. Kerkhof, J.G. Ballard; pr. Kerkhof, Joost Van Gelder; ph. Van Gelder; m. Fokke Vansaane; ed. Rene A. Hazekamp, Herbert Vandrongelen; cast. Rodney Beddat, Lorand Sarna, Ian Kerkhof, Mark Bellamy; 58m

This short Dutch combination of documentary, dramatic recreation, music video, and performance piece consists of ten vignettes, based on written facts and fictionalized accounts. This includes passages from J.G. Ballard's novel "Crash"; interviews with murderers; and a rap music video, "Murder Avenue," by the Geto Boys, inspired by Jeffrey Dahmer.

In concept, it's an intriguing look at the various subcultural interpretations, and even tributes, that have grown up around serial murderers in the effort to give form and (even celebratory?) voice to aberration. It is, however, not widely available at time of writing.

10 Rillington Place

(1970: d. Richard Fleischer) aka *Ten Rillington Place*

scr. Clive Exton; pr. Martin Ransohoff, Leslie Linder; ph. Denys Coop; m. John Dankworth; ed. Ernest Walter; cast. Richard Attenborough, Judy Geeson, John Hurt, Pat Heywood, Isobel Black, Phyllis McMahon; 111m

This is a faithful recreation of the true-life John Christie (Attenborough) case in the UK. A balding, mild-mannered married man pretends to be an abortionist in order to lure women into his house. There he gasses them to death and satisfies his compulsions with the corpse. He takes in a young couple. He kills the wife and child and manipulates the poor, mentally deficient and weak-willed husband (Hurt) into covering up the crimes. The husband is tried, convicted and executed for them.

Years later, the truth finally comes out when the killer's house is searched; the now homeless Christie is apprehended without a struggle.

More low-key than Fleischer's previous *The Boston Strangler*, this is a carefully observed character study more than a procedural. It divides its attention between the necrophile Christie, whose fragile ego demands he pretend to be something other than he is, and the simple, illiterate boarder Tim, who also has the propensity to make himself out to be more than he is. Christie recognizes this aspect of himself in the man and expertly manipulates him into taking the blame. Is there an element of projection and self-denial in his manipulative attempts? Significantly, Christie cries when Tim is convicted, both relieved and perhaps convinced of his own damnation. This is the ultimate realization of his wickedness at being able to destroy innocence at will, and himself as a monstrous patriarch seeking to escape his own impotence (he can only function with the dead — a parallel to the killer in *Citizen X*). This moment, of a killer admitting his monstrous side, is a development of the climax of *The Boston Strangler*, which had the killer's fragile ego threatened by an awareness of his actions and capabilities. In the end, when his guilt has been established, Christie quietly confesses, taking responsibility for his actions for the first time. Again there is a quiet strength in his surrender to fate and admission of defeat. There is no pretense left for the murderer.

It is a bleak view. Drained of color, its shadows and grays are testament to the decay and desolation of the human spirit. In a dilapidated, cramped house, a pitiful nothing of a man finds solace and sexual adventure in murder and manipulation. His role allows him to escape the banality that life has to offer him. Capable and intelligent, he will go to any lengths to protect

Notorious UK serial killer John Reginald Christie (Richard Attenborough, right) cleverly manipulates the hapless Tim (John Hurt) into taking the blame in *10 Rillington Place* (Columbia, 1970).

his empowerment fantasies from discovery. However, it is not the sex crimes, but the manipulation of the child-like Tim that ultimately causes his temporary near-breakdown.

The balding, short Attenborough resembles Lorre in *M*: in appearance he is far from monstrous. Indeed, he looks the part of a weak man (who calls his own wife "Mrs. Christie," revealing his resentment for women's perceived roles as sexual objects and mothers). Thus, the women he desires and kills are expectant mothers (or actual mothers) lured into his house. He poses as a benevolent yet superior man to ingratiate himself with women needing guidance and protection. He abuses the respect accorded the patriarch in society.

In reality, he is an ineffectual male.

Tim, too, is insecure about his perceived social standing and role as father and head of the family. He too wants to be an authority figure and in charge. Unlike Christie, he is capable of love for his wife and child. But he must boast at the local pub that he is a ladies man. In the end, when Christie is homeless after finally killing his wife, he too boasts in order to restore his ego and assert superiority over his fellow homeless. For him, the murder of his wife was an attempt at the ultimate psychologically restorative gesture, an attempt to free himself — although it fails miserably, as he still needs to kill. When he fails to impress even the derelicts, Christie admits his true nature and perhaps takes solace in apprehension because, for the first time, it brings with it recognition.

Serial killer John Christie (Richard Attenborough) prepares to render his latest victim uncon-scious with a lethal gas mixture (frame right) in *10 Rillington Place* (Columbia, 1970).

The film develops the killer-portrait aspect of the second half of *The Boston Strangler* (which also featured a killer forc-ing his sexual identity). The audience is effectively put in the position of the pro-filer — seeing the crime and both the envi-ronment and behavior that surrounds it. The monstrous patriarch is again the threat to the smooth functioning of patri-archy, and indeed responsible for the mis-carriage of justice. Such a patriarch is monstrous because of his ability to con-trol, manipulate and dominate those around him — to assert his perverse will over oth-ers (though when doing so can barely con-tain his sexual excitement). Such is an in-herently perverse aspect of patriarchy, in constant need of regulation and purging — and born out of the need for power, as so-cially conditioned. Thus, Fleischer stresses the cramped, claustrophobic world these people inhabit, their actions the attempt to break out of a social entrapment.

The case, one of the country's most infamous, eventually resulted in the abo-lition of capital punishment in England. Once the real Tim's innocence of the crimes he was convicted of was deter-mined, he was pardoned and re-buried on consecrated ground. With Fleischer intent on authenticity, the film was shot in the neighboring building to where the events actually took place. This block was demol-ished after the filming was complete, to make way for new council flats.

The same crew went on to make *See No Evil*.

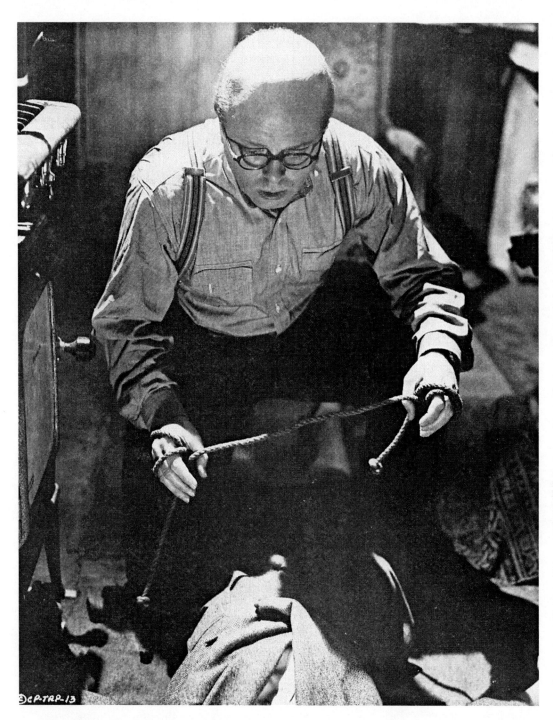

Serial killer John Christie (Richard Attenborough) prepares to strangle an unconscious victim in *10 Rillington Place* (Columbia, 1970).

Ten to Midnight

(1983: d. J. Lee Thompson)

scr. William Roberts; pr. Pancho Kohner, Lance Hool; ph. Adam Greenberg; m. Robert O. Ragland; ed. Peter Lee Thompson; art d. Jim Freiburger; cast. Charles Bronson, Lisa Eilbacher, Andrew Stevens, Gene Davis, Geoffrey Lewis, Wilford Brimley, Robert Lyons, Bert Williams; 101m

Policeman Bronson tampers with evidence in order to nab a serial killer of young women. When the suspect is considered mentally unstable, and protected by the law, Bronson takes it upon himself to goad the killer back into action. In response, the killer targets his daughter. Rather than face the prospect of the killer being released due to the insanity defense, Bronson shoots him dead in cold blood.

With Bronson cast as a cop, the film explores the legitimization of his vigilante persona as established since *Death Wish*, and its incorporation into the procedural narrative. With procedure on the side of such offenders, what opportunity is there left the moral crusader than to kill? Yet Bronson's own egotism is shown from the outset as he remarks to the press, "I want a killer, and what I want comes first." His actions are thus an effort to maintain his own ideological superiority over the killer, as much as moral outrage. The killer's actions are a deliberate challenge to his role as father and policeman — as patriarch — a sanctioned status with a responsibility he treasures and eventually distorts for his own ends.

The killer is a vile, unredeemable and arrogant youth who strips naked to commit his sex murders of young women. Inadequate with his own virginity (the murders as substitutes for intercourse), he must dominate the women who reject his advances in order to feel powerful and in charge of his own monstrous sexuality. He uses an artificial vagina as a masturbatory aid (which offends Bronson almost as much as the murders themselves) and makes obscene phone calls as a kind of foreplay. It is clear to Bronson that the killer's knife is a substitute penis, and Bronson thus becomes a kind of sanctioned castrator.

Obviously dysfunctional, the killer is made to represent an aware, "sane" murderer who knows of the insanity defense, which Bronson feels is an excuse that allows "maggots" like him to escape the death penalty

they deserve. Though his psychosis is not as explored as, say, the youthful killer of *Rampage* (with whom he shares a similar history of psychiatric treatment), the film explores the same dilemma posed to Patriarchy when faced with the monstrous son. It takes the most reactionary posture — eliminate the monstrous son and the problem goes away. Although this may not be fully legal, it is morally sanctioned. But director Thompson, rather than condone this, sees it as further evidence of a declining humanity unable to deal with its own splintering and resorting to an Old Testament justification. The vigilante cop becomes the avenger.

There is no sense of triumph at this, however, although it is all Bronson needs to validate his role as protector. Indeed, as he has been relieved of duty, his actions are a form of overcompensation, an expression of rebellion against the impotence of Patriarchy under the legal system. In this manner, the cynicism undercuts the vigilante actions rather than condones them (unlike in Joel Schumacher's films, for instance). They are the inevitable course of action for an outraged, even hypocritical humanity. Police are rendered impotent by a system of law which here serves to protect the killer from just the sort of illegal and irresponsible retributive actions that Bronson condones. This sense of the character's moral hypocrisy is developed further in *Kinjite: Forbidden Subjects*, wherein Bronson is so offended by the sexual exploitation of minors that (implied and offscreen) he uses a dildo to forcibly sodomize a male suspect. Needless to say, Thompson's irony is not subtle.

The climactic intended massacre of nurses brings to mind Chicago killer Richard Speck (whose exploits also inspired the Japanese sex-porn film *Violated Angels*). However, it is presented as a form of violent titillation, devoid of outrage and a testament to its makers' cynicism. This brooding neo-noir thriller is one of a

Top: The vigilante policeman (Charles Bronson) is ready to kill the serial killer he is after in *Ten to Midnight* (Cannon, 1983). *Bottom:* Police congregate at a suspected crime scene in *Ten to Midnight* (Cannon, 1983).

number of films Bronson made in conjunction with director Thompson (the first being *St. Ives* and the ill-fated *The White Buffalo*) and then for Cannon films. Including *Messenger of Death*, *Kinjite*, *Murphy's Law*, and *The Evil That Men Do*, these are violent, cynical thrillers exploring the depths of inhumanity people will sink to, and the option left to combat it. They cannot escape from Bronson's role as the archetypal vigilante killer in Winner's *Death Wish*, however.

A victim strikes back against the serial killer (Gene Davis) holding her captive in *Ten to Midnight* (Cannon, 1983).

Tenderness of the Wolves

(1973: d. Ulli Lommel)

scr. Kurt Raab, Lommel; pr. Rainer Werner Fassbinder; ph. Jurgen Jurges; art d. Kurt Raab; ed. Thea Eymesz; cast. Kurt Raab, Jeff Roden, Margit Carstensen, Wolfgang Schenk, Rainer Hauer, Rainer Werner Fassbinder; 86m

This is based on the true account of Fritz Haarmann, a pedophilic homosexual who raped, vampirized and cannibalized at least two dozen boys and young men in pre–Hitler Germany. A police informer, he also sold his victims' flesh on the black market. After mutilated corpses are found on the riverbanks, the trail leads to Haarmann, who is caught in the act. He was a contemporary of notorious killer Peter Kurten, who had inspired *M*.

The film is aware of its Expressionist heritage. It has self-reflexive compositions, a use of selective sound effects (the opening lone footsteps, for example), and a balding killer who brings to mind Peter Lorre in the classic *M*. The killer inhabits a sparsely populated, desolate world full of human desperation and (perhaps the greater sin) indifference. In this desolate urbanity, police remark on the insignificance of one dead, murdered body in such a world.

Tenderness is a reflective film, with minimal dialogue, in which the killer is depicted sympathetically — a manipulator certainly, but an almost tragic figure in that his emotional need for homosexual contact, and even surrender, is translated into the need to consume and kill his lovers, which ultimately dooms him. From the opening, he is shown almost as a victim himself. In bed with a naked teenager when the police burst in, he is subjected to emotional blackmail by virtue of his sexuality. But the police fail to realize or contemplate the monster he is, and indulge his amoral weaknesses in return for the information he provides. Gradually, we realize that he is not the victim, but a deceptive manipulator and the slave to desire.

At first the desire is merely illicit — for young men; but later he's shown to indulge a true monstrousness, as the killer graphically bites his victim's neck and later dismembers the body for sale and disposal. The killer believes himself the master of all, and revels in his secret identity as a means of demonstrating his superiority over the police, who consider him "nothing." Despite opportunities, however, he cannot make an emotional connection with people, and merely goes through the motions with them as a means of staying in control and protecting the false image of himself he has built up through fantasy.

Lommel thus systematically exposes the character's levels of deceptions and false fronts as covers for a sexuality that ironically makes him both horrendous and vulnerable. Despite his pretenses, he cannot control his violent sexuality (his tragic flaw?), and at the end, when police burst in as he is about to bite a victim, though caught, he still lunges to try and bite the boy. He is a slave to his insatiable sexual hunger to consume young men. On some level he seeks companionship, but is compelled to kill and disavow his need — another pretense. Beyond the pretenses, however, is such a killer knowable?

Unlike the killer in *M*, he seems less introspective over his inner compunctions, and has adapted his life to them. He has accepted his destiny and his weakness — homosexual longing. Tellingly, however, he is vulnerable to mockery for his homosexuality (as a personal insult), and so looks dejected when ridiculed by neighborhood kids, a demonstration of a vulnerable side he strives to keep hidden amidst his care-fully erected fronts. He cannot stand to be betrayed or used, as such makes him an emotional victim, and puts him in the dejected state he most abhors (but perhaps senses as inevitable at times). He compensates by indulging in black market practice and another pretense at role-playing (he pretends to be a priest collecting clothes for the needy).

It is arguable whether or not the homosexuality is a precursory aberration to homicidal proclivity, but it is clear that the murder is a substitute for orgasm, to possess the victim. Perhaps he must both destroy the object of his lust (denying it by dismembering it) and keep it with him (by ingestion). However, like the case study of such films as *Henry: Portrait of a Serial Killer*, the psychology is implied and oddly non-judgmental.

Lommel questions the complicity of others in the killer's crimes. Though some suspect, they choose to keep silent, and thus allow an abomination to occur. This inevitably brings to mind the Nazi experience; indeed, the film was reset in the immediate post–World War II years, showing the persistence of the climate of indifference to human need that had contributed to the rise of such abhorrence. Yet the killer is far from the Aryan ideal, and himself not representative of such, though the film in part addresses the moves towards post-war reconstruction, as would Von Trier's later *Zentropa*. Finally, a neighbor speaks out.

Lommel was an actor who impressed a young Fassbinder, who in turn wanted Lommel to star in his films but who had not yet made one. Lommel agreed, and Fassbinder made *Love Is Colder Than Death*, to critical hostility. Nevertheless, their association continued, and Fassbinder produced this film, Lommel's third, also starring in it as a black market dealer and the man ultimately responsible for the killer's capture. Screenwriter Raab, who had long researched the material, first approached Fassbinder to direct, but he declined and, as producer, gave Raab and Lommel complete creative control.

At its showing at the Berlin Film Festival in 1973, it was treated harshly by audiences apparently upset that Lommel had lured them into feeling sympathy for such an ultimately horrendous specimen of humanity (Frentzen, p. 30). For his part, Lommel added that he wanted to show the horror that was in every man, and that aberration is even a relative factor, perhaps the most disquieting aspect of the production. It remains Lommel's most widely known film, and his best to date in a career that shunned the mainstream and straddled exploitation and the art house.

Tenebrae

(1982: d. Dario Argento)

scr. Argento, George Kemp; pr. Claudio Argento; ph. Luciano Tovoli; spec eff. Giovanni Corridori; cast. Anthony Franciosa, John Saxon, Guiliano Gemma, Daria Nicolodi, Christian Borromeo, John Steiner; 110 (101)m

In Argento's anticipated return to the giallo after the supernatural-based flamboyance of *Suspiria* and *Inferno*, an American writer of detective fiction is on a promotional tour of Rome. It is revealed to him that a number of murders of young women are linked to the descriptions in his work. He investigates. It turns out that although a TV host has committed the murders, the protagonist has taken up the lead and become a murderer himself, acting out the misogyny for real, as if vicarious fantasy were no longer enough. A detective follows the case.

In the protagonist, Argento equates the creator (writer/director) with killer, a theme also present in Cohen's *Special Effects* and Fulci's *Cat in the Brain*. The popularity of murder stories impels the search for vicarious identification which can never be fully satisfied unless one takes a more active role. In this way the serial killer is a desired object of identification, and the murders willed by audience complicity. Argento explores the notion of personality transference from proxy to actuality (Newman, p. 106), as the writer adopts the homicidal characteristics of the murderer as a process of self-actualization: he finally puts fantasy into practice. Hence the opening passage from the character's book: that the first act of murder is a response to internal torments and proves a release, a "freedom" from personal pressures, erasing any doubts, fears and insecurities. Sex murder is addictive.

The film follows the process of personality transference between killer and writer. The killer sends letters directly to the writer and quotes from the writer's book ("There was only one answer to the fury that tormented him"). These both implicate the writer as a complicit accomplice (in effect, willing the real killers on to their crimes), and function as a means of personality recognition. The killer senses a psychological kinship with the writer and seeks to form a relationship with him. Hence, the writer here functions as the profiler figure. A flashback to a youthful imprinting—of humiliation by sexually desirable women—at first seems to belong to the killer, a gay television host. However, the memory is the writer's and may represent a symbolic shared formative experience between all those predisposed to become killers. These killers resent women's sexual power over men, and their ability to manipulate and control men because of it.

Throughout the film, men seek to sexually use women, but Argento depicts these victims as, in part, sexual provocateurs. This is not to say that they deserve what they get, only that by flaunting their sexuality they court such abuse and resentment. They would use their sexuality to manipulate men. Such is the current state of gender politics that would influence a budding killer. Women's sexual desirability gives them a power that makes them open targets for those whose quest for sensation has entered the realm of the social taboo. Even more reprehensible to the killer are lesbians, "perverts" whose sexual unattainability is the ultimate scourge. Women are not whores and virgins to the killer, but whores and perverts, contaminated by sex. The killer is a moral crusader who considers the writer the ultimate seducer.

When the writer becomes a killer, he modifies the moral pretext of the preceding type, murdering his editor, who had an affair with his girl. He then moves on to the women that have hurt his pride. His revenge murders were done in the hope that the other killer would be blamed, but as each crime is a work that bears its instigator's signature, he was unable to disguise his own agenda. The detective, aware of killer psychology, deduces that there are two types of crimes and hence more than one killer.

As usual for Argento, the murders are treated as self-contained, stylized set pieces and morbid cinematic poems which beautify acts of violence against women. With more explicitness than before, the film became a controversial talking point in Italy and was subsequently heavily cut (one scene featured a woman's severed limb gushing blood over the inside of a room), especially for the eventual US release.

The Terminal Man

(1974: d. Mike Hodges)

scr. Hodges; nvl. Michael Crichton; pr. Hodges; ph. Richard H. Kline; ed. Robert Wolfe; art d. Fred Harpman; cast. George Segal, Joan Hackett, Richard Dysart, Jill Clayburgh, Donald Moffat, Matt Clark, Michael C. Gwynne, James B. Sikking; 104m

A long-term violent criminal (Segal) has a microchip implanted in his brain, designed to curb his violence. Instead, it makes the violence a narcotic thrill, and he becomes a killer akin to an automaton, although struggling with conflicting emotions about the thrills he obtains from murder. The scientists try to control and eliminate him when it is clear that their experiment has failed.

An involving, bleak incorporation of the serial killer into technophobic science fiction, *The Terminal Man* develops themes explored also in the meditations on free will and its forcible removal/conditioning in Kubrick's *A Clockwork Orange*. It is a failed medical experiment that is ultimately responsible for the killer's descent into ever-greater violence. The brain implant designed to control him by electronic jolts proves pleasurable. The desire to do evil is in this way paralleled to physiological pleasure, and hence to narcotic addiction and ritual. This pleasure acts against the possibility of clear free will, affecting moral judgment. The serial killer functions according to an ingrained pleasure principle he cannot suppress. An attempt to interfere with natural individual psychological balance is both inhumane and futile. The fate of the individual mind is literally in the hands of the scientists, for whom the subject, referred to as "this delivery," has lost all personality or individuality beyond his function as an experiment. In this way, their experiments in behavior modification are attempts to standardize the human mind.

Correspondingly, the scientists are all callous and indifferent figures, unconcerned with the moral and ethical repercussions of their experiment. They are as devoid of a conscience as the killer, perhaps even more so. As Hardy et al. points out (*Sci-Fi*, p. 322), the scientists are shown mostly in black and white, despite the color film, a scheme reflecting their ultimately

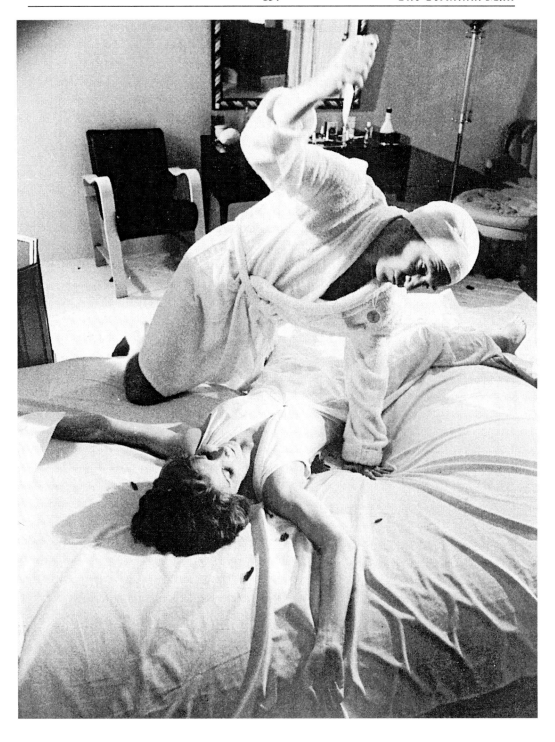

A violent offender (George Segal) is turned into a virtual killing automaton and embarks on a stabbing frenzy in *The Terminal Man* (Cannon, 1983).

limited organization of the world into clear poles. They ultimately can have no pity or understanding of the moral plight of the monster they have loosed, just that their implants have malfunctioned and the result needs to be put down before word spreads and their reputation suffers. Thus, Hodges suggests that such a killer is indeed the one a modern society deserves—technologically manufactured inhumanity. Ironically, Segal was a former computer engineer who feared that machines would take over the world. The experiment effectively turns him into a killing machine, and he stabs his victim in robotic, pointless repetition of a task. The odd symbiosis of human and implant is ultimately destructive—in contrast to the cyber-punk generation, which celebrated the fusion of man and technology.

One doctor voices an objection to the process—that it is merely a disguised lobotomy designed to make difficult patients easier to cure. Segal, who suffered blackouts when he turned violent, is given a tranquilizing spurt whenever the implant senses another blackout/seizure coming. The tranquilizer proves intoxicating, and the brain wills more seizures and their corresponding violent behavior in order to be sedated. Violence becomes orgasmic. The process drives Segal to murder and madness at the recognition of what he has become—his own worst fear, the depersonalized human machine.

The film follows the protagonist's deterioration as his moral choice and self-control are affected. It has a note of tragedy in that Segal is aware of the process but unable to stop it. He seeks refuge in a Church, but is aware only of the abandonment (or testing) by God, always a thematic duality in Hodges' work (most notably in *Prayer for the Dying* and *Black Rainbow*). His dilemma is that science has transformed Eros into Thanatos. Once he is dead, the scientists explain away his aberrance as the result of organic brain damage, and resume the search for another experimental subject, the implication being that they will loose a succession of robotic sex murderers.

Novelist Crichton was a former doctor who turned science fiction author and later director with the hit *Westworld*. He returned to medical ethics with the thriller *Coma*, and many of his subsequent novels (*Jurassic Park* included) have been made into successful films, none of which have the pessimism of Hodges' film. Although Hodges had a major hit with the thriller *Get Carter*, *Terminal Man* was harshly received by the US critics and long unreleased in his native UK. Although *Terminal Man* is not by strict definition a serial killer film, its themes have enormous bearing on the evolution of the genre, which make it worthy of inclusion here. The film's dry melancholic tone captures a mood of resignation and inevitability, which makes it a despairing film.

Terror Circus

(1973: d. Alan Rudolph) aka *Psycho Circus*; *Barn of the Naked Dead*

scr. Roman Valenti; pr. Gerald Cormier; ph. E. Lynn; spec eff. Byrd Holland, Douglas White; cast. Andrew Prine, Manuella Theiss, Sherry Alberoni, Gyl Roland, Al Cormier, Chuck Niles; 86m

Deep in the Nevada desert, a psycho (Prine) abducts women and keeps them naked and in cages in his barn. He forces them to do carnival tricks for a bizarre circus he plans to take on the road, and then graphically hacks them up with a butcher knife. His home is near a nuclear test site, and his menacing radioactivity-mutated father is kept locked up in a shed/outhouse, and taken out on occasion. Three showgirls driving to Vegas break down, and Prine offers them help.

This depiction of a hideous father and son is a supposedly startling attack on

Patriarchy. It is the notable absence of a mother — perhaps an ordering, stabilizing force ideally — which triggers the killer's aberration. His resentment for being deserted by the mother (perhaps a symbolic feminist gesture, although this is all in the interpretation of the surrounding 1970s social context) translates into his hatred and violent sexuality. He must forever punish, degrade and sexually humiliate women.

Terror Circus was Alan Rudolph's directorial debut (under the pseudonym Gerald Cromier) and is a weird horror film in the same Southern Gothic, almost apocalyptic horror-humor vein as Tobe Hooper's *The Texas Chainsaw Massacre* and *Eaten Alive*, Wes Craven's *The Hills Have Eyes*, Girdler's *Three on a Meathook* (also about father/son joint psychosis) and David Schmoeller's *Tourist Trap*. All of these subvert traditional family values, a subtext in many of the more initially disreputable horror films of the 1970s (some of which have been since given their due attention by revisionist critic Robin Wood). In some respects, notably in scenes featuring naked women forced to perform acts, *Terror Circus* may be compared to the truly nauseating *The Incredible Torture Show*.

Supposedly, this was Siskel and Ebert's favorite first effort and has a major cult following, although it's apparently hard to reconcile with Rudolph's later works. It was after this early horror experience that Rudolph went on to assist Altman on *Nashville* and become his most successful protégé, forming a reputation as an auteur.

Le Testament du Docteur Cordelier

(1959: d. Jean Renoir)

scr. Renoir; ph. Georges Leciere; ed. Renee Lichtig; cast. Jean-Louis Barrault, Michel Vitold, Teddy Bills, Jean Topart, Gaston Modot; 90m

Noted director Renoir here indirectly tackles the serial killer film in a television movie variation on *Dr. Jekyll and Mr. Hyde*. A doctor experiments on himself and transforms into a bestial creation (compared to the tramp in Renoir's classic *Boudu Saved from Drowning*) intent on liberating himself from social constraint. Initially, he uses darts on unsuspecting victims (akin to what Peter Kurten did for real), but his sadistic desires increase.

In its exploration of a man whose free will, and pleasure in sexual sadism, separates him from contemporary social constraint, the film anticipates the themes of *A Clockwork Orange* to a degree. The killer represents the worst sort of freedom from conformity, almost Sadean in his knowing, progressive defiance of constraint. But in tribute to the Stevenson original, there remains the suggestion that this liberation from constraint only frees the most bestial of motives, and that humankind, shorn of the advances of civilization, will surrender to a bestial heritage, also a theme in part in Chabrol's *Le Boucher*.

Yet for Renoir, from the bestial comes the anarchic, and that is an impulse worth celebrating. Thus, Raymond Durgnat felt that Renoir's film challenged the functions that would seek to regiment and order life. In this way, the loosed creature, Opale, exists in a kind of pre-socialization state, akin to that of the child (Durgnat, p. 339) without the training that would produce guilt at a joyfully committed sin. Socialization would function as stabilization, regulating the course of energy/freedom.

This was filmed for French television and was government financed. Renoir thought the project a means of bridging the film and television mediums, and so made the film with technicians from both sides. His use of multiple cameras allowed the actors a continuity of action which Durgnat felt freed them from directorial overreliance (p. 332). It was shown at the

1959 Venice Film Festival, and was ultimately considered a failure. It was shown on TV in 1961 after numerous disputes.

The Texas Chainsaw Massacre

(1974: d. Tobe Hooper)

scr. Kim Henkel, Hooper; pr. Hooper; ph. Daniel Pearl; m. Hooper, Wayne Bell; ed. Sallye Richardson, Larry Carroll; art d. Robert A. Burns; cast. Marilyn Burns, Alle Danziger, Paul A. Partain, William Vail, Teri McMinn, Edwin Neal, Jim Siedow, Gunnar Hansen, John Dugan, Jerry Lorenz; 83m

Following reports of the desecration of graves, four teenaged friends go back to the rural Texas where two of them (one of whom is wheelchair-bound) grew up. They pick up a peculiar hitchhiker who is a portent of the strangeness to come. Once there, at an isolated ruin of a farmhouse, they explore, and run into the killer Leatherface and his disturbed cannibal clan, the hitchhiker's family.

Despite its fearsome reputation, the film is not especially gory, and relies for its effect on the sustained atmosphere of an

A collector's item publicity photo of the demented cannibal clan from *The Texas Chainsaw Massacre* (Vortex, 1973).

The monstrous Leatherface (Gunnar Hansen) advances in *The Texas Chainsaw Massacre* (Vortex, 1973).

A young victim (Teri McMinn) hung up on a meathook in *The Texas Chainsaw Massacre* (Vortex, 1973).

out-of-control nightmare into which innocents are thrust and systematically eliminated, and tormented by the monstrous clan. Hooper's grotesque, uneasy style moves forth at an increasingly rapid pace, developing a sense of almost farcically bizarre acceleration/accumulation. Indeed, the monstrous becomes funny — the nervous laughter the only reaction left to the sustained shock of the film's dinner-party climax (itself a morbid interpretation of the Mad Hatter's tea party, and thus a nod to Lewis Carroll).

The monstrous family has been variously interpreted as a parody of the conventional television sitcom family; a perversion of the pioneer spirit that founded the country; as a symbol for the oppressed, made obsolete by progress, returning to avenge their exploitation (a theme latched onto by left-wing critics especially); and as the epitome of the destructive, animistic force in humankind. However, it is as a perversion of the operations of Patriarchy that they are best considered. The family consists of three generations of monsters, each passing the horrendous legacy of their ways to the next — hence the cook's comment that his family has always been in meat. They are grotesque caricatures, comedic, eccentric monsters, and the decision to treat them as such in no way deters from the unrelenting terror. Hooper's style interweaves the comedic and the horrific, providing an inexplicable assault from which the outraged scream of the helpless is the only release — and that too becomes the lone survivor's hysterical laughter by the film's end.

It is almost a comedy of despair in that regard, of mounting outrage, a pastiche of the fairy tale as modern nightmare. The familiar and everyday landscape becomes the perverse and the uncanny, with the serial killer clan demented innocents whose childlike manner constantly borders on the celebration of the anarchic. They are thus a threat to any form of spiritual, psychological, or physical stability: the killer as the epitome of disorder, consuming his fellows. Hooper stresses cosmological phenomenon and interpretations, suggesting the proceedings as a collective nightmare of sorts, the eruption of the unconscious.

Central to the film is the notion of the charnel house. For here the family home is transformed into a slaughterhouse. It is here, in Hooper's visualization of the forbidden room (from which Leatherface bursts out, kills, and violently closes a steel door, barring entry), that cannibalism and murder are allied to paraphilia (Brottman,

p. 123), and suggested necrophilia. The audience is manipulated into wondering what homicidal and sexual perversities are hidden within the home, and in that way the film subverts any conventional notion of safety; again, the familiar becomes the unsettling and the perversely uncanny. Audience complicity in this way is taken to provoke the subsequent shocking atrocities, a self-reflexive aspect Hooper would explore in his long-delayed sequel.

The family treats the young as disposable pieces of meat, there for their consumption, as the familiar is further twisted into the irrational. This builds to the dinner-table sequence, which is perhaps the unequalled depiction of nightmare-as-farce in the horror movie — the laughing family constantly juxtaposed with the screaming victim until the sounds merge. Indeed, it marks the beginning of a movement within the horror film to balance terror and comedy, anticipating the comic grotesquerie of Sam Raimi's early works (especially the *Evil Dead* trilogy). Hooper would subsequently try to develop this difficult tonal balance into a style, but was only infrequently successful.

This seminal horror film is based on the true-life case of serial necrophile Ed Gein, whose exploits also inspired *Psycho*, *Deranged* and *Silence of the Lambs*. It is a serial killer film more in implication than design. In part due to its title, it became the most notorious and controversial horror movie of the 1970s; and many critics were incensed when it was included in the permanent collection of the New York Museum of Modern Art. It was also screened during the Director's Fortnight at the Cannes Film Festival. It has since become one of the most analyzed of all modern horror films, especially by revisionist critics like Robin Wood, who praised the movie's subversive depiction of the monstrous Patriarchal family. This notion of the self-contained explosion of repressed urges would be a theme also developed in Wes Craven's *The Hills Have Eyes*.

The Texas Chainsaw Massacre 2

(1986: d. Tobe Hooper)

scr. L.M. Kit Carson; pr. Menahem Golan, Yoram Globus; ph. Richard Kooris; m. Hooper, Jerry Lambert; ed. Alain Jakubowicz; prod d. Cary White; cast. Dennis Hopper, Caroline Williams, Bill Johnson, Jim Siedow; 95m

This grotesque sequel has the killer clan relocated to an abandoned amusement park (thus recalling Hooper's earlier *Funhouse* and his attraction to a kind of demented carnival). The cook is now a prize-winning local chef (recalling *Motel Hell*). A country radio DJ records a murder, and a Texas agent (Hopper) believes the clan is responsible. The DJ follows the clan, who attempt to kill her, and the agent arms himself with chainsaws, ready to tackle those for whom he has been relentlessly searching and tracking for years.

The sequel develops the characters' sexual dysfunction more so than the first film. This is especially true of Leatherface, who treats his chainsaw as a substitute penis (explicitly visualized as it is held near the protagonist's crotch, threatening to penetrate her), and who in one scene has trouble starting it. Ironically, Leatherface romanticizes the DJ as a possible partner, and the film jokingly takes on a Beauty and the Beast subtext (Hartl, *film.com*).

Thus, mental aberration is rooted in sexual dysfunction, and the film attempts in part to deconstruct the nightmare of the first movie, becoming a celebration of humankind's inherent anarchic spirit. This knowing distance invariably made the sequel less gripping, though the laughter is once again despairing, and the direction apocalyptic (as the heroine becomes a chainsaw-spinning murderess, surrendering to her basic instincts, although ar-

guably provoked). In that, the film can be interpreted as charting the systematic destruction of the human spirit. Hooper admitted (*Austin Chronicle* online) that he made the sequel in part because he felt the first film's comedy had gone unrecognized.

Unlike the first film, Hooper here relies on extreme gore effects to provoke a reaction in his audience. And progressing on from the original's comedic terror, he here strives to celebrate the descent into amoral depravity and violence. The merciless ridicule of a crumbling civilization seems Hooper's indulgent aim here (a theme in much of his output). Modern America has become a rotten survivalist theme park, jokingly referred to in the film as Namland. Atrocity and incongruity pile upon each other relentlessly. The theme park aspect, a kind of Texas Chainsaw Disneyland, also self-consciously represents the commercialization of the interpersonal nightmare depicted in the first film. Thus, the descent into the killers' lair is a descent into the irrational, and is explicitly and decoratively visualized.

In the process, Hooper heightens the sense of farce and frames the monstrous family in grandiose set-design instead of the first film's squalor. Indeed, the family here is a modern success story, escaping their socioeconomic entrapment through murder and cannibalism as a Capitalist enterprise — the perversion of the grand American Dream, with the cook ironically proclaiming that they hold onto the good old ways and traditions. The US tradition here is murder, cannibalism and necrophilia. They have become the establishment, the epitome of Patriarchy, with the policeman Hopper the appointed purifier. His status as restorative agent of Patriarchy is thus also ironic and lampooned, as he is fighting a reflection of the order he aspires to.

Indeed, the film delineates Patriarchy's hierarchy within and outside the

A ghoulish spectacle as a corpse is held aloft on the back of a moving vehicle by a chainsaw wielding relative in *The Texas Chainsaw Massacre 2* (Cannon, 1986).

family as a knowing parody of the orderly functioning of society. It is clear that Hooper intends the film as a revolutionary statement (perhaps explaining the film's fate in Australia, where it was banned outright from cinema and video). The good is as monstrous as the bad, and Hooper has more sympathy for the monstrous family than before — he admires their anarchic statement of survival.

Following the original film, Hooper's career had languished. He made another Southern Gothic, *Eaten Alive*, which failed at the box office. After his stint with Spielberg on *Poltergeist*, which had the critics praising Spielberg's guiding hand rather than Hooper's, he had two big-budget flops, *Invaders from Mars* and *Lifeforce*, before agreeing to tackle a sequel to his most famous film.

Chainsaw 2 was threatened with an X rating by the MPAA, and released unrated by the distributor instead. Consequently, it played in smaller cinemas only and was refused many newsprint and TV advertising spots. Although the sequel recaptures the manic feel of the first movie, and exceeds it as grotesque comedy (more overtly), it was not a popular hit and failed to boost Hooper's career, which has continued to flounder since.

The two sequels that followed, *Leatherface* and *The Texas Chainsaw Massacre: The Next Generation*, reduced the material to the slasher formula and so are not included here. Neither of them featured Hooper, although the first film's co-screenwriter, Kim Henkel, directed the latter.

Theatre of Death

(1967: d. Sam Gallu)

scr. Ellis Kadison, Roger Marshall; pr. Michael Smedley-Astin; ph. Gilbert Taylor; cast. Christopher Lee, Lelia Goldoni, Julian Glover, Evelyn Laye, Jenny Till, Ivor Dean; 91m

In Paris, bloodless bodies of women and old tramps are discovered, and a police surgeon, lusting after a performer at a Grand Guignol theater, suspects the theater's vampiric owner (Christopher Lee), who seems to go missing. The bodies have a mark on their necks, the result of a dagger. The surgeon looks into the deaths when asked to do so by police (and thus is an early profiler-as-outsider figure).

It is the film's hybrid of vampire movie (the girlfriend's Romanian flat-mate was raised on blood in the years following World War Two) and emergent serial killer type (the incorporation of the outside agent) which in part makes it another transitional film and worthy of inclusion. It is unusually aware of the origins of the emergent movement towards explicit gore in its depictions of the operations of a Grand Guignol Theater. The recreations of gory stage acts and the audience reaction to them add a period authenticity which gives the film a longevity and interest as document beyond the vampire plot, which would be familiar to followers of Hammer horror, as the movie carefully plays with expectations of Lee's image.

Three on a Meathook

(1973: d. William Girdler)

scr, m. Girdler; pr. Lee Jones; ph. William Asman; ed. Henry Asman; cast. Sherry Steiner, Carolyn Thompson, Linda Thompson, Charles Kissinger, Hugh Smith, James Pickett; 85m

A local youth (Pickett) takes four stranded girls back to his isolated farmhouse where he lives with his domineering father. He suffers from blackouts wherein he thinks he has murdered women. The killer hangs them in the slaughterhouse, cannibalizes them and wears their skin over his own (McCarty, *Official Splatter Guide*, p. 132). His father, hiding monstrous secrets of his own, helps him out, as he has in the past. The father becomes worried when his son develops an interest in a new girl, a sympathetic waitress.

This is a movie in the vein of *Terror Circus* especially, and Tobe Hooper's Southern Gothic films. Indeed, it preceded the release of *The Texas Chainsaw Massacre*. *Three on a Meathook* is more understated (though gory) and uneven in its treatment of the comedy of terror, however, and so never achieves the sense of nightmare present in Hooper's classic. Although it can be considered an underrated item, and perhaps the least known of the films inspired in part by the real killer Ed Gein, *Meathook* lacks the style, conviction and longevity of its contemporaries. Girdler developed a minor reputation as a horror/exploitation auteur, achieving some returns with the likes of *Grizzly*, *Day of the Animals* and *The Manitou*. He also tackled the serial killer in another obscurity, *The Zebra Killer*.

There seems to be an interest in the malfunctioning of nature's interaction with humanity in his films, with the killer a decided aberration. Human relations are essentially abhorrent to Girdler, there to be perverted and expunged by superior forces, even if this means madness. The father and son relationship also ties in the film to the 1970s trend depicting the collapse of Patriarchy's traditions, as here the monstrous devours those that come into its path. The legacies of human interaction are the morbid trophies of death, decay and sex murder the killer surrounds himself with.

Tightrope

(1984: d. Richard Tuggle)

scr. Tuggle; pr. Eastwood, Fritz Manes; ph. Bruce Surtees; m. Lennie Niehaus; ed. Joel Cox; prod d. Edward Carfagno; cast. Clint Eastwood, Genevieve Bujold, Dan Hedaya, Alison Eastwood, Jennifer Beck, Marco St. John, Rebecca Perle, Regina Richardson; 114m

A New Orleans policeman (Eastwood) tracks a serial killer/strangler through the seedy nightlife of the city's French Quarter, and finds himself sexually aroused the deeper he gets into the killer's world, a world he too is familiar with, as prostitutes and lowlifes know him by sight. Indeed, it seems the killer is deliberately toying with him, killing the people the cop may have known and, in one case, using Eastwood's tie (left behind after sex) to strangle a victim. When Eastwood's daughters are threatened, he takes the case more seriously. Finally, the killer targets Eastwood's romantic interest (Bujold), a women's self defense instructor (for added irony).

This was considered a daring role for Eastwood, a long way from his *Dirty Harry* persona. Here he is more conflicted about women, even threatened by them, and is thus drawn to borderline S&M sex, handcuffing his sexual partner at one stage. In that way, his sexual desire parallels that of the killer, who is rumored to be a cop at one point. They are attracted to provocative women, the killer seeking to destroy them fully — perhaps the end result of an attraction/repulsion complex Eastwood may be headed towards: the need to dominate. Eastwood is aware of the similarities and has nightmares in which he is the killer. Perhaps this recognition is a moment of catharsis, maybe even the epiphany a patriarch needs before he succumbs to the tempting abyss of sexual homicide.

The killer has lost perspective and is an anonymous functionary of a sexual perversity akin to a contagion (it's interesting that this film emerged at the start of publicity about the AIDS crisis). This aspect, of such abhorrence being a shared quality between patriarchs, also makes for a parallel to *Cruising*. Eastwood's friendship and burgeoning romance with Bujold offers him a way out of the trap of sexual domination he has been headed towards, just as Pacino's girlfriend was a reminder of the moral order of things. And it is a trap that's all the more surprising, and dangerous, as he is the father of two young daughters. This relationship with Bujold allows Eastwood to know and respect a woman in a context beyond sexual power plays. He learns the potentially enriching qualities of male-female interaction, qualities the killer denies in his conception of a sexually disposable womanhood.

In the midst of the parallels between killer and cop is a concern for the forensic practices as the only unambiguous truth left in a morally cloudy world. Thus, the film validates the often-found convention in the serial killer film — the autopsy-room scene, where the details of the crime reveal the presence of the serial killer. Whatever his motivations, he can be ascertained and tracked by the forensic scientists (who have, since the late 1990s, become the

Detective Wes Block (Clint Eastwood) finally apprehends and fights the hooded killer who has taunted him in *Tightrope* (WB, 1984).

protagonists in serial killer films—*Kiss the Girls*—and TV programs as a new breed of profiler) who relay the information to the detectives to follow up. The details of the crime alone are the only concrete facts available.

Eastwood here is a dualistic patriarch, a father of girls who both loathes and seeks to sexually dominate women. It is suggested, therefore, that the killer is a surrogate id, doing for real what the cop may have only fantasized about. However, Eastwood is at a delicate point, that of putting his fantasies into practice—hence he playfully ties a tie around a prostitute's neck as if to strangle her as a prelude to sex. He is on the same path as the killer, and needs to purge this from his soul. His relationship with Bujold may stem in part from desire for her, and in part guilt over his own fantasies. Certainly her occupation, as counselor for sexually abused women, offers

him a psychological healing point. Thus, he is honest and confessional with her about the effect that such cases have on him—does he seek repentance?

The conflation between cop and killer, as potential doppelgangers, is signaled from the outset as we cut from the killer's sneakers to Eastwood's shoes—following in each other's footsteps. To work himself into a rage over the killer, Eastwood stares at his own reflection in the mirror. This results in a moral ambiguity which prompted some to label the film a neo-noir, an ambiguity it shares with the bleaker *Cop*. Both films are part of a noir revival in the early 1980s which sought to bring the shadowy style to a depiction of an increasingly sleazy and sexually exploitative street-life, post Schrader/Scorsese. Other films included in this mini-revival were *Angel*, *Ten to Midnight*, *The Exterminator* and *Vice Squad*. Even the infallible Dirty Harry himself had his moral sensibilities undermined in *Sudden Impact*, wherein he recognized the validity of another vigilante killer. In *Tightrope*, he finally purges the worst of himself by killing the killer (revealed as an ex-cop previously arrested by Eastwood for sex offences).

The killer leaves clues for Eastwood to follow, leading him from place to place (as Scorpio did by phone in *Dirty Harry*) in a tour of a French Quarter immersed in Mardi Gras, where masks are a common, symbolic find. Everybody conceals their own dark side and walks a tightrope between control and desire — good and evil, as the police psychiatrist explains to Eastwood at one point. These Mardi Gras scenes are oddly surrealistic, even suggestive of a kind of Hell on Earth.

Tuggle had previously scripted *Escape from Alcatraz* for Eastwood and director Don Siegel, before Eastwood agreed to star in Tuggle's directorial debut, as the actor had done for Michael Cimino in *Thunderbolt and Lightfoot*. While Eastwood drew praise from many for his willingness to test the bounds of his persona, the film was inevitably compared to the *Dirty Harry* series. Pauline Kael most notably found the film evident only of a certain self-disgust on Eastwood's part, and otherwise a mere slasher movie (Kael, pp. 238–240).

Time After Time

(1979: d. Nicholas Meyer)

scr. Meyer; stry. Kari Alexander, Steve Hayes; pr. Herb Jaffe; ph. Paul Lohmann; m. Miklos Rozsa; ed. Donn Cambern; prod d. Edward Carfagno; cast. Malcolm McDowell, David Warner, Mary Steenburgen, Charles Cioffi, Laurie Main, Andonia Katsaros, Patti D'Arbanville; 112m

Jack the Ripper (Warner) uses H.G. Wells' time machine to journey to contemporary Los Angeles, where he considers himself an amateur (showing the cynicism and lack of faith in human nature that would often surface in Meyer's films). Wells (McDowell) follows him and develops a romantic attraction for a bank clerk (Steenburgen) the Ripper intends to target next. To prove to her that he is indeed from the past, Wells takes her into the future where the next day's newspaper headline tells of her death. Together they try to alter this timeline and save her life. However, Wells is arrested as a suspect in the other sex slayings.

An excellent blend of science fiction and serial killer film, *Time After Time* neatly encapsulates the sense of outrage at the course of sex crime and social change since the original Ripper crimes. Thus, Wells is portrayed as the Utopian idealist whose hope for the future is shattered by his experience with the Ripper, whom he knows as a friend and adversary. Their rival idealism forms the film's thematic juxtapositioning, resulting in the systematic stripping away of Wells' beliefs.

As Jack escapes into the future via Wells' time machine, Wells fears that he has let a monster loose in his beloved Utopia. Once he journeys into this future, however, he realizes that it is not only unlike his views, but indeed more similar to the Ripper's. Wells may profess free love, but the result is rampant sex murder as the liberation from constraint invariably frees monstrous impulses. Ironically, and most cynically, Jack the Ripper proves to be the true visionary, with Wells left to function in reaction. Indeed, Jack proclaims that the world has surpassed even his cynical expectations, and that although in his own time he was considered a freak, by the standards of the late 1970s he is a rank amateur. He claims he is at home in this world, and that humankind has not gone forward, but back. It is thus impossible to separate the film from the tide of reactions to the escalation in violent crime over the past decades; indeed, it probably

A police officer finds and holds up Jack the Ripper's bag of weapons and surgical instruments as H.G. Wells (Malcolm McDowell, right) looks on in amazement at the implications it has for his friend in *Time After Time* (WB, 1979).

summarizes a popular view. The police in the film confirm this sense of escalation and outrage when one remarks, "First the Zodiac and now this."

McDowell is at first a naive, childlike idealist, boldly going forward into a new world (hence Meyer's later involvement with the *Star Trek* sequels). Soon booted out of a church and left homeless, he is forced to realize that Utopianism is an impossible ideal. However, he finds hope in love and heterosexual interaction with the bank clerk Steenburgen. Steenburgen too has a childlike, innocent quality, and the two of them seem out of place in the world around them. She jokes that she was all for feminine liberation, but now wonders. These two of God's children are the last hope left for a disreputable, nightmarish humanity, Meyer suggests. But as they pur-

sue romance, Warner is on the prowl, selecting random victims and then committing ferocious sex murder.

Meyer presents the struggle between McDowell and Warner not only as good and evil, but as Innocence vs. Experience. Thus, they are intercut, their fates entwined. As Wells reveals himself to his love, blood strikes the Ripper in the eye, making it look like he has cried tears of blood. Such is their respective treatment of women — Innocence to love, Experience to destroy. Sex without love is a contaminant. That is the last recourse for Wells' idealism, as he says that it is only love that makes the ages bearable.

Unusually, there is a guardedly happy ending, and love ultimately prevails. However, there is a brief instance, a knowing nod between the Ripper and his former

Jack the Ripper (David Warner) threatens his friend and nemesis H.G. Wells' new romantic interest (Mary Steenburgen) in *Time After Time* (WB, 1979).

friend, that makes the Ripper in a sense choose to die: Experience finally perhaps welcomes its demise. The triumph of Innocence is a faith in the past, as man and woman go back in time to achieve a perfect union, free from the modern hell around them. The faith in love ultimately overwhelms the cynicism. This was echoed in real life, as McDowell and Steenburgen fell in love during the making of the film and were later married.

Meyer was a novelist whose previous work had been filmed by Herbert Ross as the adventure *The Seven Per Cent Solution*, again about the fact-meets-fiction meeting of two historical (or literary) personages, this time Sherlock Holmes and Sigmund Freud. Meyer debuted as director with *Time After Time*, and went on to another

depiction of the ills of the modern world in *The Day After*, before directing two of the *Star Trek* sequels.

To Catch a Killer

(1991: d. Eric Till)

scr. Jud Kinberg; pr. Richard O. Lowry; exec pr. Jinny Schreckinger, Jud Kinberg; ph. Rene Ohashi; ed. Ralph Brunjes; cast. Brian Dennehy, Michael Riley, Meg Foster; 111m

This is an effective tele-movie about the case of John Wayne Gacy. Dennehy depicts this horrific man as a sadistic sexual predator hiding behind the facade of moral respectability. However, the film balances this character portrait with its dual focus on the well-documented facts leading to the arrogant killer's capture.

The film is intent to show the homosexual predator at work, setting his lures for younger men. It is assumed that the audience is at least partially familiar with the Gacy case, and so is aimed at the knowing. However, by deliberately choosing not to depict Gacy's homicidal actions, and favoring restraint, the film ultimately loses out on the dramatic tension it has been building towards. Thus, the intensity of the film's best scene, in which Gacy skillfully manipulates a potential victim into being handcuffed, is undercut when Gacy anticlimactically lets him go. In this case, less is not more. We never see the homicidal ferocity of the man, only his arrogant boasting, although his delight in manipulating people and keeping his secret hidden is abundantly clear. There seems no motive beyond that in his dressing as a clown to entertain children. It entertains his sense of irony and superiority, for he remarks to the investigating detective that, "Clowns can get away with murder."

The film parallels the respective lives of the killer and cop as rival patriarchs. The cop is a loving father, whereas the killer murders young boys seeking a job or guidance from him. The measure of a man is thus in the treatment of his son, whether real or symbolic. It follows strict procedural lines thereafter, as the good father is attuned to the ways of the bad and can sense the evil man's conscienceless guilt. Indeed, the policeman is a bridge between the symbolic roles of father and son — his youth is remarked on and resented by older police officers, as he represents the working best of Patriarchy's traditions. It is his capture of Gacy that enables his full transition to the role of worthy patriarch, sanctioned with the duty of chastisement.

The film is effective in depicting the cat and mouse games between the two adversaries, as the cop obtains a search warrant (finding suspicious items, including handcuffs on a torture board) and engages in follow-up procedures designed to provoke a reaction in the hulking bear of a killer. It is in the gradual revelation of details (the torture board, etc.), and their role in Gacy's private life, that the film probes the killer's monstrousness. Since the ultimate outcome is announced from the opening, the film is rather remote and suspenseless, however. Correspondingly, the gradual revelation of Gacy's past crimes brings with it no sense of necessary foreboding.

There is a passing nod to the psychic, here brought in as a last resort, who intuits Gacy's method and his conscienceless, remorseless pride at being able to trap people. And that is indeed the film's thesis of Gacy — that the torture and murder of the young men were almost secondary to their pursuit and entrapment as a means of gaining power over them before throwing it in their face. Gacy is a hunter, and this film correspondingly concentrates on that hunt and entrapment rather than the kill process. It is an interesting choice.

Despite a terrifying performance from Dennehy, the film fails to captivate as it should, leading some people to consider it a wasted opportunity. However, it is more effective than the disappointing *Hillside Stranglers*, which sought a similar exploration of arrogant killers whose egos ultimately prove their undoing.

The Todd Killings

(1971: d. Barry Shear)

scr. Dennis Murphy, Joel Oliansky; stry. Mann Rubin; pr. Shear; ph. Harold E. Stine; m. Leonard Rosenman; ed. Walter Thompson; cast. Robert F. Lyons, Richard Thomas, Belinda Montgomery, Barbara Bel Geddes, Sherry Miles, Gloria Grahame, Fay Spain, Edward Asner, Michael Conrad; 93m

This supposedly real-life based film is about a violent but somewhat charismatic sex-killer (Lyons) shielded from police by his loyal peer group. These admiring

The youthful killer (Robert Lyons) disposing of his victim in *The Todd Killings* (National General Pic., 1971).

youths, all several years younger than he, also help him hide the bodies. The killer is a 23-year-old man trapped in the glory of his high school days who now psychologically dominates and leads other similar teens, à la the cult leader Charles Manson. His sex murders are an addictive power kick for him. One youth in particular (Thomas) seems obsessed with him and his unlawful actions. Sex murder is a thrill passed on between perpetrators.

The killer is a case of arrested development. Still termed "Skipper," despite his age, he is financially dependent on a small stipend from his mother, who reinforces his ego by doting on him, even cleaning up after him. He correspondingly feels no need to pay his own way and enter the adult world. His sex murders are thrills to

him, his smugness allowing him endless self-indulgence. Though he may seem more knowledgeable and charismatic to his younger admirers, his mindset is the corruption of an adolescent longing. He therefore can target the sexual feelings of other such males and hold sway over them, indulging and validating their own desires. He is ironically the most adult presence in these teenagers' lives (as *Variety* noted), although he reinforces their immaturity. His ability to feed their burgeoning sexuality is taken as charisma.

Shear offers a "generational cross-section" of women, as *Variety* noted — of middle-aged mothers and teenaged daughters— but all in relation to the aberrant male sexuality emerging. This hints at a kind of cause and effect structure, with faulty socialization and mental imbalance clearly contributive factors to a thrill-killing mentality. Whether this thrill-killing qualifies as an anarchic statement beyond self-indulgence is another matter, however, and the film subtextually raises the anti-hero potential of such cases: the killer becomes a representative of a certain cultural, youthful grouping in a community not deprived of services or money. In that sense it arguably parodies the socialization process, and the killer's relationship to Thomas brings to mind Leopold and Loeb (as Thompson in the *New York Times* suggested).

The film was originally to have been directed by famed dramatist Abby Mann, who worked uncredited on the original script, but studio disagreements led to his removal from the project. Shear was a television director who broke into the movies briefly in the early 1970s with the hit exploitation film *Wild in the Streets* (later making the notable *Across 110th Street*). *The Todd Killings* has been compared to the much later *River's Edge*, which also explored the consequences of teenage indifference. It was considered a solid film and evidence of an emerging directorial talent now working in the mainstream.

Too Scared to Scream

(1982: d. Tony Lo Bianco)

co-d. Victor Lobl; scr. Neal Barbera, Glenn Leopold; pr. Michael Connors; ph. Larry Pizer; ed. Ed Beyer, Michael Economou; prod d. Lilly Kilvert; cast. Michael Connors, Anne Archer, Leon Isaac Kennedy, Ian McShane, Ruth Ford, John Heard, Carrie Nye, Maureen O'Sullivan, Murray Hamilton; 104m

A luxury Manhattan apartment building is beset by the murders of rich tenants. A policeman investigates and decides that the chief suspect is a doorman who lives in a lower socioeconomic field with a mute, chair-ridden mother. He sets up his female partner (Archer) as a decoy to lure the killer into action, but the assumption of the doorman's heterosexuality is constantly questioned.

This mix of police investigation, giallo (the gloved killer) and slasher film was actor Lo Bianco's directorial debut. The apartment building is a microcosm of American upper middle-class affluence and contemporary sexual politics, and the killer's actions are thus initially clothed in revolutionary guise. But the revelation of the killer as the doorman's spurned homosexual lover, who killed those tenants and women who would take his beloved's attention away from him, postulates a corruption of romantic longing as a causal factor and robs the crimes of any other subtext.

Once again, like many films of its era, it allies male desire with violence, as scenes of violence against the erotic object follow scenes of female nudity. However, in that it is a homosexual killer, the motive is resentment of others' heterosexuality. The killer therefore only targets those he considers sexual decadents, regardless of their gender (a facet he shares with slashers), and a perceived threat to his own sexual fixations on the doorman. In a peculiar (and unfortunately unexplored) nod to *Psycho*, the killer dresses up as the doorman's mother to exact final revenge. Although the killer's tortuous sexuality is suggested, it is never followed through, and the film remains an unremarkable slasher mystery.

The Toolbox Murders

(1979: d. Dennis Donnelly)

scr. Neva Friedenn, Robert Easter, Ann Kindberg; pr. Tony Didio; ph. Gary Graver; cast. Cameron Mitchell, Pamelyn Ferdin, Wesley Eure, Nicolas Beauvy, Tim Donnelly, Aneta Corsaut; 95 (92)m

This is the gruesome tale of serial killer prone to using implements from his toolbox to kill women. He is the caretaker in an apartment block where most of the murders have taken place. He blames "evil," "corrupt" women for the death of his pure daughter (a similar theme found in *The New York Ripper*).

Preempting the slasher movement (just), this is an assemblage of gruesome murder scenes (including death by power drill, hammer, screwdriver, nail gun, scissors, knife), but is otherwise a structureless depiction of the killer's psychosis (Hardy, p. 332). This is balanced with the religious monologues/sermons of a radio preacher, perhaps intended as ironic counterpoint. With much nudity, it attempts to combine the violent with the soft-core pornographic, and so treads a morally problematic ground. However, it does not achieve or maintain the self-consciously pornographic-violence-as-spectacle approach that Fulci took with *The New York Ripper*, though it is still a reportedly callous film to sit through.

There are signs that the filmmakers were striving for a certain irony (the killer singing "Sometimes I Feel Like a Motherless Child" as he murders women), but this too is evidence only of its callousness rather than a reasoned attempt to distance the viewer from the killings. Indeed, one scene, a nail-gun murder, was shown on TVs *Donahue* talk show about such violent movies, reportedly to a disgusted reception. Perhaps its novelty value today stems more from its reputation than its effectiveness.

Torso

(1973: d. Sergio Martino)

scr. Ernesto Gastaldi, Martino; pr. Carlo Ponti, Antonio Cervi; ph. Giancarlo Ferrando; cast. Suzy Kendall, Tina Aumont, Luc Meranda, John Richardson, Robert Bisacco, Angela Covello, Carla Brait, Cristina Airoldi; 90m

When a college campus is beset by sex murders, four co-eds retreat to an isolated country estate. The killer, a ferocious hooded maniac who uses a hacksaw to dismember his victims, arrives just as the group begins to erotically experiment with one another. The killer stalks them, intent on systematically eliminating them.

Despite the title implications, the actual bodily dismemberment is generally not shown, only the aftermath, with the concept instead inherent in the director's framing and fragmentation of the human body. Such a stylistic decision reflects the killer's abnormally assaultive gaze, wherein body parts are eroticized and fetishized. Indeed, the film can be treated as a self-conscious examination of the medium's fragmentation of the human body, and its particular importance in the horror film form. The killer gains sexual pleasure from bodily dismemberment, thus he is seen caressing a dead victim before lovingly dismembering her. His later actions with the body parts of other co-eds bespeak of a masturbatory infantilism, perhaps a nod to the joviality of H.G. Lewis, but without his subversive glee.

The film begins by juxtaposing a lecture in art history on the painting of saints and madonnas with soft focus scenes of a fornicating couple as a peeping tom photographs them. Ostensibly raising the interrelationship of art and sex, and suggesting its link to the Madonna-Whore complex, it is an unsubtle introduction which demonstrates Martino's style of heavy-handed juxtapositioning. Nevertheless, it suggests that high art would celebrate a woman's "purity" and low art (the film itself) her sexuality. However, as usual for any analysis of this subject after *Peeping Tom*, all male gazes seek to eroticize its object. Martino suggests that this initiates a process that leads to the desire to punish the object. Thus, the gaze seeks always to eroticize and destroy, and cinema is inherently masculine by virtue of its cut-up construction of the human body and gender identity. Still, *Variety* could find interest only in the beauty of the location work and the women.

The teen girls are part of a Bohemian lifestyle — the remnants of the hippie free love era — and Martino compares them to the local prostitutes, the difference being the latter's professionalism and work ethic. Thus, the killer's violence against the promiscuous can be interpreted as the punitive demise of a period of moral change now seeking to invalidate what it once championed. The consequences of sexual liberation are violence and sex murder. It is, of course, a conservative, reactionary posture and anticipates the teen killing of the slasher form emerging a few years later. Thus, the serial killer as sexual deviate segues into a figure akin to a punisher, chastising the sexually active for their desires and permissiveness: just as the giallo form merged murder mystery and horror.

Such a killer no longer embodies the liberation of illicit desire, and instead becomes an agent of repression. It is ironic that the professor is the killer, for the film then approaches an anti-intellectualism that would expose the art appreciator as a sexual deviate and hypocrite who considers women as disposable dolls while paradoxically championing their visual representation as the epitome of culture. Martino's film thus speaks of cultural hypocrisy. Its revelation of the killer murdering students who have blackmailed him over his sexual indiscretions recalls *Pretty Maids All in a Row.*

As such, the film has an historical value in terms of genre evolution, besides its function as a worldwide giallo release. It not only anticipates the slasher film, but also incorporates the soft-core pornography of European adult cinema into the horror genre. Much of its violence was trimmed for its US release, however. The controversial Italian giallo came to the

United States with this film, picked, along with Armando Crispino's *Autopsy*, by its distributor to introduce the form to the general American public. The same distributor, Joseph Brenner, would soon after also release Lenzi's *Eyeball*. The film's reception was soon overshadowed by the praise heaped upon the early works of Dario Argento and Fulci's own giallos. Nevertheless, the emergent giallos marked the start of the boom period in Italian horror exploitation, the "spaghetti nightmare" period. Martino is considered a minor figure in this boom, perhaps best known for *Slave of the Cannibal God*, which is remembered for its naked Ursula Andress.

Totmacher

(1995: d. Romuald Karmaker) aka *Deathmaker*

scr. Michael Farin, Karmaker; pr. Thomas Schuhly; pr. Fred Schuler; ed. Peter Przygodda; prod d. Toni Ludi; cast. Jurgen Hentsch, Gotz George, Pierre Franckh, Matthias Fuchs, H.M. Rehberg; 114m

Based on the case of real-life German homosexual killer and vampire/cannibal Fritz Haarmann (whose exploits had previously been filmed as *The Tenderness of Wolves*), *Totmacher* shows that Haarmann is caught after years of murder and mutilation, but then concentrates on the psychiatrist assigned to the case, there to determine if the killer is sane and hence able to stand trial. He interviews the killer in a small room at the mental institution where he is held.

This supposedly riveting, but generally unreleased, film has much of its dialogue reportedly taken from the transcript of the actual interview (in the same way that the film *Wannsee Conference*, about the implications of the Nazis' final solution, was based on notes taken during the actual meeting). Thus, it contains an authentically detailed description by the killer of his methods (which include forced sodomy, cannibalism, vampirism, and dismemberment), and gradually reveals his motivations (as he sees them). The film effectively puts the viewer in the position of the profiler, and explores as a case study the central dilemma of the genre regarding the killer's frame of mind and his corresponding responsibility. This was, unfortunately, unavailable at time of writing.

Touch of Death

(1988: d. Lucio Fulci)

scr. Fulci; pr. Luigi Nannerini, Antonio Lucidi; ph. Silvano Tessicini; spec eff. Angelo Mattei; cast. Brett Halsey, Ria De Simone, Pier Luigi Conti, Sasha Darwin, Zora Ulla Kesler; 91m

A serial killer murders rich women and widows who are afflicted with some kind of physical deformity.

Fulci returns to the giallo after a long absence. In the interim he had become acclaimed as an auteur and genre visionary by some, second only to Argento, and alternately considered a cynical misogynistic hack content to exploit trends set in motion by others. The film is aware of its makers reputation, a self-conscious trend that would culminate in the almost arthouse self-reflexivity of *Cat in the Brain*, almost as if the director was intent on proving himself an auteur capable of inserting personal statements into his work. Consequently, some (Hardy, p. 439) consider this movie, and Fulci's last films, as made with the critics in mind.

Touch of Death has more knowingly ironic humor than usual for Fulci, with a man given a speeding ticket by a policeman who fails to notice the propped up corpse in the passenger seat. In synopsis it recalls *The Spiral Staircase*, and can perhaps be considered another study of a killer both attracted to and repulsed by physical imperfection, though putting into practice an operation along the lines of *Monsieur Verdoux*. But, once again, misog-

yny seems to be the underlying root cause, and the gory slaughters are reportedly played for comedic effect (using Mickey Mouse music, Hardy points out).

Its callous treatment of the disabled, and its graphic violence, were considered too strong for Italian television, for which the film was originally intended. Subsequently released on video, it appealed only to the dedicated Fulci fans.

Tourist Trap

(1978: d. David Schmoeller)

scr. Schmoeller, J. Larry Carroll; pr. Carroll; ph. Nicholas von Sternberg; cast. Chuck Connors, Tanya Roberts, Keith McDermott, Dawn Jeffory, Jon Van Ness, Jocelyn Jones, Robin Sherwood; 90m

An isolated roadside museum, Slausen's Lost Oasis, is home to a homicidal owner (Connors) and his collection of telekinetic, homicidal mannequins. A group of teenagers are stranded there when their jeep breaks down. They explore and are targeted by the mannequins and the owner. The only survivor, once Connors and the dummies perish, is left in a state of mental disarray.

Offering no explanation for the mannequins' abilities, the film takes on the qualities of a subdued nightmare, slowly accumulating terror and helplessness, and most notably developing a palpable sense of the uncanny. Perhaps symbolically, the mannequins are the creations/children of the monstrous patriarch, there to consume the next generation and invoke mental chaos. However, it is unclear (or ambiguous, depending on one's opinion of the movie) as to what they represent, although they tie in to his past kills and internal projections.

Equally startling is the killer's perversely abnormal sexuality. It is revealed that he killed his wife and brother when he caught them having sex, and now resides with their corpses, two of the dummies. However, when he impersonates his dead brother, he dresses as a woman, suggesting a certain incestuous desire. It is possible that his desire for the young women wills the mannequins into life, and that he can then project his own guilt onto his creations/accomplices. He cannot part with the past and seeks to give it new form. In the end, they are inseparable and must die together. It is a sinister psychology, left unreflected.

Indeed, as he is about to kill a teenage girl, he tells her to say that she loves him and then goes into his homicidal frenzy. Sexual dysfunction and memory have fused into violent repetition. Connors is first introduced as a voyeur with a rifle, spying on the teenagers swimming nude. The gentle symbolism makes him a sex killer. But he is also a socioeconomic victim, as the new highway has all but destroyed his roadside museum (a nod to *Psycho*). Ironically, although he warns the teenagers to leave (knowing of their eventual fate at his hands), the girls joke that he is a psycho-killer, revealing an awareness of the familiarity of such convention by now in the rural nightmare horror movie. He is the bad father who lives solely in the past, in a melange of psychosis and memories. The mannequins are the forces of his memories which come alive to destroy the present.

The effect of the past on the present, and the attempt to live again, are regular Schmoeller themes, as the desire to preserve the past yields only homicidal madness. It infiltrates the voyeur-killer of *Crawlspace*, who again kills the young, and the killer of *The Arrival*, who gets younger with each murder. There is a sense of thematic progression to these films, as there is in the director's cumulative work. Sexual cruelty and the legacy of the past forever seek a homicidal reintegration. Killing, therefore, becomes a triumphant expression, an emotional (and later physical) need to be fulfilled like any other.

This tangential serial killer film is an intriguing mix of fantasy and the rural gothic of *The Texas Chainsaw Massacre*, *Eaten Alive* (especially), *Terror Circus*, and *Three on a Meathook*. Schmoeller is an underappreciated director who would go on to work primarily for Charles Band, and who repeatedly essayed the serial killer figure. Knowing Band's preference for small inanimate objects and toys coming alive, it is no surprise that he and Schmoeller should come together and team for the later hit *Puppet Master*, which continued Schmoeller's demented artist mentality. Editor Ted Nicolaou would also be a future director for Band.

The Town That Dreaded Sundown

(1977: d. Charles B. Pierce)

scr. Earl E. Smith, Pierce; pr. Pierce; ph. James W. Roberson, Jim Roberson; m. Jaime Mendoza-Nava; ed. Tom Boutross; cast. Ben Johnson, Andrew Prine, Dawn Wells, Jimmy Clem, Charles B. Pierce, Earl E. Smith; 90m

Post–World War II, the small Arkansas community of Texarkana is beset by a serial killer from within its ranks. Unable to solve the crimes, the local police seek the help of a decorated FBI agent (Johnson), but no one is able to uncover the killer. Their brief encounter with him comes about by accident more than dedicated police work. Wounded, the killer flees into the swamp.

This is an intelligent, lean, period-set serial killer thriller which emphasizes the cooperation between individuals, regardless of their place in the investigative hierarchy, for the betterment of the community. It has touches of baroque violence and the director's usual emphasis on "local color," amidst a small-town community (America in microcosm) whose innocence

The serial killer from *The Town That Dreaded Sundown* (ANE, 1977).

is shattered by the spate of serial murders. Regular voice-over narration enhances the sense of a dramatized documentary about the end of the period of post-war jubilance, as the United States, now economically prosperous, is faced with a new enemy — the killer within.

This killer, with only his boots seen, blends into the community and may even be one of its more prominent members, although this is never confirmed. He is free to prowl and terrorize, making a home in the fearsome reputation he creates for himself. Although the police are the first to respond to this threat, they wish to involve the community in an organized response. However, despite the threat, people still put themselves in places of jeopardy — the lovers' lanes. The killer grows bolder with each crime, moving ever nearer to the town itself, his crimes taunting the police and boasting of his superiority. Such crimes

are no longer an anomaly.

The director's favored natural habitats shield a sadistic killer who approaches parked lovers to shoot, kidnap, rape and murder. Nature, especially at night, is a place of menace and hostility. Although there is graphic violence, Pierce depicts the mental torture the killer inflicted on his stalked female victims, especially in one scene wherein the killer uses a trombone as a weapon. This mockingly allies his murders to musical creation (anticipating in part the murder-as-art theme which would infiltrate the genre in the 1990s). The dialogue does not flinch from descriptions of the killer's sexual atrocities, his bites into the victims' flesh, as Pierce charts the sobering effect these facts have on those who realize their threatening significance; i.e. the patriarchs, the protectors, are aware that one of their own has turned.

Pierce's semi-documentary-like account acts as a validation of sorts to his depiction of an Americana in crisis from within. This film gains from an auteurist look at Pierce's work, for the killer here is the inverse of the noble savage threatening the community in the Western *Winterhawk*, and is found regularly in the director's minor Westerns. It is as if the modern serial killer were that same noble savage corrupted by civilization. He has never fully integrated, now within and separate, and now also anonymous and seeking vengeance and expression through deliberate violence.

In so far as the killer is never caught, and by implication is free to terrorize the community forever, he is almost a supernatural force (a theme that would be developed further in *Halloween* and the slasher films, which reduce the murderer to an automaton). To counterbalance this view, Pierce stresses the strength of the investigators, who know their responsibility is to protect the community from the terrors within now that the War is over. This is confirmed in the casting choice of Ben Johnson as the specialist FBI agent, a role akin to the one he essayed in Milius' *Dillinger*. This tremendous intertextuality also implies the line of descent from gangster to serial killer as the main threat to the US community. With Johnson also the veteran of numerous Westerns, it posits the specialist FBI agent as the inheritor of the code of the Westerner, with the serial killer a new kind of outlaw. As such, the film can be considered a work in the transition of the Western. However, in that the killer escapes and is never identified, the film speaks of the need for measures greater than the code of the Westerner, as if that alone, no matter how valuable the heritage, were no longer sufficient.

The film is almost a definition of the emergent serial killer narrative in that a series of killings has stymied local police, and an outside agent is brought in to assist. It stresses the need for specialists beyond the police to deal with such horrendous and seemingly inexplicable sex crimes. The police have a respect for the outside agents, and a knowledge that teamwork is essential, as they try to decipher the killer's pattern as the key to his apprehension. Johnson is further aware of the threat posed by such a killer, and goes to a psychiatrist for a profile of the offender. Tellingly, the psychiatrist says that the killer is a highly intelligent sadist, part of the community, who will never be caught and who feels important as a result of the police attention. Thus validated, he will never stop. He kills for sexual satisfaction, even though there is no sexual act performed upon the victims. This is also an encapsulation of the popular view of the serial killer.

But amidst this oppression, Pierce interjected moments of humor, and carefully brought out the individual character traits of the locals and the community's sense of self-definition as their primary means of combating the threat — even though, ironically, the threat comes from within. In a harsh ending, he suggests there is no way to eliminate these kinds of killings from the post-war American way of life. This new kind of killing undercuts the sense of post-war celebration and sobers a jubilant America, whose demons are now domestic. The killings punctuate the manhunt narrative as structural beats.

Based on a true-life case, this is a clever if straightforward encapsulation of the serial killer formula, and an underrated film from regional director Pierce, who, despite the intriguing and equally underrated thriller *The Evictors*, was rarely able to match the efficiency he shows here. There are similar sporadic highlights throughout his mainly disappointing and middling works, notable for his concern for folk tales and his love of nature and the men who harmonize with it — here given its bleakest interpretation, as the killer secrets within nature. It is a shame that Pierce is today most associated with the surprise hit film *The Legend of Boggy Creek*, about a rural missing link.

Traces of Red

(1991: d. Andy Wolk)

scr. Jim Piddock; pr. Mark Gordon; ph. Tim Suhestedt; m. Graeme Revell; ed. Trudy Ship; prod d. Dan Bishop, Dianna Freas; cast. James Belushi, Lorraine Bracco, Tony Goldwyn, William Russ, Faye Grant, Michelle Joyner, Joe Lisi; 105m

In Palm Beach, the lover of a brash policeman (Belushi) sees him with a prostitute who ends up dead. The investigating officer declares it is one of a series. The killer sends the policeman death-threat letters before each murder, and indeed targets women the policeman knows, implicating him in the process. The policeman, who regularly takes advantage of his position to bed women, is the brother of a man running for office. More dead women turn up, and the politico becomes a suspect.

With the two brothers paralleled as suspects, the ending, with the politico a serial killer of women after being sexually abused by his mother, is a twist that needlessly complicates a partial exposure of a corrupt Patriarchy seeking to sustain itself. Thus, the good brother (Belushi) faked his own death in order to expose the bad brother and restore Patriarchy's balance. This is a common theme, and makes the surrounding plot twists merely a superficial, convoluted attempt to create a mystery. Cleverness at the plot level alone does not make for an engrossing film. Indeed, the final twist negates the film's most cynical assertion — that a serial killer policeman was buried as a hero — and restores the film to conventional banality.

This is an attempt to introduce the serial killer into film noir, as had been tried in the early 1980s, especially with *Tightrope* and *Cop*, although not as self-consciously as here. The noir ambience is furthered by the opening, which has the events narrated by the dead police officer (in a nod to *Sunset Boulevard*), although this too is in due course negated. However, its depiction of the serial killer is rooted in cliche (childhood trauma), and its plot is convoluted and hard to follow, alienating the critics even further. It was its director and screenwriter's debut work.

Trail of a Serial Killer

(1997: d. Damian Lee) aka *Papertrail*

scr. Joseph O'Brien; pr. Helder Goncalves; exec pr. Douglas Falconer, Chad McQueen; ph. Nicholas J. von Sternberg; ed. Paul G. Day; prod d. Tim Boyd; cast. Chris Penn, Michael Madsen, Jennifer Dale, Chad McQueen

A serial killer leaves notes for the investigating policeman (Penn) at the scene of the crimes, on the bodies. For ten years the cop has been following this paper trail, and is now a distraught wreck. After a four year abeyance, the murders resume and the cop is brought back into the case, and with the help of another policeman (Madsen), must reopen it. Members of a psychiatrist's extreme-fear disorder group are being killed off, and the cop searches for a connection to the psychiatrist, uncovering a killer with a multiple personality disorder.

The plot hook, of a killer striking the members of a therapy group, infiltrated the likes of *Schizoid*, *Phobia* and the dazzling *Color of Night*, which flirt with the serial killer film but never embrace it wholly, as this one strives to. Its brooding style and psychologically scarred, burned-out characters seeking purpose and meaning suggest the influence of *Seven*. It is another film to use the serial killer plot angle as a study of modern despair, where a killer seeks an interpersonal connection with his acknowledged adversary, the profiler figure (a similar plot hook used in *The Watcher*, for example).

The therapy group reflects a collection of modern phobias, but the concept lacks the sly humor that Richard Rush so expertly brought out in *Color of Night*. All characters in this modern world are desperate, at the end of their tether, and seeking resolution before they snap, as the killer has. Penn, who talks into a tape recorder and is solemn yet invigorated by the return of the killer, is a figure in the *Manhunter* mold. He is tormented by a need to know why the killer does what he does, to the point of obsession. Thus, he seeks a possible kinship with the psychiatrist, giving her the case files for her to generate her own profile of the killer, which he can to compare his own to test his accuracy.

The killer, who has multiple personalities, is obsessed with the look of fear (a nod to *Peeping Tom*). The killer's ego is reinforced by the sense of power over the victims, the ability to control their fate. This power is reinforced by killing those with a phobia to begin with, forcing them to confront and succumb to their fear. Finally, the cop must validate his own existence and conquer his fear by facing down the killer.

This offers variations on the tricks and premises of *Color of Night*. Despite the scorn heaped unfairly against that film, *Color of Night* remains the superior examination of this subgenre. Nevertheless, *Trail of a Serial Killer* is stylish in the expected brooding manner of such derivative works as *Bone Daddy* and *Resurrection*, which also strive to visualize despair, ultimately culminating in the depiction of a monstrous charnel house as symbolic of the tortured psyche epitomized by the killer. Once again, all effort revolves around deciphering and decoding the deliberate murders.

The Train Killer

(1983: d. Sandor Simo) aka *Viadukt*; *Matushka*

scr. Egon Eis, Peer J. Oppenheimer; ph. Tamas Andor; m. Zdenko Tamassy; ed. Maria Rigo, Don Stern; prod d. Pal Lovas; cast. Michael Sarrazin, Towje Kleiner, Nostanze Engelbrechy, Ferenc Bacs, Herlinde Latzko, Armin Mueller-Stahl; 95m

In Hungary, circa 1931, a man plants bombs to derail trains, and then wanders through the debris, human casualties and rescuers as a means of sexual gratification. This is based on the true story of Sylvester Matushka, one of the more peculiar serial killers in that he possessed the qualities of a mass killer by targeting trains crowded with people. He is finally identified, wandering the wreckage with post-orgasmic contentment and taking photos of the dying (for later masturbatory aids), by an adulterous lover. If not caught, he would have invariably derailed more.

From the outset, the killer is depicted as a mad visionary: he kills a woman as he watches a fire he set, claiming it a prophecy sent from God. As an adjunct to this, the film raises the possibility that the madman was thought to have been manipulated by political radicals into his course of action. A family man, with wife and daughter, he suffers the pressures of work, and suffers from a kind of class resentment the director presents as endemic in Europe at the time. His wife is an avid social climber, and he is lured into her mindset, which he resents. The forces of circumstance and mental illness act against him, and cause him to seek a grandiose form of empowerment.

This, in conjunction with his obvious psychotic need for control, causes him to derail a train on New Year's Eve. This is shot to clearly establish his sexual pleasure at the derailment — he handles the railroad tracks as if masturbating. Mass murder is a paraphilia. Although the detective on the case realizes this, his superiors do not treat this theory seriously. The detective suspects mental illness, while his superiors blame Bolshevik terrorism and seek to prove their case. Once the sexual aspect is raised, it remains undeveloped, although the killer's increasing proficiency is a sign of his sexual maturity. Finally, the boastful killer claims a higher purpose and a desire to make a name for himself — to inspire awe in the populace.

With nondescript, barely effective direction, this at first promising study of a unique and horrendous sexual dysfunction repeatedly drops its most intriguing themes. It tries for a character portrait in aberration, a recreation of period ideology and social resentments, and a procedural investigation narrative, but doesn't delve into any aspect with any convincing thoroughness. What appeal it ultimately has is therefore superficial — all promise, no delivery. As an attempt at such a paraphilia, and as the only movie about one of the more monstrous and unconventional of serial killers, it has value in the genre. However, it is a true shame that the film is not better.

Trauma

(1993: d. Dario Argento)

scr. Argento, T.E.D. Klein, Franco Ferrini, Giovanni Romoli; pr. Argento; ph. Raffaele Mertes; m. Pino Donaggio; ed. Conrad Gonzalez; prod d. Billy Jett; cast. Christopher Rydell, Asia Argento, Piper Laurie, Frederic Forrest, James Russo, Brad Dourif, Laura Johnson; 105m

This is considered by many to be "Americanized Argento," and a partial return to his giallo roots. An anorexic young woman (Asia Argento) escapes from a psychiatric hospital and befriends a young journalist. Once she is returned to her parents, she believes that her mother (Laurie) is soon killed by a stranger, a hooded serial killer known as the "Headhunter" who

strikes only when it rains. The now orphaned girl and her new friend investigate. Finally, the killer is revealed to be the mother after all. A series of electric shock treatments were performed unjustly years before on the mother, who has killed in revenge for the atrocities committed against her.

The news media keeps a running total and commentary on the killer's activity. The sensationalist media capitalize on the popular fascination with the abhorrent. The journalist must struggle with his professional obligations, his benevolent concern for the young girl, and his growing sexual attraction to her. She is an anorexic, traumatized by the apparent death of her parents, and is in a vulnerable state. Her vulnerability is a turn-on for the reporter, who's fascinated by her child-woman qualities. He is almost a violator, and so an incipient sex criminal himself. Her recognition of the horrendous mother is her rite-of-passage into mature womanhood, which needs the accompanying attentions of the male. It is not Patriarchy that is monstrous, but Matriarchy, a development of *Bird with the Crystal Plumage* and *Deep Red*, and the witches of *Suspiria*.

Also like those films, *Trauma* is a treatise on the interplay of memory, fantasy and the interpretation of the perception of the everyday. Thus, her treating doctor tries to unlock her memories of trauma by drugging her, sending her on a psychedelic trip which anticipates the surrealism of Argento's subsequent *The Stendhal Syndrome*, which also starred Asia in the role of a vulnerable woman seeking to escape the cycle of trauma. The killer is the agent of that personal trauma, possibly permitting a kind of personality transference, as is common in Argento's films.

The victims all know each other, sharing a guilty secret. Consequently, the killer is more of a revenge killer than a serial killer, there being little sexual pleasure

The serial decapitator (Piper Laurie) holds up her victim's head in *Trauma* (Overseas Film-group/ADC, 1993).

in the crimes, although the beheadings speak of a need for empowerment. Nevertheless, it is as an example of Argento's continued flirtation with the serial killer figure, but evidence of his tendency to seek a commonality between victims. Laurie's role as demented mother recalls her work in *Carrie*. Argento would treat the serial killer proper in *The Stendhal Syndrome*, a follow-up of sorts to *Trauma* (hence the reason for *Trauma*'s inclusion herein) in its depiction of a young girl rescued by a man whose designs on her serve a darker purpose.

True Crime

(1996: d. Pat Verducci)

scr. Verducci; pr. Jonathan Furie; ph. Chris Squires; ed. Gib Jaffe; prod d. John Diminico; cast. Alicia Silverstone, Kevin Dillon; 94m

When a classmate is murdered by a serial killer, a young novice detective (Silverstone) investigates the crime on her own. She decides to recreate the dead girl's movements, and meets a young man (Dillon) who likes to seduce teen girls. She follows him and takes photos. Is he the serial killer? He reveals himself as an amateur policeman also, and gains her trust. Together they set out to track the killer. A gruff policeman, who has answered her questions in the past, comes finally to her aid when Dillon turns out to be the killer after all, of course.

This film is best in its subtextual attempt to explore the sexual allure of danger and contact with a potentially malevolent pathology. It depicts an unsettling sexual ambivalence that suggests that the figure of the serial sex killer is erotically appealing to women, implying a kind of complicity which recalls Hitchcock's films. The killer thus fulfills the role of lover, to be finally put in his place by the substitute father, who restores the Patriarchal balance and chastises the young girl's initially barely realized erotic yearnings. The film suggests that such a sexual maturation in young women must be dutifully repressed by Patriarchy.

The protagonist is a devoted fan of true crime, part of the subculture that pores over the latest killer's exploits. However, she has not gone to the point of condoning or idolizing the killers, and still wishes to place herself in the role of detective or profiler and capture the offenders. Nevertheless, she represents the naive, impressionable victim of a subculture that has elevated, and even eroticized, the symbolic importance of the serial killer. But despite the erotic subtexts, the film is careful to establish her essential purity of heart. Thus, she is at first unaffected by the subculture's darker undertones, and the film neglects to develop the underlying moral ambiguities which would have made the movie a more complex assignment than the teen MTV-oriented thriller it is. As is, it is perhaps comparable to James Foley's teen *Fatal Attraction* movie *Fear*.

The naive heroine is sexually corrupted by the killer, losing her virginity to him when drunk, in the back seat of a car. She has surrendered to her illicit passions and must be rescued by the proper patriarch. Ironically, she initially feels that murder is a call for help, and that if the reasons for someone's murders are known, then the killers can be helped. The conclusion invalidates this belief, postulating the killer as a remorseless sexual manipulator and predator who seeks to destroy inno-

cence — the enemy of every young girl seeking womanhood, and hence a kind of Devil's advocate.

Tunnel Vision

(1995: d. Clive Fleury)

scr. Fleury; pr. Phillip Avalon, Australian Film Finance Corporation; ph. Paul Murphy; ed. John Scott; prod d. Phil Warner; m. David Hirschfelder, Ric Formosa; cast. Patsy Kensit, Robert Reynolds, Rebecca Rigg, Cary Day, Shane Briant; 90m

A serial killer poses his nude victims in ways that imitate the paintings of a well-known local artist. The artist comes under suspicion. A policewoman's male partner also comes under suspicion when his cheating wife's lover is also found dead. They must work together to solve the case and clear his name.

The familiar American formula (down to the autopsy room scene and the naked female cadaver) is transplanted to Sydney, Australia, without much addition or qualification. The film explores the same art world as seen in *Apology* and, in particular, *Still Life*, developing the popular 1990s theme of the serial killer as an artist, and serial murder as a valid form of artistic expression, worthy of study for its potential insights into human nature.

Considering such murder as communication invariably yields a depiction of the underground sex scene — in this case, Sydney's fetish bars. The killer is finally revealed as a sexually tormented artist surrounded by an undercurrent of sexual ambiguity, which taints even the investigating officer in her lesbian desire for her partner's wife. The taint of sexuality, at its nadir justifying murder, is another language to be effectively decoded for its private meanings, and has a corrosive effect on interpersonal relations.

The film seeks to explore the murky terrain that affects both killers and police officers by association, but is not as hard-hitting, comic or ultimately successful as *Redball*. It is guarded in its cynicism by comparison, and is interesting as a measure of the terms of acceptability of tone when dealing with such subject matter, as this film was more adept at attracting government financing than was *Redball*. It is defeated by convention.

Twin Peaks

(1989: d. David Lynch)

scr. Lynch, Mark Frost; pr. David J. Latt; ph. Ron Garcia; m. Angelo Badalamenti; ed. Duwayne R. Dunham; prod d. Patricia Norris; cast. Kyle MacLachlan, Michael Ontkean, Madchen Amick, Dana Ashbrook, Richard Beymer, Lara Flynn Boyle, Sherilyn Fenn, Warren Frost, Joan Chen, Piper Laurie, John Nance; 113m

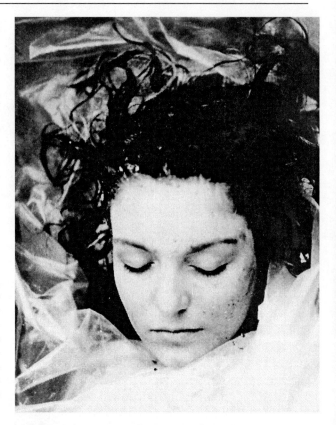

Laura Palmer (Sheryl Lee) is found dead and wrapped in plastic in *Twin Peaks* (Lynch-Frost, 1989).

Who killed Laura Palmer? The title town is beset by the murder of a teenage girl and the attempted rape/murder of another. A meticulous FBI agent (MacLachlan) is sent to investigate, and is aided by a local policeman (Ontkean). Once they have entered into the lives of the eccentric locals, a mysterious one-armed man reveals the killer as an animalistic, demonic presence named Bob who resides in a candle-lit basement lair in the local hospital.

The principle message of the film is that everyone has a secret. Thus, the detective story is the basis for an exploration of the darker yearnings and tumultuous relationships that give life and meaning to the local residents. MacLachlan plays the role like a continuation of his protagonist in Lynch's previous *Blue Velvet*, a similar exploration of the ugly sexuality that runs beneath the picturesque every-town surface. In human nature there resides a po-

tential loosed demon that embodies the monster in the basement of respectability.

Camera movements and compositions seek to explore the functioning of individuals in relation to one another as they are forced by circumstance to interact. It plays on the presence and absence of Laura as a means of exploring the diverse reactions to, and attitudes toward, such a sex murder. MacLachlan is a keen observer and recorder of details, as is the film style itself, and he embodies the narrative drive of detective cinema — the need to know, whatever the consequences.

This need is evidenced by his procedural expertise (he discovers the clues deliberately left by the killer — a letter beneath the fingernail — to establish a serial offender), and he fulfills, as outside agent, the role of the profiler, seeking insight into

The profiler (Kyle MacLachlan, left) and the detective (Michael Ontkean) behind the donuts laid out for them nightly as a treat in *Twin Peaks* (Lynch-Frost, 1989).

the mind of the killer. He gains such an insight at the end, not only into the killer but into a greater secret — the absolute truth of the connection between sexually promiscuous teenager and sex killer, a rela-tionship that is teasingly hinted at but never stated.

Did her sexual curiosity and activity summon the demonic killer to her? As Experience would seek to strip away and systematically corrupt and destroy Innocence? It is interesting that she finally reveals her secret in whispers to MacLachlan, a man depicted throughout as practically asexual. Is sexuality an evil force that taints the humanity ready to exploit it? Or is it a potentially dangerous communication between people, a hidden, secret language all to itself? Thus, the killer Bob is an otherworldly part of its semiotics— the manifestation of sexual abhorrence, a theme explored in the sequel.

This was released both as a self-contained movie on video and as a pilot episode, with a suitably altered ending withholding the killer's identity to allow episodic continuity. It indeed spawned a weird cult television series which captivated a generation and seemed for a time to signal new directions in television content and style. A movie sequel, *Twin Peaks: Fire Walk with Me*, deepened the weirdness.

Twin Peaks: Fire Walk with Me

(1992: d. David Lynch)

scr. Lynch, Robert Engels; pr. Gregg Fienberg; ph. Ron Garcia; m. Angelo Badalamenti; ed. Mark Sweeney; prod d. Patricia Norris; cast. Sheryl Lee, Ray Wise, Madchen Amick, Dana Ashbrook, Phoebe Augustine, David Bowie, Eric DaRe, Miguel Ferrer, Chris Isaak, Kyle MacLachlan, James Marshall, Jurgen Prochnow, Harry Dean Stanton, Kiefer Sutherland, David Lynch; 134m

Focusing on the final few days in the life of Laura Palmer, this is a prequel to *Twin Peaks*. Laura, who claims to be sexually abused by a mysterious Bob, leads her friend into a world of moral and sexual abandon. Meanwhile, FBI agents investigate the death of a young girl (a runaway drifter, a disposable underclass in the killer's eyes). Laura realizes that Bob is actually her father, a man consumed by his secret desires for young girls. He kills her.

This world of abandon is an ambigu-ously attractive realm (visualized brilliantly in the barroom set piece) yet run through with pain and sorrow. All of the main characters seduced by this world know of the tragedy of their loss of Innocence and surrender to Experience. Innocence slowly burns away in fantasy and desire put into practice. The conflicted sex killer, the serial killer unable to repress or regulate his desires, is the spiritual emblem of this realm. This emblem is named Bob, an Evil that resides in humans and propels them towards a netherworld of sexual wickedness. He wants to be inside his victims, systematically destroying them through a perverse sexual desire which conflicts with true love. Alternatively, the film raises the possibility that "Bob" was Laura's creation, her choice over admitting the truth — that it was her father who was abusing her.

No longer bound by the constraints of the television medium, Lynch here explores the sexual desires that lie behind the superficial appearances of people. These secret realms were only hinted at in the first film, and here they become explicit. The almost spiraling descent into weirdness is an encapsulation of the series' sense of out-of-control passions and strained human interrelationships. Only the dedicated FBI offers any challenge to the decadent world beneath appearances. They are almost angels, having the burden of weeding out the devils that seek to contaminate a flawed humanity.

This is a more bizarre and provocative work than the first *Twin Peaks*, though also more uneven and eccentric. It was critically maligned when released, and is generally not considered one of Lynch's better works, as if the premise had exhausted itself to the point of self-incineration. It had an unassailable, dedicated fan base, however.

Twisted Nerve

(1968: d. Roy Boulting)

scr. Roy Boulting, Leo Marks; stry. Roger Marshall, Jeremy Scott; pr. Boulting Brothers; ph. Harry Waxman; art d. Albert Witherick; ed. Martin Charles; m. Bernard Herrmann; cast. Hayley Mills, Hywel Bennett, Billie Whitelaw, Phyllis Calvert, Frank Finlay, Barry Foster; 118m

A psychotic young man (Bennett) from a wealthy background poses as a simpleminded, childish innocent in order to insinuate himself into the household in which he boards, in particular into the life of a young lady there (Mills). He soon kills his despised stepfather. Mills is suspicious of his involvement in the death of a banker, and investigates his past. In her absence he murders her lusting mother. When Mills returns, he can keep his secret no longer, and is about to rape and murder her when police arrive.

The film is an examination of a young man's pathological need to manipulate and mislead those around him. He is a narcissist (he caresses his own nude body in front of the mirror) who ironically pretends to be other than he is. He resents and seeks to eliminate those who would either reveal his deceptions or seek to sexually dominate him. He prefers his own touch, a sign of retarded emotional/sexual development. In return, his sexuality revolves around the power of sadistic domination, his excitement resulting in an inevitable homicidal frenzy. Thus, the film repeatedly puts him in the context of others' sexuality or absence of it, charting his control over his own desires.

These desires are bisexual in nature. On his bedside table are male bodybuilding magazines. His hatred of his stepfather may in some way be the product of repressed semi-incestuous homosexual desires which he projects rather than confronts. His seeming sexual obsession with Mills may also be a form of compensation.

His murder of her mother (rather than have sex with her) speaks to a pathology that has equated sex with murder of an object both loathed and desired. The conflict is irreconcilable. Manipulation and pretence are a means of sexual control, an identity that seeks to erect itself by governing others' reactions to it. The killer lives paradoxically in reaction to that which he seeks to control, another irreconcilable tension erupting into violent rage.

It is significant that he kills parental role models without being conflicted, but when faced with the prospect of raping and killing his desirable equal (in terms of age and generation), Mills, he is torn and reduced to confinement in a mental hospital, repeatedly muttering her name. He cannot handle the development of his erotic/homicidal projections onto a nonparental presence, although it is paradoxically a sign of his growing sexual maturity, which he longs for and rejects— such is his trap.

The killer is aware of his psychological imbalances, and has obviously researched criminal sexuality, as Mills discovers in his room a copy of sex criminal case histories, *Psychopathia Sexualis*. Perhaps he even considers himself in the same league as such killers and seeks a knowing, studied inclusion in their ranks. He is ultimately unable to reconcile his internal dilemmas and has projected them onto the erotic object, Mills.

Twisted Nerve is a film aware of its heritage. Screenwriter Marks was previously responsible for scripting the seminal *Peeping Tom*, another study of a troubled young man, and Herrmann's score is built around a tune whistled by the killer, a device used in another seminal film, *M*. Its premise, of a killer within a household, also recalls *Night Must Fall*, the remake of which just preceded this film. However, *Twisted Nerve* was considered to be an inferior item, although its virtue, as a study in the pathological need to manipulate, was submerged beneath the controversy that arose out of its leading assumption.

This British film proved controversial on release due to the connections it implies between mental retardation and serial homicide. The killer is revealed early on to have a mentally retarded brother, and that the similar chromosome in him would result in homicidal tendencies. This misapplication was decried more vehemently in the press than the more common association between schizophrenia and serial murder. Correspondingly, the producers added a disclaimer before the film, stating there was no connection between mongolism and homicidal madness, despite the association between such in the movie's startling prologue. Since this equation is really unnecessary, one suspects it was there for purely sensationalist reasons.

The producer was starlet Mills' fiancé, and he wanted to develop her image (or so *Variety* felt) as a pleasant, bright young woman capable of independence and resourcefulness in the face of adversity—a development of her precociousness as a child star. It was a nod to developing horror trends that she should face rape and murder as a consequence of these qualities. It is when she becomes a sexually desirable figure that she is placed in jeopardy, as if that were somehow inevitable.

The Two Faces of Dr. Jekyll

(1960: d. Terence Fisher) aka *House of Fright*; *Jekyll's Inferno*

scr. Wolf Mankowitz; stry. Robert Louis Stevenson; pr. Michael Carreras; ph. Jack Asher; m. Monty Norman, David Heneker; cast. Paul Massie, Dawn Addams, Christopher Lee, David Kossoff, Francis De Wolff, Pauline Shepherd; 88m

This was Hammer's first tackling of the Stevenson tale; the second was *I, Monster*. The bearded Jekyll, a dedicated scientist, experiments on himself and becomes the clean-shaven, elegant Hyde. Hyde discovers the unfaithful, duplicitous nature of Jekyll's wife, who has been having an affair with his best friend. He kills the friend, rapes the wife, and blames Jekyll for the crimes. The truth comes out when Hyde turns back into Jekyll.

The seminal twist here is that the loosed Hyde is an urbane, charming, seductive gentleman about town. In Hyde, the two conceptions of the lady-killer coincide. Released from the pretenses and repression of "civilization," the sex killer is not an animal but the epitome of class. As such, he is arguably emblematic of hypocrisy, capable of amoral, sadistic and bestial acts despite his guise, feeding on the gentlemanly aspect of Ripper lore.

Jekyll is a dedicated scientist secretly resentful of his wife's infidelities. As Hyde, he rapes her, driving her to suicide, and revenges himself for being cuckolded. Such is the collusion of pride and freedom. Indeed, he loathes his repressed weak side so much that he seeks to destroy it as a further means of fantasy empowerment, severing all ties to the mild man he was. Hyde is ever more the idealized version of Dr. Jekyll, a projection that, once it attains its own life, seeks to sever itself from its source. Evil comes from within the human desire for freedom from moral and social constraint. Correspondingly, Fisher reportedly delights in depicting the surrender to sins of the flesh (Hardy, p. 138), a stylistic choice which resulted in the US release being severely cut.

Significantly, this story of the suave killer was released the same time as *Peeping Tom* and *Psycho*, and can be seen as another effort to remove the serial killer from the monster pantheon and place him in the context of a recognizable humanity. He is an integral part of the British system, the emblem of its collapse, a monstrous patriarch seeking liberation from the Patriarchy that spawned him. Hence, there is a subversive streak in Fisher's treatment of the tale for an audience soon to enter the permissiveness of the swinging 1960s and its signposts of social collapse. It is tangentially a serial killer film, although has a bearing on the genre's evolution.

Two for the Money

(1972: d. Bernard Kowalski)

scr. Howard Rodman; pr. Aaron Spelling; ph. Archie R. Dalzell; art d. Paul Sylos; cast. Robert Hooks, Stephen Brooks, Catherine Burns, Shelley Fabares, Richard Dreyfuss, Mercedes McCambridge, Neville Brand, Walter Brennan; 73m

After a decade-long investigation into a serial killer proves a failure, the police have to admit defeat, although this attitude does not sit well with two investigating policemen. They therefore quit the force and become private detectives, attempting to do what as police they could not. They continue to pursue the case.

This unremembered tele-movie in plot demonstrates the death-of-the-mentor subtext of the serial killer film in which the normal police investigator, with stretched resources, is not good enough alone to tackle the serial killer. New dedication is needed, spring-boarding from a police basis. Ironically, it is personal obsession unencumbered by institutionalized responsibility that proves necessary. This is currently out of circulation.

The Ugly

(1997: d. Scott Reynolds)

scr. Reynolds; pr. Jonathan Dowling, in association with the New Zealand Film Commission; ph. Simon Raby; ed. Wayne Cook; m. Victoria Kelly; cast. Paolo Rotondo, Rebecca Hobbs, Jennifer Ward-Lealand, Roy Ward; 94m

A confessed serial killer has been hospitalized in a mental institution for the past five years. A new doctor is assigned, at his request, to reassess his suitability for eventual trial. An ambitious reformer, she believes she can reach the killer and even cure his affliction, and starts to visit him in the hospital. He blames the crimes on his takeover by a force he calls "the ugly" which impels him to destroy those around him. He sees this force in his own deformed reflection in the mirror. Despite warnings from the staff doctor, the new doctor believes the killer sane enough for therapy. However, she realizes that he has manipulated her and is once again becoming a violent killer prone to hallucinogenic visions, using her for his private sport.

The film explores the process whereby confession segues into deception. Thus, it questions to what extent a killer's explanation of his crimes can ever actually be considered the truth, let alone a sign of remorse or "cure." In such a case, memory, introspection and fantasy have merged in the effort to create a new identity, which in his saner moments the killer tries to project outside himself, insinuating a form of possession. As usual, it is a form of empowerment, rooted in the desire to compensate for his perceived childhood inferiority, as reinforced by a dominant parent, the mother. When he sees women his imagination takes over, and he is prone to violent flashes, a horrid potentiality. He must put these violent fantasies into reality, as if driven by them. He insists he is not a serial killer, blaming "the ugly" for the crimes, perhaps refusing to admit that such may come from within himself.

The profiler here is convinced of her abilities and her public reputation. As an outsider she is resented by the treating doctor, who considers her presence an undermining force. His warnings—that the killer will get inside her head and abuse her—prove correct. The killer is ultimately unreachable, despite her belief in the benefits of interpersonal communication. For her, this only results in nightmarish visions of her own violent death at the killer's hands. Ironically, her desire to help the killer is as selfish as the desires of his own monstrous mother, as the two women are paralleled throughout.

This debut effort follows the mainly one-on-one talks between killer and psychologist/profiler. However, it is punctuated by flashbacks to the adolescent trauma and gory violence that define the killer's life. The killer reveals that he has heard voices telling him to kill, that he was ugly and enjoyed killing. The "ugly" is, paradoxically, a liberating ideal self-image, the kind of monstrous identity explored later in *The Cell*. Every confession is accompanied by a surreal flashback to the crimes, as they were interpreted in the killer's mind as both memory and fantasy. They show that when the killer felt threatened, mocked or seemingly humiliated, the ugly would take over as a form of fantasy projection. The "ugly" is thus the sum total of all that he was made to feel as a child, twisted into retributive violence. His final victim, whom he knew, breaks his set pattern in that she was not a random victim but a figure from his own past. The implication is that her murder was his means of addressing the past, with the other murders as surrogates on the road to inner harmony — a futile search.

Like in many serial killer films, this process is rooted in childhood abnormality, particularly the once prominent notion of the schizo-affective mother, whose mixed and contradictory messages split the child's mind irreconcilably, and foster and deny incestuous union. Such a home, of course, lacks a father figure, and the mother refers to the boy's absent father as a devil, an idea that enters into his later delusions and hallucinations. The mother also beats the child in an effort to get back at the father. Finally he is driven to kill women as a means of psychological release, hoping that the corpses of his victims, which he sees as hallucinations, will leave him once he kills. He says that they do leave him, but only temporarily, returning to drive him to kill again.

The Ugly is also notable for its horrific depiction/condemnation of the New Zealand criminal psychiatric care system. The hospital is an impersonal location, with clinical blue walls testifying to a hygienic world ironically containing the most unclassifiable abnormalities of human existence. Yet these are strangely Expressionistic sets, as the walls of the killer's cell seem blood-spattered. The design enhances the sense of black comedy, where there are only the illusions of moral absolutes. It is staffed by doctors who ignore the tattooed thugs/orderlies' brutal treatment of patients. However, the film refuses to take the easy liberal option, as put forward by the new doctor, and suggests that, ultimately, such stern measures may be the only solution remaining.

Unhinged

(1982: d. Don Gronquist)

scr. Gronquist, Reagan Ramsey; pr. Gronquist; ph. Richard Blakeslee; m. Jonathan Newton; prod d. Sol Leibowitz; mkup. Janet Scoutten; cast. J.E. Penner, Laurel Munson, Sara Ansley, Virginia Settle; 79m

In rural Oregon, three women crash their car. They make their way to a nearby isolated mansion. They are welcomed and cared for by the women who live there, but soon realize that the matriarch of the household strongly resents men — ever since her husband ruined their aristocratic name by descending into crime. An outside presence stalks them. Finally, the killer is revealed to be a man in drag, prone to murdering women via scythe and machete, and keeping their body parts for a collection.

The film's portrayal of a monstrous matriarch is derivative of *Psycho*, and the notion of a hated son forced to become a woman was treated also in the contemporarily released Wes Craven film *Deadly Blessing*. *Unhinged* portrays the society of women as a monstrous, perverse abhorrence which corrupts the male and, ironically, consumes itself. The killer, whose aggressive gaze is coded as masculine, considers such young women groveling, subhuman figures, and his crimes are in part expressions against the person he has been forced to become, and the gender he has been forced to adopt. It is self-hatred and gender confusion as much as it is misogyny. However, the killer's psychology is only suggested as the film makes its way to the charnel-house finale, revealing the killer's assorted body piece trophy collection — obviously a long-term project for him.

This is a slasher film along teen-kill lines more than a serial killer movie, although it attempts the same kind of scenario as *The Texas Chainsaw Massacre*, *Tourist Trap* and other rural nightmare films of the 1970s especially. Despite this connection, it lacks humor, instead favoring a kind of accumulation of gory details, which makes it dull rather than suspenseful. Explicitly violent, *Unhinged* ran into censorship problems in Australia and the UK. However, most reviewers considered it slow and inept; consequently, it has no reputation among genre fans (except as a gory piece by a do-it-yourselfer).

Video Murders

(1987: d. Jim McCullogh)

scr. Jim McCullogh Jr.; pr. McCullogh; ph. Joseph Wilcots; m. Robert Sprayberry; cast. Foster Litton, Virginia Loridans, Alan Pierce, Eric Brown, Lee Larrimore, John Ferita; 90m

A serial killer's foremost pleasure is to lure women to his hotel room and then videotape himself raping, torturing and murdering his victims. This is a form of home snuff moviemaking practiced by the real-life sadists Leonard Lake and Charles Ng, and examined in such films as *8MM* and *52 Pick-Up*. The police establish the pattern and investigate. In the meantime, a young woman is attracted to a man and apparently decides to develop the relationship. However, she soon finds herself having to fight for her life and safety against the killer, as police close in.

Such are the perils of romance and desire in the modern world. Male predators are everywhere and could even be your next best thing: the wolf has many guises, so to speak. The killer represents the nadir of the narcissistic drive. Not only is he sexually empowered through sadistically manipulating and dominating women, but he must record the events and relive them in (presumably) masturbatory sessions, reinforcing his sense of superiority. Despite the novelty of its degree of narcissism, the film is otherwise unheralded. It is perhaps best considered a minor addition to the subgenre of snuff-movie serial killer films.

Violent Killer

(1966: d. Nagisa Oshima) aka *Violence at Noon*

scr. Taijun Takeda; nvl. Tsutomo Tamura; ph. Akira Takada; m. Hikaru Hayashi; ed. Keiichi Uraoka; prod d. Jusho Toda; cast. Kei Sato, Saeda Kawaguchi, Akiko Koyama, Matsuhiro Toura, Fumio Watanabe, Taiji Tonoyama, Sen Yano; 99m

This is set in post–World War Two Japan amidst the collapse of a collective farm, the assumed pressure provoking a man to become a serial rapist and killer. Two of his victims enter into a strange relationship with their assailant, even protecting him from the investigating police. They soon contact each other about the man.

The film, extremely quickly paced and

flashily edited (reportedly some 2000 cuts), suggested to the critics that the real crime was in the living conditions enforced upon and endured by killer and victims. The rape-murders are thus arguably more symptomatic of a desperate attempt to master circumstance by compensatory sexual empowerment. The sex is almost an incidental quality in the supposed gesture of revolution, however, it is a common language shared by everyone, and to master this language of the masses is to become powerful. Sexual sadism is a demonstration of the mastery of the will over circumstance, and a possible sociopolitical weapon. Thus he asserts to one victim that since he saved her life (by not killing her) he is God to her. His talk makes his victims subservient to rape, strangulation and necrophilia. He can rape and kill but cannot have sex with his wife when she wants it. He must be the initiator, the culturally coded male role.

The community, deep in talk over the "phantom killer," is troubled and disillusioned. The emergence of such a killer is perhaps the last stage in the collapse of the system. Ironically, the killer has found an outlet for the otherwise directionless frustration endemic in the community's lifestyle. It is a loveless existence, and so both wife and rape-victim cling to warped notions of loyalty, and protect the killer. Their acquiescence to his will deepens his fantasy of gender superiority. However, the victims' sense of shame deepens, the wife blaming herself for her husband's crimes—that if he hadn't saved her from suicide, none of it would have happened. Thus, out of resignation, she commits suicide.

Some consider this another study in compulsive behavior from Oshima, who explored compulsive sexuality in the controversial *In the Realm of the Senses*. It confirms his interest in sex as a means of communication between people, a measure of the proper functioning of cultural values, which can become the central process of self-definition in the lives of those so affected. He shares this theme in common with controversial Italian director Tinto Brass.

Virtuosity

(1995: d. Brett Leonard)

scr. Eric Bernt; pr. Gary Lucchesi; ph. Gale Tattersall; m. Christopher Young; ed. B.J. Sears, Rob Kobrin; prod d. Nilo Rodis; spec eff. L2 Communications; cast. Denzel Washington, Russell Crowe, Kelly Lynch, Stephen Spinella, William Forsythe, Louise Fletcher, William Fichtner; 105m

Sid (Crowe), a computer composite of every known serial killer, wants a life beyond the confines of a computer program. A programmer transfers him out and, via a new technology, into a semi-human form. An ex-policeman (Washington), imprisoned for killing the murderer of his wife and daughter (one of the program's composite entries), is offered a deal for release. He is brought back into the case due to his expertise with the arrogant, energetic and brilliant killer and the serial killer typology he is based on. A psychologist partners him, although he resents her presence at first.

The killer is more than human, and so cannot physically be killed in the usual way, and is capable of self-modifying his programming to become an ever more efficient serial killer (a theme also explored in the computerized killer film *Ghost in the Machine*). The theme of otherworldliness bringing with it its own higher priorities would also be explored in Leonard's *The Lawnmower Man* and *Hideaway* as an entry into an alternate, shared perception (in this case, virtual reality impinging upon the real). Imprinted with the desire and experience of the kill, it is all he lives for, and he is reduced almost to an automaton, a vain supra-human creation forever seeking

A computer amalgam takes human form as a serial killer (Russell Crowe) and asserts his will in *Virtuosity* (Paramount, 1995).

greater pleasures in murder as he evades his pursuers.

Having such a killer as a composite identity results in a self-conscious dimension, with the film about the importance of the corresponding narrative structures that have surfaced around the examination of what is a synthetic 20th century archetype. Hence his wish is finally to create "Death TV," the ultimate cultural embodiment of his homicidal fascination with murder. He is a fiction, based on reality, given its own life through technological means and loosed to perform the repetitive self-defining ritual. This ritual ironically serves to define those in opposition to him. He is the center of the world and the genre, and he knows it. Consequently, of course, such a presence taking human form is imbued with the worst of humanity — pride and vanity. He considers himself an all-powerful deity, confirming director Leonard's

thematic interest in the desire of humankind to be God. Serial murder is the end consequence of such an arrogant and vainly egotistical desire, and the powerful here has lost sight of the Good, a theme redressed in *Hideaway*. Patriarchy must protect itself from its own creations. Hence, all main characters are in some way affected by their desire to be an all-powerful creator/destroyer. Society needs a strong assessment procedure to determine its proper representatives.

Here the criminal psychologist must interview the former policeman in order to determine why he is so effective at tackling the computerized serial killer. In other words, the professional profiler must now profile the aspiring profiler rather than the killer. In this way the focus is doubled on the type of person suitable for hunting such a killer. Only those with firsthand experience of murderers (the cop's family was targeted) are suitable for their pursuit and removal. Patriarchy is forever concerned with replenishing and policing itself — so much so that its concern for the innocents of the world has suffered. In the desire to police itself, it has inadvertently loosed a monster that combines the worst of humanity with synthetic invulnerability.

The killer is the monster of the technological age and kills in the manner he has been programmed to, from role model to role model (a theme also of the copycat murderer in *Copycat*). He is an amalgam of every known violent offender. Yet he is paralleled to Washington in that both have recently been released from confinement to a new life, albeit in relation to death. Washington is the last of the true patriarchs, finally given the social sanction needed to eliminate the killer, although the killer would work to take this sanction away from his skilled nemesis, his only equal and the only partner in his dance-cart, as he puts it.

Although the film's superior computer effects (a regular aspect of Leonard's films) were praised, the movie was still considered an example of conventional Hollywood cop vs. killer action product, though jazzed up with modern trappings. Some noted the subtext of media satire (with the killer craving attention) but felt it mired in the killer's comic-bookish superhuman powers (like supervillains, he can regenerate himself). Although it may have introduced Australian actor Crowe to American audiences, *Virtuosity* did not establish him as a star — this would happen subsequently with his roles in *LA Confidential* and the Academy Award triumph of *Gladiator*. *Virtuosity*'s plot hook of a convict sent on a mission to correct an error also has its basis in Carpenter's *Escape from New York*.

Visiting Hours

(1982: d. Jean-Claude Lord)

scr. Brian Taggert; pr. Claude Heroux; ph. Rene Verzier; m. Jonathan Goldsmith; ed. Lord, Lise Thouin; art d. Michel Prouix; cast. Michael Ironside, Lee Grant, Linda Purl, William Shatner, Lenore Zann, Harvey Atkin, Helen Hughes; 105m

A television journalist returns home from a televised debate/forum on domestic brutality and is attacked by a misogynistic serial killer angered by her demonstration of independence. She survives and is taken to the hospital. Once there, however, she soon discovers that the killer has followed her and is systematically tormenting her, fixated on her. She seeks to escape his potential wrath.

If the film is taken as an intended allegory of contemporary gender politics, then the killer represents the male whose potency is threatened by increasingly high-profile women. Such a man must resort to the sadistic sexual sublimation of women in order to reinstate his lost sense of power. Hence, the killer keeps photographs of his screaming victims as souvenirs. Thus the film develops the interaction between women as a group definition formed in reaction to this male violence. It depicts inter-gender politics as a doomed, self-consuming cycle. Male violence necessitates female violence in reaction to it, which spawns greater male violence in turn, if the threat posed by suppressive masculinity is not eliminated.

This suppressive masculinity is no longer completely institutional, however, and is more of an individual aberration than an innate condition, although such a figure roams at will and has been warped by Patriarchy's malfunctioning socialization process (the alcoholic father). The killer is revealed to have seen his father rape his mother, and in so doing was imprinted with the equation of masculinity and violence as the proper expression of gender dominance. The killer resents all forms of female liberation, and even interprets prostitution as a means of sexual empowerment, thus killing them in punishment for their power over him in arousing his desires. Yet in that he is a loner he does not represent the entire functioning of Patriarchy, just that part of it that women need to assert themselves against and remove if true liberation is to be achieved.

The film can be compared to *Halloween 2*, where the supernatural killer was loose in a hospital at night. However, *Visiting Hours'* notion of the murderer as working in a tradition of sexual sublimation serves to humanize the automaton that is the (then popular) slasher killer. This has been interpreted as a knowing choice, with the film a self-aware incorporation of the genre's high points (with references to *Peeping Tom*, *Coma* and *Halloween*, among others— Nash and Ross, p. 3698). However, it is best seen as a dissection of gender roles within the genre.

The Watcher

(2000: d. Joe Charbanic)

scr. Clay Ayers, David Elliot; stry. Elliot, Darcy Meyers; pr. Elliott Lewitt, Nile Niami, Jeff Rice; ph. Michael Chapman; m. Marco Beltrami; ed. Richard Nord; prod d. Maria Rebman Caso, Brian Eatwell; cast. James Spader, Keanu Reeves, Marisa Tomei, Ernie Hudson, Chris Ellis, Robert Cicchini, Yvonne Niami, Jennifer Mc-Shane; 96m

Burnt-out detective Spader relocates to Chicago after years spent unsuccessfully tracking a Los Angeles serial killer (Reeves). The killer has developed an unhealthy attraction to him, as if the pursuit were a mutual courtship. The killer follows him to Chicago and recommences killing, sending the cop photographs of his intended victims and giving the police force 24 hours to identify and find them before they are killed. Spader is reluctantly brought back into the case, despite being high on prescription painkillers for much of the time, a fact that distresses his co-workers, who question his authority over them. One of the photographs is that of the cop's therapist (Tomei), whom the killer feels is a rival for Spader's affections and privy to an insight to which he feels he has the exclusive claim. Spader must face the killer and rescue Tomei.

The opening credits sequence sets the ominous tone (à la *Seven* and *The Bone Collector*) for the film to be a neo-noir Expressionist urban thriller — brooding yet actionful (a stylistic balance hard to achieve but fascinating when mastered). Like those films, all characters ultimately define themselves in relation to murder and the killer. The killer strives to force himself on them in order to forge a relationship. He has done so with Spader, in the process turning him into a painkiller addict and disillusioned retiree (recalling the relationship between cop and killer in *Trail of a Serial Killer*).

The killer's method is routine, and is offered as a psychological profile by Spader to his therapist. He picks and chooses women carefully, and follows and watches them for weeks in advance. Then he hides in the victim's house, surprises and subdues them, torments them (dancing with them) and kills them, strangling them with piano wire. Before killing them, he interacts with them as if they were in a kind of courtship, with murder its consummation. His psychology revolves around his need to forge a relationship, yet his sexuality does not allow a heterosexual union with his victims. Murder is a substitute, and could even be a form of projection, the victims representing a side he would repress.

In its manner, the film seeks to explore the process of obsessive male assaultive gazing, to implicate the act of watching as an illicit voyeuristic and hence erotic pleasure, bisexual in nature. It wants to be about scopophilia, hence the extreme stylization choices and the juxtapositioning of different media, but it ultimately adds nothing new to the wealth of material already examining that topic. Instead, it is better as a conventional action movie, providing a novel (though repetitive) twist on the manhunt narrative, as the victims are known and have to be found before they are killed — a search in tandem with that for the killer.

By casting Reeves as the killer, it wants to toy with his image but ultimately pulls back from subverting it totally. Thus, although Reeves is a cruel, callous and initially charming killer, and we do see him kill, he is not shown participating in any sexual contact or violation of his victims, almost as if that were too aberrant a dimension for Reeves' image to bear. However, it suggests a slyer sexuality at work in the character by stressing his almost homoerotic obsession with Spader (recalling Spader's presence with Rob Lowe in the Americanized version of *Apartment Zero*, *Bad Influence*). Reeves kills women in an attempt to forge a relationship with another man, daring that man to get to know him as a worthy adversary and potential lover, though he terms this "friend." He wants to replace Spader's lost girlfriend, who died in a fire while Spader chased Reeves away, and for whose death Spader holds himself responsible.

Typical of the post–*Manhunter* profiler, Spader is unwilling to be brought back into the case but is effectively forced to by appeals to his greater sense of responsibility. As usual, he feels both invigorated and drained (to the point of hospitalization) by the manhunt investigation. His necessary presence is partially resented by his underling, the conventional investigator, who will invariably grow to respect him. Although Spader resents it, he too has found purpose in his adversarial bond to the killer, a bond the killer feels reciprocal

and evidence of a mutual (sexual?) attraction. Killing Reeves, in a manner that allows Spader to save Tomei from a fire, provides the cathartic purge that Spader needs to progress beyond his own self-destructive infatuation. This sublimated homosexuality forms an intriguing subtext, although it is never fully confronted, losing out to straight thrills and set pieces.

Ironically, it is now the profiler figure who is the conflicted one, and not the determined killer, who sticks to his regimen and fixations as a means of self-definition. The killer's pursuit of commonality leads him to the people in Spader's life, and invariably to his therapist — as the one who holds a special insight into Spader that Reeves wants to claim all his own. Reeves obtains the therapist's tape recordings and attempts to profile the profiler, to return their "friendship" (a commonality between cop and killer that seems to springboard from that essayed between cop and thief in *Heat*). In the end, the killer voices his belief in their mutual need for each other. Although Spader claims that knowing Reeves is merely part of his job, and that he will soon move on to the next one, it is nonetheless a recognition that drives Spader to kill Reeves and free himself from such a bond. The profiler no longer wants to define himself in relation to the killer, and the only way to escape that trap is to kill the killer. Invariably, there will soon be another trap, as the role of the Patriarchy's sanctioned profiler carries with it a costly responsibility.

This is the directorial debut of a former music video maker (for alternative bands Soul Coughing, Sonic Youth and star Reeves' own band, Dogstar). It is done in a flashy MTV style that invited unfavorable comparison to David Fincher (who directed the brilliant *Seven*), who also has a background in music videos. The film's race against time scenario was also featured in *The Cell* (another film by a debuting former music video maker)—to more imaginative and critically regarded effect.

Waxworks

(1924: d. Paul Leni)

scr. Henrik Galeen; ph. Helmar Lerski; art d. Paul Leni, Ernst Stern, Alfred Junge; cast. William Dieterle, Emil Jannings, Conrad Veidt, Werner Krauss; 62m

This is a highly regarded, though now seldom seen, silent omnibus movie of three stories and a loose framing device.

Three wax statues in the ownership of a fairground wax museum are given personalized stories by a writer/poet (future director Dieterle). The last two of these three stories offer a view of the emergent serial killer as rooted in historical figures, and the individualization of atrocities once committed on a large, epic canvas.

Thus, the portrayal of Ivan the Terrible (Veidt—in a performance which supposedly impressed and influenced Sergei Eisenstein) is of a dexterous sadist who lurks unseen in a torture chamber, watching the death throes of his victims. With nightmarish, Expressionist stylization, it is an exploration of horrendous voyeurism as a function of an inherently sadistic absolute power. Given such power, a man will be seduced by evil, becoming Evil in the process, and revel in the suffering of others.

The third story, that of a dream about Jack the Ripper, can be considered a development of the preceding story. Power is achieved through the ability to force control over another's life, a desire inherently pathological. As a dream, it explores the serial killer as a historically based personage subject to interpretation and redefinition on an individualized basis as it becomes an archetypal presence. Shadowy and hallucinatory, it is the briefest section, with the Ripper not the conflicted sexual dysfunctional killer lured to innocence that he would be portrayed as in the later *Pandora's Box*, for instance. It shows the serial killer as a presence within the inner realms of human capability, even perhaps part of a collective unconscious. The serial killer is that which haunts humanity—the monster of dreams, based on historical fact and in a clear line of descent through the ages.

It was on the basis of this fantasy film that director Leni was invited to Hollywood by Carl Laemmle to work for Universal. This partnership resulted in *The Cat and the Canary*, now considered by many as a classic in suspense.

Welcome to Arrow Beach

(1974: d. Laurence Harvey) aka *Tender Flesh*

scr. Wallace C. Bennett, Jack Gross Jr.; pr. Jack Cushingham; ph. Gerald Perry Finnerman; m. Tony Camillo; cast. Laurence Harvey, Joanna Pettet, Stuart Whitman, John Ireland, Meg Foster; 99m

The only film actor Laurence Harvey ever directed was this unusual cannibal-killer tale in which a young woman survives a car crash. She is found wandering the beach and is offered shelter by a photographer (Harvey) who resides near his sister. She soon discovers the man's secret, shared by his sister, and attempts to expose him; but no one believes her, and it is up to her to prove it on her own. Despite the risk to herself, she is determined to expose the killer. The man has turned to cannibalism after a Korean War experience—his plane crashed on a deserted Pacific island and he was forced to eat the other survivors.

The film's subtext, of the consumption of human flesh perhaps invigorating and addicting the cannibal, is developed smartly in the slyly humorous *Ravenous*. However, *Arrow Beach*'s real focus is on the generation gap conflicts. The monstrous, incestuous brother and sister become substitute parents for the girl, a hippie. Thus it becomes a tale of youth seeking to expose the monstrousness of age and of the family patriarch. Although this may be a subversive intent, the film was generally considered a pretentiously handled misfire, full of jarring editing and odd inserts. Nevertheless, the theme of sexual perversion through cannibalism finds its echo in the likes of *The Texas Chainsaw Massacre*, although the theme of cannibalism by circumstance ties it closer to the likes of *Death Line* and the Italian *Cannibal Apocalypse. Arrow Beach* lacks the sly humor of the later *Motel Hell.*

The ending is clearly meant as Grand Guignol outrage — the true depths of the monstrous patriarch. Thus, a prostitute is subject to a meat cleaver, and meat hooks hold up pieces of human debris in the protagonist's charnel house. Once again, as in many of the cannibal films of the early to mid 1970s, the family home becomes the sight of a sexual nightmare of cannibalism and necrophilia.

The film saw only a brief release by Warner Bros., who withdrew it quickly, practically disowning it thereafter. Three years later it was cut by fifteen minutes and rereleased under the alternative title by the original producers. It did not fare any better. Harvey, however, died of cancer the year the film was initially released; he was only forty-five.

Werewolf of London

(1935: d. Stuart Walker)

scr. Robert Harris; pr. Stanley Bergerman; ph. Charles Stumar; m. Karl Hajos; cast. Henry Hull, Warner Oland, Valerie Hobson, Spring Byington, Lester Matthews; 75m

This is the original werewolf-as-serial-killer movie. A botanist is bitten by a werewolf and returns to his London home. He murders a prostitute but is plagued by guilt when he returns to human form. Soon London is beset by a series of violent murders, and he must struggle against a second, less conscience-affected werewolf. They battle over a rare flower capable of controlling their condition.

Significantly, and tying more into the Jekyll and Hyde mythos, the man dreads the approaching transformations, horrified by what the animal within himself can do but powerless to prevent it. This creature resembles Hyde more than a wolf, and prowls the streets in search of human flesh (tying into Ripper lore). However, his powerlessness testifies to the hold the bestial has over human nature. Once one is cursed by circumstance or nature to embrace Evil (the consumption of human flesh as a sexual perversion), one is doomed to surrender to an inherent cruelty which surpasses the otherwise benevolent spiritual motives attributed to humankind (Hardy, p. 65).

Still, the vestiges of Good cause guilt and conflict as the human and the monster increasingly coexist. The afflicted loathe their own horrendous sexuality and are driven to find some means to prevent their surrender to monstrous sexual aberration. Although the film confronts the legacy of the Ripper crimes, it still holds onto the notion that such a killer must be somehow changed from conventional humanity in order to commit such crimes. However, it begrudgingly raises the issue that such crimes are a function of a hidden, repressed human nature which can be accessed and triggered by circumstance. Thus, lycanthropy (and, by extension, serial murder) is akin to an affliction, disease or addiction (Clarens, p. 100). Guilt and self-pity result from the inability to control one's nature/affliction — the defense, in part, of the killer in *M.*

Werewolf of London predates the more widely known *The Wolf Man*, and was initially meant to star Karloff and Lugosi. Hull was a replacement, and he proved difficult by refusing to submit to lengthy makeup sessions, which led to the novelty of the beast being more recognizably human than was perhaps initially intended. The film was not a major success when released, although its reputation continues to grow.

Whatever Happened to Aunt Alice?

(1968: d. Lee H. Katzin)

scr. Theodore Apstein; nvl. Ursula Curtiss; pr. Robert Aldrich; ph. Joseph Biroc; m. Gerald Fried; ed. Frank J. Urioste; art d. William Glasgow; cast. Geraldine Page, Ruth Gordon, Rosemary Forsyth, Robert Fuller, Mildred Dunnock, Joan Huntington, Peter Brandon; 101m

A recent widow (Page), whose husband only left her a stamp collection, hires elderly women housekeepers for companionship and servitude, and then kills them for their money, bashing their heads in. To investigate a missing friend, the suspicious Gordon poses as a maid and is employed by the killer. She discovers the secret but is murdered by the killer. Relatives soon uncover the killer's garden, where she has buried the corpses. In a final irony, she learns that the stamp collection was worth over $100,000.

Page would rather murder than be poor. She delights in manipulating her housekeepers and swindling their money as a demonstration of her innate superiority. Although there is no overt sexual dimension to the crimes, and the film therefore features a repeat gimmick killer as opposed to a true serial killer, she has a fantasy image of herself, and her crimes function as a form of empowerment. She equates this empowerment with financial security—a dilemma facing many in retirement age. As such, she is the perversion of the matriarch who perceives herself abandoned by Patriarchy. But rather than rebel against that Patriarchy, she seeks those similar to herself and eliminates them so that she does not become like them; the murders are a means of escaping what she fears may be a horrendous destiny—poverty.

The threat of being left destitute is enough to initiate a retreat into a homicidal dementia, erecting the facade of preservation. She holds on to what used to give her life meaning, unable to change and so striving to preserve an ideal, eliminating any threat to her beloved financial security. Her insecurities are class-based, her self-absorbed superiority enabling all others to be disposable "lessers," her servants to do with as she will.

However, the act of murder provides her with an intense excitement (presumably more than she has achieved with her husband) and arguably replaces sex, giving her an added identity. Her role-playing with her intended victims, a trait returned by Gordon, thus has sexual undertones. Perhaps it keeps her young, as she clearly resents the younger neighbor, perhaps because it reminds her of what she could have been, or that she resents her own gender. Although this situation is replete with lesbian undertones, this aspect remains undeveloped.

This was produced by Aldrich, and in title and tone it follows on from his hit *Whatever Happened to Baby Jane?* Although some considered it further callousness (Nash and Ross, p. 3786), it was praised by *Variety* as a triumph in its own right. It is more restrained than *Baby Jane* in its approach to the grotesque, although it similarly concentrates on the manipulative and deceptive relationship between two elderly women increasingly in a state of mutual dependence.

Page may claim independence, but she needs the companionship offered by the housekeepers as much as she needs the money. She sees some of herself in Gordon's sprightly attitude, and there is, subtextually, a submerged attraction to her. One would be hard pressed to call this a lesbian undercurrent, although it is there for the arguing—an elderly woman kills those she is interested in rather than confronting her own sexual needs. Indeed, Aldrich had essayed lesbianism in the contemporary release of *The Killing of Sister George*. Page would explore sexual resentment and the yearnings of age in her subsequent role in *The Beguiled*.

When the Bough Breaks

(1993: d. Michael Cohn)

scr. Cohn; pr. Dinese Ballew, Barbara Javitz; exec pr. Barry Collier; ph. Michael Bonvillain; m. Ed Tomney; prod d. Eric Fraser; cast. Ally Walker, Martin Sheen, Ron Perlman, Rob Knepper, Scott Lawrence, Mark Donat, Christopher Doyle, Tim Halligan, Julia McCarthy; 105m

In Houston, Texas, a bag full of severed human hands is discovered; they belong to child victims, all later revealed to have been abducted from parklands. Each hand has a number tattooed on it. The police chief on the case concludes that a serial killer is responsible. He reluctantly enlists the help of an outside agent, a forensic psychologist (Walker), in order to obtain a profile of the killer. As Walker investigates, she soon discovers evidence linking the crimes to an autistic, institutionalized child. Soon Walker's relationship to the child proves the only viable lead, although her superior does not support her efforts and she receives nothing but animosity from male police officers. The main suspect is an ice cream vendor with a history of child molestation and whose house/lair is riddled with child pornography, and who dresses as a clown on occasion (à la the real John Wayne Gacy—explored also in *To Catch a Killer*). The killer, however, is the boy's father, a doctor who has abandoned the ill son to care for his twin sister. The sister has malformed hands, and the

killer, a doctor, is severing children's hands to use as a possible replacement for those on the girl, so that she may one day play the piano.

This film seems in part to have been an inspiration for the hit TV series *Profiler* (a realistic counterpart to the stylized, brooding *Millennium*), starring Walker as the killer-hunter. The movie addresses its protagonist's maternal needs, as aroused by her association with the child. Correspondingly, her presence triggers the boy's need to communicate his experiences, and his psychic link with the killer. However, the film concentrates on the female profiler in a way clearly indebted to Harris/Demme from *Silence of the Lambs*. The profiler's methods are thus paralleled to, but shown as somewhat distinct from, the usual police investigative procedures due to the presence of more intuitive work as filtered through technological means (DNA analysis and computer investigation) and victim profiles. Despite the trimmings, it follows procedural lines closely.

Perhaps most disappointingly, the style is more television movie functional, despite the occasional striking shot. Its efforts to be creepy and unsettling surface in the sporadic attempts to momentarily break the functional style and suggest another perceptual realm emerging—that reached via the kid's apparent psychic link (itself akin to multiple personality—and a parallel to that developed in Craven's *Night Visions*).

This psychic link is depicted as the corruption of a Patriarchal legacy (severed hands as hand-me-downs? = the legacy of tradition?), destroying the young men it should enrich. Indeed, the film is riddled with evidence of a crumbling macho social order, a tradition of abuse which the protagonist must go up against. Undercurrents of abuse and fear are present too, as both she and the child carry the scars (physical and metaphorical) and traumas of their formative years. Hence her bond to the child, also an isolated figure.

In contrast to the killer, Sheen represents the supposed proper functioning of such a Patriarchy, although he's at a loss to ascertain the motivations behind such a child killer — himself a perverted patriarch whose sense of loyalty to his offspring has degenerated into homicidal madness. The killer is capable of atrocity in the name of love, recalling the father in Franju's classic *Eyes Without a Face*, the inspiration for the European mad doctor/surgeon cycle. Sheen wishes initially to keep the matter in-house, among the properly ordained patriarchs. Walker is the face of the future, a young woman left to interpret and decipher the mess, recalling, in part, *Silence of the Lambs* and the subsequent *Copycat*.

When the Bough Breaks 2: Perfect Prey

(1998: d. Howard McCain)

scr. Robert McDonnell; pr. Charles Meeker, Denise Ballew, Glenn Greene; ph. Edmund Talevera; prod d. Roger Fortune; ed. Hanneh Rudkilde; m. Ennio Di Berardo; cst des. Denise Wingate; cast. Kelly McGillis, Bruce Dern, D.W. Moffett, Joely Fisher, David Keith

Kelly McGillis stars in a similar role to that vacated by Ally Walker (who went on to star in the hit TV series *Profiler*, about a female profiler). She is a Texas Ranger on stress-related personal leave who is recalled, à la *Manhunter*, to solve a murder, which she relates to others and so establishes the presence of a serial killer.

As she tracks the killer, we learn of the obsessive drive that has so affected her personal well-being, as she is forced to hunt the killer, knowing that he is the same one who once attacked her (and for which crime another killer wrongfully took credit for in an attempt at self-aggrandizement). As with her male counterparts, the way to purge her anxieties is to stop the killer,

ending the bond between them. By immersion in investigative procedure, she strives to preserve her psychological balance in the face of past trauma. The film's functional tele-movie style offers only scant attempts to probe her disturbances, however, instead focusing on her struggle to maintain a sense of the "real" amidst her intuitive visualizations of the killer's internal monstrousness and method (he feeds and cares for his victims before he watches them slowly asphyxiate). Like the profiler in *Manhunter*, she must immerse herself totally in the details.

By paralleling the profiler's investigation with the killer's work and activities, the film suggests their destinies are entwined. The profiler is a professional woman, a type resented by the killer (Keith in a role that recalls *White of the Eye*). He compensates for his perceived inferiority by sadistic torture (physical and psychological) — to cut them down a peg or two.

He is a doll collector/salesman, and his murders are the effort to transform his victims into his beloved and compliant dolls (a psychosis he shares in part with the killer in *The Cell*). It is the protagonist's refusal to be stereotyped in a male world which makes her a target for this killer, who (once again) resents his mother and puts on lipstick to talk to his victims, asking them if they are good mothers. She finally shoots him, ridding herself of the demands of the monstrous patriarch and proving herself a worthy functionary of its true operations, as she saves the victim, proving herself capable of fulfilling the male role and responsibility.

While the City Sleeps

(1956: d. Fritz Lang)

scr. Casey Robinson; nvl. Charles Einstein; pr. Bert E. Friedlob; ph. Ernest Laszlo; m. Herschel Burke Gilbert; ed. Gene Fowler Jr.; art d. Carroll Clark; cast. Dana Andrews, Rhonda Fleming,

A recent newspaper boss (Vincent Price, left) talks over his plans with a TV anchorman (Dana Andrews) in *While the City Sleeps* (RKO, 1956).

Sally Forrest, Thomas Mitchell, Vincent Price, Howard Duff, Ida Lupino, George Sanders, James Craig, John Barrymore Jr.; 100m

On the loose is "the Lipstick Killer" (a student and grocery delivery-boy, and a character based on the real William Heirens), a serial murderer who leaves messages in lipstick ("Ask Mother" being the most telling) at the crime scenes beside the sexually assaulted victims. The inheritor of a large newspaper chain (Price) offers a major promotion to any staff reporter who discovers the killer's identity. Three desperate reporters go to hazardous lengths for the job. One enlists his friend, a TV news anchor (Andrews) who baits the killer on live television into going after his own fiancée.

Here Lang explores how personal and professional integrity crumble in the face of the reward of professional self-advancement. Thus, Lang displays a cynicism more in keeping with Billy Wilder (who also criticized the morality and ethics of the journalistic establishment in the classic *Ace in the Hole*). As such, it is a late entry film noir, with all the subtleties and forcefulness of classic Lang. The reporters consider the murder story a "lulu," a hot item ripe for sensationalist exploitation, hence the decision to lead with the headline tagging the killer "the Lipstick Killer," fully aware that this may make women unduly frightened and even "guilty." Price, new to the business, resents the ridicule of others and wants to assert his dominance by making them scramble for the promotion. Thus, the film can be considered a harsh meditation on the consequences of pride and sexual resentment.

The reporter's lack of moral integrity is revealed as he and his friend plan to use a woman as bait. With one of them in an affair with the boss's wife, again as a means of self-advancement, the film explores a male code that effectively considers women disposable products, and which professional women (Lupino) must battle against. In their own way, despite their claim of benevolence (to catch the killer), they perpetrate the mentality that could allow the development of a sex killer who takes advantage of his job to attack lone, sexually desirable women. The killer's identity is revealed early. Unlike with *M*, Lang is less interested in the killer than in the moral decay of those who hypocritically seek him in the name of community benefit, but merely for profit — a theme that recalls in part the criminal posse in *M* and the mob in *Fury*.

The killer is an opportunist, motivated by hatred for his mother (anticipating *Psycho* in that regard) who dotes on him. Once his crimes are reported, he changes his means slightly, no longer leaving lipstick messages but still planting deliberate clues (he leaves a comic book, "The Strangler," at one crime scene) for the alert to decipher. He is a nobody with a soaring pride and resentment of desirable women. He so loathes being belittled on the air by Andrews that he wishes to kill out of wronged pride. An arrogant youth (in black leather, linking the film to the emergent youth rebellion movies of the late 1950s), he kills to assert his sexual personality, as he is otherwise alone and inferior and incapable of seducing the women he attacks. He is revealed to have been a fetish burglar, stealing women's underclothing (as did the real Heirens), his crimes progressing to murder as a demonstration of confidence and his perceived maturity. He gets bolder, and Andrews in-

tuits that he will strike during the day, a deliberate provocation to the authorities. When caught by the police he screams "no" repeatedly as he is dragged away like the spoilt, emotionally retarded child he is. He is caught at his game and fears the retribution to come, now that he has been trapped. He cries not out of remorse for his crimes, but at being caught.

As Andrews and the head policeman talk, Andrews (as an outside agent dragged into the investigation) is clearly the profiler. He tells the police to look for a young man, whose premeditated murder was not the first and who is clever enough to change his method to avoid being linked to past crimes. On TV he claims to have consulted a criminologist, and voices his profile of the killer over the air — a young mama's boy whose love has twisted into hate, and who is not as smart as he thinks he is. This is part of a plan, independent of the police, to goad the killer into targeting someone close to Andrews. It is a trap, but it almost results in the death of the woman.

The film was produced for United Artists before RKO agreed to distribute it, and it went on to become one of their biggest grossing releases. It was reportedly Lang's second favorite film, behind *Fury*, and has been compared to the noir triumph of *The Big Heat*.

Whisper to a Scream

(1989: d. Robert Bergman)

scr. Gerard Ciccoritti; ph. Paul Witte; m. John Beal; cast. Nadia Capone, Silvio Oliviero, Yaphet Kotto, Lawrence Bayne; 96m

An aspiring actress/stripper works for a phone sex service. She becomes concerned when someone kills women who fit the fantasy descriptions she has been using as part of the phone sex act. Is she in part complicit in these killings because she perpetrates the sexual subordination of her gender?

The killer lured by phone sex had featured in *Dead Connection* and *Out of the Dark*, both of which have a minimal recognition denied this minor effort. Once again, the film explores the consequences of male categorization of women into fantasy types, and the essential impossibility of these types existing in the real world except through fantasy projections which destroy their idealized object. Women must react to/conform to/escape from the entrapment of such restrictive and dangerous male activity, which would deny them an identity beyond that outlined as sexual fantasy, and jointly punish them for that sexuality.

White Angel

(1993: d. Chris Jones) aka *Interview with a Serial Killer*

scr. Jones, Genevieve Joliffe; pr. Joliffe; ph. Jon Walker; m. Harry Gregson-Williams; ed. John Holland; cast. Peter Firth, Harriet Robinson, Don Henderson, Anne Catherine Arton; 95m

A polite, quiet, meek and inoffensive dentist (Firth) murders blondes who wear white. Wanting to reveal his secret, and perhaps desperate for a sense of kinship with another, he becomes involved with a writer (on serial killers) who, ironically enough, has just murdered her husband and walled him up in the house. The killer proposes a partnership with the writer, for her to write his story. Thus blackmailed, she agrees, interviewing the killer on videotape.

Despite much greater production values, this can perhaps be compared with the ultra-cheap comedy of *Psychos in Love*. The collusion between killer and writer was also handled in *Rough Draft*, and the video interview was a central gimmick in *Man Bites Dog*. It aspires to the satire of the latter but sorely lacks its verve, daring and comedy.

White Angel seeks to explore the discrepancy between monstrous acts and the people who commit them. It characterizes the gender difference between killers in terms of conventional expectations of sexual depravity. The initial news reports of a female killer/mutilator therefore suggest the possibility that women are headed down a course which would see them usurp what was considered an almost exclusively male domain. That the killer prowls the streets while dressed in drag furthers the sense of gender identity transference which operates subtextually within this otherwise minor film.

The killer is correspondingly an absolute banality. However, beneath this bland surface rests a mentality that seeks forever to deceive people, playing childlike to lure them into a false sense of security. Thus, he forces his victims to face their own impending deaths (it is revealed that he videotaped his actions and forced the victim to watch — recalling *Peeping Tom*) as a demonstration of his mastery over them after all.

Perhaps in keeping with the theme of gender identity and homicide, the film is stylistically unsure of itself. It veers between stylized thriller, kitchen-sink character portrait in the established British manner, and a procedural film. Perhaps it even seeks to address in part the modern legacy of Jack the Ripper, and of the Yorkshire Ripper. However, the confusing ending, with her possibly implicated as the killer all along, negates the thematic developments that have previously emerged, although it again questions the gender implications behind serial killer pathology; maybe that alone was the whole point to this unsatisfying film.

White of the Eye

(1986: d. Donald Cammell)

scr. Donald and China Cammell; pr. Cassian Elwes, Brad Wyman; exec pr. Elliott Kastner; ph. Al Jones, Larry McConkey; m. Nick Mason,

The pensive serial killer (David Keith) from *White of the Eye* (Mrs Whites Prodn./Palisades, 1986).

Rick Fenn; ed. Terry Rawlings; prod d. Philip E. Thomas; cast. David Keith, Cathy Moriarty, Art Evans, Alan Rosenberg, Alberta Watson; 111m

Tucson, Arizona, police investigate a series of ritual murders/disembowelments. The trail leads to a hi-fi technician (Keith) who lives with his wife (Moriarty) and daughter but is propositioned by women he apparently loathes, considering himself a hunter. The man is indeed the killer, who keeps bodily trophies in his domain and, when confronted by his wife, retreats into a fantasy of himself as a native American avenging spirit of sorts, and attempts to kill her and the ex-boyfriend who comes to her aid.

This is a much more involving and stylish film than a synopsis alone indicates. The opening signals Cammell's concern for predatory animals: a pan from highway to sky to eagle is followed by a cut to Keith.

The bird's eye point of view suggests a fusion of omnipotence and alignment with a predatory sensibility — both of which are allied in the protagonist's self-image and uniquely demented spirituality (which demands ritual homicide). Distorted spatial relations abound, and Cammell uses sudden wide-angle shots (as he had in his previous *Demon Seed*) to chart the explosion of psychological space. Attention is drawn to large open spaces, with the theme of confinement being a function of ritual human interaction: such is the fate of the creature of habit, the desire to step beyond a psychological malleability that would continually re-shape them.

For Cammell, who is intent on capturing the sense of a mind in flight, the film is about a state of spiritual flux. Cammell loves to juxtapose motion and stillness. The killer considers himself a tuning fork in touch with this universal flux, and

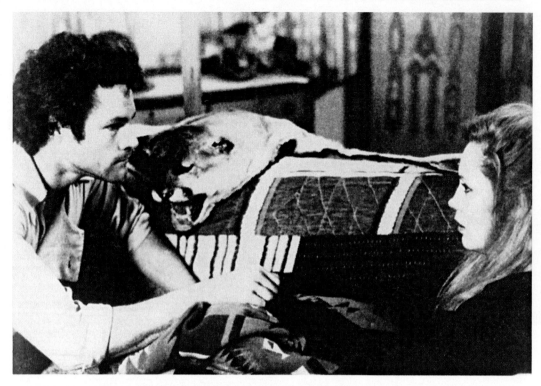

The killer's wife (Cathy Moriarty, right) realizes her predicament as she faces her menacing serial killer husband (David Keith) in *White of the Eye* (1986).

murders in ritual fashion to be in touch with the flight involved. He thinks he is blessed, chosen, untouchable, and in harmony with a higher spiritual order allied to impulse, chaos, and finally madness. This spiritual realm is one of pure power, the soul of the hunter who would keep trophies of the kill (body parts) with him.

However, this spiritual realm, which he characterizes as a black hole which sucks all life into it (a horrific interpretation of female genitalia), is one wherein men and women are opposites. The killer believes that women are the reason things turn "inside out," and so they must be eliminated. In the end he reveals his psychotic hatred of women as a force throughout the universe. Yet he still desires sexual intercourse, an irreconcilable spiritual duality. Sex drives "the chosen" men mad. His wife can only muse that she must have made him feel so alone that he turned to

homicide and delusion instead of her. She too is self-centered, except with her daughter, and that is perhaps what she learns from her husband's madness—to move beyond her regrets.

It is evident fairly early on who the killer is, and the film concentrates on building a character portrait of a man whose fantasies and memories suggest an identity other than the one he hides behind. In its exploration of the central characters, the movie explores the persistence of memory in the face of the compromise of ideals, and the perversions, regrets and missed opportunities that lie behind the image of the family. Only the killer has reconciled his present with the past, and this is ironically a sign of his madness, although he seems the most outwardly at peace as the film starts—though this is gradually undermined to stress the chaos within his soul.

Hence, the film drifts between past

and present. Flashbacks (filmed in a kind of sun-drenched, bleached Expressionism) explore the characters' meetings, psychosis, and the evolution of their self-definition. The characters are ex-hippies, and their efforts to maintain a life only speak to an elusive quality which makes them seem characters out of their time, floating in an indifferent landscape they strive to master but succumb to, destroying or denying each other. Cammell's repeated altering of the background compositions, and his disruptions of the score, indicate this. Long shots cut to jarring close-ups to shatter psychological distance, and all is modulated by match-cuts, elegant and fluid segues, as if the camera were itself in flux around the characters, à la *Performance* and *Wild Side*, where the characters seek perpetual redefinition in their relation to one another. Indeed, Cammell likes to contrast textures in a manner that recalls much avant-garde work in America in the 1960s and 1970s.

There is little psychological probing of the killer's motives, and the sense is rather that he has made a lifestyle choice to master his circumstance. Yet this makes him as indifferent to his wife as she is blind to his other side, though professing she knows him. How well can you know somebody, even if you are so close to him or her? To what extent is the self a product of sexual appetite segueing into monstrousness? These are regular themes in Cammell's unfortunately few films.

His visual style is arguably an expression of the inherent pseudo-spirituality that affects the characters (especially the killer), and the representation of the killer's perception that murder is an art form, a valid and necessary self-expression. Moments of stillness reflect the moments of objective clarity of focus in the characters' minds— before they are once again carried away. In this near-flux, the act of murder is a perceptual experience

akin to a kind of metamorphosis (and sexual ecstasy) which allows meaning and communion with nature — the ultimate perversion of the hippie ideal. It also allows the protagonist to strive to remain insular — in a sense, pure psychotic reaction.

Every camera movement that follows these moments of stillness suggests the movement towards imbalance, the flight away from certainty, and becomes foreboding. Life (and murder) is a sensual experience when presented in this style (a trick Cammell tried in the later *Wild Side*), yet still demonstrating the stagnation of interpersonal relationships since the sexual and social revolution has produced a breed of amoral killers claiming a visionary purpose. Into this, menace becomes erotic, and murder becomes the killer's form of life-enhancement. Through murder, he achieves a oneness with his higher power.

The policeman (Evans) intuits the work of a psychologically disturbed man, and even compares the body mutilations and crime scene to an artwork. Indeed, its presentation of murder (knowing of tradition, in that one scene where a woman is forced to watch herself drown alludes to *Peeping Tom*) as an act of almost hallucinatory beauty recalls the stylization of Argento and the giallo. It also anticipates the murder-as-art themes of the serial killer film since the early-to-mid–1990s. The killer's professional ambitions— to make personalized stereo units—combines the artistic and the technical. His murders, like his works, are a means of personal expression — perfect creations, the product of his higher spiritual beliefs (in a chaotic, all-consuming force beyond conventional God), which his wife hears as tangential gibberish when she finds the evidence of his killings (the trophies of his hunt and kills).

Eventually, the killer's monstrousness invades his home and threatens his wife and child. His trophies (human body parts—

recalling a flashback in which he kills a deer, mutilates it and drinks its blood) discovered, he turns psychotic, losing his balance. Marriage has ultimately become a trap for both characters, and Cammell reveals how the wife (Moriarty) is consumed by memory and regret, forever wondering if she had made the right choice, and finally faced with the terrible realization that she hadn't and must now face the consequences.

It is a stylish, even hallucinogenic film. Like *The Stepfather*, it was a genuinely disturbing thriller that was considered to have been unfairly overlooked in the wake of such "safe" thrillers as *Fatal Attraction* and *Jagged Edge*. The film, unfortunately, received scant theatrical release, being briefly shown in the United States before purchased by notorious exploitation studio/distributor Cannon Films. Thus, it was a box office failure. Not even the director's later suicide (after completing the sexually polymorphous *Wild Side*) renewed interest in this unfortunately neglected masterwork. Together with *Performance* and *Demon Seed*, it stands testament to a formidable talent who never found a solid reception.

Who Saw Her Die?

(1971: d. Aldo Lado)

scr. Francesco Barilli, Massimo D'Avak, Lado, Ruediger von Spiess; pr. Enzo Doria, Dieter Geissler; m. Ennio Morricone; ed. Jutta Brandstaedter, Angelo Curi; cast. George Lazenby, Anita Strindberg, Peter Chatel, Adolfo Celi, Dominique Boschero, Rosemarie Lindt; 90m

A child is murdered at a skiing resort. Years later an artist (Lazenby) with a daughter is in Venice. He leaves his daughter unattended while he has a sexual dalliance, and she disappears, possibly abducted by the same impulsive child killer. The little girl's body is found floating in the canals. Wracked with guilt, the father

investigates the case. He ties it to the previous case and uncovers a wealthy pedophilic lawyer, and indeed infiltrates a world of hidden, sinister desires behind the veneer of respectability. He finally uncovers the killer, a priest.

Typical of the giallo movement that emerged in Italy in the early 1970s, this is concerned with a realm of altered perceptions beneath the everyday. In this case, these perceptions are clouded by aberrant sexuality. Little girls are shown repeatedly watched by men, and every gaze or point of view shot has a predatory dimension, and is thus menacingly unstable. Correspondingly, every touch of the child by a man has pedophilic overtones. The male gaze is driven to eroticize children, and break into sudden violence to consummate the desire and remove its object in an attempt at disavowal (there is no sexual act performed on the victim, the murder being the substitute). The film cuts from the killer's point of view of children playing to a shot of meat hanging in a butcher shop. Children are disposable commodities, and Lazenby feels guilty over not supervising his daughter properly, and not recognizing the threat to her that he gradually discovers is more pervasive than he expected. It is a strangely motherless world of the perverse relationship between fathers (or substitute fathers) and daughters. It's ironic that the killer aspires to be a priest, the ultimate Father.

Lazenby moves from feelings of loss, responsibility and helplessness to outrage. The detective on the case says that for a man to do this he must be insane, and Lazenby's friend adds that this kind of killer is unlikely to be caught. This prospect angers Lazenby, who comes to believe that if he can uncover the killer then he will find redemption for his negligence. He uncovers a class of sexual perverts ready to prey on the innocent for their private gratification. The film equates the affluence and social standing of Patriarchy with sexual perversity. Pornographic imagery is a function of the perverse in that it seeks to commodify the object as both desired and disposable. It also feeds the fantasy until it must be put into reality. The killer has been so consumed by repression and fantasy that he has turned to homicide. He says he loathes girls for the whores that they become (or, rather, that male society has made them into), like his mother. In his own way, perhaps, he is saving them from the taint of adulthood, a theme also explored in many child-killer narratives, including *In the Cold Light of Day*.

This is an interesting film, one of the few to tackle the theme of pedophilia (an aspect it shares in part with *My Dear Killer*). In its depiction of an abhorrent Patriarchy, it is a curiously subversive film. Men who aspire to socially sanctioned status are secretly sexual perverts and incipient serial killers. Patriarchy has a responsibility to protect young girls, but is tormented by its simultaneous desire to exploit them, a theme of *Play Nice* also.

The Witch Who Came from the Sea

(1976: d. Matt Cimber)

scr. Robert Thom; m. Herschel Burke Gilbert; cast. Millie Perkins, Stafford Morgan, George Buck Flower, Roberta Collins

A reportedly odd cult curiosity, this rare film examines a female sex killer. A sea captain's daughter (Perkins) castrates the football players she lures, so resentful is she of male sexuality (homicidal penis envy?).

It is perhaps unusual in its wholehearted examination of male castration anxiety and the corresponding component of fear that is intertwined with heterosexual desire. Kim Newman (p. 93) reports that Cimber deliberately toys with the presumed male viewer's voyeuristic relationship to the unfolding film, intended to unsettle. The screenwriter (who was then Perkins' husband) roots the killer's pathological hatred of men in childhood abuse, when her incestuous father had a heart attack and died while molesting her. Unfortunately, this has disappeared from release.

Without Warning

(1952: d. Arnold Laven)

scr. Bill Raynor; pr. Arthur Gardner, Jules Levy; ph. Joseph Biroc; m. Herschel Burke Gilbert; ed. Arthur H. Nadel; cast. Adam Williams, Meg Randall, Edward Binns, Harlan Warde, John Maxwell, Angela Stevens, Byron Kane, Charles Tannen; 75m

A normally quiet man (Williams), the apparently typical neighbor, becomes a serial killer in reaction to his blonde wife's infidelities. He uses a pair of garden shears to murder blonde women, surrogates for the true source of his rage and resentment (a mentality that some later applied to real-life killer Ted Bundy, who murdered women who reminded him of the one girl who had rejected his advances). The efforts of two policemen to entrap him by using blonde policewomen in bars prove fruitless. Finally, dedicated forensic investigation leads to the identification of the killer.

Like the contemporary *The Sniper*, the film in part intends to be the case history of a sex murderer. It was made with the cooperation of local law enforcement operations. With much location shooting, the film strives to capture a recognizable milieu in its tackling of a modern murder phenomenon, the serial killer. Thus, is it at lengths to depict the police reaction to the crimes, and the implications to be had when they link several murders to the one offender. They have on their hands a pathological monster, a man who will never stop. However, it has a faith in ordinary, dedicated police-work's ability to triumph in the end.

This film was made by the same creative team responsible for the TV series *The Rifleman*, *Burke's Law*, and *The Big Valley*. Director Laven subsequently made many neglected features in Hollywood. The producer talked a major distribution company, UA, into releasing this low-budget independent film, which has a minor place alongside the post-noir case histories of the 1950s. It had some added novelty value at the time for its use of the then-new Los Angeles freeway system for an exciting chase conclusion. Cinematographer Biroc would go on to a lengthy collaboration with Robert Aldrich.

The Wizard of Gore

(1970: d. H.G. Lewis)

scr. Allen Kahn; pr. Lewis; ph. Alex Ameripoor, Dan Krogh; m. Larry Wellington; ed. Eskandar Ameripoor; mkup. Frank Morelli; cast. Ray Sager, Judy Cler, Wayne Ratay, Phil Laurenson, Jim Rau, John Elliot, Don Alexander; 96m

A stage magician, Montag the Magnificent, performs stage mutilations on female volunteers, murdering these hypnotized innocents, who die at a later date, thus not incriminating him in their deaths. A local TV hostess/celebrity and her journalist boyfriend investigate the baffling case and discover the magician's reliance on hypnotism and delayed affect.

This was the penultimate gore film from gore pioneer Lewis, who was responsible for the breakthrough *Blood Feast*. Its childishness and stupidity seem to suggest Lewis attempting the deliberate offensiveness that would consume the early John Waters. Indeed, the theme of illusion vs.

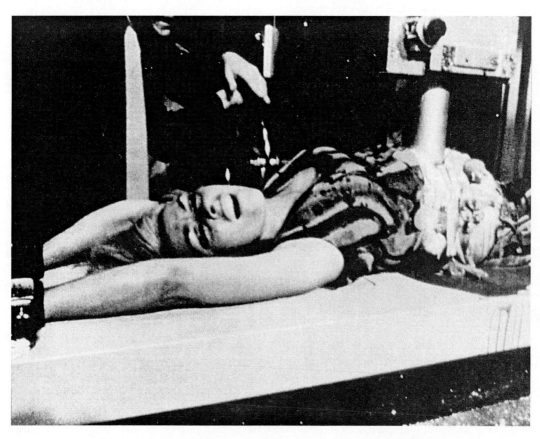

A victim of a murderous stage act in *The Wizard of Gore* (Friedman/Lewis, 1970).

Another murderous stage act from *The Wizard of Gore* (Friedman/Lewis, 1970).

reality as a scant justification for depictions of sadistic acts against women would form the basis for the reprehensible *Incredible Torture Show*.

There are numerous trashy gore scenes in the manner expected of Lewis (a woman sawed in half, a spike driven through a victim's head), but in so far as these are staged for the benefit of an appreciative audience, one senses Montag as a substitute for the director. Thus, the film can be taken as a self-reflexive treatment of Lewis' career, audience, controversial reception, growing influence, and of the accusations of moral corruption and imitation often leveled at such explicit horror. The self-reflexive component arguably raises the film from obscurity. Indeed, the film's ending, a time paradox which takes the viewer to the sit-uation at the start, suggests the genre's future repetitiveness, and is even an absurdist world view which reduces all effort to ultimate futility. Needless to say, Lewis is skillful enough to keep it a comedy, and it ironically becomes more disturbing for its slyly humorous and cynical tone, always present in Lewis' best work.

Wolf Forest

(1968: d. Pedro Olea)

scr. Juan Antonio Porto; pr. Jesus Sanchez, Imanol Olea; ph. Aurelio G. Larraya; cast. Jose Lopez Velazquez, Amparo Soler Leal, Antonio Casas, Nuria Torray, Alfredo Mayo, John Steiner; 91 (85)m

A wandering serial killer, a peddler troubled by epilepsy, targets a small European village. He eventually lures eleven women to their grisly deaths in the woods. Due to the horrific nature of the crimes, the locals come to regard the killer as a werewolf and set traps for him. Finally, he is caught in one such trap.

This is most interesting for its equation of serial killer to werewolf, and its subsequent intermingling of reality and folk tale fantasy. Its setting, an isolated village beset by a killer, recalls both *The Wolf Man* and Chabrol's *Le Boucher*, and indeed is a more common trait in European horror stories. The case has some similarities to that of nomadic killer Joseph Vacher, one of the first serial killers, and one who drifted the countryside looking for victims. However, it reportedly draws more on genuine Galician folk tales (according to Hardy, p. 194), as it's from a Basque director, an ex–film critic who turned to film fantasy.

The film won over the critics (and awards) at festivals in Chicago and the Valladoid, and apparently won additional praise for its social-realist concerns. It is reportedly dutifully solemn in approach, with attention given the prospect of community definition and the factors which would affect such a killer. However, it is hardly readily available now. It can also be compared to *It Happened in Broad Daylight* and *In the Cold Light of Day*, also about killers who lured victims into the woods, a plot hook more common in European-set thrillers.

The Wolf Man

(1941: d. George Waggner)

scr. Curt Siodmak; pr. Waggner; ph. Joseph Valentine; m. Hans Salter, Frank Skinner; cast. Lon Chaney Jr., Claude Rains, Warren William, Ralph Bellamy, Bela Lugosi, Maria Ouspenskaya, Patric Knowles; 70m

A man (Chaney Jr.) is bitten by a gypsy werewolf while rescuing a girl. He ignores warnings and soon transforms into the title beast. A Welsh village is beset by the activities of a werewolf.

This is not, in actuality, the first werewolf killer movie, as is usually thought. That honor goes to the earlier *Werewolf of London*. However, it does indicate that the werewolf's dilemma — that of an honest man who cannot control his animalistic urges, and indeed struggles perhaps in vain to understand them — is indeed allied to the serial killer's perceived compulsion to kill. It allies such a dilemma to the influence of a corruptive evil, even Satanic in origin (hence the visual stress on the pentangle motif).

Much investment was made in this film, and it proved to be another box-office horror success for Universal Studios, who knowingly chose a different visual look and design here than that used for their flop *Werewolf of London*, although it too plays on fog-enshrouded spaces. Like the beast in that earlier film, however, the man is faced with enormous guilt at the revelation of what he is capable of once transformed and in the supposed grip of an animalistic abhorrence. Such is the foundation of the werewolf legend, making it a more deliberate recognition of the human dilemma (still inherently Good) in response to multiple murder than its counterpart, the vampire (who would feel no such remorse). Chaney would play the werewolf six times, in the latter stages for comedic effect.

Screenwriter Siodmak reportedly reconstructed the legend as a combination of lycanthropic folklore, myths regarding witchcraft and witches, and Bram Stoker's *Dracula* (Nash and Ross, pp. 3893–4). Still, it is the issue of human ethics which would prove the most influential development in terms of the evolution of the serial killer genre, and which makes the werewolf myth border on tragedy, perhaps the closest that the horror field has come to it.

Critics were impressed and drew particular attention to an atmospheric set piece featuring a gypsy encampment.

Writer's Block

(1992: d. Charles Carroll)

scr. Elisa Bell; stry. Bell, Tracy Barone; pr. Vanessa Greene; ph. Tobias Schliessler; m. Nan Schwartz; ed. Tom Finan; prod d. Kathy Curtis Cahill; cast. Morgan Fairchild, Joc Regalbuto, Anthony Herrera, Debi Fares; 90m

In this tele-movie, Fairchild, a writer of mystery stories (as "Red Ribbon" tales), kills off one of her central characters, an attractive but lethal serial killer. She soon finds that someone is imitating the fictional murders for real and killing those people with whom the writer is annoyed. She faces a demented copycat/fan and starts to investigate on her own, blaming herself as essentially responsible.

This addresses the theme of the interplay of fact and fiction, as in the Stephen King novels filmed as *The Dark Half* and *Misery*. In addition, it ties into the female author's fantasies becoming reality, as in *Romancing the Stone* and *American Dreamer*. The promising theme of Fairchild's will making the killer an actuality is complimented by the killer's eventual admission that he believes himself to be the character come to life. Thus, she has taken him as her lover, an ideal role ironically, and controversially, fulfilled by the killer in her novels. The serial killer is thus a male archetype that holds its own sexual attractiveness to women, a theme also in *True Crime*.

It is also a consequence of the casual sex mentality: Fairchild is presented as a sexually independent/liberated woman whose dalliances turn dangerous— even an AIDS metaphor. She is drawn to men she does not know. The killer is the personification of the attraction to and fear of the unknown male. The film is most interesting for its positioning of this unknown man as woman's sexual fantasy, and a theme infiltrating *Looking for Mr. Goodbar*.

The Young Poisoner's Handbook

(1995: d. Benjamin Ross)

scr. Ross, Jeff Rawle; pr. Peter McAleese, Sam Taylor; ph. Hubert Taczanowski; m. Robert Lane, Frank Strobel; ed. Anne Sopel; prod d. Maria Djurkovic; art d. Matthias Kammermeier, Mark Stevenson; cast. Hugh O'Conor, Anthony Sher, Ruth Sheen, Roger Lloyd Pack, Charlotte Coleman, Paul Stacey, Tim Potter, Peter Pacey; 106m

A young man (O'Conor) obsessed with chemistry develops an interest in poisons and their workings in the human body. Angered by his mother, who admonishes him for hiding pornographic magazines (in actuality his dad's), his thoughts turn to revenge. Spurred on by a comic book war story he reads (which features the wartime use of the poison Thallium), he slowly starts to poison his own family and watch the results. The poisoning is discovered and he is put away for psychiatric treatment. There he meets a sympathetic doctor who believes he can cure the young man, and endeavors to do so. Finally the man is pronounced cured and released — back to the remains of his family, and newly married sister. He gets a factory job but resorts to his old habit, and slowly poisons his co-workers. In an effort to show otherwise, when threatened he poisons himself and lives through it to continue. When finally arrested, he sends his diary to the doctor who had pronounced him cured and "sane."

This is a brilliant cult English comedy of an unrepentant, incurable killer. It is aided by the killer's voice-over, based on the elaborate diary records he keeps of his experiences, and a narrative structure which

The budding serial poisoner (Hugh O'Conor) and the object of his erotic interest (Samantha Edmonds) in *The Young Poisoner's Handbook* (CFP, 1995).

speaks directly to Kubrick's *A Clockwork Orange*. In particular, the first act follows the young man on his criminal, homicidal path; the second act follows his treatment (which he knowingly puts himself up for); the third act follows his release and return to crime, despite the treatment.

His experiments offer an escape from his stale, stifling home environment, as do his burgeoning erotic yearnings and interest in soft porn. They are still developing fantasies he seeks to put into practice. Tellingly, and demonstrative of the film's relentlessly sly humor, he has a picture of a topless nurse, named "Nurse Esther," but he cuts out the "s" to make it "Nurse Ether." This demonstrates that his interest in chemistry and his sexuality are becoming intertwined, and that his later homicides are an expression of his perceived sexual maturity.

By the time he meets a girl who may be receptive (and gets him restricted library books for his research), he is interested only in his work. However, when a school friend expresses an interest in the girl, he poisons the friend, but still shows no direct erotic interest in the girl, though his crimes speak to a process of sexual substitution. When he finally dates her, he talks of car crash victims, revealing his morbid fascination with death and dying — a process he keenly observes, as sexual stimuli — he is in the process of sexualizing the act of slow dying.

Hence, his later efforts to poison his mother speak to his unresolved resentments and possible sublimated incestuous drives. She finds his dad's pornographic magazines and blames him for them, putting him in a bath and scrubbing him, a sexually humiliating act for the young

The serial poisoner (Hugh O'Conor) faces another of life's temptations in *The Young Poisoner's Handbook* (CFP, 1995).

man. This act of humiliation and hypocrisy is the last straw, and the young man decides to poison them in return, to punish them for their treatment of him. This punishment is a demonstration of his sexuality, a rebellion against those that would stifle it. It culminates a movement towards personal empowerment.

In the process, he no longer sees humans as worthy of life or respect, just fodder for his experiments. He therefore callously moves on to horrible atrocities to preserve his research — he puts acid in his sister's eye-drops to prevent her from prying. His immediate family never suspects him of sinister intentions, although other relatives wonder. As the dismay and uneasy comedy mount, so too does the sense of a steady descent into irony, repeatedly questioning the young man's sexuality: instead of the greatest lover, he declares (in his diary) his ambition to be the greatest

poisoner the world has ever seen. He has become a greater social problem in the meantime, and is dealt with as society feels best — incarcerated and subjected to a new treatment.

Unlike the treatment in *A Clockwork Orange*, this is designed to use dreams (which he fakes until revealing his dream of a failed experiment which, if it had worked, would presumably have marked his growth to sexual maturity) to affect true moral change instead of a conditioned response. The scenes and characters, however, refer directly to Kubrick's film, as does the choice of classical music. The treatment actually seems to work, and the protagonist shows a self-awareness and responsibility that speaks to true reform. He is such an intelligent young man that one's hopes are almost with him. Yet he seems honestly afraid of being released, as if knowing of an inevitability he finally embraces.

Once the illicit (sexual) power over others is experienced, it cannot be denied, and the protagonist, when released and mistakenly put back in the same environment, descends back into his old mindset, despite his intention for things to be different this time. He has a new handbook and a plan to destroy the world. Yet one can't help but wonder if things would have been different had he been placed anywhere instead of back home. The sense of an inevitable slide into the recesses of the human mind is complimented visually, as the shots get colder and bluer as the film proceeds, systematically drained of color, suggesting the film is in part a mildly expressionistic view of the protagonist's imbalance.

He is captured once again, and in both a scornful and responsible gesture, mails his diary to the doctor who had declared him cured. In the hospital again, he suicides, poisoning himself in a final irony — poetic justice at last. The structural descent into irony is complete. In that, Ross promises to be a worthy successor to Kubrick's cynical wit and concern for the absence of humanity. It is impossible to feel sorry for the victims in the film, and part of the movie's sly success is to make the killer's death the real loss.

The style is one of slightly caricaturish exaggeration, a form of an understated grotesque, especially in the treatment of faces. Tilted angles, shadowy compositions, bold colors and stark lighting make the film at times resemble the style of Jeunet and Caro (*Delicatessen*, *City of Lost Children*). Its period recreation and humor also warrant comparison to Bernard Rose's critically maligned *Chicago Joe and the Showgirl*, and even to the films of Peter Medak. The use of pop songs adds another means of slight undercutting, to push the viewer deeper into the descent into total irony, bordering on the absurd (and hence the tragic).

It is based on a true story, that of Graham Young, which became one of the most infamous cases in the annals of British crime since Jack the Ripper, alongside John Christie (dramatized in *10 Rillington Place*) and the Moors Murderers. In actuality, Young was a megalomaniac, a neo–Nazi obsessed with genocide, but the film wisely transforms this into a bleak satire of personal ambition (or so Ebert felt).

The Young Poisoner's Handbook was Ross' debut, and is a most assured, complex film. The actors were mainly from the stage, and Ross preserved a slight exaggeration to their performances. It was critically praised and taken as evidence of an emerging, possibly major, new director. It was also perhaps too sinister for general audience consumption, however, and remains more popular with cine-literate viewers and reviewers.

The Zebra Killer

(1974: d. William Girdler) aka *Panic City*

scr. Girdler; pr. Phillip Hazelton, Mike Henry, Gordon C. Layne; cast. Austin Stoker, James Pickett, Hugh Smith, D'Urville Martin, Charles Kissinger; 90m

In this low-budget film, Austin Stoker (best known for his work in John Carpenter's *Assault on Precinct 13*) stars as a detective on the trail of a serial killer. The killer is a Caucasian who dons black makeup in order to appear as an Afro-American. He roams the streets of San Francisco, raping and murdering women as the mood takes him. One of the victims is the detective's girlfriend. The detective enlists the help of two others to track the killer.

This curiosity from cult horror auteur Girdler (*Three on a Meathook*) is practically impossible to locate, even amongst Internet users, having never been fully released even on video. Thus, all reports are second hand. It promises to examine the racial overtones of the period, but likely treats Afro-Americans with the kind of subcultural definition that would be the fate of Native Americans in *The Manitou*. Nonetheless, Girdler has a concern for the clash of nature in conjunction with human endeavor in his later work that is missing from his earlier. The film is perhaps interesting as a measure of social change in response to increasing violence and racial issues, and as a study of a killer insecure with the cultural standing of race, paradoxically disguising himself as the Other in order to dispose of it. It is a shame that the film is unavailable, as it sounds intriguing.

Zimmer 13

(1964: d. Harald Reinl) aka *Room 13*

pr. Horst Wendland; ph. Ernst W. Kalinke; m. Peter Thomas; ed. Jutta Hering; cast. Joachim Fuchsberger, Karin Dor, Richard Haeussler, Kai Fischer; 89m

This is apparently an odd mixture of comedy and gore. A group of criminals gather in a hotel room to plan a robbery and to blackmail a politician for his previous ties to the gang twenty years ago. Meanwhile, a serial killer uses a straight razor to kill nightclubbing ladies. One cop investigates the crimes but can only find the gangsters.

Another impossibility to track down, this has not even an Internet reputation. It is perhaps interesting for its implied hierarchy of criminal endeavor, with the serial killer being the absolute nadir in a spectrum of malevolence. It is included with a question mark.

Zipperface

(1992: d. Monsour Pourmand)

scr, pr. Pourmand; ph. F. Smith Martin; m. Jim Halfpenny; ed. John Dagnen; prod d. Brian McCabe; cast. David Clover, John Dagnen, Johnny Mandel, Rikki Brando, Don Adams; 90m

In Palm City, California, a serial killer decapitates actresses/prostitutes. The female mayor puts pressure on police, and a female detective is on his trail. Although the black leather–clad killer (wearing a mask with zipper across its mouth opening) seems giallo-inspired, and anticipates the S&M killer (named "Machine") in *8MM*, the film is truly atrocious, in the manner of the cheapest home video production imitation of music video aesthetics.

Although the notion of a killer striking out against some form of socially dominant Matriarchy is suggested, it is never developed, and even undercut by the fact that the female detective needs the help of a veteran male partner. Finally, after the killer plagues a women's recreation center (run by the customary suspicious priest), the mayor shoots the killer through the mouth. The subtext is that all women must band together to eliminate the masculine monstrousness of the everyman killer. The subtext is valid, but its treatment hardly insightful or provocative.

Indeed, typical of exploitation movies, the main interest here is in the killer's method alone: he poses women in the manner of bondage photos, implying the connection between serial murder and violent pornography, and recalling the real-life case of 1950s photographer Harvey Glatman, who photographed and killed his models. A male-dominated society has been shaped by images of violence against women. But rather than truly examine these implications, the film ultimately feeds them with more violent imagery to which women must perpetually react. In that, women are allowed an identity only in response to male aberration.

The Zodiac Killer

(1971: d. Tom Hanson)

scr. Ray Cantrell, Manny Cardoza; pr. Hanson; ph. Robert Birchall, Wilson S. Hong; m. Dennis

Thomann; cast. Hal Reed, Bob Jones, Ray Lynch, Tom Pittman, Mary Darrington; 87m

In this violent, exploitative account of the true-life (but never caught) killer who terrorized San Francisco and taunted the police via letters and phone calls, the typical cat-and-mouse killer/cop games ensue.

Strangely enough, this mess was made with the assistance of *San Francisco Chronicle* reporter Paul Avery. Avery was personally involved in the reporting of the actual case after having had his life threatened by the real Zodiac on October 28, 1970. Despite this credential, the film resorts to standard gruesome-murders-by-hooded-killer theatrics. At the outset, the film announces its intention to create an awareness of a present "danger" instead of winning any commercial awards. This is a pitiful excuse for the amateurishness that follows.

Amidst murky photography (apparently intended as documentary), this look at kooks in San Francisco has the same exploitation novelty values as the numerous Manson-quickies including *The Helter Skelter Murders* made after that case broke. However, *The Zodiac Killer* does reveal all incidents as portraits of male violence against women, holding that as the root cause for social problems; but it does not explain the misogynist acts with any convincing background, beyond the expectedly crude Patriarchal legacy rhetoric. So all men are predatory and misogynistic, and opposed to young love and the hippie ideals: cultural change clashes with gender. This effectively biases the film's attempt to probe a cross section of San Franciscan class structures as affected by such a social problem.

Instead, the film emerges as a kind of reactionary sexploitation. It depicts a frustrated and useless police force desperately needing some form of outside help, even consulting a psychic for assistance. As such, it speaks of the need for a profiler to understand and contextualize such a problem, and suggests this aim as a proper function of the genre itself.

The killer is depicted as a religious lunatic intent on collecting slaves for the afterlife (as some of his notes to police actually implied). He has auditory hallucinations of the voices of the murdered throng, though otherwise there is little attempt to develop or visualize a schizophrenic perception. The film suggests him as a frustrated postman (à la the real-life Son of Sam killer, David Berkowitz) who builds his own demonic shrine (as would be later attributed to Jeffrey Dahmer). His motive is suggested to be resentment of his ill father, and thus a critique of the functioning of traditional Patriarchy. He is one of the drug-using hippie types the film wants to condemn. This stamps it as an outcry against the values of the 1960s, and just one in a rash of like-themed films of the 1970s, including *Dirty Harry* (also based on the Zodiac crimes and released the same year).

Stylistically, *The Zodiac Killer* makes use of natural light and has a feeling of rawness devoid of technical polish, perhaps intended as verite documentary or as someone's home movie. This structureless film's main point of social criticism/indictment is reserved for the end, when a voice-over from the killer remarks about how the law works to protect him. This confirms the film's overreaching intention to address current social problems.

BIBLIOGRAPHY

All individual entries from *Variety* and the *New York Times* refer to the date as given in the index to the collected volumes specified below.

All references to online sites have been accessed by a film title search at the Internet Movie Database *imdb.com* and following the related link(s) by movie title. Additional online reviews by John Hartl can be found in this manner or direct at the *film.com* website. Another Internet movie database at *allmovie.com* offers capsule summaries, mini-reviews and VHS/DVD release information about a number of the titles finished. Many fan sites offering opinions (or e-pinions as they have come to be known) can be accessed via *imdb.com* and via a "serial killer" search at any search engine, although these sites tend to relate more to actual serial killer personages; many of them offer intriguing, if disturbing (even sympathetic) glimpses into the burgeoning serial killer subculture.

A.W. "M." *New York Times*. 6/11/1951 (20:7).

Abel. "Monsieur Verdoux." *Variety*. 4/16/1947.

Archer, E. "Jack the Ripper." *New York Times*. 18/2/1960 (37:4).

Asplund, V. *Chaplin's Films*. Melbourne: Wren Publ., 1973.

Balun, C. *Lucio Fulci — Beyond the Gates*. Key West: Fantasma Books, 1997.

Beau. "Craze." *Variety*. 6/12/1974.

_____. "No Way to Treat a Lady." *Variety*. 3/13/1968.

Bergman, P., and M. Assimow. *Reel Justice: Courtroom Goes to the Movies*. Kansas City: Andrew & McNeal, 1996.

Bobb. "Psychomania." *Variety*. 2/19/1964.

Boot, A. *Fragments of Fear*. London: Creation Books, 1996.

Brog. "Man in the Attic." *Variety*. 12/23/1953.

_____. "The Sniper." *Variety*. 3/19/1952.

Brottman, M. *Meat Is Murder*. London: Creation Press, 1998.

Byro. "The Honeymoon Killers." *Variety*. 9/10/1969.

Campbell, D., C. Wilson and R. Pesaud. "Charles Manson." *Murder in Mind*. 1 (#9). Marshall Cavendish Partworks Ltd., 1997.

Canby, V. "Five Card Stud." *New York Times*. 1/8/1968 (24:1).

_____. "No Way to Treat a Lady." *New York Times*. 3/21/1968 (56:1).

Cane. "Daughter of Darkness." *Variety*. 2/04/1948.

Clagett, T.D. *William Friedkin: Films of Aberration, Obsession and Reality*. Jefferson, NC: McFarland, 1990.

Clarens, C. *Horror Movies: An Illustrated Survey*. London: Seeker & Warburg, 1968.

Clover, C. *Men, Women and Chainsaws: Gender in the Modern Horror Film*. London: BFI Press, 1992.

Crane, J.L. *Terror and Everyday Life*. Thousand Oaks, CA: Sage Publ., 1994.

Crowther, B. "Born to Kill." *New York Times*. 1/05/1947 (34:2).

_____. "Monsieur Verdoux." *New York Times*. 7/04/1964 (8:2).

_____. "The Sniper." *New York Times*. 5/10/1952 (16:2).

Douglas, J., and M. Olshaker. *Anatomy of Motive*. New York: Pocket Books, 1999.

_____, and _____. *Mindhunter*. London: Reed International Books Ltd., 1996.

Durgnat, R. *Jean Renoir*. London: Studio Vista Press, 1975.

Ebert, R. "The Cell." *Chicago Sun-Times online*. 8/18/2000.

_____. "Outside Ozona." *Chicago Sun-Times online*.

_____. *Video Companion*. London: Bloomsbury, 1997.

Edwards, P. *Shocking Cinema*. Beaconsfield: Mentmore Press, 1987.

Fhaner, B.A. (ed.). *Magill's Cinema Annual 1997*. Detroit: Gale Press, 1997.

Fleming and Manvell. *Images of Madness*. Fairleigh Dickinson. London: Ass. Univ. Press, 1985.

French, K. (ed.). *Screen Violence*. London: Bloomsbury, 1996.

Frentzen, J. "Ulli Lommel: Stranger in Paradise." *Video Watchdog*. #44. 1998.

Gilb. "Psychomania." *Variety*. 12/16/1964.

Gold. "Night Digger." *Variety*. 5/19/1971.

Good, H. *Outcasts: Image of Journalists in Contemporary Film*. London: Scarecrow Press, 1989.

Grant, B.K. "Rich and Strange: The Yuppie Horror Film," in Neale & Smith (eds.). *Contemporary Hollywood Cinema*. London: Routledge, 1998.

Gray, S. *Writers on Directors*. New York: Watson-Guptill Publ., 1999.

Greenspun, R. "Pretty Maids All in a Row." *New York Times*. 4/29/1971.

_____. "See No Evil." *New York Times*. 9/03/1971.

Guthmann, E. "American Psycho Review." *San Francisco Chronicle online*. 4/14/2000.

_____. "Strange Days Review." *San Francisco Chronicle online*. 10/13/1995.

Hall, S. *Critical Business: New Australian Cinema in Review*. Adelaide: Rigby, 1985.

Handy, D. (ed.). *Variety Film Reviews 1907–1980 Vol. 1–16*. New York: Garland Publ. Inc., 1985.

Har. "Eyeball." *Variety*. 11/01/1978.

Hardy, P. (ed.). *Aurum Encyclopedia of Horror*. London: Aurum Press, 1999.

_____. (ed.). *Aurum Encyclopedia of Science Fiction*. London: Aurum Press, 1999 (indicated in text references as *Sci-Fi*).

Harrington, R. "The Dark Half Review." *Washington Post online*. 4/23/1993.

Harvey, D. "American Psycho." *Variety online*. 1/24/2000.

Hege. "Eyes of Laura Mars." *Variety*. 8/02/1978.

Hinson, H. "The Stepfather." *Washington Post online*. 5/29/1987.

Hirsch, F. *Detours and Lost Highways: A Map of Neo-Noir*. New York: Limelight Editions, 1981.

_____. *Film Noir: Dark Side of the Screen*. New York: Da Capo Press, 1981.

Hobe. "Love from a Stranger." *Variety*. 11/05/1947.

Hooper, T., and anon. "Interview — Tobe Hooper." *Austin Chronicle online*. 11/02/1998.

Houghton, N. "Nekromantik I & II." *Redeemer*. 1 (#2). 1996. pp. 51–52.

_____. "Schramm." *Redeemer*. 1 (#3). 1996. pp. 59–60.

Howe, D. "American Psycho Review." *Washington Post online*. 4/14/2000.

_____. "Eye of the Beholder Review." *Washington Post online*. 1/28/2000.

Hunter, J. *Eros in Hell*. London: Creation Books, 1998.

_____. *House of Horror*. London: Creation Books, 1994.

Hunter, S. "Bone Collector Review." *Washington Post online*. 11/05/1999.

_____. *Violent Screen*. New York: Dell Publ., 1995.

Hutchinson, T., and R. Pickard. *Horrors: A History of Horror Movies*. London: Wattle Books, 1983.

Kael, P. *State of the Art*. New York: G.P. Dutton Press, 1985.

Kahn. "Hangover Square." *Variety*. 1/17/1945.

Kaminsky, S.M. *American Film Genres (2nd edition)*. Chicago: Nelson-Hall, 1984.

Kempley, R. "January Man Review." *Washington Post online*. 1/13/1989.

Keppel, R.D. *The Riverman*. New York: Pocket Books, 1995.

Kerekes, D. *Sex Murder Art: The Films of Jorg Buttgereit*. Cheshire: Headpress, 1994.

_____, and D. Slater. *Killing for Culture*. London: Creation Books, 1994.

Krogh, D., and J. McCarty. *The Amazing Herschell Gordon Lewis*. Albany: Fantaco Press, 1983.

Lane, B., and W. Gregg. *New Encyclopedia of Serial Killers*. London: Headline Book Publ., 1996.

Levy, E. "The Cell." *Variety online*. 8/14/2000.

Magill, F.N. (ed.). *Magill's American Film Guide Vol. 1–5*. Englewood Cliffs: Salem Press, 1983.

Matthews, J.H. *Surrealism and Film*. Ann Arbor: Univ. of Michigan Press, 1971.

McCarty, J. *The Fearmakers*. New York: St. Martin's Press, 1994.

_____. *Official Splatter Movie Guide*. New York: St. Martin's Press, 1989.

_____. *Official Splatter Movie Guide Vol. II*. New York: St. Martin's Press, 1992.

_____. *The Sleaze Merchants*. New York: St. Martin's Press, 1995.

_____. *Splatter Movies*. Albany: Fantaco Enterprises, 1981.

McDonagh, M. *Filmmaking on the Fringe*. New York: Citadel Press. 1995.

Medved, M. *Hollywood vs. America*. New York: HarperCollins, 1992.

Mezo. "It Happened in Broad Daylight." *Variety*. 7/23/1958.

Mitchell, E. "The Cell." *New York Times online*. 8/18/2000.

Muir, J.K. *Wes Craven: The Art of Horror*. Jefferson, NC: McFarland, 1998.

Murf. "The Boston Strangler." *Variety*. 10/16/1968.

_____. "Pretty Maids All in a Row." *Variety*. 3/03/1971.

Nash, J.R., and S.R. Ross. *Motion Picture Guide Vols. 1–10*. Chicago: Cinebooks, 1986.

Neale, S., and M. Smith (eds.). *Contemporary Hollywood Cinema*. London: Routledge, 1998.

New York Times Film Reviews 1913–1968 Vol. 1–6. New York: New York Times and Arno Press, 1970.

New York Times Film Reviews 1969–1970. New York: New York Times and Arno Press, 1971.

New York Times Film Reviews 1971. New York: New York Times and Arno Press, 1973.

Newman, K. *Nightmare Movies*. London: Bloomsbury, 1998.

Nichols, B. (ed.). *Movies and Methods Vol. II*. Berkeley: Univ. of California Press, 1985.

Nichols, P. *Fantastic Cinema*. London: Ebury Press, 1984.

Palmineri, L., and G. Mistretta. *Spaghetti Nightmares*. Key West: Fantasma Books, 1996.

Peary, D. *Cult Movies*. London: Vermilion Press, 1982.

Powe. "Step Down to Terror." *Variety*. 9/17/1958.

Prawer, S.S. *Caligari's Children*. Oxford: Oxford Univ. Press, 1980.

Ray, F.O. *The New Poverty Row*. Jefferson: McFarland, 1991.

Ressler, R.K. *I Have Lived in the Monster*. London: Simon & Schuster Ltd., 1997.

_____. *Whoever Fights Monsters*. London: Simon & Schuster Ltd., 1992.

Rich. "And Soon the Darkness." *Variety*. 7/22/1970.

_____. "Assault." *Variety*. 2/24/1971.

_____. "Twisted Nerve." *Variety*. 12/11/1968.

Robe. "Blade." *Variety*. 12/05/1973.

_____. "Driller Killer." *Variety*. 7/04/1979.

_____. "The Todd Killings." *Variety*. 8/18/1971.

_____. "Torso." *Variety*. 11/13/1974.

Schechter, H., and D. Everitt. *A to Z Encyclopedia of Serial Killers*. New York: Pocket Books, 1996.

"Secret Beyond the Door." *Variety*. 12/31/1947.

Sharrett, C. (ed.). *Mythologies of Violence in Postmodern Media*. Detroit: Wayne State Univ. Press, 1999.

Smith, G. "American Psycho." *Film Comment*. 36 (2). Mar-Apr. 2000.

Smith, P.J. *Desire Unlimited: The Cinema of Pedro Almodovar*. London: Verso, 1994.

Stal. "She Wolf of London." *Variety*. 4/10/1946.

Stan. "End Play." *Variety*. 12/24/1975.

Stanley, J. *Creature Features*. New York: Boulevard Books, 1997.

Stephens, B. "1980 crime movie long overdue for re-appraisal." *San Francisco Examiner online*. 5/12/1995.

Stratton, D. *The Last New Wave — The Australian Film Revival*. Melbourne: Angus & Robertson Publ., 1980.

_____. "Redball." *The Australian online*.

T.M.P. "Love from a Stranger." *New York Times*. 11/28/1947 (30:1).

Tasker, Y. *Working Girls*. London: Routledge, 1998.

Thompson, H. "The Todd Killings." *New York Times*. 10/21/1971.

Tohill, C., and P. Tombs. *Immoral Tales*. London: Titan Books, 1995.

Tone. "Whatever Happened to Aunt Alice?" *Variety*. 7/23/1969.

Tube. "Couch." *Variety*. 2/21/62.

Verr. "Possession of Joel Delaney." *Variety*. 5/17/1972.

Werb. "Lizard in a Woman's Skin." *Variety*. 4/21/1971.

Williams, L. *Hardcore*. Univ. of California Press. Berkeley. 1989.

Wilson, C., and D. Seaman. *The Serial Killers*. London: Virgin Publ. Ltd., 1997.

Wood, R. *Hollywood from Vietnam to Reagan*. New York: Columbia Univ. Press, 1986.

_____. "An Introduction to the American Horror Film" in Nichols, B. *Movies and Methods Vol. II*. pp. 195–220.

_____, & M. Walker. *Claude Chabrol*. London: November Books Ltd., 1970.

INDEX

Several names have been spelled differently in the various sources consulted, and some credit listings omit additional initials for some names in certain cases. These apparently common other spellings, additions and alternatives are noted in brackets. Numbers in **bold** refer to photographs.

Aaron, Paul 116
Abbott, Bruce 52
Abbott, John 259
Abbott, L.B. 124
Abel, Gene 375
The Abominable Dr. Phibes 38, 163
Abraham, Edward 300
Abraham, Valerie 300
Abramovitch, Barron 354
Absence of Malice 284
Absence of the Good 33, 102, 380
Absolutely Fabulous (TV) 446
Academy Awards 1, 35, 51, 291
Ace in the Hole 504
Achilli, Sante 182
Ackland, Joss 85, 87
Ackland, Noreen 341
Acosta, Rodolfo 251
Acovone, Jay 104
Across 110th Street 474
Adair, Jean 43
Adams, Andrea 382
Adams, Brandon Quinton 187
Adams, Brooke 115
Adams, Don 519
Adams, Julie 240
Aday, Meat Loaf 57, 334
The Addiction 307, 323
Addis, Keith 163
Adler, Luther 268
Adonis, Frank 157
Adorf, Mario 52
Adrian, Iris 67
The Adventures of Priscilla, Queen of the Desert 154
Afraid of the Dark 34–35, 246, 374

After Alice see *Eye of the Killer*
After Hours 409
agent/controller scenario 9–10, 10n, 303, 345, 422, 431
Agostino, Pierre 212
Aguayo, Jose F. 326
Aguilar, George 409
Ahlberg, Julie Bilson 254
Ahlberg, Mac 215, 438
AIDS 105, 159, 261, 398, 423, 467, 515
Aiello, Danny 231
Ainley, Anthony 44
Airoldi, Christina 58, 475
Alabiso, Eugene (Eugenio) 58, 407
Alaska 292
Albani, Romano 64
Albarn, Damon
Alberoni, Sherry 458
Alberstat, Philip 101
Albert, Arthur 80
Albertson, Eric 170
Albertson, Frank 356
Alcazar, Victor 326
Alda, Rutanya 111
Aldrich, Robert 423, 501, 502, 512
Alessi, Amedio 285
Alexander, Don 512
Alexander, John 43
Alexander, Kari 469
Alexander, Les 41
Alexis, Nora 191
Alford, Chuck 212
Alfredson, Daniel 272
Alghiero, Carlo 58
Alien Nation 164
Alien 3 406

aliens in films 42, 109, 110, 163, 423, 424, 429, 430
Alison, Dorothy 129, 400
Allan, Elizabeth 199
Allar, Daniel 206
Allen, Chad 351
Allen, Joan 273
Allen, Karen 104, 187, **188, 189**
Allen, Keith 326
Allen, Nancy 66, 134, 135, **135**, 250
Allen, Ronald 167
Allen, Simone 168
Allen, Stanford C. 323, 351
Allen, Tobias 91
Allen, Woody 292, 366, 408, 409
Alley, Kirstie 58
Allgood, Sara 256
Allodi, Simonetta 52
Allred, Byron 132
Almereyda, Michael 306
Almodovar, Pedro 281, 282
Altered States 307
Altman, Robert 352, 353, 459
Alvarado, Angela 409
Alvarado, Trini 184–185
Alvarez, Paco 435
Amati, Edmondo 255
Ambach, Clarissa 407
Ambler, Dail 200
Ameri, Alex 191
America see United States of America
American Dreamer 515
American Nightmare 35
American Psycho 35–37, 48, 332, 377, 391, 392
Ameripoor, Alex 512

Ameripoor, Eskander 191, 512
Ames, Leon 303
Amick, Madchen 486, 488
Amiel, Jon 94, 96
Amis, Suzy 306
amnesia 10, 10n, 51, 110, 194, 299, 346
Amor, Christine 65
Amplas, John 279, **280**
Amritraj, Ashok 419
Amsellem, George 148
Amsterdam 37, 38
Amsterdammed 37–38
Amy, George J. 131
Anciano, Dominic 374
Ancona, Amy B. 108
And God Created Woman 352
And Soon the Darkness 38, 44
And Then There Were None 428
Anders, Glenn 268
Andersen, Bibi 281
Andersen, Lotte 308
Anderson, Cletus 111
Anderson, Dave 350
Anderson, Edward 42
Anderson, Hesper 123
Anderson, Jean 316
Anderson, John 356
Anderson, Lindsay 134
Anderson, M.A. 92
Anderson, Michael 49, 50
Anderson, Pamela Lee 307, 308, 419
Anderson, Paul Thomas 445
Anderson, Rikki Louise 308
Anderson, William 235
Andor, Tamas 482
Andre, Jean 315
Andreieu, Andre 302
Andreiev, Andrei 338
Andress, Ursula 476
Andrews, Dana 503, 504, **504**, 505
Andrews, Edward 346
Andrews, Harry 321, 388
Android 33
Angel 38–40, **39**, 117, 132, 438, 468
Angel, Mikel 148, 261
Angel Heart 199
Angelli, Lou 418
Angus, Kristi 234
Anhalt, Edna 420
Anhalt, Edward 75, 77, 420
Animal Farm 295
Ann-Margret 197, 198
Anneman, Bill 97
Ansen, David 107
Ansley, Sara 492
Anspaugh, David 222, 223
Antheil, George 420
Anthony, Carl 417
Anton, Edward 215
Anton, Karl 45
Antonelli, Paul (F.) 333, 377

Antonioni, Michelangelo 53, 58
Anwar, Gabrielle 383
Apartment Zero 40–41, 259, 498
Aphex Twin (band) 144
Apology 41, 485
Applegate, Christina 437, 438
Appleyard, Vera 428
Aprea, John 42
Apstein, Theodore 501
Apted, Michael 59, 60
Aquinas, Thomas 406
Arango, Roman 281
Arcand, Denys 35, 259, 261
Archer, Anne 474
Ardant, Fanny 34
Arden, Mary 61
Argento, Asio 431, 483
Argento, Claudio 121, 455
Argento, Dario 52, 53, 58, 64, 81, 82, 121, 133, 134, 135, 136, 146, 147, 148, 156, 163, 177, 184, 245, 255, 285, 302, 314, 347, 431, 432, 455, 456, 476, 477, 483, 484, 509
Argento, Salvatore 52, 121, 177
Argenziano, Carmen 114
Arguelles, Fernando 430
Arit, Lewis 201
Arizona 81, 507
Arkansas 113, 478
Arlen, Richard 346
Armstrong, Alun 429
Armstrong, Craig 72
Armstrong, Michael 54
Armstrong, Robert 292
Arnell, Richard 54
Arnold, Mal 62, **62**
Arnold, Melbourne 361
Arnold, Tracy 203
The Arousers 41–42
Arquette, David 371
Arquette, Patricia 327
Arquette, Rosanna 163, 223
Arribas, Fernando 167
The Arrival 42–43, 100, 109, 126, 430, 478
Arsenault, Jeffrey 323
Arsenic and Old Lace 43, 121
Art of Dying 43–44, 126, 132, 151, 338, 372, 429
Arton, Anne Catherine 506
Arzner, Dorothy 264
Ascencio, Filberto 445
Ashbrook, Dana 486, 488
Ashe, Eve Brent 158
Asher, Jack 490
Ashlay, Angel 347
Ashton, John 123
Ashton, Vali 125
Asman, Henry 466
Asman, William 466
Asmodeo, James 402
Asner, Edward 472
Assante, Armand 229
Assault 44

Assault on Precinct 13 518
Asseyev, Tamara 42
Assonitis, Ovido G. 285
Asther, Nils 67
Astin, John 185
Athens 58, 59
Atkin, Harvey 496
Atkins, Christopher 125, 162
Atlanta Child Murders 44–45, 88, 123, 203, 217, 334
Attal, Yves 291
Attebury, Jim 393
Attenborough, Richard 447, **448**, **449**, **450**
Attich, Fida 286
Atwater, Edith 71
Atwill, Lionel 131, 304, 305
Auberjonois, Rene 157
Aubrey, Diane 199
Audia, April 323
Audley, Maxine 341
Audran, Stephane 78
Auer, Mischa 92
Auerbach, John 434
August, Chris 252
Augustine, Dana 47
Augustine, Phoebe 488
Aulin, Ewa 167
Ault, Marie 255
Aumont, Tina 475
Austin, Julie 162
Austin Powers (films) 422
Austin Powers: The Spy Who Shagged Me 421
Australia 138, 146, 154, 155, 225, 248, 261, 314, 373, 383, 384, 465, 485, 493
Australian exploitation 65, 249, 333, 386
Australian Film Finance Corp. 485
Australian New Wave 146, 198, 249, 333
Austria 270
Autopsy 476
Avalon, Phillip 485
The Avenger 45
The Avengers (TV) 38, 113
Avery, Paul 520
Avery, Rick 151
Avram, Chris 418
The Awful Dr. Orlof 10n, 45–46, 58, 62, 92, 98, 152, 228, 229, 263, 264
Axelrod, Lisa 90
Axelrod, Nina 103, 293, **294**
Axtell, Kirk 346
Ayers, Clay 497
Ayres, Lew 169, 170
Azevedo, Gilberto 281
Azzopardi, Mario 73

Babcock, Dwight V. 411
Baby Doll Murders 46–47
Bachaus, Jimmy 312

Bachelor, Stephanie 247
Bachmann, Lawrence P. 169
Bachus, Michael 99
Backdraft 47, 168
Bacon, Irving 407
Bacon, Kevin 102
Bacs, Ferenc 482
bad father figure *see* monstrous patriarch
Bad Influence 41, 498
Bad Lieutenant 93, 165, 293, 373
Bad Man's River 326
The Bad Seed 375
Badalamenti, Angelo 486, 488
Badger, Russ 191
Badham, Jennifer 388
Badlands 24, 138, 185, 215, 237, 238
Baer, Willi 151
Baerwitz, Jerry 208
Bafaro, Michael 253
Bahner, Blake 162
Bailey, John (R.) 88, 352
Bailey, Robin 400
Bailey-Gates, Charles 244
Baker, Dylan 82
Baker, Graham 164
Baker, Joe Don 102
Baker, Kathy 232, 288
Baker, Robert 174, 227
Baker, Roy Ward 129
Baker, Scott Thompson 332
Baker, Stanley 255
Baker, Tom 422
Balcon, Michael 255
Baldwin, Daniel 114, 115, 244
Baldwin, Declan 111
Baldwin, Earl W. 131
Baldwin, Howard 380
Baldwin, Stephen 33, 101, 102
Baldwin, William 47, 107, 108
Bale, Christian 36, 37
Ball, Joe 139
Ball, Lucille 264
Ball, Warren 97
Ballance, Jack 418
Ballard, Elise 402
Ballard, J.G. 447
Ballard, Lucien 256
Ballew, Dinese 502, 503
Ballinger, Bill S. 437
Ballis, Socrates 219
Balpetre, Antoine 264
Balsam, Martin 356
Balsam, Talia 99
Balzac 79
Bancroft, Anne 190, 251
Bancroft, Cameron 259, **260**
Band, Charles 42, 99, 101, 292, 366, 478
Band, Richard 42
Banderas, Antonio 281, 282, 313
Bandolero 174
Banes, Lionel 199
The Banker 36, 47–48, 168, 324

Banks, Leslie 292
Baragli, Nino 291
Barbachano, Paolo 119
Barbeau, Adrienne 81, 332
Barber, Glynis 142
Barber, Phil 203
Barbera, Neal 474
Barbour, Jennifer 71
Barcelona 156
Barenholtz, Barry 101
Barenholtz, Ben 48
Baril, Alain 259
Barilla, Joe 60
Barilli, Francesco 510
Barker, Clive 84, 327, 430
Barkin, Ellen 396, **397**, 398
Barn of the Naked Dead see *Terror Circus*
Barnes, Peter 388
Barnes, Priscilla 434
Barnett, Ken 116
Barnette, Alan 330
Barnikel, Philip 319
Barone, Tracy 515
Barquee, Thomas 234
Barrault, Jean-Louis 459
Barrere, Robert 316
Barrow, Carlotta 54
Barrows, Dan 141
Barry, Joan 291
Barry, Raymond J. 93
Barrymore, Ethel 425
Barrymore, John, Jr. 504
Bartel, Paul 141, **141**, 142, 252, 285, 334, 354, 366
Bartkowiak, Andrzej 192
Bartlett, Bonnie 123
Bartlett, Martine 328
Bartok, Bela 71
Bartok, Eva 61
Barton Fink 48–49, **49**, 317, 367, 396
Basic Instinct 347
Bass, Ronald 55
Bassett, Angela 436
Bassett, Craig 328
Bassier, Robert 256
Bassler, Robert 194
Basson, Giuseppe 121
Bateman, Kent 202
Bateman, Michael John 354
Bates, Alan 288
Bates, Charles 407
Bates, Kathy 408
Bates, Ralph 129, **130**
Bathory, Elizabeth 167, 264
Batman (sequels) 145
Bats 168
Battaglia, Gianlorenzo 285
Bauer, Belinda 387
Bauer, Chris 143
Bauer, Steven 419, 420
Baum, Thomas 324
Baumgarten, Alan 377
Baumgartner, Peter 228

Bautista, Aurora 326
Bava, Lamberto 285
Bava, Mario 53, 58, 60, 61, 146, 147, 198, 199, 264, 265, 281, 282, 285
Bavier, Frances 272
Baxley, Barbara 328
Baxter, Les 147, 190
Baxter, Lynsey 221
Bayne, Bruce Davis 249
Bayne, Lawrence 505
Bazelli, Bojan 236
Bazzoni, Luigi 147
Beacham, Stephanie 215, 394
Beal, John 505
Beals, Jennifer 114, 115
Bean, Orson 168
Beascoechea, Frank 71
The Beatles (band) 320
Beattie, Alan 151
Beatty, Ned 235
Beatty, Warren 443
Beauchamp, Wayne 47
Beaudelaire 264
Beauty and the Beast fairytale 166, 272, 414, 464
Beauvy, Nicolas 474
Beccaria, Mario 78
Bechard, Gorman 108, 212, 366
Beck, Christophe 73
Beck, Jennifer 467
Beck, Martha 119, 214; *see also* Fernandez, Raymond
Beckel, Graham 232
Becker, Harold 396, 398
Beckett, Jack 139
Beckles, Gordon 437
Beckley, Tony 44, 167
Beckman, John 289
Beddat, Rodney 447
Beecher, Jeremiah 261
Beecroft, David 367
Begley, Ed, Jr. 141
The Beguiled 502
Behavioral Science Unit (BSU) 22, 25n, 26, 27, 76, 85, 86, 195, 235, 275, 399, 412, 413–414; *see also* FBI
Behm, Marc 269
Bekker, Barry 382
Bel Geddes, Barbara 472
Belden, Charles S. 305
The Believers 153, 350
Bell, Arthur 107
Bell, Elisa 515
Bell, Geraint 43
Bell, James 251
Bell, Keith 193
Bell, Tobin 402
Bell, Tom 134
Bell, Wayne 139, 460
Bellamy, Mark 447
Bellamy, Ralph 514
Belli, Agostino 69
Belloc-Lowndes, Marie 255, 256, 272

Bells 49–50
Belmondo, Jean-Paul 315
Belser, Dean 73
Beltrami, Marco 286, 497
Beltran, Robert 81, 141, 409
Belushi, James 481
Belvaux, Remy 271
Belzer, Richard 424
Benigni, Roberto 291, 292
Bening, Annette 219
Benison, Peter 91, 328
Benjamin, Paul 44
Bennett, Hywel 300, 489
Bennett, Joan 398, 399, 400
Bennett, Joseph 136
Bennett, Marjorie 289
Bennett, Richard Rodney 446
Bennett, Wallace C. 499
Benson, Jay 432
Benson, Jim 41
Benson, Lucille 354
Benson, Sally 407
Bentivoglio, Fabrizio 40
Bento, Max 288
Benton, Edward 393
Benullo, David 107
Benussi, Femi 198
Benzencenet, Peter 227
Beowulf 85
Berdan, Brian 309
Berenbaum, Michael 48
Berenger, Tom 164, 165
Berens, Harols 134
Berenzier, Manuel 304
Berg, Adam 386
Berg, Peter 411
Bergan, Judith-Marie 66
Bergerman, Stanley 500
Bergin, Patrick 154, 383, 384
Bergman, Ram 53
Bergman, Robert 505
Bergqvist, Kjell 273
Berhrman, M.L. 315
Berkeley, Xander R. 241
Berkowitz, David 80, 334, 441,
    442, 520; *see also* Son of Sam
Berlin, Helene 273
Berlin, Michael 80
Berlin Film Festival 227, 455
Berman, Monty 174, 227
Bernard, James 300
Bernardi, Giuseppe 163
Bernhardt, Kevin 234
Bernstein, Charles 38–39, 42
Bernstein, Elmer 400
Bernstein, Peter 197
Bernt, Eric 494
Berridge, Louise 284
Berry, Tom 355, 374
Berryman, Michael 148
Bertolini, Angelo 246
Berwick, Wayne 285
Bessi, Roberto 99
Best Seller 33
Beswick, Martine 129, **130**, 148

Betti, Enrico 270
Betti, Laura 198
Betz, Audrey 289
Bevan, Billy 259
Beverly Hills 46, 332, 333
Beware My Lovely 50–51, 118, 250,
    251, 432
Beyda, Kent 164
Beyer, Ed 474
Beymer, Richard 103, 486
The Beyond 255
Beyond Bedlam see *Nightscare*
Beyond Re-Animator 52
Beyond the Darkness 52
Bianchi, Kenneth 211, 241; *see also*
    Hillside Stranglers
Biberman, Abner 251
Bicat, Nick 200, 374
Biderman, Ann 94
Biehn, Michael 367
Bierman, Robert 41
The Big Easy 398
The Big Heat 505
The Big Night 227
The Big Valley (TV) 512
Bigelow, Kathryn 24, 253, 436
Bigelow, Lynn 91
Bigwood, Joseph 66
Bilcock, David 146
Billingsley, Peter 118, **119**
Bills, Teddy 459
Bingham, Barbara 81
Binns, Edward 511
Birch, Derek 199
Birchall, Robert 519
Bird, Antonia 371, 372
The Bird with the Crystal Plumage
    52–53, 121, 122, 135, 136, 147,
    177, 285, 483
Birdsong, Lori 65
Birney, David 352
Biroc, Joseph 124, 501, 511
Bisacco, Robert 475
Bischoff, Samuel 437
bisexuality 75, 125, 129, 163, 192,
    204, 253, 287, 340, 378, 381,
    489, 497; *see also* homosexuality
Bishop, Carol 365
Bishop, Dan 59, 481
Bishop, Jennifer 219
Bishop, Terry 99
Bissell, Whit 173
Bissett, Jacqueline 124, 427
Bittaker, Lawrence 224, 241
Bitterman, Shem 401
Black, Isobel 447
Black, Karen 101, 148, 168, 333
Black, Stanley 174, 227
Black and White 53–54, 198
Black Angel 10n
Black Day, Blue Night 335, 410
Black Panther 54–55
Black Rainbow 458
The Black Torment 98
Black Widow 27, 55–57, **56**, 155, 351

Blackburn, Richard 141
Blackman, Honor 113
Blacktop 57
Blade (1972) 57–58, 316
Blade of the Ripper 58
Blade Runner 286, 287, 430
Bladerunner see *Blade Runner*
Blaine, Vivian 109
Blainey, Sue 154
Blair, Mark 92
The Blair Witch Project 272
Blake, Peter 300
Blake, William 276
Blakeslee, Richard 492
Blanc, Michel 291
Blanchard, Terence 441
Blane, Michel 292
Blanke, Henry 305, 345
Blanks, Jamie 24
Blatty, William Peter 149, 150
Blaylock, Leyton 92
Blewitt, David 363
Blezard, John 229
Blick, John 184
Blind Date 53, 58–59, 60
Blind Terror see *See No Evil*
blindness 34, 35, 59, 101, 155, 157,
    193, 194, 232, 233, 234, 265,
    267, 316, 381–382, 400
Blink 53, 59, 59–60, **60**
Bloch, Robert 99, 356, 362
Blocker, David 59
Blodgett, Michael 207
Bloecher, Michael 172
Blood and Black Lace 58, 60–61,
    147, 199
Blood and Wine 55
Blood Diner 64, 65, 142
Blood Feast 19, 61–64, **61**, **62**, **63**,
    101, 279, 512
Blood for Dracula 416
Blood Link 64–65, 231
Blood Salvage 65
Blood Simple 335, 353
Bloodlust 373
Bloodmoon 65
Bloodrage 66
Bloodsucking Freaks see *Incredi-
    ble Torture Show*
Bloodthirsty Butchers 66
Bloody Countess see *The Female
    Butcher*
Bloom, David 374
Bloom, Eric L. 156
Bloom, George Arthur 416
Bloom, John 55, 316
Blossier, Patrick 130
Blossom, Roberts 123
Blow Out 24, 66–67, 117, 191, 378
Blow Up 66, 121
Blown Away 168
Blue Holocaust see *Beyond the
    Darkness*
The Blue Man 375
Blue Steel 24

Blue Sunshine 57
Blue Velvet 233, 404, 486
Blue Vengeance 67, 217
Bluebeard (legend) 46, 262, 289
Bluebeard (1944) 67–68, 399
Bluebeard (1963) 68–69, **68**, 79, 289, 291
Bluebeard (1972) 69–71, **70**, 79, 422
Bluebeard's Castle 71, 345
Blumenthal, Andy 411
Bluto, John 418
Blyth, David 215
Boam, Jeffrey 115
Bochner, Hart 40, 41
Bode, Ralf 134
Bodison, Wolfgang 151, 177
Bodnia, Kim 308
Body Double 67, 165
Body of Evidence 71
The Body Snatcher 71–72, 127, 176
Boehm, Carl 281, 341, **342**, **343**
Boemler, George 169
Bogart, Peter 91
Bogner, Ludek 355, 435
Bogosian, Eric 423
Bohem, Leslie 215
Bolam, James 134
Bolger, Katy 396
Bolkan, Florinda 133, 255
Boll, Uwe 391
Bollinger, Alun 184
Bolognini, Manolo 147
Bolster, Anita 259
Bolton, Lyn 62
Bolton, Michael 208
Bonacelli, Paolo 431
Bonaduce, Danny 118
Bond, Christopher 446
The Bone Collector 27, 29n, 72–73, 74, 97, 112, 161, 206, 245, 380, 398, 406, 435, 497
Bone Daddy 73–74, 482
Bones, Ken 229
Bonet, Charlie 133
Bonet, Lisa 114
Bonezzi, Bernardo 281
Bonfire of the Vanities 439
Bonnie and Clyde 214–215
Bonuglia, Maurizio 147
Bonvillain, Michael 502
Bonvoisin, Berangere 131
Bonzel, Andre 271
Boogie Nights 445
Boomerang 15
Boone, Mark, Jr. 335
Boorman, John 149
Booth, Anthony 98
Borchers, Donald P. 38
Borden, Belinda 393
Borden, Lizzie 440
Borden, Ross 393
Borelli, Franco 227
Born to Kill 14, 72, 74–75
Bornedal, Ole 308, 327, 328

Bornstein, Charles 363
Borromeo, Christian 435
Borske, John 66
Borsos, Philip 283, 284
Bosanquet, Simon 33
Boschero, Dominique 510
Bose, Lucia 167
Bosson, Barbara 81
Boston Film Festival 370
"The Boston Strangler" *see* De-Salvo, Albert
The Boston Strangler 19–21, 21, 22, 26, 28, 38, 75–78, **76**, 77, **78**, 83, 86, 88, 112–113, 125, 126, 176, 177, 266, 267, 268, 273, 330, 437, 447, 449
Bostwick, Barry 71, 351
Boswell, Simon 136
Bota, Rick 190
Botsford, Sara 49
Bottoms, Joseph 58, 332
Bottoms, Timothy 161, 384
Le Boucher 10n, 42, 69, 78–80, 126, 165, 193, 272, 344, 459, 514
Bouchet, Barbara 133
Boudu Saved from Drowning 459
Boulting, Roy 489
Boulting brothers 489
Bound 55
Bourke, Terry 248, 249, 333, 386
Bourne, Mel 273
Boutross, Tom 478
Boutsikaris, Dennis 219
Bowen, David R. 400
Bowey, John R. 352
Bowie, David 488
Bowling, Dave 113
Boxleitner, Bruce 303
Boyack, Selina 446
Boyd, Tim 234, 380, 481
Boyden, Peter 66
Boylan, Tom 323
Boyle, Lara Flynn 486
Boyle, Peter 151, 300
Boyman, Mark 225
The Boys Next Door 80
Bozman, Ron 412
Bracco, Lorraine 481
Bradbury, Ray 247
Braddock, Reb 107
Braddon, Russell 146
Bradford, Richard 283, 316
Bradford, William 346
Bradley, Leslie 272
Brady, Scott 219
Brahm, John 194, 247, 256, 258, 259, 272
Brait, Carla 475
Bralver, Bob 285
Brammer, Sidney 92
Brams, Richard 222
Brana, Frank 346
Brancato, Chris 423, 425
Brand, Neville 139, 140, **140**, 269, 270, 491

Brandauer, James 393
Brandes, Richard 47
Brandis, Jonathan 434
Brando, Jocelyn 432
Brando, Rikki 519
Brandon, Michael 177
Brandon, Peter 501
Brandstaedter, Jutta 510
Brandt, Byron 203
Brandt, Carolyn 212
Brandt, Hank 269
Brandt, Russ 379
Braschi, Nicoletta 291, 292
Brass, Tinto 314, 315
Bratt, Benjamin 409
Braugher, Andre 181
Braun, Zev 428
Braunstein, George G. 158
Braverman, Alan M. 66
Bray, Thom 215
Brayshaw, Edward 193
Brazzi, Rossano 163, 164
Breakdance 302
Breakdown 89, 335
Breaking Point 80
Breaks, Sebastian 316
Brechtian devices 124, 365
Bregman, Martin 72, 396
Bregman, Michael 72
Brendel, Micha 395
Brenguier, Dominique 288
Brennan, Dennis 113
Brennan, Robert 65
Brennan, Sheila 427
Brennan, Walter 491
Brenneman, Amy 202
Brenner, Albert 47
Brenner, Joseph 156, 476
Brenner, Jules 203
Brent, George 425, 426, **426**
Bresin, Marty 303
Breslin, Jimmy 283, 441
Brest, Harry 60
Bretherton, David 396
Brett, Alan 394
Brett, Danielle 234
Brewster, Tony 337
Brialy, Jean-Claude 291
Briant, Shane 134, 333, 485
Bricker, George 411
Bricker, Randy 42
Bridge Across Time 81, 231, 383
Bridge on the River Kwai 430
Bridges, David 114
Briggs, Joe Bob 122
Bright, Matthew 177, 178, 179
Brimley, Wilford 118, 450
Britten, Benjamin 261
Broadway 43
Brochard, Martine 156
Brochero, Eduardo M. 58
Brock, Brian 119
Brock, Ian 435
Brodbin, Kevin 190
Broderick, Beth 409

Brody, Adrien 441, **442**
Brolin, James 75, 151, 374
Brolin, Josh 327, 328
Bronson, Charles 42, 101, 292, 366, 450, **452**, 478
Brooke, Jean 251
Brooklyn 43
Brooks, Conrad 417
Brooks, Louise 338, 339
Brooks, Mel 127, 128
Brooks, Paul 326
Brooks, Randi 93
Brooks, Richard 411
Brooks, Stephen 491
Brooks, Victor 99
Broom, Jeffrey 300
Brophy, Richard 212
Broughton, Bruce 421
Brouwer, Haig 221
Brown, Barry Alexander 441
Brown, Charles D. 176
Brown, David 242
Brown, Eric 493
Brown, Harry 420
Brown, Henry 434
Brown, L.P., III 400
Brown, Pamela 316
Brown, Penny 255
Brown, Reb 387
Brown, Sally 99
Browne, Coral 321, 388
Browne, Robert Alan 361
Browning, Tod 8, 409
Bruce, Richard Francis 404
Bruckheimer, Jerry 91, 92
Brugge, Pieter Jan 202
Brumpton, John 372
Brundin, Bo 202
Brunjes, Ralph 409, 471
Brunot, Andre 345
Brussel, Dr. James 25, 25n, 26, 270
Bryan, Dora 40, 193
Bryant, Chris 427
Bryant, Michael 388
Bryar, Claudia 361
BSU see Behavioral Science Unit
Buba, Pasquale 111, 202, 434, 438
Buchanan, Robert 147
Buck, Jules 388
A Bucket of Blood 68, 202, 390
Buckley, Martina 334
Buckman, Peter 446
Budapest 70
Buehl, Jeffrey 169
Buenos Aires 40
Buff, Conrad 232, 445
Bugliosi, Vincent 203
Buio Omega see Beyond the Darkness
Bujold, Genevieve 154, 297, 467, 468
Bukowski, Bobby 286
Bull Durham 317
Bumstead, Henry 363

Bundy, Ted 23, 25n, 36, 44, 47, 80, 91, 112, 113, 123, 137, 138, 185, 224, 241, 254, 312, 403, 415, 511
Bunuel, Luis 121
Buono, Angelo 211, 212; see also Hillside Stranglers
Buono, Cara 238
Buono, Victor 270, 271, 437
Burchiellaro, Giantito 291
Burdis, Ray 374
Burge, Roy 113
Burgess, Don 323
Burke, Barbara 227
Burke, Chris 186, 215, 394
Burke, Graham 65
Burke, John 422
Burke, John H. 315
Burke, Kathleen 304
Burke, Robert 238
Burke, Robert John 136
Burke and Hare 72, 97, 127, 129, 174, 175, 176, 230, 303
Burke and Hare 72, 176
Burke's Law (TV) 512
The Burning 429
Burns, Catherine 491
Burns, Keith Brian 53
Burns, Marilyn 139, 203, 460
Burns, Robert A. 92, 460
Burr, Jeff 434
Burr, William 434
Burrows, James 340, 341
Burstall, Tim 146, 249
Burstyn, Ellen 300
Burstyn, Thomas 151
Burt, Andrew 54
Burton, Norman 158
Burton, Richard 69, 70, **70**
Burum, Stephen H. 118
Burwell, Carter 48, 236, 363
Buscemi, Steve 48, 91
Busch, Thomas J. 206
Busey, Gary 80, 388
Busey, Jake 185
Bush, Dick 409
Bushell, David 286
Butcher, Kim 186
The Butcher Boy 220
Butkus, Dick 117
Butler, John E. 346
Butler, Michael 49, 50
Butler, William 162
Buttgereit, Jorg 30n, 52, 229, 250, 263, 264, 309, 312, 327, 395, 396
Buttolph, David 345
Buxton, Sarah 253
Byers, Mark 440
Byington, Spring 500
Byrne, Eddie 227
Byron, Carlye 440

The Cabinet of Dr. Caligari 6, 7, 9, 46, 92, 169
Cacho, Daniel Giminez 119

Cadell, Jean 261
Cadell, Simon 221
Café Flesh 41, 253
Cage, Nicolas 91, 143, 144, 145
La Cage Aux Folles 341
Cagney, James 158
Cahill, Kathy Curtis 515
Cain, Sidney 180
Caine, Michael 134, 135, **135**, 229, 230
Cairo 145
Calamari, Stephen 393
Calanai, Clara 121
Calatayud, Roman 255
Calco, Eva 251
Cale, David 169
Cale, John 35
Calendar Girl Murders 81, 99, 148, 191
Calgary 71
Calhoun, Rory, 39, 293, **294**, **296**
California 122, 138, 285, 381, 407, 408, 437, 519
Caligari see The Cabinet of Dr. Caligari
Callahan, Gene 55
Callan, Michael 346
Callaway, Clay 151
Callaway, Tom 90
Calleia, Joseph 264
Calthrop, Donald 261
Calvert, Phyllis 489
Calvert, Toni 62
Cambern, Donn 190, 469
Cameron, James 436
Cameron, Jane 337
Cameron, John 229, 388
Camille, Sharen 364
Camillo, Tony 499
Caminito, Augusto 302
Caminnecci, Pier A. 390
Cammell, China 506
Cammell, Donald 506, 507, 509, 510
Camp, Colleen 117
Campanella, Roy, II 71
Campbell, Douglas 107
Campbell, Eddie 187
Campbell, Gavin 348
Campbell, Graeme 435
Campbell, Julia 388
Campbell, Judy 437
Campbell, Martin 102, 103
Campbell, Nicholas 115, 197, 367
Campbell, Pat 350
Campbell, Stewart 215, 387
Canada 138
Canale, Gianna Maria 264
Candyman 115
Canfora, Bruno 226
Cannes Film Festival 463
Cannibal Apocalypse 500
Cannibal Holocaust 255
cannibalism 1, 20n, 27, 62, 63, 64, 67, 131, 132, 142, 156, 179, 185,

186, 187, 197, 225, 249, 270, 285, 295, 323, 326, 366, 371, 372, 401, 410, 413, 429, 453, 460, 463, 464, 476, 477, 499, 500
Cannon Films 281, 452, 510
Cannonball 142
Canter, Kieran 52
Cantrell, Ray 519
Cape Fear 103, 283
Capelier, Auguste 321
Capitalism 2, 17n, 24, 24n, 36, 48, 97, 142, 191, 270, 291, 332, 335, 391, 392, 464
Capobianco, Carmine 366
Capone, Nadia 505
Capponi, Pier Paolo 407
Capra, Frank 43
Capshaw, Kate 235
Captor, Roxanne Messina 114
The Car 50
Caraeciolo, Joseph M. 143
Cardini, Anna 52
Cardone, J. S., 312, 334, 335, 409, 410, 445
Cardone, Michael 409
Cardos, John "Bud" 42, 108
Cardoza, Manny 519
Carewe, Arthur Edmund 131
Carey, MacDonald 407
Carfagno, Edward 467, 469
Cariou, Len 246, 313
Carlen, John 138
Carleton 381
Carlin, Paul 136
Carlson, Jonathan 223
Carlson, Leslie 123
Carlsson, Ing-Marie 273
Carlyle, Phyllis 404
Carlyle, Robert 371
Carmen, Julie 216
Carmody, Don 192
Caro, Julio 82
Caronia, Vittorio 58
Carpenter, John 24, 42, 157, 173, 226, 429, 496, 518
Carpenter, Russell 246
Carradine, John 67, 68, 240
Carraro, Bill 181
Carreras, Michael 18, 134, 490
Carrey, Jim 292
Carrie 484
Carroll, Charles 515
Carroll, (J.) Larry 460, 477
Carroll, Lewis 462
Carroll, Rocky 163
Carroll-Colicchio, Jeri 441
Carruth, Milton 407
Carruthers, Lito 113
Carry On (series) 44
The Cars That Ate Paris 65
Carson, Jack 43
Carson, L.M. Kit 464
Carstensen, Margit 453
Carter, Brian Frank 366
Carter, Bruce 249

Carter, James L. 132
Carter, Ruth E. 441
Cartier, R. 45
Cartwright, Gary 337
Carver, Brent 103
Casanova 120, 192, 213, 242, 352
Casas, Antonio 513
Case of the Hillside Stranglers see *The Hillside Stranglers*
Caso, Alan 300, 434
Caso, Maria Rebman 497
Cason, Barbara 212
Cassavettes, John 225, **226**
Cassell, Jean-Pierre 288
Cassidy, Elaine 165
Cassidy, Hopalong 158
Cassidy, Joanna 254
Cassinelli, Augusto 302
Cassini, Alexander 430
Castanedo, Rafael 119
Castillo, Tony 163
Castle, Michael D. 132
Castle, William 18, 65, 321, 395
castration 125, 197, 451, 511
Castravelli, Claude 148
The Cat and the Canary 499
Cat in the Brain 81–82, 455, 477
Cat People 124
Cates, Georgina 89
Catholic issues 132, 165, 215–216, 277, 387–388
Catlett, Mary Jo 403
Catto, Max 113
Cattrall, Kim 80, 429
Cauley, Eve 163
Caulfield, Bernadette 300
Caulfield, Maxwell 80
Cavacas, John 57
Cavanagh, Paul 398
Cavani, Liliana 281
Caviezel, Jim 181, 182
Caylon, Rose 169
Cazenove, Christopher 161
Celedonio, Maria 179
Celi, Adolfo 304, 510
The Cell 27, 28n, 29n, 73, 82–85, **83**, **84**, 301, 308, 326, 327, 431, 492, 498, 503
Centerfold Girls 85
Centerfold Murders see *Centerfold Girls*
Cerami, Vincenzo 291
Cerasuolo, Ron 127
Cervi, Antonio 475
Chabrol, Claude 10n, 42, 68, 69, 78, 79, 165, 193, 289, 459, 514
Chakiris, George 337
The Challenge 410
Chamberlain, Richard 49, 50
Chamblee, Robert 240
Champagne, Andree 349
Chan, Dana 323
Chance, Larry 190
Chandler, Karen Mayo 440
Chandler, Knox 168

Chandler, Raymond 15
Chandler, Tanis 264
Chaney, Lon, Jr. 514
Chang, Gary 252
Chapa, Damien 114
Chapelier-Dehesdin, Philippe 130
Chaplin, Charles 68, 71, 79, 289, 290, **290**, 291, 292
Chaplin, Geraldine 101
Chaplin, Josephine 228
Chapman, George 384
Chapman, Lonny 327
Chapman, Michael 497
Chappaquiddick lore 66
Chappell, Crystal 246
Charbanic, Joe 497
Charles, David Orin 428
Charles, Martin 489
Charlie's Angels (TV) 250
Charlton, Robert 241
Charly 211
Charters, Rodney 363
Chase, James Hadley 321
Chase, Richard 280, 367; see also "The Sacramento Vampire"
Chatel, Peter 510
Chattaway, Jay 375
Chaucer 406
Chaykin, Maury 428
Cheek, Molly 118
Cheers (TV) 341
Chegwidden, Ann 38
Chen, Joan 486
Chenut, Jean-Marc 271
Chesier, Lewis 73
Chesney, Arthur 255
Chesser, Chris 151
Chester, Colby 351
Chevalier, Maurice 345
Chewing, Wallace 289
Chicago 60, 81, 169, 203, 380, 455, 497, 514
Chicago Bears 117
Chicago Film Festival 514
Chicago Joe and the Showgirl 518
Chikatilo, Andrei 85, 87, 185
Chiklis, Michael 367
child pornography 144, 179, 502
childhood trauma 29–30, 33, 54, 79, 83, 84, 92, 139, 151, 152, 166, 199, 205, 219, 220, 240, 241, 324, 343–344, 347, 351, 353, 354, 376, 400, 425, 492; see also monstrous patriarch
Children Shouldn't Play with Dead Things 124
Chiles, Lois 107
Chivers, Steven 136
Choi, Patrick D. 380
The Choirboys 324
Chomsky, Marvin 123
Chong, Rae Dawn 164
Chopping Mall 142
Chorney, Jo Ann 114
Chris, Marilyn 212

Christ, Jesus *see* Jesus Christ
Christian, Roger 168
Christie, Agatha 261, 428
Christie, John Reginald 180, 447, 448, 449, 450, 518
Christie, Patricia 374
Christopher, Dennis 158, 159
Christopher, Jean 349
Chubbick, Lyndon 307
Chulack, Fred A. 88
Church, Thomas Haden 402
Chute, David 90
CIA 190, 317
Cicchini, Robert 497
Ciccoritti, Gerard 505
Cimber, Matt 511
Cinema of Transgression (movement) 16n, 123, 323
Cingolani, Luigi 347
Cinieri, Cosimo 302
Cioffi, Charles 469
Cipirani, Stelvio 182
Cirillo, Patrick 151
Citizen X 85–88, **86**, **87**, 185–186, 221, 301, 447
City in Fear 88, 123, 203, 334
City of Lost Children 518
Claes, Marie-Paule 263
The Clairvoyant 88–89, 202
Clark, Bob 123, 124, 297, 296, 297, 299, 441
Clark, Carroll 503
Clark, Dick 108
Clark, Jim 94
Clark, Matt 215, 334, 456
Clark, Susan 297
Clarke, Ged 301
Clarkson, Cindy 372
Clarkson, Lana 58
Class Action 193
Class of 1984 390
Clatworthy, Robert 356
Claus, Hugo 281
Clavel, Peter 323
Clawson, Tim 236
Clay, Nicholas 316
Clay Pigeons 57, 89–90, **90**, 286, 335, 353
Clayburgh, Jill 456
Clayton, John 333
Clem, Jimmy 478
Clemens, Brian 38, 129, 400
Clemento, Steve 292
Clemm, Susanna 134
Cler, Judy 512
Clerici, Gianfranco 133, 302, 314
Clermont, Nicolas 154
Cleveland 418
Cleven, Max 323
Click: The Calendar Girl Killer 90, 99
Cline, Renee 162
Clinton, George S. 80
Cliver, Al 302

A Clockwork Orange 36, 146, 456, 459, 516, 517
Clooney, George 107
Close Encounters of the Third Kind 109
Closer and Closer 91
Clough, John Scott 379
Clouse, Robert 338
Clouzot, Henri Georges 302
Clover, Carol 157, 224
Clover, David 519
Clownhouse 311
Club 54 422, 445
Cmiral, Elia 40
Coates, Nelson 242
Cobe, Sandy 332
Coblentz, James 324
Cobo, Eva 281
Coburn, Charles 264
Cochrane, Rory 53, 163
Cocks, Jay 436
Cocteau, Jean 307
Code of Silence 208
Coe, George 170
Coen, Ethan 48
Coen, Joel 48
Coen brothers 49, 336
Coffey, Colleen 379
Cohen, Herman 101
Cohen, Larry 33, 192, 193, 278, 279, 423, 455
Cohen, Maury M. 92
Cohen, Ronald I. 103
Cohlan, Randolph 323
Cohn, Michael 502
The Cold Light of Day see *In the Cold Light of Day*
Cole, Stan 296
Coleman, Graeme 80
Coleman, Joe 91
Coleman, Lori Jane 123
Coleridge, Tania 367
Colicchio, Victor 441
Colichman, Paul 391
The Collector 242
Collectors 91
Collier, Barry 419, 502
Collinge, Patricia 407
Collins, Deborah 248
Collins, Jack T. 190
Collins, Lisa 372
Collins, Max Allan 151
Collins, Robert 428
Collins, Roberta 42, 511
Collinson, Peter 129, 134, 167, 216, 427, 428
Collyer, Pamela 148
Colombia 43
Colombier, Michel 93
Colombo, Giuseppe 431
The Color of Money 398
Color of Night 379, 481, 482
Coma 458, 497
Combs, Jeffrey 52, 185
"Come to Daddy" (song) 144

Comejo, Faustino 45
Comer, John 262
Comfort, Lance 113
Commando 390
Companeea, Jacques 345
Compulsion 15, 308
Comstock, H.W. 131
Con-Air 91–92, 203
Conaway, Jeff 47
Condemned to Live 92
Condon, Eddie 247
Cone, Buddy 367
Confessional Murders see *House of Mortal Sin*
Confessions of a Serial Killer 92–93, 206
Conlan, Joseph 292
Connell, Richard 292
Connell, Thelma 400
Connelly, Jennifer 110
Connery, Sean 235, 236, **236**
Connick, Harry, Jr. 94, **95**, 235
Connock, Jim 348
Connor, Kevin 293, 295
Connors, Chuck 269, 270, 477, 478
Connors, Michael 474
Conrad, Michael 472
Conrad, Patrick 281
Considine, John 401
Constant, Michelle 382
Constantine, Tom 148
Conti, Pier Luigi 477
Continenza, Sandro 167, 227
Contner, James A. 104
The Conversation 66, 155
Converse, Frank 129
Conway, Dan 222
Conway, Kevin 232
Cook, Bruce 117, 118
Cook, Elisha, Jr. 74, 75
Cook, T.S. 334
Cook, Wayne 491
Cooke, C.J. 325
Cooke, Malcolm 142
Coop, Denys 447
Cooper, Cami 411
Cooper, Chris 432
Cooper, Jeff 416
Cooper, Jeremy 374
Cooper, John C. 199
Cooper, Merian C. 292
Cooper's Bay 65
Coote, Greg 65
Cop 27, 41, 93–94, **94**, 103, 468, 481
Copeland, Maurice 66
Copeland, Stewart 172
Copping, Robin 146
Coppola, Francis Ford 18
Copycat 15n, 17n, 21n, 26n, 27, 29n, 67, 73, 78, 80, 91, 94–97, **95**, **96**, 102, 107, 115, 161, 163, 179, 205, 235, 241, 244, 276, 313, 496, 503

Coran, Patricia 227
Corbett, Harry H. 99
Corbucci, Enzo 147
Corby, Ellen 425, 437
Cord, Alex 386, 387
Cordio, Carlo Maria 285
Corey, Jeff 75, 176
Corll, Dean 241
Corman, Gene 354
Corman, Roger 142, 202, 304, 354, 412, 437, 440
Cormier, Al 458
Cormier, Gerald 458
Cornell, Jonas 272
The Coroner 97
Corpse Fucking Art 313
The Corpse Grinders 66, 97–98
Correll, Charles 223
Correll, Mady 289
Corri, Adrienne 441
Corridori, Giovanni 455
Corridors of Blood 200
Corrigan, Lloyd 259, 411
Corruption 98–99, 176, 441
Corsaut, Aneta 474
Corso, Eugenio 270
Corso, John W. 361
Cort, Bud 333
Cort, Robert W. 172
Cortese, Valentina 147
Cortez, Stanley 398
Corwin, Hank 309
Costanzo, Robert 246
Costigan, George 200
Costner, Kevin 409
Cotten, Joseph 407
Couch 99
Couch, Lionel 319
Countess Dracula 167
Couper, Adam 383
Courant, Curt 289
Courtenay, Tom 321, 322, **322**
Covello, Angela 475
Covent Garden 180
Cover Girl Killer 99, 148
Cox, Brian 190, 242, 273, 286, 287, 413
Cox, Christina 328
Cox, Gregory 193
Cox, Joel 118, 467
Cox, Richard 104
Cozzo, Gianni 99
Crabtree, Toni 156
Craig, Colin 227
Craig, James 504
Crank, David 194
Cranston, Joseph L. 97
"Crash" (novel) 447
Craven, Jessica 411
Craven, Matt 168
Craven, Wes 118, 160, 173, 226, 249, 303, 324, 325, 411, 412, 459, 464, 493, 502
Crawford, Anne 113
Crawlspace 43, 99–101, 228, 478

Craze 101
Craze, Galaxy 306
Creber, William 124
Crechales, Tony 219
Creelman, James A. 292
The Creeper see *Dark Side of Midnight*
Creepshow 111, 296
Cregar, Laird 194, 256, **257**, 258
Crenna, Richard 211
Crescenzi, Antonio 58
Cresciman, Vince 324
Crew, Carl 400
Cribben, Mik 325
Crichton, Michael 456, 458
Crime Time see *Crimetime*
Crimes of Passion 39, 143
Crimetime 88, 101–102, 285, 431
Crimewave 49
Criminal Law 47, 102–103, 390
The Crimson Pirate 427
Crisp, N.J. 300
Crispino, Armando 476
Cristal, Perla 45
Cromier, Gerald 459; *see also* Rudolph, Alan
Cromwell, James 423
Crone, George 251
Cronenberg, David 50, 115, 116, 188, 209, 253, 380, 402, 416, 436
Cronyn, Hume 407
Crooke, Evan 241
Crosby, Bing 129
Crosby, Cathy Lee 109
Crosby, Denise 374
Crosby, Floyd D. 42
Crosby, Gary 324
Crosby, Mary 107
Cross, Roger R. 252
Cross Country 103–104, 286, 299
Crossfire 421
Crouch, Lionel 44
The Crow 110
Crow, Sheryl 286
Crowden, Graham 316
Crowder, Tracy 440
Crowe, Christopher 330
Crowe, Russell 494, **495**, 496
Crowley, Joy 316
Crowther, Bosley 74
Croydon, John 199
Cruickshank, Art 124
Cruising 27, 41, 104–107, **105**, **106**, 125, 145, 150, 161, 235, 278, 289, 341, 370, 376, 398, 467
Crump, Owen 99
Crupa, Howard 323
Crupi, Tony 117, 118
Cry Baby 404
The Crying Game 281
Cula, Joseph M. 38
Cullen, Brett 241
Cullen, Robert 85
Culp, Joseph 42
Culp, Robert 42, 81, 303

Cuman, Maria 182
Cundey, Dean 361
Cundill, Liam 372, 382
Cunneff, Ray 367
Cunningham, Sean S. 24, 215
Cupid 363
Cupid 107
Curdled 107–108, 179
Curi, Angelo 510
Currie, Gordon 153
Curse of Frankenstein 264
Curse of Simba 201
Curse of the Full Moon 66
Curtis, Bruce Cohn 162, 164
Curtis, Jamie Lee 384, 385, 386
Curtis, Keene 57
Curtis, Patrick 422
Curtis, Tony 75, **76**, 77
Curtis, Tony (2) 217
Curtis-Cahill, Kathy 132
Curtiss, Ursula 501
Curtiz, Michael 131, 305
Cusack, John 91, 408
Cushing, Peter 98, 174, 175, 176, 217, 218
Cushingham, jack 499
Cutforth, Mark 113, 193
Cutry, Claudio M. 285
Cutting, Richard 190
Cynical Swing (band) 119
Cypher, John 57
Cyr, Miriam 423
Czerny, Henry 156

Dachman, Alan J. 191
Daddy's Deadly Darling 108
Dafauce, Felix 45
Dafoe, Willem 36, 330, 331, **331**
Dagnen, john 519
D'Agostino, Albert S. 71, 74, 176
Dahl, John 312, 335, 336, 353
Dahl, Roald 316
Dahmer, Jeffrey 92, 400, 447, 520
Dailey, Irene 328
Dale, Jennifer 481
Dali, Salvador 13n
D'Aloja, Francesca 40
Dalton, Timothy 127
Daly, Candice 252
Daly, Tyne 33
Dalzell, Archie R. 491
Damante-Shaw, Susan 346
D'Amato, Joe 52
Dameron, Lisa 320
Damon, Uma 148
Dance, Charles 151
Dance Girl Dance 264
Dance with Death 108
Dancer, Nancy 279
Dancer, Paul 80
Danforth, Logan N. 103
D'Angelo, Beverly 153
D'Angelo, Mirella 40
Daniel, Don 347
Daniell, Henry 71

Daniels, William 264
Danielson, Lynne 333
Dankworth, John 447
Danna, Jeff 435
Danna, Mychael 143, 165, 435
Danner, Blythe 129
Danning, Sybil 69
Dano, Royal 111, 240
Dante 406
Danton, Ray 85
D'Antoni, Phil 104
Danziger, Alle 460
Dara, Max 228
D'Arbanville, Patti 80, 469
Dardick, Ruth 133
Dardill, Eric 271
DaRe, Eric 488
Daring, Mason (K.) 163, 383
The Dark 42, 108–109, 189, 430
Dark City 110–111, **110**, 145, 300, 308
Dark Dancer 108
Dark Eyes of London 45
The Dark Half 111–112, **112**, 515
Dark Ride 112
Dark Side of Midnight 113
Darnell, Linda 194
Darrieux, Danielle 68
Darrington, Mary 520
Darvas, Terry 54
Darwin, Sasha 477
Da Silva, Howard 268
Dassin, Jules 15
Datcher, Alex 151
Daughter of Darkness 113
Daughton, James 58
Dauphin, Claude 345
D'Avak, Massimo 510
Davalos, Raul 409
Davenport, Nigel 341
Davey, Bert 300
Davey, Bruce 165
David, Anthea 372
David, Keith 153
David, Phil 101
David, Pierre 107, 402
Davidge, Donna 366
Davidge, Mathew 402
Davidson, James 113
Davidson, L.W. 193
Davidtz, Embeth 160
Davie, Brian 179
Davies, Jeremy 371
Davies, William 187
Davies, Windsor 348
Davis, Aaron 437
Davis, Andrew 38, 40, 208, 354
Davis, Carl 217
Davis, Charles 125
Davis, Don S. 252
Davis, Essie 383
Davis, Gene 450, **453**
Davis, Jim 219
Davis, Judy 48
Davis, Kristen 57, 300

Davison, Bruce 254
Davison, Davey 437
Davissi, Tamara 119
Dawson, Curt 279
Day, Baybi 136
Day, Cary 485
Day, Don 241
Day, Doris 352
Day, Laraine 169, 170
Day, Lawrence 35
Day, Mark 446
Day, Paul G. 481
Day, Robert 199
The Day After 471
Day of the Animals 466
Dea, Marie 345
Dead Certain 113–114
Dead Connection 114, 506
Dead of Night 299
Dead on Sight 89, 114–115
Dead Ringers 64
The Dead Zone 115–116, 209
Deadline at Dawn 10n
Deadly Blessing 226, 354, 493
Deadly Force 116–117, 372
Deadly Games 117, 133
Deadly Intruder 117–118
Deakins, Roger 48
Dean, Ivor 129, 466
De Angelis, Fabrizio 314
Dearberg, Robert 186
Dearborn, Richard 148
Death Line 500
Death Penalty see *The Satan Killer*
Death Race 2000 142, 354
Death Trap see *Eaten Alive*
Death Valley 118–119, **119**
Death Watch 59, 101
Death Wish 43, 154, 451, 452
Deathdream see *Dead of Night*
Deathmaker see *Totmacher*
Deaver, Jeffrey 72
De Beauregard, Georges 68
Debney, John 351
de Borman, John 113, 193, 301
Decae, Henri 321
Decay 119
DeChalonge, Christian 130
De Concini, Ennio 146
de Cordova, Pedro 92
DeCoteau, David 387
Dedieu, Jean Charles 142
Dedmond, Lisa 203
Dee, Ruby 44
Deeb, Hatwig 394
Deep Crimson 119–121, 214
Deep Red 53, 121–122, **122**, 147, 483
Deeply Disturbed 122–123
The Deer Hunter 43
Defait, Jean-Luc 244
DeFelice, Gregory 333
de Frank, Bob 136
deGrasse, Robert 71, 176, 247, 251

DeHartog, Jan 366
DeHaven, Carter 149, 423
Dehn, Paul 321
Dehner, John 190, 240
Dein, Edward 251
de Jesus, Louie 224
De Keyzer, Bruno 34
Delair, Suzy 302
Delaney, Delvene 146
Delaney, Kim 91, 402
DeLaurentiis, Dino 115, 194, 273
DeLaurentiis, Raffaella 47
DeLaurentiis, Suzanne 148
Delerue, Georges 340
Delia, Joe 136
D'Elia, Lucia 52
Deliberate Stranger 88, 113, 123, 203, 217, 334
Delicatessen 518
de Lint, Derek 281
Dellay, Alan 224
Delli Colli, Alessandra 314
Delligan, William 351
Delon, Nathalie 69
de Los Rios, Waldo 304
DeLouise, Michael 439
Del Rosario, Linda 313
del Ruth, Roy 9, 345
Del Ruth, Thomas 293
Delusion 89, 353
DeMartino, Alberto 64
de Mendoza, Alberto 58, 255
Dementia 13 18
Demme, Jonathan 412, 413, 414, 415, 502
Demon Seed 507, 510
DeMornay, Rebecca 42, 47, 192, 313
de Moss, Darey 337
DeMunn, Jeffrey 85
Denault, Jim 306
Dench, Judi 441
DeNiro, Robert 47, 165
Denison, Anthony John 328
Dennehy, Brian 212, 471, 472
Dennen, Barry 252
Denner, Charles 68, **68**, 315
Dennis, Jennifer Vian 335
Dennison, Tim 326
Densham, Pen 47
Deodato, Ruggero 255
DePalma, Brian 24, 53, 66, 67, 134, 135, 136, 165, 250, 361
De Paolo, Dante 61
DePrez, Therese 441
Deranged 16, 123–124, 133, 167, 202, 358, 415, 463
Derbyshire, Richard 113, 301
Dern, Bruce 503
DeRoche, Everett 249, 384
De Rouin, Colin 168
Derwin, Mark 148
De Sabata, Eliana 146
DeSade 218
DeSalvo, Albert 19, 26, 75, 90, 437

de Santis, Orqides 227
De Simone, Ria 477
DeSimone, Tom 149
Desire 124
Deskin, Andrew 35
Desormeaux, Jean 73
De Souza, Steven E. 47
Despeaux, Jean 302
Desperate Characters 349
Detective (Godard) 289
The Detective 75, 124–125, 126, 170
Detour 24
Devane, William 109, 246
Devil *see* Satan and Satanism
Devil Doll 201
The Devil 666 see *Satan Returns*
The Devil's Advocate 211
The Devil's Commandment see *Lust of the Vampire*
Devil's Playground 65
Devine, Colleen 246
Devine, Dennis 119
De Vorzon, Barry 149
de Vries, Marius 154
Dewhurst, Colleen 115
de Wolf, Karen 92
De Wolff, Francis 490
Dexter, Alan 432
de Young, Cliff 164
Diabolik 199
Diamant, Moshe 316
Diamond, David 437
Diamond, Marcia 123
Diary of a Mad Housewife 403
Diary of a Serial Killer see *Rough Draft*
Dibdin-Pitt 446
Di Berardo, Ennio 57, 503
Diberti, Luigi 431
diCaprio, Leonardo 37
DiCenzo, George 149, 203
Di Cicco, Bobby 46
Dick, Nigel 114
Dickens, Joanna 221
Dickinson, Angie 134, 135, 351
Dickinson, Desmond 167, 441
Di Concini, Ennio 69
Didden, Sjoerd 37
Didio, Tony 474
Die Hard 446
Die Screaming Marianne 395
Die Watching 125–126, 162
Diehl, John 39, 335
Dierkop, Charles 386
Diessl, Gustav 338
Dieterle, William 499
Dietrich, Erwin 228
Dietz, Frank 307
DiGiacomo, Franco 177
Dilley, Leslie 149
Dillinger 480
Dillon, Kevin 484
Dillon, Paul **60**
Diminico, John 484

Dinallo, Gregory S. 81
di Nardo, Mario 147,
Dinelli, Mel 50, 51, 425, 432
Dingle, Charles 247
Di Niese, Denyck 333
Di Palma, Carlo 291, 408
Di Paolo, Dante 147
Dirty Harry 22, 78, 125, 126–127, 137, 170, 174, 235, 252, 420, 467, 469, 520
DiSanti, John 156
Disanto, Byrnadette 434
Diskant, George E. 50
Disneyland 464
di Stefani, Marco 81
The Disturbance 127
Divine 334
Djurkovic, Maria 515
Dmytryk, Edward 16, 69, 70, 71, 79, 268, 420, 421, 422
Do the Right Thing 442, 443
Dobbs, James 219
Dobbs, Lem 110
D'Obici, Valeria 285
Dobkin, David 89
Dobson, Anita 326
Dobson, Peter 185
Docker, Peter 372
The Doctor and the Devils 72, 127–129, **128**, 176
Dr. Cook's Garden 129
Dr. Jekyll and Mr. Hyde (book) 10, 11, 459
Dr. Jekyll and Mr. Hyde (Tracy) 299
Dr. Jekyll and Sister Hyde 129–130, **130**, 142, 194, 218
Dr. Petiot 20n, 25n, 71, 130–131, 150, 291
Dr. Phibes (films) 69
Dr. Phibes Rises Again 38
Doctor X 131–132, 305
Dodd, Patrick 47
D'Offizi, Sergio 133
Dogstar (band) 498
Doherty, Matt 421
Donaggio, Pino 66, 99, 134, 313, 316, 483
Donahue (TV) 475
Donahue, Troy 90
Donat, Mark 502
Dondertman, John 168
Donnelly, Dennis 474
Donnelly, Tim 474
Donner Party incident 371
D'Onofrio, Vincent 82, **83**, **84**, 436
Donovan, Martin 40, 306, 307
Don't Answer the Phone 132–133, 334
Don't Go in the House 133
Don't Look Now 121
Don't Open the Window 167
Don't Torture the Duckling 133–134, 255

Doonan, Tony 99
doppelganger motifs 6, 8, 11, 11n, 127, 231, 468; *see also* Jekyll/Hyde motifs
Dor, Karin 519
Dorff, Matt 91
Doria, Enzo 510
Dorn, Dolores 345
Dors, Diana 101
Dotrice, Michele 38
Douglas, Gordon 124, 125, 170
Douglas, John 45, 76, 378, 412
Douglas, Michael 48
Douglas, Robyn 340
Douglas, Sarah 43
Dourif, Brad 113, 149, 157, 168, 327, 483
Dow, Nancy 219
Dowling, Jonathan 491
Down, Lesley-Anne 44
Down and Out in Beverly Hills 333
Down By Law 292
Downe, Allison Louise 61
Downey, Deborah 137
Downey, Robert, Jr. 219, 309
Downing, Aaron 366
Doyle, Chris 358
Doyle, Christopher 502
Doyle, Maxine 92
Drache, Heinz 45
Dracula (Bram Stoker book) 514
Dracula (1931) 8, 159, 304
Drago, Billy 207
Drake, Charles 432
Drake, Paul 137
Drasnin, Robert Jackson 129
Draven, Jamie 284
Dreamscape 83, 355, 434
Dreffke, Martin 108
Dressed for Death 134
Dressed to Kill 53, 67, 129, 134–136, **135**, 361
Drews, Berta 226
Dreyfuss, Richard 491
Driller Killer 136, 164, 202, 439
Driver, Charla 43
Dronot, Pierre 281
drug use 10n, 12, 64, 98, 129, 130, 142–143, 218, 436, 437
Drummond, Alice 331
Dryden, Raymond M. 117
Drye, Jenny 271
Dubin, Steve 93
Dublin 446
Dubovsky, Dana 389
Duchovny, David 236, 237, 238
Duckworth, Donna 212
Ducsay, Bob 162
Duddleston, Amy 358
Dudgeon, Neil 284
Dudikoff, Michael 285
Dudley, Anne 244
Duel 386
Duerrenmatt, Friedrich 221, 226

Dufaux, Guy 154
Duff, Howard 504
Duffy, Robert 82
Dugan, John 460
Duke, Forest 212
Dukes, David 170
Dullea, Keir 58
Dun, Tan 160
Dunaway, Faye 157, 170, 262
Duncan, Lindsay 374
Duncan, Neil 301, 429
Duncan, Patrick 254
Dunham, Duwayne R. 486
Dunk, Albert J. 225
Dunn, Andrew 200
Dunn, Michael 304, 328
Dunning, Ruth 54
Dunnock, Mildred 427, 501
Dunphy, Barbara 115, 216
DuPont, Rene 296
DuPre, Peter 156
DuPre, Susan 335
Dupuis, Matthew 374
Durkin, Bill 48
Durning, Charles 93, 387, 388
Dury, Ian 429
Duscha, Ina 45
Dust Devil 136–137, 324, 410
Dutton, Charles S. 41
Dutton, Syd 361
Duvall, Robert 124
Dye, Cameron 333
Dying Time 137–138
Dysart, Richard 456
Dzundza, George 252, 423

Early, Mary Jane 202
Easdale, Brian 341
Easter, Robert 474
Eastman, Spencer 316
Eastwood, Alison 53, 467
Eastwood, Clint 94, 126, 129, 137, 467, 468, **468**, 469
Easy Prey 138–139, 286
Easy Rider 24
Eaten Alive 65, 139–140, **140**, 270, 459, 465
Eating Raoul 141–142, **141**, 354, 366, 404, 422
Eatwell, Brian 497
Eberhardt, Norma 381
Ebert, Roger 60, 82, 231, 297, 307, 335, 518
EC comics 133, 225, 278, 295–296, 347
Eckert, John M. 225
Economou, Michael 474
Edelamn, Randy 85
Edge of Sanity 142–143, **143**
Edinburgh 72, 176
Edmonds, Don 323
Edward, Marion 384
Edwards, Ben 41
Edwards, Blake 99
Edwards, Chris 429

Edwards, Eric Alan 89
Edwards, Glynn 348
Edwards, Henry 437
Edwards, Stephan (Steve) 388, 389
Edwards, Vince 269
Egan, Eddie 334
Ege, Julie 101
Egoyan, Atom 165
Egurrola, Julieta 119
8MM 43, 126, 143–145, 168, 208, 253, 392, 406, 429, 493, 519
Eilbacher, Lisa 216, 450
Einbinder, Scott 334, 409
Einhorn, Richard 156
Einstein, Charles 503
Eis, Egon 482
Eisenstein, sergei 499
Ekins, Bud 116
Ekman, Gosta, Jr. 273
Elaine 66
Elam, Jack 416
Elcar, Dana 75
El Dorado 238
El Dorado 174
Electric Boogaloo 302
The Element of Crime 145
The Elephant Man 128
Eles, Sandor 38
Elfman, Danny 35, 177, 184, 358
Elias, Hector 116
Elizondo, Hector 334
Elliott, David 349, 497
Elliott, James 248
Elliott, John 512
Elliott, Mike 108, 168
Elliott, Sam 168
Elliott, Stephan 155
Ellis, Bret Easton 36
Ellis, Chris 497
Ellison, Joseph 133
Ellroy, James 93
Elphick, John 174
Else, Jon 241
Elsom, Isobel 262, 289
Elwes, Cary 242
Elwes, Cassian 230, 252, 506
The Embalmer 145–146
Emerson, Keith 302
Emmerich, Noah 181
Emmerich, Toby 181, 182
Empire Pictures 101
End of Days 394
End Play see *Endplay*
Endacott, Paul 301
Endplay 91, 146, 384
Engel, Alexander 390
Engelbrechy, Nostanze 482
Engels, Robert 488
English, John 346
Ennis, Michael 46
Epstein, Julius J. 43
Epstein, Philip G. 43
Eraserhead 367
Erbe, Micky 91

Ercy, Elizabeth 422
Erickson, Carl 305
Erickson, Glenn 325
Erlich, Gretel 42
Erman, John 44
Ermey, R. Lee 185, 404, 445
"erotic thriller" movement 47, 124, 125–126
Ervin, Jim 384
Erwig, Diana 416
Escape from Alcatraz 469
Escape from New York 496
Escher 298
Eshley, Norman 215, 400
Espindola, Patricia Reyes 119
Esposito, Jennifer 441
Estrada, Blanca 326
Estrin, Eric 80
The Eternal Jew 268
Eure, Wesley 474
Europe 38, 45, 145, 381, 482
European horror motifs 10n, 46, 58, 145, 148, 152, 222, 245, 250, 264, 282, 300, 347, 503, 514
Evans, Art 507, 509
Evans, Blake T. 384
Evans, David Mickey 332
Evans, Edith 101
Evans, Fiona 193
Evans, Gene 416
Everett, Gimel 208
The Evictors 480
Evigan, Greg 440
Evil Dead (trilogy) 463
Evil Eye 146–147, 199
Evil Fingers 117, 147–148, 407
Evil Judgement 148
Evil Obsession 148
Evil Spirits 148–149
The Evil That Men Do 452
Ewart, James 301
Existenz 436
The Exorcist 220, 349, 369, 370
Exorcist II: The Heretic 149
The Exorcist III 149–151, **150**, 160, 173, 289, 327
The Expert 151, 255, 390
Exquisite Tenderness 151–153, 244, 245, 246
The Exterminator 278, 468
Exton, Clive 319, 447
Eye for an Eye 151, 153–154, **153**, 156, 179, 446
Eye of the Beholder 57, 108, 154–155, 348, 420
Eye of the Killer 155–156
Eyeball 156, 476
Eyes of a Stranger 156–157, 334
Eyes of Laura Mars 157–158, 300
Eyes Wide Shut 392
Eyes Without a Face 45, 58, 98, 152, 264, 503
Eymesz, Thea 453

Fabares, Shelley 491
Fabbri, Ottavio 52
The Face at the Window 158
Fade to Black 43, 158–159, 330
Fagan, Ronald J. 81
Fahey, Jeff 222, 363
Fairbrass, Craig 326
Fairchild, Morgan 515
Fairfax, Deborah 186
Faison, Frankie 194, 412
Faithful, Marianne 101
Falconer, Douglas 481
Falk, Jonas 273
Falk, Rossella 147
Falkenberg, Paul 265
Fall Guy 10n
Fallen 150, 160–161, **160**, **161**, 173, 182, 226, 289, 333, 346, 412
Falling Down 145
Fame 302
Fancher, Hampton 286, 287
Fanci, Dan 224
Fantasia, Share 445
The Fantasist 161–162
fantasy (role of) 2, 3, 12, 12n, 18–19, 23, 28–31, 30n, 34, 35, 54–55, 60, 67, 82, 83, 84, 85, 100, 101, 102, 107, 114, 117, 121, 124, 144, 147, 159, 162, 167, 169, 183, 186, 188, 189, 198, 206, 214, 217, 222, 231, 234, 238, 244, 245, 246, 247, 249, 250, 251, 255, 259, 261, 264, 269, 275, 276, 277, 279–280, 282, 284, 285, 287, 289, 302, 312, 318, 319, 325, 327, 329, 332, 333, 338, 343, 348, 353, 354–355, 358, 361, 370, 375, 378–379, 389, 392, 396, 399, 400, 405, 420, 423, 431, 433, 434, 448, 454, 455, 468, 483, 488, 490, 491, 492, 501, 506, 508, 511, 515, 516
Fapp, Daniel L. 173
Farbrother, Pamela 186
Farentello, Nick 127
Farentino, James 365
Fares, Debi 515
Fargo 89
Farin, Michael 476
Farina, Dennis 211, 212, 273, 438
Farmer, Gary 435
Farmer, Mimsy 177
Farrell, Amy 191
Farrell, Glenda 305
Farrell, Neil 371
Farrington, Debbie 54
Farrow, Mia 400, 401, 408, 409
Fasant, I. 418
Fassbinder, R.W. 447, 453, 454
Fast, Alvin 139
Fatal Attraction 434, 485, 510
Fatal Charm 162
Fatal Exposure 162–163
Fatal Frames 163
Fathers and Sons 163, 182

A Father's Revenge 71
Faulkner, James 101
Faust, Victoria 247
Fawcett, Charles 264
Faye, Randall 158
Faylen, Frank 420
FBI 7n, 18n, 22, 25n, 26, 27, 45, 76, 85, 86, 89, 137, 138, 139, 196, 223, 224, 235, 273, 275, 301, 351, 353, 367, 371, 377, 378, 380, 389, 391, 402, 406, 412, 418, 445, 446, 478, 480, 486, 488
Fear (1990) 164
Fear (Foley) 485
Fear City 108, 132, 136, 164–165, 168, 437, 440
Fear in the Night 134
Fear No Evil 247
Febre, Louis 402
Feil, Gerald 201, 415
Feindel, Jockey A. 67
Feinstein, Alan 216
Feldman, Corey 148
Feldman, Dennis 423
Felicia's Journey 165–167
Felix, J.P. 142
Fell, Norman 440
Felperlaan, Marc 37
The Female Butcher 167, 264
female serial killer 56, 57, 108, 113, 154–155, 183–184, 282, 313, 326, 332, 347–348, 351, 353, 366, 403, 420, 421, 445
Femina Ridens see *The Frightened Woman*
Fenech, Edwige 58
Fenn, Rick 507
Fenn, Sherilyn 334, 486
Fennell, Albert 38, 129
Fenton, Frank 247
Ferdin, Pamelyn 474
Ferguson, Kathleen 325
Ferguson, Matthew 259
Ferita, John 493
Fernandes, Joao 352
Fernandez, Angel Luis 281
Fernandez, Anita 131
Fernandez, Juan 252
Fernandez, Raymond 119, 214; see also Beck, Martha
Fernandez-Mila, Miguel 58
Ferone, Pasquale 78
Ferrando, Giancarlo 475
Ferrara, Abel 93, 136, 164, 202, 307, 373, 438, 439
Ferrer, Mel 139
Ferrer, Miguel 488
Ferri, Elda 291
Ferrier, Tim 383
Ferrini, Franco 483
Ferris, Paul 422
Festa, Al 163
Fiander, Lewis 129
Fichtner, William 494

Fiedel, Brad 59, 81, 324, 438
Fiedler, John 403
Field, Chelsea 136, 419
Field, Kevin 270
Field, Sally 153
Field, Shirley Ann 341
Field, Ted 172
Field of Dreams 317
Fielder, John 94
Fielder, Pat 381
Fields, Adam 371
Fields, Joel 216
Fienberg, Gregg 114, 488
The Fiend 167
Fiends of the Nephilim (band) 137
Fiennes, Ralph 436
Fierstein, Harvey 41
The Fifth Cord see *Evil Fingers*
52 Pick-Up see *52 Pickup*
52 Pickup 429, 493
Fight Club 57, 406
film noir (and neo-noir) 10, 10n, 13n, 14n, 15, 39, 43, 44, 50, 55, 59, 74, 89, 103, 113, 155, 164, 169, 170, 173, 187, 205, 234, 251, 258, 259, 278, 299, 303, 305, 307, 312, 317, 331, 335, 353, 367, 404, 420, 421, 425, 432, 455, 468, 481, 497, 512,
Final Combination see *Dead Connection*
Final Cut 168, 270
Final Judgement 168
Final Rinse 168–169
Finan, Tom 515
Finch, Jon 180
Fincher, David 97, 145, 351, 404, 406, 498
Fine, Russell 331
Finetti, Anthony 439
Fingers at the Window 169–170
Fink, Harry Julien 126
Fink, R.M. 126
Finlan, Gary 162
Finlay, Frank 44, 297, 441, 489
Finley, William 139
Finnerman, Gerald Perry 499
Finney, Albert 319, 320, **320**
Finney, Gavin 326
Fiore, Gianni 325
Fire, Richard 203
Fireman, Joseph 132
Firestarter 390
The First Deadly Sin 170–172, **171**, 208, 334
The First Power 150, 160, 172–173, 226, 324
Firth, Colin 40, 41
Firth, Peter 506
Fischer, Kai 519
Fish, Nancy 149
A Fish Called Wanda 232
Fishburne, Lawrence 235, 236, **236**

Fisher, Albert 123
Fisher, Frances 351
Fisher, Gerry 149, 400
Fisher, Joely 503
Fisher, Steve 354
Fisher, Terence 490, 491
Fitzgerald, Anne 107
Fitzgerald, Geraldine 64
Fitzpatrick, Richard 234
Five Card Stud 173–174, 416
Flanders, Ed 149
Flannery, Erin 225
Flannery, Seamus 49
Flashdance 302, 418
Flatliners 145, 209
Flatman, Barry 138
Fleder, Gary 242, 244
Fleischer, Richard 15, 19, 38, 54,
    55, 75, 78, 176, 180, 268, 400,
    401, 437, 447, 449
Fleming, Lone 326
Fleming, Rhonda 425, 503
Flender, Rodman 367, 437, 440
The Flesh and the Fiends 72, 127,
    174–176
Flesh for Frankenstein 404, 416
Fletcher, Louise 494
Fletcher, Page 35
Fleury, Clive 485
Fliesler, Joseph R. 338
Flood, Gerald 186
Florance, Sheila 146
Florey, Robert 303, 304
Florimont, Eugene 418
Flower, George Buck 511
Fluegel, Darlanne 80, 374, 418
Flynn, John 33, 34
Foden, Tom 82, 358
Fog see *A Study in Terror*
The Fog 226
Foley, James 485
Foley, John M. 264
Folk, Robert 409
Follow Me Quietly 176–177
Fonda, Henry 20, 21, 26, 28, 75,
    76, **78**, 177
Fonda, Peter 306, **306**
Fondato, Marcelo 60
Fonseca, Gregg 438
Fontaine, Jean 417
Forbes, Michelle 236, 238, 284
Forbstein, Leo F. 131
Force, Lewis 200
Forced Entry see *Last Victim*
Ford, Derek 98, 441
Ford, Donald 98, 441
Ford, Maria 168, 440
Ford, Ruth 474
Ford, Wallace 407
Foree, Ken 162
Foreign Legion 118
Foreman, Carl 430
Foreman, Ron 261
Foriscot, Emilio 58
Formosa, Ric 485

Forrest, Brett 301
Forrest, Christine 111, 279
Forrest, Frederic 123, 483
Forrest, Sally 504
Forrest, Steve 238, 345
Forstater, Mark 161
Forster, Robert 47, 48, 334, 335
Forsyth, Rosemary 501
Forsyth, Stephen 198
Forsythe, William 378, 494
Fort Apache the Bronx 420
Fort Smith 113
Fortunato, Ron 163
Fortune, Roger 503
Fos, Antonio 326
Foster, Barry 180, 489
Foster, Byron J. 97
Foster, Gloria 44
Foster, Jodie 195, 196, 223, 408,
    412, 413, **414**, 415
Foster, Meg 146, 375, 377, 434,
    471, 499
Foster, Norman 71
Foster, Preston S. 131
Four Flies on Grey Velvet 53, 177
The 400 Blows 179
Fowler, Gene, Jr. 503
Fowler, Marjorie 272
Fox, Angel 42
Fox, James 34
Fox, John 382
Fox, Michael J. 184, **184**, 185, **185**
Fox, Robbie 421
Fox, Sidney 303
Fox, Ted 252
Foxcroft, Lex 248
Fraisse, Robert 85
Fraker, William A. 240
Frakes, Randall 389
France 38, 68, 315, 345
Franciosa, Anthony 455
Francis, Carole 99
Francis, Freddie 18, 101, 127, 128,
    129, 319
Franckh, Pierre 476
Franco, Jess 10n, 45, 46, 58, 62,
    98, 100, 167, 228, 229, 234, 281,
    282, 326, 390, 391
Franco, Ramon 116
Franju, Georges 45, 46, 58, 98,
    503
Frank, Ben 132
Frank, David M. 207
Franke, Christopher 151
Frankenheimer, John 137, 270,
    352, 425, 429
Frankenstein 131, 304
Frankenstein Created Woman 129
Franklin, Billy 393
Franklin, George 225
Franklin, Pamela 38
Franklin, Richard 249, 333, 361,
    362, 384, 386
Franklyn, John 38
Franz, Arthur 420

Franz, Dennis 66, 134, 361
Frappier, Roger 259
Fraser, Brad 259
Fraser, Duncan 374
Fraser, Eric 502
Fraser, Hugh 229
Fraser, John 394, 441
Frazier, Jimmy B. 151
Freaks 383
Freas, Dianna 481
Freda, Riccardo 264, 265
Freebie and the Bean 125
Freeman, J.E. 94
Freeman, Jonathan 380
Freeman, Morgan 27, 44, 57, 170,
    242, **242**, **243**, 244, 380, 404,
    405, 406
Freeman, Robert 261
Freemasons 297
Freeway 156, 177–179, **178**, 179,
    286, 438
Freeway 2 179–180
Fregonese, Hugo 272
Freiburger, Jim 450
Freilino, Brian 250
French, Edward 325
The French Connection 104
Frenzy 180–181, **181**
Frequency 161, 181–182
Fresnay, Pierre 302
Fresnell, Robert, Jr. 272
Freticelli, Franco 121, 291
Freud, Sigmund 111, 218, 297, 471
Freund, Karl 303
Frey, Sammi 55
Friberg, Ulf 273
Fricker, Brenda 421
Friday the 13th 24, 193, 215
Friday the 13th Part 3D 416
Fried, Gerald 381, 501
Friedenn, Neva 474
Friedhofer, Hugo 354
Friedkin, William 104, 105, 106,
    107, 149, 277, 341, 367, 368, 369,
    370, 371
Friedlob, Bert E. 503
Friedman, David F. 61
Friedman, Peter 59
Fries, Tom 81
Friese-Greene, Claude 437
The Frightened Woman 38,
    182–184
The Frighteners 184–186, **184**, **185**
Frightmare 186–187, 215, 216, 270,
    325, 394, 422, 423
Frisina, Hibah Sherif 300
Frisk 107
Fritz, Walter 67
Frizzi, Fabio 81
Frobe, Gert 226
From Beyond 152
From Dusk Till Dawn 107
From Hell 187
Fromkess, Leon 67
Frost, Mark 486

Frost, Sadie 101
Frost, Warren 364, 486
Fryer, Robert 75
Fuchs, Herbert 228
Fuchs, Matthias 476
Fuchsberger, Joachim 519
Fuest, Robert 38, 44, 129, 167, 216
The Fugitive 446
Fuhrer, Martin 446
Fujimoto, Tak 412
Fulci, Lucio 35, 58, 81, 82, 133, 134, 146, 156, 163, 202, 255, 285, 302, 314, 315, 387, 418, 440, 455, 475, 476, 477
Full Moon (studio) 42
Fuller, Fleming B. 353
Fuller, Parmer 325
Fuller, Robert 501
Fulton, Red 132
Fun 179
Funhouse 139, 464
Furie, Jonathan 484
Furrer, Urs 129
Fury 505
Fusco, Maria Pia 69
F/X 386

G-String Murders (novel) 247
Gabel, Martin 268
Gacy, John Wayne 80, 91, 92, 185, 212, 334, 471, 472, 502
Gaillard, Jacques 68, 78
Galeen, Henrik 499
Galik, Denise 340
Gallego, Gina 116
Galligan, Zach 107, 355
Gallo, Fred 246
Gallo, Vincent 179
Galloway, Sheri 92
Gallu, Sam 466
The Game 406
A Game of Death 293
Gammell, Robin 73
Gammon, James 82
Gandolfini, James 143, 144, 160
Gannon, Dennis 301
Gantillon, Simon 345
Ganzino, Davide 409
Gaos, Lola 167
Garcia, Andy 232, 233, **233**, 234, 283
Garcia, Angel 127
Garcia, Ron 486, 488
Garciadiego, Paz Alicia 119
Gardner, Arthur 381
Garfield, Allen 33, 325, 417
Garfield, Brian 432
Garfield, John David 394
Garland, Glenn 53, 168
Garnes, Earl 337
Garofalo, Janeane 89, 286, 287
Garrett, Berkley 92
Garrett, Hank 80
Garrett, Leif 47
Garris, Mick 363, 364, 365

Garrity, Joseph T. 172
Garroni, Andrew 151, 277
Gaslini, Giorgio (George) 123, 418
Gassner, Dennis 48
Gastaldi, Ernesto 58, 475
Gatsby, Jill 151
Gaudio, Tony 262
The Gauntlet 50
Gavin, John 356
Gay, John 328
Gazzara, Ben 441
Geary, Karl 306
Gedrick, Jason 47, 435
Geels, Laurens 37
Geeson, Judy 326, 447
Gein, Ed 16, 36, 123, 358, 415, 463, 466
Geissler, Dieter 510
Geleng, Antonello 431
Gelin, Daniel 288
Gelin, Xavier 288
Gell, Frank 161
Geller, James J. 262
Gemma, Guiliano 455
Gendron, Pierre 67
Generation X 35, 238, 259, 306, 308, 377, 435
Genn, Leo 186, 255
Genoves, Andre 78
Gentner, Richard 238
Gentry, Curt 203
George, Christopher 346
George, Clara 328
George, Gotz 476
George, Linda Day 346
George, Susan 229, 422
Georgiadis, A. 326
Georgiadis, P. 326
Gerber, Fred 91
Gere, Richard 193
Germany 5, 9, 270, 453
Gerolmo, Chris 85
Gerrard, Henry 292
Gerrish, Flo 132
Gersak, Savina 285
Gershon, Gina 53
Gerstad, Harry 425
Gertsman, Manny 411
Gerzo, Bunther 251
Get Carter 458
Gethers, Stephen 211, 212
Geto Boys (band) 447
Ghost in the Machine 187–190, **188**, **189**, 215, 494
giallo films 35, 37, 38, 53, 58, 61, 64, 121, 133, 134, 135, 146, 147, 148, 156, 163, 177, 183, 184, 193, 200, 255, 277, 282, 285, 302, 314, 315, 347, 351, 407, 418, 432, 440, 455, 474, 476, 477, 483, 509, 510, 519
Gianasi, Rick 163
Giannini, Giancarlo 194
Gianviti, Roberto 133, 407
Gibb, Cynthia 230

Gibbons, Cedric 169, 317
Gibbons, Rodney 374
Gibbs, Ann 354
Gibson, Thomas 259
Gicca, Enzo 270
Gielgud, John Sir 297
Gien, Joseph 324
Gilbert, Herschel Burke 503, 511
Gilbert, Ron 216
Gilberti, Nina 378
Gilford, Gwynne 158
Gill, John 319
Gillen, J. 123
Gillette, Pierre 315
Gillin, Hugh 361
Gilling, John 174, 175, 176
Ginn, Jeff 73
Ginnever, Jodi 107
Ginsberg, Claire 285
Ginsburg, Robert 246
Giovannini, Giorgio 147
Giraud, Roland 288
Girdler, William 459, 466, 467, 518, 519
The Girl in Black Stockings 190
Girl in the Red Velvet Swing 15
Gislason, Tomas 145
Gittens, George 251
Gjurokovic, Natasha 350
Gladiator 496
Gladwin, Joe 319
Glas, Uschi 407
Glasgow, William 501
Glasser, Isabel 151, 152
Glatman, Harvey 132, 264, 519
Glatstein, Bert 99
Gleason, James 43
Gleason, Paul 316
Gleason, Russell 92
Glen or Glenda 417
Glendinning, Hone 158
Glenn, Scott 47, 330, 409, 410, 412, **414**, 418
Glennon, James 223
Glickenhaus, James 418, 419; *see also* Shapiro/Glickenhaus
Glickenhaus, Jesse Cameron 418
Glimcher, Arne 235
The Glimmer Man 117, 190–191, 378
Globus, Yoram 207, 281, 464
Glover, Danny 445, 446
Glover, John 41
Glover, Julian 466
Glynn, Carlin 316
Goblin (band) 121, 347
Godard, Jean-Luc 289
Goddard, Bill 197
The Godfather 147
Godfrey, Derek 193
Godfrey, Peter 190
Goebbels, Josef 268
Goff, John F. 323
Goi, Michael 148
Golan, Menahem 207, 281, 464

Goldberg, Jason 262
Goldblum, Jeff 163, 208, 209, 288
Golden, Robert 430
Goldenberg, Billy 44, 203
Goldenberg, William 85
Goldeneye 103
Goldenthal, Elliot 202, 219
Goldfinger 113
Goldman, William 328
Goldner, Lynn 335
Goldoni, Lelia 466
Goldsmith, Jerry 102, 124, 361
Goldsmith, Jonathan 496
Goldstein, Eric 307
Goldstein, Leonard 251
Goldstein, William 411
Goldwyn, Samuel 387
Goldwyn, Tony 242, 481
Golia, David 387
Golin, Larry 114
Golin, Steve 114
Gomez, Andreas Vicente 281
Gomez, Nick 67
Gonclaves, Helder 481
Gone in 60 Seconds 238
Gonzales, Conrad M. 40, 483
Gonzalez, John 43
Good, Peter B. 162
The Good Son 375, 434
Goodlet, Ken 146
Goodman, David Zelag 157
Goodman, Gregory 114
Goodman, John 48, **49**, 160, 396, 398
Goodman, John B. 407
Goodwin, Ron 180
Goorwitz, Allen *see* Garfield, Allen
Gorcey, David 430
Gorcey, Leo 430
Gord, Ken 428
Gordon, Bert I. 269
Gordon, Dorothy 199
Gordon, Gavin 305
Gordon, Keith 134, 135
Gordon, Mark 481
Gordon, Ruth 501
Gordon, Stuart 42, 152, 292
The Gore-Gore Girls 191–192
Gorini, Arianna 61
Gorman, Cliff 39, **39**
Gornick, Michael 279
Gorshin, Frank 169
Goth culture 137, 149, 307, 402
Gothard, Michael 229
Gothic 127
Gottlieb, Mallori 107
Gould, Elliott 325
Goyer, David S. 110
Grabol, Sofie 308
Grade, Lew 349
Graham, Lauren 327
Graham, William A. 81
Grainer, Ron 319
Grammon, Francis 46

Granger, Farley 418
Granillo, Guillermo 119
Granstedt, Greta 381
Grant, Cary 43
Grant, Faye 231, 481
Grant, Lee 496
Grant, Monty 217
Grant, Richard E. 221
Grass, Steve 162
Grau, Jorge 167
Graumann, Walter 293
Graver, Gary 90, 148, 149, 386, 387, 474
Gray, Bruce 197
Gray, Charles 321
Gray, John 190
Gray, Rebecca 97
Gray, William 103
Grayson, Diane 400
Grazer, Brian 47, 358, **360**
Greece 58
Green, Bruce S. 216
Green, Hilton A. 361, 363
Green, Lewis 114, 313
Green Bush, Billy 123, 367
Greenan, David 415
Greenberg, Adam 450
Greenberg, Ed 396
Greenberg, Jerry 134
Greenberg, Stephen 310
Greenburg, Dan 300
Greene, Danford B. 240, 340
Greene, Ellen 163, 238
Greene, Eve 74
Greene, Glenn 502
Greene, Vanessa 515
Grefe, William 219
Gregg, Christina 99
Gregory, Laura 429
Gregson, John 321
Gregson-Williams, Harry 506
Grey, Frances 284
Gribble, David 330
Grice, Grimes 349
Grier, David Alan 179, 330
Grier, Pam 402, 420
Gries, Tom 203
Griest, Kim 273
Griffin, Ted 371
Griffith, Hugh 101
Griffith, Melanie 164, 165
Griffith, Tracy 172
Griffiths, Leon 174
Griggs, Jeff 80
Grimaldi, Dan 133
Grimm, Douglas K. 249
Grip of the Strangler see The Haunted Strangler
Grisham, John 154, 310
Grizzard, George 123
The Grizzly 466
Grodnik, Daniel 310
Gronquist, Don 492
Groom, Jim 326
Groom, Sam 117

Gross, Arye 401
Gross, Frank 432
Gross, Holger 207
Gross, Jack, Jr. 499
Gross, Steve 42
Grossman, Karen 285
Grossmann, Georg 6
Grot, Anton 131, 305
Grumann, Francis 137
Grundgens, Gustav 265
Guardino, Harry 126
Guerrieri, Lorenza 182
Guerrini, Giacomo 52
Guerrini, Mino 147
Guest, Cliff 127
Guffey, Burnett 420
Guida, Wandista 264
Guilfoyle, Paul 176, 219
Guilty as Charged 330
Guilty as Sin 192–193
Guinness, Alec 330
Guintoli, Neil 206
Gulager, Clu 81
Gulino, Christina 366
Gull, William 230
Gun Crazy 24, 138
Gunn, James 74, 247
Gunn, Joseph 216
Guns of Navarone 430
Gunton, Bob 190
Gurevitch, Steve 234
Guzman, Luis 72
Gwynne, Fred 408
Gwynne, Michael C. 456

Haag, Romy 281
Haarmann, Fritz 6, 10n, 29, 271, 453, 476
Haas, Lukas 246
Haber, David M. 123
Hack, Shelley 432
Hackett, Joan 456
Hackford, Taylor 211
Haden, Sara 411
Haeussler, Richard 519
Hagen, Ross 90
Haid, Charles 93
Haines, Donald 430
Haines, Francis 429
Hainey, Daniel 35
Hairspray 404
Haitkin, Jacques 378, 411
Hajos, Karl 500
Hale, Binnie 261
Hale, Jonathan 346
Hale, Ken 203
Haley, Mike 212
Halfpenny, Jim 519
Hall, Arch, Jr. 97
Hall, Conrad 55, 232
Hall, Huntz 430
Hall, Kenneth J. 125
Hall, Melanie 366
Hall, Peter 313

Hall, Philip Baker 153
Hall, Scott H. 62
Hall, Zooey 217
Haller, Barbara 226
Haller, Ernest 304
Hallier, Lori 328
Halligan, Dick 164
Halligan, Tim 502
Halloween 24, 157, 202, 386, 395, 415, 480, 497
Halloween 2 497
hallucination 59, 111, 122, 127, 215, 220, 228, 240, 247, 282, 307, 363, 379, 399, 431, 491, 492, 499, 509, 510, 520
Halsey, Brett 81, 477
Halsey, Clayton 125
Halsey, Colleen 421
Halsey, James 44
Halsey, Michael 350
Halsey, Richard 421
Halsted, Dan 177
Haman, Richard Y. 293
Hamill, Mark 285
Hamill, Pete 428
Hamilton, Hale 292
Hamilton, Murray 75, 328, 474
Hamilton, Patrick 194
Hamlisch, Marvin 231
Hammer, Robert 132
Hammer films 44, 46, 98, 129, 134, 142, 167, 175, 194, 201, 299, 422, 466, 490
Hammill, Ellen 133
Hammond, Peter 227
Hamori, Andras 313
Hampshire, Susan 319
Hampton, Janice 187, 403
Hampton, Sanford 384
Hamsher, Jame 309
Hanan, Michael 363
Hanbury, Victor 113
Hancock, Sheila 319
Hanczakowski, Agatha 208
Hand of Death 193
The Hand That Rocks the Cradle 42
The Handmaid's Tale 253
The Hands of Orlac 132
Hands of the Ripper 129, 193–194
Handy, James 53
Haney, Daryl 108
Hangover Square 194
Hanks, Tom 201, 202
Hanley, Chris 35, 177, 179
Hanley, Daniel 47
Hanna, Ed 197
Hannah, John 168
Hannay, Charles 333
Hannay, David 333
Hannibal 1, 20n, 27, 57, 125, 194–197, **195**, **196**, 413, 415
Hansel and Gretel fairytale 187
Hansen, Gunnar 460, **461**
Hansen, James 323

Hansen, Lisa (M.) 377, 378
Hansen, Robert 292
Hanson, Curtis 41, 42
Hanson, Tom 519
Happiness 261
Happy Face Murders 197–198, 324, 333
Hardcore 39, 43, 143, 164, 168, 253, 278
Harding, Ann 261
Harding, John Wesley and the Sons of Bitches (band) 335
Hardware 136, 430
Hardwicke, Sir Cedric 256, 264
Hardy, Robin 161, 162
Hark, Tsui 338
Harkins, John 367
Harmody, Ron 158
Harmon, Mark 123
Harmon, Robert 312
Harper 329
Harper, Tess 102
Harrelson, Woody 309
Harris, Brad 270
Harris, Burtt 104
Harris, Ed 153, 235, 236
Harris, Jack H. 157
Harris, James B. 93, 94
Harris, Jared 306
Harris, Jo-Ann 117
Harris, Lynn 404
Harris, Moira 161
Harris, Robert 500
Harris, Thomas 29n, 114, 273, 327, 402, 412, 502
Harrison, Gregory 428
Harrison, John K. 49
Harrison, Kathleen 317
Harron, Mary 35, 36, 37
Hart, Christina 203
Hart, Christine 269
Hartford-Davis, Robert 98, 167
Hartkoxicz, Irek 334
Hartley, Hal 307
Hartman, Phil 421
Hartsniker, Tanneke 37
Harvey 13
Harvey, Laurence 499, 500
Harwood, Ronald 127, 128
Hasler, Emil 265
Hasselhoff, David 81
Hatchet for a Honeymoon 198–199
The Hatchet Man see *Nature of the Beast*
Hatfield, Hurd 75
Hathaway, Henry 14, 173
Hathcock, Jeff 323
Hauer, Rainer 453
Hauer, Rutger 73, 429
The Haunted Strangler 199–200, 258
Hauser, Wings 43, 44, 116, 117, 337, 338, 372, 393
Hausmanis, Andris 352
The Hawk 200

Hawkins, Jack 388
Hawkins, Timothy 156
Hayashi, Hikaru 493
Hayers, Sidney 44
Hayes, Isaac 168
Hayes, Robert 332
Hayes, Steve 469
Hayman, David 200
Haynes, Jayne 335
Haynie, Jim 230
Hays Code 2, 14n, 18, 74
Haysbert, Dennis 286
Hayward, Chad 248
Hayward, Lillie 176
Hazekamp, Rene A. 447
Hazelton, Phillip 518
He Kills Night After Night After Night 200–201, 348
He Knows You're Alone 201–202, 334
Head, Edith 247
Headless Eyes 202
Heald, Anthony 143, 412
Healy, Cindy 393
Healy, Matt 89
Heard, Howard 409
Heard, John 474
Hearn, George 446
Hearst, Patty (Patricia) 403,404
Heat 202–203, 276, 498
Heath, C. Ernst 57
Heath, Hilary 102
Heath, Laurence 293
Heatherton, Joey 69
Hebb, R.R. 299
Heche, Anne 358, 359, 361
Heckart, Eileen 328, 329
Hedaya, Dan 177, 467
Hedley, Jack 314
Hedlund, Brett 234
Heidnik, Gary 244
Heim, Alan 94
Heirens, William 13, 13n, 55, 504, 505
The Heiress 51
Helfrich, Mark 438
Helgenberger, Marg 197, 198, 423, 424
Heller, Jack 99
Heller, Otto 341
Hellraiser 81
Helm, Anne 99
Helmond, Katherine 246
Helps, James 326
Helter Skelter 88, 123, 203
The Helter Skelter Murders 520
Hembrow, Mark 333
Hemingway, Mariel 283
Hemmings, David 121, **122**, 297, 298, **298**
Henderson, Don 506
Henderson, Ena 162
Hendricks, Evelyn 320
Hendrickson, Stephen 153
Heneker, David 490

Hengge, Paul 407
Henkel, Kim 460, 466
Henley, Elmer Wayne 91, 241
Henley, Jack 430
Henman, Ray 248
Henricksen, Lance 215, 232, 233, 310, 311, **311**, 354
Henriksen, Scott 401
Henry see Henry: Portrait of a Serial Killer
Henry, Buck 141
Henry, Leonard 158
Henry, Mike 518
Henry, Noble 234
Henry, Victor 422
Henry: Portrait of a Serial Killer 55, 69, 92, 93, 112, 132, 167, 202, 203–206, **204**, **205**, 207, 235, 263, 271, 277, 278, 288, 301, 398, 403, 429, 454
Henry: Portrait of a Serial Killer 2 — Mask of Sanity 92, 217, 206–207
Hensleigh, Jonathan 91
Henstridge, Natasha 423, 424
Hentsch, Jurgen 476
Herbert, Percy 167
Hering, Jutta 407, 519
Hernandez, Rubio 323
Hero and the Terror 207–208, **208**, 262
Heroux, Claude 496
Herrera, Anthony 515
Herrero, Jorge 390
Herrington, Rowdy 230, 231, 438
Herrman, Edward 118
Herrmann, Bernard 194, 316, 356, 358, 363, 489
Hershenson, Joseph 432
Hertzberg, Paul 377, 378
Herzbrun, Bernard 247
Herzner, Norbert 244
Hesch, Gottlieb 338
Heschong, Albert 71
Heslenfeld, Arnold 221
Hess, Oliver 33
Hessler, Gordon 304
Hewett, Robert 146
Hewitt, Jon 372, 373
Heyman, David 371
Heyward, Louis M. 304
Heywood, Pat 447
Hickey, William 75, 396
Hickox, Anthony 234
Hickox, Douglas 234
Hicks, Catherine 118
Hickson, Joan 261
The Hidden 430
Hideaway 208–211, **210**, 494, 495
Hieronymous, Richard 261
Higby, Mary Jane 212
Higgins, Douglas 138, 151
High Noon 430
High Road to China 172
Highlander 381

Hill, Debra 115
Hill, Dennis 92
Hill, Douglas 200, 348
Hill, James 441
Hill, Leonard 216
Hill, Michael 47
Hilliard, Richard 365
Hillman, William 346
The Hills Have Eyes 118, 459, 464
Hillside Stranglers 128, 133, 217; *see also* Bianchi, Kenneth and Buono, Angelo
The Hillside Stranglers 133, 211–212, 217
Hilton, George 58
Hinde, Madeline 167
Hines, Gregory 330, **331**
Hines, Suzanne 179
Hiney, William 81
Hinman, W.B. 346
Hipp, Paul 163
Hirsch, Paul 66
Hirschfelder, David 485
Hitchcock, Alfred 12, 13, 14, 15, 16, 17, 18, 19, 53, 73, 136, 146, 180, 181, 255, 256, 258, 259, 262, 272, 287, 356, 358, 359, 361, 362, 395, 407, 408, 427, 432, 434, 485
Hitchcock, Patricia 356
Hitchcock's Mystery Magazine (journal) 386
The Hitcher 312, 335
Hitler, Adolf 322
Hitzig, Rupert 325
Hobbs, Julian P. 91
Hobbs, Rebecca 491
Hobby, Amy 306
Hoblit, Gregory 160, 161, 181, 182
Hobson, Valerie 500
Hodge, Kate 124
Hodges, Ken 44, 388, 427
Hodges, Mike 456, 458
Hodiak, John 262
Hoenack, Jeremy 112
Hoenig, Dov 110, 202, 273
Hoesli, John 400
Hoey, Dennis 411
Hofflund, Judy 143
Hoffman, David 57
Hoffman, Margaret 289
Hoffman, Thom 221
Hoffmann, G.G. 390
Hoffmeyer, Stig 308
Hogan, Susan 138
Hoimark, Peter 145
Hoist, Per 145
Holbeck, Joachim 308, 327
Holcombe, W.L. 365
Holden, Marjean 440
Holder, Chris 118
Holland 38
Holland, Byrd 458
Holland, John 190, 506
Holland, Tom 162, 325, 361, 362

Hollywood 42, 43, 48, 92, 125, 141, 202, 206, 259, 268, 309, 315, 327, 331, 386, 394, 398, 401, 421, 422, 424, 445, 496, 512
Hollywood Madam see Lady in Waiting
Hollywood Strangler see Don't Answer the Phone
The Hollywood Strangler Meets Skid Row Slasher 212
Holman, Clare 34
Holmes, Gerry 328
Holmes, Jack H. 164
Holmes, Taylor 50
Holocaust 2000 65
Holten, Bo 145
Holton, Nigel 307
Holyfield, Evander 65
Homicidal 18, 65
Homicide: Life on the Street (TV) 373
homosexuality 14, 27, 36, 41, 80, 86, 103, 104, 105, 106, 107, 125, 127, 133, 134, 146, 156, 174, 206, 239, 255, 259, 284, 311, 321, 336, 340–341, 361, 371, 378, 388, 398, 453, 454, 455, 456, 472, 474, 476, 485, 489, 498, 501–502
Honess, Peter 153
Honeycutt, Kirk 168
The Honeymoon Killers 64, 119, 212–215, **213**
Hong, James 55
Hong, Wilson S. 519
Hong Kong 338, 393, 394
Honnold, Nancy 269
Hooks, Robert 491
Hool, Lance 450
Hooper, Tobe 108, 124, 139, 140, 240, 270, 295, 424, 459, 460, 462, 463, 464, 465, 466
Hoosiers 223
Hootkins, William 136
Hoover, Richard 327
Hope, Harry 270
Hope, Margot 316
Hopkins, Anthony 194, **195**, **196**, 235, 412, 413, **414**, 415
Hopkins, John 296
Hopkins, Miriam 394
Hopper, Dennis 24, 55, 464
Hordern, Michael 349
Horie, George 252
Horneff, Wil 187, **188**
Horner, Chris 303
Horner, Harry 50, 51, 251
Horoks, Zbigniew 131
Horror Express 326
The Horror of Party Beach 365
Horror Show 215
Horvitch, Andy 80
Hoskins, Bob 165, 166
Houck, Joy N., Jr. 320
Houde, Germain 352

Hough, John 225
Houle, Norman 394
House 215
House of Fright see *The Two Faces of Dr. Jekyll*
House of Mortal Sin 187, 215–216, 387–388, 394
House of Usher 264
House of Wax 305, 345, 390
House of Whipcord 187, 215
House III see *Horror Show*
Houseman, John 49, 50
Houston 502
Houston, Donald 441
Houston, Renee 174
Houston Astros 317
Hoven, Adrain 390
Howard, Andy 384
Howard, Clint 47
Howard, Duke 409
Howard, Esther 74
Howard, James Newton 153, 235, 330
Howard, Jeffrey 445
Howard, John 262
Howard, Paul 315
Howard, Ron 47
Howard, Sandy 38, 80, 116, 352
Howard, Trevor 101
Howell, Hoke 90
Howes, Reed 417
Howitt, Louise 248
Howland, Chris 390
Hoy, Maysie 177
Hoy, William 72
Hsu, V. 337
Hubbs, Gil 81
Hubley, John 268
Hubley, Season 352, 434
Hudson, Ernie 497
Hudson, Gary 156, 402
Hudson, Rock 351, 352
Hudson Hawk 439
Huff, Shawn 33
Huggins, Erica 187, 403
Huggins, Jere 367
Hughes, Albert 187
Hughes, Allan 187
Hughes, David 326
Hughes, Helen 225, 496
Hughes, Prince 347
Hull, Henry 500
Hull, Josephine 43
Hume, Alan 229
Hummel, Richard K. 246, 378
Humphries, Tessa 333
Huneck, John 47
Hungary 143, 482
Hunnicutt, Gayle 427
Hunt, Helen 222, 223
Hunt for the Night Stalker 212, 216–217
Hunter, Clark 89
Hunter, Holly 94
Hunter, John 103

Hunter, Martin 236
Hunter, Tab 42, 334
Huntington, Joan 501
Hurd, Gale Anne 445
Hurley, Elizabeth 326
Hurley, Joseph 356
Hurndall, Richard 217
Hurst, Brandon 303
Hurt, John 340, **341**, 447, **448**
Hurt, William 110
Hurwitz, Tom 241
Hussein, Waris 349
Hussey, Olivia 364, 365
Huston, John 303
Hutchings, Jeanine 300
Hutchinson, Bill 146
Hutchinson, Josephine 432
Huth, Harold 436
Hutton, Brian G. 170, 171, 172
Hutton, Lauren 164
Hutton, Timothy 111, **112**
Hyams, Peter 411
Hyde, Jacquelyn 109

I Come in Peace 430
I Confess 292, 387
I Dismember Mama 217, 417
I Know What You Did Last Summer 327
I, Monster 98, 142, 217–218, 490
I Spit on Your Grave 136, 157
I, Vampiri see *Lust of the Vampire*
Ibold, Douglas 330
Ice House 218–219
Images 403
Imi, Tony 215
Imperiolo, Michael 331, 441
impotence 87, 261, 277, 447
Impulse 64, 219
In Cold Blood 89
In Dreams 208, 219–220
In the Cold Light of Day 93, 133, 221–222, 227, 511, 514
In the Company of Darkness 222–223
In the Deep Woods 223–224
In the Folds of the Flesh 183
In the Heat of the Night 330
In the Realm of the Senses 494
incest 35, 54, 146, 193, 203, 224, 225, 228, 235, 295, 336, 347, 348, 349, 350, 352, 364, 365, 387, 416, 478, 488, 489, 492, 499, 511
Incredible Torture Show 224–225, 459, 513
Incubus 225–226, **226**
Inferno 455
Ingails, Joyce 116
Ingle, John 434
Ingvordsen, J.C. 67
Inspector Morse (TV) 284
Interview with a Serial Killer see *White Angel*

Invaders from Mars 465
The Invisible Man 10, 11, 29n
Iregua, Victor 227
Ireland, John 225, 270, 499
Ironside, Michael 35, 103, 299, 496
Irwin, Ashley 151
Irwin, Mark 115, 418
Isaac, James 215
Isaacks, Levie 114, 151, 310
Isaacs, Bud S. 203
Isaak, Chris 488
Iscove, Robert 301
Isham, Mark 242
The Island of Dr. Moreau (1996) 137
Isobel, Katherine 244
It Happened in Broad Daylight 222, 226–227, 514
It Happened One Night 415
The Italian Job 428
Ivan the Terrible 499
Ivanek, Zeljko 194
Ives, Burl 129

Jack, Wolfman 293
Jack the Ripper (and Ripper lore) 1, 5, 6, 8, 11, 22, 24, 26, 46, 57, 71, 72, 81, 98, 109, 127, 129, 142, 162, 165, 176, 180, 187, 193, 194, 199, 208, 218, 227, 228, 229, 230, 231, 255, 256, 262, 263, 266, 297, 298, 299, 305, 308, 339, 340, 382, 383, 384, 388, 389, 411, 416, 417, 425, 429, 437, 441, 469, 470, 471, 499, 500, 506, 518
Jack the Ripper (1958) 227
Jack the Ripper (1971) 227–228
Jack the Ripper (1976) 46, 100, 228–229
Jack the Ripper (1988) 229–230
Jack the Ripper Goes West see *Silent Sentence*
Jacks, Robert L. 272
Jack's Back 230–231, **231**, 439
Jackson, Gerald 66
Jackson, Gordon 321
Jackson, Peter 184, 186
Jackson, Mark 156
Jackson, Samuel L. 149
Jacobi, Joelle 246
Jacobs, Emma 301
Jacobs, Joel 127
Jacobs, Mike, Jr. 125
Jacoby, Hans 226
Jade 371
Jaeckel, Richard 109
Jaffa, Rick 153
Jaffe, Gib 484
Jaffe, Herb 293, 469
Jaffe, Robert 293
Jaffe, Steven-Charles 293, 436
Jagged Edge 193, 510
Jahn, Robert 66

Jakubowicz, Alain 464
James, Brion 148, 215, 241, 310
James, Ken 355
James, Steve 207
Jannings, Emil 499
Janos, Victor 249
Janowitz, Hans 6–7, 7n
Jansen, Adolf 265
Jansen, Pierre 68
Janssen, David 88
Janssen, Famke 163, 379
The January Man 231–231
Der Januskopf 11
Japan 493
Jarchow, Stephen 391
Jarmusch, Jim 292
Jarre, Maurice 41, 173, 321
Jason, Rick 340
Javitz, Barbara 419, 502
Jaws 81, 109
Jean, Vadim 326
Jean-Baptiste, Marianne 82
Jeavons, Colin 394
Jeffory, Dawn 477
Jeffries, Philip 283
Jekyll and Hyde motifs/mythos 6,
     7n, 10, 11–12, 17, 20n, 29, 64, 98,
     111, 112, 129, 130, 142, 143, 194,
     218, 230, 231, 240, 346, 408,
     459, 490, 500
Jekyll and Hyde 230
Jekyll and Hyde (book) 10
Jekyll's Inferno see *The Two Face
     of Dr. Jekyll*
Jelinski, Manfred (O.) 312, 395
Jenkins, Gordon 170
Jenkins, Rebecca 428
Jenkins, Richard 396
Jennifer 8 34, 60, 93, 220, 232–
     234, **233**
Jensen, Dave 430
Jensen, Peter 325
Jessop, Peter 186, 394
Jesus Christ 126, 175, 176, 209,
     284, 380, 388, 389, 393, 425
Jesus of Montreal 261
Jett, Billy 285, 483
Jeunet and Caro 518
Jewell, Isabel 42, 74, 251
Jewett, Tom 117
Jewison, Norman 231
Jeynes, Roderick 48
Jill Rips see *Jill the Ripper*
Jill the Ripper 234–235
Jiminez, Neil 208
Jing, Wong 393
Jinks, Dan 72
Joan of Arc 43
Jodts, Let 263
Joffe, Charles 408
Johns, Mervyn 215
Johnson, Arte 148
Johnson, Ben 478, 480
Johnson, Bill 464
Johnson, Chris 67

Johnson, Clark 355
Johnson, Don 192, 193
Johnson, James 66
Johnson, Kari 382
Johnson, Laura 303, 483
Johnson, Laurie 38
Johnson, Michelle 190
Johnson, Noble 292
Johnson, Penny 324
Johnson, Shelley 230
Johnson, Todd 252
Johnston, Tucker 65
Johnstone, Nahanni 428
Jolie, Angelina 72
Joliffe, Genevieve 506
Jolley, Stan 416
Jolliffe, Brock 355
Jones, Al 506
Jones, Allan 118
Jones, Angela 107
Jones, April Campbell 353
Jones, Bob 520
Jones, Carolyn 139
Jones, Chris 506
Jones, Donald 261, 301
Jones, Freddie 44
Jones, James Earl 44
Jones, Jeffrey 371
Jones, Jocelyn 477
Jones, Lee 466
Jones, Steven A. 203
Jones, Tommy Lee 157, 309
Jones, Trevor 110, 208, 396
Jones, Tyler 391
Jonfield, Peter **298**
Jordan, Bobby 430
Jordan, James Carrol 418
Jordan, Joanne Moore 217
Jordan, Lawrence 160
Jordan, Neil 208, 219, 220
Jordan, Richard 216, 283, **284**
Joseph, Karen 353
Joyce, Yootha 316
Joyner, Michelle 481
Judd, Ashley 154, 202, 242, **242**,
     244
Julia, Raul 157
June 255
June, Ray 317
Junge, Alfred 499
Jurassic Park 458
Jurgensen, Randy 104
Jurges, Jurgen 453
Just Cause 235–236, **236**
Justice, Katherine 173
Jympson, John 180

Kaczender, George 352
Kaczmarek, Jan A.P. 337
Kadison, Ellis 466
Kael, Pauline 214, 469
Kafka, Franz 409
Kahn, Allen 512
Kaiser, Joel 113

Kalifornia 103, 236–238, **237**, 238,
     240, 335
Kalin, Tom 331
Kalinke, Ernst W. 519
Kallberg, Kevin 33
Kaller, Berwick 66
Kalsch, Ken 136
Kaman, Steve 67
Kamen, Michael 115, 181
Kaminski, Janusz 367
Kammermeier, Matthias 515
Kampendonk, G. 45
Kandel, Aben 101
Kane, Byron 511
Kane, Carol 331, 332
Kane, Mike 103
Kanter, Peter 389
Kaper, Bronislau 169
Kaplan, Corey 300
Kaplan, Martin 438
Kaproff, Dana 118
Karlatos, Olga 302
Karlen, John 112
Karloff, Boris 71, 199, 200, 264,
     422, 423, 500
Karmaker, Romuald 476
Karnowski, Tom 350
Karr, Tom 123
Kasdan, Mark 102
Kasem, Casey 109
Kastle, Leonard 119, 212, 214
Kastner, Elliott 118, 506
Katkin, Brian 97
Katsaros, Andonia 469
Katzenbach, John 235, 283
Katzin, Lee H. 501
Katzman, Sam 430
Kauderer, Emilio 418
Kaufman, Susan 201
Kava, Caroline 71
Kavanagh, John 161, 446
Kavner, Julie 408
Kawaguchi, Sueda 493
Kaye, Artie 157
Kazan, Elia 15
Kazan, Nicholas 160
Kazann, Zitto 418
Keach, James 351
Keach, Stacy 240, 384, 385, **385**,
     386
Keane, Kerrie 225
Kearney, Philip 354
Keefe, Tom 206
Keen, Malcolm 255
Keeter, Worth 419, 420
Kehoe, Jack 293
Keitel, Harvey 108, 231
Keith, Carlos 71; see also Lewton,
     Val
Keith, David 503, 507, **507**, **508**
Keith, Katterina 57
Keith, Sheila 186, 187, 215, 216
Kell, Joseph 73, 107
Kellaway, Roger 108
Keller, Almanta 314

Keller, David Henry 67
Keller, Harry 432
Keller, Walter E. 71, 74
Kellerman, Sally 75, 78
Kellin, Mike 75
Kellogg, John 416
Kelly, Claire 38, 134
Kelly, Craig 326
Kelly, Mary 382
Kelly, Monika 97
Kelly, Victoria 491
Kelly's Heroes 170
Kelman, Rickey 432
Kelsh, Ken 238
Kemp, Elizabeth 88, 201
Kemp, George 455
Kemp, Martin 124
Kemp, Michael 65
Kemper, Ed 23, 80, 95, 107, 179, 241
Kemper, Victor J. 44, 340
Kempner, Brenda 167
Kempster, Victor 309
Kendal, Suzy 44, 52, 101, 475
Kennedy, Burt 240
Kennedy, George 75
Kennedy, John F. assassination 22, 241; funeral 76
Kennedy, Leon Isaac 474
Kensit, Patsy 485
Kent, Jean 199
Kent, Rolfe 114
Kenyon, Sandy 42
Keppel, Bob 123
Kerkhof, Ian 447
Kern, David 375
Kern, Richard 323
Kern, Robert J. 317
Kerns, Joanna 328
Kerr, Bill 215
Kerridge, Linda 158
Kershner, Irvin 157
Kerwin, William 62
Kesler, Zora Ulla 477
Kesner, Jillian 386
Kessel, Joseph 321
Kesselring, Joseph 43
Keuhnelian, Janice 163
Kewley, Michael 337
Key, Allison 54
Keyes, Irwin 66
Keyworth, Ben 34
Khanjian, Arsinee 165
Khondji, Darius 219, 404
Khoury, Ziad El 244
Kidder, Margot 71
Kiersch, Fritz 162
Kikoine, Gerard 142, 143, 149
Kiley, Richard 420
Kilik, Jon 163, 441
Killer: A Journal of Murder 238, 238–240
The Killer Inside Me 240, 386
Killer's Delight see *Dark Ride*
Killing Hour see *The Clairvoyant*

The Killing Jar 241
The Killing of America 23n, 241
The Killing of Sister George 502
Kilmer, Val 202
Kilpatrick, Lincoln 116
Kilvert, Lilly 436, 474
Kimbal, Russell 346
Kimmel, Anne 141
Kinberg, Jud 471
Kindberg, Ann 474
King, George 158
King, Ivan 113
King, Kandice 388
King, Lance 388
King, Martin Luther assassination 22
King, Perry 88, 349
King, Robb Wilson 222
King, Rufus 398
King, Stephen 43, 111, 115, 116, 364, 515
Kingdom of the Spiders 109
Kingsford, Walter 169
Kingsley, Ben 446
Kinjite: Forbidden Subjects 451, 452
Kinninmont, Tom 155
Kinski, Klaus 45, 99, 100, 228
Kirkland, Sally 439
Kirpaul, Amanda I. 334
Kirshner, Mia 259
Kirst, H.H. 321
Kirwin, William 349
Kish, Bert 57
Kiss Me Monster 391
Kiss of Death 14, 158, 159
Kiss the Girls 26n, 27, 116, 224, 242–244, **242**, **243**, 468
Kissinger, Charles 466, 518
Kitay, David 323
Klarr, Jack 316
Klass, David 242
Klawitter, Michael 72
Klein, T.E.D. 483
Kleiner, Towje 482
Kleinman, A. 250
Kline, Kevin 231, 232
Kline, Richard (H.) 75, 456
Klinger, Kevin 137
Kljakovic, Miljen Kreka 423
Klugman, Jack 124
Knell, Catalaine 379
Knepper, Rob 502
A Knife for the Ladies 416
Knight, Esmond 145
Knight, H.A. 326
Knight, Jack 378
Knight, Marcie 219
Knight, Shirley 99
Knight Moves 153, 244–246, **245**
Knightriders 67
Knowles, Patric 514
Kober, Jeff 46, 172
Kobrin, Rob 493
Kobritz, Richard 164

Koch, Hawk 181
Koch, Howard W. 190
Koefoed, Christopher 388
Koenig, Ken 249
Koepp, David 40, 41
Koffler, Pamela 331
Kohane, Lisa 349
Kohlberg, Stanford S. 61–62
Kohner, Pancho 450
Kohnhurst, Michael 206
Kolik, Jon 441; see also Kilik, Jon
Kolker, Henry 67
Koltai, Lajos 235
Komenich, Rick 206
Kong, Jackie 64
Koons, Robert 374
Koontz, Dean R. 208, 211
Kooris, Richard 464
Kopelson, Arnold 404
Korda, David 151
Korean War 365, 499
Korn, Iris 108
Koromzay, Alix 327
Kortner, Fritz 338
Koscina, Sylvia 418
Kossoff, David 490
Kosteck, Martin 411
Koster, Henry 13
Koteas, Elias 160, **160**
Kottenbrook, Carol 334
Kotto, Yaphet 173, 352, 505
Kouf, Jim 91
Kovacs, Laszlo 94
Koval, Paul 355
Kowalski, Bernard 491
Koyama, Akiko 493
Kozak, Lana 354
Kracauer, S. 70
Krafft-Ebing 5, 259
Kraft, Scott 91
Kramer, Stanley 51, 78, 268, 420, 421
Krampf, Gunther 338
Kramreither, Anthony 35
Krane, Jonathan D. 162
Krause, Brian 307
Krauss, Werner 499
The Krays 374, 425
Kress, Frank 191
Kretschmann, Thomas 431
Krevoy, Brad 33
Kriel, Anneline 372
Krim, Viju 224
Krish, John 334
Krish, Justin 200
Kristofferson, Kris 337
Krogh, Dan 512
Kroonenburg, Pieter 103
Kruze, John 44
Kubrick, Stanley 36, 456, 516, 517, 518
Kuchar, George 396
Kuchuck, Danny 67
Kuehl, William L. 99
Kuepper, Rob 33

Kulzer, William 409
Kumar, Barin 411
Kupferschmidt, John 263
Kurant, Willy 241
Kuras, Ellen 441
Kurson, Jane 133
Kurta, Paul 423
Kurten, Peter 6, 8, 96, 266, 268, 453, 459
Kurtz, Swoozie 334
Kusaba, Craig 409
Kuskowski, Allan 137
Kuveiller, Luigi 121, 255, 314
Kuvin, Howard 123
Kyle, Brenda R. 246

LA Confidential 42, 496
Labern, Arthur 180
Lacambre, Daniel 42
Lacey, Catherine 422
Lacone, Jeremy 72
Ladd, Diane 55
Lado, Aldo 510
Lady from Shanghai 164
Lady in a Cage 293
Lady in Cement 125
Lady in Waiting 246
Lady in White 246–247, 374
Lady of Burlesque 14n, 199, 247–248, **248**, 258, 272, 340, 440
Lady Stay Dead 248–249, 261
Laemmle, Carl 499
Laemmle, Carl, Jr. 303
LaFleur, Art 254, 367
Lahti, Christine 208
Lai, Me Me 145
Laine, Jimmy 136
Lake, Alan 348
Lake, Florence 394
Lake, Leonard 493; *see also* Ng, Charles
Lake, Ricki 403
Lake Havesa 81
Lally, Mick 161
LaLoggia, Frank 246, 247
Lam, Allan 393
La Marca, Andrew G. 246
Lamb, John Lowry 350
Lambert, Ed 300
Lambert, Christopher 244, **245**, 380, 381
Lambert, Jerry 464
Lambert, Mary 440
Lambert, Steve 93
Lambroschini, Julien 431
LaMotta, Jake 67
Lancaster, Burt 427
Lanchester, Elsa 425
Landis, John 179
Landon, Richard 190
Landres, Paul 381, 411
Landru see *Bluebeard* (1963)
Landry, Margaret 251
Lane, Diane 244

Lane, James 301
Lane, Priscilla 43
Lane, Robert 515
Lang, Fritz 6, 8n, 14, 70, 265, 267, 268, 269, 398, 400, 427, 503, 504, 505
Lang, K.D. 154
Lang, Katherine Kelly 324
Langan, Glenn 194
Lange, Arthur 247
Langedyk, Jack 148
Langencamp, Heather 411
Langenfeld, Sara 64
Langton, Brooke 253
Lanoe, Henri 315
Lansbury, Angela 446
Lansford, Roy 288
Lanyer, Charles 432
LaPaglia, Anthony 421, 441
Larch, John 126
Larquey, Pierre 302
Larraine, Les 325
Larraya, Aurelio G. 513
Larrimore, Lee 493
Larry, Sheldon 428
Larsen, Kaj 273
Larson, Richard W. 123
LaRue, Lash 337
Las Vegas 458
Laser Moon 249, 333
La Shelle, Joseph 194
Laskus, Jacek 434
Laso, Mara 45
Lassander, Dagmar 182, 198
Lassgard, Rolf 273
The Last Emperor 35
Last House on Dead End Street 249–250
Last House on the Left 249, 250
Last Victim 250
Laszlo, Ernest 268, 503
Latifah, Queen 72
Latimer, Cherie 42
Latt, David J. 486
Latzko, Herline 482
Laufer, Paul 82
Laughing Policeman 125
Laughton, Charles 14
Laurel, Bobby 387
Laurence, Ashley 107
Laurence, Mitchell 434
Laurenson, James 44
Laurenson, Phil 191, 512
Lauria, Dan 328
Laurie, Piper 483, 484, **484**, 486
Laustsen, Dan 308, 327
Lautore, Ronald M. 211
La Vallee, Bill 367
Lavanant, Dominique 291
Laven, Arnold 511, 512
Laverick, June 174
Lavia, Gabriele 121
LaVine, Ronald 123
Lavista, Raul 251
Law, John Philip 427

The Lawnmower Man 82, 188, 209, 211, 494
Lawrence, Arthur 341
Lawrence, Diarmuid 284
Lawrence, Gail 277
Lawrence, Marc 108
Lawrence, Scott 502
Lawrence, Toni 108
Lawrence of Arabia 321
Laws, Andrew 286
Lawson, Tony 219
Lawton, Charles 169
Lax, Leo 45
Laye, Evelyn 466
Layne, Gordon C. 518
Lazard, Justin 423, 424
Lazenby, George 510
Leach, Rosemary 200
Leal, Amparo Soler 513
Leatherface 466
Leatherwoman see *Jill the Ripper*
Leavenworth Prison 238
Leaver, Philip 227
Lebenzon, Chris 91
Le Blanc, John 440
Leciere, Georges 459
Leder, Paul 46, 47, 217, 417
Lederer, Charles 169, 170
Lederer, Francis 381
Lederer, Franz 338
Ledingham, David 168
Le Duke, Harrison 249
Lee, Christopher 217, 218, 466, 490
Lee, Cosette 123
Lee, Damian 481
Lee, Gypsy Rose 247
Lee, Pinkie 247
Lee, Rowland V. 261
Lee, Sheryl **486**, 488
Lee, Spike 441, 442, 443, 444, 445
Lee, Virginia 440
Leekley, John 222
The Legend of Boggy Creek 481
Legend of Lylah Clare 423
Leguizamo, John 323, 441, **442**, 443, **443**, 444
Lehrer, Wayne 418
Leibowitz, Armond 423
Leibowitz, Sol 492
Leigh, Janet 361, 362, 363
Leigh, Jennifer Jason 47, 156
Leigh, Norman 116
Leigh, Suzanna 167
Leigh-Hunt, Barbara 180
Leighton, Michael (W.) 240, 337
Leipzig, Matt 440
Le Mat, Paul 118
Le Mesurier, John 227
Lemmo, James 164, 375, 378
Lemmons, Kasi 412
Lemoine, Michel 390
Leni, Paul 499
Lenney, Sean 97
Lenz, Kay 164, 299, 437, 438, 440

Lenzi, Umberto 156, 407, 476
Leonard, Brett 82, 188, 208, 209, 211, 494, 495, 496
Leonard, David 306
Leonard, Elmore 387, 428, 429
Leonard, Joshua 389
Leonard, Queenie 256
Leonard, Robert Sean 238
Leonardi, Marco 431
Leonetti, Matthew F. 423, 436
The Leopard Man 251, 411
Leopold, Glenn 474
Leopold and Loeb 15, 308, 474
Lepel, Bernd 101
Le Picard, Marcel 430
Lepurier, Denise 68
Lepurier, Dian 68
Lerner, Michael 48
Leroux, Maxime 288
Leroy, Philippe 182
Lerski, Helmar 499
Leslie, William 99
Lester, Henry E. 441
Lester, Mark L. 389, 390
Lester, Richard 320
Lethal Weapon 190
Leto, Jared 36, 445
Lett, Dan 328
Leung, Ivy 393
LeVay, Sylvester 216, 223
Levels, Calvin 44, 254
Levin, Ira 129
Levine, Steve 288
Levine, Ted 202, 412, 413, 445
Levinson, Carri 206
Levinson, Mark 238
Levitt, Zane W. 333
Levy, Jules (V.) 381, 511
Levy, Michael 153
Levy, Shuki 353
Lewis, Christopher 382
Lewis, Gary 350
Lewis, Geoffrey 333–334, 450
Lewis, Gwen 156
Lewis, H.G. 19, 61, 63, 64, 66, 97, 191, 192, 279, 347, 366, 475, 512, 513
Lewis, Jerry 292
Lewis, Joseph H. 24
Lewis, Juliette 236, 237, **237**, 238, 309, 436
Lewis, Linda 382
Lewis, Richard B. 47, 434
Lewis, Robert 289
Lewis, W. Michael 241
Lewitt, Elliott 497
Lewton, Val 71, 72, 74, 251
Leyh, Blake 430
Lichtig, Renee 459
Liddle, George 110
Lieberman, Charlie 203
Lieberman, Jeff 57
Life in the Balance 251–252
Life Is Beautiful 292
Lifeforce 424, 465

The Lift 37
Lillard, Matthew 403
Lim, Kay Tong 330
Limbic Region 115, 252
Lind, Kevin 333
Linder, Leslie 400, 447
Lindfors, Viveca 149, **150**, 415
Lindley, John 432
Lindsay, Frederic 234
Lindsay, Mark 241
Lindsay, Robert 277
Lindt, Rosemarie 510
Lindup, David 427
Link 386
The Link see *Blood Link*
Linke, Paul 293, **294**
Linkman, Ludwig 45
Linn, Michael 419
Linson, Art 202
Liotta, Ray 194
Lippert, Randy 401
Lipstadt, Aaron 337
"lipstick killer" see Heirens, William
Lipton, Peggy 162
Liquid Dreams 252–253, 334
Liquid Sky 143
Lisi, Joe 481
Lisi, Virna 69
Lissek, Leo 65
Listen 249, 253–254
Lithgow, John 66, 67, 160
Littaye, Guy 78
Litto, George 66, 134, 316
Litton, Foster 493
Litvak, Anatole 13, 71, 321
Live! from Death Row 254–255
Live Wire 168
Lively, Gerry 337
Livesy, Roger 226
Lizard in a Woman's Skin 255
Ljotka, Daniel 42
Lloyd, Norman 268
Lloyd, Russell 64
Lloyd, Sue 98
LoBianco, Tony 71, 212, **213**, 214, 474
Lobl, Victor 474
Locke, Bruce 384
The Locket 258
Lockhart, June 117, 411
Locklin, Loryn 324
Lodge, David 98, 142, 167
Lodge, John 304
The Lodger (1926) 129, 180, 255–256, 262
The Lodger (1944) 14n, 129, 194, 199, 227, 247, 256–259, **257**, 264, 272, 340
Loeb, Lisa 402
Logan, Phyllis 127
Loggia, Robert 361, 375
Lohmann, Dietrich 244
Lohmann, Paul 469
Lom, Herbert 115, 304

Lombardo, Lou 231
Lomma, Jeannie M. 379
Lommel, Ulli 453, 454, 455
London 11, 72, 98, 134, 167, 180, 187, 200, 201, 218, 227, 259, 262, 264, 298, 313, 383, 411, 429, 430, 437, 500
London, Andrew 292, 361
London Blackout Murders 259
Long, Audrey 74
Long, Stanley 422
Long, Stephen 192, 273
Longmire, Susan 409
Longo, Malisa 81
Longworth, David 374
Lonnen, Ray 302
Lonnerheden, Hans 272
Lonsdale, Peter 384
Look Back in Anger (play) 319
Looking for Mr. Goodbar 42, 193, 515
Loomis, Rod 230
Lopez, Jennifer 82, 85
Loquasto, Santo 408
Lord, Jean-Claude 496
Lord, Justine 200
Lords, Traci 249, 404
Lorenz, Jerry 460
Loridans, Virginia 493
Loring, Teala 67
Lorre, Peter 7, 43, 79, 258, 265, **266**, 267, **267**, 268, 448
Lorys, Diana 45
Los Angeles 113, 190, 230, 268, 354, 366, 367, 375, 402, 430, 445, 469, 497, 512
Losey, Joseph 268, 269, 421
Lotti, Angelo 407
Lottimer, Ed 437, 440
Lottman, Evan 192
Louzil, Eric 409
Louzon, Gary 332
Lovas, Pal 482
Love and Human Remains 35, 103, 259–261, **260**, 306, 336, 277, 435
The Love Butcher 261
Love from a Stranger (1936) 261–261
Love from a Stranger (1947) 262
Love in Cold Blood see *Ice House*
Love Is Colder Than Death 454
Love Lies Bleeding 208, 262–263
Lovecraft, H.P. 52
Lovejoy, Ray 288
Lovelock, Ray 302
Lovett, Robert Q. 365
Lovick, Josanne B. 57
Low, Warren 173
Lowe, Arthur 388
Lowe, Rob 498
Lowe, Susan 404
Lowensohn, Elina 306, 307
Lower, Tony 138
Lowry, Hunt 438

Lowry, Richard O. 471
Lubin, Hedda 191
Lucas, Henry Lee 92, 204, 206, 400
Lucas, Joshua 36
Lucchesi, Gary 232, 494
Lucidi, Antonio 477
Lucker 124, 163–164
Ludi, Toni 476
Ludwig, Pamela 285, 337
Lugagne, Francoise 68
Lugosi, Bela 71, 303, 430, 500, 514
Luisi, James 112, 158
Lumaldo, Miguel Angel 40
Lumet, Sidney 192
Lumley, Joanna 446
Lund, Deanna 386
Lund, Kevin 57
Lundell, Marjie 351
Lundgren, Dolph 234
Lundigan, William 176
Luner, Jamie 389
Lunn, Kitty 156
Lupino, Ida 50, 51, 504, 505
Lured 264, 345
Lurie, Evan 291, 331
Lurie, John 89
Lust of the Vampire 264–265
Lustig, Dana 53
Lustig, William 35, 42, 116, 133, 151, 202, 277, 278–279, 375, 376, 377, 418, 419
Luther, Igor 221
Lynch, Brad 288
Lynch, David 128, 247, 287, 307, 336, 374, 486, 488
Lynch, Kate 138
Lynch, Kelly 494
Lynch, Paul 35, 103, 299
Lynch, Ray 520
Lyndon, Barre 194, 256
Lynn, Carol 90
Lynn, E. 458
Lyon, Ronald 88
Lyonne, Natasha 179
Lyons, Robert (F.) 384, 450, 472, **473**

M (1933) 6, 7, 8, 9, 11, 22, 29, 43, 79, 96, 102, 164, 255, 258, 259, 265–268, **266**, **267**, 271, 291, 324, 363, 399, 409, 421, 448, 453, 454, 489, 500, 505
M (1951) 51, 268–269
M, Beatrice 312
M, Monika 312, 395
Maas, Dick 37
Maass, John 107
Maazel, Lincoln 279
MacAdam, Elisa 331
Macat, Julio 333, 421
Macauley, Richard 74
Macchi, Egisto 281
MacDonald, Philip 71, 262
Macdonald, Richard 232

MacGregor, Scott 134
Machon, Karen 57
MacKenzie, Jack 381
Mackintosh, Woody 170
MacLachlan, Kyle 486, **487**, 488
MacLaine, Shirley 349
Maclean, Robert K. 102
MacNeill, Peter 328
MacRae, Meredith 417
Macrae, Michael 351
Macy, William H. 114, 115, 358
The Mad Bomber 269–270
The Mad Butcher 168, 270–271, 437
Mad Jake see *Blood Salvage*
Maddalena, Marianne 324, 411
Madden, Brent 162
Madden, David 172
Madigan, Amy 111
Madin, Christopher 200
Madonna 408
Madou, Malou 271
Madrid, Jose 227
Madsen, David 94
Madsen, Michael 114, 388, 389, 423, 424, 481
Maehl, Ross A. 351
Mafia 119, 165
Maganini, Elena 203
Magar, Guy 434
Magee, Patrick 167
Magree, Frank 372
Mahal, Taj 334
Mahler, Gustav 212
Mahoney, John 48
Main, Laurie 354, 469
Maisner, Andrew 418
Major, Grant 184
Malco, Paolo 285, 314
Malden, Karl 345
Malick, Terence 24
Malik, Art 284
Malkin, Sam 435
Malkovich, John 91, 232, 408
Mallaby, George 146
Mallalieu, Aubrey 158
Malo, Rene 138
Mamet, David 194
The Man 51
Man, Si 393
Man Bites Dog 27, 271–272, 287, 366, 506
Man Hunt 400
Man in the Attic 272
Man on the Balcony 272–273
Manasse, George 57, 201
Manasse, Massimo 285
The Manchurian Candidate 425
Mancina, Mark 91
Mancini, Henry 164, 180
Mancuso, Frank, Jr. 423
Mandel, Johnny 519
Mandell, Daniel 43
Mander, Miles 169
Manes, Fritz 467

Manfredini, Harry 114, 215
Mangine, Joseph 54
Manhattan 474
Manhunt: Search for the Night Stalker see *Hunt for the Night Stalker*
Manhunter 10n, 11n, 20n, 21, 25n, 27, 29n, 42, 73, 80, 83, 94, 156, 202, 207, 223, 232, 244, 272, 273–277, **274**, **275**, 324, 325, 350, 377, 378, 402, 410, 413, 414, 482, 498, 503
Mania see *The Flesh and the Fiends*
Maniac (1963) 18
Maniac (1980) 132, 133, 202, 217, 277–279, **278**, 347, 377
Maniac Cop 116, 279, 324, 377
Manifest Destiny 251, 371
Manino (Mannino), Vincenzo 302, 314
The Manitou 466, 519
Mankowitz, Wolf 490
Mankuma, Blu 80, 292
Mann, Abby 44, 124, 474
Mann, Anthony 176
Mann, Edward 240, 268
Mann, Michael 192, 202, 273, 276, 277
Mann, Steve 246
Mannino, Vincenzo (aka Manino, Vincenzo) 314
Manos, Mark 252, 333, 334
Mansard, Claude 68
Mansfield, David 119
Mansfield, Scott 117
Mansian, Steve 346
Manson, Charles 19, 22, 22n, 88, 203, 403, 473, 520
Mantegna, Joe 153
Mantooth, Randolph 81
Manuel, Dennis 246
Manzatt, Russell V. 285
Manzie, Jim 434
Manzo, Bianca 148
Maranne, Cindy 418
March or Die 118
Marchione, Luigi 39
Marcoux, Ted 187
Marcus, Andrew 35
Marcus, Paul 155
Mardi Gras 279, 469
Mardi Gras Massacre 279
Margo 251
Margolin, Alan 224
Margulies, David 134
Margulies, Michael D. 123
Margulies, William 190
Marielle, Jean Pierre 177
Marinano, Rensso 227
Marino, Dean Richard 162
Marino, Juan 346
Marion, Charles 430
Marion, Frances 261
Mark, Laurence 55

Mark, Stephen 440
Mark, Tony 148
Markell, Bob 129
Marker, Harry 425
Markowitz, Russell D. 379
Marks, Julian 91, 328
Marks, Leo 341, 489
Markwell, John 34
Marley, John 57
Marley, Peverell 345
Marli, Adalberto-Maria 315
Marlowe, Derek 229
Marlowe, Faye 194
Marlowe, Linda 200
Marquette, Jacques 437
Married with Children (TV) 438
Marrow, Hyla 277
Marsh, Stephen 39
Marsh, Terence 160
Marshal, Alan 317
Marshal, Ruth 259
Marshall, James 488
Marshall, Roger 466, 489
Marshek, Archie 292, 328
Martelle Randonnee 155
Martin 9, 28, 85, 107, 111, 132,
    249, 279–281, **280**, 306, 307,
    323, 333, 337, 338
Martin, Alan 326
Martin, Conrado San 45
Martin, Dean 173, 174
Martin, D'Urville 518
Martin, Eugenio 167, 326
Martin, F. Smith 519
Martin, Greg 43
Martin, Marion 247
Martin, Pamela 401
Martin, Quinn 293
Martin, Richard 251
Martin, Yvonne 345
Martinez, A. 216
Martinez, Nacho 281
Martino, Lea 285
Martino, Luciano 58
Martino, Sergio 58, 475, 476
Marvin, Lee 251
Marvin, Richard 33
Marx, Solly 415
Marx, Timothy 85
Marz, Carolyn 136
Mas, Juan A. 97
Mascara 281
Masefield, Joseph 133
Mashelski, Thomas 409
Mask of Zorro 103
Mason, Andrew 110
Mason, Connie 62
Mason, James 296, **297**
Mason, Melinda 172
Mason, Nick 506
Massacesi, Aristide 52; *see also*
    D'Amato, Joe
Massachusetts 71
Massari, Lea 315
Massey, Anna 180, 341, **343**

Massey, Raymond 43
Massey, Walter 148
Massie, Paul 490
Masters, Ben 123
Masterson, Mary Stuart 88
Masterson, Peter 88, 316
Mastorakis, Nico 58, 59
Mastrantonio, Mary Elizabeth
    231
Mastroianni, Armand 88, 89, 201,
    202
Masur, Richard 283
Matador 20n, 155, 281–283, 366
Mather, Aubrey 256
Mather, Jack 123
Mathews, James 419
Mathieson, John 194
Mathis, Samantha 36
Matley, Doug 419
Matlock (TV) 197
Matonak, Ron 42
Matshikiza, John 136
Mattei, Angelo 477
Matthews, Lester 259, 500
Mattison, James 301
Matushka see *The Train Killer*
Matushka, Sylvester 482
Matzdorff, Michael 366
Maur-Thorp, Sarah 142
Max, Arthur 404
Max, Ron 250
Maximilliene 302
Maxwell, Edwin 305
Maxwell, Roberta 363
May, Bradford 292
May, Brian 65, 384
May, Curt 66
May, Jack 200
Mayer, Louis B. 319
Mayfield, Les 363
Mayhew, Peter 199
Maylam, Tony 429
Maynard, Mimi 347
Maynard, Richard 81
Maynard, William 409
Mayne, Ferdinand 244
Mayniel, Juliette 68
Mayo, Alfredo 513
Mayo, Virginia 148
Mazey, Nina 127
Mazurka, Mike 85
McAleese, Peter 515
McAnally, Ray 229
McArdle, Kip 212
McArthur, Alex 242, 367, **368**,
    369
McAuliffe, Nicola **128**
McBrearty, Dan 35
McBride, Chi 185
McBride, Ian 35
McBride, Michele 353
McCabe, Anne 168
McCabe, Brian 519
McCain, Howard 503
McCambridge, Mercedes 491

McCann, Sean 102, 138
McCarthy, Francis 324
McCarthy, John 259
McCarthy, Julia 502
McCarthy, Kevin 333
McCarthy, Matt 215
McCauley, John 117
McClellan, Gordon 380
McClory, Belinda 373, 372
McClory, Sean 272
McClure, Ernest 66
McCole, Stephen 350
McCollum, Chuck 347
McConkey, Larry 506
McCowan, Jack 123
McCowen, Alec 180
McCraw, Charles 240
McCrea, Joel 292, 293
McCullogh, Jim 493
McCullogh, Jim, Jr. 493
McDaniel, Donna 39
McDermott, Keith 477
McDonagh, Neal 371
McDonald, Christopher 80
McDonald, Michael J. 108
McDonald, Peter 165
McDonald, Rodney 124
McDonell, Fergus 319
McDonnell, Gordon 407, 432
McDonnell, Robert 350, 503
McDormand, Francis 89
McDowall, Betty 227
McDowall, Roddy 173, 174, 351
McDowell, Malcolm 151, 152,
    262, 263, 469 470, **470**, 471
McElroy, Alan B. 299
McEnery, John 394
McGann, Paul 34
McGee, Jerry 66
McGee, Vic 417
McGill, Bruce 347
McGillis, Kelly 503
McGillivay, David 186, 187, 200,
    215, 387, 394, 395, 423
McGinley, Patrick 161
McGinnis, Niall 437
McGlone, Mike 72
McGowan, Dorrell 219
McGowan, Jack 279
McGowan, Stuart 218
McGrath, Jim 380
McGrath, Martin 383
McGraw, Ali 300
McGregor, Ewan 154, 327
McGuffie, Bill 98
McGuire, Dorothy 425, 426, **426**
McGuire, Michael 57, 340
McHattie, Stephen 118, **119**
McHeady, Robert 123
McHugh, Frank 305
McIlwraith, David 197
McIntire, John 356
McIntire, Tim 240
McKay, Craig 412
McKenna, Siobhan 113

McKenna's Gold 430
McKinney, Austin 261
McLaughlin, James 169
McLean, David 437
Mcleod, Eric 82
McLeod, Mary 259
McLerie, Allyn 345
McMahon, Louis 365
McMahon, Phyllis 447
McMillan, Kenneth 88, 340
McMillan, Weston 292
McMinn, Teri 460
McMuster, Niles 224
McNamara, William 94
McNaughton, John 92, 203, 205, 206
McQueen, Chad 481
McQuinn-Mason, Edward 384
McRae, Peter A. 142
McRaney, Gerald 138, 320
McReary, Lew 286
McShane, Ian 474
McShane, Jennifer 497
McSweeney, John, Jr. 129
Mean Season 48, 102, 283–284, **284**
Meaney, Colm 91
Meat Loaf 334; *see also* Aday, Meat Loaf
Mechoso, Julio Oscar 245
Medak, Peter 374, 388, 423, 424, 425, 518
Medford, Harold 345
Medina, Patricia 345
Medoff, Mark 41
Medwin, Michael 319
Meeker, Charles 503
Meeker, Ralph 124
Megginson, Robert T. 325
Meheux, Phil 41, 102, 187
Melbourne 372
Melies, G. 5
Mell, Marisa 407
Melle, Gil 123, 211
Mellor, James 200
Melnick, Mark 324
Mendenhall, David 437
Mendoza-Nava, Jaime 478
Menjou, Adolphe 420, 421
Menke, Sally 327
mental illness 11, 12, 13, 13n, 17, 50, 101, 127, 149, 169, 170, 220, 240, 266, 269, 288, 289, 324, 358, 362, 367, 369, 379, 391, 415, 420, 430, 483; *see also* multiple personality disorder, schizophrenia
Mention, Michel 269
Meranda, Luc 475
Mercado, Hector 347
Merchant, Tom 352
Merhi, Joseph 43, 44
Meril, Macha 121
Merrick, Ian 54
Merrill, Dina 164

Merritt, George 217
Merrow, Jane 193
Mertes, Raffaele 483
Mery-Clark, Laurence 127
Messenger of Death 452
Messiah 284–285
Mesta, J. Daniel 445
Metcalf, Laurie 59
Metcalfe, Tim 236, 238, 240
Metesky, George 25
Metoyer, Julius 409
Metty, Russell 432
Metzler, Jim 299
Mexico 120
Meyer, Carey 430
Meyer, Nicholas 469, 470, 471
Meyers, Darcy 497
Meyers, Janet 383
MGM 200, 354
Miami Vice (TV) 277
Michael, Ryan 354
Michaelis, Dario 264
Michaels, David 391
Michelet, Michel 264, 268
Michelot 345
Mickery, Lizzie 284
Microwave Massacre 285
Midnight Cowboy 354
Midnight Horror see *Midnight Killer*
Midnight Killer 285
Midnight Ride 285–286
Midsomer Murders (TV) 284
Mier, Felipe 137
The Mighty Quinn 288
Mihalka, George 325, 355, 356, 374, 375
Mikels, Ted V. 64, 66, 97, 98, 270, 446
Milchan, Arnon 94, 202, 438
Miles, Kevin 146
Miles, Sherry 472
Miles, Sylvia 365
Miles, Vera 356, 361, 362
Milford, Penelope 64, 206
Milian, Tomas 133
Milicevic, Ivana 350
Milius, John 480
Milkes, Gary 114
Millbern, David 391
Millbrook, Les 74
Millennium (TV) 1, 115, 325, 355, 502
Miller, A.C. 131
Miller, Bruce 328
Miller, Colleen 432
Miller, Dennis 313
Miller, J.B. 203
Miller, Jason 149
Miller, Jeff 155
Miller, Penelope Ann 334
Miller, Robin 365
Miller, Seton I. 416
Miller, W. Peter 310
Millian, Cindy 127

Millichamp, Stephen 384
Milligan, Andy 64, 66, 98, 270, 446
Milling, William 325
Milling, William P. 415
Millington, Mary 348
Mills, Alec 65
Mills, Alley 44
Mills, Hayley 489, 490
Mills, Mort 356
Milne, Bernadette 99
Minard, Michael 423
The Minus Man 90, 286–288
Mir, Irene 227
Miranda, John 66
Miranda, Robert 124
Mirkovich, Steve 91
Mirman, Brad 244, 380
Mirren, Helen 200, 373
Misch, Laura 279
Misery 111, 515
Mishkin, William 66
Mission Impossible (TV) 232
Mr. Frost 288–289, 326
Mitchell, Cameron 60–61, 64, 474
Mitchell, Donna 364
Mitchell, Elizabeth 181
Mitchell, Sanford 97
Mitchell, Silas Weir 33
Mitchell, Thomas 504
Mitchum, Robert 14, 173, 174, 285, 286
Mittleman, Phil 246
Miyahara, Matt 445
Mizrahi, Tony 384
Modesto, Sam 52
Modot, Gaston 459
Moen, Paul 434
Moffat, Donald 456
Moffett, D. W. 503
Mohr, Gerald 420
Mokae, Zakes 136, 418
Mokri, Amir 153
Mokrosinsky, Peter 272
Mole, Charlie 113, 301
Molina, Alfred 208, 209
Molina, Antonio 227
Molina, Jacinto 227
Molyneaux, William C. 129
Monahan, Lee 137
Moncada, Santiago 198
Mondey, Fawnia 354
Mones, Paul 163
Monese, Alessandro 163
Money Train 434
Monkey Shines 112
Monreale, Cinzia 52
Monroe, Marilyn 159
Monsieur Verdoux 68, 71, 79, 213, 289–291, **290**, 322, 392, 408, 477
The Monster 291–291
The Monster of Venice see *The Embalmer*
monstrous patriarch in films 33,

83, 84, 108, 129, 137, 152, 169, 172, 188, 195, 196, 211, 215, 234, 269, 295, 308, 336, 375, 412, 432–433, 439, 448, 449, 458–459, 477, 503; *see also* patriarchy
Montagu, Ivor 255
Montalban, Ricardo 251
Montero, Edward L. 108
Montero, Roberto 418
Montesano, Vittorio 148
Montevideo 285
Montgomery, Belinda 415, 472
Montgomery, Robert 317, **318**, 319, 320
Monti, Silvia 255
Monton, Vincent 384
Montone, Rita 277
Montreal 148
Montreal World Film Festival 401
Moody, Lynne 44
Mooradian, George 350
Moorcroft, Judy 296
Moore, Alan 187
Moore, Charles Philip 108
Moore, Duke 417
Moore, James 113, 417
Moore, John Jay 396
Moore, Julianne 194, 195, **196**, 276, 277, 358
Moore, Mavor 292
Moore, Randy 411
Moore, Sheila 374
Moore, Teddi 297
Moore, Tim 230
Moors Murderers 518
Morales, Jose 281
Morant, Richard 229
Moraz, Patrick 432
Morelli, Frank 512
Morgan, Alexandra 117
Morgan, Glen 80
Morgan, Michele 68
Morgan, Ralph 92
Morgan, Stafford 511
Moriarty, Cathy 507, **508**, 510
Moriarty, Michael 64
Morin, Catherine 315
Morley, Karen 268
Morley, Robert 441
Morneau, Louis 168
Morricone, Ennio 52, 64, 69, 147, 177, 255, 315, 367, 431, 510
Morrill, John A. 108, 394
Morris, John 127
Morris, Phil 89
Morris, Reginald (Reg) 49, 138, 296
Morrissey, Chris 445
Morrissey, Paul 404; *see also* Warhol/Morrissey films
Morrison, Sammy 430
Morse, Barry 49, 113
Morse, Susan E. 408
Mortal Sins 292

Mortensen, Viggo 358, 359, 374
Mortimer, Trisha 186
Moss, Lou 60
The Most Dangerous Game 47, 292–293
Most Wanted 293
Il Mostro see *The Monster*
Motel Hell 142, 293–296, **294**, **296**, 464, 500
Mountjoy, Eunice 300
Mowbray, Alan 264
Ms .45 136, 164, 165
MTV 90, 127, 381, 485, 498
Muckler, Craig 285
Mueller, Max 395
Mueller-Stahl, Armin 482
Mulcahy, Russell 160, 249, 333, 380, 381, 386
Mulkey, Chris 187, 230
Mull, Martin 108
Mullally, Don 305
Mullavey, Greg 217
Mullen, M. Favit 107
Muller, Paul 81, 264
Muller, Wolfgang 312, 395
Mullin, Mark 241
Mullins, Bartlett 341
Mulroney, Dermot 94
multiple personality disorder 10, 19, 75, 136, 211, 324, 352, 353, 356, 358, 394, 481, 482, 502
The Mummy 159
The Mummy (new) 388
Munchkin, Richard W. 148
Mundhra, Jag 332
Munro, Caroline 277, 323
Munro, Lochlyn 57
Munson, Laurel 492
Murawski, Bob 151
Murder-as-art theme 21n, 67, 95, 96, 101, 149, 162–163, 163, 202, 245, 405, 435, 479, 485
Murder Blues see *Dead Certain*
Murder by Decree 20n, 25n, 26, 230, 296–299, **297**, **298**, 441
Murder by Night 299–300
Murder by Phone see *Bells*
Murder Elite 300
Murder in Mind 300
Murder in My Mind 301
Murder in the Red Barn 158
Murder: Live from Death Row (TV) 254
Murder Lust 301
Murder My Sweet 421
The Murder of Mary Phagan 71
Murder on Line One 301
Murder Rock 302, 314, 418, 440
Murder She Wrote (TV) 197
The Murderer Lives at Number 21 302
Murderock see *Murder Rock*
Murderous Vision 303
Murders in the Rue Morgue (1932) 303–304, 345

Murders in the Rue Morgue (1971) 304
Murders in the Zoo 304–305
Murlawski, John 382
Murman, George 13; *see also* Heirens, William
Murnau, F.W. 6, 11
Murphy, Audie 51
Murphy, Dennis 472
Murphy, Don 309
Murphy, Fred 316
Murphy, John 326
Murphy, Michael 411
Murphy, Paul 485
Murphy's Law 452
Murray, Billy 98
Murray, Graeme 244
Murton, Peter 349
Musante, Tony 52, 53, 124
Musuraca, Nicholas 425
Musy, Mario 198
mutilation (inc. dismemberment) 6, 10n, 20n, 27, 40, 42, 52, 58, 62, 63, 67, 84, 86, 108, 113, 123, 124, 127, 131, 132, 149, 156, 165, 168, 190, 204, 224, 228, 234, 235, 249, 263, 270, 279, 284, 288, 311, 312, 314, 315, 317, 347, 366, 382, 391, 394, 396, 400, 404, 416, 453, 454, 475, 476, 477, 509, 510
Mutter (band) 395
Muzquiz, Carlos 251
Muzyk, Christina 445
My Bloody Valentine (band) 307
My Bloody Valentine 375
My Dear Killer 511
Mycroft, Walter C. 437
Myers, David 116
Myers, Mike 421, 422
Myers, Stanley 58, 186, 215, 328, 394
Myerscough-Jones, David 200
Mystery of the Wax Museum 68, 132, 305

Nadeau, Elyane 279
Nadel, Arthur H. 511
Nadja 306–307, **306**, 323
Naked City 15
Naked Souls 307–308
Namibia 137
Nance, John 441
Nannerini, Luigi 81, 477
Napier, Alan 194
Napier, Charles 323, 324, 384
Napoli, Lisa 323
Naschy, Paul 227, 228
Nash, Jason 354
Nash, Marilyn 289
Nassar, Debbie 440
Nasso, Julius R. 190
Natalucci, Giovanni 99
Nathan, Robert 223
Nathanson, Michael 94

Nathanson, Rick 324
Nation, Terry 38
National Theatre (London) 313
Nattevagten 308–309, 327
Natural Born Killers 24, 37, 80, 108, 138, 237, 255, 271, 309–310, **310**, 403, 431
Nature of the Beast 103, 286, 310–312, **311**
Naulin, John (A.) 230, 332
Navajo Indians 410
Nazis and Nazism 71, 100, 131, 152, 183, 265, 268, 293, 321, 322, 367, 426, 427, 454, 476, 518
Neal, Edwin 460
Neal, Patricia 316
Nebenzal, Seymour 265, 268
Necoechea, Miguel 119
Necronomicon 391
Necrophagus see *Lucker*
necrophilia 6, 20n, 46, 52, 69, 82, 120, 123, 124, 128, 146, 163, 168, 180, 184, 186, 191, 203, 207, 224, 228, 241, 249, 263, 264, 270, 277, 281, 282, 305, 307, 308, 312, 319, 327, 328, 332, 347, 349, 350, 358, 364, 365, 366, 378, 395–396, 400, 410, 420, 423, 447, 463, 464, 475, 494, 500
Needs, James 129
Neer, Kay 261
Negret, Francois 288
Neil, Debra 211
Nekromantik (films) 30n, 52, 124, 229, 263, 309, 312, 396
Nekromantik 2 312–313, 332, 348, 395, 420
Nelligan, Kate 408
Nelson, Danny 65
Nelson, Earle Leonard 14, 15, 219, 408
Nelson, Herbert 320
Nelson, Judd 278, 375, 376, **376**, 377, 378
Nelson, Shane 337
Nelson, Willie 337
Nemec, Joseph C., III 164
Nepomniaschy, Alex 303
Neri, Francesca 194
Nero, Franco 147
Nesbitt, Derren 348
Nettleton, John 38
Neufeld, Martin 374
Neuman, Jeffrey R. 313
Neumann, Dorothy 354
Neumann, Mathias 391
Neuville, Ernest 345
Neuwirth, Bebe 335, 336, 441, **443**
Nevada 458
Never Cry Devil see *Night Visitor*
Never Pick Up a Stranger see *Bloodrage*
Never Talk to Strangers 313

Neville, John 441
New England 71
New Mexico 251, 335
New Orleans 380, 467
New York City (NYC) 48, 57, 66, 104, 118, 125, 137, 163, 190, 202, 305, 323, 334, 347, 375
The New York Ripper 82, 302, 314–315, 387, 475
New Zealand 492
Newbrook, Peter 98
Newcomb, James E. 247
Newman, Lionel 75, 272
Newman, Thomas 430
Newman, Serge 45
Newton, Jonathan 492
Newton, Linda 333
Ng, Charles 493; *see also* Lake, Leonard
Ng, Francis 393
Niami, Nile 380, 497
Niami, Yvonne 497
Nicholas, Kim 219
Nichols, Barbara 346
Nichols, Lisa 301
Niciphor, Nick 162
Nico, William 289
Nicolaou, Ted 411, 478
Nicolini, Angelo 431
Nicolodi, Daria 121, 455
Nicols, Barbara 151
Niehaus, Lennie 467
Niekirk, Sidney 148, 386
Nielson, Donald 54, 55
Nietzsche 371
Night After Night After Night see *He Kills Night After Night After Night*
The Night Caller 315
Night Cries 315–316
The Night Digger 316
Night Game 316–317
Night Must Fall (1937) 259, 262, 316, 317–319, **318**, 394, 427, 489
Night Must Fall (1964) 18, 316, 319–320, **320**
Night of Bloody Horror 320–321
Night of the Generals 70, 71, 79, 291, 321–323, **322**, 330
Night of the Hunter 14, 173
Night of the Living Dead 159
Night Owl 307, 323, 338
The Night Porter 183, 281
Night Ripper 323
Night Shadow 323
The Night Stalker 323–324
Night Visions 303, 324–325, 502
Night Visitor 325
Nightmare 325–326, 416
Nightmare Concert see *Cat in the Brain*
Nightmare Hotel 326
Nightmare on Elm Street 327, 412
Nightscare 326–327

Nightwatch (1994) see *Nattevagten*
Nightwatch (1998) 309, 327–328, 351
Niles, Chuck 458
Nilsen, Des 41
Nilsson, Stefan 272–273
99 and 44/100% Dead 270
The Ninth Configuration 149, 151
Nitzsche, Jack 104
Niven, Kip 300
No Escape 103
No One Could Protect Her 328
No Way to Treat a Lady 75, 158, 328–330, **329**
Noble, Patsy Ann 97
Noiret, Philippe 321
Nolan, William F. 81
Nolte, Nick 327
Noonan, Tom 202, 273
Nord, Richard 423, 497
Norfolk 393
Norman, Monty 490
Norris, Aaron 384
Norris, Chuck 207, 208, **208**
Norris, George T. 201
Norris, Patricia 486, 488
North, Sheree 293
Norton, Bill L. 300
Norton, Dee Dee 92
Norton, Terri 136
Norton, William 217
Nosferatu 6, 7, 338
Not Without My Daughter 154
Nouri, Michael 246, 355
Novack, Shelly 293
Novak, Danny 73
Novak, Frank 310
Novello, Ivor 255
Noyce, Philip 72, 73
Nuchtern, Simon 415, 416
Nunn, Bill 242
Nye, Carrie 474
Nyman, Michael 371

Oakland, Simon 356
O'Bannon, Rockne S. 164
Obel, Michael 308, 327
Ober, Arlon 141
Oberon, Merle 256, 258
O'Bradovich, Bob 224, 250
O'Brien, Joseph 481
O'Brien, Patrick 375
O'Brien, Richard 110
O'Brien, Seamus 224
O'Brien, Timothy 319
O'Connor, Diane Patrick 253
O'Connor, Glynnis 123
O'Connor, Kevin 423
O'Connor, Pat 231
O'Connor, Robin 348
O'Conor, Hugh 515, **516**, 517
Odd, David 284
O'Donnell, Sylvia 54
O'Fallon, James 81

Off Limits 190, 227, 330–331, **331**
The Office Killer 331–332
Ogilvy, Ian 422
O'Halloran, Jack 207, **208**
Ohashi, Rene 471
O'Heaney, Caitlin 201
O'Keefe, Dennis 251
O'Keefe, Doug 57
O'Keefe, Michael 164
O'Keefe, Miles 377
Oklahoma 383
Oland, Bill 423
Oland, Warner 500
Oldfield, Mike 149
Oldman, Gary 102, 194, 195
Olea, Imanol 513
Olea, Pedro 513
O'Leary, Jack 118
Oliansky, Joel 472
Oliver, Gordon 425
Oliviero, Silvio 505
Olmos, Edward James 252
Olsen, Wes 113
Olvis, William 337
Oman, Chad 91
O'Mara, Kate 98
The Omen 349, 375, 394
On Deadly Ground 190, 191
One Flew Over the Cuckoo's Nest 415
O'Neal, Ryan 340, **341**
O'Neil, Barbara 398
O'Neill, Ed 72
O'Neill, Robert Vincent 38, 40, 116, 117
Ontkean, Michael 486, **487**
Open House 332–333
Opera 432
Oppenheimer, Peer J. 482
O'Quinn, Terry 55, 432, **433**, 434
Oregon 492
Organic Theatre Company (Chicago) 206
Orlandi, Nora 58
Ormonde, Czenzi 432
Ormsby, Alan 123, 124
Ornitz, Arthur J. 349
Ornstein, Michael 337
O'Ross, Ed 347
Orr, Buxton 199
Orser, Leland 72, 380, 404
Ortolani, Riz 407
Orton, Ray 334
Osbiston, Alan 321
Osborne, William 187
Osco, Bill 400
Oshima, Nagisa 493, 494
Ossenfort, Kurt 306
Osth, Robert 133
O'Sullivan, Maureen 474
The Other Sister 237
O'Toole, Peter 321, 322, **322**, 388, 389
O'Toole, Stanley 65
Ouimette, Stephen 156

Ouspenskaya, Maria 514
Out of the Body 197, 333
Out of the Dark 333–334, 506
Out of the Darkness 334
Outside Ozona 57, 132, 249, 286, 312, 333, 334–335, 353, 410, 445
Oxenberg, Catherine 391

Pabst, G.W. 6, 7, 338
Pacey, Peter 515
Pacheco, Godofredo 45
Pacific Heights 153
Pacino, Al 104, **105**, **106**, 202, 396, **397**, 398, 467
Pack, Charles L. 99
Pack, Roger Lloyd 515
Page, Geraldine 501, 502
Page, Grant 384
Paglia, Mark 248
Pagliai, Ugo 163
Paine, Cathey 203
The Paint Job see *Painted Heart*
Painted Heart 335–337, 435, 440
Painter, Andrew 314
Painter, Chris 162
Pair of Aces 173, 337
Paiva, Nestor 176
Palance, Jack 101, 272
Pale Blood 337–338, 372, 394
Palk, Tony 44
Palm, Anders 113, 114, 193, 301
Palm Beach 481
Palm City 519
Palmer, Anthony 316
Palmer, Byron 272
Palmer, Keith 229
Palmer, Lilli 304
Paltrow, Gwyneth 404, 406
Pamphili, Mirelia 182
Pan, Kant 221
Pandora's Box 6, 8, 162, 259, 338–340, 499
Panic City see *The Zebra Killer*
Panic in the Streets 15
Pantoliano, Joe 283, 401
Panzram, Carl 238, 239
Paoli, Dennis 292
Paolone, Catherine 378
Papadelis, Anne-Marie 58
Papamichael, Phedon 437, 440
Papas, Irene 133
Paper Chase 50
Paperhouse 247
Papertrail see *Trail of a Serial Killer*
Pappaert, Nelly 271
Pappas, George 170
Paquette, Andre 155
Paramount 358
Paranoiac 18
Pare, Michael 387, 391, 392, 393
Paredes, Marisa 119
Parello, Chuck 206
Parents 372
Paris 67, 304, 345, 466

Parisot, Dean 435
Parker, Brian 409
Parker, Cecil 441
Parker, Clifton 113
Parker, Jean 67
Parker, Norman 88
Parker, Sarah Jessica 438, **439**
Parker, Scott 201
Parkins, Barbara 81
Parks, Richard 41
Parmet, Phil 53
Parry, Mark 168
Parslow, Philip L. 372
Parsons, Nancy 293, **294**
Parsons, Steve 429
Partain, Paul A. 460
Partners 315, 340–341, **341**
Partridge, Ross 53
Partridge Family (TV) 118
Pastorelli, Robert 335, 336, 438
Patriarchal Capitalism see Capitalism
Patriarchy 2, 28, 31, 36, 57, 65, 73, 74, 80, 100, 104, 105, 106, 108, 114, 116, 118, 137, 138, 144, 158, 161, 163, 172, 178, 179, 181, 182, 183, 189, 193, 194, 207, 209, 216, 218, 221, 223, 224, 243, 247, 263, 280, 286, 300, 313, 315, 316, 324, 325, 328, 336, 337, 340, 341, 348, 352, 353, 356, 370, 372, 375, 376–377, 384, 394, 395, 411, 412, 419, 420, 424, 425, 432, 435, 438, 439, 449, 451, 459, 463, 464, 467, 472, 481, 483, 485, 491, 495, 496, 497, 498, 501, 502, 503, 511, 520; see also Capitalism, monstrous patriarch
Patrick 386
Patrick, Dorothy 176
Patrick, Gail 304
Patterson, David J. 103
Patterson, Lee 227
Pattinson, Michael 252
Patton, Will 94, 223, 335, 336
Paul, Alexandra 353
Paul, Richard 141
Paul, Rick 203, 206
Paull, Morgan 158
Pavey, Stan 113
Paxton, Bill 44
Paymer, David 334
Pays, Amanda 330
Peach, Patrick 353
Peacock, Michael 134
Peacocke, Thomas 292
Pearce, Guy 371
Pearl, Daniel 460
Pearson, Brian 155
Pease, Patsy 201
Peckinpah, Sam 93, 401
Pedas, Jim 48
Pedas, Ted 48
pedophilia 133, 178, 196, 217, 220,

221–222, 226, 265, 348, 372, 387, 453, 510, 511
Peeping Tom 16, 18n, 22, 44, 45, 67, 71, 100, 126, 134, 163, 167, 276, 281, 301, 338, 341–345, **342**, **343**, 346, 354, 358, 390, 422, 423, 427, 429, 436, 475, 482, 489, 490, 497, 506, 509
Pelegrin, Ines 156
Pelletier, David 234
Pember, Ron 297
Pembroke, George 67
Penhalington, Susan 215
Penn, Chris 481, 482
Penn, William 92
Penner, J.E. 492
Pennies from Heaven (TV) 166
Penzer, Jean 315
People Under the Stairs 411
Pepin, Richard 43, 44
Pepler, Martin 49
Peploe, Mark 34, 35
Peranio, Vincent 403
Percy, Lee 241
Pereira, Hal 328
Perez, Jose 251
Performance 509, 510
Perkins, Anthony 142, 143, **143**, 223, 224, 281, 356, **357**, 359, 361, 362, 363, 364
Perkins, Frank 99
Perkins, Millie 511
Perle, Rebecca 467
Perlman, Ron 401, 502
Perrin, Bryce 371
Perry, Felton 44, 378
Perry, Fred C. 58
Perry, Steve 117, 235
Personal Column 264, 345
Persons, Johanna 303
Peskanov, Alexander 88, 201
Peskanov, Mark 201
Peters, Jon 157
Peters, Rick 197
Peters, Werner 52
Petersen, William 273, **274**, **275**, 277, 350
Peterson, Amanda 162
Peterson, Clark 107
Petiot, Marcel 131
Petit, Paul 127
Pettet, Joanna 321, 499
Pettiet, Christopher 379
Pettillo, Alan 134
Peyser, John 85
Peysher, Ernie 224
Pfieffer, Deedee 215
Phantom of the Opera 418
The Phantom of the Opera 248
Phantom of the Rue Morgue 9, 304, 345–346
The Phantom Speaks 346
Phelps, Nigel 72, 219
Phillips, Alex, Jr. 158
Philips, Lee 365

Phillips, Lou Diamond 172, 173
Phillips, Mark 366
Phillips, Stu 394
Phobia 379, 481
Phoenix, Joaquin 89, **90**, 143, 144
The Photographer 346
Piana, Dennis M. 396
Piana, Nina 396
Piazzolli, Roberto D'Ettore 285
Picardo, Robert 230
Piccioni, Piero 227
Pickett, James 466, 518
Picnic at Hanging Rock 65
Piddock, Jim 481
Pieces 325, 346–347
Piedmont, Leon 283
Pieges see *Personal Column*
Pielmeier, John 197
Pierce, Alan 493
Pierce, Charles B. 478, 479, 480, 481
Pierce-Roberts, Tony 111
Pierson, Carl 67
Pigot, Neil 372
Pileggi, Mitch 324, 411, **412**
Pilgaard, Ulf 308
Pinchuk, Sheldon 299
Pinewood Studios 180
Pinori, Giuseppe 302
Pintoff, Ernest 57, 58
Piper, Kelly 277
Pitt, Brad 236, 237, **237**, 238, 404, 405, **405**, 406
Pittman, Tom 520
Pittsburgh 279,280
Pivar, Ben 411
Pizer, Larry 474
Place, Patricia 353
Platoon 330
Platt, Joseph 247
Play Nice 347–348, 352, 420, 511
Playbirds 348
The Playgirl Killer 348–349
Pleasence, Donald 163, 174, 175, 321, 322, 408
Plessner, Amotz 53
Plumeri, Terry 367, 379
Plumeri, Tony 168
Plummer, Amanda 168, 177, 421
Plummer, Christopher 296, **297**, 321, 427, **428**
Poe, Edgar A. 303, 304, 345, 390
Poelvoorde, Benoit 271
Poelvoorde-Pappaert, Jacqueline 271
Pogany, Gabor 69
Pogue, Charles Edward 363
Poison Ivy 438, 440
Polcelli, Franca 270
Poledouris, Basil 403, 445
Polis, Joel 402
Polito, Jon 48, 88
Polito, Sol 43
Poll, Martin 349, 350
Pollack, Sydney 284

Pollak, Kevin 334
Pollard, Michael J. 42, 43, 325, 429
Pollini, Francis 351
Pollock, Dee 50
Polone, Gavin 143
Poltergeist 140, 411, 465
Polyester 445
Ponte, Gideon 35
Ponti, Carlo 68, 475
Poole, Duane 351, 409
Poor Albert and Little Annie see *I Dismember Mama*
Pope, Dick 374
Poplin, Jack 99
Porel, Marc 133
Porky's 297
pornography 30, 30n, 35, 36, 43, 46, 62, 63, 67, 80, 82, 122, 124, 126, 143, 144, 145, 148, 168, 201, 212, 228, 249, 250, 253, 277, 278, 282, 312, 314, 316, 338, 341, 344, 348, 365, 366, 367, 373, 386, 391, 396, 400, 401, 417, 423, 424, 429, 436, 444, 446, 455, 475, 476, 502, 511, 515, 516, 519
Portal, Michel 131
Porter, Don 411
Porter, Eric 193
Porter, Shea 409
Porter, Steven M. 39
Portishead (band) 307
Porto, Juan Antonio 513
Positively True Adventures of the Alleged Texas Cheerleader-Murdering Mom 403
The Possession of Joel Delaney 349–350
Post, Ted 129
Postlethwaite, Pete 101, 429
Postman Always Rings Twice 55
Postmortem 350–351, 380, 406
Potter, Tim 515
Pottle, Harry 296
Pounder, CCH 364
Pourmand, Monsour 519
Powder 311
Powell, Michael 16, 17, 19, 71, 341, 343, 344, 345, 427
Powell, Reg 47
Power, Derek 108
Powers, Tom 346
Powladge, David 353
Powley, Bryan 261
Pratt, Anthony 316
Pratt, Vicky 57
Pravda, Hanna-Maria 38
A Prayer for the Dying 292, 387, 458
Praying Mantis 57, 351
Predator 109, 430
Preissel, Miriam L. 246
Premier Productions 354
Preovolos, Nicholas T. 418
Presnell, Robert, Jr. 251

Pressman, Edward R. 35
Presson, Jason 246
Pretty Maids All in a Row 351–352, 476
Pretty Poison 214
Pretty Woman 48
Prettykill 352–353
Preuss, Ruben 114
Prey of the Chameleon 57, 353–354
Price, Henri 212
Price, Jonathan 119
Price, Richard 396, 398
Price, Vincent 38, 69, 504, **504**
Priest 371
Priestley, Jack 170, 328
Priestley, Jason 154
Prieto, Aurore 131
Primal Fear 161
Prime Suspect (TV) 200, 284, 373
Prime Time Murder see *Stringer*
Prince, William 57, 88
Prine, Andrew 85, 458, 478
Prior, David A. 419
Prior, Ted 419
"Prisoner" (song) 157
Private Parts 141, 354
Probyn, Brian 134
Prochnow, Jurgen 488
Profile for Murder 354–355
profiler figure 1, 2, 8n, 19, 20n, 21, 25–28, 25n, 28n, 29–31, 34, 37, 38, 45, 47, 48, 49, 50, 53, 57, 71, 72, 73, 74, 75, 76, 77, 83, 84, 85, 88, 89, 91, 94, 95, 96, 97, 111, 115, 130, 138, 145, 156, 159, 161, 164, 168, 173, 177, 191, 194, 197, 198, 203, 207, 221, 223, 224, 227, 232, 233, 242, 245, 252, 258, 263, 273–275, 276, 283, 286, 288, 292, 293, 303, 306, 314, 315, 317, 324, 326, 327, 331, 334, 345, 350, 353, 355, 367, 377, 378, 379, 380, 381, 382, 383, 388, 389, 402, 412, 413, 419, 421, 429, 430, 446, 449, 466, 477, 480, 481, 485, 486, 491, 492, 495, 498, 503, 505, 520
Profiler (TV) 1, 115, 325, 502, 503
PROFILER program 26; *see also* VICAP
Prosperi, Franco 147
prostitutes 35, 39, 40, 64, 93, 98, 101, 129, 135, 142, 166, 175, 202, 218, 227, 228, 246, 250, 256, 263, 277, 279, 308, 316, 321, 322, 323, 324, 325, 327, 330, 338, 339, 352, 353, 372, 383, 386, 408, 409, 416, 417, 419, 424, 437, 438, 441, 445, 456, 467, 468, 497, 500, 519
Protosevich, Mark 82
Prouix, Michel 103, 496
Provis, George 101

Proyas, Alex 110
Pryce, Jonathan 127, **128**
Pryor, Bryn 97
Przygodda, Peter 476
Psychic 89, 355–356, 375, 380
Psychic-link films 64, 89, 156, 157, 163, 164, 173, 208, 219, 225, 300, 325, 333, 356, 366, 411, 412, 502
psychics 20, 20n, 37, 75, 85, 88, 109, 115, 116, 121, 156, 164, 173, 209, 300, 303, 324, 333, 337, 355, 440, 472
Psycho (1960) 12, 16, 17, 19, 22, 43, 70, 89, 129, 133, 134, 140, 148, 167, 190, 281, 295, 320, 326, 329, 353, 354, 356–358, **357**, 361, 365, 395, 415, 437, 463, 474, 478, 490, 493, 505
Psycho (1998) 358–361, **359, 360**
Psycho 2 361–362, 363, 386
Psycho 3 356, 362, 363
Psycho 4: The Beginning 363–365
Psycho Circus see *Terror Circus*
Psychomania 365
Psychopathia Sexualis (book) 489
Psychos in Love 108, 212, 366, 506
Puberty Blues 65
Puente, Jesus 198
Pughe, George 437
Puig, Raul 107
Pulp Fiction 48, 108
Pupkewitz, David 101
Puppet Master 478
Purdom, Edmund 147, 346
Purdy-Gordon, Carolyn 42
Pure Killjoy 366–367
Purl, Linda 496
Putnam, Mark 168
Pyle, Denver 173
Pym, Walter 146
Pyun, Albert 350, 351

Quabins, Faith 269
Quaid, Dennis 181, 182, 355, 445
Quarry, Robert 148
Quasimodo 182
Quastel, Jonas 253
Quayle, Anthony 297, 441
Queen, Ellery 441
Queer as Folk (TV) 284
Quentin, John 431
Quigley, Linnea 163
Quinn, Aidan 59, 60, 219
Quinn, Eileen 200
Quinn, Francesco 113

Raab, Kurt 453, 454, 455
Rab, Leonid 176
Rabier, Jean 68, 78
Rabin, Trevor 91, 190
Raby, Simon 491
Racette, Francine 177
Radd, Ronald 427
Rae, Dan 429

Rafelson, Bob 55, 57
Rafferty, James 323
Ragalyi, Elemer 313
The Rage: Carrie 2 438, 440
Ragland, Robert O. 117, 352, 450
Raho, Umberto 52
Railsback, Steve 117, 203
Raimi, Sam 49, 463
The Rain Killer 367
Rainer, Klaus 52
Rains, Claude 514
Raising Cain 67
Raley, Ron 142
Raman, Gordon 202
Ramirez, Juan 222
Ramirez, Richard 212, 216, 217
Ramos, Rudy 332
Rampage 107, 151, 280, 367–371, **368, 369**, 451
Rampling, Charlotte 281
Ramsay, Anne 168
Ramsay, Bruce 107
Ramsay, Todd 149, 286
Ramsey, Reagan 492
Ranahan, Patrick 252
Rand, Patrick 367
Randall, Dick 346
Randall, Gary 367
Randall, Meg 511
Randall, Stacie 148
Randell, Ron 190
Ransford, Maurice 194
Ransley, Peter 200
Ransohoff, Martin 192, 400, 447
Ransom, John 179
Rao, N. 125
Raposo, Joe 349
Rassimov, Ivan 58
Ratay, Wayne 512
Rathbone, Basil 169, 261, 262
Rau, Jim 512
Ravel, Jean 69
Raven, Elisa 212
Raven, Mike 217
Ravenous 371–372, 410, 499
Rawle, Jeff 515
Rawley, Fabienne 101
Rawlings, Terry 507
Rawlinson, A.R. 158
Rawlinson, Brian 400
Ray, Aldo 85
Ray, David 57
Ray, Eric J. 366
Ray, Nicholas 128
Raye, Martha 289
Raymond, Emily 262
Rea, Chris 103
Rea, Stephen 85, 86, **86**, 87, **87**, 127, **128**, 219
Read, Ian 199
Reading, Tony 229
Re-Animator 152
Rear Window 73, 137
Reardon, Dan 168
Reason to Die 372

Rebhorn, James 201
Red Cat in a Labyrinth of Glass 156
Red Dragon see *Manhunter*
Red Lips see *Sadisterotica*
Red Rain see *Jack's Back*
Red Rock West 89
Redball 372–373, 486
Redford, J.A.C. 138
Redford, Robert 288
Redgrave, Michael 398, 399
Redler, Dan 354
Redman, Anthony 164
Redmond, Liam 113
The Reds (band) 273
Reed, Alistair 316
Reed, Hal 520
Reed, Joel M. 224
Reed, Laura 439
Reed, Lenii 445
Reed, Maxwell 113
Reed, Roland D. 92
Reed, Shanna 47
Reed, Tom 303
Reeder, Mark 312
Reefer Madness 417
Rees, Angharad 193
Rees, Betty Anne 346
Reese, Michelle 324
Reeve, Christopher 73, 292
Reeves, Keanu 497, 498
Reeves, Michael 98, 169, 218, 422
The Reflecting Skin 374
Regalbuto, Joe 515
Regan, Pat 434
Regehr, Duncan 47
Regnoli, Piero 264
Rehberg, H.M. 476
Reid, Beryl 127
Reid, James 33
Reid, Roy 417
Reilly, John C. 327
Reineke, Gary 49
Reiner, Carl 60
Reinl, Harald 519
Reis, Terence 382
Reishl, Geri 217
Reisz, Karel 18, 134, 319, 320
Relative Fear 374–375
Relentless 278, 375–377, **376**, 378, 418
Relentless 2 377–378
Relentless 3 378–379
Relentless 4 379
Remar, James 59, 104, 151, 152, 162, 324, 340, 358
Remick, Lee 124, 125, 328
Renan, Sheldon 23n, 241
Rendelstein, Les 354
Rennahan, Ray (aka Renuhan, Ray) 305
Reno, John 67
Renoir, Jean 459
Renoir, Pierre 345
Renuhan, Ray (aka Rennahan, Ray) 131

Renzetti, Joe 303, 418
Renzi, Eva 52
Reservoir Dogs 271
Resino, Andrea 227
Reskin, David 90
Resnikoff, Robert 172
Ressel, Franco 61
Ressler, Robert 2, 3, 22, 45, 76, 372, 378
Resurrection 284, 325, 380–381, 406, 482
The Return of Dracula 92, 381–382, 408, 432
Return of the Family Man 382
Return to Paradise 89, 434
Revell, Graeme 187, 238, 363, 436, 481
Revenge 383
Revere, Anne 398
Reville, Alma 407
Rexrode, Cecyle Osgood 92
Reynaud, Janine 390, 391
Reynolds, Harry 194
Reynolds, Robert 485
Reynolds, Scott 491
Rhames, Ving 91
Rhodes, Jennifer 417
Rhys, Paul 262
Ricci, Bill 133
Rice, Frank 191
Rice, Jeff 497
Rich, Eli 301
Rich, Lee 235
Richard, J. 418
Richards, Ann 262
Richards, Dick 118
Richards, Sylvia 398
Richardson, David M. 80, 391
Richardson, Henry 101, 114
Richardson, Ian 110
Richardson, Jay 418
Richardson, John 156, 475
Richardson, Regina 467
Richardson, Robert 309
Richardson, Sallye
Richardson, Tony 134
Richert, Ted 156
Richmond, Anthony B. 371
Richter, Deborah 47
Rickman, Alan 231
Ricochet 160
Ridges, Stanley 346
Ridley, Philip 374
Riesner, Dean 126
The Rifleman (TV) 512
Rigand, George 156
Rigg, Rebecca 485
Rigo, Maria 482
Rijn, Brad 423
Riley, Michael 471
Rinaldi, Antonio 198
Rinaldi, Mary 163
Rinder, Laurin 241
Ringuette, Lory-Michael 122
Ringwald, Molly 331

Riparetti, Anthony 350
Ripper see Jack the Ripper
The Ripper (1986) 382–383
The Ripper (1997) 227, 383–384
Ripper Man 384
Ripstein, Arturo 119, 121
Risher, Sara 59
Ritter, Magdalena 273
Rivera, Geraldo 254
River's Edge 117, 474
RKO 176, 505
Roach, Bert 303
road movie 103, 237, 238, 286, 335
Roadgames 362, 384–386, **385**
Roadhouse 231, 439
Robards, Jason, Jr. 44, 304
Robbins, Eva 281
Roberson, James W. 478
Roberson, Jim 478
Roberts, Arthur 346
Roberts, Davie 66
Roberts, Doris 212, 328
Roberts, Eric 310, 311, 391
Roberts, Lynne 346
Roberts, Marguerite 173
Roberts, Michael D. 254
Roberts, Rick 259, 374
Roberts, Tanya 250, 477
Roberts, William 450
Robinson, Andrew (Andy) 44, 126, 162
Robinson, Bob 192
Robinson, Bruce 219, 220, 232
Robinson, Casey 503
Robinson, Cathy 253
Robinson, Harriet 506
Robinson, Jack T. 375
Robinson, Jay 340
Robinson, John 94
Robinson, Matt 349
Robinson, Phil Alden 377
Robson, Mark 251
Rocco, Alex 246
Rocky IV 234
Rodan, Allison 289
Rodat, Robert 383
Roddenberry, Gene 351, 352
Roden, Jeff 453
Rodenkirchen, Franz 312, 395
Roderick-Jones, Alan 116
Rodis, Nilo 494
Rodman, Howard 491
Rodriguez, Marco 402
Rodriguez, Miguel 40
Roe, Willy 348
Roehm, Edward 261
Rogers, Eric 44
Rogers, Lorraine 365
Rogers, Peter 44
Rohner, Clayton 307
Rojas, Mimi 156
Roland, Gyl 458
Rolfing, Tom 201
Rolling Thunder 33, 133

Rollins, Jack 408
Rolsky, Robert M. 351
Romahn, Michael 395
Romalo, Frank 62
Roman, Leticia 147
Roman, Ruth 219, 416
Romancing the Stone 515
Romanini, Mario 148
Romano, Andy 253
Romano, Renato 52, 147
Romans, Pierre 131
Romay, Lina 228
Rome 70, 455
Romero, George (A.) 9, 28, 109, 111, 124, 139, 279, 296, 323
Romoli, Giovanni 483
Romper Stomper 373
Romvari, Jozsef 85
Ronan, Danny 325
Ronane, John 427
Rooker, Michael 72, 111, 112, 203, **204, 205**, 206, 396, 398
Room 13 see *Zimmer 13*
Roots of Evil 386–387
Rope 14, 15
Roquevert, Noel 302
The Rosary Murders 387–388
Rose, Bernard 247, 518
Rose, George 227
Rose, Sherman 381
Rosell, Jose 281
Rosemary's Baby 101
Rosen, Barry 138
Rosen, Charles 88
Rosen, Larry 418
Rosen, Phil 430
Rosenbaum, Mark 216, 223
Rosenberg, Aaron 124, 125
Rosenberg, Alan 507
Rosenberg, C.A. 277
Rosenberg, Philip 192, 231
Rosenberg, Scott 91
Rosenbloom, David 181, 222
Rosenburg, George 58
Rosenman, Leonard 88, 472
Rosenstock, Harvey 238, 242
Rosenwald, Francis 176
Rosher, Charles 351
Ross, Anita 134
Ross, Benjamin 515, 518
Ross, Charles 270
Ross, Herbert 471
Ross, Howard 314
Ross, Jacquie Freeman 65
Ross, Katherine 108
Ross, Kelly 219
Ross, Kenneth G. 333
Ross, Rebecca 307
Ross, Sandi 234
Rossberg, Susanna 281
Rossetti, Marco 52
Rossi, F. 418
Rossi, Leo 55, 375, 377, 378, 379
Rosten, Leo 264
Rostov 86

Rote, Ed W. 430
Roth, Chris 108
Roth, Christopher 389
Roth, Leon 217
Roth, Richard 273
Rothman, John 94
Rothman, Marion 75
Rothrock, Cynthia 153
Rothschild, Jon 325
Rothstein, Richard 118
Rotondo, Paolo 491
Rottweiller 420
Rotundo, Nick 103
Rotunno, Giuseppe 431
Rough Draft 102, 388, 506
Roundtree, Richard 47, 325
Rourke, Mickey 88, 158
Roven, Charles 160
Rowe, Tom 252, 292
Rowley, Kevin 284
Roy, Esperanza 326
Roya, David 323
Royal Shakespeare Company 313
Rozsa, Miklos 398, 469
Rubell, Paul 82
Ruben, Albert 88
Ruben, Andy 437, 440
Ruben, Joseph 375, 432, 434
Ruben, Katt Shea 108, 437, 438, 440
Rubin, Gregg 366
Rubin, Jennifer 391
Rubin, Lance 293
Rubin, Mann 170, 472
Rubini, Michael 273
Rubinstein, Donald 279
Rubinstein, John 240
Rubinstein, Keith 80
Rubinstein, Richard T. 279
Rudkilde, Hanneh 503
Rudolf, Gene 93
Rudolph, Alan 458, 459
Ruehl, Mercedes 286, 287
Rugerrio, Gene 269
Ruggles, Charles 304
Ruhmann, Heinz 226
Rules of Engagement 371
The Ruling Class 388–389, 425
Run for the Sun 293
Running Scared 190
Ruscio, A. 116
Rush, Jordan 313
Rush, Richard 482
Rush, Tony 262
Russ, Tim 114
Russ, William 481
Russell, John L.
Russell, Karen 113
Russell, Ken 39, 143
Russell, Kurt 47, 283
Russell, Ray 225
Russell, Rosalind 317, **318**
Russell, Theresa 55, 56, **56**, 57
Russia 86
Russo, Aaron 340

Russo, James 483
Rustan, Mardi 139
Rustic, Carl 60
Rutowski, Richard 177, 309
Ruymen, Ayn 354
Ryan, John P. 430
Ryan, Michael 437
Ryan, Robert 50, 51
Ryann, Janna 302
Rydell, Christopher 483
Ryon, Rex 230

Sabatini, Antonio 177
Sabato, Antonio 407
Sabrina 219
Sacchetti, Dardano 285, 314
Sacramento Vampire 367; *see also* Chase, Richard
Sacrifice 47, 103, 389–390
Sadean/Romantic themes 46, 162, 228, 234, 265, 282, 390, 425
sadism and sadists 12, 23, 34, 46, 73, 89, 98, 99, 149, 152, 165, 180, 187, 211, 212, 215, 216, 224, 229, 269, 286, 293, 298, 299, 303, 304, 305, 314, 319, 342, 390, 394, 415, 423, 459, 471, 479, 480, 489, 493, 499, 503, 513
Sadisterotica 68, 390–391
Safan, Craig 158
Saffran, Jason 241
Safra, Michel 345
Sagebrecht, Marianne 136
Sager, Ray 35, 512
Saiger, Susan 141
Saigon 330
Saigon see *Off Limits*
St. Gerard, Michael 430
St. Ives 452
St. John, Marco 467
St. John, Nicholas 136, 164
St. Jon, Philip 320
Sakata, Harold 219
Salcedo, Pepe 281
Salerno, Enrico Maria 52
Salfas, Stan 89, 430
Salgado, Maria Rosa 226
Salkind, Alexander 69
Salo: 120 Days of Sodom 183
Salomon, Mikael 47, 93
Salon Kitty 183
Salt, Jennifer 334
Salt Lake City 34
Salter, Hans 262, 514
Salva, Victor 310, 311
Salvati, Sergio 99
Salvay, Bennett 310
Salven, David 367
Sam the Sham (band) 438
Sampson, Robert 42
Sampson, Tim 409
San Francisco 113, 122, 252, 420, 518, 520
Sanchez, Jesus 513
Sanchez-Short, Elba 383

Sanciriaco, Manuel Cano 198
Sanctimony 391–393, 407
Sandell, William 190
Sanders, George 194, 256, 264, 504
Sanders, Jay O. 242
Sanders, Lawrence 170
Sanders, Ronald 115
Sandrock, Steve 382
Sands, Julian 127
Sanford, Isabel 346
Sanger, Jonathan 127
Sangster, Jimmy 227
Santa Monica 109, 367
Santa Rosa 408
Santoni, Reni 126
Santos, Joe 57
Saperstein, Richard 404
Sarandon, Susan 231
Sarde, Alain 130
Sarlui, Eduard 316
Sarna, Lorand 447
Sarossy, Paul 165, 259
Sarrazin, Michael 281, 482
Sartamaran, Enrich 348
Sasdy, Peter 193
Sassone, Oley 379
Sassoon, Catya 108
Satan and Satanism 172, 209, 211, 216, 217, 288, 325, 348, 370, 393, 429, 514
The Satan Killer 393
Satan Returns 393–394
Sato, Kei 493
Satorius, James 104
Saturday Night Live (TV) 422
Satwell, Paul 74
Saulnier, Jacques 68
Savage Intruder 394
Savalas, Telly 351
Savini, Tom 124, 277, 279, 382, 383
Saxon, Edward 412
Saxon, John 42, 46, 65, 147, 455
Sayer, Diane 437
Sayre, Stephen 393
Scaglione, Michael 42
Scalia, Pietro 194
Scanner Cop 402
Scanners 50, 115, 188, 402
Scantlebury, Glen 91
Scardino, Don 104, 201
Scarlet Street 400
Scarpelli, Henry 250
Scarpulla, Clare 353
Scarwid, Diana 363
Scavolini, Romano 325, 416
Schach, Max 261
Schaefer, Armand 346
Schafer, Natalie 398
Schary, Dore 425
Schechter, Harold 91
Scheider, Roy 316
Schell, Johnny Lee 334
Schemmel, Sandy 113

Schenk, Aubrey 190
Schenk, Wolfgang 453
Schenkel, Carl (aka Shenkel, Carl) 151, 152, 153, 244, 245
Scherre, Martine 263
Schien, Loren 285
Schiff, Paul 187
Schifman, Aron 148
Schifrin, Lalo 81, 126, 283, 351
Schiller, Fanny 251
Schivazappa, Piero 182, 183
Schizo (1977) 187, 394–395
Schizo (1981) see *Nightmare*
Schizoid 379, 481
schizophrenia 82, 85, 111, 121, 122, 127, 136, 149, 169, 179, 209–211, 225, 230, 240, 269, 309, 358, 370, 379, 388, 389, 394, 425, 431, 432, 490, 520
Schlamme, Thomas 421
Schlesinger, John 134, 153, 154, 350, 446
Schlesinger, Katherine 446
Schlesinger, Tobias A. 252
Schliessler, Tobias 515
Schlom, Herman 74, 176
Schmitz, Gundula 395
Schmoeller, David 42, 43, 99, 100, 101, 270, 459, 477, 478
Schmoeller, Gary 42, 350
Schneider, Aaron 242
Schneider, Barry 116
Schneider, Bonnie 301
Schneider, Harold 55
Schnerr, Charles 97
Schoedsack, Ernest B. 292
Schoelen, Jill 432
Schrader, Chieko 241
Schrader, Leonard 241
Schrader, Paul 33, 39, 89, 124, 164, 241, 277, 348, 438, 468
Schrader/Scorsese *see* Schrader, Paul and Scorsese, Martin
Schrager, Rudolph 289
Schramm 30n, 229, 309, 395–396
Schreckinger, Jinny 471
Schreyer, John F. 190
Schroeder, Michael 333, 334, 377
Schubert, Franz 281
Schubert, Karin 69
Schuck, John 57
Schudsonn, H.D. 117
Schuhly, Thomas 476
Schulenberg, Robert 141, 333
Schuler, Fred 476
Schultz, Albert 355
Schultz, Harry 136
Schumacher, Joel 143, 145, 154, 209
Schurman, Petra 407
Schurr, Arthur 168
Schuster, Thomas 364
Schwalm, Thomas 161
Schwartz, Nan 515
Schwartzenberger, Xavier 395

Sciacqua, Duane 386
Sciagna, Duane 148
science fiction 82, 111, 145, 231, 301, 308, 337, 367, 421, 458, 469
scopophilia 35, 44, 342, 343, 344, 346, 498
Scorsese, Martin 39, 89, 103, 132, 164, 212, 277, 345, 348, 409, 438, 468
Scotland 350
Scotland Yard 45, 101, 194, 228, 229, 262, 264
Scott, Allan 427
Scott, Campbell 446
Scott, Carey 384
Scott, Darin 434
Scott, Elisabeth A. 307
Scott, Gary 116
Scott, George C. 143, 149, **150**
Scott, Gordon L.T. 334
Scott, Ian 66
Scott, Jeremy 489
Scott, John 101, 441
Scott, John (2) 485
Scott, Laurie 434
Scott, Randolph 304
Scott, Ridley 1, 89, 194, 367, 413
Scott, Simon 99
Scott, Susan 418
Scott, T.J. 57
Scoutten, Janet 492
Scream 327, 366
Screamplay 396
Scrim, Angus 163
Scully, Terry 200
Sea of Love 112, 206, 264, 304, 396–398, **397**, 438
Seabrook, Melinda 253
Seagal, Steven 190, 191
Seaman, David 273
Sears, B.J. 208, 494
Sears, Phil 384
Seattle International Film Festival 363, 370
Sebetsky, Don 387
Seconds 352
Secret Beyond the Door 70, 262, 398–400
Secret Life of Jeffrey Dahmer 400
Sedaka, Neil 349
Seder, Eugene 396
Seder, Rufus Butler 396
See No Evil 35, 38, 400–401, 449
Sefan, Craig 38
Segal, George 328, 329, 456, **457**, 458
Segan, Allison Lyon 383
Seguin, Francois 259
Seine river 304
Seixas, Charles 234
Sekula, Andrezej 35
Self Storage 401
Selkirk, Jamie 184
Sellar, Joanne 136
Sellars, Randolph 353

Selleck, Tom 293
Selznick, David O. 427
Semilian, Julian 107, 402
Semler, Dean 72
Sena, Dominic 236, 238
Sendel, Max A. 349
Sera, Ian 346
Serandrei, Mario 147
serial killer: defined 1, 2, 22, 24; as noble savage 238, 480; as revolutionary 6n, 27, 126, 136, 187, 217, 309, 332, 333, 402, 430, 435, 474, 494; subculture 16n, 25, 25n, 91, 108, 197, 272, 309, 403, 435, 447, 453, 485; as tragic figure 30n, 42, 80, 121, 396, 453, 454, 458, 514, 518; as visionary 191, 309, 406, 435, 469, 482, 509; *see also* childhood trauma, female serial killer
Serial Killer 402
Serial Killing 4 Dummies 402–403
Serial Mom 403–404
Serna, Assumpta 281
Serna, Pepe 240
Serpico 125, 422
Serralonga, Jorge 255
Serrano, Julieta 281
Serrault, Michel 131
Sersen, Fred 256
Setbon, Philip 288
Seton, Bruce 261
Settle, Virginia 492
Seven 17n, 21, 27, 29n, 72, 73, 74, 94, 137, 143, 144, 145, 170, 208, 211, 242, 244, 245, 284, 300, 317, 380, 393, 394, 404–406, **405**, 407, 413, 481, 497, 498
Seven Orchids Stained in Red 407
The Seven Per Cent Solution 297, 471
Severance, Joan 354
Sevi, Mark 377, 379, 402
Sevigny, Chloe 36
Sewell, Rufus 110, **110**
Seymour, Henry 101
Seymour, Jane 57, 229, 351
Shadow, John 346
Shadow Hunter see *Shadowhunter*
Shadow of a Doubt 14, 15, 180, 219, 259, 268, 381, 407–408, 427, 432, 434
Shadowhunter 137, 335, 409–410
Shadows and Fog 408–409
Shadows Run Black 409
Shaffer, Anthony 180
Shaine, Rick 59, 202, 273
Shakespeare 350, 364
Shakleton, Allan 321
Shalhoub, Tony 48
Shampoo 443
Shaner, Michael 151
Shanker, Mark 170
Shanks, Susan 148

Shanley, John Patrick 231
Shapiro, Colin 382
Shapiro, Neil 323
Shapiro/Glickenhaus 377; *see also* Glickenhaus, James
Sharif, Omar 321, 322
Sharkey, Ray 367, 377
Sharp, Anthony 215
Shatner, William 219, 496
Shaver, Helen 337
Shavick, James 354, 391
Shaw, Crystal 249
Shaw, Edward S. 193
Shaw, Larry 328
Shaw, Peter 427, 446
Shaw, Roland 134
Shaw, Sebastian 437
Shaw, Stan 164
Shawn, Dick 39, **39**
Shaye, Robert 59
She-Wolf of London 411
Shear, Barry 472, 473, 474
Shearer, Moira 341
Shearmur, Edward 423
Sheedy, Ally 164
Sheen, Charlie 80, 334, 350
Sheen, Martin 44, 115, 334, 502, 503
Sheen, Ruth 515
Sheldon, Lynette 224
Sheldon, Ralph 422
Shellen, Stephen 435
Shelton, Deborah 124
Shelton, Lois 118
Shelton, Robert 416
Shenar, Paul 116
Shenkel, Carl see Schenkel, Carl
Shepherd, Pauline 490
Shepherd, Simon 301
Sheppard, Delia 386
Sher, Anthony 515
Sheridan, Dani 422
Sherman, Cindy 331, 332
Sherman, Gary 303
Sherman, George 259
Sherwood, Robin 261, 477
Shew, Jonathan 114
Shields, Brooke 177
Shiesser, Dave 316
Ship, Trudy
Shipton, Susan 165
Shirley's World (TV) 349
Shmale, Dan 162
Shocker 150, 160, 173, 215, 346, 411–412, **412**
Shonteff, Lindsay 200, 201
Shopping 430
Shore, Howard 82, 192, 404, 412
Shostrom, Mark 116
Showtime cable channel 446
Shrake, Bud 337
Shreve, Leo H. 99
Shryack, Dennis 49, 50, 207
Shumaker, James 47, 108
Shyman, James 418

Sicari, Joseph R. 340
Sidney, Sylvia 262
Siedow, Jim 460, 464
Siegel, Don 22, 50, 126, 469
Siegel, Sol C. 328
Siemazko, Casey 335
Sienkiewicz, Bill 85
Sigel, Newton Thomas 160
Sighvatsson, Joni 114
Sikking, James B. 456
Silence of the Lambs 1, 10n, 16, 20n, 25n, 26, 27, 29n, 47, 57, 72, 83, 91, 94, 114, 123, 129, 195, 197, 223, 235, 275, 276, 313, 355, 358, 367, 392, 394, 402, 412–415, **414**, 418, 463, 502, 503
Silent Madness 415–416
Silent Sentence 173, 227, 416–417
Silva, Maria 45
Silver, Alain 325
Silver, Amanda 153
Silver, Ron 53
Silverman, Joel 393
Silverstone, Alicia 208, **210**, 484
Silvi, Roberto 313
Sim, Alastair 388
Sim, Gerald 129, 180, 229
Simenon, Georges 251
Simo, Sandor 482
Simon, Juan Picher 346
Simon, Marty 374
Simon, Michel 226
Simonelli, Giovanni 81
Simpson, O.J., trial 154
Simpson, Robert 124
Sinatra, Frank 124, 125, 170, 171, **171**, 172
Sinde, Jose Maria Gonzalez 167
Singh, Tarsem 82
Sinise, Robert L. 62
The Sinister Urge 417
Sinkovics, Geza 418
Siodmak, Curt 259, 514
Siodmak, Robert 264, 345, 425, 427
Sirk, Douglas 264
Sirtis, Marina 58
Siskel and Ebert 459; *see also* Ebert, Roger
Sissel, Sandi 222
Sissman, Rob 65
Sisto, Jeremy 208, **210**
666 Satan Rebirth see *Satan Returns*
Sizemore, Tom 202, 309, 436, 438
Sjowall, Maj 273
Skerritt, Tom 81, 115, 244
Sketches of a Stranger 417
Skiba 323
Skiles, M. 437
Skinner, Frank 514
Skirball, Jack H. 407
Skouras, D.T. 58
Skousen, Camilla 308
Slade, Jack 174

Slash Dance 302, 418, 440
The Slasher 418
slasher figure and films 17, 23, 24, 25n, 35, 38, 47, 65, 109, 117, 118, 133, 156, 157, 158, 159, 165, 173, 193, 201, 207, 215, 250, 323, 325, 333, 334, 347, 362, 363, 365, 382, 396, 409, 415, 416, 418, 419, 427, 429, 466, 469, 474, 475, 476, 480, 493, 497
Slasher Is a Sex Maniac see The Slasher
Slaughter, Tod 158, 446
Slaughter of the Innocents 377, 418–419
Slave of the Cannibal God 476
Sledge Hammer 419
Sleeping with the Enemy 434
Sleepwalkers 364, 365
Slesar, Henry 304
Slezak, Walter 74
Sliver 253, 429
Sloane, Bernard 151
Slobotkin, Trace 402
Sloman, Roger 221
Slovakia 372
Sluizer, Georges (George) 101, 102, 328
Small, Michael 55
Small Town in Texas 240
Smart, Rufus 136
Smedley-Astin, Michael 466
Smerczak, Ron 382
Smight, Jack 328, 329, 330
Smith, Bud 104
Smith, Charles Martin 168
Smith, Constance 272
Smith, Earl E. 478
Smith, Frazer 337
Smith, Howard 375, 436
Smith, Hugh 466, 518
Smith, Jack Martin 75, 124
Smith, John Patrick 114
Smith, John Victor 349
Smith, Keith 366, 388
Smith, Kent 425
Smith, Kurtwood 114
Smith, Liz 40
Smith, Mitchell 389
Smith, Paul 346
Smith, Richard 41
Smith, Rusty 401
Smith, Sharon 325
Smith, Shawnee 138
Smith, Thaddeus 384
Smith, Tony 154
Smithee, Alan 88, 162, 215, 334
Smokler, Peter 241
The Snake Pit 13n
Snapdragon 419–420
Sneagle, Brian 123
Sneakers 232
The Sniper 16, 51, 268, 420–421, 511
Snuff 321

snuff movies 43, 44, 143, 144, 145, 163, 204, 235, 250, 288, 338, 423, 428, 429, 436, 493
Snukal, Robert 310
Snyder, Drew 108
Snyder, Suzanne 352
So I Married an Axe Murderer 421–422
Soavi, Michele 418
socialization 17, 30, 33, 34, 58, 79, 93, 104, 176, 199, 336, 400, 401, 426, 443, 459, 474, 496
Soderbergh, Steven 327
Soelberg, Lane 366
Soh, John 417
Sohm, Willi 45
Soho 200, 201, 227, 437
Solar, Silvia 156
Soler, Juan Alberto 227
Soleri, Varo 182
Solomon, Christian Halsey 35
Solomon, Maribeth 91
Solon, Ewen 227
Solondz, Todd 261
Someone to Watch Over Me 367
Somers, Brendan 101
Somers, Suzanne 403
Sommer, Josef 387
Sommers, Stephen 388
Son of Sam 96, 283, 334, 377, 441, 442, 444, 520; *see also* Berkowitz, David
Son of the Pink Panther 292
Sondergaard, Gale 394
Sondheim, Stephen 446
Sonic Youth (band) 498
Soodor, Taavo 156
Sopel, Anne 515
Sorbo, Kevin 418
The Sorcerers 169, 307, 422–423
Sorel, Jean 255
Sorel, Sonia 67
Sorenson, Soren Krag 308
Sorvino, Mira 441
Sorvino, Paul 104
Sotos, Jim 250
Soul Coughing (band) 498
South, Leonard J. 180
South Africa 137, 382
Southern Illinois University at Carbondale 313
Southon, Mike 168
Soylent Green 401
Spacey, Kevin 404
Spader, James 230, **231**, 497, 498
Spain 46, 282
Spain, Fay 472
Spangler, Larry G. 416
Sparke, Jackie 127
Spaulding, Tom 417
Speakman, Jeff 151
Special Effects 43, 423, 429, 455
Species 424
Species 2 423–425
Speck, Richard 107, 179, 451

Speed 168
Speer, Martin 112
Spellbound 13, 13n
Spelling, Aaron 491
Spencer, Bud 177
Spencer, James 187
Spencer, John 371
Spencer, Norris 194
Spheeris, Penelope 80
Spider Baby 149
Spiegel, Sam 321
Spielberg, Steven 104, 140, 465
Spielbergian fantasy 246
Spier, Carol 115
Spina, Mark Grillo 285
Spinell, Joe 104, 170, **171**, 277, 278, **278**
Spinella, Stephen 371, 494
Spino, Anthony 93
Spinotti, Dante 59, 202, 273
The Spiral Staircase (1946) 51, 157, 345, 425–427, **426**, 432, 477
The Spiral Staircase (1976) 427–428, **428**
Spiridakis, Tony 401
Spisak, Neil 202, 316
Split Images 428–429
Split Second 109, 145, 429–430
Spooks Run Wild 430
Sprang, John 409
Spratling, Tony 142
Sprayberry, Robert 493
spree killer 23–24, 117, 138, 237, 286, 309, 310, 354, 393
Spring, Tim 372
Squires, Chris 484
Stacey, Bill 384
Stacey, Paul 515
Stack, Robert 293
Staenberg, Zach 440
Stafford, Baird 325
Stafford, Brendan J. 300
Stagefright 418
Stakeout 60
Staley, Lora 35
Stand By Me 247
Standinger, Hannes 71
Stanley, John 64, 378
Stanley, Richard 136, 137, 430
Stannard, Eliot 255
Stanton, Harry Dean 313, 488
Stanwyck, Barbara 247
Stapel, Huub 37
Star Time 430–431
Star Trek (films) 470
Star Trek (TV) 352
Star Wars: The Phantom Menace 154
Stark, Don 252
Starkweather, Charles 185
Starling, Boris 284
Starman 42
Starr, Irving 169
Starrett, Jack 240
Starz! cable channel 383

Stathis, Jimmy 137
Staton, Rick 91
Stavin, Mary 124, 332
Stay Tuned 411
Steadman, Robert (Bob) 81, 389
Stearn, Andrew 36
Steckler, Ray D. 212
Steel, Amy 347
Steel, Dawn 160
Steeman, S.A. 302
Steen, Jessica 435
Steenburgen, Mary 469, 470, 471, **471**
Stefano, Joseph 356, 358, 363, 364, 365
Steibel, Warren 212
Steiger, Rod 231, 328, **329**, 330
Stein, Ken 367
Stein, Peter 324
Steiner, John 455, 513
Steiner, Max 292
Steiner, Sherry 466
Steinkamp, William 242
Steinmetz, Richard 252
Steinmetz, Tom 384
Stell, Aaron 240, 420
Stella, Stefania 163
The Stendhal Syndrome 53, 431–432, 483, 484
Step Down to Terror 408, 432
The Stepfather 51, 155, 432–434, **433**, 510
Stepfather 2 434
Stepfather 3 434–435
Stephens, Jason Robert 119
Stephens, Robert 34
Sterling, Tisha 240
Stern, Don 482
Stern, Erik 261
Stern, Ernst 499
Stern, Merril 331
Stern, Sandor 138
Stern, Tina 155
Sternad, Rudolph 420
Sterzengbach, Benno 45
Stevens, Andrew 450
Stevens, Angela 511
Stevens, Dana 59
Stevens, Inger 173
Stevens, Keith 50
Stevens, Kimberly 148
Stevens, Mark 143
Stevens, Onslow 99
Stevens, Robert M. 164, 403
Stevenson, Mark 515
Stevenson, Robert (Louis) 11, 230, 459, 490
Stewart, Catherine Mary 355
Stewart, David A. 101
    ⸱t, Frank 366
    James 85
    Iohn 90
    atrick 127
    ona 349
        441

Stigmata 394
Stiliadis, Nicolas 435
Still Life see *Still Life: The Fine Art of Murder*
Still Life: The Fine Art of Murder 41, 245, 336, 435–436, 485
Stine, Harold (E.) 99, 472
Stivaletti, Sergio 431
Stock, Nigel 321
Stockdale, Gary 440
Stockholm 273
Stockwell, Dean 307
Stoker, Austin 518
Stoker, Bram 514
Stole, Mink 252, 403, 404
Stoler, Shirley 212, 213, **213**, 214
Stone, Dee Wallace 185
Stone, Oliver 24, 37, 80, 108, 177, 309, 310, **310**
Stone, Peter 235
Stone, Sharon 81
Stone, Stuart 402
Stopkewich, Lynne 80
Stoppa, Franca 52
Storaro, Vittorio 52, 147
Stormare, Peter 143
Storti, Raymond 119
Story, David 219
Story, Robert 219
Storym, Lesley 437
Stossel, Ludwig 67
Stott, Ken 284
Stowe, Madeleine 59, 60, **60**
Stradling, Harry 169
Straight on Till Morning see *Dressed for Death*
Strange Days 59, 253, 436
The Strangler (1941) 436–437
The Strangler (1964) 18, 437
Stratton, David 373
Strauss, Arthur 244
Strauss, Richard 281
Straw Dogs 401
Strayer, Frank R. 92
Street Smart 164
Streets 437–438, 440
Streisand, Barbra 157
Strentch, Gary 114
Stricklyn, Ray 381
Striking Distance 230, 231, 337, 438–439, **439**
Strindberg, Anita 510
Stringer 439
Stringer, Michael 117
Stripped to Kill 99, 108, 168, 191, 253, 437, 438, 440
Stripped to Kill 2 440
Striptease 440
Stritch, Elaine 427
Strobel, Frank 515
Stroller, Louis A. 72, 396
Stromberg, Hunt 247, 264, 317, 319
Strong, Shelly 241
Stroud, Chuck 85

Stroud, Don 240
Strudwick, Shepperd 365
Stuart, Jeb 235, 445, 446
Stubblefield, Bruce 440
Studi, Wes 202, 241
A Study in Terror 98, 297, 441
Stumar, Charles 500
Stumper, Johnny 67
Styles, Mark 323
Subotsky, Milton 217
Sudden Impact 235, 469
Suhestedt, Tim 481
Suhrstedt, Tim 337
Sukowa, Barbara 331
Sullivan, Jennifer 90
Sullivan, Ron 202
Sullivan, Susan 88
Sullivan, Susan Jennifer 112
Summer of Sam 96, 441–445, **442**, **443**, **444**
Sumpter, Donald 54, 200
Sundance Film Festival 372, 431
Sunset Boulevard 394, 481
Superstar Female Serial Killer 445
Suran, Mark 60
The Surgeon see *Exquisite Tenderness*
Surtees, Allan 301
Surtees, Bruce 126, 363, 467
Suspicion 262, 399
Suspiria 121, 302, 455, 483
Sutherland, Donald 47, 85, 86, **87**, 160, 297, 387
Sutherland, Edward 304
Sutherland, Kiefer 110, 153, **153**, 156, 177, **178**, 179, 488
Suvari, Mena 242
Swackhamer, E.W. 81
Swain, Jack 293
Swanson, Kirsty 401
Swanson, Ted Adams 446
Swanton, Scott 81
Swayze, Patrick 231, 439
Sweeney, Mark 488
Sweeney, Mary 306
Sweeney Todd 305, 446
Sweeney Todd, the Demon Barber of Fleet Street 158, 446
Sweet, Freddy 250
Sweet Kill see *The Arousers*
Swenning, William 217
Swerdlow, Ezra 231
Swift, David 54
Switchback 235, 312, 445–446
Swordfish 238
Sydney 485
Sylbert, Paul 66
Sylbert, Richard 340
Sylos, Paul 491
Syrewicz, Stanislas 161
Szalay, Attia 57
Szollosi, Tom 73

Taav, Michael 335, 337, 435
Tabar, Juna 167

Tabet, Sylvio 158
Taczanowski, Hubert 515
Taggart, Rita 215
Taggert, Brian 496
Takada, Akira 493
Takeda, Taijun 493
Tal, Omer 246
Talalay, Rachel 187, 189, 190, 440
Talazac, Odette 302
Talbot, Kenneth 193
Tale of Sweeney Todd 446
Talevera, Edmund 503
Talgorn, Frederic 142
Tally, Ted 412, 415
Tamasini, George 356
Tamassy, Zdenko 482
Tamerlis, Zoe 423
Tamura, Tsutomo 493
Tan, Birke 440
Tan, Yuen King 393
Tank Girl 190
Tannen, Charles 511
Tannen, William 207, 208, 262
Tannura, Philip 261
Tapping, Amanda 57
Tarantino, Quentin 107, 108, 271, 309
Tard, Jean Baptiste 154
Tarlov, Mark 94, 403
Tarnoff, John 310
Tarren, Jenny 334
Tarver, John P. 402
Tarzan and the Lost City 246
Tarzana, Herman 60
Tasker, Robert 131
Tate/LaBianca murders 22
Tatopoulos, Patrick 110
Tattersall, David 91
Tattersall, Gale 208, 494
Tavelia, Dino 145
Tavier, Vincent 271
Tax, Yan 281
Taxi Driver 55, 66, 165, 168, 240
Taylor, Barbi 384
Taylor, Gilbert 180, 466
Taylor, Jack 346
Taylor, Jud 88, 334
Taylor, Lili 238
Taylor, Lisa 157
Taylor, Marjorie 157
Taylor, Rocky 301
Taylor, Rod 432
Taylor, Ronnie 396
Taylor, Sam 515
Taylor, Stan 216
Teakle, Spencer 99
Teale, Owen 200
Teefy, Maureen 430
Tejada-Flores, Miguel 355
Telefon 50
Telfer, James 40
Tell Them Willie Boy Is Here 410
Temerson, Jean 345
Temple, Tim 65
Temple, William A. 310

Ten Monologues from the Lives of Serial Killers 447
10 Rillington Place 25n, 38, 54, 176, 177, 180, 447–449, 448, 449, 450, 518
Ten to Midnight 43, 89, 132, 278, 437, 450–452, 452, 453, 468
Tenderness of the Wolves 6, 10n, 271, 453–455, 476
The Tenderness of Wolves see Tenderness of the Wolves
Tenebrae 53, 82, 314, 455–456
Tenny, Del 365
Tenser, Tony 422
Tent, Kevin 418
The Terminal Man 37, 456–458, 457
Terror Circus 65, 85, 108, 458–459, 466, 478
Terrorvision 411
Terry, Allen 323
Terry, Philip 74
Tesh, John 411
Tessicini, Silvano 477
Le Testament du Docteur Cordelier 459–460
Tewes, Lauren 156
Texarcana 478
Texas 335, 460, 502
The Texas Chainsaw Massacre 16, 36, 63, 65, 108, 123, 124, 139, 140, 295, 358, 415, 460–464, 460, 461, 462, 466, 478, 493, 500
The Texas Chainsaw Massacre: The Next Generation 466
The Texas Chainsaw Massacre 2 139, 209, 464–466, 465
Thayer, Brynn 207
Theatre of Death 466
Theiss, Manuella 458
Thelma and Louise 180
Theroux, Justin 36
They Walk Alone (play) 113
Thibeau, Jack 330
Thibeault, Debi
Thicke, Alan 81
Thief 202
Thieltges, Gary 141
Thin Man 170
The Thing (remake) 429
Thirard, Armand 302
This Is Spinal Tap 271
Thom, Robert 511
Thomann, Dennis 519–520
Thomas, Dylan 72, 127, 128
Thomas, Henry 197, 363, 364, 365
Thomas, Larry 323
Thomas, John 177
Thomas, Peter 519
Thomas, Philip E. 507
Thomas, Richard 472, 473, 474
Thomas, Scott 374
Thomerson, Tim 125, 158, 439
Thomopoulos, Tony 438

Thompson, Carolyn 466
Thompson, Gary Scott 429
Thompson, Hilary 112
Thompson, J. Lee 437, 450, 451, 452
Thompson, Jamie 377
Thompson, Jim 240
Thompson, Kevin 331
Thompson, Linda 466
Thompson, Peter Lee 450
Thompson, Walter 472
Thompson, William C. 417
Thompson-Baker, Scott 332
Thomson, Alex 316
Thomson, Helen 65
Thomson, R.H. 73
Thoolen, Gerard 221
Thorn, Frankie 252
Thornton, Malcolm 446
Thorp, Roderick 124
Thorpe, George 113
Thorpe, Richard 317, 319
Thouin, Lise 496
Three on a Meathook 459, 466–467, 478, 518
Thunderbolt and Lightfoot 469
Thundercrack! 396
Thunderheart 410
Thurman, Uma 232, 233, 234
Tichy, Gerard 346
Tickner, Clive 429
Ticotin, Rachel 91
Tidy, Frank 283
Tierney, Lawrence 66, 74, 75
Tietz, Fred 168
Tiffin, Pamela 147
Tightrope 27, 94, 103, 227, 234, 467–469, 468, 481
Till, Eric 471
Till, Jenny 466
Tilly, Meg 361, 362
Time After Time 25n, 182, 231, 297, 308, 469–471, 470, 471
A Time to Kill 145, 154
Times Square 66
Tingwell, Charles 146
Tiomkin, Dimitri 407
Tisier, Jean 302
To Catch a Killer 212, 217, 471–472, 502
To Die For 101, 403
To Kill a Mockingbird 247
To Live and Die in LA 277, 370
Tobin, Bud 348
Toda, Jusho 493
Todd, Ann 167
Todd, Sweeney see Sweeney Todd
The Todd Killings 25n, 472–474, 473
Tokuda, Marilyn 252
Toll, Gerry 224
Tolo, Marila 69
Tom, David 434
Tom Jones 320

Tomassi, Vincenzo 81
Tombello, Allen 148
Tomei, Marisa 497, 498
Tomita, Tamlyn 241
Tomlin, Lily 408
Tomney, Ed 252, 502
Tonoyama, Taiji 493
Tony Rome 125, 170
Too Scared to Scream 474
The Toolbox Murders 474–475
Toole, Otis 92, 206
Toomayan, Alan 141
Topart, Jean 459
Topper, Burt 18, 437
Torn, Rip 44, 337
Tornberg, Ralph 46
Toronto 37
Torray, Nuria 513
Torso 58, 156, 347, 475–476
Torvay, Jose 251
Totheroh, Roland 289
Totmacher 476–477
Tottenham, Merle 317
Touch of Death 477
Touch of Evil 251
Tougas, Ginger 335
Touliatos, George 292
Toura, Matsuhiro 493
Tourist Trap 43, 65, 100, 140, 217, 270, 459, 477–478, 493
Tourneur, Jacques 251
Tover, Leo 272
Tovoli, Luciano 455
Tower, Richard 131
Tower, Wade 382
Towles, Tom 203
Town That Dreaded Sundown 25n, 85, 478–481, **479**
Townsend, Layton 309
Townsend, Leo 251
Traces of Red 481
Tracy, Lee 131
Tracy, Marlene 217
Tracy, Spencer 299
Trail of a Serial Killer 379, 481–482, 497
The Train Killer 482–483
Tranquili, Silvano 167
transcendence 10n, 12, 29, 36, 41, 59, 83, 111, 131, 152, 172, 230, 276, 312, 379, 410, 413, 423, 431
transformation motifs (inc. meta-morphosis) 10, 10n, 11–12, 29, 98, 129, 130, 172, 215, 251, 258, 413, 509, 514
transgression motifs 37, 62, 75, 129, 131, 143, 193, 194, 230, 263, 264, 283, 301, 308, 328, 350, 352, 364, 365, 387, 416, 478, 488, 489, 492, 499, 511
nsvestites and transsexuals 40, ⁹9, 134, 136, 200, 281, 358, 364, ⁴15
⁴32, 483–484, **484**
⁻nder 321

Travanti, Daniel J. 235
The Travelling Executioner 330
Travers, Henry 407
Travis, Len 354
Travis, Neil 44
Travis, Nancy 421
Travolta, John 66
Treas, Terri 347, 420
Trebor, Robert 334
Trench, John 113
Trenchard-Smith, Brian 197, 249, 333, 386
Trentham, Barbara 349
Trevarthen, Noel 98
Treviglio, Leonardo 285
Trevino, Jorge 251
Trevor, Clare 74, 75
Trevor, William 165
Trigg, Derek 136
The Trigger Effect 442
Trinity Brown 386
Tripplehorn, Jeanne 331
Trog 101
Trosper, Elizabeth 409
Troupe, Al 285
Trube, Harry John 402
True Believer 434
True Crime 484–485, 515
Truffaut, François 179
Truman, Tim 222
Tsioisias, Nicholas 127
Tsu, Irene 419
Tubor, Morton 354
Tucker, Robert 168
Tucson 507
Tuggle, Richard 467, 469
Tulane, Dirkan 301
Tulsa 383
Tunnel Vision 485–486
Turman-Foster 283
Turner, Guinevere 35
Turner, Kathleen 403
Turner, Simon Fisher 306
Turner, Tim 199
Turney, Nadyne 42
Turpin, Gerry 127
Turturro, John 48, **49**
Tusell, Felix 156
Tushingham, Rita 134
Twelve Angry Men 371
Twiggy 127, **128**
Twilight Zone (TV) 164
Twin Peaks 27, 486–488, **486**, **487**
Twin Peaks: Fire Walk with Me 488
Twisted Nerve 300, 489–490
The Two Faces of Dr. Jekyll 98, 490–491
Two for the Money 491
2000 Maniacs 63
Tyler, Walter 173
Tyrell, Susan 39, 240
Tyson, Barbara 380

U-Turn 89, 335
Ubeda, Diego 227

Udy, Claudia 35
The Ugly 491–492
UK *see* United Kingdom
Ulmer, Edgar G. 24, 67, 68
Ulrich, Kurt 45
Uncle Sam 279
Under Siege 388
Underwood, Blair 235, 236
Uner, Kubilay 107
Unhinged 354, 492–493
United Kingdom (UK/England) 101, 180, 230, 300, 326, 338, 344, 383, 389, 427, 428, 429, 447, 449, 458, 493
United States of America (US) 46, 70, 93, 118, 143, 154, 231, 292, 326, 330, 345, 349, 350, 362, 381, 382, 383, 386, 391, 393, 446, 456, 476, 479, 510
Unmasked Part 25 see *Hand of Death*
Upton, Mike 97
Uraoka, Keiichi 493
Urban Legend 24, 115
Urich, Robert 299
Urioste, Frank J. 501
Urquiza, J. Gomez 251
Utah 190, 418
Utt, Kenneth 412

Vaccaro, Brenda 170
Vacher, Joseph 514
Vachon, Christine 331
Vadim, Jean 352
Vadim, Roger 351
Vail, William 460
Vajda, Ladislao 226
Valcke, Serge-Henri 37
Valenti, Raf 52
Valenti, Roman 458
Valentine, Joseph 407, 514
Valladoid festival 514
Valle, Ricardo 45
Valli, Alida 163
Vampire of Dusseldorf *see* Kurten, Peter
vampirism 6, 7–8, 9, 9n, 10, 28, 42, 92, 96, 163, 167, 279, 306, 307, 323, 337–338, 367, 371, 374, 381–382, 420, 453, 466, 476, 477, 514
van Bergen, Ingrid 45
Vance, Brenda 323
Vance, James 381
van den Berg, Rudolf 221
Vandenbroeck, Willy 271
Van Den Steenhoven, Jules 101
Vandervlis, Diana 190
Van de Sande, Theo 172
Vandevelde, Helga 263
Vandewoestijne, Johan 263
Van Dien, Casper 391, 392
Van Doren, Mamie 190
Vandronglen, Herbert 447
Van Druten, John 317

Vanelli, Ross 168
Van Every, Dale 303
Van Gelder, Joost 447
Van Gogh art 321
Van Haren Noman, Eric 207
The Vanishing 102, 328
Van Ness, Jon 477
Vanni, Renata 246
Vannicola, Joanne 259
Van Ow, Anita 226
Van Patten, Joyce 99
Van Pernis, Mona 382
Van Rooyen, Johan 382
Vansaane, Fokke 447
Van Sant, Gus 358, **359**, **360**, 361
Vansier, Gerald 148
Van Suyt, Nick 263
Van Valkenburgh, Deborah 367
Varnals, Wendy 98
Varney, Jim 151
Vash, Karl 265
Vaughn, Ralph Pruitt 65
Vaughn, Robert 88
Vaughn, Vince 82, 89, **90**, 358,
    359, 361
Vayer, Tomas 69
Veber, Francis 315, 340
Vegas *see* Las Vegas
Veidt, Conrad 499
Velazquez, Jose Lopez 513
Veloz, David 309
Velvet, Vickie 445
Ven de Ven, Monique 37
Veneta 445
Venice, California 42, 437
Venice, Italy 510
Venice Film Festival 460
Venora, Diane 202
Ventanonoi, John 354
Ventimiglia, Baron 255
Verducci, Pat 484
Vermeiren, Misjel 281
Verne, Jules 347
Verneuil, Henri 315
Vernon, Howard 45
Vernon, Jackie 285
Vernon, John 123
Vertical Limit 103
Verzier, Rene 103, 496
Vetchinsky, Alex 441
Viadukt see The Train Killer
VICAP 26, 59, 76, 419
Vice Squad 39, 44, 89, 117, 164,
    278, 303, 468
Vicente, Mark 246
Video Murders 493
Videodrome 116, 253
Vienna 271
Vietnam War 51, 299, 322, 331
Vig, Tommy 250
Vigilante 151
vigilantism 43, 44, 132, 136, 145,
    151, 153–154, 174, 175, 235, 255,
    338, 372, 377, 390, 393, 405,
    451, 452, 469

Viharo, Robert 324
Villa Rides 174
Vince, Pruitt Taylor 164
Vince, Robert 88
Vincent, Allen 305
Vincent, Virginia 381
Vint, Jesse 108
Violated Angels 451
Violence at Noon see *Violent Killer*
Violent Killer 493–494
The Violent Years 417
Virginia 393
Virtuosity 26n, 82, 97, 188, 209,
    211, 430, 494–496, **495**
Visart, Natalie 247
Visiting Hours 152, 496–497
Visovich, Randal 325
Vitale, Sam 387
Vitold, Michel 459
Vlessing, Mark 101
Vogel, Jack 90
Voight, Jon 202
Volk, Pal G. 43
Vollbrecht, Karl 265
Vollert, Alois 312
Von Bagendorff, Leopold 315–316
Von Brandenstein, Patrizia 235
Von Fuerstenberg, Ira 147
Von Gober, Ron 119
Von Gustorf, Florian Koerner 395
Von Harbou, Thea 265
Von Ornsteiner, Joel 418
Von Spiess, Ruediger 510
Von Sternberg, Nicholas (J.) 477,
    481
Von Stroheim, Erich 345
Von Trier, Lars 145, 454
Von Wiese, Ursuls 228
Vosloo, Arnold 372, 388
Vosper, Frank 261

Wade, Russell 71
Wadleigh, Michael 137
Waggner, George 514
Wagner, Christian A. 207
Wagner, Fritz Arno 265
Wagner, Natasha Griegson 163
Wagner, Raymond 207
Wahloo, Per 273
Wait Until Dark 24, 35, 401
Waite, Ric 33
Wajda, Laszlo 338
Wakhevitch, G. 345
Waldau, Nicolai Coster 308
Walden, Chris 300
Walden, Dana 46
Waldman, Marion 123
Walken, Christopher 115, 116
Walker, Ally 502, 503
Walker, Andrew Kevin 143, 208,
    211, 404, 406
Walker, Gerald 104
Walker, Jon 506
Walker, Kathryn 57
Walker, Pete 98, 129, 134, 167,

186, 187, 200, 215, 387, 388, 394,
    395, 422, 423, 428
Walker, Polly 156
Walker, Rob 326
Walker, Stuart 10, 500
Wall Street 48
Wall Street culture 36, 37
Wallace, Art 129
Wallace, Edgar 46, 53, 158, 407
Wallace, Joshua 388
Wallis, Hal B. 173
Walsh, Dermot 174
Walsh, Fran 184
Walsh, Gwynyth 252
Walsh, J.T. 47, 335
Walsh, Kate 206
Walsh, M. Emmett 88, 123, 241,
    374
Walsh, Ned 197
Walston, Ray 65
Walter, Ernest 447
Walter, Jessica 187
Walter, Tracey 252, 334
Walters, Martin 352
Walton, Fred 387
Wanamaker, Sam 427
Wannsee Conference 476
Wanted Dead or Alive 303
The War Wagon 174
Warbeck, David 101, 163
Ward, Cotter 393
Ward, Edward 317
Ward, Fred 330
Ward, Roger 248
Ward, Roy 491
Ward, Vincent 220
Ward-Lealand, Jennifer 491
Warde, Harlan 511
Wardell, Frederick 241
Wardell, Gareth 234
Warden, Jack 192
Warfield, Emily 337
Warhol actors 323
Warhol Factory 142
Warhol/Morrissey films 404, 416
Warner, Allyn 215
Warner, David 299, 307, 469, **471**
Warner, Natasha Gregson 163
Warner, Pam 177
Warner, Phil 485
Warner, Robert 123
Warnow, Stan 212
Warren, F. Brooke 158
Warren, Lesley Ann 41, 93
Warwick, John 158
Warwick, Norman 127, 129
Washbourne, Mona 319
Washington, Dennis 330
Washington, Denzel 72, 73, 160,
    160, 161, **161**, 494, 496
Wasserman, Lee 434
Watanabe, Fumio 493
The Watcher 27, 72, 73, 82,
    482, 497–499
Watergate disillusio

Waters, John 146, 334, 403, 404
Waterston, Sam 403
Watkin, Pierre 346
Watkins, John L. 325
Watson, Alberta 507
Watson, Jack 341, 394
Watson, John 47
Watts, Queenie 394
Watts, Roy 38, 116
Waxman, Harry 489
Waxworks 499
Wayans, Keenan Ivory 190, 191
Wayne, David 268
Wayne's World 422
WB 43, 90
Weatherwax, Paul 50
Weaver, Robert A. 320
Weaver, Sigourney 94, 95, **96**
Webb, J. Watson, Jr. 256
Webb, James R. 345
Webb, Roy 71, 425
Webb, William 47
Webber, Liz 156, 326
Webber, Lou Ann 285
Weber, Jake 82
Weber, Steven 222
Webster, Jon 374
Wechsier, Lazar 226
Wechsler, Nick 163
Wedekind, Franz 338
Weeks, Ada-May 289
Weeks, Stephen 217
Weigand, Al 119
Weigel, Teri 47
Weill, Kurt 408, 409
Weine, Robert 6
Weiner, John 67
Weintraub, Bruce 104
Weintraub, Jerry 104
Weis, Jack 279
Weisburg, Rochelle 136
Weiss, Michael T. 179
Weist, Gary 134
Welch, Raquel 69
Welcome to Arrow Beach 63,
    499–500
Weller, Peter 41
Welles, Orson 164, 289, 291
Wellington, Larry 512
Wellman, William 247, 248, 258
Wells, Dawn 478
Wells, H.G. 297, 469, 470
Wendigo myth 371, 410
Wendland (Wendlandt), Horst
    407, 519
Wenger, Clifford 90
Wengraf, John 381
werewolf motifs 10, 11, 228, 249,
    251, 411, 500, 514
erewolf of London 10, 500–501,
    14
   icke, Otto 265
      Cary 43
       334
        383

West, Simon 91, 92
Westbrook, James 393
Westerner's code / legacy 93, 118,
    173, 174, 251, 337, 480
Westerns 118, 137, 173, 174, 326,
    337, 371, 410, 416
Westworld 458
Whale, James 10
What Dreams May Come 220
Whatever Happened to Aunt Alice?
    149, 501–502
Whatever Happened to Baby Jane?
    501
Whatham, Charles 300
Wheatley, David 333, 377
Wheeler, Lyle 194
Wheeler, W. (Whitney) Brooke
    33, 402
When a Stranger Calls 387
When Harry Met Sally 366
When the Bough Breaks 223,
    502–503
*When the Bough Breaks 2: Perfect
    Prey* 503
Where Eagles Dare 170
While the City Sleeps 503–505,
    504
Whinnery, Barbara 99
Whirry, Shannon 246
Whisper to a Scream 505–506
Whistance-Smith, Steve 428
Whitaker, David 348
White, Cary 337, 464
White, Charlotte 320
White, Douglas 458
White, Ethel Lina 425
White, Michael 236
White, Nick 113
White, Peter 57
White, Randall 382
White Angel 506
The White Buffalo 452
White Heat 158, 159
White of the Eye 119, 126, 410, 503,
    506–510, **507**, **508**
Whitechapel 227
Whitehead, O.Z. 50
Whitelaw, Billie 174, 180, 300, 489
Whiteman, Frank 217
Whitlock, Albert 361
Whitman, Stuart 118, 139, 190,
    499
Whitmore, Stanford 108
Whittaker, David 129
Whitting, Barbara 50
Whittredge, J.R. 71
Whitty, (Dame) May 317, **318**
Who Saw Her Die? 510–511
Whorf, Richard 262
The Wicker Man 161, 162
Wickes, David 229, 230
Wicking, Charles 304
Widmark, Richard 158
Wiederhorn, Ken 156
Wilcots, Joseph 493

Wilcox, Clayton 417
Wilcox, Richard Kent 292
Wild in the Streets 474
Wild Side 509, 510
*The Wild Wild World of Jayne
    Mansfield* 347
Wilde, Andrew 301
Wilde, Cecilia 366
Wilden, Gregory 47
Wilder, Billy 504
Wilder, Christopher 138
Wilder, James 353
Wilder, John 293
Wilder, King 316
Wilder, Thornton 407
Wilding, Chris 252
Wilding, Gavin 253
Wiley, Jan 411
Wiley, Martin 313
Wilkes, Donna 39, **39**
William, Warren 514
Williams, Adam 511
Williams, Barbara 73
Williams, Bert 450
Williams, Billy Dee 164
Williams, Caroline 434, 464
Williams, Elmo 176
Williams, Emlyn 317, 319
Williams, Gary 261
Williams, Grant 99
Williams, Heathcote 221
Williams, Ian 65
Williams, Jack Eric 325
Williams, James 50
Williams, Jimmy 352
Williams, Michael 299
Williams, Patrick 293
Williams, Peter 348
Williams, Rhys 272
Williams, Sherman 107, 238
Williams, Steven Lloyd 108
Williams, Wayne 44, 45
Williamson, Daryl 90
Williamson, Kevin 366
Williamson, Mykelti 91, 172, 202,
    423
Williamson, Nicol 55, 149
Willieim, Ladislav 388
Willis, Bruce 438, 439, **439**
Wilson, Georges 133
Wilson, Ian 38
Wilson, Ilona 269
Wilson, Keith 334
Wilson, Neil 129
Wilson, Owen 286, 288
Wilson, Reno 388
Wilson, Scott 89, 149, 151
Wimble, Chris 102
Wimbury, David 232
Wimmer, Kurt 374
Winans, Sam 47
Wincott, Jeff 354
Wincott, Michael 436
Windsor, Barbara 441
Windsor, Marie 190, 420

Wingate, Ann 200
Wingate, Denise 503
Winger, Debra 55, 56, **56**
Winn, Kitty 293
Winner, Michael 154, 452
Winning, David 354
Winterhawk 480
Wise, Ray 491
Wise, Robert 14, 71, 72, 74
Wisman, Ron 91
Wissner, Gary 143
The Witch Who Came from the Sea 511
Witeman, Frank 417
Witherick, Albert 489
Witherspoon, Reese 36, 177
Without Warning 511–512
Witness for the Prosecution 193
Witte, Paul 505
Witter, Karen 333
Wizan, Joe 242
The Wizard of Gore 512–513, **512**, 513
Wodoslawsky, Stefan 374
Wolf, Nancy 203
Wolf Forest 92, 513–514
The Wolf Man 500, 514, 514–515
Wolfe, Donald 394
Wolfe, Robert 456
Wolfen 137
Wolk, Andy 481
Wolski, Dariusz 110
Woman in the Window 400
Wonacott, Edna Mae 407
Wong, James 80
Woo, John 338, 394
Wood, Annabella 66
Wood, Edward D., Jr. 417
Wood, John 85
Wood, Oliver 133, 212, 445
Wood, Robin 106, 157, 187, 459, 463
Wood, Sarah 133
Wood, Tom 401
Woodbine, Bokeem 177, 389
Woodlawn, Holly 323
Woods, Barbara A. 108
Woods, James 93, **94**, 238, 240
Woodward, Edward 284
Wooley, Peter 211
Wooley, Stephen 219
Woolf, Charles 354
Woolrich, Cornell 10, 251
Workman, Nanette 148
World Series (baseball) 181

World War One 51
World War Two 71, 131, 170, 259, 437, 454, 466, 493
Worlock, Frederick 259, 262
Woronov, Mary 141, **141**, 142
Worrall, Bruce 354
Worth, Nicholas 132
Worthy, Athena 440
Wozciechowski, Michael 241
Wray, Ardel 251
Wray, Fay 131, 292, 293, 305
Wright, Steven J. 419
Wright, Teresa 407, 408
Wrightman, Robert 434
Writer's Block 91, 355, 515
Wunstorf, Peter 80
Wyeth, Katye 134
Wyldeck, Martin 319
Wyler, William 242
Wylie, Philip 304
Wyman, Brad 177, 179
Wyner, Joel 253
Wynn, Keenan 109, 240, 351
Wynne, Gilbert 200
Wynorski, Jim 234
Wynters, Charlotte 346

X-Files (TV) 425

Yablans, Irwin 158
Yang, Janet 238
Yanne, Jean 78
Yanni, Rossana 390
Yano, Sen 493
Yarbrough, Jean 411
Yarra river 372
Yates, Marjorie 54
Yau, Chingamy 393
Yavneh, Cyrus 337
Yee, Derek-James 122
Yellen, Gaye 320
Yen, Donnie 393
Yeoman, Robert 367
Yoakam, Dwight 286
York, John J. 91
York, Michael 383
York, Susannah 352
Yorkshire Ripper 506
Young, Aida 193
Young, Bruce A. 59
Young, Christopher 94, 111, 232, 494
Young, Collier 50
Young, Felicity 99
Young, Graham 518

Young, Jerry 293
Young, Karen 102, 316
Young, Kendal 44
Young, Laura 97
Young, Terence 24
Young and Innocent 180
The Young Poisoner's Handbook 37, 287, 422, 515–518, **516**, **517**
Yuzna, Brian 52, 292

Zabriskie, Grace 367
Zaccariello, Giuseppe 182
Zahavi, Natan 53
Zaillian, Steve 194
Zaloom, George 363
Zand, Michael 347
Zane, Billy 211, 212
Zann, Lenore 35, 496
Zappa, Moon 80
Zappari, Bernardino 121
Zarpas, Chris 89
Zavaglia, Richard 41
Zaza, Paul 35
Z'Dar, Robert 119, 324
Zea, Kristi 412
The Zebra Killer 466, 518–519
Zedd, Nick 323
Zeffirelli, Franco 364
Zeltser, Leon 53
Zemeckis, Robert 184
Zeno, Ron 122
Zentropa 145, 454
Zerbe, Anthony 115
Zerra, Ronald 156
Zetlin, Barry 33
Zielinski, Jerzy 231
Zielinski, Rafal 179
Ziller, Paul 80, 356
Zimmer, Hans 47, 194
Zimmer 13 519
Zimmerman, Robert 415
Zimmerman, Vernon 158
Zipperface 519
Zito, Joseph 66
Zittrer, Carl 123
Zivetz, Carrie 333
Zodiac Killer 22, 126, 149, 252, 470, 520
The Zodiac Killer 519–520
Zomer, Wim 37
Zsiba, Peter 133
Zsigmond, Vilmos 66
Zucco, George 264
Zuniga, Daphne 353
Zurli, Guido 270